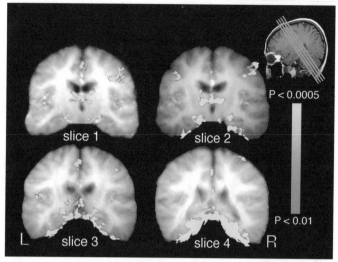

Color Plate 2.1 The increase in brain activity measured by functional magnetic resonance imaging (fMRI) to seeing pictures of scenes, compared to the activity from looking at a fixation mark without seeing any pictures. These records are the averages for six participants. The scale on the right indicates that red represents lower activation and yellow represents higher activation. The location of the four brain slices are indicated by the green lines cutting through the brain, with slice 1 being the one closer to the front of the brain. (See Chapter 2, page 49.)

(From Brewer, J. G., Zhao, Z., Desmond, J. E., Glover, G. H., & Gabrieli, J. D. E., 1998, "Making Memories: Brain Activity That Predicts Whether Visual Experience Will Be Remembered or Forgotten." *Science, 281,* 1185–1187.)

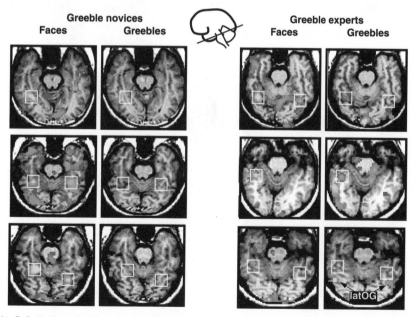

Color Plate 3.1 Brain activation caused by seeing faces and Greebles for Greeble novices (left two columns) and Greeble experts (right two columns). Records for three different participants are shown. The location of the fusiform face area (FFA) is indicated by the white squares. As in the records in Color Plate 2.1, yellow indicates higher activation. Comparing the right column for Greeble experts to the right column for Greeble novices shows that becoming a Greeble expert causes an increase in FFA activation for Greebles. (See Chapter 3, page 93.)

(From Gauthier, I., Tarr, M. J., Anderson, A. W., Skudlarski, P., & Gore, J. C., 1999, "Activation of the Middle Fusiform 'Face Area' Increases With Expertise in Recognizing Novel Objects." *Nature Neuroscience, 2,* 568–573.)

www.wadsworth.com

www.wadsworth.com is the World Wide Web site for Wadsworth and is your direct source to dozens of online resources.

At *www.wadsworth.com* you can find out about supplements, demonstration software, and student resources. You can also send email to many of our authors and preview new publications and exciting new technologies.

www.wadsworth.com
Changing the way the world learns®

ABOUT THE AUTHOR

E. Bruce Goldstein is Director of Undergraduate Programs in Psychology and is a member of the cognitive psychology group in the Department of Psychology at the University of Pittsburgh. He has received the Chancellor's Distinguished Teaching Award for his classroom teaching and textbook writing. He received his bachelor's degree in chemical engineering from Tufts University and his PhD in experimental psychology from Brown University, and he was a postdoctoral fellow in the biology department at Harvard University. Bruce has published papers on a wide variety of topics, including retinal and cortical physiology, visual attention, and the perception of pictures. He is the author of *Sensation and Perception*, 6th edition (Wadsworth, 2002), and the editor of the *Blackwell Handbook of Perception* (Blackwell, 2001). He currently teaches undergraduate courses in cognitive psychology, sensation and perception, and the psychology of visual art and graduate courses in the teaching of psychology.

Cognitive Psychology

Connecting Mind, Research, and Everyday Experience

E. Bruce Goldstein

University of Pittsburgh

THOMSON

WADSWORTH

Australia • Canada • Mexico • Singapore • Spain
United Kingdom • United States

THOMSON

WADSWORTH ™

Publisher/Executive Editor: *Vicki Knight*
Acquisitions Editor: *Marianne Taflinger*
Technology Project Manager: *Darin Derstine*
Assistant Editor: *Jennifer Keever*
Editorial Assistants: *Nicole Root, Justin Courts*
Marketing Manager: *Chris Caldeira*
Marketing Assistant: *Laurel Anderson*
Advertising Project Manager: *Brian Chaffee*
Project Manager, Editorial Production: *Paul Wells*
Print/Media Buyer: *Rebecca Cross*
Permissions Editor: *Kiely Sexton*
Production Service: *Scratchgravel Publishing Services*

Text Designer: *Cheryl Carrington*
Art Editor: *Lisa Torri*
Photo Researcher: *Laura Molmud*
Copy Editor: *Mary Anne Shahidi*
Illustrator: *Rolin Graphics*
Compositor: *Scratchgravel Publishing Services*
Cover Designer: *Cheryl Carrington*
Cover Image: *Jennifer Durrant,* Sweet Pea Painting *(1978–1979),
Tate Gallery, London/Art Resource, NY*
Cover Printer: *Phoenix Color Corp*
Printer: *R R Donnelley*

Printed in the United States of America

3   4   5   6   7   08   07   06   05

For more information about our products, contact us at:
**Thomson Learning Academic Resource Center
1-800-423-0563**

For permission to use material from this text or product,
submit a request online at http://www.thomsonrights.com.
Any additional questions about permissions can be submitted
by email to thomsonrights@thomson.com.

Library of Congress Control Number: 2003116810

ISBN 0-534-57726-1

**Thomson Wadsworth
10 Davis Drive
Belmont, CA 94002-3098
USA**

Asia
Thomson Learning
5 Shenton Way #01-01
UIC Building
Singapore 068808

Australia/New Zealand
Thomson Learning
102 Dodds Street
Southbank, Victoria 3006
Australia

Canada
Nelson
1120 Birchmount Road
Toronto, Ontario M1K 5G4
Canada

Europe/Middle East/Africa
Thomson Learning
High Holborn House
50/51 Bedford Row
London WC1R 4LR
United Kingdom

Latin America
Thomson Learning
Seneca, 53
Colonia Polanco
11560 Mexico D.F.
Mexico

Spain/Portugal
Paraninfo
Calle Magallanes, 25
28015 Madrid, Spain

Dedicated to my wife, Barbara, and

my editor, Marianne, for their unwavering support,

and to the many students and teachers of cognitive psychology

whose input helped shape the creation of this book

BRIEF CONTENTS

Contents

CHAPTER 5 SENSORY MEMORY, SHORT-TERM MEMORY, AND WORKING MEMORY 135

The following experiments are described in the text, beginning on the page indicated. The icons in the left margin indicate that a figure or table illustrates:

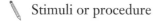 Stimuli or procedure

Results

Neuropsychological case studies are listed in the section, Applications and Everyday Experiences, on page xxxvi.

Cognitive Psychology Experiments Illustrated

CHAPTER 6   LONG-TERM MEMORY: BASIC PRINCIPLES

Chapter 7 Everyday Memory and Memory Errors

Chapter 9   Visual Imagery

Chapter 11   Problem Solving

Chapter 12   Reasoning and Decision Making

Demonstrations and "Do This"

The text contains the following demonstrations and "do this" suggestions (the latter are marked here by ∗). Both demonstrations and suggestions encourage students to go beyond just reading the text.

APPLICATIONS AND EVERYDAY EXPERIENCES

The following tables list places in the text that refer to people's experiences and real-world events. Additional connections to students' experiences are listed in the section, Demonstrations and "Do This," on page xxxii.

Neuropsychological case studies are indicated by 🗣 .

Chapter 1 Introduction	
Example	Illustrates
Sarah walks through campus	Cognition in everyday experience / 1
Cognition in the news	Cognition in everyday life / 2
Trevor returns to his old neighborhood as an adult	The complexity of cognitive mechanisms / 4
A psychological "Rip Van Winkle"	Changes that occurred due to the cognitive revolution / 14
Ways students study and what happens on exams	How to apply cognitive principles to using the "Test Yourself" questions / 19

Chapter 2 Cognition and the Brain: Basic Principles	
Example	Illustrates
Juan turns off his alarm in the morning	Connection between what happens in the brain and behavior / 24
Perseveration in a patient with prefrontal lobe damage	Localization of function in the brain / 28
Remembering a phone number or a place you have been before	How synaptic changes are responsible for memory / 35
Person with prospagnosia, who can't recognize faces	Modular organization of brain (inferotemporal cortex) / 40
Person with motion agnosia, who can't perceive motion	Modular organization of brain (medial temporal area) / 41
Speaking difficulties of a patient with Broca's aphasia	Modular organization of the brain (Broca's area) / 41

Applications and Everyday Experiences

Applications and Everyday Experiences

Chapter 4 Attention *(continued)*

Example	Illustrates
Teenagers playing video games	Effect of practice on attentional processing / 111
Observing a person learning to drive	Effect of practice on a task, and on attention / 113
Musician playing without thinking	Automatic processing / 115
Sam driving his car (reprise)	Automatic vs. controlled processing / 116
Encountering construction while driving and talking to someone in the car	Effect of task difficulty on divided attention / 118
Talking on a cell phone while driving	How using attentional resources on one task can affect performance on another task / 118
"Animal" in the woods (from Chapter 3)	Spread of attention throughout an object / 129
Patients with unilateral visual neglect	A disorder of attention / 129

Chapter 5 Sensory Memory, Short-Term Memory, and Working Memory

Example	Illustrates
My students create a "top ten" list for memory	The uses of memory / 136
Clive Wearing, who lost ability to form long-term memories from temporal lobe damage	How memory is essential to life / 137
Rachel orders a pizza on the phone	Operation of different stages of the modal model of memory / 140
The trail left by a sparkler	Persistence of vision; sensory store / 140
How a movie projector operates	Persistence of vision; sensory store / 142
Ways to remember a cognitive psychology lecture	Visual, phonological, and semantic coding / 149
The pizza shop changes its phone number, and Rachel has difficulty remembering the new one	Proactive interference / 151
Patient H.M. (continued from Chapter 2)	Evidence for different mechanisms for STM and LTM / 154
Patient K. F. (poor STM)	Dissociation between STM and LTM / 155
Reading a book; doing a puzzle	Components of working memory / 162
Looking for a restaurant in a new city	Operation of the central executive / 163

Applications and Everyday Experiences

Example	Illustrates
Jimmy G., who has Korsakoff's syndrome	Debilitating effect of being unable to form new LTMs / 179
"Lennie" from the film *Memento*	Less severe memory loss; distinction between losing STM and losing ability to form new LTMs / 181
What a student remembers just after he sits down in class	What is in STM and LTM; difference between recent and more distant LTMs / 182
Cindy says, "Jim and I saw the new James Bond movie last night."	Interaction between working memory and LTM; different kinds of information contained in LTM / 183
A series of statements about events and facts someone has remembered	Distinction between episodic and semantic memory / 185
Daniel Schacter's golf partner, with Alzheimer's	Deficient episodic memory; intact semantic and procedural memory / 186
Jon, with hippocampus damage due to birth problems	Deficient episodic memory; semantic memory in normal range / 187
Italian woman, with brain damage due to encephalitis	Episodic memory functioning; semantic memory deficient / 187
Knowing capital of United States; that people sometimes put ketchup on hot dogs; what a screen pass is in football	Connections between semantic and episodic memory / 188
How advertisements affect us	Implicit memory; propaganda effect / 191
Riding a bike; tying shoes	Examples of procedural memory / 192
Student whose mother cooks a lot of chicken	Connections strengthen encoding of LTMs / 197
Creating memory for a phone number	Synaptic strengthening during learning / 205
H.M. again	Role of hippocampus in memory / 207
Knowing answer to exam question/person's name, but being unable remember it	Retrieval failure / 209
Author forgets that he was going to take a tape on amnesia to school	Retrieval cue provided by place / 209
Student description of memories flooding back when visited grandmother's house	Retrieval cue provided by place / 209
Students studying in different places	State-dependent learning and studying / 214
What memory tells us about studying (section with many examples)	Section on improving effectiveness of studying by applying principles from memory research / 216

Chapter 8   Knowledge

Example	Illustrates
Imagine yourself in another town, where you have never been before	Categories provide knowledge about the world / 266
Seeing a person with his or her face painted black and gold	How categories ("football fan") can help us make sense of the world / 267
How U.S. students and members of Itza culture use categories, like "trees" and "birds"	Effect of culture on levels of categorization; how experience affects categorization / 283
Remembering where car is parked and properties of cars	Idea proposed by constructivist researchers to deal with rapid learning / 301

Chapter 9   Visual Imagery

Example	Illustrates
What do you experience when answering some questions such as "Are an elephant's ears round or pointy?"	Mental imagery / 310
How Paul McCartney used auditory imagery to compose the song "Yesterday"; how scientists have used imagery	Practical aspects of mental imagery / 310
Flashing lights on a mainframe computer	Nature of an "epiphenomenon" / 318
How an automobile appears in your visual field as you walk toward it	Relationship between viewing distance and the ability to perceive details / 321
M.G.S., who had part of occipital lobe removed to treat epilepsy	Occipital lobe is important for imagery / 329
A number of patients with neglect and other conditions that affect perception, imagery, or both	Relationship between perception and imagery / 330
A number of ways to use imagery to improve your memory (methods of loci and pegword)	Practical application of imagery / 341

Chapter 10   Language

Example	Illustrates
Various uses of human language	Characteristics of language; how human language differs from animal communication / 346
How a foreign language sounds like an unbroken string of words, to someone who doesn't know it	The role of meaning in solving the problem of speech segmentation / 351

Chapter 10   Language *(continued)*

Example	Illustrates
Susan says, "My mother is bugging me."	Using context of sentence to determine meaning / 355
Excerpt from *Through the Looking Glass* ("'Twas brillig and the slithy toves")	How syntax can create meaning / 360
How the reader may have interpreted a garden-path sentence	Characteristics of garden-path sentences / 360
Analogy between how we parse a sentence and parsing a visual scene (from Chapter 3)	Why researchers use garden-path sentences to determine how people understand language / 362
Quote from *New York Times* interview of George Foreman	Using our knowledge of the world to create anaphoric inference / 370
Examples of sentences about Sharon getting a headache	Different strengths of causal inference / 371
Passage from *Anna Karenina*	How real-world knowledge can help create causal inference / 371
Passage about Mary ordering in a restaurant	Making global connections / 373
A number examples of conversations	Grice's cooperative principle and conversational maxims / 377
Examples of indirect statements	Characteristics of indirect statements / 378
Examples of how U.S. and Chinese people use indirect statements	Cultural differences in use of indirect statements / 380
How American and Chinese group objects; how different cultures categorize colors	Link between language and thought / 381

Chapter 11   Problem Solving

Example	Illustrates
Anecdote about Nobel laureate Richard Feynman's thought processes	Describing the process of thinking can be humorous / 387
What students in my class think are "problems"	The definition of "problem" / 388
Being late for class	The definition of "problem" / 388
Various problems and their solutions (Duncker candle, Maier two-string, Luchins's water-jug; triangle problem, chain problem)	Principles of insight, restructuring, and mental set proposed by the Gestalt psychologists / 392
Initial steps in solving the Tower of Hanoi problem; how a person might arrange to get his or her car fixed	Means-end analysis / 399

Chapter 11   Problem Solving

Example	Illustrates
More problems and their solutions (hobbits-orcs, mutilated-checkerboard, Russian village, Duncker's radiation problem, monk-and-mountain problem)	Problem solving as search; using analogy to solve problems / 400
Impossible board problem	Value of creating a mental picture of the problem before starting / 416
Homemaker with frontal lobe damage, who had trouble preparing meals	Role of frontal lobe in problem solving / 421

Chapter 12   Reasoning and Decision Making

Example	Illustrates
Examples of everyday reasoning	Reasoning is involved in many cognitive processes / 428
Susan graduates from college; Richard is vice president of a bank	Difference between inductive and deductive reasoning / 428
Numerous examples of concrete versions of syllogisms	Validity of syllogism is determined by its form; content of syllogism can bias judgment of validity / 431
Problem involving visualizing positions of balls on a pool table	How people solve a problem by imagery, rather than applying rules / 438
Attending a "mixer" of the Artists, Beekeepers, and Chemists society	Basic principles behind using mental model approach to reasoning / 438
A discussion between an experimenter and a participant in a cross-cultural study	Basing conclusions about validity on empirical evidence vs. theoretical evidence; cross-cultural differences in reasoning / 440
Thinking about lending a friend money	Conditional syllogisms / 443
Various concrete versions of Wason four-card problem	How person's knowledge of world affects ability to solve a problem; permissions schemas / 449
A number of observations and conclusions (about crows being black; chances of the Red Sox winning the pennant; the sun rising)	Nature of inductive reasoning; differences in the strength of inductive arguments / 454
How Cheng and Holyoak came up with the idea for their cholera experiment	How inductive reasoning can be used to create hypothesis for scientific experiments / 456
Sarah thinks about what will be on Professor X's exam; Sam decides to buy from mail-order company Y	Inductive reasoning in everyday life / 457

One reason that teaching cognitive psychology is challenging is illustrated by the following paradox: An aspect of cognitive psychology that makes the field fascinating to researchers is that mental processes cannot be measured directly but must be inferred from things we can measure, such as behavior and physiological responding. However, this aspect of cognitive psychology is the very thing that makes this subject foreboding to students. Many students perceive cognitive psychology as too abstract and theoretical, and as not connected to everyday experience. Thus, the challenge is to present the subject in a way that is understandable and relevant even though students' perception of cognitive psychology as abstract and theoretical is, to some degree, accurate. My way of doing this is to follow two closely related maxims: (1) be concrete, and (2) make connections.

In writing this book, I have taken these two maxims seriously. The ideas of being concrete and making connections are the guiding principles behind my approach. This preface outlines a number of the ways this book makes cognitive psychology more real to students.

Using Examples from Life to Illustrate Cognitive Principles

One way to help students see the connections between cognitive psychology and experience is to use examples from life to illustrate cognitive principles. This is accomplished in the 125 examples—an average of about 10 per chapter—that are listed in the "Applications and Everyday Experiences" section on page xxxvi. Here are a few of them:

- Looking up a phone number to order pizza (to illustrate operation of the modal model of memory). Later, the pizza shop changes its phone number (proactive interference). (Chapter 5)

- Story about false identifications of people in criminal investigations (memory errors). (Chapter 7)

- Imagining oneself in another town, where things are different from at home, yet there is a lot that seems familiar (functions of categories). (Chapter 8)

- Familiar excerpt from *Through the Looking Glass* (how syntax can create meaning). (Chapter 10)

Describing Experiments So Students Know Where Results Came From

Another way of making the material more concrete is to present the findings of cognitive psychology not as "facts," but as outcomes of experiments, which are explained in enough detail so students will have a feel for what the researchers did. Some of these explanations are brief, such as Levin and Simons' (1997) change blindness experiment. Other examples are presented in more detail, such as Schneider and Shiffrin's (1977) classic experiments on automatic and controlled processing. The book contains 165 of these descriptions, an average of about 13 per chapter, with most of the examples accompanied by figures illustrating the procedures or the results of the experiment. Of course there are references to many other experiments as well, but these 165 experiments have been selected to be described in more detail (see the "Cognitive Psychology Experiments Illustrated" section on page xxi for a list of these experiments).

The techniques of presenting concrete illustrations from life and showing how results are obtained in the laboratory make cognitive psychology more "real" to students. But just using examples and describing experiments is not enough. For students to connect to the material, and to remember it later, they need to take the step from being passive readers to being actively involved.

Using Demonstrations to Help Students Connect to the Material

Getting students to break out of the passive mode of reading, with highlighter in hand, is not easy to accomplish, but there are features in this book that are designed to help achieve this goal. One of these features is Demonstrations. Demonstrations are integrated into the flow of the text, rather than being isolated in boxes and they are simple and easy to do. Each chapter also includes a number of suggestions to do or try. The 65 demonstrations and "Do this" suggestions help create a book that says to the students, "Here is something you can be involved with." (See page xxxii for a listing of the "Demonstrations and 'Do This'" suggestions for each chapter.)

Helping Students Connect to the Material Through "Test Yourself" and "Think About It" Questions

The idea of having the student be actively involved in the material is also encouraged by Test Yourself questions, which appear in the middle and at the end of each chapter, and which are designed to get students to access the information they have just read. Here are some examples of Test Yourself questions:

■ The idea that there are two different types of memory, one short-term, and the other long-term, is supported by experiments that measured the serial position curve, and by experiments that investigated the form of the memory code. Describe these experiments and the reasoning behind them. (Chapter 5)

- What evidence supports the statement that "meaning makes it easier to perceive letters in words, and words in spoken sentences"? (Chapter 10)

A brief section called "Knowing, Learning, and Remembering" is included just before the first Test Yourself questions in Chapter 1. This section provides some hints on how to use the Test Yourself feature most effectively, and also refers students to the end of Chapter 6, where they can read about how they can use laboratory findings about memory to increase the effectiveness of their studying. In addition, there is a feature called Think About It, at the end of each chapter, which uses "thought" questions and "doable" projects as a way to take students beyond the material in the chapter. Here are two examples of items from Think About It.

- *Thought question:* In Christopher Nolan's film *Memento*, the main character, "Lennie," is described as having lost his short-term memory. From Lennie's behavior, it is obvious that he can remember only what has happened for the most recent 1–3 minutes. What is wrong with Nolan's description of Lennie's condition, and how would you change it to match how psychologists conceive of memory? (Chapter 5)

- *Project:* Do a survey to determine people's conception of "typical" members of various categories. For example, ask a number of people to name, as quickly as possible, three typical "animals," "vehicles," or "foods." What do the results of this survey tell you about what level is "basic" for different people? What do the results tell you about the variability of different peoples' conception of categories? (Chapter 8)

Creating Coherence Through Clear, Connected Writing

My overarching goal in writing this text has been to create coherence at all levels by making connections among ideas that extend across paragraphs, across sections within a chapter, and across chapters. My goal is to make one thought flow from another—in other words, to tell a story. In a good story, readers often wonder what will happen next. This book is written is such a way that while students may not know exactly what is going to happen next, they will see how one idea follows from another.

Connections also occur across chapters, with the initial chapters designed to create a foundation for what is going to happen later. For example, as Chapter 1 introduces the history of cognitive psychology, it also introduces the idea that we cannot directly observe the operation of the mind, so we must infer its operation from the results of behavioral and physiological experiments. Chapter 2 introduces the basic concepts of cognitive neuroscience in just the amount of detail necessary for students to be able to understand the discussions of physiology in the chapters that follow. Chapter 3, on perception, focuses on one topic within perception—perceiving objects—in order to introduce a number of basic principles that not only are important for perception, but that are also central to cognition in general. These principles are: (1) the invisibility of many of our cognitive processes; (2) how we use heuristics to draw conclusions; (3) how cognition is based on representation; and (4) how brain functioning is adapted to the environment. So, as Chapters 1, 2, and 3 discuss history, brain functioning, and perception, they are also serving the larger purpose of setting the stage for the chapters that follow, on attention and memory. As the book continues, links are often made across chapters to help students become aware that principles we are discussing in one area also apply to the field as a whole.

Making Sure the Writing Is Clear, by Class Testing

While all of the features of this book have been designed to teach cognitive psychology to students in an accessible way that makes the subject clear and interesting, the real test of teaching is provided by the students themselves. I know from my experience in teaching that I have created test questions that seem perfectly clear to me but which end up being interpreted in creative, new ways by students. I have also had the uncomfortable experience of presenting a lecture that I thought explained a principle with great clarity, only to find that it was confusing to many of my students.

So the best-laid plans in teaching can be derailed by a failure to take the students' perspective into account. To prevent this from happening in this book, I used a near-final draft of the manuscript as the text for one section of my course and asked students to indicate which parts of each chapter were hard to understand or needed clarification. I received over 2,500 specific comments from 150 students. I didn't act on every suggestion students made, but when I received comments about a particular place in a chapter from a number of students, I looked at that material very closely and usually did whatever was necessary to make it more understandable (for example, by rewording, or adding an example or a figure). The result is, I believe, a presentation that will enable students to spend less time trying to figure out what is being said and more time learning the material.

Reviewed for Teachability, Accuracy, and Coverage

The final text was shaped not only by feedback from students but also by feedback from over 50 reviewers. These reviewers included both teachers of cognitive psychology, who read the chapters paying particular attention to "teachability," and experts in various content areas, who evaluated the chapters for accuracy and coverage.

Supporting the Text With a Good Illustration Program

A powerful way to make material clear to students is to include illustrations in the form of graphs to make experimental results easier to "see," diagrams to make theoretical models more concrete, and tables to present complex material in an organized way. To this end, there are over 300 graphs and diagrams and 20 tables. The guiding principle behind each of the figures and tables was to include them only if they made it easier to understand the text.

Supporting the Text With the Opportunity to Participate in Experiments

In order to provide the opportunity for students to experience being in cognitive psychology experiments for themselves, students automatically receive access to CogLab with every copy of the book. CogLab is a set of over 40 online experiments that students can run themselves, compare their data to the class average, export their data to a statistical spreadsheet, compare their results to the original experiment, or use it in other ways as determined by the class instructor. At the end of each chapter in the text, there are titles of the CogLab experiments that are relevant to that chapter.

Supporting the Text With Concept Maps

The *Concept Maps and CogLab Online Manual*, which is packaged with the text, includes 59 concept maps that provide visual representations of the way the material in the text is organized. Each box in the concept maps is accompanied by questions that can be answered in the space provided to the right of the box. These questions are cross-referenced to page numbers in the text, to help students easily review the relevant material. The maps and accompanying questions, along with the Test Yourself questions in the text, provide two ways for students to check their understanding.

Achieving a Balance Between Cutting-Edge Research and Classic Studies

So far, I have been focusing on how this book uses a variety of pedagogical tools. But what about the actual content of the book? One principle I followed in deciding what material to include was that it is important to include both cutting-edge research and classic studies. The colored bars in the histogram in Figure P.1 on the next page show that cutting-edge research is cited heavily (15 percent of the references are from 2000–2004, and 32 percent are from 1990–1999). The gray bars show that the 165 experiments that are described in more detail, and are often accompanied by a figure, are distributed between early and more recent research, with many of the studies being from the 1950s, 1960s, and 1970s.

Taking a Multilevel Approach to Content

Another principle I followed was the idea that to fully understand how the mind operates, it is necessary to study it both behaviorally and physiologically. The importance of recent work in physiology is underscored by the separate chapter on basic physiological principles and by including physiological material in every chapter. This material has been integrated into the text whenever possible, rather than always being placed it at the end of a chapter.

One of the advantages of integrating physiology and behavior is the way they can support each other when both behavioral and physiological results suggest the same

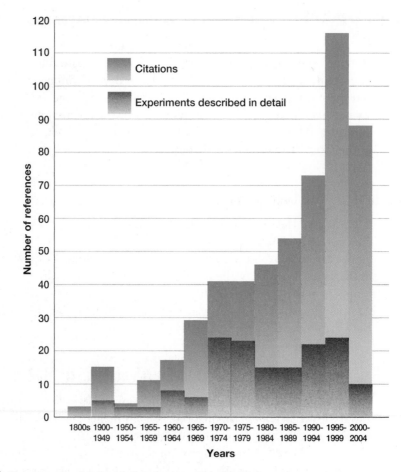

Figure P.1 Histogram showing the citations to research in this book.

conclusion. (Or when the physiology and behavior don't support each other, this makes for an interesting discussion, as occurs in a few places in the text.) Here are a few examples of situations in which behavioral and physiological results are discussed together in the text:

- *Brain activity and remembering.* Behavioral: Some words are remembered 20 hours after studying them; others are forgotten. Physiological: fMRI recordings shows that words that were remembered caused more brain activation as they were being studied than words that were forgotten (Davachi et al., 2003). (Chapter 1)

- *Emotions and memory.* Emotional pictures cause greater activation of the amygdala, and are more likely to be remembered than non-emotional pictures (Hamann et al., 1999). A patient with amygdala damage does not exhibit enhanced memory for emotional events, as normal participants do (Cahill et al., 1995). (Chapter 7)

■ *Relationship between visual imagery and perception.* Activity in the visual cortex, measured by fMRI, increases when a person perceives an actual stimulus, and similar activation occurs when a person imagines the stimulus (LeBihan et al., 1993). (Chapter 9)

Nowhere is the synergy between behavior and physiology more clear than in the 20 neuropsychological case studies that are described in the text (indicated by a brain icon in the "Applications and Everyday Experiences" section, beginning on page xxxvi). Students find case studies fascinating, and they provide yet another way of moving from abstract concepts to concrete examples. For example, the chapter on long-term memory describes a case in which a person lost his semantic memory but retained his episodic memory and another case in which the person's semantic memory remained intact, but her episodic memory was lost. Examples such as these not only reinforce an argument that originated from behavioral research (that it is valuable to distinguish between semantic and episodic memory), but also provide a real-life perspective on the terms "semantic" and "episodic."

Finally, descriptions of recent research involving cross-cultural approaches to cognition have been included in the chapters on knowledge, language, and reasoning. This research is relevant to cognitive psychology as a whole because it demonstrates the importance of recognizing that if the study of the mind is limited to mainly American and Western European college students, then the conclusions we reach may not hold for "the mind" in general but may be valid only for people of a specific population.

The bottom line regarding the content of this book is that it covers the basics of the field in a balanced way by considering both early and recent research, behavioral and physiological approaches, and emerging areas such as cross-cultural cognition.

A Message to the Student

Although most of this preface has been directed to instructors, I want to close by adding a few words to the students who will be reading this book. As you begin reading, you probably have some ideas about how the mind works from things you have read, from other media, and from your own experiences. In this book you will learn what we actually do and do not know about the mind, as determined from the results of controlled scientific research. Thus, if you thought that there is a system called "short-term memory" that can hold information for short periods of time, then you are right, and when you read the chapters on memory you will learn more about this system and how it interacts with other parts of your memory system. If you thought that some people can accurately remember things that happened to them as very young infants, you will see that there is a good chance that these reports are inaccurate. In fact, you may be surprised to learn that even more recent memories that seem extremely clear and vivid may not be entirely accurate due to basic characteristics of the way the memory system works.

But what you will learn from this book goes much deeper than simply adding more accurate information to what you already know about the mind. You will learn that there is much more going on in your mind than you are conscious of. You are conscious of experiences such as seeing something, remembering a past event, or thinking about how to solve a problem—but behind each of these experiences lies a myriad of complex and largely invisible processes. Reading this book will help you appreciate some of the "behind the scenes" activity in your mind that is responsible for everyday experiences such as perceiving, remembering, and thinking.

You will see as you read this book that cognitive psychologists have uncovered many of the hidden processes of the mind, and you will also see that there is a tremendous amount that remains to be learned. I hope you will find this book to be clear and interesting, and that you will sometimes be fascinated or surprised by some of the things you read. If you have any questions or comments about anything in the book, please feel free to contact me at bruceg@pitt.edu.

ACKNOWLEDGMENTS

The starting point for a textbook like this one is an author who has an idea for a book, but other people soon become part of the process. First, the editor provides, among other things, guidance regarding what kind of book teachers want. Then reviewers provide feedback about chapters as they are written. Finally, when the manuscript is completed, the author's illusion that the book is "finished" is quickly smashed, as the production process begins and a new group of people take over to turn the manuscript into a book. What this all means is that this book has been a group effort and that I had lots of help, both during the process of writing and after submitting the final manuscript. I would therefore like to thank the following people for their extraordinary efforts in support of this book.

- Marianne Taflinger, my editor, for her encouragement at the beginning of this project and for her support as I wrote it. Marianne was my editor for the fourth, fifth, and sixth editions of *Sensation and Perception*, and I am happy to note that this is the first book we have created together from the ground up. My experience in working with Marianne over the years, as our relationship has continually evolved, is one reason that this book is dedicated to her.

- Vicki Knight, of Wadsworth's psychology group, for her leadership of the psychology list, and for her friendship.

- Anne Draus of Scratchgravel Publishing Services, who brought together all of the various components of this book, while at the same time providing the support and understanding that helped me get through the sometimes trying process of transforming the manuscript and rough sketches of the art program into a finished book. It was a pleasure working with you, Anne!

- Lisa Torri, for her direction of the art program. I consider myself extremely lucky to have worked with Lisa on four previous books, and I was delighted when I heard that she was on board for this one as well. I am grateful both for her expertise in handling the art program and for the gentle touch she brings to dealing with what is a complex process, especially for the first edition of a book.

- Justin Courts, for dealing so expertly with my requests when I contacted the office, and for his contagious enthusiasm for the power of technology. I also thank Nicole Root, who served in the same capacity during the early years of this project.

- Vernon Boes, for coordinating the design of the book, for helping us create the cover we wanted all along, and for his cryptic and entertaining email messages.

- Cheryl Carrington, for her elegant and functional design.

- Paul Wells, production project manager, for getting all of the pieces together on schedule, even when I wanted to make a few more changes.
- Jennifer Keever, who edited the supplements (*Instructor's Manual* and *Concept Maps and CogLab Online Manual*). I thank her for her impressive attention to detail and for being fun to work with.
- Mary Anne Shahidi for her expert copy editing.
- Laura Molmud for her photo research and Kiely Sexton for obtaining permissions.
- Chris Calderia and Lori Grebe Cook, marketing managers, for creating clear and informative marketing materials.
- Brain Chaffee, advertising project manager, for his elegant writing and for supporting this book by creating materials that tell cognitive psychology instructors why this book will work in their classes.
- Lisa Maxfield for her work on the demanding task of creating an instructor' manual.
- Randall Baker of Blue Heron electronic art studio for creating and executing the "concept maps" that accompany this book, and for doing what was needed to make them "work," even when I wrote too much text and there wasn't enough space.

In addition to the help I received from all of the above people on the editorial and production side, I received a great deal of help from teachers and researchers who gave me feedback on what I wrote, made suggestions regarding new work in the field, and provided illustrations for the text. I thank the following people for their help in these areas:

Thomas Alley
Clemson University

Gerry Altmann
University of York

Cheryl Anagnopoulos
Black Hills State University

Chris Ball
College of William & Mary

Ute Bayen
University of North Carolina

Sheila Black
University of Alabama

James Brewer
Johns Hopkins University

Richard Catrambone
Georgia Tech

Steven Christman
University of Toledo

James Chumbley
University of Massachusetts

William Collins
University of Michigan

Brian Crabb
Western Washington University

Tim Curran
University of Colorado

Lila Davachi
New York University

Robert Durham
University of Colorado–Colorado Springs

Martha Farah
University of Pennsylvania

Julie Fiez
University of Pittsburgh

Ira Fischler
University of Florida

Greg Francis
Purdue University

Jane Gaultney
University of North Carolina,
Charlotte

Isabel Gauthier
Vanderbilt University

Gabriel Kreiman
California Institute of Technology

Linda Henkel
Fairfield University

Robert Hines
University of Arkansas at Little Rock

Audrey Holland
University of Arizona

Keith Holyoak
University of California, Los Angeles

Peter Howell
University College London

Kathy Johnson
Indiana University–Purdue University
Indianapolis

Beena Khurana
Cornell University

Derek Mace
Pennsylvania State University,
Behrend

Barbara Malt
Lehigh University

Lisa Maxfield
California State University,
Long Beach

Richard Mayer
University of California, Santa Barbara

James L. McClelland
Carnegie-Mellon University

Jeff Mio
Cal Poly Pomona

Kristy Neilson
Marquette University

Charles Perfetti
University of Pittsburgh

John Philbeck
George Washington University

Gabriel Radvansky
University of Notre Dame

Eric Reichle
University of Pittsburgh

Lisa Saunders
University of Oregon

Christian Schunn
University of Pittsburgh

Bennett Schwartz
Florida International University

Carl Scott
University of St. Thomas

Aimée Surprenant
Purdue University

Greg Simpson
University of Kansas

Annette Taylor
University of San Diego

Natasha Tokowicz
University of Pittsburgh

Jyotsna Vaid
Texas A&M

Douglas Waring
Appalachian State University

Tessa Warren
University of Pittsburgh

The following people responded to a Wadsworth survey of cognitive psychology teachers, which was conducted a number of years ago. As I was beginning this project in 1999, I relied heavily on the results of this survey to shape the content and approach of this book. Although these people did not know that their responses would, years later, be used to help create a new cognitive psychology text, I would like to thank them for providing valuable information about their courses, about what they wanted in a cognitive psychology text, and about their conceptualization of the field of cognitive psychology. I hope that many of you will see that some of the things you suggested became part of this book. If anyone's name is misspelled (which occasionally occurs due to errors in entering the handwritten survey responses into the computer), please let me know at bruceg@pitt.edu so the spelling can be corrected in the next printing. Note that university affiliations are those at the time of the survey and may have changed.

Herve Abdi, University of Texas, Dallas
Jennifer Ackil, Gustavus Adolphus College
David Albritton, University of Pittsburgh
Mark Alcorn, University of Northern Colorado
Joel Alexander, Western Oregon University
Gordon A. Allen, Miami University
Tom R. Alley, Clemson University
Julie A. Allison, Pittsburg State University
Paul C. Amrhein, University of New Mexico
Richard Anderson, Bowling Green State University
Pam Ansburg, Slippery Rock University
Tim Babler, Edgewood College
Andrea Backscheider, University of Notre Dame
Maryann Baenninger, The College of New Jersey
Susan Baillet, University of Portland
Carl Bartling, McNeese State University
Ute J. Bayen, University of North Carolina
John Bechtold, Messiah College
Andrew Becker, Monmouth College
Robert C. Becklen, Ramapo College of New Jersey
Susan E. Beers, Sweet Briar College
Denise Beike, University of Arkansas
Martha Ann Bell, Virginia Technical University
Timothy A. Bender, SW Missouri State University
Jane Berry, University of Richmond
Dorrit Billman, Georgia Institute of Technology

Dawn Blasko, Pennsylvania State University, Erie
Stephen Blessing, University of Florida
Michael Bloch, University of San Francisco
Richard A. Block, Montana State University
David B. Boles, Rensselaer Polytechnic Institute
Marilyn Boltz, Haverford College
Terri Bonebright, DePauw University
Gary Bradshaw, University of Illinois
Paul Van Den Broek, University of Minnesota
Alan S. Brown, Southern Methodist University
Tracy Brown, University of North Carolina, Asheville
James P. Buchanan, University of Scranton
Stephen Buggie, University of New Mexico
Danuta Bukatko, College of the Holy Cross
Dan Burns, Union College
Gregory Burton, Seton Hall University
Darrell Butler, Ball State University
Linda Buyer, Governors State University
Thomas Capo, SUNY at Fredonia
Mark Casteel, Pennsylvania State University, York
Claude G. Cech, University of Southern Louisiana
Stephen Chew, Samford University
Christine Chiarello, University of California, Riverside
James I. Chumbley, University of Massachusetts
James Craig Clarke, Salisbury State University

Dov Cohen, University of Illinois

David B. Conner, Truman State University

Paul F. Cunningham, Rivier College

Thomas F. Cunningham, St. Lawrence University

Laura DaCosta, University of Illinois at
Springfield

Donna Dahlgren, Indiana University Southeast

Darlene DeMarie-Dreblow, Muskingum College

Rayne Sperling Dennison, West Virginia
University

Peter Derks, William and Mary University

Ann Sloan Devlin, Connecticut College

Patricia deWinstanely, Oberlin College

R. Dale Dick, University of Wisconsin, Eau Clare

Don Diener, University of Nevada

Wallace E. Dixon, Jr., Heidelberg College

James Dooley, Mercy College

Barbara Dosher, University of California, Irvine

Gina Dow, Dension University

James Duke, Linfield College

John Dunlosky, University of North Carolina,
Greensboro

Dana Dunn, Moravian College

Robert Durham, University of Colorado,
Colorado Springs

Frank Durso, University of Oklahoma

Lani Van Dusen, Utah State University

Alan Eby, Eastern Mennosite University

Nina Eduljee, St. Joseph's College

David G. Elmes, Washington & Lee University

Laurel End, Mount Mary College

Corinne S. Enright, University of Wisconsin,
Stout

Anders K. Ericsson, Florida State University

Monica Fabiani, University of Missouri,
Columbia

Ramona Fears, University of Evansville

Alan Ferris, Mount Marty College

Phil Finney, Southeast Missouri State University

Ronald Fisher, Florida International University

Charles L. Folk, Villanova University

Peter Foltz, New Mexico State University

Gary B. Forbach, Washburn University

Bradley K. Fox, Mt. Vernon Nazarene College

Gregory Francis, Purdue University

Christina Frederick, Southern Utah University

Glenn Gamst, University of La Verne

Mark Garrison, Kentucky State University

Jane F. Gaultney, University of North Carolina,
Charlotte

Mary Gauvain, University of California,
Riverside

Michael Gayle, SUNY at New Paltz

Nancy R. Gee, SUNY, Fredonia

John Geiger, Marycrest International University

Janet M. Gibson, Grinnell College

Douglas J. Gillen, New Mexico State University

Elizabeth Glisky, University of Arizona

Judith Goggin, University of Texas at El Paso

Hank Gorman, Austin College

Gail Gottfried, Occidental College

Kerry Green, University of Arizona

Jennifer Griffin, Thiel College

Scott Gronlund, University of Oklahoma

Bea Grosh, Millersville University

David E. Grover, Indiana University Purdue

Lisa Hager, Midway College

Cathy Hale, University of Puget Sound

Lynda Hall, Ohio Wesleyan University

Don Hall, Radford University

Andrea Halpern, Bucknell University

John Halpin, Eureka College

Aura Hanna, Virginia Commonwealth University

Heidi Harley, New College of University of
South Florida

Catherine L. Harris, Boston University

Richard Harris, Kansas State University

Frank Hassebrock, Denison University

Tonia S. Heffner, University of Tennessee at
Chattanooga

Myra Heinrich, Mesa State University

Diana Heise, Millsaps College

Monton Heller, Winston-Salem State University

Linda Henkel, University of North Florida

Douglas Herrmann, Indiana State University

Thomas J. Hershberger, Chatham College

Tom Hewett, Drexel University

James V. Hinrichs, University of Iowa

Susan Holleran, Oakwood College

Arlene Horne, New Mexico Highlands University

John Horner, The Colorado College

David T. Horner, University of Wisconsin Oshkosh

Joseph Hosie, New York University

James H. Howard, Catholic University

Lumei Hui, Humboldt State University

Ray Hyman, University of Oregon

Lisa Isenberg, University of Wisconsin, River Falls

Lorna Hernandez Jarvis, Hope College

Timothy Jay, North Adams State College

Douglas N. Johnson, Colgate University

Kathy Johnson, Indiana University–Purdue University Indianapolis

Helen J. Kahn, Northern Michigan University

George Kallingal, University of Guam

Richard A. Kasschau, University of Houston

Beena Khurana, Cornell University

In-Kyeong Kim, La Sierra University

Gary Klatsky, SUNY, Oswego

Nancy Knous, NW Oklahoma State University

Barbara Koslowski, Cornell University

Kenneth Kotousky, Carnegie Mellon University

Richard Krinsky, University of Colorado

Neal Kroll, University of California, Davis

Kevin R. Krull, University of Houston

V. K. Kumar, West Chester University

Geoffrey Lasky, Adelphi University

Gary D. Laver, California Polytechnic University, San Luis Obispo

Adrienne Lee, New Mexico State University

Dan Levin, Kent State University

Susan Levine, University of Chicago

Diana Lewis, Elms College

Jill Lohmeier, University of Alabama in Huntsville

Robert Lorch, University of Kentucky

Andrew Lotto, Loyola University Chicago

Eugene A. Lovelace, Alfred University

B. Lucero-Wagoner, California State University, Northridge

Mark R. Ludorf, Stephen F. Austin State University

John Lutz, East Carolina University

Mary Jean Lynch, North Central College

Jan H. Lynch, Roanoke College

Leslie A. MacGregor, Berry College

Neil Macmillan, Brooklyn College

William A. Mahler, Concordia College

Barbara Mailhiot, Angelo State University

Ruth Maki, Texas Tech University

Margo Malakoff, Harvey Mudd College

Peter A. Mangan, University of Virginia

Chris Mann, Woodbury University

Michael Marcell, College of Charleston

Paul D. Markel, Minot State University

Robert P. Markley, Fort Hays State University

William Marks, University of Memphis

Richard L. Marsh, University of Georgia

Chad J. Marsolek, University of Minnesota

Charles F. Matter, University of Wisconsin, Green Bay

Gail Mauner, University of Buffalo

Lisa Maxfield, California State University, Long Beach

Frank McAndrew, Knox College

Benjamin Miller, Salem State College

Kevin Morrin, Indiana-Purdue University

Andrea Groves Mudd, Silver Lake College

Neil W. Mulligan, Southern Methodist University

Sharon A. Multer, Western Kentucky University

John Murray, Georgia Southern University

Ian Neath, Purdue University

Leanne Neilson, California Lutheran University

Douglas L. Nelson, University of South Florida

Kristy A. Nielson, Marquette University

B. Nodine, Beaver College

Kent L. Norman, University of Maryland

A. Norvilas, Saint Xavier University
Laura Novick, Vanderbilt University
Michael W. O'Boyle, Iowa State University
Stephan Ohlsson, University of Illinois at Chicago
Robert E. Otis, Ripon College
Scott Ottaway, Western Washington University
Hajime Otuni, Central Michigan University
Ken Paap, New Mexico State University
Robert G. Pachella, University of Michigan
Janet Parker, Florida International University
Ralph Parsons, Carroll College
Stephen T. Paul, Mississippi State University
Jennifer P. Peluso, Emory University
Robert Peterson, Illinois State University
Colin Phillips, University of Delaware
Joan Piroch, Coastal Carolina University
David B. Pisoni, Indiana University
David J. Pittenger, Marietta College
Richard Platt, St. Mary's College of Maryland
John Polich, University of California, San Diego
Derek Price, Wheaton College
Robert Radtuc, Southern Illinois University
Gabriel Radvansky, University of Notre Dame
Gary E. Raney, University of Illinois at Chicago
Alliston K. Reid, Wofford College
Kirsten Rewey, Saint Vincent College
Charles L. Richman, Wake Forest University
Lance Rips, Northwestern University
Bret Roark, Oklahoma Baptist University
A.E. Roberts, Cataluba College
Doug Rohrer, GWU
Miguel Roig, St. John's University
Matt Rossano, Southeastern Louisiana University
Kevin Sailor, Lehman College
James R. Sawusch, SUNY at Buffalo
Steven Schandler, Chapman University
A. R. Schmauder, University of South Carolina
Stephen R. Schmidt, Middle Tennessee State University
Laura F. Schneider, Texas Wesleyan University
Gregory Schraw, University of Nebraska
P. Schulman, SUNY Institute of Technology

Miriam W. Schustack, California State University, San Marcos
Wendy Schweigert, Bradley University
Carl Scott, University of St. Thomas
Jay A. Seitz, York College, CUNY
Michele E. Shady, SUNY, Geneseo
Eldar Shafir, Princeton University
James Shaneau, Kansas State University
Matthew Sharps, California State University, Fresno
Raymond Shaw, Merrimack College
Tim Shearon, Albertson College of Idaho
Alice Sheppard, University of Maine, Presque Isle
Wendy E. Shields, University of Montana
T. C. Sim, Sam Houston State University
Valerie Sims, Cedar Crest College
Patricia Siple, Wayne State University
Louisa M. Slowiaczek, University of Albany–SUNY
David Smith, Middleburg College
Janet V. Smith, Pittsburg State University
Brenda Smith, Westmont College
Michael Stadler, University of Missouri
Margo A. Storm, Temple University
Walter L. Stroud, Mars Hill College
Padmanabhan Suderan, University of Wisconsin
John R. Surber, University of Wisconsin, Milwaukee
Aimee Surprenant, Purdue University
Dan Swift, University of Michigan, Dearborn
Linda K. Swindell, Anderson University
Holly A. Taylor, Tufts University
Annette Kujawski Taylor, University of San Diego
Thomas Thieman, College of St. Catherine
Robin Thomas, Miami University
Margaret Thomas, University of Central Florida
Burt Thompson, Niagara University
Joseph B. Thompson, Washington & Lee University
Pamela S. Tidwell, Auburn University at Montgomery
Sharon Tkacz, Kent State University

Thomas R. Tradasso, The University of Chicago
David Trafimow, New Mexico State University
Anne Treisman, Princeton University
R. Treman, Wayne State University
Pamela Tsang, Wright State University
Marilyn L. Turner, Wichita State University
Barbara Tversky, Stanford University
Kathy VanGiffen, California State University,
    Long Beach
Cyma VanPetten, University of Arizona
Edward Vela, California State University, Chico
Paul Verhaeghen, Syracuse University
Peter Vishton, Amherst College

Walter F. Wagor, Indiana University East
X. T. Wang, University of South Dakota
Douglas A. Waring, Appalachian State University
Charles A. Weaver III, Baylor University
Robert C. Webb, Suffolk University
John Webster, Towson University
Tony Whetstone, East Carolina University
Hedy White, Western Carolina University
Lynn Winters, Purchase College, SUNY
William Wozniak, University of Nebraska at
    Kearney
Nukhet D. Yarbrough, Coe College
David Zehr, Plymouth State College

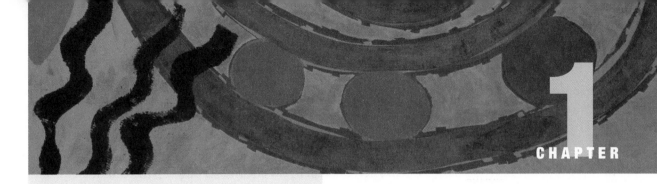

CHAPTER 1

Introduction to Cognitive Psychology

Some Questions We Will Consider

✔ What does the field of cognitive psychology include?

✔ How is cognitive psychology relevant to my life?

✔ Are there practical applications of cognitive psychology?

✔ How is it possible to study the inner workings of the mind, when we can't really see the mind directly?

■   ■   ■

Sarah is walking across campus. She stops for a moment to talk with a friend about the movie they saw last night, but can't talk for long, because she has an appointment with her advisor to plan her schedule for next term, so she says goodbye and heads off in the direction of her advisor's office.

This minor event in Sarah's life is not particularly exciting. It is just one of many things that happened to her on a typical day. But if we stop for a moment to consider what's involved in this simple sequence of behaviors, we see that beneath the simplicity lies mental processes such as the following:

- Perception: Sarah is able to see her way through campus, to recognize her friend, and to hear her speak.

- Attention: As she walks across campus, she focuses on only a portion of her environment, but seeing her friend captures her attention.

- Memory: Sarah remembers her friend's name, that she has an appointment, and how to get to her advisor's office. She finds it interesting that although she and her friend saw the same movie, they remember different things about it.

- Language: She talks with her friend about the movie they saw last night.

- Reasoning and decision making: Sarah needs to decide which courses to take. This is not a major decision but a big decision soon looms on the horizon, because Sarah needs to decide what to do after graduation. Should she go to graduate school or start looking for a job?

Not only is it easy to provide examples of cognition in everyday experience, but it is also easy to find examples in the news.

- Perception: Thousands of deaf people have had a cochlear implant operation that enables them to hear. Researchers are also working to develop devices that would provide sight to the blind.

- Attention: Researchers testify at a hearing of the New York State legislature that cell phones distract attention from driving. The legislature agrees and bans the use of cell phones while driving in New York

- Memory: Memory researchers search for ways to prevent the memory losses that are associated with aging.

- Memory: Research studies show that a large number of innocent people have been convicted of crimes based on faulty memory by eyewitnesses at crime scenes.

- Problem solving and reasoning: A panel of experts ponders evidence to determine the cause of the power blackout that hit tens of millions of people in the United States and Canada in August 2003. → woods! [A'daeks, WA)

Each of the items on the preceding lists are aspects of **cognition***—the mental processes that are involved in perception, attention, memory, problem solving, reasoning, and making decisions. **Cognitive psychology** is the branch of psychology concerned with the scientific study of cognition.

---

*Key terms that appear in color in the text are defined in the Glossary at the end of the book.

How can we go beyond simply labeling different aspects of cognition, as we did for Sarah's walk across campus and the examples of cognition in the news? The first step is to realize that many of the processes involved in cognition are complex and often hidden from view.

The Complexity of Cognition

Many of the cognitions we listed to describe Sarah's behavior occurred without much effort on her part. She easily perceived the scene around her and recognized her friend. It took a little more effort to remember some of the details of the movie she saw the night before, but she accomplished this without much difficulty. However, when cognitive psychologists have looked more closely at processes such as these, they have found that beneath this ease and apparent simplicity lie complexities that may not be initially obvious.

To illustrate some of these complexities, let's consider attention. As Sarah walked through campus, her eyes were flooded with images, but she attended closely to just a few. Thus, in the scene shown in Figure 1.1, Sarah was aware of her friend, whom she saw approaching on the sidewalk, but she was hardly aware of the person approaching on her right, who actually looms much larger, but whom she doesn't know. This situation enables

Figure 1.1 Sarah is walking toward her friend, who is waving in the distance. She is aware of her friend, but has little awareness of the stranger who is passing on her right, even though he is much closer.

us to pose the following question: Even though both people are clearly present in Sarah's field of view, what causes her to be very aware of her friend, but hardly aware of the person she doesn't know?

Another hint at the complexity of attention is given in the following demonstration.

◣ Demonstration

Naming Colors

Turn to Color Plate 1.1, inside the front cover. Your task is to name, as quickly as possible, the color of ink used to print each of the circles. For example, starting in the upper left corner, and going across, you would say, "red, blue. . ." and so on. Time yourself (or a friend whom you have enlisted to do this task), and determine how many seconds it takes to report the colors of all of the circles. Then repeat the same task for Color Plate 1.2, remembering that your task is to specify the color of the *ink*, not the color name that is spelled out. ■

If you found it harder to name the colors of the words than the colors of the circles, then you were experiencing the **Stroop effect,** which was first described by J. R. Stroop in 1935. This effect, in which the names of the words interferes with the ability to name the colors of the ink, is caused by people's inability to avoid paying attention to the words, even though they are instructed to ignore them. Thus, while our example involving Sarah showed we can focus attention on certain things and ignore others, the Stroop effect shows that some stimuli can affect our behavior by forcing themselves on our consciousness, even if we are actively trying to ignore them.

Another example of the complexity of cognition is provided by the following situation. Trevor went to grade school in a suburb of St. Louis, but his family moved to Portland, Oregon, many years ago, and he has only dim memories of his grade school days. After many years, he returns to St. Louis to attend a professional conference, and decides to visit his old neighborhood. Much to his surprise, as soon as he starts approaching his old grade school, memories for things he hadn't thought about for decades come flooding back. Trevor's experience demonstrates that although it is sometimes difficult to remember things, returning to the place where the memories were originally formed can reveal the memories that were there all along. What is behind this interesting property of memory? This is another problem for cognitive psychologists to solve.

These examples illustrate that experiences that involve attention and memory (and other cognitions, as well) involve "hidden" processes that we may not be aware of. We can think about these hidden processes by drawing an analogy between the way the mind works and what happens as an audience watches a play at the theater. The audience is aware of the drama created by the characters in the play. But there is a lot going on backstage that they are unaware of. Some actors are changing costumes, others are listening for their cues, and stagehands are moving sets into place for the next scene change. Just as a great deal of activity occurs backstage in a play, a great deal of "backstage" activity goes on in your mind.

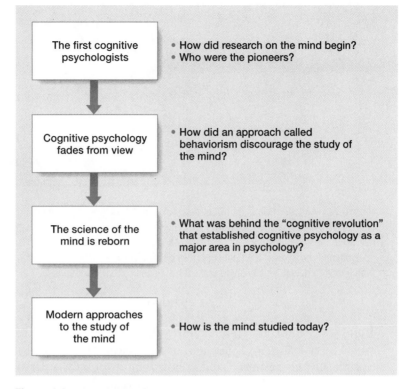

Figure 1.2 Flow diagram for this chapter.

One of the goals of this book is to show you how cognitive psychologists have revealed the hidden processes that occur "behind the scenes." This chapter is the beginning of a story of cognitive psychology research that began over 100 years ago, even before the field of psychology was formally founded. To give us perspective on where cognitive psychology is today, it is important to see where it came from, and so we will begin by describing some of the pioneering early research on the mind that began in the 19th century (Figure 1.2). We then consider what happened in the first half of the 20th century, when studying the mind became unfashionable; what happened in the second half of the 20th century, when the study of the mind began to flourish again; and how present-day research on the mind is approached by psychologists and by researchers in other fields.

The First Cognitive Psychologists

Cognitive psychology research began in the 19th century at a time when there was no field called cognitive psychology—or even, for that matter, psychology. In 1868, eleven years before the founding of the first laboratory of scientific psychology, Franciscus Donders, a Dutch physiologist, did one of the first cognitive psychology experiments.

(a) Press *J* when light goes on.   (b) Press *J* for left light, *K* for right.

Figure 1.3 A modern version of Donders' (1868) reaction time experiment. (a) the simple reaction-time task; and (b) the choice reaction-time task. For the simple reaction time task, the participant pushes the J key when the light goes on. For the choice reaction time task the participant pushes the J key if the left light goes on, and the K key if the right light goes on. The purpose of Donders' experiment was to determine the time it took to decide which key to press for the choice reaction-time task.

Donders' Reaction-Time Experiment   Donders conducted research on what today would be called **mental chronometry**, measuring the time-course of cognitive processes. Specifically, he was interested in how long it took for a person to make a decision. He determined this by using a measure called **reaction time**, the time between presentation of a stimulus and a person's response to the stimulus.

Donders measured two types of reaction time. To determine **simple reaction time**, he asked participants to make a response, such as pushing a button, as quickly as possible after seeing a flash of light (Figure 1.3a). To determine **choice reaction time**, he asked participants to push one of two buttons in response to a flash of light. They were to push one button if the light was on the left, and another button if the light was on the right (Figure 1.3b).

The rationale behind Donders' simple reaction-time experiment is shown in Figure 1.4a. The process begins with presentation of the stimulus (the light). This is followed by the participants' mental response to the stimulus (perceiving the light), which leads to the participants' response (pushing the button). The reaction time (dashed line) is the time between the stimulus and the behavioral response.

A similar diagram for the choice RT experiment is shown in Figure 1.4b. In this diagram, the mental response includes not only perceiving the light but also deciding which button to push. Donders reasoned that the choice reaction time would be longer than the simple reaction time, because of the time it takes to make the decision. Thus, the difference in reaction time between the simple and choice conditions would indicate how long it took to make the decision.

Donders found that it took one-tenth of a second longer to respond in the choice reaction-time condition, so he concluded that it took one-tenth of a second to decide which

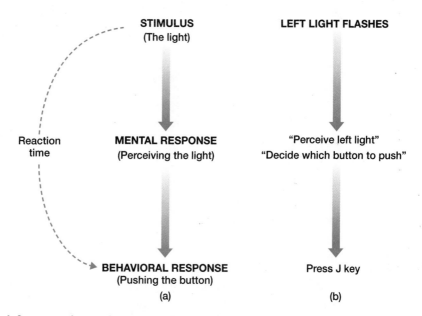

Figure 1.4 Sequence of events between presentation of the stimulus and the behavioral response, in Donders' experiment. The dashed line indicates that Donders measured reaction time, the time between presentation of the light and the participant's response. (a) simple reaction-time task; (b) choice reaction-time task.

button to push. His experiment is important both because it was one of the first cognitive psychology experiments, and also because it illustrates something extremely important about studying the mind—the mental response (perceiving the light, and deciding which button to push, in this example) cannot be measured directly, but must be inferred from the participants' behavior. We can see why this is so by noting the dashed line in Figure 1.4a, which indicates that, when Donders measured the reaction time, he was measuring the relationship between the presentation of the stimulus and the participant's response. He did not measure the mental response, but inferred how long it took, by measuring the reaction time. The fact that mental responses can't be measured directly, but must be inferred, is a principle that holds not only for Donders' experiment, but for all research in cognitive psychology.

Helmholtz's Unconscious Inference   Hermann von Helmholtz was another 19th-century researcher who was concerned with studying the operation of the mind. Helmholtz, who was Professor of Physiology at the University of Heidelberg (1858) and Professor of Physics at the University of Berlin (1871), was one of the preeminent physiologists and physicists of his day. He made basic discoveries in physiology and physics, and also developed the ophthalmoscope (the device that an optometrist or ophthalmologist uses to look into your eye) and proposed theories of object perception, color vision,

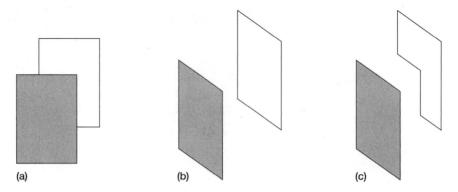

Figure 1.5 The display in (a) looks like (b) a gray rectangle in front of a light rectangle; but it could be (c) a gray rectangle and a six-sided figure that are lined up appropriately.

and hearing. One of the conclusions he reached from his research on perception is a principle called the theory of **unconscious inference,** which states that some of our perceptions are the result of <u>unconscious assumptions</u> that we make about the environment.

The theory of unconscious inference was proposed to account for our ability to create perceptions from stimulus information that can be seen in more than one way. For example, what do you see in the display in Figure 1.5a? According to the theory of unconscious inference, we infer that Figure 1.5a is a rectangle covering another rectangle, because of experiences we have had with similar situations in the past. Our inference is called unconscious because it occurs without our awareness or any conscious effort. Most people perceive a gray rectangle in front of a white rectangle, as shown in Figure 1.5b. But as Figure 1.5c indicates, this display could have been caused by a six-sided white shape positioned to line up with the upper right-hand corner of the gray rectangle. Helmholtz's idea that we infer much of what we know about the world, was an early statement of what is now considered to be a central principle of modern cognitive psychology.

The First Psychology Laboratories   People like Donders and Helmholtz, who were investigating the mind in the 19th century, were usually based in departments of physiology, physics, or philosophy, since there were no psychology departments at the time. But in 1879 Wilhelm Wundt founded the first laboratory of scientific psychology at the University of Leipzig, with the goal of studying the mind scientifically. He and his students carried out reaction-time experiments, measured basic properties of the senses, particularly vision and hearing, and developed a technique called **analytic introspection.**

Analytic introspection is a procedure in which trained participants describe their experiences and thought processes in response to stimuli presented under controlled conditions. For example, in one experiment, Wundt asked participants to describe their experience of hearing a five-note chord played on the piano. Wundt was interested in whether they heard the five notes as a single unit or if they were able to hear the individual notes.

Wundt made a tremendous contribution to psychology by training PhD's who established psychology departments at other universities, many in the United States. Thus, by the beginning of the 20th century, psychology was taking hold in the United States, with much of the research being inspired by Wundt's interest in understanding mental functioning. However, by the second decade of the 20th century, events were about to occur that would shift the focus of psychology away from the study of mental processes and toward the study of observable behavior.

THE DECLINE AND REBIRTH OF COGNITIVE PSYCHOLOGY

At the beginning of the 20th century, psychology was firmly established at a number of universities in the United States, and was spreading rapidly. Research in most of these departments was conducted in the tradition of Wundt's laboratory, with its emphasis on uncovering the hidden processes of the mind. This emphasis was to change, however, because of the efforts of John Watson, who received his PhD in psychology in 1904 from the University of Chicago.

The Rise of Behaviorism

The story of how John Watson founded an approach to psychology called behaviorism is well known to introductory psychology students. We will briefly review it here because of its importance to the story of cognitive psychology. Early in his career, Watson experienced dissatisfaction with the method of analytic introspection. His problems with this method were that it produced extremely variable results from person to person, and that these results were difficult to verify because they were interpreted in terms of invisible inner mental processes. One of Watson's most famous papers, "Psychology as the behaviorist views it," set forth the goals of a new approach to psychology, which Watson called behaviorism.

> Psychology as the Behaviorist sees it is a purely objective, experimental branch of natural science. Its theoretical goal is the prediction and control of behavior. Introspection forms no essential part of its methods, nor is the scientific value of its data dependent upon the readiness with which they lend themselves to interpretation in terms of consciousness. . . . What we need to do is start work upon psychology making behavior, not consciousness, the objective point of our attack. (Watson, 1913, pp. 158, 176)

There are three key parts of this quote: (1) Watson rejects introspection as a method, (2) he eliminates consciousness as a topic for study, and (3) he suggests that psychology's main topic for study should be behavior. In another part of this paper, Watson also proclaims that "psychology must discard all references to consciousness; when it need no longer delude itself into thinking that it is making mental states the object of observation"

(p. 163). Watson's goal was to eliminate the mind as a topic of study in psychology, and to replace it with the study of directly observable behavior.

Over a period of about 20 years after the publication of Watson's paper, behaviorism gradually became the dominant force in American psychology. Watson's most famous experiment was the "little Albert" experiment, in which Watson and Rosalie Rayner (1920) caused a 9-month-old boy named Albert to become frightened of a rat by presenting a loud noise every time the rat (which Albert had liked) came close to Albert. Watson used this result to argue that behavior can be analyzed without any reference to the mind. He was not concerned with what was going on inside little Albert's head, either physiologically or mentally. His main concern was how pairing noise with the rat affected Albert's behavior.

One of the most influential psychologists of the 20th century, B. F. Skinner, furthered Watson's "anti-mind" manifesto through his research on operant conditioning, which focused on determining how behavior is strengthened by presentation of positive reinforcers, such as food, or withdrawal of negative reinforcers, such as a shock. For example, Skinner showed that reinforcing a rat for pressing a bar will maintain or cause an increase in the rat's rate of bar pressing. Notice that Watson and Skinner were both measuring behavior, but instead of using behavior to infer what was going on in the person's or animal's mind, they were interested in studying behavior in its own right.

Skinner's ideas about operant conditioning influenced an entire generation of psychologists and dominated psychology in the United States during the 1940s, 1950s, and into the 1960s. Psychologists applied the techniques of conditioning to things like classroom teaching and treating psychological disorders. They were also finding practical applications for conditioning, many of which are still used today. However, beginning in the 1950s, changes began to occur in psychology, which would eventually lead to the rebirth of interest in the mind.

The Decline of Behaviorism

One of the important events that led to the decline of behaviorism was the publication of Skinner's book *Verbal Behavior*, in 1957 (see time line in Figure 1.6). In this book, Skinner explained that children learn language by imitation and reinforcement. They imitate speech that they hear, and correct speech is rewarded. But Noam Chomsky (1959), a linguist from the Massachusetts Institute of Technology (MIT), published a scathing review of Skinner's book, in which he pointed out that children say many sentences that they have never heard ("I hate you mommy," for example), and that during the normal course of language development, they go through a stage in which they use incorrect grammar, such as "the boy hitted the ball," even though this incorrect grammar has never been reinforced.

Chomsky saw language development as being determined not by imitation or reinforcement, but by an inborn program that holds across cultures. Chomsky's analysis led psychologists to reconsider the idea that language and other complex behaviors such as

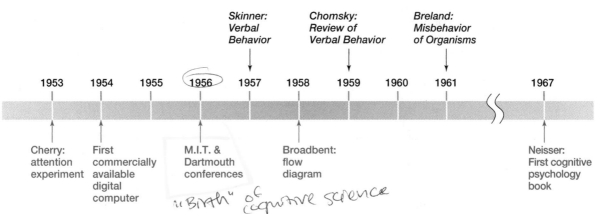

Figure 1.6 Time line, showing events associated with the decline of behaviorism (above the line) and events that led to the development of the information-processing approach to cognitive psychology (below the line).

problem solving and reasoning can be explained by operant conditioning, and they began to realize that to understand complex cognitive behaviors it is necessary to consider not only the relation between stimulation and its consequences, but to also consider how the mind works.

Another event that led people to question behaviorism was the publication in 1961 of a paper titled "The Misbehavior of Organisms" by two of Skinner's students, Keller Breland and Marian Breland. The title of their paper was, significantly, a takeoff on the title of Skinner's 1938 book *The Behavior of Organisms*, in which Skinner described how behavior can be controlled by presenting reinforcements.

Drawing on their experience in using operant conditioning to train animals for circuses, TV, and film stunts, the Brelands described a number of situations in which their attempts to condition an animal's behavior ran head-on into the animal's built-in instincts. For example, according to the theory of operant conditioning, rewarding a behavior should increase its frequency. However, when the Brelands attempted to train a raccoon to drop two coins in a piggy bank by rewarding this response with food, the raccoon did not cooperate. After the raccoon was rewarded with food for dropping two coins into the bank, it took the next two coins and began rubbing them together, just as they do to remove the shells of newly caught crayfish. Eventually, the coin-rubbing response overpowered the coin-dropping response and the Brelands had to abandon their attempt to condition the raccoon. The Brelands used this and other examples to emphasize the importance of biologically programmed behavior.

While some researchers were questioning the ability of reinforcement to explain complex behaviors, such as the development of language in humans, and biologically programmed behaviors, such as the "coin-rubbing" of Breland's raccoons, other researchers were developing an alternative approach, based on the idea that the mind is a processor of information.

The Rise of the Information-Processing Approach

In the 1950s, a new approach, called the **information-processing approach**, was developed, which focused on how the mind processes information (see Figure 1.6). An early experiment that used this approach was done by the English psychologist Colin Cherry (1953), who was interested in determining how well people can pay attention to some information when other information is presented at the same time. He asked participants to listen to two different messages, one presented to the left ear and the other presented to the right ear, and asked the participants to repeat, out loud, one of the messages.

Cherry found that participants were able to focus on the message they were repeating, but could take in very little information from the other message. The importance of Cherry's experiment is that it demonstrated that people can focus on one message and ignore another one that is presented at the same time, and it also introduced a procedure for studying the way people process information.

At about the time Cherry and others (Mowbray, 1953) were studying how people process information, another important development occurred. In 1954 IBM introduced a new device to the general public, called the digital computer. Herb Simon and Alan Newell obtained one of these computers and used it to develop a program called *logic theorist*, which was able to prove mathematical theorems (Newell and Simon, 1956).

Newell and Simon described their logic theorist program at two conferences in 1956, one at MIT on applying information theory to perception, language, and thinking, and another at Dartmouth University on the design of thinking machines. What was notable about these conferences was that they brought together researchers from many different fields who interested in the study of the mind at a time when behaviorism was still the dominant force in psychology. Although those in attendance may not have realized it at the time, the conferences were so influential that scientific historians have called 1956 the "the birthday of cognitive science" (Bechtel et al., 1998; Neisser, 1988).

While Newell and Simon were programming the computer to do tasks that are normally done by humans, such as solving logic problems, other researchers were using the computer in another way. They noted how computers processed information by transforming it through a sequence of stages (Figure 1.7a), and how programs written for computers showed information flowing from one stage to the next (Figure 1.7b). Inspired by the way computers processed information through a sequence of stages, these researchers began applying similar principles to the study of the mind. This way of thinking about the mind led an English psychologist, Donald Broadbent (1958), to introduce a flow diagram (see Figure 1.8) to represent what happens in the mind of a person as he or she directs attention to one stimulus in the environment—much as Cherry's participants did when they focused their attention on the message presented to one ear. This flow diagram is notable because it was the first one that depicted the mind as processing information in a sequence of stages. You will see many more flow diagrams like this throughout this book because they have become one of the standard ways of depicting the operations of the mind.

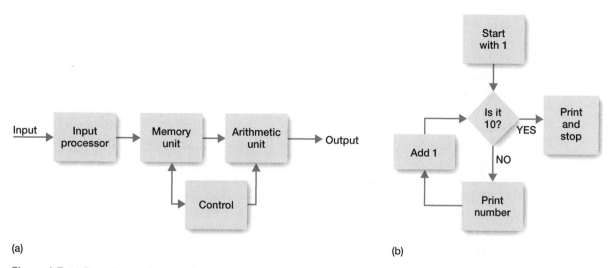

(a)

(b)

Figure 1.7 (a) Flow diagram for an early computer; (b) flow diagram for an early computer program.

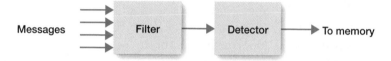

Figure 1.8 Broadbent's flow diagram depicting mental processes that occur as a person pays attention to one stimulus in the environment. This diagram shows that many messages enter a "filter" that selects the message to which the person is attending for further processing by a detector and then storage in memory. We will describe this diagram more fully in Chapter 4.

Was There a Cognitive Revolution?

Many accounts of the development of the information-processing approach say that in the 1950s and 1960s, a "cognitive revolution" occurred that reintroduced the study of the mind to psychology. This description sounds as if cognitive psychology came riding in on a horse to vanquish the behaviorist foe. As it turns out, a change did take place in psychology, which resurrected the study of the mind, but it wasn't quite as dramatic as the word "revolution" implies. It was a slow process that occurred over a few decades, and that involved not just one or two key people, as did behaviorism under the influence of Watson and Skinner, but many people who came from different backgrounds and had different interests.

But although the change from behaviorism (with its focus on behavior) to cognitive psychology (with its focus on mental processes) was not perhaps as dramatic as the term "revolution" might imply, there was no doubt that something important had happened in psychology in the decades following the 1956 conferences. We can appreciate this by imagining a psychological Rip Van Winkle, who falls asleep in his laboratory in 1960 and wakes up 25 years later. Just before falling asleep he would probably have heard the clicking sounds of rats pushing the bars of Skinner boxes, and may have been thinking about how the rat's behavior was being controlled by reinforcements. If he did have any thoughts about what was going on in the rat's (or a human's) mind, he kept them to himself because most of his fellow psychologists would surely ridicule any talk of "thoughts" or "mind."

Upon awakening in 1985, our psychologist would find his Skinner boxes gone, and would observe a scene that he might find difficult to comprehend—humans sitting at computer terminals, responding to stimuli flashed on computer screens. Even more amazing, he would find that the experiment he is watching is designed to study how information is processed as it flows though different stages in the person's mind. There's little doubt that our psychological Rip Van Winkle would have found these changes to be revolutionary.

Although the birth date of cognitive psychology has been designated as 1956, the birth of this new discipline wasn't obvious at the time. A textbook on the history of psychology published in 1966 makes no mention of cognitive psychology (Misiak & Sexton, 1966), and it wasn't until 1967 that the first cognitive psychology textbook appeared (Neisser, 1967). Nonetheless, all through the 1960s and 1970s a new breed of psychologist had begun conducting experiments in perception, attention, memory, language, and problem solving, and were interpreting their results in terms of the flow of information within the mind. It soon became evident that the information-processing approach worked, and so more and more psychologists became interested in using it, and by the 1980s, American psychology had evolved from being a behaviorist world to a cognitive one. It happened gradually, more like an *evolution* than a *revolution*, but looking back on it, the net result was revolutionary.

MODERN APPROACHES TO THE STUDY OF THE MIND

Now that we have described the history of cognitive psychology, let's take a brief look at how cognitive psychology is studied today. The basic principle of using behavior to infer mental processes, as Donders did, is a principle that still guides present-day research. In addition, modern researchers can use another measure, physiological responding, to study mental processes. The fact that modern research studies the mind by measuring both behavior and physiological responding is an important development in cognitive psychology because it is based on the idea that we can approach the study of the mind in a number of different ways.

Behavioral and Physiological Approaches to Cognition

An important characteristic of the present-day study of cognition is the use of both behavioral and physiological approaches to the study of the mind. The **behavioral approach to the study of the mind** involves measuring behavior and explaining cognition in terms of behavior. For example, in Donders' experiment he measured behavior (reaction time) and explained his result in terms of behavior (the longer reaction time in the "choice" condition is the extra time it takes to make a decision).

The **physiological approach to the study of the mind** involves measuring both behavior and physiology and explaining cognition in terms of physiology. For example, let's assume that we decide to repeat Donders' experiment in a modern laboratory so we can measure reaction time, as he did, and can also measure a person's brain activity as they respond to the stimuli. Figure 1.9 updates the diagram of Figure 1.4, taking these physiological measurements into account. The diagram still includes the relationship between the stimulus and behavior (relationship A) that was included in Figure 1.4, but adding the physiological response creates two additional relationships: the relationship between the stimulus and the physiological response (relationship B) and between the physiological response and behavior (relationship C).

To understand what these relationships mean, let's consider how they might be measured in Donders' reaction-time experiment. Let's assume, for the purposes of this example, that we can measure the parts of the brain that are activated by Donder's task. (We will see in Chapter 2 that we can actually do this by using a technique called *brain imaging*.) We still

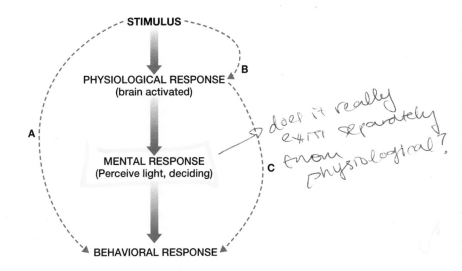

Figure 1.9 Updated sequence of events between stimulus and response, taking into account the physiological response. A, B, and C show relationships that can be measured. The mental response must be inferred from these relationships.

measure relationship A by determining the reaction time. We measure relationship B by flashing the light and determining which areas of the brain are activated. We measure relationship C by looking at how this brain activation is related to the person's response.

Comparing the results in the choice reaction-time task to the results in the simple reaction-time task should tell us something about what is happening in the brain as a person is making the decision about which button to push. Thus, taking a physiological approach to Donders' experiment might enable us to offer a physiological explanation, such as "making a choice between two lights activates a particular area of the brain that is not activated when a person is responding to just one light." The premise behind many modern cognitive psychology experiments is that using both behavioral and physiological approaches can result in a better understanding of cognition than using either one alone.

To provide an example of the modern approach to the study of the mind, we will briefly describe an experiment that uses both the behavioral and physiological approaches to investigate processes involved in memory.

A Modern Memory Experiment

The experiment we are going to describe, by Lila Davachi, Jean Mitchell, and Anthony Wagner (2003), is typical of many modern cognitive psychology experiments in that it studies a cognitive phenomenon (in this case, memory) using both behavioral and physiological approaches. We will describe the behavioral and physiological parts of this experiment separately, and will then show how they can both be included in a diagram like the one in Figure 1.9.

The Behavioral Approach
The basic design of the behavioral part of Davachi's experiment is shown in Figure 1.10. In the learning part of the experiment, the participants

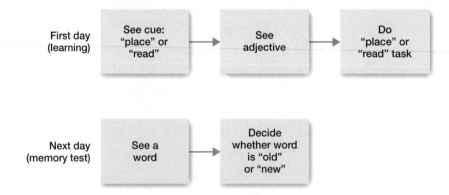

Figure 1.10 Design of Davachi et al. (2003) experiment. There were two parts to this experiment. The first part, learning, was followed one day later by a memory test. Note that the participants' brain activity was measured during the learning task using a technique called *functional magnetic resonance imaging*. This technique for measuring brain activity will be explained in more detail in Chapter 2.

first saw a cue word, either *place* or *read*, and then saw an adjective. Seeing the cue word *place* meant that they were to create an image in their mind of a place described by the adjective. For example, for the word "dirty" they might imagine a garbage dump. Seeing *read* meant that they were to pronounce the word backward in their mind (not out loud). For example, for the word "happy" they would imagine saying "ip-pah." The idea behind these different tasks was to cause participants to process the words differently in the two conditions. Each participant saw 200 words preceded by the *place* cue and 200 words preceded by the *read* cue.

One of the purposes of this experiment was to show how the type of task the participants did as they were learning the words affected their ability to remember the words later. (Note that there were other purposes to this experiment, as well, but we are going to focus on the difference in memory that occurred for the two different kinds of cues.)

In the test part of the experiment, which occurred after a delay of 20 hours, participants saw each of the 400 words they had seen in the learning part of the experiment, plus 400 new words that they had not seen. Their task was to indicate if the word was "old" (it was one of the words presented earlier) or "new." The results of the test, shown in Figure 1.11, indicate that participants correctly identified 54 percent of the old words for which they had created images of places (the *place* task), but only 30 percent of the words that they had mentally pronounced backward (the *read* task). The dashed line indicates the percentage of new words that the participants mistakenly identified as being old.

Better memory for words that are associated with a meaningful task has been found in many previous experiments, as we will see in Chapter 6. Thus, this part of the experiment confirms the results of previous behavioral experiments that have concluded that

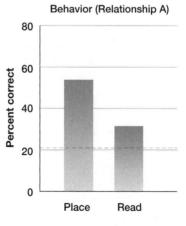

Figure 1.11   The results for the behavioral part of the Davachi et al. (2003) experiment. This graph indicates the relationship between how the participants reacted to the stimulus (*place* or *read*) during learning and their performance in the memory test. This corresponds to Relationship A in Figure 1.9.

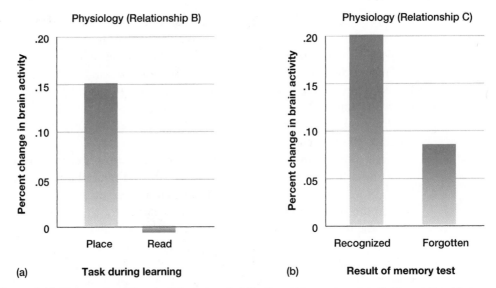

Figure 1.12 The results of the physiological part of the Davachi experiment. Left: The relationship between how the participants reacted to the stimulus during learning (*place* or *read*) and the physiological response (Relationship B). Right: The relationship between the physiological response and the behavioral response (whether the person recognized or forgot the word) (Relationship C).

processing words in a meaningful way enhances memory compared to processing words in terms of their physical characteristics, such as their sound.

The Physiological Approach

The physiological part of the experiment was done at the same time as the behavioral part because as the participants were presented with the cues and the words, the responses of different areas of their brain was being measured by a brain scanner. (The technique used, called *functional magnetic resonance imaging*, will be described in Chapter 2.) Davachi was interested in the relationship between this brain activity measured during learning and the participants' memory 20 hours later. (Brain activity was not measured during the memory test.)

Figure 1.12a shows that for an area of the brain called the *perirhinal cortex* (an area located inside the brain that belongs to a cluster of areas that are involved in memory), the *place* task caused an increase in brain activity, but the *read* task did not. Figure 1.12b shows that there was more activity in the perirhinal cortex for words that were remembered 20 hours later than there was for words that were forgotten. This result enabled Davachi to explain memory physiologically by stating that memory is better if the perirhinal cortex is activated when the word is being learned.

Combining the Behavioral and Physiological Approaches

Now that we have described the experiment, let's return to the diagram in Figure 1.9. Relationship A, the relationship between the stimulus and memory, was determined in the behavioral part of the experiment for the *place* and *read* tasks, with the result shown in Figure 1.11. Relationship B, the relationship between the stimulus and brain activity, was determined in the physiological part of the experiment (Figure 1.12a), as was relationship C, between brain activity and memory (Figure 1.12b).

As we survey the field of cognitive psychology in this book, we will see that most of the early experiments and many recent experiments have studied cognitive processes by measuring only behavior. We will also see that an increasing number of present-day experiments also include the measurement of physiological responses.

Interdisciplinary Approaches to the Study of the Mind

Although this book is titled *Cognitive Psychology* and much of the research you will read about in these pages has been carried out by people who call themselves psychologists, people from many disciplines are involved in the study of the mind. This was apparent in 1956 when people from many different disciplines gathered at MIT and Dartmouth to talk about what was to become a new beginning for the study of the mind. The interdisciplinary approach to the study of the mind is also apparent today in a new field called **cognitive science,** which refers to the study of the mind as carried out by many different disciplines. Cognitive science includes cognitive psychology and also research on the mind within the fields of computer science, linguistics, neuroscience, anthropology, artificial intelligence, and philosophy. The wide net of disciplines that are involved in the study of the mind reinforces the idea that the mind can be studied from a large number of different perspectives.

Knowing, Learning, and Remembering: Strategies for Successful Learning

As you start your cognitive psychology course and this book, one of your goals is probably to do well in the course and perhaps learn something along the way! Of course, one key to doing well is to be able to remember the material that you hear in lectures and read in this book.

Since cognitive psychology has to do with the study of the mind, you might think that it would have something to say about the best way to accomplish this. You will see, as you read the chapters on memory, that cognitive psychology has quite a lot to say about the best way to remember, and at the end of Chapter 6 there is a section that summarizes some basic principles of memory as applied to studying.

You might want to preview the material in Chapter 6 (see pages 216–219), but it is worth emphasizing a few basic principles now, at the beginning of the book, that might help you learn the material in this book and the course. We will focus on three basic principles.

Principle 1: It is important to know what you know.

A lament that professors often hear from students is, "I came to the lecture, read the chapters a number of times, and still didn't do well on the exam." Sometimes this statement is followed by " . . . and when I walked out of the exam I thought I had done pretty well." If this is something that you have experienced, then the root of the problem may be that you didn't have a good awareness of what you knew about the material and what you didn't know. The problem is that if you think you know the material but actually don't, you might stop studying or might continue studying in an ineffective way, with the net result being a poor understanding of the material and an inability to remember it accurately, come exam time.

Principle 2: Don't mistake ease and familiarity for knowing.

One of the main reasons that students may think they know the material, even when they don't, is that they mistake familiarity for understanding. Here is how it works: You read the chapter once, perhaps highlighting as you go. Then later, you read the chapter again, perhaps focusing on the highlighted material. As you read it over, the material is familiar because you remember it from before, and this familiarity might lead you to think, "OK, I know that." The problem is that this feeling of familiarity is not necessarily equivalent to knowing the material and may be of no help when you have to come up with an answer on the exam. In fact, familiarity can often lead to errors on multiple-choice exams, because you might pick a choice that looks familiar, only to find later that it was something you had read, but it wasn't really the best answer to the question.

Principle 3: The pathway to learning is often paved with mistakes.

This principle may sound counterintuitive, but research has shown that one of the most effective ways to learn material is to attempt to retrieve that material, even if you fail the first time or two. As you will see in Chapter 6, retrieval refers to the act of remembering material that is in your memory. Thus, when you unexpectedly see a person you just met at a party last night, but can't remember his or her name (even though you know you know it, and may even remember it later), you are having a retrieval problem. However, trying to retrieve the name, finding out what it is, and then trying to retrieve it again later greatly increases the chances that you will remember the person's name when you meet again next week.

The same principle holds for studying the material in this book. Reading a chapter once is a good idea, but then simply doing things that increase your familiarity with the material without pushing yourself to practice retrieving it is not the most effective way to study. So rather than reading the chapter a second time, try answering the "Test Yourself" questions that are included in every chapter. (Most chapters have two sets of these questions, one in the middle of the chapter, and one at the end.) The key is to try answering them before you look back at the book to find the answer. If you find you don't know the material, that's good information because it tells you what to study, and whether you realize it or not, the very act of *trying* to answer a question increases the chances you will be able to answer it when you try again later. The reason answering questions works is that *generating* material is a more effective way of getting information into memory than simply *reviewing* it.

After you have tried to generate an answer, go back over the material, perhaps following some of the principles at the end of Chapter 6. Keep in mind that an effective strategy is to rest (take a break or study something else) before studying more and then retesting yourself. Research has shown that memory is better if studying is spaced out over time, rather than being done all at once. Repeating this process a number of times— attempting retrieval, checking back to see if you were right, waiting, attempting retrieval again, and so on—is a more effective way of learning the material than simply looking at it and getting that warm, fuzzy feeling of familiarity, which may not translate into actually knowing the material when you are faced with questions about it on the exam.

 Test Yourself 1.1

1. Why could we say that Donders and Helmholtz were cognitive psychologists, even though in the 19th century there was no field called cognitive psychology? Describe Donders' experiment and the rationale behind it, and Helmholtz's theory.
2. When was the first laboratory of scientific psychology founded and how important was the study of mental functioning in psychology at the end of the 19th century and beginning of the 20th?
3. Describe the rise of behaviorism, especially the influence of Watson and Skinner. How did behaviorism affect research on the mind?
4. Describe the events that helped lead to the decline of behaviorism and the events that were important in establishing the information-processing approach to psychology.
5. What was the "cognitive revolution"? How long did the revolution last, and what did it accomplish?
6. Distinguish between the behavioral approach and the physiological approaches to the study of cognition.
7. How was memory studied behaviorally and physiologically by Davachi and coworkers? How can this experiment fit into the same scheme as Donders' reaction-time experiment?
8. What is cognitive science and how is cognitive psychology related to it?

1. Check the newspaper or newsmagazines for stories that are related to cognitive psychology. Some examples: stories about memory research ("Scientists race to find memory-loss cure"); stories about memory in court testimony ("Defendant says he can't remember what happened"); and stories about decisions people make ("Survey shows many people choose not to receive flu shots").

2. The idea that we have something called "the mind" that is responsible for our thoughts and behavior, is reflected in the many ways that the word *mind* can be used. For example, consider "She is out of her mind" or "Do you mind if I borrow your notes?" See how many examples you can think of that illustrate different uses of the word *mind*, and decide how relevant each is to what you will be studying in cognitive psychology (as indicated by the table of contents of this book).

3. Donders compared the results of his simple and choice reaction-time experiments to infer how long it took to make the decision as to which button to push, when given a choice. But what about other kinds of decisions? Design an experiment to determine the time it takes to make a more complex decision. Then relate this experiment to the diagrams in Figures 1.4 or 1.9.

Key Terms

Analytic introspection
Behavioral approach to the study of the mind
Behaviorism
Choice reaction time
Cognition
Cognitive psychology
Cognitive science

Information-processing approach
Mental chronometry
Physiological approach to the study of the mind
Reaction time
Simple reaction time
Stroop effect
Unconscious inference

CogLab To experience these experiments for yourself, go to http://coglab.wadsworth.com. Be sure to read each experiment's setup instructions before you go to the experiment itself. Otherwise, you won't know which keys to press.

Primary Lab

Stroop effect How reaction time to naming font colors is affected by the presence of conflicting information from words (p. 4).

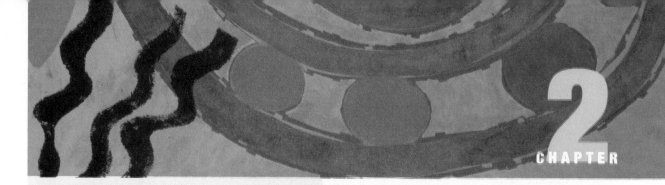

CHAPTER 2

Cognition and the Brain: Basic Principles

Some Questions We Will Consider

✔ How can memory be explained by the firing of neurons?

✔ What percentage of my brain do I actually use?

✔ How is it possible to tell what's happening in the brain while someone is thinking?

■　　■　　■

At 7:00 AM, in response to hearing the familiar but irritating sound of his alarm clock, Juan swings his arm in a well-practiced arc, feels the contact of his hand with the snooze button, and in the silence he has created, turns over for 10 more minutes of sleep. How can we explain Juan's behavior in terms of physiology? What is happening inside Juan's brain that makes it possible for him to hear the alarm, take appropriate action to turn it off, and know that he can sleep a little longer and still get to his early-morning class on time?

We can give a general answer to this question by considering some of the steps involved in Juan's action of turning off the alarm. The first step in hearing the alarm occurs when sound waves from the alarm enter Juan's ears and stimulate receptors that change the sound energy into electrical signals (Figure 2.1a). These signals then reach the auditory area of Juan's brain, which causes him to hear the ringing of the bell (Figure 2.1b). Then signals are sent to the motor area of the brain, which controls movement. The motor area sends signals to the muscles of Juan's hand and arm, and the muscles carry out the movement that turns off the alarm (Figure 2.1c).

But there is more to the story than this sequence of events. For one thing, Juan's decision to hit the snooze button of his alarm is based on his knowledge that this will silence the alarm temporarily, and that the alarm will sound again in 10 minutes. He also knows that if he stays in bed for 10 more minutes, he will still have time to get to his class. A more complete picture of what's happening in Juan's brain when the alarm rings would, therefore, have to include processes involved in retrieving knowledge from memory and making decisions based on that knowledge. Thus, a seemingly simple behavior such as turning off an alarm in the morning involves a complex series of physiological events.

Students often wonder why they need to know about principles of nervous system functioning for a course in cognitive psychology. The answer to this question is contained in our discussion of the physiological approach to cognition in Chapter 1. One of the main points of that discussion was that we can achieve a fuller understanding of cognition by studying it both behaviorally and physiologically. Thus, as we describe how cognitive psychologists have studied the mind in the chapters that follow this one, we will be looking both at behavior and at physiology.

The purpose of this chapter is to give you the basic background you will need to understand the physiological material on perception, attention, memory, language, decision making, and problem solving that we will be covering in the chapters that follow. We will describe some basic principles of nervous system functioning and we will then look at some of the methods that cognitive neuroscientists use to study the physiology of cognition (Figure 2.2).

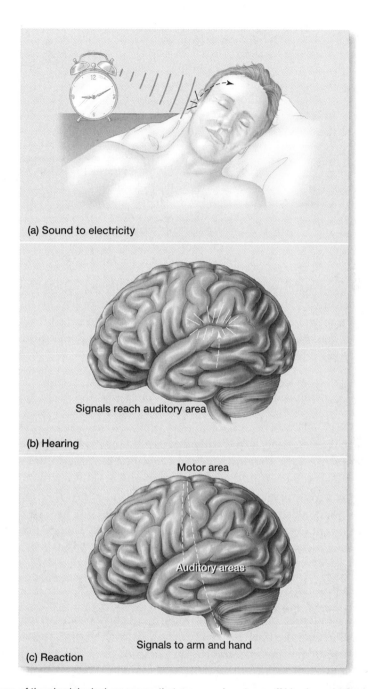

(a) Sound to electricity

Signals reach auditory area

(b) Hearing

Motor area

Auditory areas

Signals to arm and hand

(c) Reaction

Figure 2.1 Some of the physiological processes that occur as Juan turns off his alarm. (a) Sound waves are changed to electrical signals in the ear and are sent to the brain; (b) Signals reaching the auditory areas of the brain cause Juan to hear the alarm; (c) Signals sent from the auditory areas to the motor area cause signals to be sent from the motor area to muscles in Juan's arm and hand. (Note that the actual pathways from ear to auditory areas and from auditory areas to the motor area are much more complex than shown here.)

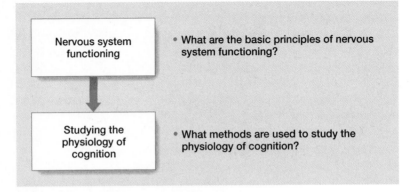

Figure 2.2 Flow diagram for this chapter.

In order to help you relate some of the principles and methods that we will be presenting in this chapter to research in cognitive psychology, a number of "Physiological Previews" have been included in this chapter. These previews provide a capsule summary of material on the link between physiology and cognition that is covered in more detail later in the book.

THE MIND'S COMPUTER

In the first American textbook of psychology, Harvard psychologist William James (1890) described the brain as the "most mysterious thing in the world" because of the amazing feats it achieves and the intricacies of how it achieves them. One thing that contributes to the mysteriousness of the brain is its complexity. It is made up of billions of interconnected cells called neurons, and as we will see below, these interconnections are an important part of the mechanism that creates our mental processes. Before describing neurons, we will consider the overall layout of the brain.

Layout of the Brain

The picture of the brain in Figure 2.3 shows the surface of the brain's outer covering, which is called the **cerebral cortex**. The cerebral cortex is only 3mm thick, but this thin layer of neurons contains the mechanisms responsible for most of our higher mental functions, such as perception, language, thinking, and problem solving. The cerebral cortex is divided into four lobes: the **temporal lobe** (important for language, memory, hearing, and vision), the **occipital lobe** (the first place in the cerebral cortex where visual information is received), the **parietal lobe** (where signals are received from the touch system and which is also important for vision and attention), and the **frontal lobe** (which serves higher functions such as language, thought, memory, and motor functioning).

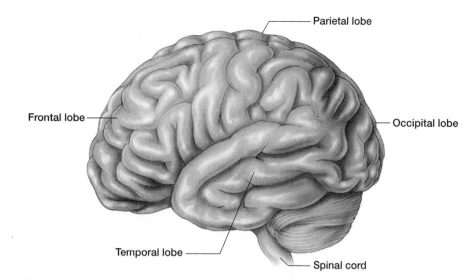

Figure 2.3 The human brain, showing the four major lobes.

Beneath the cerebral cortex are **subcortical structures,** which also play important roles in cognition, especially in the processing of information for memories and the creation of emotions (Figure 2.4). Some of the important subcortical structures are the

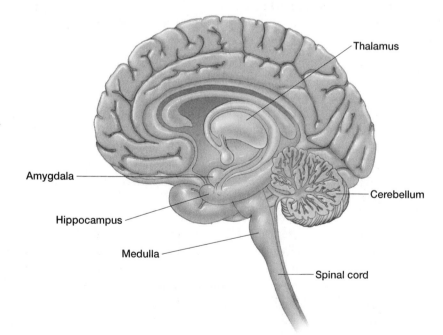

Figure 2.4 Cross-section of the human brain, showing a number of the subcortical structures that are important for cognition.

hippocampus, which is important for forming memories, the **amygdala,** which is important for emotions and emotional memories, and the **thalamus,** which is important for processing information from the senses of vision, hearing, and touch.

Neurons Are the Building Blocks of the Nervous System

For many years, the nature of the brain's tissue was a mystery. Looking at the interior of the brain with the unaided eye gave no indication that it is made up of billions of smaller units. The existence of these units was confirmed by the Italian anatomist Camillo Golgi (1844–1926), who developed a chemical technique that stained some neurons but left most unstained, thereby revealing the structure of single neurons in pictures like the one in Figure 2.5. **Neurons** are cells that are specialized to receive and transmit information in the nervous system.

The key components of neurons are shown in Figure 2.6a. The **cell body** contains mechanisms to keep the cell alive; **dendrites** branch out from the cell body to receive electrical signals from other neurons; and the **axon,** or **nerve fiber,** is a tube filled with fluid that conducts electrical signals. Neurons that are specialized to receive information from the environment are called **receptors** because they have receptor structures in the place of the cell body. There are receptors that are specialized to respond to light energy (vision), mechanical deformation (touch, pain), pressure changes in the air (to create hearing), molecules in the air (smell), and molecules in liquid (taste).

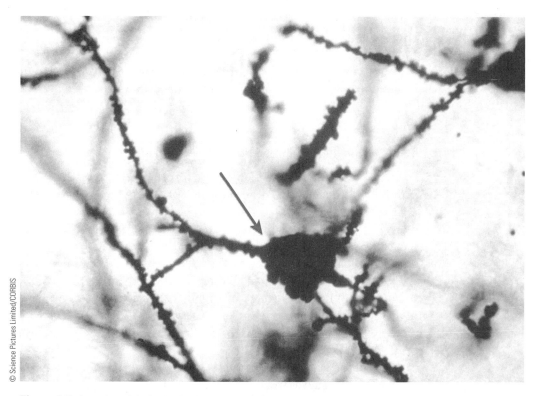

Figure 2.5 A portion of the brain that has been treated with Golgi stain shows the shapes of a few neurons. The arrow points to a neuron's cell body. The thin lines are dendrites or axons (see Figure 2.6).

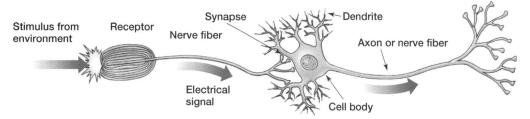

Figure 2.6 Basic components of the neuron. The neuron on the left contains a receptor, which is specialized to receive information from the environment (in this case, pressure that would occur from being touched on the skin). This neuron synapses on the neuron on the right, which has a cell body instead of a receptor.

Electricity in the Nervous System

The operation of the nervous system is based on signals that originate in the receptors when stimuli from the environment are transformed into electricity.

Receptors Transform Environmental Energy Into Electrical Energy

Transduction is the transformation of one form of energy into another form of energy. An example of transduction is the sequence of events that occurs when you touch the "Withdrawal" button on the screen of the ATM machine at the bank. The pressure exerted by your finger is transduced into electrical energy, which is then transduced into mechanical energy to push your money out of the machine.

In the nervous system, transduction occurs when environmental energy is transformed into electrical energy. For example, consider the eye in Figure 2.7. Light energy enters the front of the eye through the pupil, and electrical energy leaves the back of the eye in the neurons that make up the optic nerve. It is in the **retina,** a network of neurons that line the back of the eye, that light energy that enters the eye is transformed into the electrical energy that leaves the eye.

Since the process of transduction is not important for understanding cognition, we will not consider it again as we describe the links between physiology and cognition. What is important is that transduction leads to the generation of electrical signals called *action potentials*, which *have* been linked to cognition.

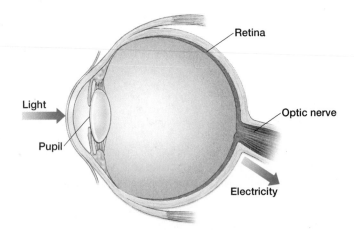

Figure 2.7 The eye, showing the location of the retina lining the back of the eye, and how light enters the front of the eye through the pupil, and electricity leaves the back, in the optic nerve.

Action Potentials Transmit Information Down the Axon

Action potentials are recorded by using tiny wires called **microelectrodes** that are placed in or near an axon, and that pick up the electrical signals that travel down the axon (Figure 2.8a). When the axon's electrical signals are displayed on a device called an oscilloscope, we see that the inside of the neuron becomes positive for about 1 millisecond and then returns to its original level (Figure 2.8b). Changing the time scale on our display

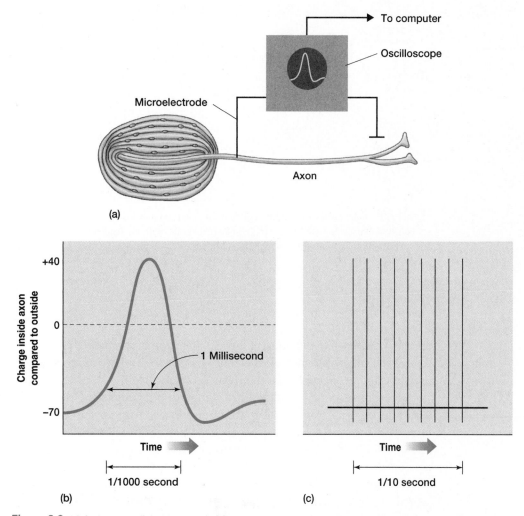

(a)

(b)

(c)

Figure 2.8 (a) Action potentials are recorded from neurons with tiny microelectrodes that are positioned inside or right next to the neuron's axon. These potentials are displayed on the screen of an oscilloscope and are also sent to a computer for analysis. (b) An action potential recorded by a microelectrode looks like this. The inside of the axon becomes more positive, then goes back to the original level, all within 1 millisecond (1/1,000 second). (c) A number of action potentials displayed on an expanded time scale, so a single action potential appears as a "spike."

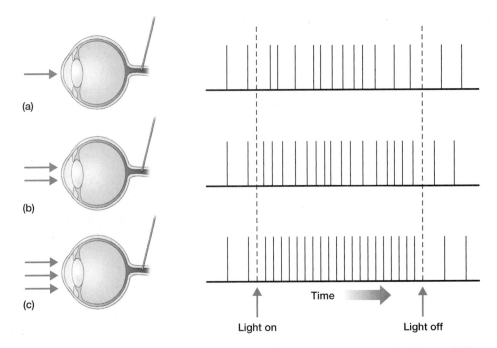

Figure 2.9 Records showing action potentials in a neuron that responds to light entering the eye. (a) Presenting light causes an increase in firing; (b) increasing the light intensity increases the rate of firing further; and (c) even more light results in a high rate of firing.

creates a display like the one in Figure 2.8c in which the nerve impulses look like lines, or "spikes." Using this time scale makes it possible to display a number of action potentials as they pass by the electrode on their way down the axon.

Neurons respond to increases in stimulation by increasing the rate of nerve firing, as shown in Figure 2.9. Thus, at low stimulus levels, firing occurs slowly (Figure 2.9a), but increasing the stimulus intensity causes an increase in the rate of nerve firing (Figures 2.9b and c). Notice that although the rate of nerve firing increases as stimulus intensity increases, the size of the action potentials remains the same. This is an important property of action potentials because it means that information about stimulus intensity is represented not by the *size* of action potentials, but by their *rate of firing*.

Another property of action potentials is that they are **propagated**—once a signal is generated at one end of the axon it travels to the other end. This property of traveling from one end of the axon to the other without getting smaller enables signals to be transmitted over large distances in the nervous system.

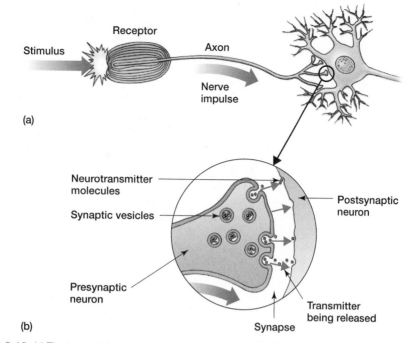

Figure 2.10 (a) The axon of the neuron with the receptor reaches the cell body of another neuron. (b) The synapse is the space between the end of one neuron (the presynaptic neuron) and the next neuron (the postsynaptic neuron). Neurotransmitter molecules are released when an action potential reaches the synaptic vesicles of the presynaptic neuron.

HOW NEURONS COMMUNICATE

Early physiologists wondered what happens to action potentials once they reached the end of the axon. One explanation was that neurons make direct contact with each other so that a signal reaching the end of one neuron passes directly to the next neuron. However, that turned out not to be the case because for most neurons, there is a space, called the synapse, between the end of the axon and the next neuron (Figure 2.10a).

Neurons Communicate by Releasing Neurotransmitters at the Synapse

How are the electrical signals generated by one neuron transmitted across the synapse? Early in the 1900s, it was discovered that the action potentials themselves do not travel across the synapse. Instead, they trigger a chemical process that bridges the gap between neurons. When the potentials reach the end of the *presynaptic neuron* (the neuron sending

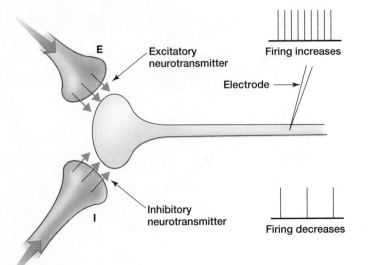

Figure 2.11 Release of excitatory neurotransmitter (top synapse) causes an increase in firing measured by the electrode in the axon of the postsynaptic neuron. Release of inhibitory neurotransmitter (bottom synapse) causes a decrease in the firing. A given neuron can receive both excitatory and inhibitory inputs. The firing rate of the neuron is determined by the amount of excitatory and inhibitory transmitter it receives.

the signal), they cause structures called synaptic vesicles to open up and release molecules called neurotransmitters (Figure 2.10b).

Neurotransmitter molecules travel across the synapse to the postsynaptic membrane and cause a change in the membrane of the postsynaptic neuron. As we will see, this change can cause either an increase or a decrease in the neuron's rate of firing.

Excitation and Inhibition Interact at the Synapse

The two scenarios that can occur when neurotransmitters are released are shown in Figure 2.11. The transmitter released at the top synapse of Figure 2.11 is an excitatory neurotransmitter because it increases the chances that the next (postsynaptic) neuron will fire, and is therefore associated with increased nerve firing. The transmitter released at the bottom synapse is called an inhibitory neurotransmitter because it decreases the chances that a neuron will fire, and is therefore associated with decreased nerve firing. Thus, some neurotransmitters cause excitation in the postsynaptic neuron, which tends to increase the rate of nerve firing in this neuron, and some neurotransmitters cause inhibition, which tends to decrease the rate of nerve firing in the neuron. The interplay between excitation and inhibition that occurs at the synapse plays an important role in neural information processing, as we will see below.

Physiological Preview: THE SYNAPSE AND COGNITION
How Memories Are Stored at Synapses

You have an experience and then you remember it later. How was the experience you remembered recorded in your brain? One answer to this question is that memories are stored at synapses because when a particular experience causes particular neurons to fire, this firing causes changes in the structure at the neurons' synapses (Figure 2.12) (Toni et al., 1999), and these structural changes cause increased nerve firing. Thus, a particular experience is represented in the nervous system by the enhanced firing of a number of neurons. According to this idea, remembering a phone number or experiencing a place you've been to before as feeling familiar involves activation of the same group of neurons that fired when you originally learned the phone number or experienced the place. (From Chapter 6, page 203.)

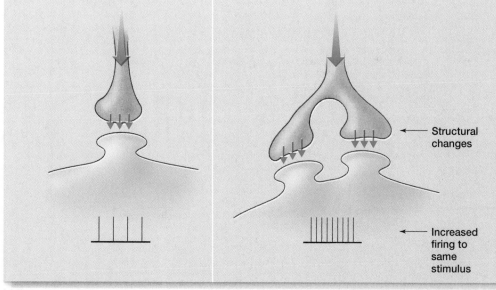

(a) Before experience   (b) After experience

Figure 2.12 (a) A particular experience causes a neuron to fire and transmitter to be released. The record indicates the rate of nerve firing measured in the postsynaptic neuron due to this initial experience. (b) After continued firing occurs due to repetitions of the experience, structural changes at the synapse occur that result in increased firing to the same stimulus. These changes in the neuron's firing rate provide a neural record of the experience. The record for a particular experience would involve many neurons.

How Neurons Process Information

Neurons do not operate alone. The brain contains 180 billion neurons, 80 billion of which are involved in cognitive processes (Kolb & Wishaw, 1990). Each of these billions of neurons receives signals from about 1,000 other neurons, so there are more synapses in the brain than the number of stars in the Milky Way! We will now consider how the processing of information by the nervous system is based on interactions between these neurons.

Neurons Process Information by Interacting With Each Other

To understand how the nervous system works, we need to understand how neurons interact with one another. These interactions take place at the synapses where one neuron releases its neurotransmitter onto another neuron and neural processing occurs. **Neural processing** is the interaction of a number of neurons that cause a target neuron or group of neurons to respond to specific stimuli. Neural processing is accomplished by **neural circuits,** which are groups of interconnected neurons.

To understand neural processing and neural circuits, we will consider the simple neural circuit in Figure 2.13a, which consists of five receptors that all synapse onto neuron A. Synapsing of a number of neurons onto a single neuron, as in Figure 2.13a, is

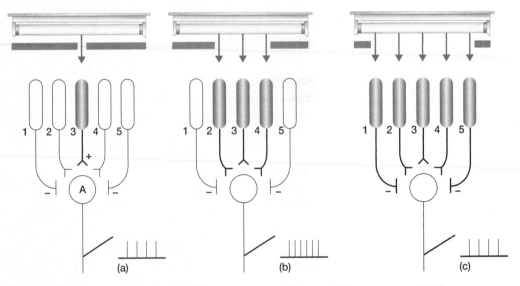

Figure 2.13 How a neural circuit works. "Y" synapses are excitatory and "T" synapses are inhibitory. (a) When receptor 3 is stimulated by light, excitatory neurotransmitter is released onto neuron A, and action potentials are recorded from A's axon. (b) When receptors 2, 3, and 4 are stimulated neuron A receives more excitatory neurotransmitter and firing increases. (c) When all five neurons are stimulated, excitatory transmitter is released from 2, 3, and 4, but the release of inhibitory neurotransmitter from neurons 1 and 5 causes a decrease in firing. This circuit therefore causes neuron A to fire best to a bar of light of medium length.

called **convergence.** The synapses associated with receptors 2, 3, and 4 are excitatory, so stimulating these receptors will cause the release of excitatory transmitter and an increase in firing of neuron A. The synapses associated with receptors 1 and 5 are inhibitory, so stimulating these receptors will cause the release of inhibitory transmitter and a decrease in firing of neuron A.

For the purposes of our example, let's assume that these receptors respond to light, so if we shine a small spot of light onto receptor 3, neuron A will fire, as shown in Figure 2.13a. If we now stimulate receptors 2, 3, and 4 together, so the light forms a short bar, then neuron A fires more rapidly, because it is now receiving excitatory signals from three receptors (Figure 2.13b). However, when we stimulate all five of the receptors, the firing of neuron A decreases, because now neurons 1 and 5 are releasing inhibitory transmitter onto A, which decreases A's rate of firing (Figure 2.13c).

The neural processing we have described for the circuit in Figure 2.13 shows how convergence, excitation, and inhibition can result in a neuron that responds best to a specific stimulus—in this case, a short bar of light. Figure 2.14 shows how a neuron in the cat's visual system responds as we increase the size of a spot of light. Initially, the neuron's response increases as we increase the spot size (Figures 2.14a and b), but the response decreases once the spot gets too large (Figures 2.14c and d). This is similar to what happened in the neural circuit in Figure 2.13. Even though many more receptors are involved for the cat's neuron, the principle is the same: When the spot is small, mainly excitatory synapses are involved. However, when we increase the size of the spot, inhibitory synapses cause a decrease in firing.

Research on neurons further along in the visual system has revealed that as we move up the visual pathways, neurons become more specialized. David Hubel and Thorsten

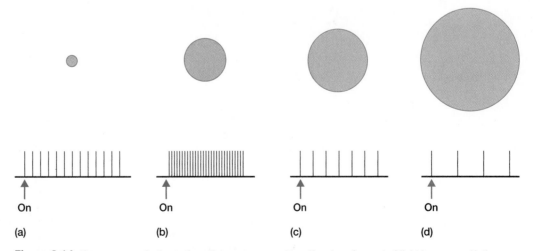

(a) (b) (c) (d)

Figure 2.14 How a neuron in the cat's optic nerve responds as the size of a spot of light increases. Notice that the best response occurs to the medium-sized spot of light in (b), but decreases when the spot is made larger, as in (c) and (d). (Adapted from Hubel & Wiesel, 1961.)

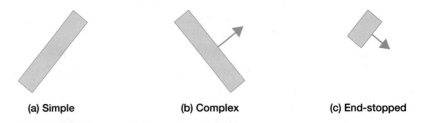

(a) Simple   (b) Complex   (c) End-stopped

Figure 2.15 Stimuli that cause neurons in the cortex to fire. (a) Simple cells respond to bars of light with a particular orientation; (b) complex cells respond to oriented bars of light that are moving in a particular direction; (c) end-stopped cells respond best to moving bars of light of a particular length that are moving in a specific direction.

Wiesel (1965) won the Nobel Prize for their research on the visual system. They found neurons that respond best to a bar of light with a particular orientation, called simple cells (Figure 2.15a), neurons that respond best to bars of light of a particular orientation that were moving across the retina in a specific direction, called complex cells (Figure 2.15b), and neurons that respond best to an oriented bar of light with a specific length, moving in a specific direction, called end-stopped cells (Figure 2.15c). Table 2.1 summarizes the properties of these three types of neurons.

Neurons such as simple, complex, and end-stopped cells, which fire in response to specific features of the stimuli, are called feature detectors. There are neurons in other areas of the cortex that respond best to even more complex stimuli. For example, some neurons in the temporal lobe respond best to complex geometrical stimuli (Figure 2.16a), to common objects in the environment such as buildings (Figure 2.16b), and to faces (Figure 2.16c) (Kremer et al., 2000; Perret et al., 1992; Tanaka, 1993).

Table 2.1	PROPERTIES OF NEURONS IN THE VISUAL CORTEX	
Type of Cell	Best Stimulus	Example of Best Stimulus
Simple	Oriented bar of light.	Bar oriented at 45 degrees.
Complex	Oriented bar of light moving in a specific direction.	Vertical bar moving to the right.
End-stopped	Oriented bar of light, with a specific length, moving in a specific direction. Also responds to moving corners.	Short horizontal bar moving up.

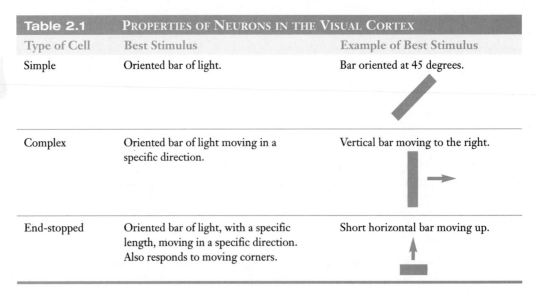

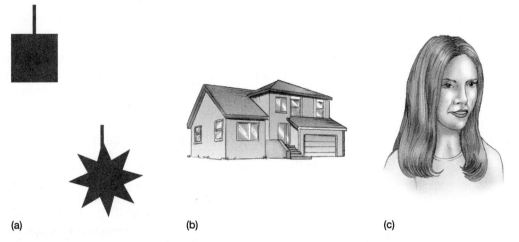

(a)   (b)   (c)

Figure 2.16 Neurons have been found in the temporal cortex that respond to (a) complex geometrical figures; (b) common objects in the environment; and (c) faces.

It may seem amazing that neural processing that is based just on convergence, excitation, and inhibition could result in neurons that respond best to stimuli as complex as houses or faces, but remember that the brain contains billions of neurons and huge numbers of interconnections. The complexity of these interconnections creates the neural processing that results in neurons that respond best to complex stimuli.

 Test Yourself 2.1

1. How does the example of Juan turning off his alarm clock support the idea that even simple behaviors involve a complex series of physiological events?
2. The organization of the brain can be described in terms of lobes in the cerebral cortex and subcortical structures. What functions are associated with each of the four lobes and three subcortical structures described in the text?
3. What are neurons? What is the difference between the structure of receptors and other neurons?
4. What is transduction, and what are the properties of the action potentials that occur in nerve axons?
5. What is a synapse, and how do neurons communicate with each other by releasing excitatory and inhibitory neurotransmitter at the synapse?
6. How do convergence, excitation, and inhibition work to create neural processing that can cause a particular neuron to respond best to a small spot of light? Describe neurons in the visual system that respond to complex stimuli.

Cognition and the Brain: Basic Principles

HOW NEURONS ARE ORGANIZEDY BY FUNCTION

We have seen how excitatory and inhibitory interconnections between neurons can result in neurons that respond to specific types of stimuli. We will now see that neurons with similar functions are located in specific areas of the brain.

Groups of Neurons With Similar Functions Are Organized Into Modules

If we zoom in on specific areas of the brain and determine the properties of neurons in these areas, we find that neurons in different areas respond best to different kinds of stimuli. What this means is that specific areas of the brain serve different functions. This property of different functions being found in different areas is called **localization of function** and brain areas that are specialized for specific function are called **modules** for that function (Figure 2.17).

An example of a module is the **inferotemporal (IT) cortex,** which is rich in neurons that respond to forms like the ones in Figure 2.16. The presence of these neurons (plus other evidence) has led researchers to conclude that the IT cortex is a module for form perception. The additional evidence involves the finding that people who have suffered damage to this area and some surrounding areas have difficulty recognizing objects. In one particularly striking condition, called **prospagnosia,** the affected person cannot recognize the faces of familiar people. A person with prospagnosia might not even be able to recognize close friends, members of their own family, and even the reflection of their own face in the mirror (Burton et al, 1991; Hecaen & Angelerques, 1962; Parkin, 1996). It is important to note that even though the IT cortex has been called a module for form, this

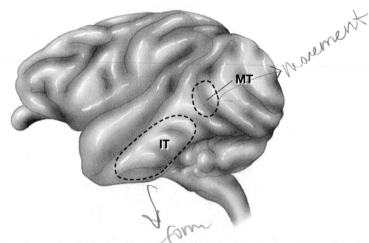

Figure 2.17 Side view of a monkey brain showing the locations of the inferotemporal (IT) and medial temporal (MT) areas.

Physiological Preview: MODULES IN THE BRAIN
An Area for Language in the Frontal Lobe

There are a number of areas in the brain that are specialized for processing language. One of them, called **Broca's area,** is located in the frontal lobe (Figure 2.18). Damage to Broca's area causes a condition called **Broca's aphasia,** in which a person has great difficulty speaking. This difficulty is caused not by an inability to use the lips, tongue, and mouth to produce language, but rather by an inability to process language. An example is provided by the following response of a 30-year-old man who had suffered damage to Broca's area due to a stroke, when he was asked, "Were you in the Coast Guard?": "No, er, yes, yes. . . . Ship. Massachu . . . cetts . . . coast guard . . . years." At this point he raised his hand twice to signify that he was in the Coast Guard for 19 years. He was still able to understand language, but couldn't put his thoughts into words (Gardner, 1974). In Chapter 10 we will see that other brain areas are also involved in understanding and producing language (Wernicke's area, shown in the figure, is one of them). (From Chapter 10, pages 347–348.)

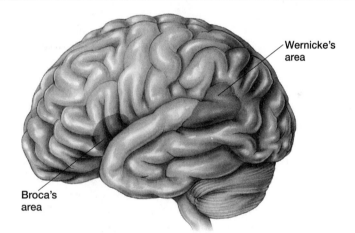

Figure 2.18 Location of Broca's and Wernicke's areas, which are both involved in the processing of speech and language.

doesn't mean that it is the only area of the brain involved in form perception. As we will see, most of our cognitive abilities involve many areas of the brain.

The **medial temporal (MT) area,** which is located above the IT cortex, is an example of a module that is specialized for perceiving visual movement. Evidence supporting this idea includes the fact that the majority of neurons in this area respond to moving stimuli, and cases in which damage to this area affects motion perception. In one of these cases, a 43-year-old woman lost the ability to perceive movement when she suffered a stroke that damaged the MT cortex. Her inability to perceive motion, called **motion agnosia,** made it difficult for her to pour tea or coffee into a cup because the liquid appeared to be frozen, so she couldn't perceive the fluid rising in the cup and had trouble knowing when to stop pouring. It was also difficult for her to follow dialogue because she couldn't see movements of a speaker's face and mouth (Zihl et al., 1983, 1991).

HOW THE ENVIRONMENT IS REPRESENTED IN THE NERVOUS SYSTEM

We know that neurons that respond to specific types of stimuli are found together in the same area of the brain. From what we know about the IT cortex, we would expect that when Susan looks at Bill, there will be a lot of neural activity in her IT cortex, and especially in the place within the IT cortex that is rich in neurons that respond best to faces.

But how does Susan know that the face she is seeing is Bill's? The answer to this question is that the firing of neurons in Susan's IT cortex must contain information that stands for, or *represents*, "Bill's face." The information contained in the way neurons fire to Bill's face (or to any other object or experience) is called the **neural code** for that object or experience.

Experiences Are Represented by a Neural Code

How is our experience represented by a neural code? To answer this question, we will use the example of how Bill's face is represented in Susan's IT cortex, although the answer we will arrive at is true for all experiences, not just for seeing faces. One possible way that faces could be represented by neural firing is based on the existence of neurons called feature detectors that respond to complex stimuli, as in Figure 2.16. We know that there are feature detectors that respond to faces, but are there neurons that respond only to Bill's face, so when they fire Susan knows she is looking at Bill?

This way of representing Bill's face won't work for a number of reasons. For one thing, there are just too many different faces and other objects in the environment to assign specific neurons to each one. Also, while there are neurons that respond only to specific types of stimuli, like faces, even these neurons respond to a number of different faces. Thus, a neuron that responds to Bill's face would also respond to Roger's and Samantha's faces as well.

The answer to the problem of neural coding is to be found not by considering how one very specialized type of neuron fires, but by considering how groups of neurons fire. For example, let's consider how the five neurons in Figure 2.19 fire to a number of different faces. Bill's face causes all five neurons to fire, with neuron 1 responding the most and neuron 3 responding the least. Roger's face also causes firing in all five neurons but the pattern is different, with neuron 5 responding the most and neuron 1 the least. All five neurons also fire to Samantha's face, but with a pattern that differs from the firing to either Bill's or Roger's faces. Thus, each face is represented by a specific pattern of firing

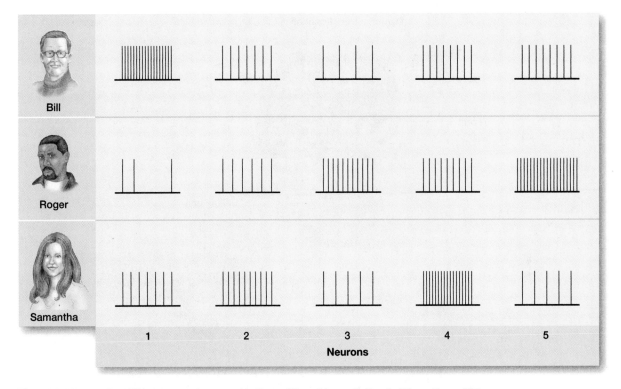

Figure 2.19 How five different neurons respond to three different faces. Notice that the pattern of firing across the five neurons is different for each face.

across a number of neurons. This solution to the problem of neural coding is called dis-tributed coding because the code that indicates a specific face is distributed across a number of neurons.

Although we have used faces to illustrate how distributed coding works, the principle of distributed coding also applies to other cognitive capacities. For example, it is likely that specific memories are represented by the pattern of firing of a large number of neurons.

A Particular Stimulus Creates Distributed Activity in the Brain

We've seen that a specific stimulus, like Bill's face, can be represented by the pattern of firing across a number of neurons. We now broaden our perspective from groups of neurons to the entire brain. When we do this, we see is that even seemingly simple cognitions involve the activation of many areas of the brain.

As an example of how activation can be spread over many areas, let's consider a simple situation. A person who is sitting at a table sees a green ball roll by (Figure 2.20) (see Hubel, 1985). From what we know about the operation of the visual system, the ball activates the visual area in the occipital lobe and also activates other areas of the brain as well.

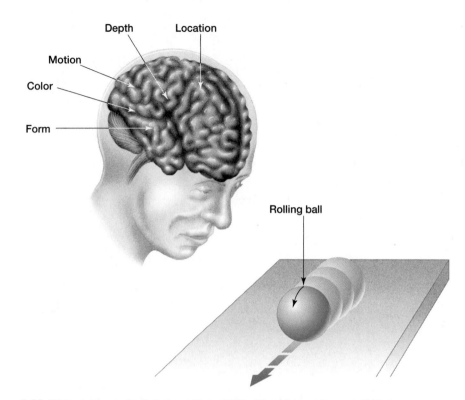

Figure 2.20 When a green ball rolls by, a number of different cortical areas are activated.

Each quality of the ball activates a different area, so its form is represented by the firing of neurons in IT cortex, and its motion by neurons in MT cortex. In addition, other areas are activated by the ball's color and by its distance. This simultaneous activation of a number of areas is called **distributed activation of the brain.**

TECHNIQUES FOR STUDYING THE PHYSIOLOGY OF COGNITION

The principles of nervous system operation that we have described were determined using a variety of different methods, many of which we will encounter again as we describe experiments on the physiology of cognition. We will describe a number of these methods, beginning with one that has been central to much of our basic knowledge about the physiology of the nervous system—recording from single neurons.

Recording From Single Neurons

A great deal of our knowledge about the nervous system has been determined by recording from single neurons, a procedure that is called **single-unit recording.** Single-unit recording is important because it provides information about what the individual units of

Physiological Preview: DISTRIBUTED ACTIVITY IN THE BRAIN
How Memory Creates Activity Throughout the Brain

Which areas of the brain are involved in storing memories of experiences and then in retrieving them later? The answer to this question is that many different areas of the brain serve the many different aspects of memory. Memories that last only a short time, as when you look up a phone number and then forget it right after making your call, involve the prefrontal cortex (Courtney et al., 1998; Fiez, 2001) (Chapter 5). Memories that last a longer time involve a number of structures in the medial temporal lobe (Brewer et al., 1998; Wagner et al., 1998). (Chapter 6). Emotional memories activate the amygdala (Harmann, 1999) (Chapter 7). Thus, when Roger unexpectedly encounters his old girlfriend, Gloria, the memories triggered by this encounter activate a number of areas that are distributed across his brain (Figure 2.21). (From Chapter 5, page 175; Chapter 6, page 208; Chapter 7, page 253.)

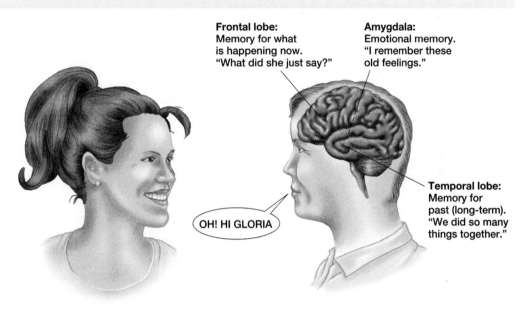

Frontal lobe:
Memory for what is happening now.
"What did she just say?"

Amygdala:
Emotional memory.
"I remember these old feelings."

Temporal lobe:
Memory for past (long-term).
"We did so many things together."

OH! HI GLORIA

Figure 2.21 When Roger unexpectedly encounters his old girlfriend Gloria, different types of memories cause activation of a number of different areas of Roger's brain.

the nervous system are doing. For example, consider what you would perceive if you walked into a huge room in which there are thousands of people, all talking at once about a political speech they have just heard. The "crowd noise" that you hear tells you little about what is going on in the room, other than perhaps the crowd's general level of excitement. However, listening to what individual people are saying provides more specific information about peoples' reactions to the speech.

SINGLE-UNIT RECORDING
How Attention Affects the Firing of Single Neurons

When we focus our attention on something, we usually become more aware of what is happening at the place where we are attending. The relation between attention and the responding of single neurons has been demonstrated by the results of experiments on monkeys that have revealed neurons in the cortex that fire less rapidly when the monkeys are not paying attention to a stimulus and more rapidly when the monkeys are paying attention to the stimulus. The record in Figure 2.22a depicts how one of these neurons fires when a monkey is looking at the X but is not paying attention to the light that is off to the side. The record in Figure 2.22b depicts how the same neuron fires when the monkey is still looking at the X but is performing a task that requires attention to the light. The neuron's firing increases when the monkey is paying attention to the light, even though it is still looking at the X, as before (Colby et al., 1995). (From Chapter 4, page 125.)

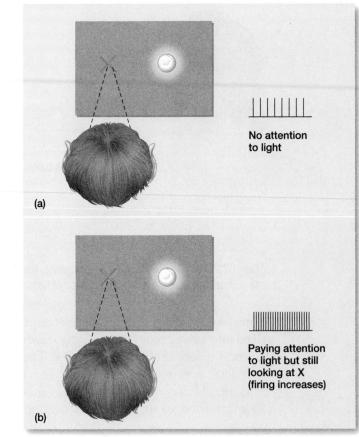

No attention
to light

(a)

Paying attention
to light but still
looking at X
(firing increases)

(b)

Figure 2.22 (a) When a monkey is looking at the X and is not paying attention to the flashing light that is off to the side, a neuron in the cortex fires slowly; (b) when the monkey pays attention to the light (while still looking at the X), firing of the neuron increases.

Just as listening to individual voices provides valuable information about what is happening within a crowd, recording from single neurons provides valuable information about what is happening in the brain. It is, of course, important to record from as many neurons as possible, since, just as individual people may have different opinions about the speech, different neurons may respond differently to a particular stimulus or situation.

We have described how single-unit activity is measured with microelectrodes (see page 31) and how these measurements have led to the discovery that many neurons are tuned to specific stimuli (see page 38). While single unit recording is an extremely valuable tool, one of its disadvantages is that it is suitable for use only on animals. Although on a few rare occasions, single-unit recording has been done on humans as part of a neurosurgical procedure, most of the measurements of human brain activity have used other methods, such as the event-related potential and brain imaging.

Event-Related Potential

The **event-related potential (ERP)** is a response of many thousands of neurons to a specific stimulus or event. This response is recorded with disc electrodes placed on a person's scalp (Figure 2.23). When a stimulus is presented, the electrodes record voltage changes

(a)

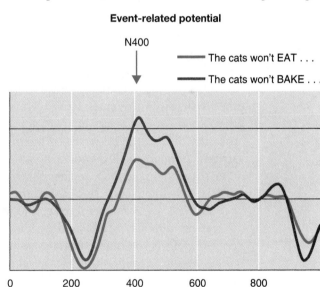

(b)

Figure 2.23 The event-related potential (ERP) is recorded with electrodes on the surface of the scalp. (a) This person is wearing an electrode cap that contains 129 electrodes. Each electrode records activity from the many thousands of neurons that are located near the electrode. (b) The ERP response consists of a number of waves, labeled N for negative, which is up in these records, and P for positive. The number indicates when the wave peaks. This example shows the negative N400 wave, which peaks 400 msecs after the stimulus is presented. The dark record indicates that the N400 wave becomes larger when a word is presented that doesn't fit the meaning of the sentence. (Reprinted from *Trends in Cognitive Sciences*, Volume 1, Issue 6, Osterhout et al., "Event-Related Potentials and Language," Figure 1, Copyright © 1997 with permission from Elsevier.)

in the brain generated by the thousands of neurons under the electrodes. The record of the response shows that presenting the word *eat* or *bake* causes positive potential at about 200 msec (note that positive is down), followed by a larger negative potential, which is called N400 because the response is negative and occurs 400 msec after the word is presented. This series of electrical responses is the event-related potential.

The property that makes the ERP especially valuable for cognitive psychology is that different components of the response indicate different aspects of cognitive processing. For example, the ERP indicated by the green line is the response to the word *eat* in the sentence *The cats won't eat*. However, when the sentence is changed to read *The cat won't bake*, the N400 response to the word *bake* becomes larger than it was to the word *eat*. This change in the size of the ERP response to a word that does not fit the meaning of a sentence is telling us that information about a word's meaning is registered in the brain within 400 msec. The ERP can, therefore, tell us *when* particular cognitive activity is occurring in the brain. In addition, the position on the scalp of the electrodes that pick up the largest response provides an estimate of *where* this activity is occurring in the brain.

Brain Imaging

One of the most widely used techniques for measuring brain activity in humans is **brain imaging,** which allows us to determine which areas of the brain are activated as awake humans carry out various cognitive tasks.

One of these techniques, **positron emission tomography (PET),** was introduced in the 1970s (Hoffman, et al., 1976; ter-Possin et al., 1975). PET takes advantage of the fact that blood flow increases in areas of the brain that are activated by a cognitive task. To measure blood flow, a low dose of a radioactive tracer is injected into a person's bloodstream. (The does is low enough so it is not harmful to the person.) The person's brain is then scanned by the PET apparatus, which measures the signal from the tracer at each location in the brain (Figure 2.24). Higher signals indicate higher levels of brain activity.

PET provides a way to determine which areas of the brain are being activated by a particular stimulus or task. To determine how a particular task, which we will call the *target task*, affects the brain, researchers use the **subtraction technique.** Using this technique, *baseline activity* is first measured while a person carries out a control task and then *stimulation activity* is measured while the person carries out the target task. Brain activity associated with the target task is determined by subtracting the baseline activity from the stimulation activity.

An example of how this technique was actually used is provided by an experiment by Steven Petersen and coworkers (1988), who determined which brain areas were activated by saying a word. First they determined which areas of the brain were activated when the person saw the word flashed on the screen. This provided a measure of *baseline activity*. They then determined which areas were activated when the person saw the word and then *said* the word. This provided a measure of *stimulation activity*. The activity that occurred

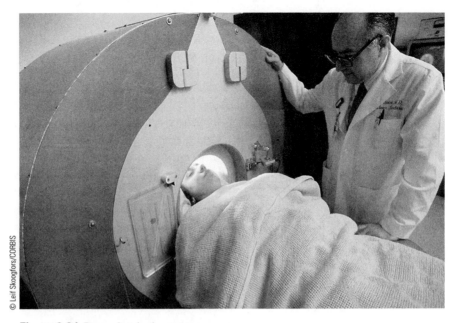

Figure 2.24 Person in a brain scanner.

due to saying the word was then determined by subtracting the baseline activity (the response to seeing the word) from the stimulation activity (the response to seeing and saying the word).

Recently, another neuroimaging technique called **functional magnetic resonance imaging (fMRI)** has been introduced. Like PET, fMRI is based on the measurement of blood flow. An advantage of fMRI is that blood flow can be measured without radioactive tracers. It does this by using the fact that hemoglobin, which carries oxygen in the blood, contains a ferrous molecule and therefore has magnetic properties. Thus, if a magnetic field is presented to the brain, the hemoglobin molecules line up like tiny magnets.

fMRI indicates the presence of brain activity because the hemoglobin molecules in areas of high brain activity lose some of the oxygen they are transporting. Losing oxygen increases the hemoglobin's response to a magnetic field so these molecules respond more strongly to the field. The fMRI apparatus determines the relative activity of various areas of the brain by detecting changes in the magnetic response of the hemoglobin. The subtraction technique described previously for PET is also used for fMRI but because fMRI doesn't require radioactive tracers and because it is more accurate, this technique has become the primary method for localizing brain activity in humans.

Color Plate 2.1 (inside front cover) shows a record from an fMRI experiment in which brain activity was measured as a person viewed pictures (Brewer et al., 1998). Brain activation is indicated by the colored areas. These records illustrate distributed activation of the brain because a single stimulus activates a number of areas (see page 43).

BRAIN IMAGING

How Creating a Visual Image Affects the Brain

Looking at a tree causes electrical activity in the visual receiving area of your cortex (Figure 2.25a). But what happens when you just imagine the tree by closing your eyes and creating a mental image of it? Research using functional magnetic resonance imaging (fMRI), shows that imagining an object, like the tree, activates the same area of the brain that is activated when the object is actually seen (Figure 2.25b) (Kosslyn & Thompson, 2000). This result tells us that there are important similarities between what happens in the brain when we imagine seeing something and when we actually see it. (From Chapter 9, page 328.)

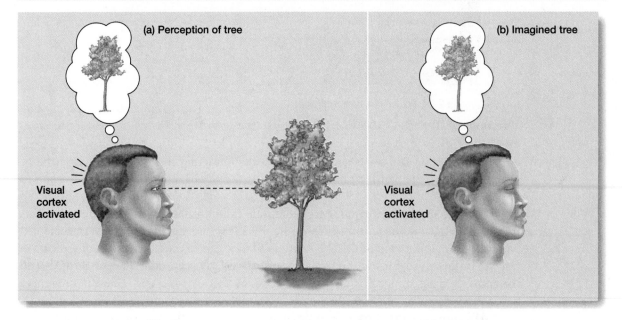

Figure 2.25 (a) Looking at a tree causes activity in the occipital cortex; (b) imagining a tree also activates this area.

Brain Lesioning

One way to determine the function of a particular area of the brain is to determine how removing that area affects behavior. This technique is called **brain lesioning,** where lesioning is removal of a portion of the brain.

Brain lesioning is used only rarely in humans in situations in which a portion of the brain is removed to obtain a therapeutic result. One of the most famous of these cases is the case of patient H.M., who had his hippocampus and some surrounding areas removed

Chapter 2

(see Figure 2.4), in an attempt to stop his severe epileptic seizures. While this operation did reduce H.M.'s seizures, it also had the unfortunate side effect of causing him to lose his ability to form new memories, a result that the neurosurgeons had no way of foreseeing, based on the knowledge available at that time (Scoville & Milner, 1957). Because of these effects, this operation has never been repeated but studies of H.M.'s memory loss have taught us a great deal about the role of the hippocampus in memory. We will describe the case of H.M. in more detail in Chapter 6.

Neuropsychology

Neuropsychology is the study of the behavioral effects of brain damage in humans. This brain damage is generally caused by accidents or by a stroke in which the blood supply to an area of the brain is disrupted. The basic idea behind neuropsychology is that we can understand how a system operates by studying dissociations—situations in which one function is absent while another function is present.

To help us understand dissociations, we will consider the example of a broken television (Parkin, 1996). One observation about broken televisions is that they can lose their color but still have a picture. This situation, when one function (color) is absent and the other (picture) is present, is called a single dissociation. The existence of a single dissociation indicates that the two functions involve different mechanisms, although they may not operate totally independently of one another.

Demonstrating a single dissociation involves just one TV, like the one we just described with a picture but no color. Now let's consider a situation in which we have two TV sets. A has no sound but has a picture. B does have sound but has no picture. A double dissociation occurs when we can demonstrate that one function is absent and the other is present in one TV (A: no sound, but the picture is OK) and that the opposite can also occur in another TV (B: sound OK, but there is no picture) (Table 2.2a). When a double dissociation occurs, this means that the two functions—sound and picture, in this example—involve

Table 2.2a	DOUBLE DISSOCIATION: TWO BROKEN TVS	
	Function 1: Sound	Function 2: Picture
Broken TV "A"	OK	No
Broken TV "B"	No	OK
Table 2.2b	DOUBLE DISSOCIATION: TWO PEOPLE WITH BRAIN DAMAGE	
	Function 1: Short-Term Memory	Function 2: New Long-Term Memories
Alice (temporal lobe damage)	OK	No
Bert (frontal lobe damage)	No	OK

NEUROPSYCHOLOGY
How Brain Damage Affects the Ability to Recognize Living and Nonliving Things

The idea of modularity states that areas of the brain are specialized to carry out specific tasks. For example, we know that areas in the temporal lobe are specialized for recognizing objects. But neuropsychological research with brain damaged patients has revealed that specialization is even more specific than this. Some patients with damage to their inferotemporal area of the temporal lobe have difficulty naming tools but can name living things. There are other patients with damage in nearby areas who have the opposite problem: they can name tools but have difficulty naming living things (Caramazza, 2000). The idea that there are different brain areas for recognizing different kinds of objects was originally suggested by studying brain damaged patients and has now been confirmed by the results of fMRI research (Martin & Chao, 2001). (From Chapter 8, page 304.)

different mechanisms and that these mechanisms operate independently of one another. This makes sense for our television example because the television picture is created by the picture tube and the sound is created by the amplifier and speakers.

This same reasoning can be applied to cases of human brain damage. For example, let's consider a hypothetical situation in which Alice, who has suffered damage to her temporal lobe, can remember what just happened (her short-term memory is intact), but can't transfer any of his experience into long-lived memories (she can't form new long-term memories). Bert, who has had damage to his frontal lobes, has the opposite problem: He can't remember what has just happened, but can form new long-term memories (Table 2.2b). These two cases, which are analogous to our two TVs, represent a double dissociation and indicate that forming short-term memories and forming new long-term memories are served by different mechanisms that are independent of one another. Notice that in order to demonstrate a double dissociation it is necessary to find two people with opposite problems.

Test Yourself 2.2

1. What is a brain module? Why are the IT cortex and MT cortex considered to be brain modules?
2. How is a specific stimulus, such as Bill's face, represented by the firing of neurons? How does a specific cognitive function (such as memory) activate the brain? Be able to distinguish between distributed coding and distributed activation of the brain.

3. Describe how the following techniques have been used to study brain function: (1) single-unit recording; (2) event-related potentials; (3) brain imaging; (4) brain lesioning; and (5) neuropsychology. Be sure to understand the basic principle behind each process, particularly the subtraction technique (for brain imaging) and dissociations (for neuropsychology).

Think About It

1. In this chapter, we call the brain the mind's computer. What are computers good at, that the brain is not? How do you think the brain and the mind compare in terms of complexity? What advantage does the brain have over a computer?

2. People generally feel that they are experiencing their environment directly, especially when it comes to sensory experiences such as seeing, hearing, or feeling the texture of a surface. However, our knowledge of how the nervous system operates indicates that this is not the case. Why would a physiologist say that all of our experiences are indirect?

3. When brain activity is being measured in an fMRI scanner, the person's head is surrounded by an array of magnets and must be kept perfectly still. In addition, the operation of the machine is very noisy. How do these characteristics of brain scanners limit the types of behaviors that can be studied using brain scanning?

4. It has been argued that we will never be able to fully understand how the brain operates because doing this involves using the brain to study itself. What do you think of this argument?

KEY TERMS

Action potential
Amygdala
Axon
Brain imaging
Brain lesioning
Broca's aphasia
Broca's area
Cell body
Cerebral cortex
Complex cells
Convergence
Dendrites
Dissociations
Distributed activation of the brain

Distributed coding
Double dissociation
End-stopped cells
Event-related potential (ERP)
Excitation
Excitatory neurotransmitter
Feature detectors
Frontal lobe
Functional magnetic resonance imaging (fMRI)
Hippocampus
Inferotemporal cortex
Inhibition
Inhibitory neurotransmitter
Localization of function

Medial temporal area
Microelectrodes
Modules
Motion agnosia
Nerve fiber
Neural circuits
Neural code
Neural processing
Neurons
Neuropsychology
Neurotransmitter
Occipital lobe
Parietal lobe
Positron emission tomography (PET)

Propagated
Prospagnosia
Receptors
Retina
Simple cells
Single dissociation
Single-unit recording
Subcortical structures
Subtraction technique
Synapse
Temporal lobe
Thalamus
Transduction

CogLab To experience these experiments for yourself, go to http://coglab.wadsworth.com. Be sure to read each experiment's setup instructions before you go to the experiment itself. Otherwise, you won't know which keys to press.

Primary Lab

Receptive fields   A receptive field of a visual neuron is the area on the retina that influences the activity of that neuron. In this lab you can map the receptive fields of some neurons (p. 38).

Related Lab

Brain asymmetry   How speed of processing for shapes and words may be different in the left and right hemispheres.

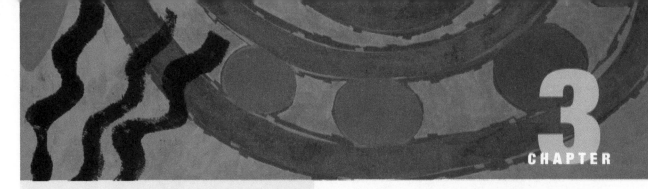

Perception

Some Questions We Will Consider

✔ Why does something that is so easy, like looking at a scene and seeing what is out there, become so complicated when we look at the mechanisms involved?

✔ Why is recognizing an object so easy for humans, but so difficult for computers?

✔ How is our knowledge of the world, which we use for perceiving, stored in the brain?

■ ■ ■

One of the things that makes many movies exciting is the amazing special effects, such as those in films like *The Lord of the Rings* (Figure 3.1). The special effects in movies may amaze us, but you don't have to go to a movie to see amazing visual effects—you are experiencing them right now, as you read this book or when you look up to perceive whatever is around you. **Perception**, the conscious experience that results from stimulation of the senses, may not seem particularly special because all we have to do is look around, listen, or touch something, and perception just "happens"

Figure 3.1 This scene from the film *The Lord of the Rings: The Fellowship of the Ring* involves special effects similar to those that are found in many films. Although the boats, carrying members of the "Fellowship," look extremely small compared to the two gigantic statues that flank the Great River, the statues used to create this scene were actually models about 8 feet high. As spectacular as these special effects are, the processes involved in creating our perception of a normal scene in the environment is far more complex and miraculous than the process involved in creating any movie special effects. (From *The Lord of the Rings™: the Fellowship of the Ring™*. Copyright MMI, New Line Productions, Inc.™ The Saul Zaentz Company d/b/a Tolkien Enterprises under license to New Line Productions, Inc. All rights reserved. Photo by Pierre Vinet. Photo appears courtesy of New Line Productions, Inc.)

with little effort or our part. However, the mechanisms responsible for your ability to perceive are far more amazing than the technology used to create even the most complicated special effects.

Because of the ease with which we perceive, many people don't see the feats achieved by our senses as complex or amazing. "After all," the skeptic might say, "for vision, a picture of the environment is focused on the back of my eye, and that picture provides all the information my brain needs to duplicate the environment in my consciousness." But the idea that perception is not that complex is exactly what misled computer scientists in the 1950s and 1960s into proposing that it would take only about a decade or so to create "perceiving machines" that could negotiate the environment with humanlike ease.

These predictions, made over 40 years ago, have yet to come true, even though a computer defeated the world chess champion in 1997. From a computer's point of view, perceiving a scene is more difficult than playing world-championship chess. One of the

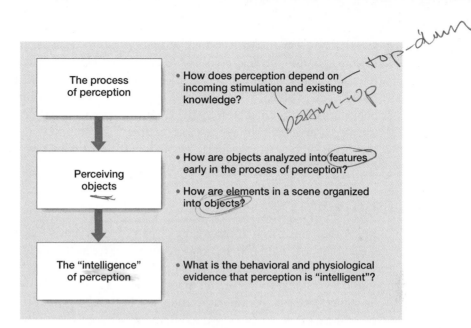

Figure 3.2 Flow diagram for this chapter.

goals of this chapter is to make you aware of the processes that are responsible for creating our perceptions.

The plan of this chapter is shown in Figure 3.2. We first describe how the process of perception depends both on the incoming stimulation and knowledge we bring to the situation. Following this introduction, we will devote the rest of the chapter to answering the question, "How do we perceive objects?"

One reason that we will be focusing on object perception is that perceiving objects is central to our everyday experience. Consider, for example, what you would say if you were asked to look up and describe what you are perceiving right now. Your answer would, of course, depend on where you are but it is likely that a large part of your answer would include naming the objects that you see. ("I see a book. There's a chair against the wall. . . .")

Another reason for focusing on object perception is that it enables us to achieve a more in-depth understanding of the basic principles of perception than we could achieve by covering a number of different types of perception more superficially. After describing a number of mechanisms of object perception, we will consider the idea that perception is "intelligent." We will see that behavioral and physiological evidence supports this idea.

What Happens During the Process of Perception?

Although perception seems to just "happen," it is actually the end result of a complex process. We can appreciate the complexity involved in seemingly simple behaviors by returning to our example of Juan and the alarm clock from the beginning of Chapter 2. We saw that one way to describe Juan's situation was to consider how neurons in his ear and brain respond to the ringing of his alarm. But we also saw that things become more complicated when we consider that Juan's response to his alarm (hitting the snooze button and going back to sleep) is determined by knowledge that he brings to the situation. His behavior is determined both by the ringing of the alarm clock and his knowledge that he can sleep longer and still get to class on time. We will now consider another behavior that may seem simple but which also involves hidden complexities.

Roger Misperceives a Street Sign

Roger is driving through an unfamiliar part of town. He is following directions, which indicate that he should turn left on Washington Street. It is dark and the street is poorly lit, so it is difficult to read the street signs. Suddenly, just before an intersection, he sees the sign for Washington Street and quickly makes a left turn. However, after driving a block, he realizes he is on Washburn Avenue, not Washington Street. He feels a little foolish because it isn't that hard to tell the difference between *Washington Street* and *Washburn Avenue*, but the sign really did look like it said *Washington* at the time.

We can understand what happened in this example by considering some of the events that occur during the process of perception. The first event in the process of perception is reception of the stimulus. Light from a streetlight is reflected from the sign into Roger's eye (Figure 3.3). We can consider this step "data in" since a pattern of light and dark enters Roger's eye and creates a pattern on his retina.

Before Roger can see anything, this information on his retina has to be changed into electrical signals (see transduction, page 30), transmitted to his brain, and processed (Figure 3.4). During processing, various mechanisms work toward creating a conscious perception of the sign (see neural processing; neural coding, pages 36 and 42). But just saying that "processing" results in conscious perception of the sign does not tell the entire story, as we will see next.

The Role of Data and Knowledge in Perception: Bottom-Up and Top-Down Processing

Up to this point, saying that the "data comes in and is processed," could be describing what happens in a computer. In the case of human perception, the computer is the brain, which contains neurons and synapses instead of solid-state circuitry. This analogy between the digital computer and the brain is not totally inaccurate, but it leaves out something that is extremely important. Roger's brain contains not only neurons and synapses but also *knowledge*, and when the incoming data interacts with this knowledge, the resulting response is different from what would happen if the brain were just a computer that responded in an automatic way to whatever stimulus patterns it was receiving.

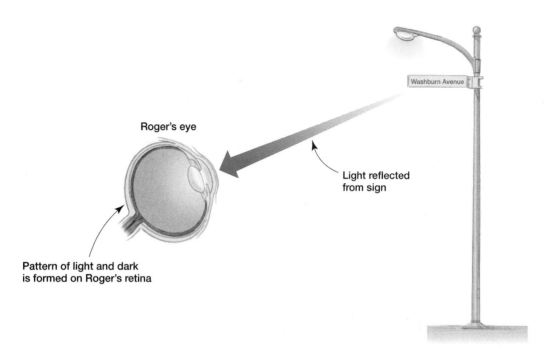

Figure 3.3 Light from the streetlight is reflected from the sign into Roger's eye, which creates a pattern representing the street sign on Roger's retina.

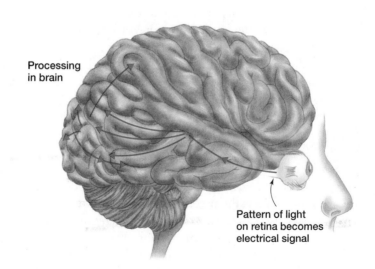

Figure 3.4 The pattern on the retina is transformed into electrical signals, which are transmitted to the brain and processed.

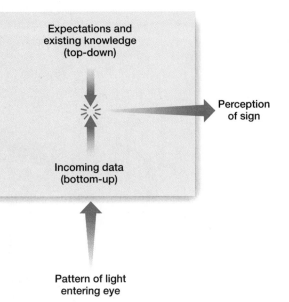

Figure 3.5 Roger's perception of the sign is created by the processing of the incoming data provided by the pattern of light entering his eye (bottom-up processing) *plus* the influence of existing knowledge and expectations (top-down processing).

Before Roger even saw the sign, his brain contained knowledge about driving, street signs, how to read a map, and how to read letters and words, among other things. In addition, the fact that he was looking for Washington Street and was expecting it to be coming up soon played a large role in causing him to mistakenly read *Washington* when the actual stimulus was *Washburn*. Thus, if Roger had not been expecting to see *Washington*, he might have read the sign correctly. However when the incoming data collided with his expectation, *Washburn* turned into *Washington*.

Psychologists distinguish between the processing that is based on incoming data and the processing that is based on existing knowledge by distinguishing between bottom-up processing and top-down processing. **Bottom-up processing** (also called *data-based processing*) is processing that based on incoming data. This is always the starting point for perception because if there is no incoming data, there is no perception. In our example, the incoming data is the pattern of light that enters Roger's eye (Figure 3.5). **Top-down processing** (also called *knowledge-based processing*) refers to processing that is based on knowledge. Knowledge doesn't have to be involved in perception but, as we will see, it usually is—sometimes without our even being aware of its presence.

Roger's experience in looking for a street sign on a dark night illustrates how these two types of processing can interact. The following demonstration illustrates what happens when incoming data is affected by knowledge that has been provided just moments earlier.

unless hallucinating, visualizing...

Figure 3.6 Picture for "perceiving a picture" demonstration. See text for instructions. (Adapted from "The Role of Frequency in Developing Perceptual Sets," by B. R. Bugelski et al., 1961, *Canadian Journal of Psychology, 15*, pp. 205–211, Copyright © 1961 by the Canadian Psychological Association.)

◥ Demonstration

Perceiving a Picture

After looking at the drawing in Figure 3.6, close your eyes, then turn to the next page in the book without looking at the page. Then open and shut your eyes rapidly to briefly expose the picture in Figure 3.8. Decide what the picture is based on this brief exposure. Do this now, before reading further. ■

What did you see when you looked at Figure 3.8? Did it look like a rat (or a mouse)? If it did, you were influenced by the clearly rat- or mouse-like figure you saw in Figure 3.6. But people who first observe Figure 3.12 instead of Figure 3.6 usually identify Figure 3.8 as a man. (Try this demonstration on someone else.) This demonstration, which is called the rat-man demonstration, shows how recently acquired knowledge ("that pattern is a rat") can influence perception.

In this example, the pattern of lines in Figure 3.8 is the data that is the starting point for bottom-up processing. The expectation created by first looking at Figure 3.6 is the knowledge that is associated with top-down processing. Just as Roger's expectation that he would soon see *Washington* created top-down processing that influenced his perception, your expectation that a particular pattern of lines is a picture of a rat may have influenced your perception.

Another example of an effect of top-down processing is provided by an experiment by Stephen Palmer (1975), in which he presented a context scene such as the one on the left of Figure 3.7 and then briefly flashed one of the target pictures on the right. When Palmer asked participants to identify the object in the target picture, they correctly identified an object like the loaf of bread (which is appropriate to the kitchen scene) 80 percent of the time, but correctly identified the mailbox or the drum (two objects that don't fit into the scene) only 40 percent of the time. This experiment shows how a person's knowledge of the context provided by a particular scene can influence perception.

As you read later chapters in this book, you will see that there are numerous situations in which incoming data interacts with a person's knowledge. This occurs for attention, memory, language, and most of the other types of cognition we will be discussing. In this

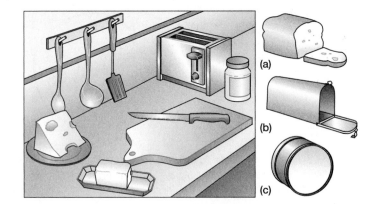

Figure 3.7 Stimuli like those used in Palmer's (1975) experiment, which showed how context can influence perception. (Reprinted from "The Effects of Contextual Scenes on the Identification of Objects," by S. E. Palmer, 1975, *Memory and Cognition, 3,* pp. 519–526, Copyright ©1975 with permission from the author and the Psychonomic Society Publishers.)

chapter, we will focus on perception by looking at what cognitive psychologists have discovered about how both bottom-up and top-down processes operate as we perceive objects. We are going to start by describing how incoming stimuli are analyzed by the visual system. This analysis occurs rapidly and without our awareness and provides an example of the bottom-up processing that occurs at the beginning of the process of perception.

ANALYZING OBJECTS INTO COMPONENTS: THE FIRST STEP IN THE PERCEPTUAL PROCESS

Our lack of awareness of the processes that create perception is particularly true at the very beginning of the perceptual process, when the incoming data is being analyzed. Early in the process of object perception objects are analyzed into smaller components, called features. We will describe the **feature approach to object perception** by first describing a simple model for recognizing letters, then describing how physiological and behavioral evidence supports the idea that features are important in perception. Finally, we will describe two theories of object perception that are based on the idea that objects are analyzed into features early in the perceptual process.

A Model for Recognizing Letters

Figure 3.9 shows a simple model, which illustrates how the analysis of features can lead to the recognition of letters. We will describe how it works by considering the way the model responds to presentation of the letter *A*. The first stage of this model, called the **feature analysis stage**, consists of a bank of **feature units,** each of which responds to a specific

Figure 3.8 (Adapted from "The Role of Frequency in Developing Perceptual Sets," by B. R. Bugelski et al., 1961, *Canadian Journal of Psychology, 15,* pp. 205–211, Copyright © 1961 by the Canadian Psychological Association.)

feature. The *A* activates three of these units—one for "line slanted to the right," one for "line slanted to the left," and one for "horizontal line." Thus, in this stage, the *A* is broken down into its individual features.

The second stage, called the **letter-analysis stage,** consists of a bank of **letter units,** each of which represents a specific letter. Just six of these letter units are shown here, but in the complete model there would be one unit for each letter in the alphabet. Notice that each letter unit receives inputs from the feature units associated with that letter. Thus, when the letter *A* is presented, the *A*-unit receives inputs from three feature units. Other letters that have features in common with the *A* also receive inputs from feature units that are activated by the *A*.

The basic idea behind feature analysis is that activation of letter units provides the information needed to determine which letter is present. All the visual system has to do is

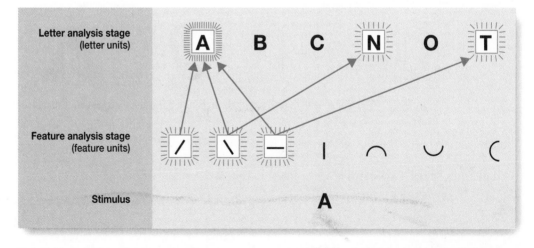

Figure 3.9 A model for recognizing letters by analyzing their features. The stimulus, *A,* activates three feature-units. These feature-units cause strong activation of the *A* letter-unit and weaker activation of units for letters such as the *N* and the *O,* which lack some of *A*'s features. The *A* is identified by the high level of activation of the *A* letter-unit.

Figure 3.10 Different kinds of *A*'s that share features.

determine which unit is activated most strongly. In our example, the units for *A*, *N*, and *T* are activated, but because the *A* receives inputs from three feature units and the *T* and *N* receive inputs from only one, the *A*-unit is activated more strongly, indicating that *A* was the letter that was presented.

The idea that objects are analyzed into features is especially appealing because it helps explain how we can recognize all of the patterns in Figure 3.10 as being the letter *A*. Analyzing letters into features makes it possible to identify many of these *A*'s as being the same letter, even though they look different, because underneath their differences, each *A* contains many of the same features.

The feature analysis model we have described is a simple one that would have trouble identifying more unconventional looking letters like the ones in Figure 3.11 as *A*'s, and would also have problems telling the difference between letters with similar features that are arranged differently, like *L* and *T*. To tell the difference between the L and the T, a more complex model is required. Furthermore, a feature analysis model designed to consider objects in addition to letters would have to be even more complex. Thus, the point of presenting the model in Figure 3.9 is not to present a model that would actually work under real-world conditions, but to illustrate the basic principle behind feature analysis— feature units are activated and these units send signals to other, higher-order, units.

Figure 3.11 The simple feature analysis model in Figure 3.9 would have difficulty identifying all of these as *A*'s.

Evidence for Feature Analysis

The idea of feature-based perception is supported by both physiological and behavioral evidence.

eg cells in low-level visual areas that respond to specific inputs...

Neural Feature Detectors The neural feature detectors that we introduced in Chapter 2 provide a physiological basis for feature analysis. There are simple feature detectors that respond to oriented lines like the ones in the model, and there are also more complex feature detectors that respond to combinations of these simple features (see Figure 2.16).

Figure 3.12 The "man" stimulus for the rat-man demonstration. (Adapted from "The Role of Frequency in Developing Perceptual Sets," by B. R. Bugelski et al., 1961, *Canadian Journal of Psychology, 15,* pp. 205–211, Copyright © 1961 by the Canadian Psychological Association.)

Visual Search Experiments   The feature approach has been studied behaviorally using a technique called **visual search** in which participants are asked to find a target stimulus among a number of distractor stimuli. In one of the early visual search experiments, Ulric Neisser (1964) asked participants to find a target letter among a number of "distractor" letters. Try this yourself by looking for the Z in Figure 3.13a and then try to find it in Figure 3.13b. Neisser's participants detected the Z more rapidly in the first list than in the second one. It's easy to see why, by noting that the Z shares no features with the distractors in Figure 3.13a, but has many features in common with the distractors in Figure 3.13b.

We can explain Neisser's behavioral result in terms of physiology by noting that the Z in the left column will cause feature detectors that respond to horizontal lines and slanted lines to fire, but the distractors will cause a different group of feature detectors to fire. Thus, in the list on the left, presence of the Z is clearly signaled by the firing of the "slanted line" and "horizontal line" detectors. However, in the list on the right, both the Z and some of the distractors activate the same detectors, so the neurons activated by the Z will not be that different from the neurons activated by the distractors.

Following Neisser's lead, Ann Treisman (1986) also has used visual search to study feature analysis. However, instead of just showing that letters can be detected faster if their features are different from the distractors, she asked the question: "How does the speed that a target can be detected depend on how many distractors are present?" The following demonstration is based on Treisman's procedure.

ODUGQR	IVMXEW
QCDUGO	EWVMIX
CQOGRD	EXWMVI
QUGCDR	IXEMWV
URDGQO	VXWEMI
GRUQDO	MXVEWI
DUZGRO	XVWMEI
UCGROD	MWXVIE
DQRCGU	VIMEXW
QDOCGU	EXVWIM
CGUROQ	VWMIEX
OCDURQ	VMWIEX
UOCGQD	XVWMEI
RGQCOU	WXVEMI
GRUDQO	XMEWIV
GODUCQ	MXIVEW
QCURDO	VEWMIX
DUCOQG	EMVXWI
CGRDQU	IVWMEX
UDRCOQ	IEVMWX
GQCORU	WVZMXE
GOQUCD	XEMIWV
GDQUOC	WXIMEV
URDCGO	EMWIVX
GODRQC	IVEMXW

(a)	(b)

Figure 3.13 Stimulus for Neisser's (1964) visual search experiment.

■ Demonstration

Visual Search

■ In Figure 3.14, find the letter *O* in the display on the left and then in the display on the right.

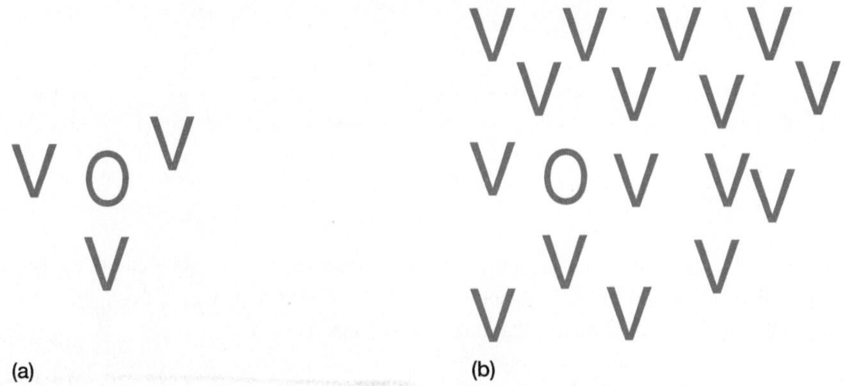

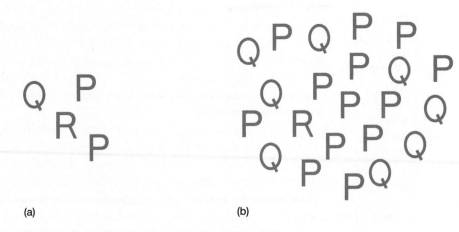

Figure 3.14 Find the *O* on the left and then on the right.

Figure 3.15 Find the *R* on the left and then on the right.

■ In Figure 3.15, find the letter *R* in the display on the left and then in the display on the right. ■

The usual result for these visual search tasks is that the *O*'s on the left and right both exhibit an effect called **pop-out**—we see them almost instantaneously, even when there are many distractors, as in the display on the right. However, the usual result for the *R*'s is different. The *R*'s don't pop out, and it usually takes longer to find the *R* when there are more distractors, as on the right.

Results from controlled experiments using stimuli like the ones in Figure 3.14 and 3.15 are shown in Figure 3.16. Notice that the function for the *O*'s search times is flat, indicating that the *O* is detected rapidly no matter how many distractors are present. In contrast, the function for the *R* increases as the number of distractors increases, indicating that it takes longer to find the *R* when there are more distractors.

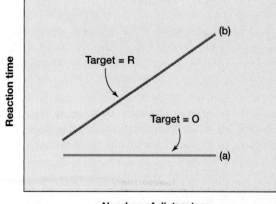

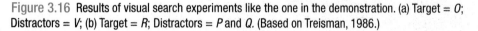

Figure 3.16 Results of visual search experiments like the one in the demonstration. (a) Target = *O*; Distractors = *V*; (b) Target = *R*; Distractors = *P* and *Q*. (Based on Treisman, 1986.)

Why are the results for the *O* and the *R* different? According to Treisman (1986), the difference occurs because of the features of the target letter and distractor letters. In Figure 3.14 the *O*'s feature of *curvature* differs from the *V*'s feature of *straight lines*. If the target's features are different from the distractor's features, the target "pops out," whether there are few distractors or many distractors.

However, in Figure 3.15 the *R* has features in common with the distractors. The *R* has straight lines like the *P*, slanted lines like the *Q*, and a curved line like both the *P* and the *Q*. These shared features prevent pop-out, and so it is necessary to scan each letter individually to find the target, just as you would have to scan the faces in a crowd to locate one particular person. Because scanning is necessary, adding more distractors increases the time it takes to find the target, as shown in curve (b) in Figure 3.16.

By determining which features cause the "pop-out" effect in search tasks, Treisman and other researchers have identified a number of basic features, including curvature, tilt, line ends, movement, color, and brightness (Beck, 1982; Julesz, 1984; Treisman, 1986, 1995). Treisman's research led her to propose a theory of feature analysis called feature integration theory.

CogLab
Visual Search

Feature Integration Theory (FIT)

Figure 3.17 shows the basic idea behind feature integration theory (FIT; Treisman, 1986). According to this theory, the first stage of perception is the preattentive stage, so named because it happens automatically and doesn't require any effort or attention by the perceiver. In this stage, an object is analyzed into its features.

The idea that an object is automatically broken into features seems counterintuitive because when we look at an object, we see the whole object, not an object that has been divided into its individual features. The reason we aren't aware of this process of feature

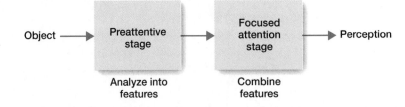

Figure 3.17 Flow diagram for Treisman's (1986) feature integration theory (FIT). According to this theory, objects are first analyzed into features in the preattentive stage, and then these features are combined into an object that can be perceived in the focused attention stage.

analysis is that it occurs early in the perceptual process, before we have become conscious of the object. To provide some perceptual evidence that objects are, in fact, analyzed into features, Treisman and H. Schmidt (1982) did an ingenious experiment to show that early in the perceptual process features may exist independently of one another.

Treisman and Schmidt's display consisted of four objects flanked by two black numbers (Figure 3.18). She flashed this display onto a screen for one-fifth of a second, followed by a random-dot masking field designed to eliminate any residual perception that may remain after the stimuli are turned off. Participants were told to report the black numbers first and then to report what they saw at each of the four locations where the shapes had been.

In 18 percent of the trials, participants reported seeing objects that were made up of a combination of features from two different stimuli. For example, after being presented with the display in Figure 3.18, in which the small triangle was red and the small circle

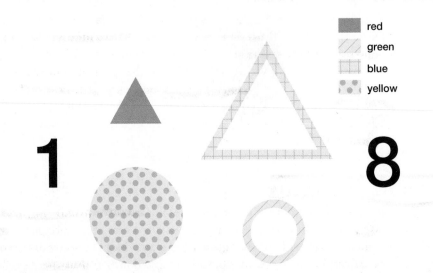

Figure 3.18 Stimuli for Treisman and Schmidt's (1982) illusory conjunction experiment. The geometrical figures were different colors, as indicated by the key. The numbers were black. (Adapted from Treisman et al., 1982.)

Figure 3.19 The results of the illusory conjunction experiment suggest that very early in the perceptual process, features that make up an object are "free floating." This is symbolized here by showing some of the features of a cell phone as existing separately from one another at the beginning of the perceptual process.

was green, they might report seeing a small red circle and a small green triangle. These combinations of features from different stimuli are called **illusory conjunctions.** Illusory conjunctions can occur even if the stimuli differ greatly in shape and size. For example, a small blue circle and a large green square might be seen as a large blue square and a small green circle.

According to Treisman, these illusory conjunctions occur because at the beginning of the perceptual process each feature exists independently of the others. That is, features such as "redness," "curvature," or "tilted line" are not, at this early stage of processing, associated with a specific object (Figure 3.19). They are, in Treisman's (1986) words, "free floating" and can therefore be incorrectly combined in laboratory situations when briefly flashed stimuli are followed by a masking field.

One way to think about these features is that they are components of an "alphabet" of vision. At the very beginning of the process of perception these components of perception exist independently of one another, just as the individual letter tiles in a game of Scrabble exist as individual units when the tiles are scattered at the beginning of the game. However, just as the individual Scrabble tiles are combined to form words, the individual

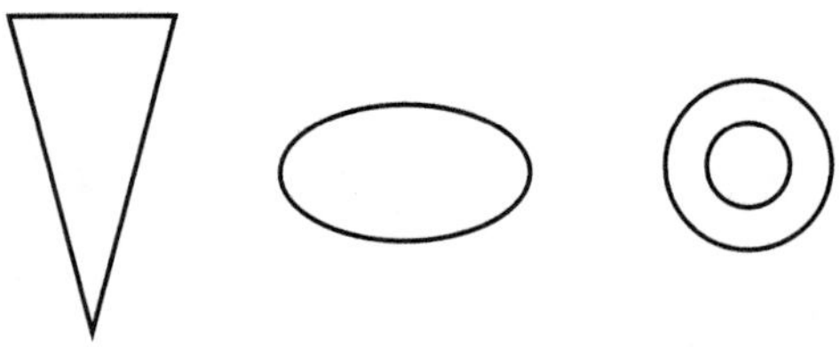

Figure 3.20 Three stimuli used by Treisman to illustrate how top-down processing can influence the combining of features. (From Treisman & Schmidt, 1982.)

features combine to form perceptions of whole objects. According to Treisman's model, these features are combined in the second stage, which is called the **focused attention stage.** Once the features have been combined in this stage, we perceive the object.

During the focused attention stage, the observer's attention plays an important role in combining the features to create the perception of whole objects. To illustrate the importance of attention for combining the features, Treisman repeated the illusory conjunction experiment using the stimuli in Figure 3.18, but she instructed her participants to ignore the black numbers and to focus all of their attention on the four target items. This focusing of attention eliminated illusory conjunctions so that all of the shapes were paired with their correct colors.

The feature analysis approach proposes that at the beginning of the process of perception, the stimulus is analyzed into elementary features, which are then combined to create perception of the object. This process involves mostly bottom-up processing because knowledge is not involved. In some situations however, top-down processing can come into play. For example, when Treisman did an illusory conjunction experiment using stimuli such as the ones in Figure 3.20 and asked participants to identify the objects, the usual illusory conjunctions occurred, so the orange triangle would, for example, sometimes be perceived to be black. However, when she told participants that they were being shown a carrot, a lake, and a tire, illusory conjunctions were less likely to occur, so subjects were more likely to perceive the triangular "carrot" as being orange. Thus, in this situation, the participants' knowledge of the usual colors of objects influenced their ability to correctly combine the features of each object. Top-down processing comes into play even more in the focused attention stage because the observer's attention can be controlled by meaning, expectations, and what the observer is looking for, as when Roger was watching for a particular street sign.

Next we will consider another feature-based approach to perception similar to the preattentive stage of feature integration theory in that it is a bottom-up process that involves combining features to form objects.

Recognition-by-Components Approach

In the **recognition-by-components (RBC) approach** to perception, the features are not lines, curves, or colors, but are three-dimensional volumes called **geons.** Figure 3.21a shows a number of geons, which are shapes such as cylinders, rectangular solids, and pyr-

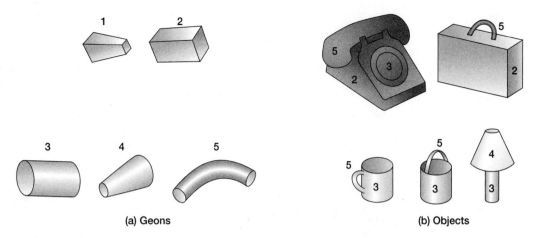

(a) Geons   (b) Objects

Figure 3.21 (a) Some geons; (b) some objects created from the geons on the left. The numbers on the objects indicate which geons are present. (Adapted from "Recognition-by-Components: A Theory of Human Image Understanding," by I. Biederman, 1987, *Psychological Review, 24,* 2, pp. 115–147, Figures 3, 6, 7, and 11, Copyright © 1987 with permission from the author and the American Psychological Association.)

amids. Irving Biederman (1987), who developed RBC theory, has proposed that there are 36 different geons, and that this number of geons is enough to enable us to construct a large proportion of the objects that exist in the environment. Figure 3.21b shows a few objects that have been constructed from geons.

An important property of geons is that they can be identified when viewed from different angles. This property, which is called **view invariance,** occurs because geons contain **view invariant properties**—properties such as the three parallel edges of the rectangular solid in Figure 3.21 that remain visible even when the geon is viewed from many different angles.

You can test the view-invariant properties of a rectangular solid yourself by picking up a book and moving it around so you are looking at it from many different viewpoints. As you do this, notice what percentage of the time you are seeing the three parallel edges. Also notice that occasionally, as when you look at the book end-on, you do not see all three edges. However, these situations occur only rarely, and when they do occur it becomes more difficult to recognize the object. For example, when we view the object in Figure 3.22a from the unusual perspective in Figure 3.22b, we see fewer basic geons and therefore have difficulty identifying it.

Two other properties of geons are discriminability and resistance to visual noise. **Discriminability** means that each geon can be distinguished from the others from almost all viewpoints. **Resistance to visual noise** means that we can still perceive geons under "noisy" conditions. For example, look at Figure 3.23. The reason you can identify this object (what is it?)—even though over half of its contour is obscured—is because you can still identify its geons. However, in Figure 3.24, in which the visual noise is arranged so the geons cannot be identified, it becomes impossible to recognize that the object is a flashlight.

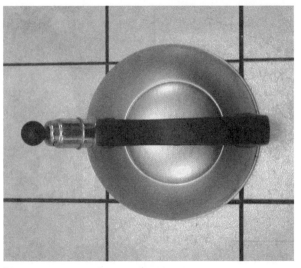

(a)

(b)

Figure 3.22 (a) A familiar object; (b) the same object seen from a viewpoint that obscures most of its geons and therefore makes it harder to recognize.

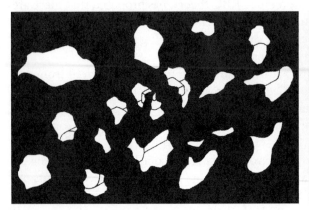

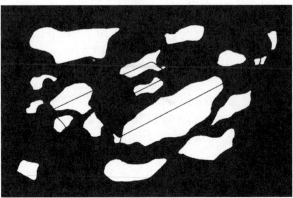

Figure 3.23 What is the object behind the mask? (Reprinted from "Recognition-by-Components: A Theory of Human Image Understanding," by I. Biederman, 1987, *Psychological Review, 24,* 2, pp. 115–147, Figure 26, Copyright © 1987 with permission from the author and the American Psychological Association.)

Figure 3.24 The same object as in Figure 3.23 (a flashlight) with the geons obscured. (Reprinted from "Recognition-by-Components: A Theory of Human Image Understanding," by I. Biederman, 1987, *Psychological Review, 24,* 2, pp. 115–147, Figure 25, Copyright © 1987 with permission from the author and the American Psychological Association.)

The basic message of RBC theory is that if enough information is available to enable us to identify an object's basic geons, we will be able to identify the object (also see Biederman & Cooper, 1991; Biederman et al., 1993; Biederman, 2001). A strength of Biederman's theory is that it shows that we can recognize objects based on a relatively small number of basic shapes. For example, we easily recognize Figure 3.25a, which has

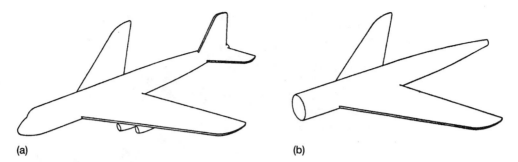

(a)   (b)

Figure 3.25 An airplane, as represented by (a) nine geons; (b) three geons. (Reprinted from "Recognition-by-Components: A Theory of Human Image Understanding," by I. Biederman, 1987, *Psychological Review, 24,* 2, pp. 115–147, Figure 13, Copyright © 1987 with permission from the author and the American Psychological Association.)

nine geons, as an airplane, but even when only three geons are present, as in Figure 3.25b, we can still identify an airplane.

Both feature-integration theory (FIT) and recognition-by-components (RBC) theory are based on the idea the idea of early analysis of objects into parts. These two theories explain different facets of object perception. FIT theory is more concerned with very basic features like lines, curves, colors, and with how attention is involved in combining them, whereas RBC theory is more about how we perceive three-dimensional shapes. Thus, both theories explain how objects are analyzed into parts early in the perceptual process.

There is, however, more to perceiving objects than analyzing them into parts. We will now consider another aspect of object perception, which focuses not on analysis that occurs early in the perceptual process, but on how we organize elements of the environment into separate objects.

Test Yourself 3.1

1. Describe the role of bottom-up and top-down processing on Roger's search for Washington Street, in the rat-man demonstration, and in Palmer's kitchen experiment.

2. What is the basic idea behind the feature analysis approach to perception? Describe the feature analysis model for recognizing letters. How do parts of this model relate to what we know about physiology?

3. Describe how Neisser and Treisman used visual search to provide evidence for the feature analysis approach to perception. Be sure to understand how Treisman used visual search to identify visual features.

4. Describe Treisman's feature integration theory. How do her experiments on illusory conjunctions support the idea that features are "free floating" in the preattentive stage? What is the focused attention stage, and what is the evidence that attention is important for combining the features?

5. Describe Biederman's recognition-by-components theory. How is it similar to Treisman's theory and how is it different?

R. C. James

Figure 3.26 What is this? The process of grouping the elements of this scene together to form a perception of an object is called perceptual organization. (The object is a Dalmatian.)

PERCEPTUAL ORGANIZATION: PUTTING TOGETHER AN ORGANIZED PERCEPTUAL WORLD

What do you see in Figure 3.26? Take a moment and decide before reading further.

If you have never seen this picture before, you may just see a bunch of black splotches on a white background. However, if you look closely you can see that the picture is a Dalmatian, with its nose to the ground. Once you have seen this picture as a Dalmatian, it is hard to see it any other way. Your mind has achieved **perceptual organization**—the organization of elements of the environment into objects—and has perceptually organized the black areas into a Dalmatian. But what is behind this process? The first psychologists to study this question were a group called the **Gestalt psychologists,** who were active in Europe beginning in the 1920s.

The Gestalt Approach to Perception

Early in the 1900s, perception was explained by an approach called **structuralism** as the adding-up of small elementary units called **sensations.** According to this idea, we see the two glasses in Figure 3.27a because hundreds of tiny sensations, indicated by the dots in

(a)   (b)

Figure 3.27 (a) Two overlapping wine glasses; (b) each dot represents a sensation. According to the structuralist approach, these individual sensations are combined to result in our perception of the glasses.

Figure 3.27b, add up to create our perception of the glasses. But the Gestalt psychologists took a different approach. Instead of looking at the glasses as a collection of tiny sensations, they considered the overall pattern created by the glasses. According to the Gestalt approach, the pattern in Figure 3.27b can potentially be perceived as representing a number of different objects, as shown in Figures 3.28a, b, and c. But even though many different objects could have created the pattern in Figure 3.27a, the fact that we automatically see the picture as two separate glasses, as in Figure 3.28a, caused the Gestalt psychologists

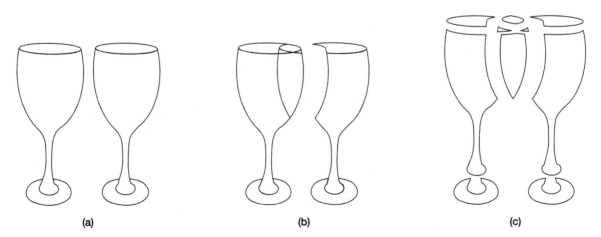

(a)   (b)   (c)

Figure 3.28 Each of the objects in (a), (b), and (c) could have resulted in the perception in Figure 3.27a if arranged appropriately in relation to one another. The Gestalt psychologists pointed out that we see the pattern as two glasses, as in (a), and proposed "laws of perceptual organization" to explain why certain perceptions are more likely than others.

to ask what causes us to organize our perception in this way. The Gestalt psychologists felt that this question could not be answered in terms of elementary sensations. Instead, they proposed that the mind groups patterns according to rules that they called the laws of perceptual organization.

The Gestalt Laws of Perceptual Organization   The **laws of perceptual organization** are a series of rules that specify how we perceptually organize parts into wholes. Let's look at six of the Gestalt laws.

■ **Pragnanz**   *Pragnanz*, roughly translated from the German, means "good figure." The **law of Pragnanz**, the central law of Gestalt psychology, which is also called the **law of good figure** or the **law of simplicity**, states: *Every stimulus pattern is seen in such a way that the resulting structure is as simple as possible.* The familiar Olympic symbol in Figure 3.29a is an example of the law of simplicity at work. We see this display as five circles and not as other, more complicated shapes such as the ones in Figure 3.29b. We can also apply this law to the wine glasses in Figure 3.28. Seeing the pattern as two glasses as in Figure 3.28a is much simpler than seeing it as the more complex objects in Figures 3.28b and c.

■ **Similarity**   Most people perceive Figure 3.30a as either horizontal rows of circles, vertical columns of circles, or both. But when we change some of the circles to squares, as in Figure 3.30b, most people perceive vertical columns of squares and circles. This perception illustrates the **law of similarity**: *Similar things appear to be grouped together.* This law causes the circles to be grouped with other circles and the squares to be grouped with other squares. Grouping can also occur because of similarity of lightness (Figure 3.31), hue, size, or orientation.

■ **Good Continuation**   We see the electric cord starting at A in Figure 3.32 as flowing smoothly to B. It does not go to C or D because that path would involve making sharp turns and would violate the **law of good continuation**: *Points which, when connected, result in straight or smoothly curving lines, are seen as belonging together, and the lines tend to be seen as following the smoothest path.* Because of the law of good continuation we see one cord going from the clock to B and another one going from the lamp to D.

is this empirically tested??

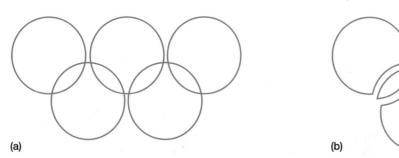

(a)   (b)

Figure 3.29 Law of simplicity. We see five circles as in (a), not the more complex array of nine objects, as in (b).

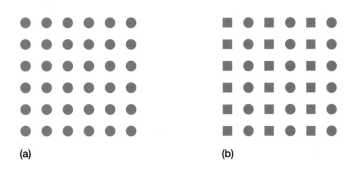
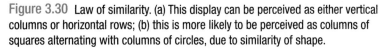

(a)   (b)

Figure 3.30 Law of similarity. (a) This display can be perceived as either vertical columns or horizontal rows; (b) this is more likely to be perceived as columns of squares alternating with columns of circles, due to similarity of shape.

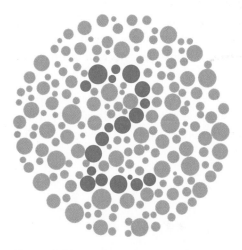

Figure 3.31 Grouping due to similarity of lightness. The darker circles form a group that stands out from the lighter circles.

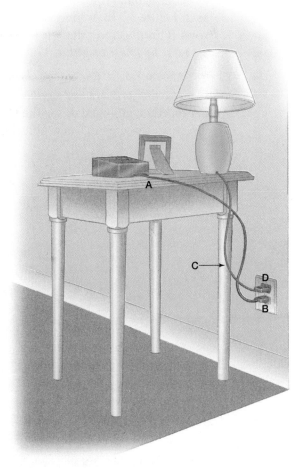

Figure 3.32 Good continuation. We perceive both electrical cords as following a smooth path to the electrical outlet.

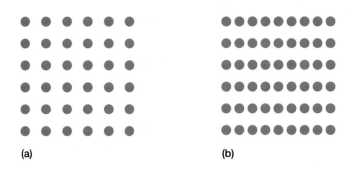

(a)   (b)

Figure 3.33 Law of nearness. The pattern in (a) is perceived as vertical columns or horizontal rows, but when the dots are near each other, as in (b), the perception changes to horizontal rows.

■ **Proximity or Nearness** Figure 3.33a is the pattern from Figure 3.30a that can be seen as either horizontal rows or vertical columns or both. By moving the circles closer together, as in Figure 3.33b, we increase the likelihood that the circles will be seen in horizontal rows. This illustrates the **law of proximity** or **nearness**: *Things that are near to each other appear to be grouped together.*

■ **Common Fate** The **law of common fate** states: *Things that are moving in the same direction appear to be grouped together.* Thus, when you see a flock of hundreds of birds all flying together, you tend to see the flock as a unit, and if some birds start flying in another direction, this creates a new unit (Figure 3.34).

Figure 3.34 The birds that are moving together, in the same direction, are perceived as a group. In this example, the birds on the right that have broken off from the main group have formed a new perceptual group because of their common direction of movement. This illustrates the law of common fate.

■ **Familiarity** According to the **law of familiarity,** *things are more likely to form groups if the groups appear familiar or meaningful* (Helson, 1933; Hochberg, 1971). You can appreciate how meaningfulness determines perceptual organization by doing the following demonstration.

◣ Demonstration

Finding Faces in a Landscape

Consider the picture in Figure 3.35. At first glance this scene appears to contain mainly trees, rocks, and water. But on closer inspection you can see some faces in the trees in the background, and if you look more closely, you can see that a number of faces are formed by various groups of rocks. See if you can find all 12 faces that are hidden in this picture. ■

In this demonstration some people find it difficult to perceive the faces at first, but then suddenly they succeed. The change in perception from "rocks in a stream" or "trees in a forest" into "faces" is a change in the perceptual organization of the rocks and the trees. The two shapes that you at first perceive as two separate rocks in the stream become perceptually grouped together when they become the left and right eyes of a face. In fact, once you perceive a particular grouping of rocks as a face, it is often difficult *not* to perceive them in this way—they have become permanently organized into a face. This effect

Figure 3.35 *The Forest Has Eyes* by Bev Doolittle (1985). Can you find 12 faces in this picture?

of meaning on perceptual organization is an example of the operation of top-down processing in perception.

Perceptual organization also occurs for hearing, and **speech segmentation,** the organization of sounds of speech into individual words, provides another example of how perceptual organization is influenced by meaning. Try the following demonstration.

Demonstration

Organizing Strings of Sounds

Read the following words: Anna Mary Candy Lights Since Imp Pulp Lay Things. Now that you've read the words, what do they mean? ■

If you think that this is a list of unconnected words beginning with the names of two women, Anna and Mary, you're right; but read this series of words a little faster, ignoring the spaces between the words on the page, and see if you can hear a connected sentence that does not begin with the names Anna and Mary. (For the answer, see page 97—but don't peek until you've tried reading the words rapidly.)

If you succeeded in creating a new sentence from the series of words, you did so by changing the perceptual organization of the sounds, and this change was achieved by your knowledge of the meaning of the sounds. Just as the perceptual organization of the forest scene in Figure 3.35 depended on seeing the rocks as meaningful patterns (faces), your perception of the new sentence depended on knowing the meanings of the sounds you created when you said these words rapidly.

Another example of how meaning is responsible for organizing sounds into words is provided by these two sentences.

- Jamie's mother said, "Be a *big girl* and eat your vegetables."
- The thing *Big Earl* loved most in the world was his car.

"Big girl" and "Big Earl" are both pronounced the same way so hearing them differently depends on the overall meaning of the sentence in which these words appear. This example is similar to the familiar "I scream, you scream, we all scream for ice cream" that many people learn as children. The sound stimuli for "I scream" and "ice cream" are identical, so the different organizations must be achieved by the meaning of the sentence in which these words appear.

Speech segmentation is something that we do all the time as we understand normal speech. This is so because although you might think that there are spaces between the words you are hearing, there are either no physical breaks in the sound or the breaks that do occur that don't necessarily correspond to the breaks we perceive between words (Figure 3.36). The fact that the speech signal is continuous becomes obvious when you listen to someone speaking a foreign language. To someone unfamiliar with that language, the

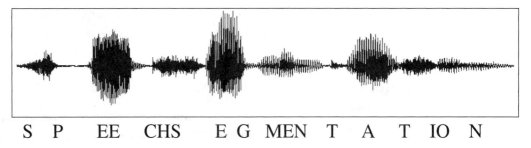

S P EE CHS E G MEN T A T IO N

Figure 3.36 Sound energy that results from saying the two words "Speech Segmentation." Notice that it is difficult to tell from this record where one word ends and the other begins. (Speech signal courtesy of Lisa Saunders.)

words seem to speed by in an unbroken string. However, to a speaker of that language who understands what the words mean, the words seem separate, just as the words of your native language seem separate to you.

The Gestalt Laws Provide "Best Guess" Predictions About What Is Out There

The purpose of perception is to provide accurate information about the properties of the environment. The Gestalt laws provide this information because they reflect things we know from long experience in our environment and because we are using them unconsciously all the time. For example, the law of good continuation reflects the fact that we know that many objects in the environment have straight or smoothly curving contours so when we see smoothly curving contours, such as the electrical wires in Figure 3.32, we correctly perceive the two wires.

Despite the fact that the Gestalt laws usually result in accurate perceptions of the environment, sometimes they don't. We can illustrate a situation in which the Gestalt laws might cause an incorrect perception by imagining the following: As you are hiking in the woods, you stop cold in your tracks because not too far ahead, you see what appears to be an animal lurking behind a tree (Figure 3.37). The Gestalt laws of organization play a role in creating this perception. You see the two dark shapes to the left and right of the tree as a single object because of the Gestalt law of similarity (since both shapes are dark, it is likely that they are part of the same object). Also, good continuation links these two parts into one, since the line along the top of the object extends smoothly from one side of the tree to another. Finally, the image resembles animals you've seen before. For all of these reasons, it is not surprising that you perceive the two dark objects as part of one animal.

Since you fear that the animal might be dangerous, you take a different path and as your detour takes you around the

Figure 3.37 What lurks behind the tree?

Figure 3.38 It is two strangely shaped tree stumps, not an animal!

tree, you notice that the dark shapes aren't an animal after all, but are two oddly shaped tree stumps (Figure 3.38). So in this case, the Gestalt laws have misled you.

The fact that perception guided by the Gestalt laws results in accurate perceptions of the environment most of the time, but not always, means that instead of calling the Gestalt principles *laws*, it is more correct to call them *heuristics*. A heuristic is a "rule of thumb" that provides a best-guess solution to a problem. Another way of solving a problem, an algorithm, is a procedure that is guaranteed to solve a problem. An example of an algorithm is the procedures we learn for addition, subtraction, and long division. If we apply these procedures correctly, we get the right answer every time. In contrast, a heuristic may not result in a correct solution every time.

To illustrate the difference between a heuristic and an algorithm, let's consider two different ways of finding a cat that is hiding somewhere in the house. An algorithm for doing this would be to systematically search every room in the house (being careful not to let the cat sneak past you!). If you do this, you will eventually find the cat, although it may take a while. A heuristic for finding the cat would be to first look in the places where the cat likes to hide. So you check under the bed and in the hall closet. This may not always lead to finding the cat, but if it does, it has the advantage of being faster than the algorithm.

The fact that heuristics are usually faster than algorithms helps explain why the perceptual system is designed in a way that sometimes produces errors. Consider, for example, what the algorithm would be for determining what the shape in Figure 3.37 really is. The algorithm for perceiving these shapes would involve walking around the tree so you can see if from different angles, and perhaps taking a more close-up look at the objects behind the tree. While this may result in an accurate perception, it is potentially risky (what if the shape actually *is* a dangerous animal?), and slow. The advantage of our Gestalt-based heuristics is that they are fast, and correct most of the time.

The Intelligence of Object Perception

We have seen that the beginning stage of object perception involves largely bottom-up processing but that as perception proceeds past the feature-analysis stage, top-down processing becomes more important.

The influence of knowledge and the top-down processing that accompanies knowledge means that it would not be inaccurate to describe perception as being "intelligent." This intelligence becomes apparent when we bring our knowledge to bear on the creation of faces in the rocks and trees of Figure 3.35, but we could argue that there is a certain intelligence behind even simpler processes, such as grouping by similarity and nearness. The idea that these simple grouping processes could involve intelligence is perhaps not obvious because they seem so automatic. In fact, people often react to some of the Gestalt laws as if they are simply common sense. Our skeptic from the beginning of the chapter, who thought perception was simple, might say, "Of course things that are close to each other will become grouped. I don't think there's much intelligence involved in that."

It is easy to understand why someone might say this because these groupings usually happen so easily and naturally that it doesn't appear that much of anything is going on. It is a case of perception just "happening." But in reality there is a lot going on because the Gestalt laws are based on characteristics of our environment. Of course, grouping is easy because our perceptual system is tuned into the way things are usually arranged in our environment, so it responds by creating the appropriate perception when these arrangements occur.

This idea that the perceptual system is tuned to the way things are usually arranged in our environment brings us back to the fact that perception is usually easy for people but difficult for computers. The computer's difficulty stems from a lack of this perceptual intelligence that humans take for granted. Let's consider a few of the things about perception that make perceiving particularly difficult for computers.

Why Computers Have Trouble Perceiving Objects

We can understand why it has been difficult to program computers to perceive, by considering a few of the problems that the computer must deal with in order to accurately perceive a scene.

The Stimulus on the Receptors Is Ambiguous
Objects seen from just one viewpoint result in ambiguous information on the receptors. For example, you might think that the scene in Figure 3.39a is a circle of rocks, but viewing it from another angle reveals its true configuration (Figure 3.39b). This ambiguity occurs because a particular image on the retina can be caused by an infinite number of different objects. This fact, called the **inverse projection problem,** is illustrated by Figure 3.40. This figure shows a square stimulus (solid lines) that is creating a square image on the retina. It also shows, however, that there are a number of other stimuli (dashed lines) that could create exactly the same image on the retina. A larger square that is farther away, a trapezoid that is tilted, as well as an infinite number of other objects, can create the same retinal image as the square. Thus, any image on the retina can be created by an infinite number of objects. This creates serious problems for a computer, but humans usually perceive the correct object and not any of the other potential objects that might cast the same image on the retina.

Objects Need to Be Separated
It is often difficult to determine where one object ends and another begins. This is part of the problem of object segregation we discussed

(a)   (b)

Figure 3.39 An environmental sculpture by Thomas Macaulay. (a) When viewed from exactly the right vantage point, the stones appear to be arranged in a circle. (b) Viewing the stones from another angle reveals a truer picture of their configuration.

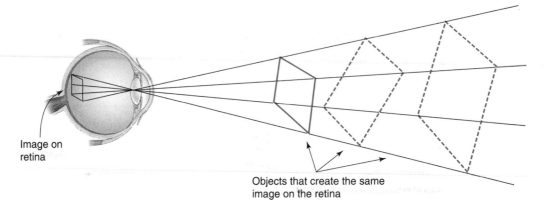

Image on retina

Objects that create the same image on the retina

Figure 3.40 The principle behind the inverse projection problem. The small rectangular stimulus (solid lines) creates a rectangular image on the retina. However, this image could also have been created by the larger, more distant, rectangle, by the tilted trapezoid (dashed lines), or many other stimuli. This is why we say that the image on the retina is ambiguous.

earlier. For example, in Figure 3.41, how do we know that the intersection at (a) is the corner of object 1, but the intersection at (b) is created by objects 1 and 2 together? Although computers have been programmed successfully to answer this kind of question for problems involving blocks, it is still difficult for a computer to answer it for more complex natural objects.

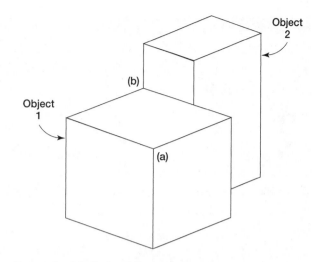

Figure 3.41 To correctly perceive this display, it is necessary to determine where one object ends and the other begins.

Figure 3.42 A computer would have a difficult time determining what this object is. Humans can easily tell that it is an animal hiding, probably a member of the cat family.

Parts of Objects Can Be Hidden   It is difficult to determine the shapes of objects that are partially hidden. Imagine, for example, how difficult it would be to program a computer to be able to identify the hidden object in Figure 3.42, something we can do with little effort.

The Reasons for Changes in Lightness and Darkness Can Be Unclear   In a scene such as the one in Figure 3.43, it is necessary to determine which changes in lightness and darkness are due to properties of objects in the scene and which are due to changes in illumination. It is easy for us to tell that the border between area (a) and area (b) is due to a change in the illumination, caused by the shadow. We can also tell that the border between (a) and (c) occurs because the panel at (a) is made of lighter material than the one at (c). These judgments, which we make with ease, would not be easy for a computer, because it is difficult for the computer to tell which borders are caused by shadows and which are caused by other differences between parts of a scene.

These are only a few of the problems facing computer vision The situation becomes even more

Figure 3.43 For this scene, it would be difficult for a computer to sort out which changes are due to properties of different parts of the scene and which are due to changes in illumination.

complex when we consider the many varied shapes we see in the real world. (For more detailed discussions of the problems involved in computer vision, see Barrow & Tannenbaum, 1986; Beck et al., 1983; C. Brown, 1984; McArthur, 1982; Poggio, 1984; Srinivasan & Ventatesh, 1997.)

The reason for this brief foray into computer vision is to make the point that humans are presented with the same information as the computer, in the form of a two-dimensional image of the scene on our retina, yet we are able to solve the foregoing problems and translate the images into correct perceptions of the scenes much more easily than even the most powerful computer. Although we are sometimes fooled (perhaps object 2 in Figure 3.41 is not really a rectangular solid), most of the time we are able to deal effortlessly with the complexities of object perception and to arrive at correct perceptions of objects and the scenes in which these objects exist.

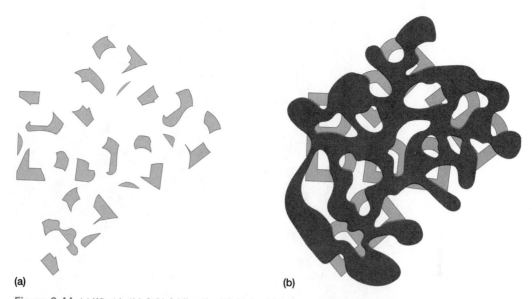

Figure 3.44 (a) What is this? (b) Adding the ink blot, which covers only the open areas in the other pattern, reveals the presence of six *B*'s. (Reprinted from "Asking the 'What for' Question in Auditory Perception," A. Bregman, in *Perceptual Organization*, M. Kubovy & J. R. Pomerantz, Eds., 1981, pp. 99–119. Copyright © 1981 with permission from Lawrence Erlbaum Associates, Inc.

The built-in intelligence of the human perceptual system is one of the things that gives humans the advantage over computers when it comes to perception. We have already seen some examples of this intelligence in the Gestalt laws of organization, which are more accurately described as heuristics rather than laws. Let's consider a few more examples of how heuristics shape our perceptions.

More Heuristics for Perception

What do you see when you look at Figure 3.44a? Most people see a bunch of meaningless fragments. However, when you look at 3.44b you may see six "B's," even though the fragments are identical to the ones in (a). The addition of the inkblot in (b) activates a perceptual heuristic called the occlusion heuristic, which states that when a large object is partially covered by a smaller one, we see the larger one as continuing behind the occluder. This rule, like the Gestalt principle of good continuation, prevents us from seeing things in our environment as being chopped into pieces when they are partially obscured by other objects (Figure 3.45).

The following demonstration illustrates another perceptual heuristic.

Figure 3.45 In the distance, the Cathedral of Learning on the campus of the University of Pittsburgh rises from behind a tree. Because of the occlusion heuristic, we perceive this building as continuing behind the tree. Similarly, we don't see the person in the foreground (your author) as being chopped into little pieces by the fence, but we see his body as continuing behind the fence.

◥ Demonstration

Shape From Shading

What do you perceive in Figure 3.46? Do some of the discs look like they are sticking out, like parts of three-dimensional spheres, and do others appear to be indentations? If you do see the discs in this way, notice that the ones that appear to be sticking out are arranged in a square. After observing this, turn the page over so the black dot is on the bottom. Does this change your perception? ■

You can see from the explanation in Figure 3.47 that if we are assuming that light is coming from above (which is usually the case in the environment), then patterns like the circles that are light on the top would be created by an object that bulges out, but a pattern

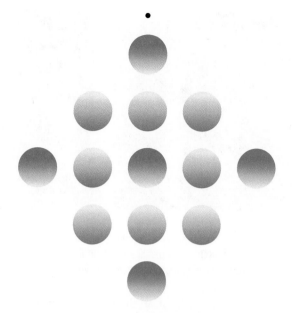

Figure 3.46 Rounded shapes jutting out or indentations? Follow the directions in the "Shape From Shading" demonstration.

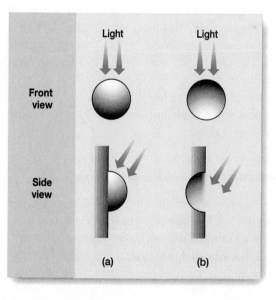

Figure 3.47 Explanation behind your perception of the display in Figure 3.46. Light coming from above will illuminate (a) the top of a shape that is jutting out, and (b) the bottom of an indentation. Because we assume that light is coming from above, the pattern of shading determines whether we see the shapes as "innies" or "outies."

(a)   (b)

Figure 3.48 These may appear to be two different photographs, but the one on the right is simply the one on the left printed upside down. If the one on the left looks like ridges in the sand and the one on the right looks like steps, it is because the light-from-above heuristic is influencing your perception.

like the circles that are light on the bottom would be created by an indentation in a surface. The assumption that light is coming from above has been called the **light-from-above heuristic** (Kleffner & Ramachandran, 1992). Apparently, people make the light-from-above assumption because most light in our environment comes from above. This includes the sun as well as most artificial light sources.

Another example of the light-from-above heuristic at work is provided by the two pictures in Figure 3.48. You may perceive the picture in Figure 3.48a as a series of rounded edges in the sand separated by flat "valleys," and the picture in Figure 3.48b as "steps" with the sun shining on the part you would step on if your were to climb them. [Note that the picture in (b) is sometimes perceived as ridges in the sand separated by valleys, as in (a).] But if you turn the book upside down, your perceptions of (a) and (b) will switch in accordance with the assumption that light is coming from above because (b) is simply (a) printed upside down.

Where Does Our Perceptual Intelligence Come From?

There is no doubt that our advantage over computers comes from the knowledge we possess and the intelligent nature of the perceptual process. Sometimes, however, this knowledge gets us into trouble, as Roger found out when he misread the street sign. But most of the time this knowledge is exactly what enables us to come up with correct perceptions of our environment, even when the stimuli on which we base our perceptions are ambiguous.

Where does the knowledge that is important for achieving accurate perceptions come from? We can approach this question both behaviorally and physiologically. The behavioral approach is the most straightforward because it is based on the fact that beginning just after we are born, we are constantly acquiring knowledge and learning things about our environment. This knowledge is stored in the brain as memories for experiences and for a huge number of facts, ranging from the things we learned in school ("George Washington was the first president of the United States") to things we have observed about the nature of our environment ("Light usually comes from above").

The physiological approach to our question is not quite as straightforward. Clearly, all of those memories for facts and experiences must be stored in the brain (we will discuss how this is achieved in Chapter 6), but there is also another way that the brain contributes to the intelligence of perception. The brain contains specialized circuits, which create neurons that respond to faces and other objects in the environment (see section on neural processing, Chapter 1, p. 36). These specialized circuits can be considered a form of built-in perceptual intelligence because they turn the brain into a processor that is adapted to what the person encounters in the environment.

How Do Neurons Become Specialized to Respond to Aspects of Our Environment?

Neurons can become specialized through the mechanism of evolution, which has occurred over the extremely long time that it takes a species to evolve, and through mechanisms related to experience, which can occur over relatively brief time periods during the life of a particular individual.

Specialization Through Evolution

Why do some neurons respond best to specific stimuli? One answer to this question is that the nervous system may have evolved to respond to situations and stimuli that are commonly found in the environment. According to the **theory of natural selection,** genetically based characteristics that enhance an animal's ability to survive, and therefore reproduce, will be passed on to future generations. Thus, a person whose visual system contains neurons that fire to important things in the environment (like specific orientations and faces) will be more likely to survive transmit their genetic makeup to their offspring than will a person whose visual system does not contain these specialized neurons. Through this evolutionary process, the visual system may have been shaped to contain neurons that respond to faces and other important perceptual information. In line with this idea, there are neurons in the visual cortex of the newborn monkey that respond to the direction objects are moving and to the relative depths of objects, two qualities that are important for the monkey's survival (Chino et al., 1997).

Specialization Through Experience

While it may be important for the visual system to have some specialized neurons at birth, it is also important that the visual system be able to adapt to the specific environment within which a person or animal lives. There is, in fact, a great deal of evidence that the nervous system achieves this adaptation to the environment through a mechanism called **experience-dependent plasticity,** which causes neurons to develop so they respond best to the types of stimulation to which the person has been exposed.

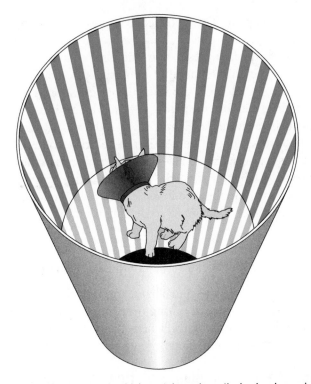

Figure 3.49 Cats raised in this environment, which contains only verticals, develop a visual cortex that contains only neurons that respond to vertical or near-vertical orientations. The cat is wearing the ruff to prevent it from turning the verticals into horizontals by tilting its head. (Reprinted from "Development of the Brain Depends on the Visual Environment," by C. Blakemore & G. G. Cooper, 1970, *Nature, London, 228*, pp. 477–478, Copyright © 1970 with permission from Nature Publishing Group.)

The idea of experience-dependent plasticity was first suggested by experiments on animals. For example, if kittens are raised in an environment that contains only verticals (Figure 3.49), most of the neurons in their visual cortex respond best to verticals (Blakemore & Cooper, 1970). Since this early demonstration of experience-dependent plasticity, many more experiments have demonstrated this effect in animals (Freedman et al., 2001; Merzenich et al., 1998), and recently this effect has been demonstrated in humans as well.

The demonstration of experience-dependent plasticity in humans is based on the finding that there is an area in the temporal lobe called the **fusiform face area (FFA)** that is rich in neurons that are activated when a person looks at faces. To determine whether this response to faces might be due to experience-dependent plasticity, Isabel Gauthier and coworkers (1999) used functional magnetic resonance imaging (fMRI) to measure the level of activity in the FFA in response to faces and to objects called Greebles—families of computer-generated "beings" that all have the same basic configuration but differ in the shapes of their parts (Figure 3.50). The results for this part of the experiment, shown in the left pair of bars in Figure 3.51, indicate that the FFA neurons responded well to faces but poorly to Greebles.

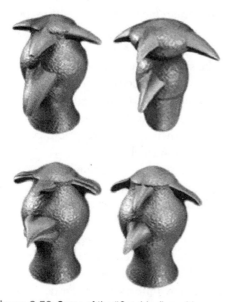

Figure 3.50 Some of the "Greebles" used by Gauthier et al. (1999). (Reprinted from "Activation of the Middle Fusiform 'Face Area' Increases with Expertise in Recognizing Novel Objects," by I. Gauthier et al., from *Nature Neuroscience, 2*, pp. 568–573. Copyright © 1999 with permission of the author and Nature Publishing Group.)

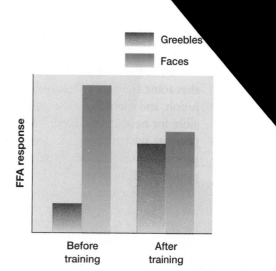

Figure 3.51 Results of Gauthier et al.'s (1999) Greeble experiment. The FFA response is the brain activity in the fusiform face area as measured by fMRI, as participants view Greebles (dark bars) or faces (colored bars). The left pair of bars indicates that before training, the faces cause a large response in the FFA, and the Greebles cause a very small response. The right pair of bars indicate that after training, the FFA is activated both by faces and by Greebles. See Color Plate 3.1 (inside cover) for pictures that show the areas of the brain that were activated by the Greebles and by the faces in the two conditions. (From Gauthier et al., 1999.)

A picture of the brain activation caused by the faces and Greebles is shown in the left two columns in Color Plate 3.1, inside the front cover. The small white squares indicate the location of the FFA. The color inside the FFA on the left indicates that faces activate neurons in the FFA. The lack of color on the right indicates that Greebles do not activate the FFA.

Gauthier then gave her participants extensive training in "Greeble recognition" over a 4-day period. After these training sessions, the participants had become "Greeble experts," so they were able to assign names to particular Greebles, just as people are able to assign names to other people's faces.

The right pair of bars in Figure 3.51 and the two right columns in Color Plate 3.1 show how becoming a Greeble expert affected the responding of neurons in the participants' FFA. Figure 3.51 shows that after the training, the FFA responded almost as well to Greebles as to faces. The colors inside the squares in the far right column in the color plate indicate that the Greebles now activate the FFA. Apparently, the FFA contains neurons that respond not just to faces, but to other complex objects as well. The particular objects to which the neurons respond best is established by experience with the objects. In fact, Gauthier has also shown that neurons in the FFA of people who are experts in

ng cars and birds respond well not only to human faces, but to cars (for the car
nd to birds (for the bird experts) (Gauthier et al., 2000).

answer to the question "How do neurons become specialized?" seems to be
specialized neurons might be built into the system through the process of evo-
that others are created by experience-dependent plasticity, which makes it pos-
urons to match their tuning to what occurs in the environment. We can ap-
at this means for perception by remembering our discussion of top-down
n page 60, in which we noted the role of knowledge in perception. Now we
see that there are two ways to think about knowledge in the brain.

The brain can be thought of as a storehouse that contains all the knowledge we have
accumulated, ranging from things we have learned through years in school to something
we may have learned just moments ago. But results like the Greeble experiment indicate
that we can think of the brain not only as a place to store knowledge, but also as a device
that has been designed to process incoming information intelligently. It accomplishes this
"intelligent processing" through specialized circuits that have been created both by evolution and by experience-dependent plasticity. What this means is that even in situations
in which there is no obvious "knowledge" involved in determining a particular perception,
the way the brain is designed increases the chances that what we perceive will provide accurate information about what is out there in the environment.

WHY PERCEPTION IS THE GATEWAY TO COGNITION

Perception is our "window on the world" that enables us to experience what is "out there"
in our environment. Thus, perception is the first step in the process that eventually results
in all of our cognitions. Paying attention, forming and recalling memories, using language, and reasoning and solving problems all depend—right at the beginning—on perception. Without perception, these processes would be absent or greatly degraded.
Therefore it is accurate to say that perception is the gateway to cognition.

We can also say that the *study* of perception is also the gateway to the *study* of cognition because many of the principles that have emerged from the study of perception are
also important for other types of cognition as well. Here are some of the principles from
this chapter that we will also encounter in the chapters on attention, memory, language,
and thinking:

■ **Invisible Processing** The mental and neural processing that results in our conscious experience of the environment is often invisible. For example, we are unaware of the neural
impulses that create our perceptions, and we are also unaware of mental processing such
as the analysis of objects into features. Similar "invisible" processes occur for all other
types of cognition as well. One of the messages of this book is that we are only aware of
the "tip of the iceberg," and that most of the processing that is responsible for cognition
occurs invisibly, behind the scenes, outside of our consciousness.

■ **Representation** Our perceptions are based not on direct contact with objects but on representations of objects. Thus, when we look at a tree, our perception of the tree is based on the image of the tree on our retina and on the neural impulses generated by the tree in our visual system. Representations are also involved in all other cognitive processes. For example, if a few days after seeing the tree the person remembers standing in a field looking at it, this memory is based on a representation of the tree and of the experience of looking at the tree that has been stored in the person's brain.

■ **Bottom-Up and Top-Down Processing** Just as our perceptions are created by interactions between information we are taking in at a particular point in time and information that is already stored in the system, so are our memories, thoughts, and other cognitive processes.

■ **Heuristics and Knowledge** Just as our perceptual system often uses heuristics— rules of thumb that produce a best guess answer to a problem—so do other cognitive processes. We use heuristics to help us to remember (Chapter 7), to understand language (Chapter 10), and to solve problems (Chapter 11).

■ **Behavioral and Physiological Approaches** In this chapter, we focused mainly on the behavioral level of perception, but we also looked at the role of neurons in creating this behavior and especially how knowledge that we gain from experiences is stored. In the chapters that follow, we will continue to consider both behavioral and physiological approaches to studying cognition.

 Test Yourself 3.2

1. What idea about perception that was popular early in the 1900s did the Gestalt psychologists disagree with? What are the Gestalt laws of organization? How has the law of meaningfulness been applied both to vision and hearing?
2. Why is it suggested that the Gestalt laws should be called heuristics rather than laws? What is a heuristic? An algorithm? What are the advantages of heuristics for perception?
3. What are two heuristics for perceptual organization that have been proposed by modern perceptual psychologists?
4. Why do we say that human perception is "intelligent"?
5. What makes perception difficult for computers?
6. What is the occlusion heuristic? The light-from-above heuristic? How are these heuristics relevant to the "intelligence" of perception?
7. What are two possible mechanisms to explain how neurons become tuned to the environment?
8. What is experience-dependent plasticity? Describe how the Greeble experiment supports the idea of experience-dependent plasticity.

1. Describe a situation in which you initially thought you saw or heard something, but then realized that your initial perception was in error. What was the role of bottom-up and top-down processing in this process of first having an incorrect perception and then realizing what was actually there?

2. According to the feature analysis approach, our perceptual system analyzes objects into simple features. Look around in your environment and see if you can describe objects in terms their features. How well do you think objects can be described by their features? In addition to oriented lines and curves, what features might be needed to fully describe objects? How well do you think the feature-analysis approach would work if you went out into the woods, where there are more natural objects and fewer objects made by humans?

3. Try observing the world as though there were no such thing as top-down processing. For example, without the aid of top-down processing, seeing a restaurant's restroom sign that says "Employees must wash hands" could be taken to mean that we should wait for an employee to wash our hands! If you try this exercise, be warned that it is extremely difficult because top-down processing is so pervasive in our environment that we usually take it for granted.

KEY TERMS

Algorithm
Bottom-up processing
Common fate, law of
Discriminability
Experience-dependent plasticity
Familiarity, law of
Feature analysis stage
Feature approach to object perception
Feature integration theory
Feature units
Focused attention stage
Fusiform face area
Geon
Gestalt psychologists
Good continuation, law of
Good figure, law of
Heuristic

Illusory conjunctions
Inverse projection problem
Laws of perceptual organization
Letter units
Letter-analysis stage
Light-from-above heuristic
Natural selection, theory of
Nearness, law of
Occlusion heuristic
Perception
Perceptual organization
Pop-out
Pragnanz, law of
Preattentive stage
Proximity, law of
Rat-man demonstration
Recognition-by-components approach

Resistance to visual noise
Sensations
Similarity, law of
Simplicity, law of
Speech segmentation

Structuralism
Top-down processing
View invariance
View invariant properties
Visual search

CogLab To experience these experiments for yourself, go to http://coglab.wadsworth.com. Be sure to read each experiment's setup instructions before you go to the experiment itself. Otherwise, you won't know which keys to press.

Primary Labs

Visual search Visual searching for targets that are accompanied by different numbers of distractors (page 67).

Related Labs

Apparent motion How flashing two dots one after another can result in an illusion of motion.

Mapping the blind spot Map the blind spot in your visual field that is caused by the fact that there are no receptors where the optic nerve leaves the eye.

Metacontrast masking How presentation of one stimulus can impair perception of another stimulus.

Muller-Lyer illusion Measure the size of a visual illusion.

Signal detection Collect data that demonstrate the principle behind the theory of signal detection, which explains the processes behind detecting hard-to-detect stimuli.

Answer to Demonstration on Page 80

An American delights in simple play things.

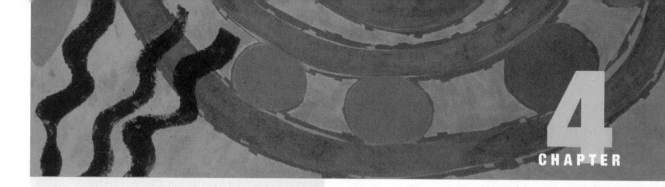

Attention

Some Questions We Will Consider

✔ Is it possible to focus attention on just one thing, even when there are lots of other things going on at the same time?

✔ Under what conditions can we pay attention to more than one thing at a time?

✔ What does attention research tell us about the effect of talking on cell phones while driving a car?

■   ■   ■

As Sam drives down the street, he is anticipating his goal: a lunch date with his friend Susan. He listens to a CD and takes in the street scene but isn't thinking much about his driving. Just as he passes a movie theater he sees a ball bouncing in front of his car, followed by a young boy who is chasing it. He shoots a glance to the left lane, swerves into it, hits his brakes, and succeeds in avoiding the boy. "That was a close call," he thinks.

When he arrives at lunch, the restaurant is crowded and noisy. "Did you see the *Star Wars* promotion in front of the theater?" Susan asks. "Two guys fighting with light sabers." "Must have missed it," Sam says, and realizes that the boy had run out in front of his car just as he was passing the theater.

Attention is the process of concentrating on specific features of the environment, or on certain thoughts or activities. This focusing on specific features of the environment usually leads to the exclusion of other features of the environment (Colman, 2001; Reber, 1995). We can see how this applies to Sam's experience by noting that as he drives, his attention is directed to his lunch date. He also pays some attention to the music from his CD and to what is happening in the street, but his driving is on "automatic."

When the boy runs in front of the car, things change. The emergency captures Sam's attention, and he concentrates exclusively on his driving in order to avoid the boy. He becomes unaware of the music and the street scene, and therefore misses the *Star Wars* promotion entirely. Later, in the restaurant, Sam's attention to Susan enables him to make out what she says, even though many other conversations are happening simultaneously.

From these examples, we can see that not all instances of attention are the same. Although listening to lyrics on a CD, focusing on avoiding an accident, and paying attention to what a person is saying in a noisy restaurant all may involve focusing on specific features of the environment, thoughts, or activities, they seem different and probably involve different mechanisms. The fact that we can cite so many different behaviors as examples of attention has led attention researchers to see attention not as being a single concept, but as comprising a large number of different psychological phenomena (Luck & Vecera, 2002; Styles, 1997).

Whatever attention is, it is clear that it plays a central role in determining our daily experiences. Consider, for example, the following *objects* of Sam's attention: *his lunch date, music, what is happening in the street, driving, avoiding the boy,* and *what Susan is saying*. This list is nothing less than a description of Sam's experience. As we will see in this chapter, attention is central to many aspects of cognition. Attention is involved in perception (paying attention to something increases the chances you will perceive it), in memory (you are more likely to remember something later if you were paying attention to it when it first occurred); in language (it is difficult to have a conversation if you aren't paying attention); and in solving problems (your success in solving the problem may depend on what aspect of the problem captures your attention).

In this chapter, we will consider a number of aspects of attention in approximately the order they have concerned attention researchers (Figure 4.1). We begin by considering the process of selective attention—our ability to attend to one message and ignore other, competing, messages (as when Sam listens to Susan in the restaurant and ignores the other conversations). We will consider two approaches to selective attention: (1) Models of attention that liken attention to a filter that selects some messages and rejects others, and (2) an approach that looks at how our ability to focus on one thing depends on the nature of the task we are dealing with. In addition to focusing on one thing, we often want to pay attention to a few things at once, as Sam was doing just before the boy appeared. This is

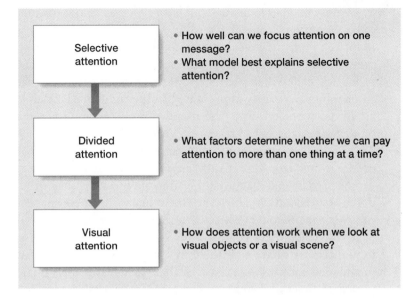

Figure 4.1 Flow diagram for this chapter.

called <u>divided attention</u>. We will consider when divided attention is possible, and when it is not. Finally, we will examine recent research on how attention operates as we look at a visual scene.

SELECTIVE ATTENTION: FOCUSING ON ONE THING

Much of the early research on attention used <u>auditory stimuli</u> and focused on the process of **selective attention**—the ability to focus on one message and ignore all others. This research began with experiments that indicated that if we are paying attention to one message it is difficult or impossible to take in the information in another message that is presented at the same time. You can demonstrate this to yourself as follows.

◼ Demonstration

Hearing Two Messages at Once

Enlist the help of another person. Select two books on different topics that you have not read before. Your task is to read one of these selections to yourself while the person reads the other selection out loud. Do this for about a minute and note how well you are able to remember both passages. ◼

Were you able to understand both passages? Experiments in which people are asked to pay attention to one of two simultaneously presented messages show that it is possible to focus on one message, but that not much information is obtained from the other message. One of the first of these experiments was done by Colin Cherry (1953), who used a procedure called **dichotic listening** in which one message was presented to the left ear and another message was presented to the right ear. Participants were instructed to pay attention to one message (the attended message) and to ignore the other one (the unattended message) and to repeat the attended message out loud, as they were hearing it. This procedure of repeating a message out loud is called shadowing. The shadowing procedure is used to ensure that the participant is paying attention to the attended message.

As participants shadowed the attended message, they still received the other message in the unattended ear. However, when they were asked what they heard in the unattended ear, participants could only say that they heard the message and could identify it as a male or female voice. They could not report the content of the message. Other dichotic listening experiments have confirmed this lack of awareness of most of the information in the unattended ear, with one showing that participants were unaware of a word that was repeated 35 times in the unattended ear (Moray, 1959).

Cherry's experiment is often described as a demonstration of the **cocktail party phenomenon**—the ability to pay attention to one message and ignore all other messages—because it resembles what people routinely achieve in a noisy party when they focus on one message and ignore all the others. Cherry's finding is particularly significant because it led Donald Broadbent to propose his **filter model of attention.**

Broadbent's Filter Model

Donald Broadbent's (1958) filter model is one of the classic theories in psychology because it was the first to describe the human as an information processor, and it was the first to depict the course of this information processing with a flow diagram. Broadbent's model, which was designed to explain selective attention, states that information passes through the following stages (Figure 4.2). *both the flow diagram...*

1. The *sensory store*, which holds incoming information for a short period of time and transfers all of it to the filter. (The sensory store will be described in more detail in the next chapter.)

KNOW

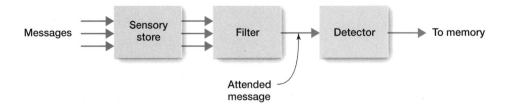

Figure 4.2 Flow diagram of Broadbent's filter model of attention.

2. The *filter* identifies the attended message based on its physical characteristics—things like the speaker's tone of voice, pitch, speed of talking, and accent—and lets only this message pass through the detector in the next stage. All other messages are filtered out. The exact brain mechanism for achieving this filtering is still being studied. We will describe some physiological research on attention later in the chapter, but we will focus mainly on research that takes a behavioral approach to studying attention.

3. The *detector*, where the information is processed to determine higher-level characteristics of the message such as its meaning. Since only the important, attended information has been let through the filter, the detector processes all of the information that enters it.

4. *Short-term memory*. The output of the detector enters the memory system, where it can be used immediately or moved into long-term memory for later use. We will describe short- and long-term memory in more detail in the next chapter.

Broadbent's model is called an **early-selection model,** because the filtering step occurs before the incoming information is analyzed to determine its meaning. One way to think about the filter is to consider a sieve at use at the beach, trapping the coarse grains of sand and letting through the small grains (Figure 4.3a). The filter in Broadbent's model filters messages in a similar way but instead of filtering based on the size of particles, it filters based on physical characteristics of the message, such as the speaker's pitch or rate of speaking (Figure 4.3b).

Most of the early research on selective attention used auditory stimuli such as stories, letters, or words. This research also made use of the fact that we have two ears, so that it

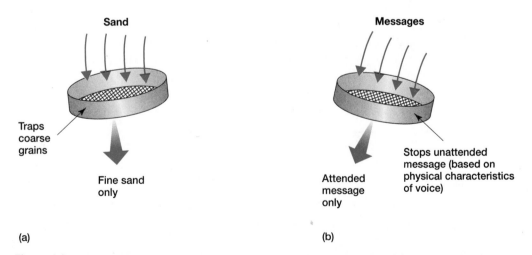

Figure 4.3 (a) A sieve that lets through small grains of sand and keeps coarse sand from getting through, based on the physical characteristic of the size of the sand particles; (b) Broadbent's model of attention lets through the attended message and keeps the unattended message from getting through, based on physical characteristics of the message, such as the pitch of a person's voice.

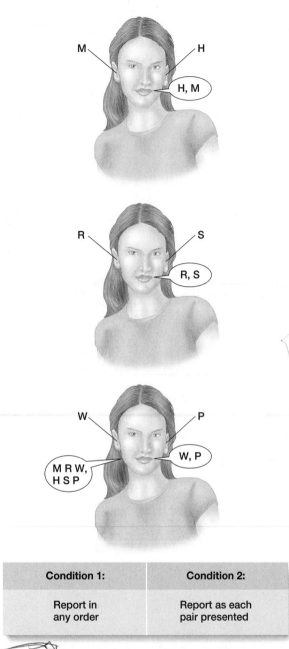

Condition 1:	Condition 2:
Report in any order	Report as each pair presented

Figure 4.4 In Broadbent's (1958) "split-scan" experiment, letters are presented simultaneously to the left and right ears. For example, *M* is presented to the right ear and *H* is presented to the left ear. The participant's task is to repeat the letters in any order after a number of letters have been presented (Condition 1), or to repeat them in pairs, as they are presented (Condition 2).

is possible to present one message to the left ear and another message to the right ear. As we will see, researchers thought of the left and right ears as separate *channels*, and they were concerned with how people take in information from these two channels under different conditions.

An example of this dual-channel research is Broadbent's (1958) "split-scan" experiment (Figure 4.4). Letters were presented to the left and right ears in pairs. For example, *H* was presented to the left ear and *M* was simultaneously presented to the right ear, then *S* and *R*, then *W* and *P*. The participant's task was to repeat the six letters immediately after hearing all six.

In Condition 1, participants were asked to report the letters in any order. When given these instructions, they tended to report all the letters that were presented to one ear (*H, S, P*) and then all the letters that were presented to the other ear (*M, R, W*). The reason they did this, according to Broadbent, is because switching back and forth between channels is hard so it is easier to report the information first from one channel and then from the other. In this condition, participants reported 65 percent of the letters correctly.

In Condition 2, participants were told to report pairs of letters in the order each *pair* was presented. This task, which required participants to respond "H, M; R, S; W, P" for the example in Figure 4.4, was more difficult than the other task because to do it, participants had to switch back and forth between channels as the letters were being presented. In this condition, participants reported only 20 percent of the letters correctly. Broadbent concluded from this result that it is difficult to switch attention between channels.

Broadbent's theory was an extremely important achievement in cognitive psychology because it analyzed human thought processes in terms of information being processed through a sequence of stages. Broadbent's theory was also important because it stimulated a great deal of re-

Broadbent: all unattended info gets filtered out @ beginning

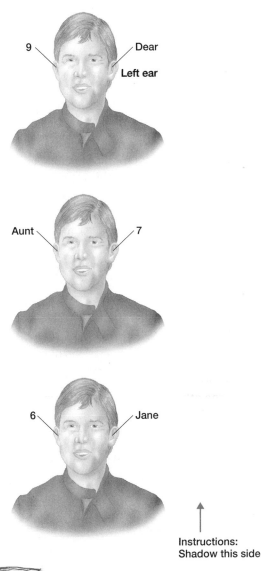

**Instructions:
Shadow this side**

Figure 4.5 In Gray and Weddeburn's (1960) "Dear Aunt Jane" experiment, the message "Dear Aunt Jane" starts in the left ear, jumps to the right ear and then goes back to the left. Participants were told to shadow the message presented to the left ear.

search on attention. However, some of this research posed problems for Broadbent's theory. For example, Neville Moray (1959) used the dichotic listening procedure and had his participants shadow the message from one ear. But when Moray presented the listener's name to the other, unattended ear, about a third of the participants detected it (also see Wood & Cowan, 1995).

Moray's participants had recognized their name even though, according to Broadbent's theory, it should have been filtered out. (Remember that the filter is supposed to let through only one message, based on its physical characteristics.) Clearly, the person's name had not been filtered out and, most important, had been analyzed enough to determine its meaning. You may have had an experience similar to what Moray demonstrated in the laboratory if, as you were talking to someone in a noisy room, you have suddenly heard someone saying your name.

Following Moray's lead, a number of other researchers did experiments that raised further problems for the filter theory. As you read the description of each experiment keep in mind that although the experiments may differ, they all make a similar point: *Information presented to the unattended ear is processed enough to provide the listener with some awareness of its meaning.*

J. A. Gray and A. I. Wedderburn (1960) did the following experiment, which is sometimes called the "Dear Aunt Jane" experiment, as an undergraduate research project at the University of Oxford. As in Cherry's dichotic listening experiment, the participants were told to shadow the message presented to one ear. As you can see from Figure 4.5, the attended (shadowed) ear received the message "Dear 7 Jane" and the unattended ear received the message "9 Aunt 6." However, rather than reporting the "Dear 7 Jane" message that was presented to the attended ear, participants reported hearing "Dear Aunt Jane."

Saying "Aunt" means that their attention had jumped to what was supposed to be the unattended message, because they were taking the *meaning* of the words into account. Notice that even though Broadbent had shown that it is difficult to switch between channels, the meaning of the words presented in the *Dear Aunt Jane* experiment caused participants to switch channels anyway.

Anne Treisman (1964), who was also at the University of Oxford at the time, did a similar experiment. Different messages were presented to both ears, and the participant was instructed to shadow the message in the left ear. However, as participants shadowed the left-ear message, the sentence that started in the left ear switched to the other, unattended, ear. For example, the beginning of the sentence ("I saw the girl") was presented to the left ear, and the rest of the sentence ("jumping in the street") was continued in the right ear.

This switch in meaning caused most participants to switch to the right ear for a word or two before switching back to the left ear. The crucial result of this experiment is that the participants' attention shifted from one ear to the other based on the meaning of the message. This indicates, like Gray and Wedderburn's result, that participants can become aware of the meaning of the unattended stimulus. Because these results can't be easily explained by Broadbent's filter theory, Treisman proposed another theory, which she called the attenuation theory of attention.

Treisman's Attenuation Theory

Treisman's theory was proposed to account for the fact that information from the unattended ear, like the person's name in Moray's experiment or words that create meaningful phrases in Gray and Wedderburn's or Treisman's experiments, sometimes got through to consciousness. (Remember that according to Broadbent all of the unattended information should have been filtered out right at the beginning, as indicated in Figure 4.2.)

Treisman proposed that selection occurs in two stages (Figure 4.6). Instead of a filter, Treisman substituted an attenuator. The attenuator analyzes the incoming message in terms of (1) its physical characteristics—whether it is high-pitched or low-pitched, fast or slow, (2) its language—how the message groups into syllables or words, and (3) its meaning—how sequences of words create meaningful phrases. Note that this is similar to what Broadbent proposed but with the addition of language and meaning as information that can be used to separate the messages. However, the analysis of the messages is carried out

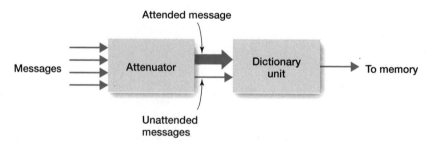

Figure 4.6 Flow diagram for Treisman's attenuation model of selective attention.

only as far as is necessary to identify the attended message. For example, if there are two messages, one in a male voice and one in a female voice, then analysis at the physical level is adequate to separate the low-pitched male voice from the higher pitched female voice. If, however, the voices are similar, then it might be necessary to use the message's meaning to separate the two messages.

Once the attended and unattended messages are identified, both the attended and unattended messages are let though the attenuator, but the attended message emerges at full strength, and the unattended messages are attenuated—they are still present, but are weaker than the attended message. Since the unattended message gets through the attenuator, Treisman's model has been called a "leaky filter" model.

The final output of the system is determined in the second stage when the message is analyzed by the **dictionary unit,** which contains stored words, each of which have thresholds for being activated (Figure 4.7). A threshold is the smallest signal strength that can just be detected. Thus, if the threshold is low for a particular word, very weak signals can be detected, but if it is high, signals need to be stronger to be detected. According to Treisman, words that are common or especially important, such as the listener's name, have low thresholds, so even a weak signal in the unattended channel can activate that word, and we hear our name from across the room. Uncommon words or words that are unimportant to the listener have higher thresholds, so it takes the strong signal of the attended message to activate the words. The final result, therefore, is that the strong attended message gets through, plus important parts of the weaker unattended message. Treisman's model, like Broadbent's, is often called an early-selection model because the attended message can be separated from the unattended message early in the information-processing system. However, since further selection can also occur later, Treisman's model could also be classified as an intermediate-selection model. *Johnson says NO!*

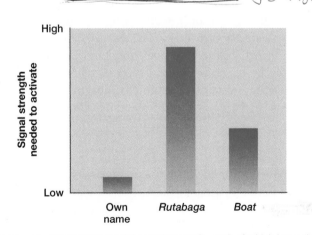

Figure 4.7 The dictionary unit of Treisman's model contains words, each of which has a threshold for being detected. This graph shows the thresholds that might exist for three words. The person's name has a low threshold, so it will be easily detected. The thresholds for the words *rutabaga* and *boat* are higher, since they are used less or are less important to this particular listener.

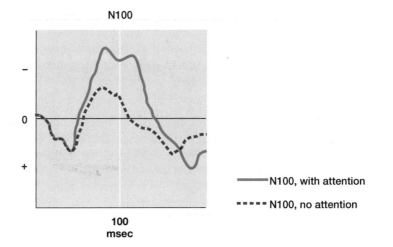

N100

100 msec

━━━ N100, with attention

▪▪▪▪▪ N100, no attention

Figure 4.8 Event-related potential (ERP) recorded when a person is selectively attending to a message (solid line) and when the person is not selectively attending (dashed line). The N100 wave, a negative wave that peaks at 100 msec, is larger when the person is paying attention. (Reprinted from "Electrical Signs of Selective Attention in the Human Brain," by S. A. Hillyard et al., 1973, *Science, 182,* pp. 177–180. Copyright © 1973 AAAS.)

Physiological evidence for early selection has been provided by research using the event-related potential (ERP) (Figure 4.8). As we saw in Chapter 2, the ERP is an electrical response recorded with electrodes on the scalp that has a number of waves, some of which have been related to different aspects of mental processing. The earliest wave, N100, reflects processing that occurs within the first 100 msec after the stimulus is presented. Figure 4.8 shows that the size this wave increases when a listener selectively attends to a message (Hillyard et al., 1973; also see Hillyard & Anllo-Vento, 1998; Luck et al., 1997). The fact that selective attention affects a very early component of the ERP supports the idea of early selection (also see Chun & Wolfe, 2001).

While there are both behavioral and physiological results to support early-selection theories, other results support theories that are called late-selection models because they propose that selection of stimuli for final processing doesn't occur until after the information has been analyzed for its meaning (Deutsch & Deutsch, 1963; Norman, 1968).

Late-Selection Models

The evidence for late-selection models is based on experiments that show that words presented in the unattended channel can be processed to the level of their meaning. Donald MacKay (1973) showed this by using ambiguous sentence that can be taken more than one way, such as

They were throwing stones at the bank.

In this example, "bank" could be a river bank or a financial institution.

In an initial control experiment, MacKay presented the ambiguous sentences and determined which meanings participants picked. In the selective attention experiment, he used only ambiguous sentences for which each meaning was equally likely.

In the selective attention experiment, participants shadowed the ambiguous sentence, which was being presented in the attended ear, while simultaneously a biasing word was presented to the unattended ear. For example, as the participants were shadowing "They were throwing stones at the bank," they were simultaneously presented with either the word "river" or "money" in the unattended ear.

After hearing a number of the ambiguous sentences, participants were presented with pairs of sentences such as

They threw stones towards the side of the river yesterday.
They threw stones at the savings and loan association yesterday.

When they indicated which of these two sentences was closest in meaning to one of the sentences they had heard previously, MacKay found that the meaning of the biasing word had affected the participants' choice. For example, if the biasing word was "money," participants were more likely to pick the second sentence. This occurred even though participants reported that they were unaware of the biasing words that were presented to the unattended ear. Since the meaning of the unattended word ("money") was affecting the participant's judgment, this word must have been processed to the level of meaning. *meaning right away,*

Figure 4.9 symbolizes the differences *vs.* between the early- and late-selection approaches to selective attention in terms of *later* what characteristics of messages are processed. According to the early-selection view, only the physical characteristics of the message are processed before selection occurs. According to the late-selection view, both the physical characteristics and the meaning are processed before selection occurs. Because there is evidence to support both views, how can we choose between them?

One answer has been to propose that the information that gets processed during a selective-attention task is determined by

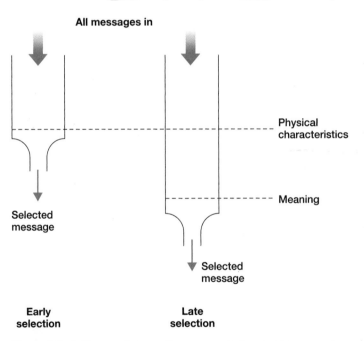

All messages in

Physical characteristics

Meaning

Selected message

Selected message

Early selection

Late selection

Figure 4.9 A difference between the early- and late-selection approaches to selective attention is the characteristics of the messages that are used to accomplish selection. Early selection (Broadbent's approach) is based on physical characteristics. Late selection (MacKay's approach) is based on meaning. Treisman's attenuation model falls in between these two because selection can be based on physical characteristics, meaning, or both.

the nature of the task facing the person (Kahaneman, 1973; Lavie, 1995). Nilli Lavie (1995) proposed that the crucial variable is task load—how much of the person's cognitive resources are used to accomplish a task.

Selection and Task Load

Lavie described a *high-load task* as one that is difficult, requiring most of the person's cognitive resources, and a *low-load task* as one that is easier, so some cognitive resources remain that can be used for other tasks. He makes the following predictions regarding selection under high- and low-load conditions: Under high-load conditions all cognitive resources are devoted to the selection task, so only the selected items will be processed. In contrast, low-load conditions do not require all of the person's cognitive resources, so some additional information can be processed.

A way to test this idea is provided by the flanker-compatibility task (Lavie, 1995). Figure 4.10a shows stimuli for the low-load condition in an experiment by Shawn Green and

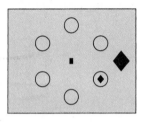

(a) Low load

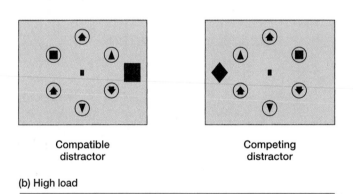

Compatible   Competing
distractor   distractor

(b) High load

Figure 4.10 The Green and Bavelier (2003) flanker compatibility experiment. (a) In the low-load condition, there is only one target (inside the circle); (b) in the high-load condition, there are six targets. The shapes on the far left or right are distractor shapes that the participant is told to ignore. Note that in the displays on the left, the distractor is the same as the target (compatible-distractor condition), and on the right the distractor is different from the target (competing distractor). (From "Action Video Game Modifies Visual Selective Attention," by C. S. Green & D. Bavelier, *Nature, 423,* 6939, pp. 534–537, Copyright © 2003 by C. S. Green et al. Reprinted with permission of the authors and Nature Publishing Group.)

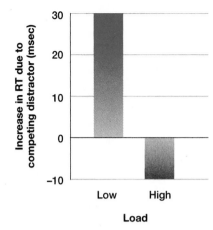

Figure 4.11 Results of the Green and Bavelier experiment, showing that the competing distractor has more of an effect on performance in the low-load condition. (From Green & Bavelier, 2003.)

Daphne Bavelier (2003) that used this task. The subjects' task was to decide as quickly as possible whether one of the shapes in the display was a target shape (either a square or a diamond), while ignoring the distractor shape presented outside the ring. The distractor shape was either *compatible* (the same shape as the target inside the ring, as in the left display in Figure 4.10a) or *competing* (the other shape; right display in Figure 4.10a).

The key finding for stimuli like the ones in Figure 4.10a is that participants responded more slowly if a competing distractor was present. This result is shown by the left bar in Figure 4.11, which indicates that the presence of the competing distractor increased the time it took to identify the target. The fact that the competing distractor affected reaction time indicates that the distractor was being processed, even though the participant was told to ignore the distractor. However, if the task is made more difficult by adding more shapes inside the circles, as shown in the display marked *high load* (Figure 4.10b), the competing distractor does not slow down responding (right bar in Figure 4.11).

Why do you think processing of the distractor would be decreased in the high-load condition? Think about a task you have done that is extremely difficult—perhaps solving a complex math problem or trying to decipher the symbolism in a literary passage. If the task was difficult enough, you probably had to focus all of your attention on it, ignoring everything else that was going on around you. This is apparently what happened in the high-load condition of Green and Bavelier's experiment. Participants had to focus all of their attention on finding the target among all of the extra shapes, and so did not process the competing distractor.

Results such as these provide a different way to think about the experiments that examined whether selection is early or late. According to Lavie (1995), the experiments that support the idea of early selection involve high-load tasks that require most of the participant's resources, so the attended message is processed and the unattended one isn't. However, experiments that support the idea of late selection involve low-load tasks that require less of the participant's resources, so both the attended message and some of the unattended message are processed. By pointing out that task load can affect performance when a person is presented with more than one message, Lavie showed how results that appeared contradictory (some supporting early selection, and others supporting late selection) can all be explained by the same general principle.

The idea of looking at how task load affects attention is important not only because of what it tells us about the problem of early versus late selection, but because it has enabled researchers to pose other questions as well. For example, one question that has generated a great deal of interest in recent years is, "What are the effects of playing video games?" Some research has considered whether playing violent video games has the negative effect of increasing the tendency for those who play them to become more violent (Anderson & Bushman, 2001; Sherry, 2001). But looking at video games from

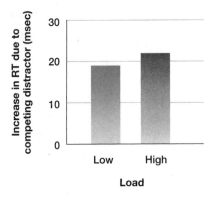

Figure 4.12 Results of the Green and Bavelier experiment for participants who have had a great deal of experience playing video games. For these participants the competing distractor has the same effect on the low- and high-load conditions. (From Green & Bavelier, 2003.)

another perspective, attention researchers have asked whether playing video games might increase players' attentional resources.

To determine how practice at playing video games affects a person's ability to pay attention to more than one thing at a time, Green and Bavelier (2003) repeated the flanker-compatibility task we have just described, but with experienced video-game players. Their results, shown in Figure 4.12, show that increasing load has little effect on these participants. Apparently, practice playing video games can enhance the ability to process visual information, so even when the load is increased, these players can still process additional information. (Note that Green and Bavelier also did control experiments that showed that their results could not be explained by the possibility that people who have high attentional capacities may be more likely to play video games.)

Test Yourself 4.1

1. How has the dichotic listening procedure been used to demonstrate the cocktail party phenomenon? What did this procedure tell us in Colin Cherry's experiment about how well people can focus on the attended message and how much information can be taken in from the unattended message?

2. Describe Broadbent's model of attention. Why is it called an early-selection model? What was the split-scan experiment, and what did it show?

3. What were the results of experiments by Moray ("words in the unattended ear"), Grey and Wedderburn ("Dear Aunt Jane") and Treisman ("I saw a girl jumping in the street . . ."), and why do they cast doubt on Broadbent's filter model of attention?

4. Describe Treisman's attenuation theory. How does it deal with the fact that we are sometimes aware of messages that are presented to the unattended channel?

5. Describe the experiment in which ambiguous sentences were used to provide evidence for the late-selection model of attention. Be sure you understand why the result of this experiment supports late-selection theory.

6. How has the early- versus late-selection debate been recast by Lavie's ideas about how task load affects selective attention?

7. What is the evidence that training can increase people's ability to deal with high-task loads?

Divided Attention: Paying Attention to More Than One Thing

Our emphasis so far has been on attention as a mechanism for focusing on one message, but we often want to spread our attention over a number of tasks. Can we do more than one thing at a time? Although you might be tempted to answer "no" based on the fact that it is difficult to listen to two conversations at once, there are many situations in which people can pay attention to a number of things simultaneously, a condition called **divided attention**. For example, people can simultaneously drive, have conversations, listen to music, and think about what they're going to be doing later that day. The ability to divide attention depends on a number of factors, including (1) practice, (2) the difficulty of the task, and (3) the type of task.

The Effect of Practice

Recently, as I was standing on the curb waiting for the "walk" signal, I observed a woman driving a car marked "AAA Driving School." I was impressed both by how slowly she was driving and by the intense look of concentration on her face. She was paying very close attention to her task and it clearly was not easy for her. Many people have had this experience when learning to drive, but later, with practice, they find that driving becomes much easier.

Research on divided attention has shown that with practice, people can learn to do two fairly difficult things simultaneously. When two college students first arrived at Elizabeth Spelke's laboratory (Spelke et al., 1976), they could easily read short stories and take dictation (writing words that were spoken to them), but couldn't do both at the same time. However, after 85 hours of practice spread over 17 weeks, they were able to read a story rapidly and with good comprehension while simultaneously categorizing dictated words (for example, classifying "chair" as "furniture").

Divided attention was demonstrated in another way by Walter Schneider and Richard Shiffrin (1977) using the procedure illustrated in Figure 4.13. At the beginning of a trial, participants saw a *memory set* that consisted of characters (letters or numbers) (Figure 4.13a). They then saw a quick succession of 20 *frames* (Figure 4.13b). Each frame had four positions, and at each position, there was either a random dot pattern, or a target (one of the characters from the memory set) or a distractor (a character from the *distractor set*). The distractors were from a different category than the characters in the memory set so if the characters in the memory set were numbers, the distractors were letters.

Another characteristic of the stimuli was that if a particular letter or number was a target, it was never used as a distractor on another trial, and similarly, distractors were not used as targets. Because of this consistency of targets and distractors, Schneider and Shiffrin called this way of presenting stimuli the *consistent mapping condition*.

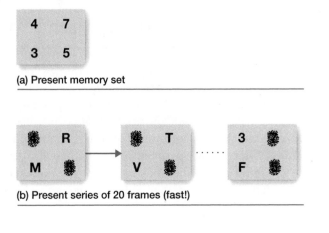

(a) Present memory set

(b) Present series of 20 frames (fast!)

(c) Was target from memory set present in a frame?

Figure 4.13 Consistent mapping condition for Schneider and Schiffrin's (1977) experiment.

As the 20 frames were being presented, the participants' task was to detect and identify a target, if one was presented in one of the frames (Figure 4.13c). In half of the trials, a single target was presented in one of the 20 frames. In the other half, no target was presented. (We can see from the example that the target *3* did appear in one of the frames on this particular trial.) This was not an easy task because the frames were presented very rapidly. For example, when the frame duration was 120 msecs, all 20 frames were presented within 2.4 seconds.

At the beginning of the experiment, the participants' performance was only 55 percent correct, and it took 900 trials for performance to reach 90 percent (Figure 4.14). Participants reported that for the first 600 trials they had to keep repeating the target items in the memory set in order to remember them. However, participants reported that after about 600 trials, the task had become automatic: the frames appeared and they responded without consciously thinking about it. What this means, according to Schneider and Shiffrin (1977), is that the many trials of practice resulted in **automatic processing,** a type of processing that occurs (1) without intention (it automatically happens without the person intending to do it), and (2) using few cognitive resources.

Another demonstration of automatic processing is the Stroop effect, in which the names of words interferes with the ability to name the color of ink used to print the words (For example, if the word "RED" is printed in blue ink the task is to say "blue"). (We presented the Stroop as a demonstration on page 4. If you didn't do it earlier, refer to Color Plates 1.1 and 1.2, and try it now.)

The reason the Stroop effect demonstrates automatic processing is that reading the words occurs automatically, without the person's intention to do so. Note that although reading the words uses few cognitive resources, it does use enough resources to slow down the speed of saying the colors.

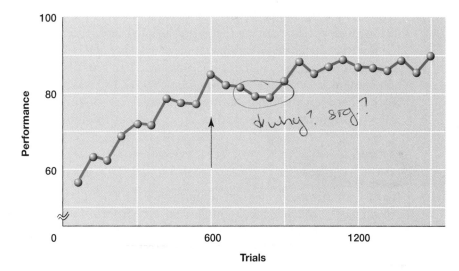

Figure 4.14 Improvement in performance with practice in Schneider and Schiffrin's experiment. The arrow indicates the point at which participants reported that the task had become automatic. (Reprinted from "Controlled and Automatic Human Information Processing: Perceptual Learning, Automatic Attending, and a General Theory," by R. M. Shiffrin & W. Schneider, *Psychological Review, 84,* pp. 127–190. Copyright © 1977 with permission from the American Psychological Association.

Automatic processing often occurs outside of the laboratory for tasks that are well practiced. For example, skilled musicians often report that they read music or play from memory automatically, without thinking about which notes they are playing or which fingers they are using. In fact, if they do start thinking about these things, they start making errors. What things do you do that are so well practiced that they are "on automatic"?

Let's now return to the laboratory and again consider Shiffrin and Schneider's participants, who after a great deal of practice were able to perform their task automatically with 90 percent accuracy. Two of the variables that Schneider and Shriffin changed for each trial were (1) the number of characters in the memory set, and (2) the number of characters in each frame. There could be 1 or 4 characters in the memory set and 1, 2, or 4 characters in each frame (in the example in Figure 4.13, there are 4 characters in the memory set and 2 in the frames). We might suppose that increasing the number characters in the memory sets and the frames would make the task more difficult but doing this had little effect on the participants' performance. They performed with over 90 percent accuracy no matter how many characters were in the memory set or the frames.

What this result means, according to Schneider and Shiffrin, is that their participants were able to carry out a number of tasks in parallel. Practice had enabled the participants to divide their attention so even if 4 targets and 4 frame items were presented, they could deal with all of this information simultaneously. In fact, they had become so good at the task, that it had become automatic and therefore required little attention at all.

We can relate the results of Schneider and Shiffrin's experiment back to the example from the beginning of the chapter, in which Sam was able to simultaneously drive, listen to his CD player, and perhaps do other things as well. He was able to do this because he had so much practice driving that it had become automatic.

But what about the situation that occurred when the boy ran out in front of Sam's car? As soon as that happened, being on "automatic" no longer worked. Sam had to devote all of his attention to dealing with the emergency, and so was no longer able to divide his attention between a number of tasks. Schneider and Schiffrin considered what happens when task difficulty increases by including another condition in their experiment.

The Effect of Task Difficulty

If a task is difficult, divided attention is sometimes not possible. This is illustrated by the second part of the Schneider and Shiffrin experiment in which the participants' task was made more difficult by making the following changes: (1) The characters in the memory set and the distractor set were all letters, and (2) a particular character could be in the memory set in one trial and in the distractor set in another trial (Figure 4.15). Schneider and Shiffrin called this more difficult task the *varied mapping condition* because participants didn't know whether a particular letter was going to be a distractor or in the memory set from trial to trial. This contrasts with the *consistent mapping condition* we described earlier, in which a particular letter or number could either be in the memory set or in the distractor set, but never in both.

The varied mapping condition was so difficult that the participants never achieved the automatic processing that they had in the consistent mapping condition. The processing for the varied mapping condition is described as **controlled processing** because the par-

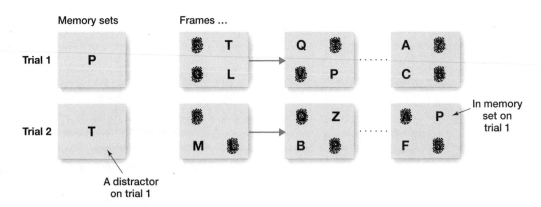

Figure 4.15 Varied mapping condition for Schneider and Shiffrin's (1977) experiment. This is more difficult than the consistent mapping condition because all the characters are letters and also because a character that was a distractor on one trial (like the T) can become a target on another trial, and a character that was in the memory set on one trial (like the P) can become a distractor on another trial.

ticipants had to pay close attention at all times and had to search for the target among the distractors in a much slower and more controlled way.

Remember that for the consistent mapping condition, increasing the number of characters in the memory set or the distractor set had no effect on performance. However, for the varied mapping condition, increasing the number of characters in the memory and distractor sets caused a large decrease in performance. For example, when there were 4 characters in the memory set and 4 characters in the distractor set, participants could do the task only if the presentation of the distractors was slowed to 400 msecs for each one. (In the consistent mapping condition, each distractor appeared for only 120 msec.) Furthermore, even at this slower speed, their performance dropped to about 50 percent correct (in the consistent condition, performance was over 90 percent, even for the faster presentation). See Table 4.1 for a summary of the consistent and varied mapping conditions of Schneider and Shiffrin's experiment.

The varied mapping condition is an example of a situation in which the task was made so difficult that even after extensive practice, divided attention was still not possible. However, sometimes increasing the difficulty of one task may not completely eliminate divided attention but may simply decrease performance on another task. Sherman Tyler and coworkers (1979) conducted such an experiment by giving participants two tasks: (1) an anagram task, in which they had to unscramble letters to form a word, and (2) a reaction-time task, in which participants had to push a button every time they heard a brief tone. In the "hard" anagram condition (i.e., unscramble *croodt*), Tyler's participants took longer to react to the tone than in the "easy" anagram condition (i.e., unscramble *dortoc*) (Figure 4.16). One way to explain this result is that the hard anagrams had used up more of the participant's cognitive resources, leaving fewer resources for the reaction-time task. (Note: The answer to both tasks is "doctor.")

Table 4.1	SUMMARY OF RESULTS INVOLVING CONSISTENT MAPPING AND VARIED MAPPING		
Condition	Memory Set and Distractor Set	Processing	Effect of Increasing Memory or Distractor Sets
Consistent mapping	Always different because if one is numbers, the other is letters.	• Difficult at the beginning, during learning. • Becomes automatic processing after practice.	No effect.
Varied mapping	Both are letters. A particular letter can be in the memory set in one trial, and then switch to the distractor set in a later trial.	Controlled processing.	Slower presentation needed. Performance decreases, even for slower presentation.

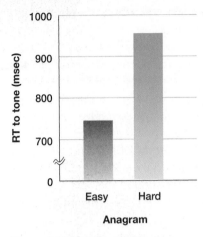

Figure 4.16 Results of Tyler et al.'s (1979) divided-attention experiment. The anagram task designated as hard increased the reaction time to the tone.

Tyler's result is an example of a hard task and an easy one competing for a person's attention. As long as the hard task isn't too hard, the person can do both tasks simultaneously. However, when task difficulty increases, performance decreases on the easier, or less important, task. Our example of what happened when the boy ran out in front of Sam's car illustrates this phenomenon, and you may have experienced something similar (although perhaps not as exciting) when driving and talking with a passenger at the same time. It may be easy to talk and drive at the same time when traffic is light. But when traffic is heavy, and you see a flashing light that announces "Construction Ahead," you might have to stop your conversation to devote all of your cognitive resources to driving.

A recent newsworthy example of cognitive capacity on the road is a problem that appears to be created by people talking on cellular phones while driving. An article in the *New York Times* titled "Road Daze: A Hand on the Wheel and an Ear to the Phone" (Hafner, 1999) cites numerous situations in which talking on cellular phones while driving has been associated with accidents. These anecdotal reports are supported by a survey of accidents and cellular phone use in Toronto, which indicates that the risk of a collision when using a cellular phone is four times higher than the risk when a cellular phone was not being used (Redelmeier & Tibshirani, 1997).

Perhaps the most significant result of the Toronto study from the point of view of cognitive capacity is that hands-free cell phone units offered no safety advantage. This finding is supported by the results of an experiment by David Strayer and William Johnston (2001), in which participants who were involved in a simulated driving task were required to apply the brakes as quickly as possible in response to a red light (Figure 4.17a).

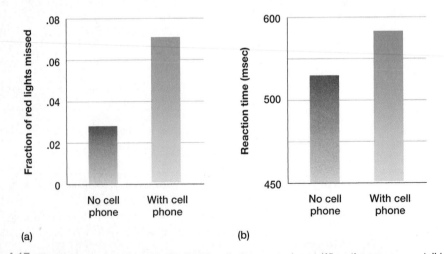

Figure 4.17 Result of Strayer and Johnston's (2001) cell-phone experiment. When the person was talking on the cell phone, they (a) missed more red lights, and (b) took longer to apply the brakes.

Doing this task while talking on a cell phone caused the participants to miss twice as many of the red lights compared to when they weren't talking on the phone, and increased the time it took to apply the brakes (Figure 4.17b). In agreement with the results of the Toronto study, the same decrease in performance occurred when participants used a "hands-free" cell phone device as when they were holding the cell phone. Strayer and Johnston concluded from this result that the cognitive task of talking on the phone uses resources that would otherwise be used for driving the car (also see Haigney & Westerman, 2001; Lamble et al., 1999; Spence & Read, 2003; Violanti, 1998). Because of results such as these, a number of states have passed laws banning cell phone use while driving (Whitaker, 2003).

The Effect of Task Type

Another factor that plays a role in determining whether divided attention is possible is task type. This is illustrated by the following demonstration

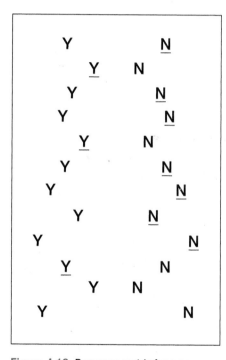

Figure 4.18 Response matrix for response-dependent attention demonstration. (Reprinted from "Spatial and Verbal Components of the Act of Recall," by L. Brooks, *Canadian Journal of Psychology, 22,* pp. 349–368. Copyright © 1968 by the Canadian Psychological Association.)

◼ Demonstration

Response-Dependent Attention

Memorize the sentence below and then without looking at it, consider each word in order and say "yes" if it is a noun and "no" if it isn't a noun.

John ran to the store to buy some oranges.

Now try the same task for the sentence below. After memorizing the sentence, look at Figure 4.18 and as you remember each word in the order it appears in the sentence, point to the Y if the word is a noun and to the N if it isn't (move down a row in the display in Figure 4.18 for each new word).

The bird flew out the window to the tree.   ◼

Did you notice any difference in the difficulty of these two tasks? Participants in Lee Brooks's (1968) experiment, on which this demonstration is based, found it harder when they had to say *yes* or *no* than when they had to point to *yes* or *no*. This occurs because the verbal response (saying *yes* or *no*) matches the verbal task of remembering the sentence and therefore competes with it. However, the spatial response (pointing to *yes* or *no*) does not match the verbal task. Thus, responding is harder when similar types of tasks compete for cognitive resources.

Brooks also did another experiment you might want to try. Brooks's participants visualized a block letter, like the *F* in

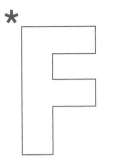

Figure 4.19. Starting at the corner marked by the * they visualized each corner in turn and said *yes* if the corner was an outside corner and *no* if it was an inside corner. (Try this, but remember that you need to *visualize* the *F*, rather than simply looking at the picture of the *F*.) In another condition, participants responded by pointing to *Y* or *N* (as in Figure 4.18). Try this too. Which task is easier, and why? [Hint: In this case, the memory task is spatial and the tests are either verbal (*yes/no*) or spatial (pointing).] What do this result and the result of the demonstration that used sentences say about task conditions that would make divided attention easier? Harder?

So far in this chapter, we have been concerned with peoples' ability to selectively focus their attention on one task or stimulus and with their ability to divide their attention among a number of different tasks or stimuli. In the rest of this chapter, we are going to consider some of the processes that occur as we visually observe objects in the environment.

Figure 4.19 Visual stimulus for Brooks's (1968) spatial visualization experiment. See text for instructions. (From Brooks, 1968.)

VISUAL ATTENTION: SEEING THINGS IN THE ENVIRONMENT

Look around you right now. What do you see? It is likely that your response to this question involves describing the overall scene and some of the objects in it. You may have noticed that you were able to take in the overall scene very quickly, but that you had to pay special attention to the specific things that you wanted to see in more detail.

Evidence that people can quickly take in whole scenes comes from experiments that show that people can describe the overall gist of a picture even if it is flashed for only a fraction of a second (Biederman, 1981). In a recent experiment, Fei Fei Li and coworkers (2002) showed that we can take in information from a photograph even if we aren't focusing our attention on it. Li's participants were asked to focus their attention at the center of a display where five letters would be flashed (Figure 4.20). Their task was to decide, as quickly as possible, whether all five letters were the same or whether one of the letters was different. Almost immediately after the letters appeared, a photograph of an environmental scene was flashed off to the side, appearing at a different position on each trial. Even though the participants' attention was directed away from the photograph by the letter task, and even though the photograph was visible for only 27 msec., participants were able to correctly indicate whether an animal was present in the photograph in 76 percent of the trials (50 percent would be chance performance, since animals were present in half of the pictures).

The fact that people can very quickly take in whole scenes creates the impression that we are aware of most of the characteristics of our environment. However, this turns out not to be true when we consider smaller details. A phenomenon called *change blindness* demonstrates that we are often unaware of many of the details in the environment.

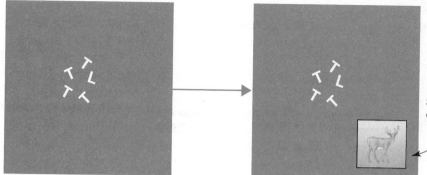

Figure 4.20 Display similar to those used by Li et al. (2002). One task in this experiment was to decide whether the five letters in the center were the same. Immediately after the letters appeared, a photograph that could contain an animal was flashed off to the side for 27 msec. and participants indicated whether or not an animal was present.

Scene that might contain an animal

◣ Demonstration

Change Blindness

CogLab

Change Detection

When you have read these instructions, look at the picture in Figure 4.21 for just a moment. Then turn the page and see if you can determine what's different about Figure 4.22. Do this now. ■

Figure 4.21 Stimulus for change-blindness demonstration. See text for instructions.

Were you able to see what was different in the second picture? People often have trouble detecting the change even though it is obvious when you know where to look. (Try again, paying attention to the lower left portion of the picture.) When Ronald Rensink and coworkers (1997) did a similar experiment under more controlled conditions, they found that people needed to alternate back and forth between two pictures a number of times to detect differences.

This difficulty in detecting changes in scenes is called **change blindness** (Rensink, 2002). It is caused by a failure to pay attention. The importance of attention is demonstrated by the fact that when Rensink added a cue indicating which part of a scene had been changed, participants detected the changes much more quickly (also see Henderson & Hollingworth, 2003; Rensink, 2002).

The change-blindness effect also occurs when the scene changes in different shots of a film. Figure 4.23 shows successive frames from a video of a brief conversation between two women. The noteworthy aspect of this video is that changes take place in each new shot. In Shot B, the woman's scarf has disappeared; in Shot C, the other woman's hand is on her chin, although moments later, in Shot D, both arms are on the table. Also, the plates change color from red in the initial views to white in Shot D.

Although participants who viewed this video were told to pay close attention to the film, only 1 of 10 participants claimed to notice any changes. Even when the participants were shown the video again and were warned that there would be changes in "objects,

Figure 4.22 Stimulus for change-blindness demonstration.

body position, or clothing," they noticed fewer than a quarter of the changes that occurred (Levin & Simons, 1997).

This lack of awareness may seem like a bad thing, but we apparently function quite well without being aware of every detail in our environment. One reason for this is that we are so familiar with our environment that if we "fill in the blanks" based on our past experiences, we can predict approximately what will be in a particular scene. Thus, if we briefly see a scene that includes a gas station, we will know that it is extremely likely that there are gas pumps in front of the station, even if we weren't paying attention to that part of the scene. (This phenomenon is an example of the intelligence of perception we discussed beginning on page 82 of Chapter 3.)

If our perceptual system was required to register all of the details in a scene, it might become overloaded very rapidly. So instead of constantly being aware of everything, we

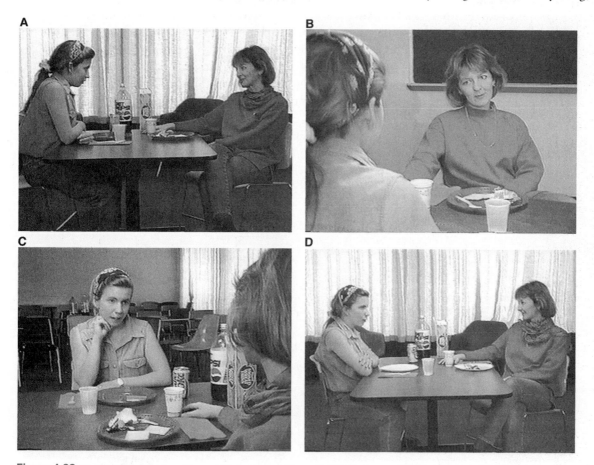

Figure 4.23 Successive shots in a film used in Levin and Simons's (1997) change-blindness experiment. (From "Failure to Detect Changes in Attended Objects in Motion Pictures" by D. Levin & D. Simons, 1997, *Psychonomic Bulletin and Review, 4,* pp. 501–506. Copyright © 1997 with permission of the Psychonomic Society Publications.)

have a general awareness of the scene and when we need to see specific details, we direct our attention to them. This idea has led some researchers to liken attention to a spotlight scanning for details in a scene.

The Spotlight of Visual Attention

The **spotlight model of attention** conceives of visual attention as having an effect that is similar to a spotlight which, when directed at different locations, increases the efficiency for which signals at that location can be processed (Norman, 1968; Posner et al., 1980).

In one of the early experiments designed to answer the question "Does attention to a specific location improve processing of a stimulus presented at that location?" Michael Posner and coworkers (1980) used a **precueing procedure,** in which participants were presented with a visual cue that told them where to direct their attention.

Figure 4.24 shows the stimulus setup used for the precueing procedure. Participants looked at a small square that was flanked by two lights on each side. Initially none of the lights were turned on, but at the beginning of a trial, the participants saw a cueing signal inside the square that indicated which light was going to be turned on (Figure 4.24a). One second later, one of the lights was illuminated (usually the one that was indicated by the cueing signal, but occasionally a light at another position was illuminated) and the participants' task was to push a button as quickly as possible (Figure 4.24b).

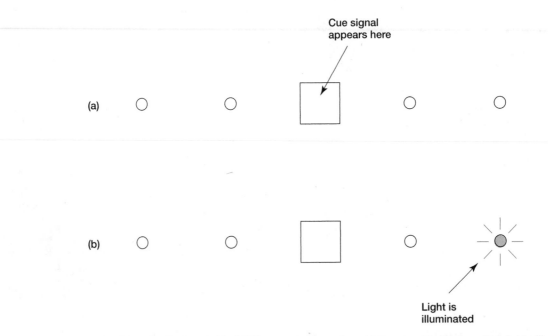

Figure 4.24 Stimuli for Posner et al.'s (1980) precueing procedure. (a) Cue signal indicating which light will flash appears within the square; (b) one light is illuminated. Usually the light illuminated was the one indicated by the cue, but sometimes it wasn't. (From Posner et al., 1980.)

The result of this experiment was that participants responded faster when the light appeared at the location indicated by the cueing signal than when it appeared at the different locations, even though they had always kept their eyes fixed steadily on the small box. This supports the idea that information processing is more efficient at the place where attention is directed.

This idea is supported by physiological evidence such as an experiment by Carol Colby and coworkers (1995), in which they trained a monkey to keep its eyes fixated on a dot marked *Fix* (see Figure 4.25) while a peripheral light is flashed at a location off to the right. In the "fixation only" condition (Figure 4.25a), the monkey's task is to look at the fixation light and to release its hand from a bar when the light dims. In the "fixation and attention" condition (Figure 4.25b), the monkey must still keep its eyes fixed on the fixation light but must release the bar when the peripheral light dims. Thus, in this condition, the monkey had to pay attention to what was happening at the light's location.

As the monkey was performing these tasks, Colby recorded from a neuron in the parietal cortex that fired to the peripheral light. The records in Figure 4.25 show that this neuron responded well to the peripheral light when the monkey was paying attention to it, but responded poorly when the monkey wasn't paying attention. Remember that the image on the monkey's retina was always the same because the monkey was always looking directly at the fixation point. Thus, the greater response when the monkey was paying attention to the peripheral light must be caused not by any change of the stimulus on the monkey's retina, but by the monkey's attention to the light. Because the retinal stimulus (the incoming data) remains the same in both the attended and nonattended trials, what does this result say about the role of top-down processing?

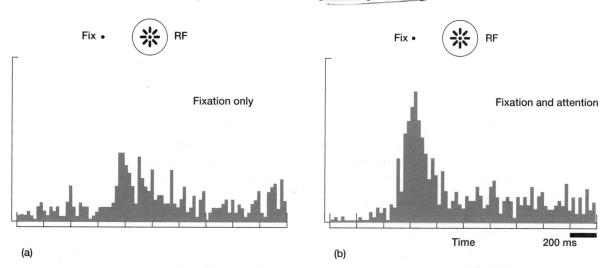

(a) (b)

Figure 4.25 Top: Stimuli for Colby et al.'s (1995) selective-attention experiment. The monkey always looked at the dot marked *Fix*. A light was flashed inside the circle marked *RF*. Below: (a) Nerve firing when the monkey was not paying attention to the light; (b) firing when the monkey was paying attention. (Reprinted from "Oculocentric Spatial Representation in Parietal Cortex," by C. L. Colby et al., *Cerebral Cortex, 5,* pp. 470–481. Copyright © 1995, with permission from Oxford University Press.)

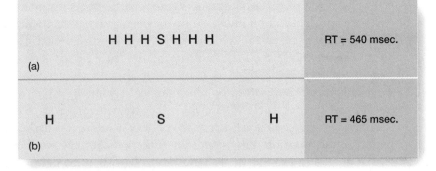

Figure 4.26 Flanker-compatibility task used to test the "spotlight" approach to attention. Participants pay attention to a target stimulus at *S* and are told to ignore flanker stimuli like the *H*'s. (a) Flankers close to the target; (b) flankers farther away. Reaction times are the results of Eriksen and Eriksen's (1974) experiment. (From Eriksen & Eriksen, 1974.)

The spotlight idea is also supported by experiments using the flanker-compatibility task (see page 110). The basic idea behind this procedure is to have a participant focus attention by responding to a target stimulus, such as the *S* in Figure 4.26a, while also presenting competing flanker stimuli, such as the *H*'s, at other locations. The *H*'s compete because they are associated with a different response than the target stimulus. If the correct response to the *S* is moving a lever to the right, the correct response to the *H* would be moving the lever to the left. Because the *S* is the target, the correct response is to move the lever to the right.

The question in the competing-response experiment is "Does the presence of a competing letter, like the *H*, cause slower responding compared to a control condition in which compatible letters are present?" If the *H*'s do cause slower responding, then we can conclude that they were identified, even though the participant was directing attention to the target.

When Barbara Eriksen and Charles Eriksen (1974) used this procedure, they found that competing flanker letters did increase reaction time, *and* that the flankers had less effect if the spacing between the letters was increased so that the distractors were moved away from the target (Figure 4.26b). According to the spotlight idea, flankers caused a longer RT when they were close to the center of attention because they were close to the attentional "spotlight," and the flankers had less effect when they were moved away because they were farther from the spotlight.

The idea of a spotlight provided a good way to describe the process of visual attention (Figure 4.27a) and led to many experiments and to some proposed modifications of the spotlight idea. One proposal was the **zoom lens model** of attention, which proposed that attention could be spread over a larger area or could be focused onto a smaller area (Eriksen & Yeh, 1985; Eriksen & St. James, 1986). According to this idea, attention enhances processing the most when the "beam" of attention is more zoomed in so it is narrowly

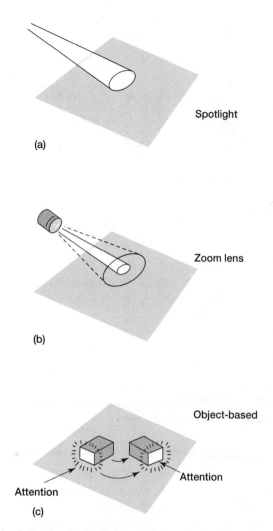

Figure 4.27 Three models of attention. (a) Spotlight model: Attention is focused on one area; (b) zoom lens model: A "spotlight" in which the area of attention can be varied to be small or large; (c) object-based attention: Attention is focused on an object and moves with the object.

focused, but some enhancement still occurs when attention is zoomed out so it is spread out over a larger area (Figure 4.27b).

Both the spotlight and zoom lens models describe **location-based attention.** That is, they describe attention as operating on whatever stimuli are at a particular location. However, there is also evidence of **object-based attention.** According to this idea, the enhancing effect of attention can be located on a particular object rather than at a particular location (Figure 4.27c).

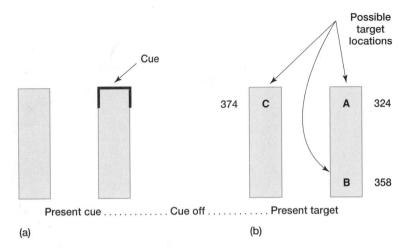

Figure 4.28 Stimuli for Egly et al.'s (1994) object-based attention experiment. (a) Cue signal appears at the top or bottom of one of the rectangles to indicate where the target will probably appear; (b) target appears at one of the ends of the rectangle. Numbers indicate reaction times in msecs for when the cue appeared at the top of the right rectangle.

Object-Based Visual Attention

The idea that attention is associated with objects has been supported by the fact that when attention is directed to one *place* on an object, the enhancing effect of this attention spreads throughout the object.

Enhancement Spreads Throughout an Object

The idea that the effect of attention spreads throughout an object was demonstrated in the experiment diagrammed in Figure 4.28 (Egly et al., 1994). In this experiment the participant first saw two side-by-side rectangles followed by a cue signal that indicated where the target would probably appear (Figure 4.28a). After the cue, the participant pressed a button when the target appeared anywhere in the display (Figure 4.28b). Reaction time was fastest when the target appeared at A, where the cue signal predicted it would appear. However, the most important result of this experiment is that participants responded faster when the target appeared at B, which is in the same rectangle as A, than when it appeared at C, which is in the neighboring rectangle. Notice that B's advantage occurs even though B and C are the same distance from A. Apparently, the enhancing effect of attention had spread within the rectangle on the right so even though the cue was at A, some enhancement occurred at B, as well.

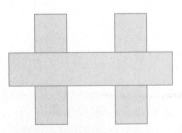

Figure 4.29 Stimuli in Figure 4.28 but with a horizontal bar added (Moore et al., 1998).

The same result occurs even if the rectangles are occluded by a horizontal bar, as shown in Figure 4.29 (Moore et al., 1998). The fact that attention can affect the whole object, even if it is occluded by other objects, is important because occlusion such as this occurs in the real world all the time. For example, remember our "animal" lurking behind the tree in Figure 3.37. Because attention spreads behind the tree, our awareness spreads throughout the object, thereby enhancing the chances we will recognize the interrupted shape as an animal. (Also see Baylis & Driver, 1993; Driver & Baylis, 1989, 1998; and Lavie & Driver, 1996, for more demonstrations of how attention spreads throughout objects.)

Object-based attention has also been demonstrated by neuropsychological studies of people with a condition called unilateral neglect, which affects their attentional mechanisms.

Neglect Can Occur for Locations and for Objects

People with **unilateral neglect** have usually suffered damage to an area in their right parietal lobe. This damage causes people to ignore stimuli in the left half of their visual field (Behrmann & Tipper, 1994; Robertson & Rafal, 2000).

vs. not being able to see

Figure 4.30 shows an example of a drawing of a flower made by a patient with unilateral neglect. The patient reacts as if only half of the object is there, even though he or she can see perfectly well on the "absent" side. Unlike a person who is blind on one side of the visual field because of damage to the primary visual receiving area, the patient with unilateral neglect will not turn his or her head to scan the missing area of their environment. In fact, these patients often will not eat food from the left side of their plate, or shave the left side of their face. They act as if half of the world doesn't exist.

Testing many of these patients indicates that their neglect often represents a lack of attention to the left side of space. But neglect occurs not only based on location in space, but also on location on a particular object. Stephen Tipper and Marlene Behrmann (1996)

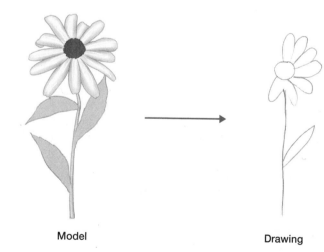

Model   Drawing

Figure 4.30 When patients with unilateral neglect are told to copy the model on the left, they produce drawings like the one on the right, in which the left side of the flower (or other model object) is missing.

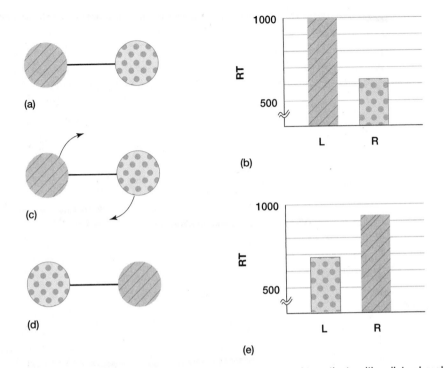

Figure 4.31 Barbell stimuli that Tipper and Behrmann (1996) presented to patients with unilateral neglect. (a) Target lights flashed in the left or right circle resulted in reaction times shown in (b). The reaction times were slower for the left side, which the patient usually neglected. (c) The pattern is rotated until the circles are reversed, as shown in (d), and the reaction times are also reversed, as shown in (e). This shows that the patient's attentional problem traveled with the object.

demonstrated this by presenting a barbell pattern to a person with neglect (Figure 4.31a). A target light flashed in either in the left circle or the right circle signaled the person to push a button as rapidly as possible. The results, shown in Figure 4.31b, indicate that the reaction time was longer when the target was flashed on the left rather than on the right. This is what we would expect because the left-side neglect would cause less efficient processing on the left side. (Even though these participants had trouble reporting what they saw on the left side, they could respond to brief flashes presented to that side, although much more slowly than a normal participant.)

In the second part of the experiment, the participants observed the same barbell pattern, but after one second it began rotating (Figure 4.31c) until the circle originally on the left was on the right (Figure 4.31d). Once it reached this position, the target was flashed within one of the circles. The results, in Figure 4.31e, show that the participants now responded more slowly when the target was flashed on the right side. Apparently, the inhibition of responding caused by the patient's left-side neglect traveled with the circle as it rotated to a new position.

From all of the research on visual attention, we can conclude that attention can be based both on where a person is looking in the environment (that is, it can be location based) and on where a person is looking on an object (object based). One way to think about how attention operates in the environment is to imagine a spotlight that scans different locations, which would be particularly important in static environments or scenes that contain few objects, and another mechanism that locks onto objects and follows them when they move, which would be particularly important in environments with many objects and movement (Behrmann & Tipper, 1999; Luck & Vecera, 2002).

THE ROLE OF ATTENTION IN COGNITION

At the beginning of the chapter we noted that attention is central to many aspects of cognition. To end the chapter, let's look at this idea again as well as how attention relates to the idea of top-down and bottom-up processing that we introduced in Chapter 3.

Attention as Top-Down Processing

How does attention fit into the distinction between bottom-up and top-down processing? (See Chapter 3, page 60.) Sometimes attention is associated with bottom-up processing. For example, automatically turning your head in the direction of a flash of light or a loud noise could be considered bottom-up because it is an automatic response that does not depend on a person's knowledge. (Although perhaps you might argue that some knowledge does come into play because our attentional system has evolved to alert us to stimuli that could possibly be important or dangerous. See page 91 for a discussion of this idea as applied to perception.)

But even in the case of a light flash or loud noise, top-down processing takes over as you search for the meaning of the flash or noise. When you think, "What was that about?" and begin looking around for explanations, your attention to different things in the environment is driven by a search for meaning that is definitely an example of top-down processing.

Much of our attention is driven by meaning and the knowledge we bring to a situation. Suddenly hearing your name in a noisy room is an example of attention driven by meaning. Any time a stimulus is attended because of its meaning, top-down processing is involved. Meaning not only attracts our attention but often guides our attention. For example, think about a time you were searching for the solution to a problem. One way to think about this process is that you may have been focusing your spotlight of attention onto different strategies, things you have learned in the past, or aspects of the problem that might lead you to the solution. Anytime you are engaged in a search process such as this, attention is involved. In fact, attentional processes that involve top-down processing are involved in many different cognitive processes.

Attention as Linked to Other Cognitive Processes

Looking back on the previous chapter on perception reveals some interesting interconnections between perception and attention. We saw that attention is involved in integrating elementary visual features (Treisman's feature integration theory). In this chapter we have presented evidence that attention is necessary for perception (change blindness) and that attention can affect what we perceive (spotlight of attention, object-based attention).

These connections between attention and perception are not really surprising. Even though we have discussed perception and attention in separate chapters, there is no such neat separation between them in real life. As we move through the world, what we perceive depends on what we attend to, and what we attend to depends on perceptual characteristics of the environment.

But these interconnections don't occur only for perception and attention. We have already introduced the idea that attentional processes play a role in solving problems. And another cognitive process, memory, has played an important role in some of the experiments we have described in this chapter. For example, Schneider and Shiffrin's participants had to remember the items in the memory set so they could compare them to what they saw in the frames that followed. As we discuss memory in the next chapter, we will see that the way we attend to specific stimuli or events is one of the major things that determine what we will remember later. We will also revisit many of the basic principles that we listed at the end of Chapter 3. Principles like invisible processing, representation, and using both behavioral and physiological approaches have continued to be important as we have discussed attention, and we will encounter them again as we begin our discussion of memory in the next chapter.

 Test Yourself 4.2

1. How did the results of Spelke's experiment and Schneider and Shiffrin's experiment provide support for the idea that divided attention is possible, and that it can be accomplished through automatic processing? What is the Stroop effect, and how does it demonstrate automatic processing?
2. What changes did Schneider and Shiffrin make in their experiment that decreased their participants' ability to divide their attention and to achieve automatic processing? Be sure you understand the differences between the consistent mapping and the varied mapping conditions.
3. What is the evidence that when task difficulty is increased, divided attention can occur, but performance is decreased on one of the tasks? (Review the anagram experiment and the effect of using a cell phone while driving.)
4. How does the response required by two tasks (spatial vs. verbal) affect the ability to divide attention between them?
5. What is the evidence that indicates that people can take in the "gist" of a scene very rapidly, but that becoming aware of details requires some attention? What is the ar-

gument for the idea that our lack of awareness of details of the environment may not be such a bad thing?

6. What does in mean to say that visual attention is like a spotlight directed to a specific location in space, and how do the results of precueing and response competition experiments support this idea? How is the zoom-lens model both similar to and different from the spotlight model?

7. How has physiological research shown that focusing attention on a particular stimulus can affect neural firing for that stimulus?

8. Research has shown that attention can enhance responding when it is directed at specific locations in space and also when it is directed at specific places on an object. What is the evidence for object-based attention? When would location-based attention be most important? When would object-based attention be most important?

Think About It

1. Pick two items from the following list and decide how difficult it would be to do both at the same time. Some things are difficult to do simultaneously because of physical limitations. For example, it is not possible (or at least extremely dangerous) to type on your computer and drive at the same time. Others things are difficult to do simultaneously because of cognitive limitations. For each pair of activities that you pick, decide why it would be easy or difficult to do them simultaneously. Be sure to take the idea of cognitive load into account.

Driving a car	Talking on a cell phone
Reading a book for pleasure	Flying a kite
Doing math problems	Walking in the woods
Talking to a friend	Listening to a story
Thinking about tomorrow	Writing a paper for class
Rock climbing	Dancing

2. Find someone who is willing to participate in a brief "observation exercise." Cover a picture (preferably one that contains a number of objects or details) with a piece of paper and tell the person that you are going to uncover the picture and that their task is to report everything that they see. Then uncover the picture very briefly (less than a second) and have the person write down, or tell you, what they saw. Then repeat this procedure, increasing the exposure of the picture to a few seconds so the person can direct their attention to different parts of the picture. Perhaps try this a third time, allowing even more time to observe the picture. From the person's responses, what can you conclude about the role of attention in determining what a person is aware of in their environment?

3. How does the attention involved in carrying out actions in the environment differ from the attention involved in scanning a picture for details, as in the previous "observation exercise" above?

4. As you sit in a stadium watching a football game, there is a lot going on in the game, in the stands, and on the sidelines. Which things that you might look at would involve object-based attention, and which would involve location-based attention?

5. It has been argued that talking on a cell phone while driving is really not that different than listening to the radio or talking to a passenger in the car. What arguments can you think of that (a) support this idea, and (b) argue against it?

KEY TERMS

Attention

Attenuation theory of attention

Automatic processing

Change blindness

Cocktail party phenomenon

Controlled processing

Dichotic listening

Dictionary unit

Divided attention

Early-selection model

Filter model of attention

Flanker-compatibility task

Late-selection model of attention

Location-based attention

Object-based attention

Precueing procedure

Selective attention

Shadowing

Spotlight model of attention

Task load

Unilateral neglect

Zoom lens model

CogLab To experience these experiments for yourself, go to http://coglab.wadsworth.com. Be sure to read each experiment's setup instructions before you go to the experiment itself. Otherwise, you won't know which keys to press.

Primary Labs

Change detection	A task involving detecting changes in alternating scenes (p. 121)
Spatial cueing	How cueing attention affects reaction time to the cued area. Evidence for the spotlight model of attention (p. 128).
Stroop effect	How reaction time to naming font colors is affected by the presence of conflicting information from words (p. 114 and Chapter 1, p. 4).

Related Labs

Attentional blink	How paying attention to one stimulus affects the ability to attend to a subsequent stimulus.
Simon effect	How speed and accuracy of responding is affected by the location of the response to a stimulus.

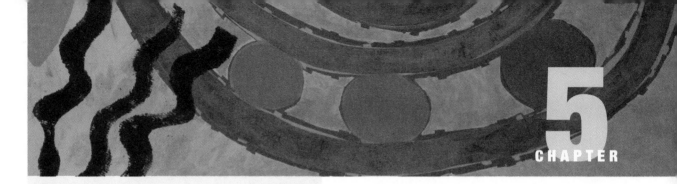

5

CHAPTER

Sensory Memory, Short-Term Memory, and Working Memory

Some Questions We Will Consider

✔ Why can we remember a telephone number long enough to place a call, but then we forget it almost immediately?

✔ Is there a way to increase the ability to remember things that have just happened?

✔ Do we use the same memory system to remember things we have seen and things we have heard?

■　■　■

Everything in life is memory, save for the thin edge of the present.
(Gazzaniga, 2000)

The thin edge of the present is what is happening right at this moment, but a moment from now the present will become the past, and some of the past will become stored in memory. What you will read in this chapter and the two that follow supports the idea that "everything in life is memory" and shows how our memory of the past not only provides a record of a lifetime of events we have experienced and knowledge we have learned, but can also affect our experience of what is happening right at this moment.

WHAT IS MEMORY?

The definition of **memory** provides the first indication of its importance in our lives: *Memory is the processes involved in retaining, retrieving, and using information about stimuli, images, events, ideas, and skills after the original information is no longer present.* The fact that memory retains information that is no longer present means that memory can serve as a form of "mental time travel," enabling us to bring back many different things that have happened in the past. We can use our memory "time machine" to go back just a moment—to the words you read at the beginning of this sentence—or many years—to events as early as a birthday party in early childhood.

What Are the Purposes of Memory?

Memory is important not only for recalling events from the distant past, but also for dealing with day-to-day activities. When I asked students in my cognitive psychology class to make a "Top 10" list of what they use memory for, they came up with over 30 different uses, most of them related to day-to-day activities. The top five items on their list, involved remembering the following things.

1. material for exams
2. their daily schedule
3. names

4. phone numbers
5. directions to places

What would your list include? As a student, remembering material for exams is probably on your list, but it is likely that people from different walks of life, such as business executives, construction workers, homemakers, nurses, or football players, would create lists that would differ from the ones created by college students in ways that reflect the demands of their particular lives. Remembering the material that will be on the next cognitive psychology exam might not make a football player's list, but remembering the playbook might.

One reason I ask students to create their "memory list" is to get them to think about how important memory is in their day-to-day lives. But the main reason is to make them aware of how many important functions they *don't* include on their lists, because they take them for granted. A few of these things include labeling familiar objects (you know you are reading a "book" because of your past experience with books), having conversations (you need memory to keep track of the flow of a conversation), knowing what to do in a restaurant (you need to remember a sequence of events, starting with being seated and ending with paying the check and leaving a tip), and finding your way to class.

The list of things that depend on memory is an extremely long one because just about everything we do depends on remembering what we have experienced in the past. But perhaps the most powerful way to demonstrate the importance of memory is to consider what happens to people's lives when they lose their memory. Consider, for example, the case of Clive Wearing (Annenberg, 2000).

Wearing was a highly respected musician and choral director in England who, in his 40s, contracted viral encephalitis, which destroyed parts of his temporal lobe that are important for forming new memories. Because of his brain damage, Wearing lives totally within the most recent one or two minutes of his life. He remembers what just happened and forgets everything else. When he meets someone, and the person leaves the room and returns three minutes later, Wearing reacts as if he hadn't met the person earlier. Because of his inability to form new memories, he constantly feels he has just become conscious for the first time.

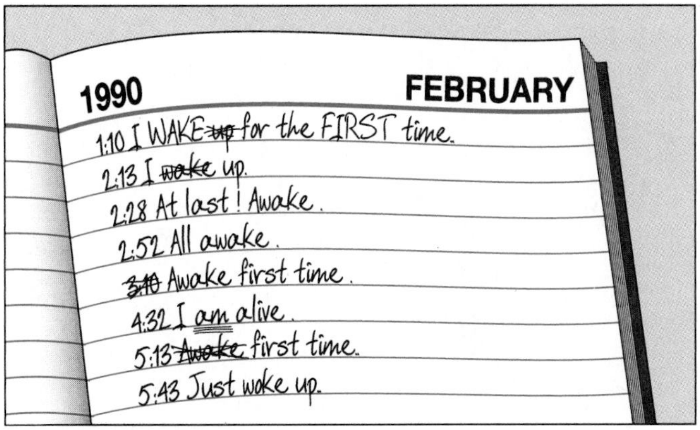

This feeling is made poignantly clear by Wearing's diary, which contains hundreds of entries like "I have woken up for the first time" and "I am alive" (Figure 5.1). But Wearing has no memory of ever writing anything except for the sentence he has just written. When questioned about

Figure 5.1 Clive Wearing's diary looked like this. Sometimes he would cross out previous entries, because he could only remember writing the most recent entry.

previous entries, Wearing acknowledges that they are in his handwriting, but because he has no memory for writing them, he denies that they are his. It is no wonder that he is confused, and not surprising that he describes his life as being "like death." His loss of memory has robbed him of his ability to participate in life in any meaningful way, and he needs to be constantly cared for by others.

The Plan of This Chapter

The goal of this chapter is to begin describing the basic principles of memory so we can understand both cases like Clive Wearing's and also the basic principles behind normal memory processes (Figure 5.2). We begin by describing a model of memory that is called the *modal model*. This is an information-processing model, which contains a number of

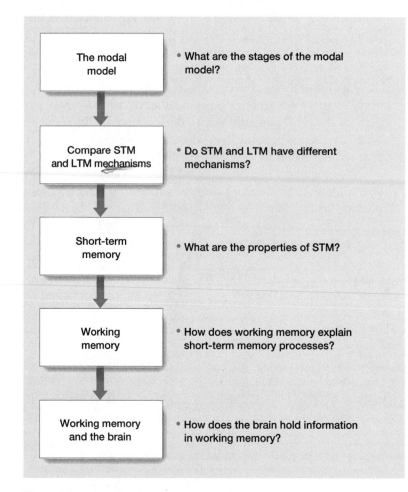

Figure 5.2 Flow diagram for this chapter.

stages, beginning with ones that hold information for only a short time (sensory memory and short-term memory) and ends with one that can hold information for extremely long periods of time (long-term memory).

After introducing the modal model, we will consider evidence for the idea that the short-term and long-term components of the modal model involve different mechanisms. We then focus on the short-term component, first looking at properties of short-term memory and then at research that has led to a more modern way of looking at the short-term stage of memory, which is called working memory. Finally, we will describe research on where some of the mechanisms of working memory are located in the brain. This chapter therefore focuses mainly on the short-term component of the memory system. In Chapters 6 and 7 we will consider the longer-term components.

Introduction to the Modal Model of Memory

In 1968 Richard Atkinson and Richard Shiffrin proposed a model of memory that included stages with different durations (Figure 5.3). The model has been so influential that it is called the **modal model of memory.** The various stages of the model are called the **structural features** of the model. There are three major structural features: (1) **sensory memory,** an initial stage that holds information for seconds or fractions of a second; (2) **short-term memory (STM),** which holds information for only 15–30 seconds; and (3) **long-term memory (LTM),** which can hold information for years or even decades.

Atkinson and Shiffrin also describe the memory system as including **control processes,** which are active processes that can be controlled by the person and may differ from one task to another. An example of a control process is **rehearsal**—repeating a stimulus over and over, as you might repeat a telephone number in order to hold it in your mind after looking it up in the phone book. Other examples of control processes are (1) strategies you might use to help make a stimulus more memorable, such as relating the *e.g.* numbers in a phone number to a familiar date in history, and (2) strategies of attention that help you selectively focus on other information you want to remember.

e.g. mnemonics —

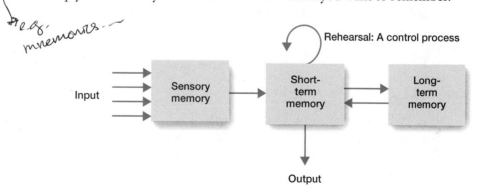

Output

Figure 5.3 Flow diagram for Atkinson and Shiffrin's (1968) model of memory. This model, which is described in the text, is called the *modal model* because of the huge influence it has had on memory research.

To illustrate how the structural features and control processes operate, let's consider what happens as Rachel looks up the number for Mineo's Pizza in the phone book (Figure 5.4). When she first looks at the book, all of the information that enters her eyes is registered in sensory memory (Figure 5.4a). But Rachel focuses on the number for Mineo's using the control process of selective attention, so the number enters STM (Figure 5.4b) and Rachel uses the control process of rehearsal to keep it there (Figure 5.4c).

After Rachel has dialed the phone number, she may forget it because it has not been transferred into long-term memory. However, she decides to memorize the number so next time she won't have to look it up in the phone book. The process she uses to memorize the number, a control process we will discuss in Chapter 6, transfers the number into long-term memory, where it is stored (Figure 5.4d). A few days later, when Rachel's urge for pizza returns, she remembers the number. This process of remembering information that is stored in long-term memory is called retrieval because the information must be retrieved from LTM so it can reenter STM to be used (Figure 5.4e). Retrieval is another control process that we will describe in Chapter 6.

One thing that becomes apparent from our example is that the components of memory do not act in isolation. Long-term memory is essential for storing information but before we can become aware of this stored information, it must be moved into STM. STM is where information resides as we are working with it, as Rachel was doing when she first looked up the phone number and when she later retrieved it from LTM.

We have described the broad outline of the model, but what about the details? As we delve deeper into the modal model, we will see that each stage handles information differently, and that our ability to remember depends on how these stages work together. We begin by describing sensory memory.

What Is Sensory Memory?

Sensory memory is the retention, for brief periods of time, of the effects of sensory stimulation. We can demonstrate this brief retention for the effects of visual stimulation with two familiar examples: the trail left by a moving sparkler and the experience of seeing a film.

The Sparkler's Trail and the Projector's Shutter

It is dark, sometime around the Fourth of July, and you place a match to the tip of a sparkler. As sparks begin radiating from the hot spot at the tip, you sweep the sparkler through the air, and create a trail of light (Figure 5.5). Although it appears that this trail is created by light left by the sparkler as you wave it through the air, there is, in fact, no light along this trail. The lighted trail is a creation of your mind because everywhere the sparkler goes you retain a perception of its light for a fraction of a second. This retention of the perception of light in your mind is called the persistence of vision.

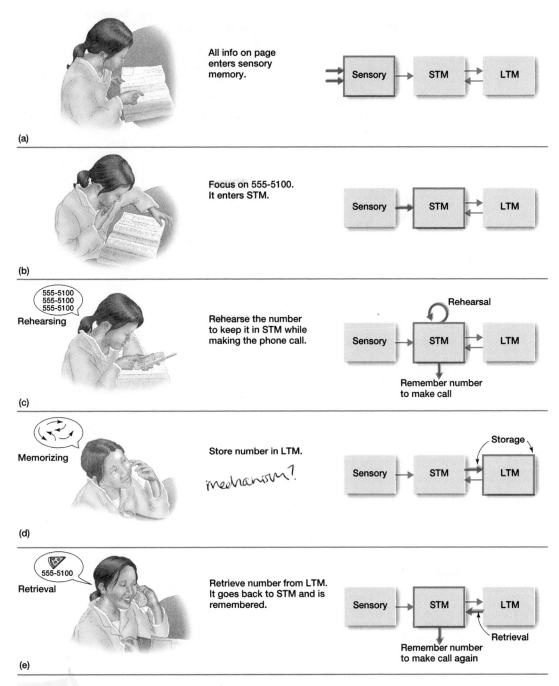

Figure 5.4 What happens in different parts of Rachel's memory as she is (a and b) looking up the phone number, (c) calling the pizza shop, and (d) memorizing the number. A few days later, (e) she retrieves the number from long-term memory to order pizza again. Darkened parts of the modal model indicate which processes are activated for each action that Rachel takes.

Figure 5.5 (a) A sparkler can cause a trail of light when it is moved rapidly. (b) This trail occurs because the perception of the light is briefly held in the mind.

Perceptual trail

Something similar happens while you are watching a film in a darkened movie theater. You may see actions moving smoothly across the screen, but what is actually projected is quite different. We can appreciate what is happening on the screen by considering the sequence of events that occur as a film is projected. First, a single film frame is positioned in front of the projector lens, and when the projector's shutter opens, the image on the film frame is projected onto the screen. The shutter then closes, so the film can move to the next frame without causing a blurred image, and during that time, the screen is dark. When the next frame has arrived in front of the lens, the shutter opens again, flashing the next image onto the screen. This process is repeated rapidly, 24 times per second, so 24 still images are flashed on the screen every second, with each image separated by a brief period of darkness (see Table 5.1).

CogLab
Apparent
Movement

Table 5.1	Persistence of Vision in Film	
What Happens?	**What Is on the Screen?**	**What Do You Perceive?**
Film frame 1 is projected.	Picture 1	Picture 1
Shutter closes and film moves to the next frame.	Darkness	Picture 1 (persistence of vision)
Shutter opens and film frame 2 is projected.	Picture 2	Picture 2*

*Note that the images appear so rapidly (24 per second) that you don't see individual images, but see a moving image created by the rapid sequence of images.

A person viewing the film sees the progression of still images as movement and doesn't see the dark intervals between the images because the persistence of vision fills in the darkness by retaining the image of the previous frame. If the period between the images is too long, the mind can't fill in the darkness completely, and you perceive a flickering effect. This is what happened in the early movies when the projectors flashed images more slowly, causing longer dark intervals. This is why these early films were called "flickers," a term that remains today, when we talk about going to the "flicks."

Sperling's Experiment: Measuring the Visual Icon

The persistence of vision effect that adds a trail to our perception of moving sparklers and fills in the dark spaces between frames in a film has been known since the early days of psychology (Boring, 1942). This lingering of the visual stimulus in our mind was studied by Sperling (1960) in a famous experiment in which he flashed an array of letters, like the one in Figure 5.6a, on the screen for 50 milliseconds (50/1,000 sec) and asked his participants to report as many of the letters as possible. This procedure was called the whole-report procedure because participants were told to base their report on the whole display.

Sperling's participants were able to report an average of only 4 or 5 of the 12 letters in the display, but they often commented that they had seen all of the letters at first, but the letters had faded away as they were reporting them. What were the participants seeing before the letters faded? To answer this question, Sperling used the procedure shown in Figure 5.6b.

Sperling flashed an array of 12 letters as before, but immediately after they were extinguished he sounded a tone that told the participant which row of letters to report. A high-pitched tone indicated that the participant should report the letters in the top row, a medium-pitched tone signaled the middle row, and a low-pitched tone signaled the bottom row. Note that since the tones were presented *after* the letters were turned off, the participant's attention was directed not to the actual letters, which were no longer present, but to whatever trace remained in the participant's mind after the letters were turned off. This procedure was called the partial-report procedure because participants were asked to direct their attention to just part of the display.

The results showed that no matter which row the participants were instructed to report, they remembered an average of about 3.3 of the 4 letters (82 percent) in that row. Starting with the fact that his participants were able to remember 82 percent of he letters no matter which row they reported, Sperling was able to calculate how many letters were available to participants from the entire 12-item display just after the display was turned off. Assuming that 82 percent of the entire display was available, Sperling's calculation, $12 \times 0.82 = 9.8$, indicated that about 10 letters were available from the whole display.

We have already noted that Sperling's participants could report only 4 or 5 letters when tested using the whole-report procedure because as they were reporting these 4 or 5 letters, the other letters had faded. To determine the time course of this fading, Sperling

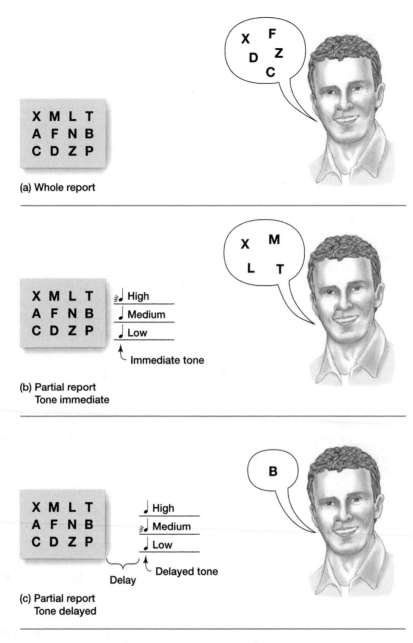

Figure 5.6 Procedure for three of Sperling's (1960) experiments. (a) Whole report procedure: Person saw all 12 letters at once for 50 msec. and reported as many as he or she could remember. (b) Partial report: Person saw all 12 letters, as before, but immediately after they were turned off, a tone indicated with row the person was to report; (c) Partial report, delayed: Same as (b), but with a short delay between extinguishing the letters and presentation of the tone.

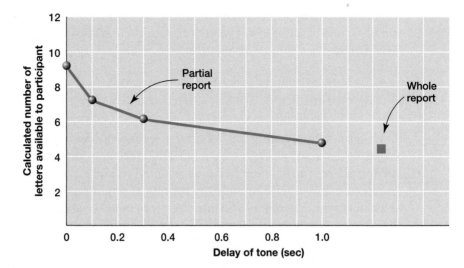

Figure 5.7 Results of Sperling's (1960) partial-report experiments. The decrease in performance is due to the rapid decay of iconic memory (called *sensory memory* in the modal model).

repeated the partial-report procedure but instead of presenting the cue tones immediately after the letters were extinguished, he delayed presentation of the tones so he could determine what a person could report from each row at various times after the display had been extinguished (Figure 5.6c).

The result of the partial-report experiments showed that the participants' memory dropped rapidly, so that by 1 second after the flash, they could report just slightly more than 1 letter in a row, or a total of about 4 letters for all three rows—the same number of letters they reported using the whole-report technique. Figure 5.7 plots this result in terms of the number of letters available to the participants from the entire display, which Sperling determined by multiplying the average number of letters reported for 1 row times 3.

Sperling concluded from these results that a short-lived sensory memory registers all or most of the information that hits our visual receptors but that this information decays within less than a second. This brief sensory memory for visual stimuli is called iconic memory or the visual icon (*icon* means "image"), and corresponds to the sensory memory stage of Atkinson and Shiffrin's model. Other research, using auditory stimuli, has shown that sounds also persist in the mind. This persistence of sound, which is called echoic memory, lasts for a few seconds after presentation of the original stimulus (Darwin et al., 1972).

Thus, sensory memory can register huge amounts of information (perhaps all of the information that reaches the receptors), but it retains this information for only seconds or fractions of a second. There has been some debate regarding the purpose of this large but rapidly fading store (Haber, 1983), but many cognitive psychologists believe that the sensory store is important for (1) collecting information to be processed; (2) holding the information briefly while initial processing is going on; and (3) <u>filling in the blanks</u> when stimulation is intermittent. We now turn to the next boxes in the modal model, short-term memory, and long-term memory.

How Can We Distinguish Between Short-Term and Long-Term Memory?

Short-term memory and long-term memory are the central parts of the modal model. When we described what happened in Rachel's memory system as she ordered a pizza, we saw that there is a rich interaction between STM and LTM. However, the way they are represented as two separate boxes in the model implies that they are two different types of memory with different properties. Certainly, our everyday experience seems to indicate that there is one type of memory for remembering telephone numbers you have just looked up in the phone book and another type for remembering the phone number a few days later or remembering what you did last summer. But could there be just one type of memory in which some information decays rapidly and some remains for long periods? Although this is a possibility, there is good evidence to support the idea that STM and LTM are two different types of memory. We begin describing this evidence by considering a classic experiment that measured the relationship between a word's position in a list and the chances that the word will be remembered later.

The Serial-Position Curve

CogLab
Serial Position

How well can you remember a list of words? The following demonstration is based on a classic experiment in memory research (Murdoch, 1962).

◼ Demonstration

Remembering a List

Get someone to read the stimulus list (see end of chapter, on p. 178) to you at a rate of about one word every two seconds. Right after the last word, write down all of the words you can remember.

◼

You can analyze your results by noting how many words you remembered from the first five entries on the list, the middle five, and the last five. Did you remember more words from the first or last five than from the middle? Individual results vary widely, but when Murdoch did this experiment on a large number of participants and plotted the percentage recall for each word versus the word's position on the list, he obtained the serial-position curve shown in Figure 5.8, which indicates that memory is better for words at the beginning or end of the list.

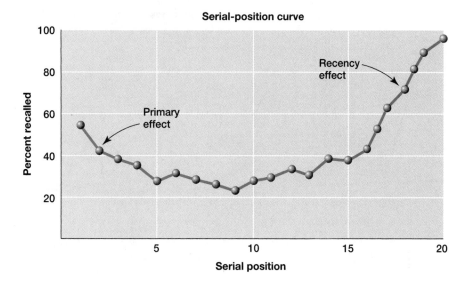

Figure 5.8 Serial-position curve (Murdoch, 1962). Notice that memory is better for words presented at the beginning of the list (primacy effect) and at the end (recency effect). (Reprinted from "The Serial Position Effect in Free Recall," by B. B. Murdoch, *Journal of Experimental Psychology, 64,* pp. 482–488. Copyright © 1962 with permission from the American Psychological Association.)

To understand why the words' position in the list should matter let's first consider the better memory for words at the end of the list. This is called the **recency effect** because these are the words that were presented most recently. One possible explanation for the better memory for words at the end of the list is that the most recently presented words are still in STM. To test this idea, Murray Glanzer and Anita Cunitz (1966) repeated Murdoch's experiment but had their participants count backwards for 30 seconds right after hearing the last word. This counting prevented rehearsal and allowed time for information to be lost from STM. The result was what we would predict: The delay caused by the counting eliminated the effect (Figure 5.9a). Glanzer and Cunitz therefore concluded that the recency effect is due to storage of recently presented items in STM.

But what about the words at the *beginning* of the list? Superior memory for stimuli presented at the beginning of a sequence is called the **primacy effect.** A possible explanation of the primacy effect is that these words have been transferred to LTM. One piece of evidence supporting this idea is that the participants in Glanzer and Cunitz's experiment continued to remember these words even after they had finished counting backwards for 30 seconds.

One reason that the words presented earlier in the list could have been transferred into LTM is that participants had more time to rehearse them. Glanzer and Cunitiz tested this idea by presenting the list at a slower pace, so there was more time between each word and participants had more time to rehearse. Just as we would expect if the primacy effect

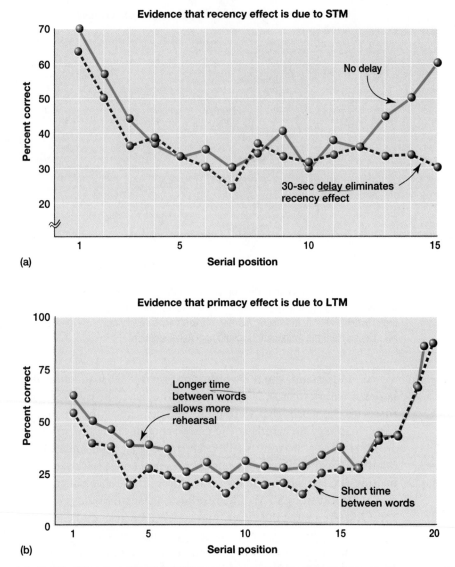

Figure 5.9 Result of Glanzer and Cunitz's (1966) experiment. (a) The serial-position curve has a normal recency effect when the memory test is immediate (solid line), but no recency effect occurs if the memory test is delayed for 30 seconds (dashed line). (b) Memory for earlier words is better when words are presented more slowly (solid line). (Reprinted from *Journal of Verbal Learning and Verbal Behavior, 5*, M. Glanzer & A. R. Cunitz, "Two Storage Mechanisms in Free Recall," pp. 351–360, Figures 1 & 2, copyright © 1966, with permission from Elsevier.)

is due to rehearsal, increasing the time between each word increased memory for the early words (see dotted curve in Figure 5.9b). Table 5.2 summarizes the results of the serial position experiments we have just described.

Table 5.2	PRIMACY AND RECENCY EFFECTS	
Effect	Why Does It Occur?	How Can It Be Changed?
Recency Effect Better memory for words at the end of the serial-position curve.	Words are still in STM.	To decrease, test after waiting 30 seconds after end of the list so information is lost from STM (see Figure 5.9a).
Primacy Effect Better memory for words at the beginning of the serial-position curve.	Words are rehearsed during presentation of the list so they get into LTM.	To increase, present the list more slowly so there is more time for rehearsal (see Figure 5.9b).

Differences in Coding

Another way to distinguish between STM and LTM is to consider the way information is coded in STM and LTM. Coding refers to the way information is represented. Remember, for example, our discussion in Chapter 2 of how a person's face can be represented by the pattern of firing of a number of neurons. Determining how a stimulus is represented by the firing of neurons is a physiological approach to coding. We can also take a mental approach to coding by asking how a stimulus or an experience is represented in the mind. For example, imagine that you have just finished listening to your cognitive psychology professor give a lecture. We can describe different kinds of mental coding that occur for this experience by considering some of the ways you might remember what happened in class.

Imagining what your professor looks like, perhaps by conjuring up an image in your mind, is an example of visual coding. Remembering the sound of your professor's voice is an example of auditory coding, which is called phonological coding. Finally, remembering what your professor was talking about is an example of coding in terms of meaning, which is called semantic coding (see Table 5.3).

Research on how information is coded in memory has demonstrated all of these kinds of coding for both STM and LTM, but has shown that the most common type of coding for short-term memory is phonological coding and the most common type of coding in long-term memory is semantic coding. *interesting. – why?*

Table 5.3	TYPES OF CODING
Type of Coding	Example
Visual	Image of a person
Phonological	Sound of the person's voice
Semantic	Meaning of what the person is saying

Coding in Short-Term Memory   One of the early experiments that investigated coding in STM was done by R. Conrad in 1964. In Conrad's experiment, participants saw a number of target letters flashed briefly on a screen, and were told to write down the letters in the order they were presented. Conrad found that when participants made errors, they were most likely to misidentify the target letter as another letter that *sounded like* the target. For example, "F" was most often misidentified as "S" or "X," two letters that sound similar to "F." Thus, even though the participants *saw* the letters, the mistakes they made were based on the letters' *sound*.

From these results Conrad concluded that the code for STM is phonological (based on the *sound* of the stimulus), rather than visual (based on the *appearance* of the stimulus). This conclusion fits with our common experience with telephone numbers. Even though our contact with them in the phone book is visual, we usually remember them by repeating their sound over and over rather than by visualizing what the numbers look like in the phone book (also see Wickelgren, 1965).

Do Conrad's results mean that STM is always coded phonologically? Not necessarily. Some tasks, such as remembering the details of a diagram or an architectural floor plan, require visual codes (Kroll, 1970; Posner & Keele, 1967; Shepard & Metzler, 1971a). This use of visual codes in STM was demonstrated in an experiment by Guojun Zhang and Herbert Simon (1985), who presented Chinese language symbols to native-speaking Chinese participants. The stimuli for this experiment were "radicals" and "characters" (Figure 5.10a). *Radicals* are symbols that are part of the Chinese language and that are not associated with any sound. *Characters* consist of a radical plus another symbol, and do have a sound.

When participants were asked to reproduce a series of radicals presented one after another, or a series of characters, they were able to reproduce a string of 2.7 radicals, on the

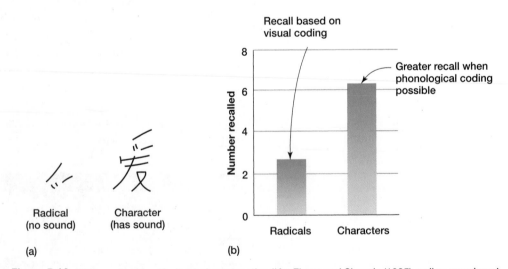

Figure 5.10 (a) Examples of *radical* and *character stimuli* for Zhang and Simon's (1985) coding experiment. (b) Results showing evidence for visual coding (left bar) and phonological coding (right bar).

average, and a string of 6.4 characters, on average (Figure 5.10b). The participants' ability to remember the radicals must be due to *visual* coding, since the radicals have no sound or meaning. The participants' superior memory for the characters is most likely due to the addition of phonological coding, since each character is associated with a sound.

Thus, information can be coded in STM both visually and phonologically. In addition, there is also evidence for semantic coding in STM. This is illustrated by an experiment in which Delos Wickens and coworkers (1976) had three different groups of participants (the "fruit" group, the "meat" group, and the "professions" group) listen to three words, count backwards for 15 seconds, and then remember the three words. They did this for a total of four trials, with different words presented on each trial.

Table 5.4 shows the experimental design of Wickens's experiment for the three groups of participants. Looking down the "fruit" column indicates that the fruit group was asked to remember names of fruits for all four trials. The meat group was asked to remember meats for the first three trials and then was switched to fruit on trial 4, and the professions group was asked to remember professions for the first three trials, and then was switched to fruit on trial 4.

The results for these three groups are indicated in Figure 5.11. There are two important things to notice about these results. First, participants in three all groups remembered about 87 percent of the words on trial 1 (Figure 5.11a), and the performance for all three groups dropped on trials 2 and 3 (Figures 5.11b and c), so by trial 3 they remembered only about 30 percent of the words. The decrease in performance on the second and third trials is caused by an effect called proactive interference (PI)—information learned previously interferes with learning new information.

The effect of proactive interference is illustrated by what might happen when a frequently used phone number is changed. Consider, for example, what might happen when Rachel calls the number 521-5100, she had memorized for Mineo's Pizza, only to get a recording saying that the phone number has been changed to 522-4100. Although Rachel tries to remember the new number, she makes mistakes at first because proactive interference is causing her memory for the old number to interfere with her memory for the new

Table 5.4	WICKENS'S EXPERIMENT DEMONSTRATING SEMANTIC CODING IN STM		
	Groups		
	Fruit	Meat	Profession
Trial 1	banana, peach, apple	salami, pork, chicken	lawyer, firefighter, teacher
Trial 2	plum, apricot, lime	bacon, hot dog, beef	dancer, minister, executive
Trial 3	melon, lemon, grape	hamburger, turkey, veal	accountant, doctor, editor
Trial 4	orange, cherry, pineapple (same category)	**orange, cherry, pineapple** (switch category)	**orange, cherry, pineapple** (switch category)

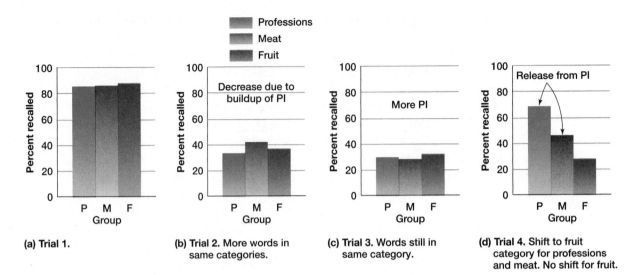

Figure 5.11 Results of Wickens et al.'s (1976) proactive inhibition experiment. (See Table 5.4 for design). (a) Initial performance on trial 1. (b and c) On trials 2 and 3 performance for all groups (professions, meat, and fruit) drops due to proactive interference. (d) On trial 4, performance recovers for the professions and meat group due to release from proactive interference.

number. The fact that the new number is similar to the old one adds to the interference and makes it harder to remember the new number.

The decrease in performance on trials 2 and 3 of Wickens's experiment was caused by proactive interference because the new items on each trial were from the same category as those on the previous trials. Participants in the fruit group heard only names of fruits for the first 3 trials, those in the meat group heard only names of meats, and those in the professions group heard only names of professions. But on the fourth trial, all of the groups heard names of fruits. Performance remained low for the participants who had been hearing the names of fruits because proactive interference continued for that group, but performance increased for the professions group because shifting to fruits eliminated the proactive interference that had built up on trials 1–3 for the names of professions (Figure 5.11d). The resulting increase in performance is called **release from proactive interference,** or release from PI.

Figure 5.11d also indicates that the release from PI is not as pronounced for the switch from meats to fruits because meats and fruits are more similar to each other than are professions and fruits. Can you relate these results to Rachel's problem in remembering the new number for the pizza shop? Would the switch have been easier or harder for Rachel if the new phone number had been very different from the old one?

What does release from PI tell us about coding in STM? The key to answering this question is to realize that the release from PI that occurs in the Wickens experiment depends on the words' categories (fruits, meats, professions). Because placing words into categories involves the *meanings* of the words, the results of the Wickens experiment demonstrate the operation of *semantic coding* in STM.

Coding in Long-Term Memory

Although *some* semantic coding does occur in STM, semantic coding is the *predominant* type of coding in LTM. Semantic encoding is illustrated by the kinds of errors that people make in tasks that involve LTM. For example, remembering the word "tree" as "bush" would indicate that the meaning of the word "tree" (rather than its visual appearance or the sound of saying "tree") is what was registered in LTM.

Jacqueline Sachs (1967) demonstrated the importance of meaning in LTM by having participants listen to a tape recording of a passage like the one in the following demonstration. Try this yourself.

Demonstration

Reading a Passage

Read the following passage.

> There is an interesting story about the telescope. In Holland, a man named Lippershey was an eyeglass maker. One day his children were playing with some lenses. They discovered that things seemed very close if two lenses were held about a foot apart. Lippershey began experimenting and his "spyglass" attracted much attention. He sent a letter about it to Galileo, the great Italian scientist. Galileo at once realized the importance of the discovery and set about to build an instrument of his own.

Now cover up the passage and indicate which of the following sentences is identical to a sentence in the passage and which sentences are changed.

1. He sent a letter about it to Galileo, the great Italian scientist.
2. Galileo, the great Italian scientist, sent him a letter about it.
3. A letter about it was sent to Galileo, the great Italian scientist.
4. He sent Galileo, the great Italian scientist, a letter about it.

Which sentence did you pick? Sentence 1 is the only one that is identical to one in the passage. Many of Sachs's participants (who heard a passage about two times as long as the one you read) correctly identified (1) as being identical and knew that (2) was changed, but a number identified (3) and (4) as matching one in the passage, even though the wording was different. The participants apparently remembered the sentence's meaning and not its exact wording.

But just as STM can be encoded in a few different ways, so can LTM. For example, you use a visual code when you recognize someone based on his or her appearance, and you are using a phonological code when you recognize them based on the sound of his or her voice.

In Chapter 2 we saw that a technique used in neuropsychology is identifying dissociations—situations in which one function is absent but others are present. This technique has been used in memory research to differentiate between STM and LTM by studying people with brain damage that has affected one of these functions while sparing the other.

People With Functioning STM but Poor LTM

Clive Wearing, the musician who lost his memory due to viral encephalitis, is an example of a person who has a functioning STM but is unable to form new LTMs. Another case of functioning STM but absent LTM is the case of H.M., who became one of the most famous cases in neuropsychology when surgeon's removed his hippocampus (see Figure 5.12) in an attempt to eliminate epileptic seizures that had not responded to other treatments (Scoville & Milner, 1957).

The operation eliminated H.M.'s seizures, but unfortunately also eliminated his ability to form new LTMs. Thus, the outcome of H.M.'s case is similar to that of Clive Wearing's, except Clive Wearing's brain damage was caused by disease and H.M.'s was caused by surgery. H.M.'s unfortunate situation occurred because in 1953 the surgeons did not realize that the hippocampus is crucial for the formation of LTMs. Once they realized the devastating effects of removing the hippocampus, H.M.'s operation was never repeated. However, H.M. has been studied for over 50 years and has taught us a great deal about memory. The property of H.M.'s memory that is important for distinguishing between STM and LTM is the demonstration that it is possible to lose the ability to form new LTMs while still retaining STM. This loss of one ability while the other remains intact is a single dissociation. To determine a double dissociation we need to find another person who has the opposite problem (i.e., good LTM, poor STM). *so, is STM NOT localized in hippocampus?*

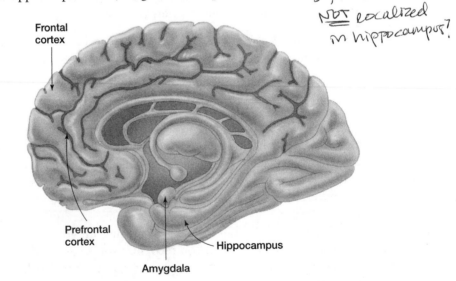

Frontal cortex

Prefrontal cortex

Hippocampus

Amygdala

Figure 5.12 Cross-section of the brain showing some of the key structures that are involved in memory.

People With Functioning LTM but Poor STM T. Shallice and Elizabeth Warrington (1970) describe K.F., a patient with normal LTM but poor STM. One indication of K.F's problems with STM is her reduced digit span—the number of digits a person can remember. You can determine your digit span by doing the following demonstration.

◼ Demonstration

Digit Span

Using an index card or piece of paper, cover all of the numbers below. Move the card down to uncover the first string of numbers. Read the numbers, cover them up, and then write them down. Then move the card to the next string and repeat this procedure until you begin making errors. The longest string you are able to reproduce without error is your digit span.

2149
39678
649784
7382015
84261432
482392807
5852981637

If you succeeded in remembering the longest string of digits, you have a digit span of 10. The typical span is between 5 and 8 digits. Patient K.F. had a digit span of 2 and, in addition, the recency effect in her serial-position curve, which is associated with STM, was reduced.

Table 5.5, which indicates which aspects of memory are impaired and which are intact for Clive Wearing, H.M., and K.F., demonstrates that a double dissociation exists for STM and LTM. In Chapter 2 we saw that this means that the two functions are caused by different mechanisms, which act independently. *think about this...*

The evidence we have described involving coding, the serial-position curve, and neuropsychological case studies provides good reasons to differentiate between STM and LTM. We will see that this distinction has proven to be an extremely valuable way to approach the study of memory. In the remainder of this chapter we will describe the properties of STM and then focus on working memory, which is an updated way of looking at short-term memory.

Table 5.5	A DOUBLE DISSOCIATION FOR STM AND LTM	
	STM	**LTM**
Clive Wearing and H.M.	OK	Impaired
K.F.	Impaired	OK

1. Why can we say that "memory is life"? Answer this question by considering what memory does for people with the ability to remember, and what happens when this ability is lost, as in cases like Clive Wearing (p. 137).

2. Describe Atkinson and Shiffrin's modal model of memory both in terms of its structure (the boxes connected by arrows) and the control processes. Then describe how each part of the model comes into play when you decide you want to order pizza but can't remember the phone number of the pizzeria.

3. What do seeing the trail left by a moving sparkler and watching a film have in common? How are both related to the modal model of memory?

4. Sperling showed that we can see 9 or 10 out of 12 letters right after they are briefly flashed, but we can report only about 4 of these letters just a short time later. How did he show this? How is this result related to the modal model?

5. The idea that there are two different types of memory—one short-term and the other long-term—is supported by experiments that measured the serial-position curve and by experiments that investigated the form of the memory code. Describe these experiments and the reasoning behind them.

6. The proactive interference experiment described in the chapter is presented as evidence for a particular type of coding in short-term memory. What type of coding was demonstrated? Why does the conclusion hold for STM, even though the experiment took much longer than the 30–60 seconds that information is usually held in STM?

7. Studying the behavior of people with brain damage has provided further evidence for the idea of two types of memory. Describe the cases of Clive Wearing, H.M., and K.F. in terms of their symptoms and how we can draw general conclusions about memory from these symptoms. Why can we draw stronger conclusions about memory by considering more than one case?

WHAT ARE THE PROPERTIES OF SHORT-TERM MEMORY?

As we think about memory, considering both what psychologists have learned about it and how we use it every day, it is easy to downplay the importance of STM compared to LTM. In my class survey of the uses of memory, my students focused almost entirely on how memory enables us to hold information for long periods, such as remembering directions, people's names, or material that might appear on an exam. Certainly, our ability to store information for long periods is important, as attested by cases such as H.M. and Clive Wearing, whose inability to form LTMs makes it impossible for them to function independently. But, as we will see, STM (and working memory) is also crucial for normal functioning. Consider, for example, the following sentence.

The human brain is involved in everything we know about the important things in life, like football.

How do we understand this sentence? First, the beginning of the sentence is stored in STM. Then we read the rest of the sentence and determine the overall meaning by comparing the information at the end of the sentence to the information at the beginning.

But what if we couldn't hold the beginning of the sentence in STM? If the information in the first phrase faded before you completed the sentence, you might think that the topic of the sentence is football and wouldn't realize that the sentence is really about the brain.

Holding small amounts of information for brief periods is the basis of a great deal of our mental life. Everything we think about or know at a particular moment in time involves STM because short-term memory is our window on the present. (Remember from Figure 5.4e that Rachel remembered the phone number of the pizzeria by transferring it from LTM to STM.) Early research on STM focused on answering the following two questions: (1) How much information can STM hold? and (2) How long can STM hold this information?

What Is the Capacity of Short-Term Memory?

One measure of the capacity of STM is the digit span of 5–8 items (or more for some people). A famous paper by George Miller (1956), who was one of the pioneers in the development of modern cognitive psychology, begins with the title "The Magical Number Seven, Plus or Minus Two," and goes on to present evidence that we can hold 5–9 items in our short-term memory.

One of the things Miller grapples with in his discussion of STM is the problem of defining exactly what an *item* is. Although the answer to this question might seem obvious if we simply consider the memory span for digits, it becomes more complicated when we consider trying to remember the following words: team, noise, room, crowd, training, screening, football, film.

How many units are there in this list? There are 8 words, but if we group them differently, they can form the following 4 pairs: football team, training film, crowd noise, screening room. We can take this one step further by arranging these groups of words into one sentence: The *football team* viewed the *training film* about *crowd noise*, in the *screening room*.

Is this stimulus 8 items, 4 items, or 1 item? Miller introduced the concept of **chunking** to describe the fact that small units (like words) can be combined into larger meaningful units, like phrases or sentences. A **chunk** has been defined as a collection of elements that are strongly associated with one another but are weakly associated with elements in other chunks (Gobet et al., 2001). Thus the word *noise* is strongly associated with the word *crowd* but is not as strongly associated with the other words, such as *film* or *room*.

Research has shown that chunking in terms of meaning can increase our ability to hold information in STM. Thus, we can recall a sequence of 5–8 unrelated words, but arranging the words to form a meaningful sentence so that the words become more strongly associated with one another increases the memory span to 20 words or more (Butterworth et al., 1990).

K. Anders Ericcson and coworkers (1980) demonstrated an effect of chunking by showing how a college student with average memory ability was able to achieve amazing feats of memory. Their participant, S.F., was asked to repeat strings of random digits that were read to him. Although S.F. had a typical memory span of 7 digits, after 230 one-hour sessions, he was able to repeat sequences of up to 79 digits without error. How did he do it? S.F. used chunking to recode the digits into larger units that formed meaningful sequences. For example, 3492 became "3 minutes and 49 point 2 seconds, near world-record mile time," and 893 became "89 point 3, very old man." This example illustrates how STM and LTM can interact with each other, because S.F., who was a runner, created his chunks based on his knowledge of running times that were stored in LTM.

Another example of chunking that is based on an interaction between STM and LTM is an experiment by William Chase and Herbert Simon (1973a, 1973b) in which they showed chess players pictures of chess pieces on a chess board for 5 seconds. The chess players were then asked to reproduce the positions they had seen. Chase and Simon compared the performance of a chess master who had played or studied chess for over 10,000 hours to the performance of a beginner who had less than 100 hours of experience. The results, shown in Figure 5.13a, show that the chess master placed 16 pieces out of 24 correctly on his first try, compared to just 4 out of 24 for the beginner. Moreover, the master required only four trials to reproduce all of the positions exactly, whereas even after seven trials the beginner was still making errors.

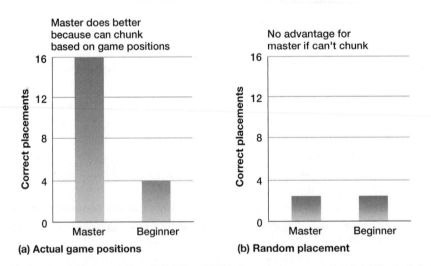

Figure 5.13 Results of Chase and Simon's (1973a, 1973b) chess memory experiment. (a) Master is better at reproducing actual game positions. (b) Master's performance drops to level of beginner when pieces are arranged randomly.

We know that the master's superior performance was caused by chunking because it occurred only when the chess pieces were arranged in positions from a real chess game. When the pieces were arranged *randomly*, however, the chess master performed as poorly as the beginner (Figure 5.13b). Chase and Simon concluded that the chess master's advantage was due not to a more highly developed short-term memory, but to his ability to group the chess pieces into meaningful chunks. Because the chess master had stored many of the patterns that occur in real chess games in LTM, he saw the layout of chess pieces not in terms of individual pieces but in terms of 4 to 6 chunks, each made up of a group of pieces that formed familiar, meaningful patterns. When the pieces were arranged randomly, the familiar patterns were destroyed and the chess master's advantage vanished (also see DeGroot, 1965; Gobet et al., 2001).

Chunking is an essential feature of STM because it enables this limited capacity system to deal with the large amount of information involved in many of the tasks we perform every day, such as chunking letters into words as you read this, remembering the first three numbers of familiar telephone exchanges as a unit, and transforming long conversations into smaller units of meaning.

What Is the Duration of Short-Term Memory?

CogLab

Brown-Peterson

How long does information stay in short-term memory if we are prevented from rehearsing it? In a famous experiment carried out independently by John Brown (1958) in England and Lloyd Peterson and Margaret Peterson (1959) in the United States, participants were given a task similar to the one in the following demonstration.

◪ Demonstration

Remembering Three Letters

You will need another person to serve as a participant in this experiment. Tell the person that you are going to read them three letters followed by a number. Once they hear the number they should start counting backwards by 3's from that number, and then when you say "Recall" they should write down the three letters that they heard at the beginning. Once they start counting, time 20 seconds and say "Recall." Note their accuracy and repeat this procedure for a few more trials, using a new set of letters and a new three-digit number on each trial.

Trial 1:	B F T	100
Trial 2:	Q S D	96
Trial 3:	K H J	104
Trial 4:	L W G	50
Trial 5:	C M Y	52
Trial 6:	Z F H	75
Trial 7:	F N C	120

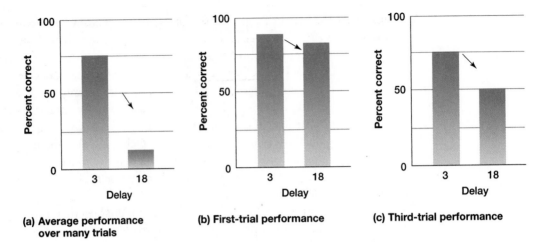

(a) Average performance over many trials

(b) First-trial performance

(c) Third-trial performance

Figure 5.14 Results of Peterson and Peterson's (1959) duration of STM experiment. (a) The result originally presented by Peterson and Peterson, showing a large drop in memory for letters for a delay of 18 seconds between presentation and test; (b) analysis of Peterson and Peterson's results by Keppel and Underwood, showing little decrease in performance on trial 1, and (c) more decrease by trial 3.

Peterson and Peterson found that their participants were able to remember about 80 percent of the letters after a 3-second delay (left bar in Figure 5.14a), but could remember an average of only 10 percent of the three-letter groups after an 18-second delay (right bar in Figure 5.14a). Peterson and Peterson initially interpreted this result as demonstrating that STM decays within 18 seconds. According to this interpretation, participants forgot the letters because of the passage of time. However, when Keppel and Underwood (1962) looked closely at Peterson and Peterson's results, they found that if they just considered the participants' performance on the first trial, there is little falloff between the 3-second and the 18-second delay (Figure 5.14b). However, when they analyzed the results for the third trial, they began seeing a drop-off in performance between the 3-second and the 18-second delay (Figure 5.14c).

The fact that memory for the letters becomes worse after a number of trials (also see Waugh & Norman, 1965) suggests that the difficulty may have been caused by proactive interference. [Remember from our description of Wickens's experiment (see Figure 5.11 and Table 5.4) that proactive interference occurs when material that was presented earlier interferes with memory for new information.] The rapid fading of memory observed in Brown's and Peterson and Peterson's experiments was therefore actually caused not by decay, but by interference.

What does it mean that the *reason* for the decrease in memory is proactive interference, rather than decay? Because there is a great deal of interference in our everyday experience, it doesn't really matter that PI causes the memory decrease, and we can still conclude that the effective duration of STM, when rehearsal is prevented, is about 15–20 seconds.

Problems With the Modal Model

Atkinson and Shiffrin's model of memory has served the study of memory well because by breaking the process of memory into stages, it generated a huge amount of research on each stage and on how the stages interact with one another. There are, however, some results that pose problems for the model. The model does not account for how a person such as K.F. who had a very small digit span could have poor STM but normal LTM. According to the model, all information must pass through STM to reach LTM. But how could this work for K.F., if her STM is defective? Shallice and Warrington (1970), who studied K.F., suggested that the Atkinson and Shiffrin model is oversimplified and that perhaps there may be another pathway that enables information to enter LTM without passing through STM.

In addition, other research has shown that STM is not just a single process but consists of a number of different processes, perhaps corresponding to the way information is coded into STM (remember that there is evidence for visual, phonological, and semantic encoding in STM; Freedman & Martin, 2001). Some of the most influential evidence for this idea has been provided by Alan Baddeley, who has shown that the short-term process consists of a number of specialized components.

One of the first experiments that suggested that the short-term process consists of a number of components was the observation by Baddeley and Hitch (1974) that under some conditions participants could do two tasks at once. You can demonstrate this to yourself with the following demonstration.

◣ Demonstration

Reading Text and Remembering Numbers

Keep these numbers in your mind (7, 1, 4, 9) as you read the following passage.

> *Baddeley reasoned that if STM had a limited storage capacity of about the length of a telephone number, filling up the storage capacity should make it difficult to do other tasks that depend on STM. But he found that participants could hold a short string of numbers in their memory while carrying out another task, such as reading or even solving a simple word problem. How are you doing with this task? What are the numbers? What is the gist of what you have just read?* ■

Because Baddeley's participants were able to read while simultaneously remembering numbers, he concluded that the short-term process must consist of a number of components that can function separately. In the foregoing example, the digit span task in which you held numbers in your memory is handled by one component while comprehending the paragraph is handled by another component. Based on results such as this, Baddeley decided that the name of the short-term process should be changed from short-term memory to *working memory*.

WORKING MEMORY: THE MODERN APPROACH TO SHORT-TERM MEMORY

Baddeley (2000) defines working memory as follows: *Working memory is a limited capacity system for temporary storage and* manipulation *of information for complex tasks such as comprehension, learning, and reasoning.* From this definition we can see that working memory differs from STM in two ways:

1. Working memory consists of a number of parts.
2. Its function is not just to briefly *store* information but to *manipulate* information to help us carry out complex cognitive tasks.

Thus, the emphasis of the working memory concept is not on how information is briefly retained but on how information is manipulated to achieve complex cognitions such as thinking and comprehension (Baddeley, 2000).

The Three Components of Working Memory

Working memory accomplishes the manipulation of information through the action of three components: the *phonological loop*, the *visuospatial sketch pad*, and the *central executive* (Figure 5.15).

The Phonological Loop   The phonological loop holds verbal and auditory information. Thus, when you are trying to remember a telephone number or a person's name, or to understand what your cognitive psychology professor is talking about, you are using your phonological loop (Figure 5.16a). This loop is divided into two parts:

1. Storage—a place that holds the memory trace. The trace fades in about 2 seconds unless it is refreshed by rehearsal. This is the passive part of the phonological loop.
2. Rehearsal—the part of the phonological loop responsible for the repetition that refreshes the memory trace. This is the active part of the phonological loop.

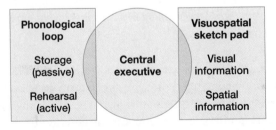

Baddeley's working memory model

Figure 5.15 Diagram of the three main components of Baddeley and Hitch's (1974; Baddeley, 2000) model of working memory: the phonological loop, the visuospatial sketch pad, and the central executive.

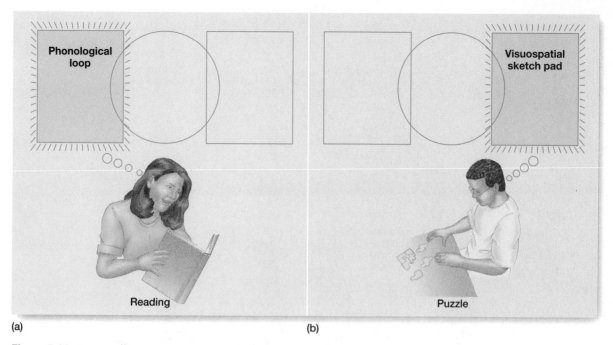

Figure 5.16 Tasks handled by components of working memory. (a) The phonological loop handles language. Reading is shown here, but the phonological loop also handles information that is received verbally, as when listening to someone speak. (b) The visuospatial sketch pad handles visual and spatial information.

The Visuospatial Sketch Pad   The **visuospatial sketch pad** holds visual and spatial information. When you form a picture in your mind or do tasks like solving a puzzle or finding your way around campus, you are using your visuospatial sketch pad (Figure 5.16b). As you can see from the diagram, the phonological loop and the visuospatial sketch pad are attached to the central executive.

The Central Executive   The **central executive** is where the major work of working memory occurs. The central executive pulls information from long-term memory and coordinates the activity of the phonological loop and visuospatial sketch pad by focusing on specific parts of a task and switching attention from one part to another. For example, imagine that you are driving in a strange city, and a friend in the passenger seat is reading you directions to a restaurant. As your phonological loop takes in the verbal directions, your sketch pad is helping you visualize a map of the streets leading to the restaurant (Figure 5.17). These two kinds of information are coordinated and combined by the central executive to create a coherent episode that we might title "Finding the Restaurant."

As we describe working memory, keep in mind that it is a hypothesis about how the mind works that needs to be tested by doing experiments. A number of experiments have been conducted to test the idea that the phonological loop and visuospatial sketch pad deal with different types of information.

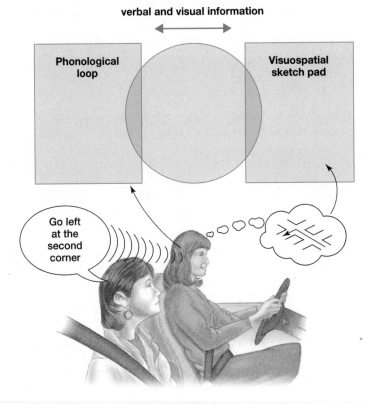

Figure 5.17 Tasks processed by the phonological loop (hearing directions) and visuospatial sketch pad (visualizing the route) being coordinated by the central executive.

Operation of the Phonological Loop

Three phenomena support the idea of a system specialized for language: the *phonological similarity effect*, the *word-length effect*, and *articulatory suppression*.

Phonological Similarity Effect   The **phonological similarity effect** occurs when letters or words that sound similar are confused. Remember Conrad's experiment in which he showed that people often confuse similar-sounding letters, such as "T" and "P." Conrad interpreted this result to support the idea of phonological coding in STM. In present-day terminology Conrad's result would be described as a demonstration of the phonological similarity effect that occurs as words are processed in the phonological loop of working memory. Here is another demonstration of the phonological similarity effect:

CogLab

Phonological
Similarity
Effect

◣ Demonstration

Phonological Similarity Effect

Task 1: Slowly read the following words. Look away and count to 15. Then write them down.

mac, can, cap, man, map

Task 2: Now do the same thing for these words.

pen, pay, cow, bar, rig

     Which of the two tasks was more difficult? Many people find that they confuse the similar-sounding words in Task 1 and that it is easier to remember the different-sounding words in Task 2. This confusion of words in Task 1 is an example of the phonological similarity effect.

Word-Length Effect   The **word-length effect** refers to the finding that memory for lists of words is better for short words than for long words.

◣ Demonstration

Word-Length Effect

Task 1: Read the following words, look away, and then write down the words you remember.

beast, bronze, wife, golf, inn, limp, dirt, star

Task 2: Now do the same thing for the following list.

alcohol, property, amplifier, officer, gallery, mosquito, orchestra, bricklayer

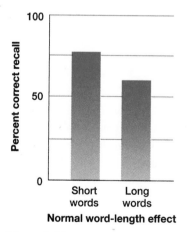

Figure 5.18 How word length affects memory, showing that recall is better for short words (Baddeley et al., 1984).

Each list contains eight words but according to the word-length effect the second list will be more difficult to remember because the words are longer. Results of an experiment by Baddeley and coworkers (1984) that illustrate this advantage for short words is shown in Figure 5.18. The word-length effect occurs because the larger words fill up the capacity of the phonological loop, and so rehearsal is less effective for the longer words because of the extra time needed to rehearse them.

    The limited capacity of the loop explains the initially surprising finding that American children have a larger digit span than Welsh children. Before you conclude that American children are smarter than Welsh children, consider that the names of numbers in Welsh (un, dau, tri, pedwar, pump, chwech . . .) are longer than the names of the numbers in

English (one, two, three, four, five, six . . .). Since it takes longer to pronounce Welsh numbers, fewer can be held in the phonological loop, and the memory span for these numbers is therefore less (Ellis & Hennelly, 1980).

In another study of memory for verbal material, Baddeley and coworkers (1975) found that people are able to remember the number of items that they can pronounce in about 1.5–2.0 seconds (also see Schweickert & Boruff, 1986). Try counting out loud, as fast as you can, for two seconds. According to Baddeley, the number you reach should be close to your digit span.

Articulatory Suppression   A phenomenon called articulatory suppression occurs when a person repeats an irrelevant sound such as "the" while hearing words to remember. Saying "the, the, the, the . . ." impairs memory for the words by interfering with operation of the phonological loop (Baddeley et al., 1984; Murray, 1968). The following demonstration, which is based on an experiment by Baddeley and coworkers (1984), illustrates an effect of articulatory suppression:

◼ Demonstration

Repeating "The"

Task 1: Repeat the word "the" out loud (i.e., "the, the, the . . .") as you read the following list. Then turn away and recall as many words as you can.

automobile	mathematics
apartment	syllogism
basketball	Catholicism

Task 2: Now do the same thing for the following list.

story	ant	towel
car	coffee	swing

According to the word-length effect, the second list should be easier to recall than the first because the words are shorter (see Figure 5.18). Remember that one of the advantages of shorter words is that they leave more space in the phonological loop for rehearsal. However, Baddeley et al. (1984) showed that articulatory suppression caused by saying "the, the, the . . ." reduces performance on both lists and reduces the advantage for short words (Figure 5.19a). This occurs because repeating "the, the, the . . ." prevents rehearsal in the phonological loop (Figure 5.19b).

What about the effect of saying "the, the, the . . ." on the phonological similarity effect, in which similar sounding words are confused? If participants *hear* a list of words while saying "the, the, the . . .," the phonological similarity effect still occurs because even though the phonological loop is dealing with "the, the, the . . .," asking participants to

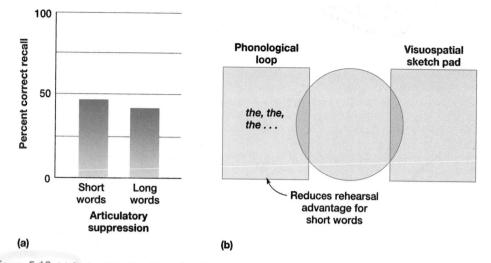

(a)

(b)

Figure 5.19 (a) Saying "the, the, the . . ." abolishes the word-length effect, so there is little difference in performance for short words and long words (Baddeley et al., 1984). (b) Diagram of how working memory explains this result by proposing that saying "the, the, the . . ." reduces rehearsal in the phonological loop.

listen to the words causes the words to enter the phonological loop directly (Figure 5.20a). Once in the phonological loop these words can be confused based on their sound, so the phonological similarity effect still occurs.

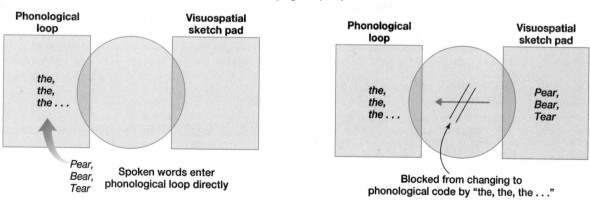

Effect of saying "the, the, the . . ."

(a) Phonological similarity effect occurs if words are heard

(b) No phonological similarity effect if words are read

Figure 5.20 Working memory and the effect of saying "the, the, the . . ." on the phonological similarity effect. (a) Phonological similarity effect still occurs for spoken words because listening causes words to enter phonological loop directly. (b) The effect does not occur for visually presented words because they are prevented from being recoded verbally in the phonological loop.

Table 5.6	EFFECT OF SAYING "THE, THE, THE . . ." ON THE PHONOLOGICAL SIMILARITY EFFECT FOR AUDITORY AND VISUAL PRESENTATIONS	
Presentation	Effect?
Auditory (hear word list)	**No** Phonological similarity effect still occurs (see Figure 5.20a)
Visual (read a word list)	**Yes** Phonological similarity effect no longer occurs (see Figure 5.20b)

However, if participants *read* a visually presented list of words while saying "the, the, the . . .," the phonological similarity effect does *not* occur, because the words are initially registered in the visuospatial sketch pad and saying "the, the, the . . ." prevents them from being changed to a phonological code by the phonological loop (Figure 5.20b). Without a phonological code, similar-sounding words can't be confused based on their sound so the phonological similarity effect is eliminated. Table 5.6 summarizes the effects of saying "the, the, the . . ." on the phonological similarity effect.

The Visuospatial Sketch Pad

When we discussed divided attention in Chapter 4 (see page 113), we described some experiments by Lee Brooks (1968) in which participants were asked to do two tasks at once. In one experiment, participants were asked to indicate whether each word in a sentence they had memorized was a noun by either saying *yes* or *no* (task 1), or by pointing to *Y* or *N* in a visual display (task 2) like the one in Figure 4.18 (see Figure 5.21a). In another experiment, participants were asked to indicate whether each corner of a block letter "F" that they were imagining was an outside corner by either saying *yes* or *no* (task 3) or pointing to *Y* or *N* (task 4) (see Figure 5.21b).

The important result for our purposes is that for both of these experiments the task was easier if the stimulus that participants was holding in their mind and the operation they were performing on that stimulus involved *different* capacities. Thus, in the first experiment, in which the stimulus was *verbal* (a memorized sentence), the *spatial task* (task 2) was easier, but in the second experiment, in which the stimulus was *spatial* (an imagined letter), the *verbal task* (task 3) was easier. We can explain these results in terms of the phonological loop and the visuospatial sketch pad by recognizing that verbal tasks depend on the phonological loop and spatial tasks depend on the visuospatial sketch pad. Thus, for task 1 in the first experiment, when the stimulus and task were both verbal (Figure

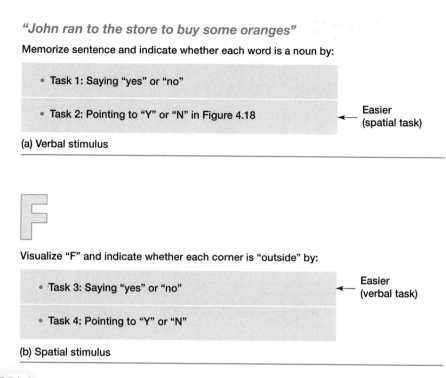

"John ran to the store to buy some oranges"

Memorize sentence and indicate whether each word is a noun by:

- Task 1: Saying "yes" or "no"

- Task 2: Pointing to "Y" or "N" in Figure 4.18 ← Easier (spatial task)

(a) Verbal stimulus

Visualize "F" and indicate whether each corner is "outside" by:

- Task 3: Saying "yes" or "no" ← Easier (verbal task)

- Task 4: Pointing to "Y" or "N"

(b) Spatial stimulus

Figure 5.21 Summary of the results of Brooks's (1968) experiment described in Chapter 4. (a) The tasks involving the verbal stimulus. Task (2), which involves a spatial response, is easier. (b) The tasks involving the spatial stimulus. Task (3), which involves a verbal response, is easier.

5.22a), the phonological loop was overloaded and the task became difficult. But for task 2 in the first experiment, when the stimulus was verbal and the task was spatial (Figure 5.22b), the loop and sketch pad shared responsibility and the task became easier. Figures 5.22c and d show the spatial stimulus in the sketch pad for tasks 3 and 4 of experiment 2. Fill in the tasks and results for each diagram to match the information in Figure 5.21b.

All of these demonstrations show that working memory is set up to process phonological and visual-spatial information separately so it can handle *different* types of information that are presented simultaneously, but that working memory has trouble handling *similar* types of information that are presented simultaneously.

Before leaving the loop and the sketch pad, let's consider an experiment by M. A. Brandimonte and coworkers (1992) that illustrates the principles we have been discussing in a different way. Brandimonte briefly presented a picture of an object like the one in Figure 5.23a and then briefly presented a picture of part of the object, as in Figure 5.23b. The participants' task was to subtract the second picture from the first and indicate what the new picture represented. Remember that the pictures were not present while the participants

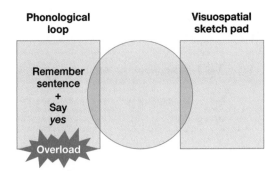

Phonological loop   **Visuospatial sketch pad**

Remember
sentence
+
Say
yes

Overload

(a) Task 1

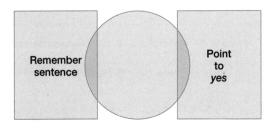

Remember
sentence

Point
to
yes

(b) Task 2: Easier

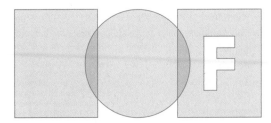

(c) Task 3: You fill in the task and result

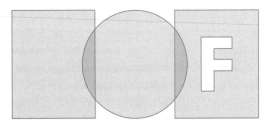

(d) Task 4: You fill it in

Figure 5.22 The results of Brooks's (1968) experiments from Figure 5.21, explained in terms of working memory. When the stimulus is verbal, (a) task 1, which requires a verbal response, is difficult because the phonological loop has to process both the verbal stimulus and verbal response. (b) Task 2, which requires a visual response, is easier because processing is divided between the phonological loop and the visuospatial sketch pad. (c and d) Fill in these diagrams for tasks 3 and 4 in Figure 5.21b.

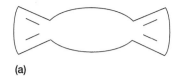

(a)

(b)

Figure 5.23 Stimuli used in Brandimonte et al.'s (1992) experiment. (a) The initial stimulus; (b) part that the participant is asked to mentally subtract from the initial stimulus. (Reprinted from "Influence of Short-Term Memory Codes on Visual Image Processing: Evidence from Image Transformation Tasks," by M. A. Brandimonte, *Journal of Experimental Psychology: Learning, Memory and Cognition, 18,* pp. 157–165. Copyright © 1992 with permission from the American Psychological Association.)

carried out the subtraction task so the subtraction had to be done in their minds. In the example in Figure 5.23, the initial picture is a piece of candy, and after subtraction, it becomes a fish. Brandimonte then had another group of participants do the same task while saying "la, la, la. . . ."

Based on what you know about operation of the phonological loop and visuospatial sketch pad, how do you think saying "la, la, la . . ." would affect participants' performance on the subtraction task? One way to answer this question is to reason that saying "la, la, la . . ." would not affect participants' performance because the words "la, la, la . . ." are processed by the phonological loop and the visual images are processed by the visuospatial sketch pad, so they wouldn't interfere with one another. However, as it turns out, saying the words *improved* participants' performance on the subtraction task.

Why did the *la, la, la* group do better? The key to answering this question is to realize that in the first part of the experiment there are two ways that the participants can memorize the objects. They can name them (verbal coding) so the object in Figure 5.23a would become the word "candy," or they can create visual images of them (visual coding) so the object would be a "picture" in the participants' minds.

The working memory diagram in Figure 5.24 shows that saying "la, la, la . . ." fills up the phonological loop and so prevents the image in Figure 5.23a from being coded phonologically. Consequently, the participants must code the objects visually in the sketch pad (Figure 5.24). Because the subtraction task in the second part of the experiment is easier when starting with a visual image, being forced to use the sketch pad improves performance. Thus, the Brandimonte experiment shows how performance can be enhanced when activity in one component of working memory forces participants to use the system that is most well-suited to the task.

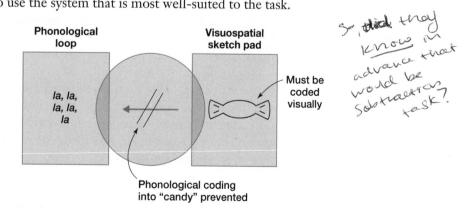

Figure 5.24 Explanation of the Brandimonte result in terms of working memory. Saying "la, la, la . . . ," prevents the initial stimulus from being recoded verbally by the phonological loop. Therefore, it must be coded visually by the visuospatial sketch pad.

Status of Research on Working Memory

One of the characteristics of a good theory is that it suggests new experiments. Atkinson and Shiffrin's modal model did this, and so has Baddeley's working memory model. But just as Baddeley's early observations led to a rethinking of the STM part of the modal model, other observations (including some made by Baddeley) have raised questions about the working memory model.

For example, there are patients with brain damage whose memory spans have been reduced to just one or two digits, indicating that the phonological loop is severely impaired. However, these same patients can repeat back sequences of 5 or 6 words if the words form a sentence (Vallar & Baddeley, 1984; Wilson & Baddeley, 1988). How can this memory for sentences occur if the phonological loop is impaired? One possibility is that perhaps long-term memory (which is not impaired in these patients) helps out for meaningful material like sentences. Results such as these have led Baddeley (2000) to propose that there are additional components in the working memory system that communicate closely with long-term memory. It is likely that future research on working memory will be concerned with the connection between working memory and long-term memory (see Ericsson & Kintsch, 1995).

More research is also needed to better determine how the central executive works. You may have noticed that we said little about the central executive. One reason for this is because the central executive's task of coordinating and controlling the two subsystems is very complex, and only recently have researchers begun studying the ways that the central executive operates (see Andrade, 2001; Baddeley, 1996).

WORKING MEMORY AND THE BRAIN

Early physiological studies of the short-term component of memory demonstrated that behaviors that depended on working memory can be disrupted by damage to specific areas of the brain, especially the prefrontal cortex (PF cortex; see Figure 5.12). The PF cortex receives inputs from the sensory areas, which are involved in processing incoming visual and auditory information. It also receives signals from areas involved in carrying out actions and is connected to areas in the temporal cortex that are important for forming long-term memories (see Figure 2.3 for location of the temporal lobe). Thus the "wiring diagram" of the PF cortex is exactly what we would expect for the operation of a memory system like working memory that has to take incoming information from the environment and pass some of this information on to longer-term storage.

The Delayed-Response Task in Monkeys

Early work on the physiology of working memory used a task called the **delayed-response task,** which required a monkey to hold information in working memory during a delay period. Figure 5.25 shows the setup for this task. The monkey sees a food reward in one of

Monkey observes food Delay Response

Figure 5.25 The delayed-response task being administered to a monkey.

two food wells. Both wells are then covered, a screen is lowered during a delay, and then the screen is raised and the monkey obtains the food if it reaches for the correct food well.

Monkeys can be trained to accomplish this task but if their PF cortex is removed, their performance drops to chance level so they pick the correct food well only about half of the time. This result supports the idea that the PF cortex is important for holding information for brief periods of time. In fact, it has been suggested that one reason we can describe the memory behavior of very young infants (younger than about 8 months of age) as "out of sight, out of mind" (so when an object that the infant can see is then hidden from view, the infant behaves as if the object no longer exists) is that their frontal and prefrontal cortex does not become developed until about 8 months (Goldman-Rakic, 1992). The idea that PF cortex is important for working memory is also supported by experiments that have looked at how single neurons in PF cortex respond during a brief delay.

Neurons That Hold Information

One of the requirements for any physiological system for memory is the ability to record and hold information after the original stimulus is no longer present. Shintaro Funahashi and coworkers (1989) conducted an experiment in which they recorded from neurons in a monkey's PF cortex while it carried out a delayed-response task. For the task, the monkey first looked steadily at a fixation point, X, while a square was flashed at one position on the screen (Figure 5.26a). In this example, the square was flashed in the upper left corner (on the other trials the square would be flashed at different positions on the screen). This causes a small response in the neuron.

After the square went off, there was a delay of a few seconds. The nerve firing records in Figure 5.26b show that the neuron was firing during this delay. This firing is the neural record of the monkey's working memory for the position of the square. After the delay,

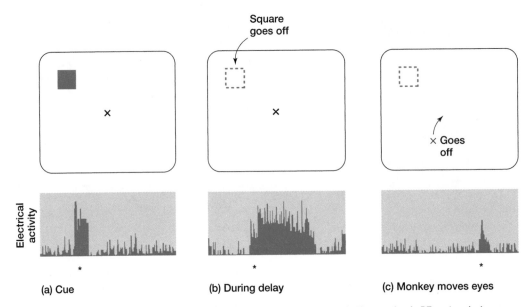

Square
goes off

Goes
off

Electrical
activity

(a) Cue (b) During delay (c) Monkey moves eyes

Figure 5.26 Results of an experiment showing the response of neurons in the monkey's PF cortex during an attentional task. Neural responding is indicated by an asterisk (*). (a) A cue square is flashed at a particular position, causing the neuron to respond. (b) The square goes off, but the neuron continues to respond during the delay. (c) The fixation X goes off and the monkey demonstrates its memory for the location of the square by moving its eyes to where the square was. (Adapted from "Mnemonic Coding of Visual Space in the Primate Dorsolateral Prefrontal Cortex," by S. Funahashi et al., *Journal of Neurophysiology, 61,* pp. 331–349. Copyright © 1989 with permission from the American Physiological Society.)

the fixation X goes off. This is a signal for the monkey to move its eyes to where the square had been flashed (Figure 5.26c). The monkey's ability to do this provides behavioral evidence that it had, in fact, remembered the location of the square.

The key result of this experiment was that Funahashi found neurons that responded when the square was flashed *in a particular location* and that the neurons continued responding during the delay. For example, some neurons responded only when the square was flashed in the upper right corner and then during the delay, and other neurons responded only when the square was presented at other positions on the screen and then during the delay. The firing of these neurons indicates that an object was presented at a particular place, and this information remains available for as long as these neurons continue firing.

Research has also found neurons in other areas of the brain that respond during the delay in a working memory task. Neurons with these properties have been found in the primary visual cortex, which is the first area of the brain that receives visual signals (Super et al., 2001), and the inferotemporal cortex, which is a visual area responsible for perceiving complex forms (Desimone et al., 1995). Thus, although the PF cortex may be the brain area that is most closely associated with working memory, other areas are also involved in working memory.

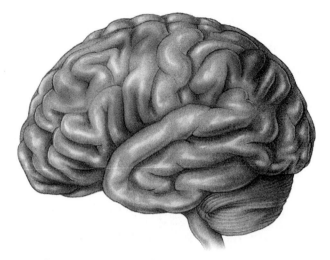

Figure 5.27 Some of the areas in the cortex that have been shown by brain-imaging research to be involved in working memory. (Adapted from Fiez, 2001.)

Brain Imaging in Humans

The conclusion that many brain areas are involved in working memory has been confirmed by research using imaging techniques such as PET and fMRI to measure brain activity in humans. These studies show that as a person carries out a working memory task, activity occurs in the prefrontal cortex (Courtney et al., 1998) and in other areas as well (Fiez, 2001; Olesen et al., 2003) (Figure 5.27). As we continue our study of the physiology of memory in the next chapter, we will see that a similar situation exists for long-term memory: One or two structures are especially important for long-term memory tasks, but many structures, distributed across the brain, are involved as well.

 Test Yourself 5.2

1. How has the capacity of STM been measured? In answering this question, consider why it is easier to remember a word that contains 10 letters (*experiment*) than the same 10 letters arranged randomly (*xetpmieren*).
2. How has the duration of STM been measured? In answering this question, be sure you understand the Peterson and Peterson experiment in terms of their results, their interpretation of the mechanism behind these results, and the newer interpretation proposed by Keppel and Underwood.
3. Why has "working memory" replaced the modal model's "short-term memory" as a way of describing memory that lasts only a short time? What is the advantage of the working memory concept?

4. The working memory model contains three components. What are they, and how has their operation been investigated using (1) the phonological similarity effect, (2) the word-length effect, and (3) articulatory suppression?

5. One of the characteristics of Baddeley's working memory model is that it enables us to consider how the mode of presentation (visual or auditory) affects memory. When do visual and auditory presentations result in the same results? Describe experiments that show how the visual and auditory mechanisms can interact.

6. The physiology of working memory has been studied using (1) brain lesions in monkeys, (2) neural recording from monkeys, and (3) brain imaging in humans. What do the results of each of these procedures tell us about working memory and the brain?

Think About It

1. As Tina slowly moves a sparkler in a circle, Cedric sees a short trail left by the sparkler. Tina starts moving the sparkler faster and faster in this circular motion, until when she is twirling it at about 3 revolutions per second, Cedric exclaims, "I see a circle!" What does Cedric's observation demonstrate about the duration of the persistence of vision?

2. Analyze the following in terms of how the various stages of the modal model are activated, using Rachel's pizza-ordering experience in Figure 5.4 as a guide: (1) listening to a lecture in class, taking notes, or reviewing the notes later as you study for an exam; (2) watching a scene in a James Bond movie in which Bond captures the female enemy agent whom he had slept with the night before.

3. Adam has just tested a woman who has brain damage and he is having difficulty understanding the results. When he reads a list of words to her, she can't remember any of them when she is tested immediately after hearing the words, but her memory gets better if she is tested after a delay. Interestingly enough, if the woman reads the list herself, she remembers well at first, so the delay is not necessary. Can you explain these observations using the modal model? The working memory model? Can you think of a new model that might explain this result better than those two?

KEY TERMS

Articulatory suppression
Central executive
Chunk
Chunking
Coding
Control processes
Delayed-response task

Digit span
Echoic memory
Iconic memory
Long-term memory
Memory
Modal model of memory
Partial-report procedure

Persistence of vision
Phonological coding
Phonological loop
Phonological similarity effect
Primacy effect
Proactive interference
Recency effect
Rehearsal
Release from proactive interference
Retrieval
Semantic coding

Sensory memory
Serial-position curve
Short-term memory
Structural features
Visual coding
Visual icon
Visuospatial sketch pad
Whole-report procedure
Word-length effect
Working memory

CogLab To experience these experiments for yourself, go to http://coglab.wadsworth.com. Be sure to read each experiment's setup instructions before you go to the experiment itself. Otherwise, you won't know which keys to press.

Primary Labs

Apparent movement	How the perception of movement can be achieved by flashing still images (p. 142).
Partial report	The partial report condition of Sperling's iconic memory experiment (p. 143).
Serial position	How memory for a list depends on an item's position on the list (p. 146).
Memory span	How memory span depends on the nature of stimuli that are presented (p. 155).
Brown-Peterson	How memory for trigrams fades (p. 159).
Phonological similarity	How recall for items on a list is affected by the how similar the items sound (p. 164).

Related Labs

Irrelevant speech effect	How recall for items on a list is affected by the presence of irrelevant speech.
Modality effect	How memory for the last one or two items in a list depends on whether the list is heard or read.
Operation span	Measuring the operation-word-span, a measure of working memory.
Position error	What happens when trying to remember the order of a series of letters.

Sternberg search	A method to determine how information is retrieved from short-term memory.
Suffix effect	How adding an irrelevant item to the end of a list affects recall for the final item on the list.

Stimulus List for "Remembering a List" Demonstration (p. 146)

1. barricade
2. children
3. diet
4. gourd
5. folio
6. meter
7. journey
8. mohair
9. phoenix
10. crossbow
11. doorbell
12. muffler
13. mouse
14. menu
15. airplane

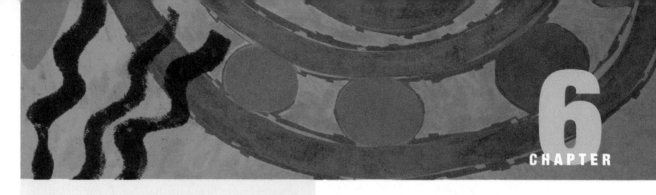

Long-Term Memory: Basic Principles

Some Questions We Will Consider

✔ What is the best way to store information in long-term memory?

✔ What are some techniques we can use to help us get information out of long-term memory when we need it?

✔ How is it possible that a lifetime of experiences and accumulated knowledge can be stored in neurons?

■   ■   ■

Jimmy G. had been admitted to the Home for the Aged accompanied by a transfer note that described him as "helpless, demented, confused, and disoriented." As neurologist Oliver Sacks talked with Jimmy about events of his childhood, his experiences in school, and his days in the Navy, Sacks noticed that Jimmy was talking as if he were still in the Navy, even though he had been discharged 10 years earlier. Sacks (1985) recounts the rest of his conversation with Jimmy as follows:

"What year is this, Mr. G?" I asked, concealing my perplexity under a casual manner.

"Forty-five, man. What do you mean?" He went on, "We've won the war, FDR's dead, Truman's at the helm. There are great times ahead."

"And you, Jimmy, how old would you be?"

Oddly, uncertainly, he hesitated a moment, as if engaged in calculation.

"Why, I guess I'm nineteen, Doc. I'll be twenty next birthday."

Looking at the gray-haired man before me, I had an impulse for which I have never forgiven myself—it was, or would have been, the height of cruelty had there been any possibility of Jimmy's remembering it.

"Here," I said, and thrust a mirror toward him. "Look in the mirror and tell me what you see. Is that a nineteen-year-old looking out from the mirror?"

He suddenly turned ashen and gripped the sides of the chair. "Jesus Christ," he whispered. "Christ, what's going on? What's happened to me? Is this a nightmare? Am I crazy? Is this a joke?"—and he became frantic, panicky.

"It's okay, Jim," I said soothingly. "It's just a mistake. Nothing to worry about. Hey!" I took him to the window. "Isn't this a lovely spring day. See the kids there playing baseball?" He regained his color and started to smile, and I stole away, taking the hateful mirror with me.

Two minutes later I reentered the room. Jimmy was still standing by the window, gazing with pleasure at the kids playing baseball below. He wheeled around as I opened the door, and his face assumed a cherry expression.

"Hiya, Doc!" he said. "Nice morning! You want to talk to me—do I take this chair here?" There was no sign of recognition on his frank, open face.

"Haven't we met before, Mr. G?" I said casually.

"No, I can't say we have. Quite a beard you got there. I wouldn't forget you, Doc!"

. . .

"You remember telling me about your childhood, growing up in Pennsylvania, working as a radio operator in a submarine? And how your brother is engaged to a girl from California?"

"Hey, you're right. But I didn't tell you that. I never met you before in my life. You must have read all about me in my chart."

"Okay," I said. "I'll tell you a story. A man went to his doctor complaining of memory lapses. The doctor asked him some routine questions, and then said, 'These lapses. What about them?' 'What lapses?' the patient replied."

"So that's my problem," Jimmy laughed. "I kinda thought it was. I do find myself forgetting things, once in a while things that have just happened. The past is clear, though." (Sacks, 1985, p. 14)

Jimmy G. suffers from **Korsakoff's syndrome,** a condition caused by a prolonged deficiency of vitamin B1, usually as a result of chronic alcoholism. The deficiency leads to the destruction of areas in the frontal and temporal lobes, which causes severe impairments in memory. The damage to Jimmy G.'s memory makes it impossible for him to assimilate or retain new knowledge. He cannot recognize people he has just met, follow a story in a book, find his way to the corner drugstore, or solve problems that take more than a few moments to figure out.

Jimmy's problem is similar to Clive Wearing's, from Chapter 5. He is unable to form new long-term memories and his reality therefore consists of some memories from long ago plus what has happened within the last 30–60 seconds.

Another person who couldn't form new long-term memories was "Lennie," the fictional character played by Guy Pearce in the film *Memento*. (Although Lennie's problem was identified in the film as a loss of short-term memory, his short-term memory was fine because he could remember what had just happened to him. His problem was that he couldn't transfer his short-term memories into long-term memories.) Lennie's problem was apparently not as severe as Clive Wearing's or Jimmy G's because he was able to function in the outside world, although with some difficulty. To compensate for his inability to form new memories, Lenny recorded his experiences with a Polaroid camera, and had key facts tattooed onto his body (Figure 6.1).

Memento still photo © CORBIS SYGMA

Figure 6.1 Guy Pearce's character "Lennie" from the film *Memento*. To deal with his memory problem, he had key facts he wanted to remember tattooed on his body.

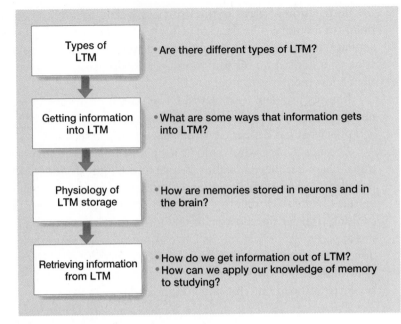

Figure 6.2 The flow diagram for this chapter.

The severe disabilities suffered by all of these people illustrate the importance of being able to retain information about what has happened in the past. The purpose of this chapter is to begin looking at how long-term memory operates. We will do this by following the plan shown in Figure 6.2. First we will consider some of the basic characteristics of LTM, which includes the idea that LTM may consist of a number of mechanisms that are designed to handle different types of information. We will then consider how information becomes stored in long-term memory, and some of the physiological mechanisms responsible for this storage. Finally, we will describe some of the factors involved in retrieving information from LTM. The principles introduced in this chapter lay the groundwork for the next chapter, in which we will continue our discussion of LTM by considering everyday applications of memory, and why we make errors of memory.

INTRODUCTION TO LONG-TERM MEMORY

One way to describe LTM is as an "archive" of information about past events in our lives and knowledge we have learned. What is particularly amazing about this storage is how it stretches from just a few moments ago to as far back as we can remember. The large time span of LTM is illustrated in Figure 6.3, which shows what a student who has just taken a seat in class might be remembering about events that occurred at various times in the past.

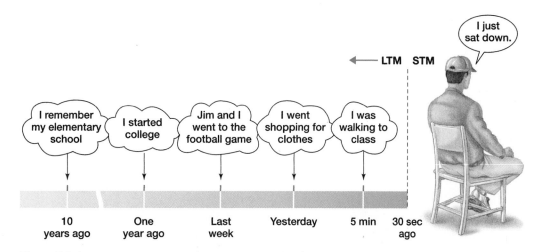

Figure 6.3 Long-term memory covers a span that stretches from about 30 seconds ago to your earliest memories. Thus, all of this student's memories, except the memory "I just sat down," would be classified as long-term memories.

His first recollection—that he has just sat down—would be contained in his short-term/working memory because it happened within the last 30 seconds. But everything before that—from his recent memory that 5 minutes ago he was walking to class, to a memory from 10 years earlier of the elementary school he had attended in the third grade—is part of long-term memory.

Although all of these memories are contained in LTM, they aren't all the same. More recent memories tend to be more detailed, and much of this detail and often the specific memories themselves fade with the passage of time and as other experiences accumulate. Thus, on October 1, 2004, this person would probably not remember the details of what happened while walking to class on October 1, 2003, but would remember some of the general experiences from around that time. One of the things that we will be concerned with in this chapter and the next one is why we retain some information and lose other information.

But simply considering LTM as an "archive" that retains information from the past leaves out an important function of LTM. LTM works closely with working memory to help us create our ongoing experience. Consider, for example what happens when Tony's friend Cindy says, "Jim and I saw the new James Bond movie last night." As Tony's working memory is holding the exact wording of that statement in his mind, it is simultaneously accessing information from long-term memory, which helps him understand what Cindy is saying and helps him draw conclusions that go beyond her statement. Thus, Tony's ability to understand the sentence depends on retrieving, from LTM, the meanings of each of the words that make up the sentence, and, as shown in Figure 6.4, his LTM also contains a great deal of additional information about movies, James Bond, and Cindy.

Figure 6.4 Tony's STM, which is dealing with the present, and his LTM, which contains knowledge relevant to what is happening, work together as Cindy tells him something.

Although Tony might not consciously think about all of this information (after all, he has to pay attention to the next thing that Cindy is going to tell him), it is all there in his LTM and adds to his understanding of what his is hearing, and his interpretation of what that might mean.

LTM therefore provides both an archives that we can refer to when we want to remember events from the past, and a wealth of background information that we are constantly consulting, often without even being aware of it. The first step in understanding how LTM operates is to describe the different types of information that LTM handles.

WHAT IS LONG-TERM MEMORY?

A good place to begin our description of LTM is by distinguishing between two types of LTM, declarative memory and implicit memory. **Declarative memory** is our conscious recollections of events or facts that we have experienced or learned in the past. **Implicit memory** (or **nondeclarative memory**) is memory that occurs when a past experience influences behavior, but we are not aware of the experience that is influencing the behavior (Figure 6.5).

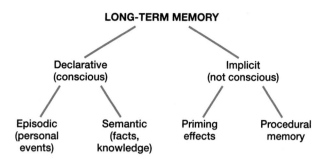

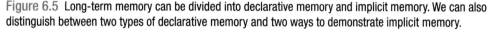

Figure 6.5 Long-term memory can be divided into declarative memory and implicit memory. We can also distinguish between two types of declarative memory and two ways to demonstrate implicit memory.

Declarative Memory

When a person says "I remember visiting my grandfather's house when I was 10," this recollection is an example of declarative memory because it involves a conscious recollection of something that happened to the person in the past. Another example of declarative memory is facts we remember about the world, such as how an automobile engine works, the names of famous impressionist painters, or the difference between a blue jay and a finch. Although recollections of events and facts are both considered declarative memories (because we are conscious of them), Endel Tulving (1972) differentiates between the two. Tulving calls memories of events in our lives *episodic memories*, and memories for facts *semantic memories*.

Two Types of Declarative Memory Episodic memory is memory for specific events that have happened to the person having the memory. These events are usually remembered as a personal experience that occurred at a particular time and place. Semantic memory is memory for knowledge about the world that is not tied to any specific personal experience. This knowledge can be things like facts, vocabulary, numbers, and concepts. In contrast with episodic memory, remembering these things does not create the feeling of reliving a personal experience.

Distinguishing Between Episodic Memory and Semantic Memory Using the definitions of episodic and semantic memories above, try to classify the following statements as either episodic or semantic.

1. I remember taking a test in cognitive psychology last week.
2. I remember seeing a volcano erupt in Hawaii last summer.
3. I remember that the University of California at Davis is near Sacramento.
4. I remember learning that the University of California at Davis is near Sacramento when Matt was telling me about his girlfriend, who is a graduate student there.

5. Bill Clinton won the 1992 presidential election.
6. I was watching TV when they interrupted my favorite program and announced the Supreme Court's decision about the Florida results in the 2000 presidential election.
7. I remember the words *boat*, *cheese*, *salamander*, and *house* from the list you read. There were others, but that's all I can remember.

Here are the answers:

1. Episodic, because it describes something that happened that the person remembers as an event in his or her life. Notice that the cognitive psychology test that the person remembered can also be defined by time (last week) and place (in the classroom).
2. Episodic, for the same reasons as sentence 1.
3. Semantic. The fact that the University of California at Davis is near Sacramento exists independently of any person's experience. Facts are things that other people also know and that might be found in reference books.
4. Episodic. This would be an episodic memory because it involves a recollection of specifically when the person learned about the location of the University of California at Davis.
5. Semantic. This is a statement of fact that could appear in a newspaper article or a book describing the 1992 election. Anytime a person remembers a fact without relating it to a personal experience that occurred at a specific time and place, the fact is a semantic memory.
6. Episodic. This statement about an election is different than the one in sentence 5 because it refers specifically to something that happened to the person who is having the memory.
7. Episodic. This is tricky because it sounds like the person could be remembering facts, but these words are a person's answers to a memory test in which she was asked to repeat back a list of words that he or she had just read. If the person remembers reading the words in the list, this qualifies as an episodic memory.

The distinction between episodic and semantic memory has proven useful for describing research on LTM. We will now consider the evidence that supports the idea that episodic and semantic memories may be served by different mechanisms.

Evidence for Different Mechanisms for Episodic and Semantic Memory Although it is possible to classify some memories as episodic and others as semantic, we can still ask whether there is any evidence to support Tulving's idea that episodic memory and semantic memory are served by different mechanisms. Neuropsychological research on participants with different kinds of brain damage provides evidence for these differences.

Daniel Schacter (1996) provides anecdotal evidence for differences between episodic and semantic memory with his description of a round of golf with Fredrick, a man in the early stages of **Alzheimer's disease,** a degeneration of the brain that eventually results in severe memory deficits. Fredrick remembered the rules of golf, such as how to keep score and golf course etiquette, so his semantic memory was intact. However, the effect of his disease on his episodic memory became evident when Fredrick teed off and then, when Schacter and another golf partner took a little longer than usual to hit their balls, insisted, rather angrily, that he be given a chance to hit his ball as well. He had forgotten the very recent episode of teeing off on that hole, and after returning to the clubhouse couldn't remember anything about the 18 holes of golf he had just played.

Another example of intact semantic memory but defective episodic memory is provided by Jon, a 16-year-old boy who weighed less than 3 pounds when he was born prematurely and who suffered from damage to his hippocampus and other temporal lobe structures. Because of this damage, Jon was unable to remember what he had done during the day and everyday events such as telephone conversations, messages, and visitors. However, despite these problems with episodic memories, Jon was able to enter a mainstream school, and to read and write and understand factual knowledge at levels within the normal range (Vargha-Khadem et al., 1997).

Fredrick and Jon both have intact semantic memories and poor episodic memory. The "complement" to Fredrick and Jon is an Italian woman who was in normal health until she suffered an attack of encephalitis at the age of 44 (DeRenzi et al., 1987). The first signs of a problem were headaches and a fever, which were later followed by hallucinations lasting for five days. When she returned home after a 6-week stay in the hospital, she had difficulty recognizing familiar people; had trouble shopping, because she couldn't remember the meaning of words on the shopping list or where things were in the store; and had become unable to recognize famous people or recall facts such as the identity of Beethoven or the fact that Italy was involved in World War II.

Despite this severe impairment of memory for semantic information, the woman's episodic memory for events in her life was preserved. She could recount what she had done during the day and things that had happened weeks or months before.

Table 6.1 summarizes the cases we have described. These cases, taken together, demonstrate a double dissociation between episodic and semantic memory, which supports the idea that memory for these two different types of information probably involves different mechanisms. (See Chapter 2 for a discussion of double dissociations.)

Table 6.1	DISSOCIATIONS OF EPISODIC AND SEMANTIC MEMORY	
	Semantic	Episodic
Fredrick (the golfer)	OK	Poor
Jon	OK	Poor
Italian woman	Poor	OK

Although the double dissociation shown in Table 6.1 supports the idea of separate mechanisms for semantic and episodic memory, not all researchers agree that a double dissociation has been demonstrated. For example, Larry Squire and Stuart Zola-Morgan (1998) argue that just because Jon has been able to perform adequately in school doesn't mean that his semantic memory hasn't been affected by his brain damage and that perhaps his semantic memory needed to be tested by other, more sensitive, measures. (Also see Tulving & Markowitsch, 1998, for more on this controversy.)

Evidence for separate mechanisms has also been provided by the results of brain-imaging experiments. These experiments have shown that episodic tasks, like studying and remembering a list of words, and semantic tasks, like indicating whether a word refers to something that is living or nonliving, activate different areas of the brain (Duzel et al., 1999; also see Nyberg et al., 1996).

Although the issue of whether episodic and semantic memories involve different, independent mechanisms is still being discussed among memory researchers, most think that it is often useful to distinguish between the two. They also point out, however, that episodic and semantic information often occur together in our everyday experience.

How Episodic and Semantic Information Can Occur Together in Everyday Experience   There are a number of the ways that episodic and semantic memories are linked to one another.

- Episodic memories have been called the "gateway" to semantic memory (Squire and Zola-Morgan, 1998) because new information is always presented initially as part of some event in the person's life. Thus, at some point earlier in your life, you learned that Washington, DC, was the capital of the United States. Perhaps you learned this in the first grade, or your parents told you, or you saw it on television. Remembering this initial learning experience would be an episodic memory, but even if you are unable to remember the specific learning experience, the semantic information that you learned remains.

- Episodic memories can be used to infer semantic information. For example, if someone asked you whether people put ketchup on hot dogs, you might answer "yes" because you remember the last time you were at a baseball game and saw a person at the condiment stand squirting ketchup onto their hot dog.

- Semantic knowledge can influence the formation of episodic memories, such as when our factual knowledge biases our memories for events in our lives. For example, someone who has a detailed knowledge of the rules of football (semantic) would probably remember the details of a particular football game that they attended (episodic) differently than someone who lacked this knowledge (see Figure 6.6).

Although there are interactions between episodic and semantic memories and sometimes the borderline between them can be fuzzy, making a distinction between them has

Semantic knowledge can influence formation of episodic memory

Figure 6.6 How a person's knowledge can influence their episodic memory. Even though two people have seen the same football game, they remember different things about it because of their differing knowledge of the game of football.

proven helpful in understanding memory. In this chapter and the next one, we will focus our attention on episodic memory. In Chapter 8 we will focus on how people draw knowledge from semantic memory.

Implicit Memory

CogLab

Implicit Learning

Declarative memories enable us to consciously relive past experiences (episodic memory) or to remember facts we have learned (semantic memory). But we are not conscious of implicit memory. Implicit memory occurs when an experience affects a person's behavior, even though the person is not aware that he or she had those experiences. This effect was first demonstrated in patients with brain damage who couldn't form new long-term memories. Elizabeth Warrington and Lawrence Weiskrantz (1968) tested five patients with Korsakoff's syndrome (like Jimmy G., whom we described at the beginning of the chapter), by presenting incomplete pictures such as the ones in Figure 6.7 (Gollin, 1960). The participant's task was to identify the picture. The fragmented version in Figure 6.7a was

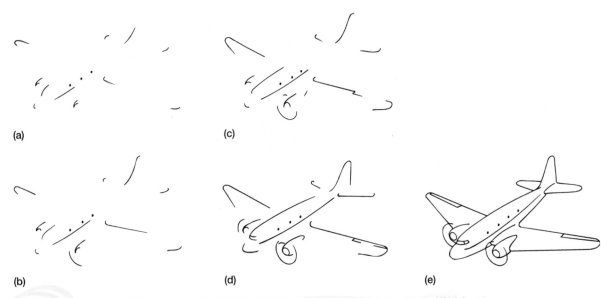

(a)

(b)

(c)

(d)

(e)

Figure 6.7 Incomplete pictures developed by Gollin (1960) that were used by Warrington and Weiskrantz (1968) to study implicit memory in amnesiac patients. (Reprinted from *Nature, London, 217,* March 9, 1968, E. K. Warrington, & L. Weiskrantz, "New Method of Testing Long-Term Retention with Special Reference to Amnesic Patients," pp. 972–974, Fig. 1. Copyright © 1968 with permission from Nature Publishing Group.)

presented first, and then participants were shown more and more complete versions (b, c, d, and e) until they were able to identify the picture.

The results, shown in Figure 6.8, indicate that by the third day of testing these participants were able to identify the pictures with fewer errors than they could at the be-

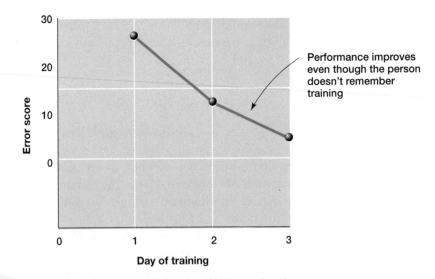

Performance improves even though the person doesn't remember training

Figure 6.8 Results of Warrington and Weiskrantz's (1968) experiment.

ginning of training, even though they had no memory for any of the previous day's training. The improvement of performance represents an effect of implicit memory because the patients learned from experience, but couldn't remember having had this experience.

The procedure used in this experiment is called repetition priming because an initial presentation of the stimulus (the priming stimulus, which is the airplane pictures in this example) affects the person's response involving the same stimulus when it is presented later. This procedure has also been used to demonstrate implicit memory in normal participants. For example, participants might be presented with a list of words, one of which is *perfume*, in the first part of the experiment. Then, in the second part of the experiment, they are asked to complete a word fragment such as "p_ _ _um_," or a word stem such as "per____" with the first word that comes to mind (Roediger et al., 1994). The results of this kind of test show that seeing the word in part 1 increases the chances of producing that word in part 2 ("per____" could also be completed by other words, such as *perfect*, *pertain*, *percolator*, and so on) or increases the speed with which the word is produced.

Remember from our definition of implicit memory that participants are not supposed to be aware of the initial presentation of the stimulus that is affecting their later behavior. This is easy to demonstrate in the brain-damaged participants because they have no memory that they have ever seen the priming stimulus before, even though they have become better at responding to it. However, normal participants could potentially remember the initial presentation of the priming stimulus (such as perfume) as they are being asked to create a word from "per____."

Researchers use the following procedures to lessen the chances that this might happen.

1. The test does not directly test memory by asking a person to remember a word they had seen or heard. Instead, the person is asked a question ("What is this a picture of?") or a problem to be solved ("Make a word from these letters").
2. Participants are instructed to answer a question or solve a problem as rapidly as possible by saying the first answer that comes to mind. This decreases the chances that they will take the time to consciously recollect whether or not they had previously seen the word.

An example of a situation in which implicit memory may be affecting our behavior without our awareness is when we are exposed to advertisements that may extol the virtues of a product or perhaps just present the product's name. Although we may believe that we are unaffected by some advertisements, they can be having an effect just because we are exposed to them.

This idea is supported by the results of an experiment by T. J. Perfect and C. Askew (1994), who had participants scan articles in a magazine. Each page of print was faced by an advertisement, but participants were not told to pay attention to the advertisements. However, when they were asked to rate the advertisements on a number of dimensions such as how appealing, eye-catching, distinctive, and memorable they were, they gave higher ratings to the ones they had been exposed to than to other advertisements that they had never seen. This result qualifies as an effect of implicit learning because when the participants were asked to indicate which advertisements had been presented at the beginning of the experiment, they recognized only an average of 2.8 of the original 25 advertisements.

This result is related to the **propaganda effect**, in which participants are more likely to rate statements they may have read or heard before as being true, simply because they have been exposed to them before. This effect can occur even if the person is told that the statements are false when they first read or hear them (Begg et al., 1992). Experiments that demonstrate the propaganda effect provide evidence for a statement that has, on occasion, been made in reference to political advertising that people will believe just about anything if they hear it repeated often enough.

The propaganda effect provides a hint of the importance of implicit memory because it demonstrates how events that are outside of our awareness can influence our behavior. Later in our discussion of LTM, especially in Chapter 7, we will see how implicit memory can lead to errors of memory. We will see, for example, how eyewitnesses to crimes have identified people as having been at the crime scene not because they were actually there, but because the eyewitnesses had seen them somewhere else at another time so they seemed familiar.

Procedural memory is our memory for how to carry out highly practiced skills, and we include it under implicit memory because people often find it difficult to explain how they carry out skilled behaviors. Consider, for example, riding a bike. Can you explain how you keep your balance? Or how about tying your shoes? Tying your shoes is so easy for most people that they do it without even thinking about it. But if you think you are aware of how you do it, describe which lace you loop over the other one, and then what you do next. Most people have to either tie their shoes or visualize tying their shoes before they can answer this question.

Riding a bike and tying your shoes are both motor skills because they involve movement and muscle action. But you have also developed many purely cognitive skills that qualify as involving procedural memory. Consider, for example, your ability to read the sentences in this book. Can you describe the rules you are following for putting the words together into sentences and the sentences together into meaningful thoughts? Unless you've studied linguistics, you probably don't know the rules, but that doesn't stop you from being a skilled reader.

Neuropsychological research shows that procedural memory can remain even when episodic or semantic memory is lost. For example, Schacter's golf partner had lost much of his ability to access episodic memories but still knew how to drive a golf ball down the fairway. Similarly, even though the Italian woman had lost much of her semantic memory for facts, she was still able to perform housework such as operating the washing machine and ironing.

How Does Information Become Stored in Long-Term Memory?

One of your goals in reading this chapter is probably to transfer the information you are reading into long-term memory so you can remember it later, for the exam. The process of acquiring information and transforming it into memory is called **encoding.**

Notice that the term *encoding* is similar to the term *coding* that we discussed in Chapter 5. Some authors use these terms interchangeably. We will use the term *coding*, as we did in Chapter 5, to refer to the *form* with which information is represented. For example, a word can be coded visually, or by its sound, or by its meaning. We will use the term *encoding* to refer to the *process* used to get information into LTM. For example, a word can be encoded by repeating it over and over, by thinking of other words that rhyme with it, or by using it in a sentence. One of the main messages in this chapter is that some methods of encoding are more effective than others.

Once you have used an encoding process to store information in your LTM you need to be able to withdraw this information later when you want to remember the name of an acquaintance or answer a question on an exam. This process of recovering previously encoded information is called **retrieval** (Brown & Craik, 2000). Thus, memory involves encoding and storing of information in memory and then retrieving it later. We will see that these processes are not independent of each other. For example, the way information is encoded can determine how easily it can be retrieved later. We will describe the processes involved in encoding and retrieval by focusing on declarative memory.

Maintenance Rehearsal and Elaborative Rehearsal

One way to learn something is to rehearse it. We saw in Chapter 5 that rehearsal can be used to keep information in STM or working memory, as when you repeat a phone number you have just looked up in the phone book. Although rehearsal can keep information in working memory, rehearsal doesn't guarantee that information will be transferred into LTM. You know this from your experience in rehearsing a telephone number and then forgetting it right after you place the call. When you rehearse a telephone number in this way you are usually just repeating the numbers without any consideration of meaning or making connections with other information. This kind of rehearsal, called **maintenance rehearsal,** does help *maintain* information in memory, but it is not an effective way of *transferring* information into long-term memory.

Another kind of rehearsal, **elaborative rehearsal,** occurs when you think about the meaning of an item or make connections between the item and something you know. We can demonstrate that elaborative rehearsal is a good way to establish long-term memories by describing an approach to memory called levels-of-processing theory.

Levels-of-Processing Theory

In 1972 Fergus Craik and Robert Lockhart proposed the idea of levels of processing (LOP). According to levels-of-processing theory, memory depends on how information is encoded. Another way of saying this is that memory depends on how information is programmed into the mind. The following demonstration serves as an introduction to the idea that there are different ways to program information into the mind.

◣ Demonstration

Remembering Lists

Part 1 Cover up the list below and then uncover each word one by one. Count the number of vowels in each word and then go right on to the next one.

> chair
> mathematics
> elephant
> lamp
> car
> elevator
> thoughtful
> cactus

Now cover the list, and then count backwards by 3's from 100. When you get to 76, write down the words you remember. Do that now.

Part 2 Cover up the list below and uncover each word one by one as you did in the previous part. This time, visualize how useful the item might be if you were stranded on an uninhabited island.

> umbrella
> exercise
> forgiveness
> rock
> hamburger
> sunlight
> coffee
> bottle

Cover the list and count backwards by 3's from 99. When you reach 75, write down the words you remember. Do that now. ■

Which procedure resulted in better memory, counting the number of vowels or visualizing an item's function? Most of the experiments that have asked this kind of question have found memory to be superior when a meaningful connection has been made between an item and something else. Thus, memory for words is better when the words are processed by relating them to other knowledge, such as how useful an object might be on an uninhabited island, than when processed based on a nonmeaningful characteristic such as the number of vowels. Craik and Lockhart's levels-of-processing theory states that memory depends on the **depth of processing** that an item receives. They describe depth of processing by distinguishing between shallow processing and deep processing.

Shallow processing involves little attention to meaning. Shallow processing occurs if attention is focused on **physical features** such as the number of vowels in a word or whether the word is printed in lowercase or capital letters. It also occurs during maintenance rehearsal, in which an item is repeated to keep it in memory but without considering its meaning or its connection with anything else.

Deep processing involves close attention, focusing on an item's meaning and relating it to something else. Considering how an item might be useful in a particular situation or creating an image of the item in relation to another item would create deep processing. This way of processing an item occurs during elaborative rehearsal.

Levels-of-processing theory makes the following two predictions.

1. Deep processing takes longer than shallow processing.
2. Deep processing results in better memory than shallow processing.

These predictions have been confirmed in a number of experiments. Consider, for example, the experiment by Fergus Craik and Endel Tulving (1975) diagrammed in Figure 6.9a. In the first part of the experiment they asked participants a question. To achieve different levels of processing they asked three different types of questions:

1. A question about physical features of the word (shallow processing).
   Example: Is the word printed in capital letters?
2. A question about rhyming (deeper processing).
   Example: Does the word rhyme with *train*?
3. A fill-in-the-blanks question (deepest processing).
   Example: Does the word fit into the sentence "He saw a _____ on the street"?

After each question, the participant saw a word and answered the question, and the time needed to answer the question (reaction time) was measured. Examples of words and answers for our example questions above are:

Example 1. word: boat; answer: none
Example 2. word: pain; answer: yes
Example 3. word: car; answer: yes

After participants responded to these questions, they were given a memory test to see how well they recalled the words. The results are shown in Figure 6.9b. As predicted from the theory, deep processing is associated with longer reaction times and better memory.

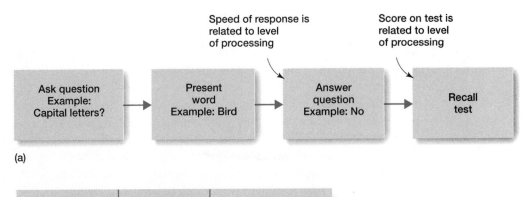

(a)

Question	Reaction time (msec)	Memory performance (%)
Capital letter?	550	15
Rhyme?	630	47
Fill-in-blank	730	81

(b)

Figure 6.9 (a) Sequence of events in Craik and Tulving's (1975) experiment. (b) Results of this experiment. Deeper processing (fill in the blanks) is associated with longer reaction times to answer the question about a word, and better memory for the word.

The power of deep processing has been illustrated in another way in an experiment by Thomas Hyde and James Jenkins (1969), which asked the question, Will deep processing cause better memory even if people don't realize that their memory will be tested? One group of participants rated words for how pleasant they were, and another group counted the number of *E*'s in each word. Some participants in each group were told that they would be asked to recall the words later and some participants were not warned that they would be tested later.

The results showed that the participants' knowledge that they would be tested had no effect on their performance but that the depth of processing did. Thus, participants who rated the words' pleasantness but didn't know they would be tested later, did better than participants who counted the number of *E*'s and knew they would be tested later. Deep processing causes good memory whether or not people know that they will be tested later.

Levels-of-processing theory generated a great deal of research when it was first introduced, but the theory's popularity has decreased because many researchers felt that "depth of processing" was not adequately defined. Stating that takes longer and results in better memory does not really define deep processing, but indicates the *result* to be expected from deep processing. The concept, these researchers argue, needs to be defined independently from its result.

Also, deep processing doesn't always take longer than shallow processing. For example, we can determine whether an automobile is a type of transportation or a vegetable faster than we can determine the number of vowels in the word. In addition, memory performance is not always determined just by whether processing is deep or rehearsal is elaborative. Later in this chapter we will see that sometimes the key factor in determining memory performance is not depth of processing but is the relationship between how information is encoded and how it is retrieved later.

Additional Factors That Aid Encoding

Although LOP theory is no longer the central focus of memory research that it was in the 1970s, its enduring contribution is the idea that memory is affected by the way information is programmed into the mind. This is illustrated by (1) how memory is affected by forming connections with other information and (2) how information to be remembered is organized.

Forming Connections With Other Information

If you were given the task of remembering the word *chicken*, which sentence do you think would result in the best memory?

1. She cooked the chicken.
2. The great bird swooped down and carried off the struggling chicken.

Craik and Tulving (1975) found that memory is much better if the word is presented within the complex sentence. Their explanation for this result is that the complex sentence creates more connections between the word to be remembered and other things, and these other things act as *cues* that help us retrieve the word when we are trying to remember it. Consider, for example, your response to each of the sentences about the chicken. If reading them resulted in images in your mind, which image was more vivid—a woman cooking, or a giant bird carrying a struggling chicken?

Apparently, most of the participants in Craik and Tulving's experiment found the giant-bird sentence to be more memorable, but this wasn't true for one student in my class, who reported that since her mother cooks a lot of chicken, she thought of her mother when reading the shorter sentence. Thus, for this student, the image of her mother cooking formed a stronger connection than the image of the swooping bird.

The idea that imagery can help create connections that will enhance memory was tested by Gordon Bower and David Winzenz (1970), who presented a list of 15 pairs of nouns, such as *boat* and *tree*, to participants for 5 seconds each. One group was told to silently repeat the pairs as they were presented, and another group was told to form a mental picture in which the two items were interacting. When participants were later asked to recall as many of the words as possible, the participants who created the images

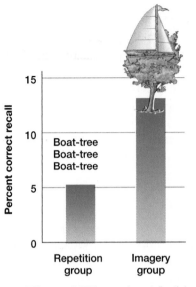

Figure 6.10 Results of the Bower and Winzenz (1970) experiment. Participants in the repetition group repeated word pairs. Participants in the imagery group formed images representing the pairs.

remembered more than twice as many words as the participants who just repeated the word pairs (Figure 6.10).

Another example of how memory is improved by connections is provided by the self-reference effect: Memory is better if you are asked to relate a word to yourself. T. B. Rogers and coworkers (1979) demonstrated this by using the same procedure Craik and Tulving had used in their depth-of-processing experiment. Just as in Craik and Tulving's experiment, Rogers' participants were presented with a cue question and then a word, and were asked to apply the cue question to the word and answer "yes" or "no" (Figure 6.11a). The words in the Rogers experiment were adjectives such as "shy" and "outgoing."

One of the questions in the Rogers experiment was "Is the word long?" and another was "Does the word describe you?" The results for the words that resulted in a "yes" response, shown in Figure 6.11b, indicate that participants were almost three times more likely to remember words that they rated as describing themselves than they were to remember words that they rated for length.

Why were participants more likely to remember words they had connected to themselves? We can answer this question in terms of depth of processing by saying that making a judgment about whether the word describes you results in deeper processing than judging whether the word is long or short. But another possible explanation is that the self provides information, or *cues*, that become linked to the word and that make it easier to remember later. This is similar to the example in which the information provided by the giant swooping bird provided a cue that helped remember the word *chicken*. Cues such as this, that help us remember information that has been stored in memory, are called

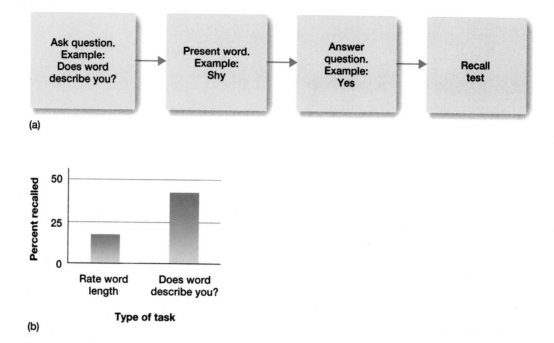

Figure 6.11 (a) Sequence of events in Rogers et al.'s (1979) self-reference experiment. This is the same as the design of Craik and Tulving's (1975) experiment shown in Figure 6.9, but the questions refer to the person being tested. (b) Results of the experiment.

retrieval cues. The fact that the way we encode information can create retrieval cues that help us remember the information later illustrates the close link between how information is encoded and our ability to retrieve it later. We will consider the idea of retrieval cues in more detail later in the chapter.

Organizing Information
File folders, computerized library catalogs, and tabs that separate different subjects in your notebook are all designed to organize information so that it can be accessed more efficiently. The memory system also uses organization to access information. This has been shown in a number of ways.

Demonstration

Reading a List

Get paper and pen ready. Read the following words, then cover them and write down as many as possible.

apple, desk, shoe, sofa, plum
chair, cherry, coat, lamp, pants
grape, hat, melon, table, gloves

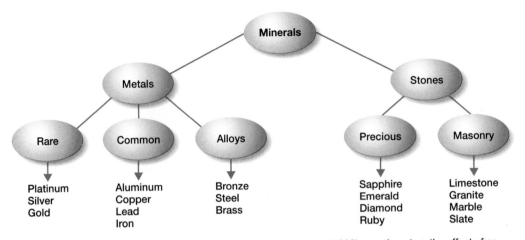

Figure 6.12 The organized tree for "minerals" used in Bower et al.'s (1969) experiment on the effect of organization on memory. (Reprinted from *Journal of Verbal Learning and Verbal Behavior, 8,* Bower et al, "Hierarchical Retrieval Schemes in Recall of Categorized Word Lists," pp. 323–343, Copyright © 1969, with permission from Elsevier.)

After creating your list of remembered words, look at your list and notice whether similar items (for example, apple, plum, cherry; shoe, coat, pants) are grouped together. If they are, your result is similar to the result of research that shows that participants spontaneously organize items as they recall them (Jenkins & Russell, 1952). One reason for this result is that remembering words in a particular category may serve as a retrieval cue for other words in that category. So remembering the word "apple" helps you retrieve "grape" or "plum" and therefore creates a recall list that is more organized than the original list that you read.

If words presented randomly become organized in the mind, what happens if words are presented in an organized way from the beginning, during encoding? Gordon Bower and coworkers (1969) answered this question by presenting material to be learned in a "tree," which organized a number of words according to categories. For example, one tree organized the names of different minerals by grouping together precious stones, rare metals, and so on (Figure 6.12).

One group of participants studied trees for "minerals," "animals," "clothing," and "transportation" for one minute each and were then asked to recall as many words as they could from all four trees. In the recall test, participants tended to organize their responses in the same way that the trees were organized, first saying "minerals," then "metals," then "common," and so on. Participants in this group recalled an average of 73 words from all four trees.

Another group of participants also saw four trees, but the words were randomized, so that each tree contained a random assortment of minerals, animals, clothing, and transportation. These participants were able to remember only 21 words from all four trees. Thus, organizing material to be remembered results in substantially better recall. Perhaps

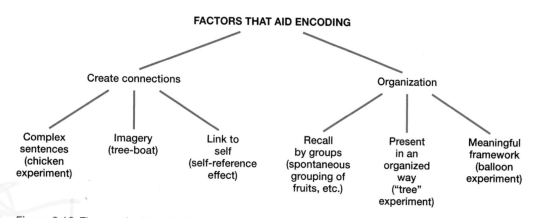

FACTORS THAT AID ENCODING

Create connections

- Complex sentences (chicken experiment)
- Imagery (tree-boat)
- Link to self (self-reference effect)

Organization

- Recall by groups (spontaneous grouping of fruits, etc.)
- Present in an organized way ("tree" experiment)
- Meaningful framework (balloon experiment)

Figure 6.13 The organized tree for the material about encoding presented in this chapter. Also see Concept Map 6.4 in the booklet *Concept Maps and CogLab Online Manual*, which accompanies this text.

this is something to keep in mind when creating study materials for an exam. You might, for example, find it useful to organize material you are studying for your cognitive psychology exam in trees like the one in Figure 6.13. (Also see the concept maps in the booklet *Concept Maps and CogLab Online Manual* that accompanies this text.)

If presenting material in an organized way improves memory, we might expect that preventing organization from happening would reduce the ability to remember. This effect was illustrated by John Bransford and Marcia Johnson (1972), who asked their participants to read the following passage:

> If the balloons popped, the sound wouldn't be able to carry since everything would be too far away from the correct floor. A closed window would also prevent the sound from carrying, since most buildings tend to be well insulated. Since the whole operation depends on the steady flow of electricity, a break in the middle of the wire would also cause problems. Of course, the fellow could shout, but the human voice is not loud enough to carry that far. An additional problem is that the string could break on the instrument. Then there would be no accompaniment to the message. It is clear that the best situation would involve less distance. Then there would be fewer potential problems. With face to face contact, the least number of things could go wrong. (p. 719)

What was that all about? If you had a problem understanding the passage, you're not alone, because so did Bransford and Johnson's participants. But most important, their participants also found it extremely difficult to *remember* this passage.

To make sense of this passage, reread it while looking at Figure 6.14. When you do this, the passage makes more sense, and participants who saw this picture before they read the passage remembered twice as much from the passage as participants who did not see

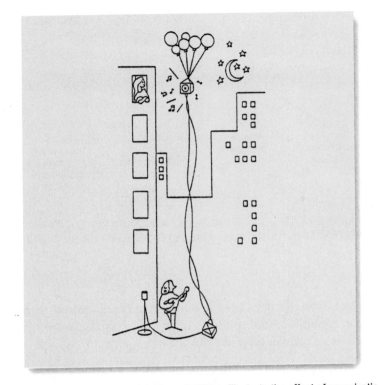

Figure 6.14 Picture used by Bransford and Johnson (1972) to illustrate the effect of organization on memory. (Reprinted from *Journal of Verbal Learning and Verbal Behavior, 11*, J. D. Bransford & M. K. Johnson, "Contextual Prerequisites for Understanding: Some Investigations of Comprehension and Recall," pp. 717–726, Copyright © 1972, with permission from Elsevier.)

the picture or participants who saw the picture after they read the passage. The key here is *organization*. The picture provides a meaningful framework that helps organize the information from the passage in memory. The result of this organization is a passage that is both easier to comprehend and easier to remember later.

but ies→multiple (visual) vs. just one 'code'

 ## Test Yourself 6.1

1. Researchers have proposed that there are a number of different kinds of LTM. Be able to distinguish between declarative and nondeclarative memory, and within declarative memory, between episodic and semantic memory.
2. How have neuropsychological case studies and brain-imaging experiments distinguished between episodic and semantic memory?
3. What type of memory effect occurs when a person can't remember the experience that caused a memory? What type of memory is associated with this effect, and how has it been studied using neuropsychological case studies and in priming experiments

in normal participants? How might this type of memory influence our response to advertisements and political speeches?

4. What is procedural memory, and how have neuropsychological case studies been used to distinguish it from episodic and semantic memory?

5. What is the difference between elaborative rehearsal and maintenance rehearsal in terms of (1) the procedures associated with each type of rehearsal, and (2) their effectiveness for creating long-term memories?

6. What is levels-of-processing theory? How has it been tested? How does it relate to the difference between maintenance and elaborative rehearsal?

7. Give examples of how memory for a word can be increased by (1) using it in a sentence, (2) creating an image, and (3) relating it to yourself. What do each of these procedures have in common?

8. What are some examples from the text that support the statement: "Organization and good memory go hand in hand"?

WHERE ARE MEMORIES CREATED AND STORED IN THE BRAIN?

You can mentally travel back in time to when you got up this morning, or to last New Year's Eve, or to your early days in grade school, because information about these events is stored somewhere in your brain. What form does this storage take? How can a record of what happened to you in the fifth grade be stored in neurons? One way researchers have tried to answer these questions is to look at what happens at synapses in the brain.

Information Storage at the Synapse

Remember from Chapter 2 that synapses are the small spaces between the end of the presynaptic neuron and the cell body or dendrite of the postsynaptic neuron (Figure 2.10) and that when signals reach the end of the presynaptic neuron, they cause a release of neurotransmitter onto the postsynaptic neuron. It is here, at the synapse, that the physiology of memory begins, according to an idea first proposed by the Canadian psychologist Donald Hebb.

Memories Are Represented by Changes at the Synapse   Hebb (1948) introduced the idea that learning and memory are represented in the brain by physiological changes that take place at the synapse. Let's assume that a particular experience causes nerve impulses to travel down the axon of presynaptic neuron A, and when these impulses reach the synapse, neurotransmitter is released onto postsynaptic neuron B (Figure 6.15a). Hebb's idea was that this activity strengthens the synapse by causing structural changes, greater transmitter release, and increased firing (Figures 6.15b and c). Hebb also proposed that all of these changes at the synapse provide a neural record of the experience that caused nerve impulses to travel down neuron A in the first place. Memory, according to this idea, is represented by changes at the synapse.

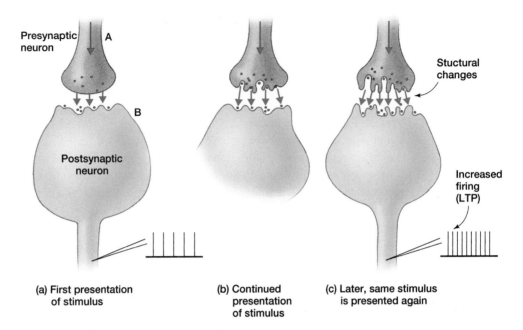

Figure 6.15 What happens at a synapse as (a) a stimulus is first presented. The record next to the electrode indicates the rate of firing in the axon of the postsynaptic neuron. (b) The stimulus is repeated. Structural changes are beginning to occur. (c) After many repetitions, more complex connections have developed between the two neurons, which causes an increase in the firing rate, even though the stimulus is the same one that was presented in (a).

Hebb's idea that synaptic changes provide a record of experiences is still the starting point for modern research on the physiology of memory. Researchers that followed Hebb's lead have shown that activity at a synapse does, in fact, lead to structural changes at the synapse and to enhanced firing in the postsynaptic neuron. This enhanced firing is called **long-term potentiation (LTP)** because it has been shown to last for periods of days or weeks in laboratory experiments. Researchers speculate that LTP may last even longer in the living, functioning brain and that this would provide a physiological mechanism for the long-term storage of memories.

One of the pioneers in identifying the changes in the synapse that are associated with long-term potentiation is Eric Kandel (2001), who received the 2000 Nobel Prize in Physiology and Medicine for his work. Kandel and others (Abel & Lattal, 2001; Malenka & Nicoll, 1999) have shown that LTP is easiest to generate in regions of the brain responsible for learning and memory, particularly the hippocampus, which we will see plays a major role in forming LTMs.

In our example in Figure 6.15, we used just two neurons—neuron A synapsing onto neuron B. However, the actual situation in the brain is much more complex than this because even simple experiences cause many thousands of neurons to fire. Realizing this,

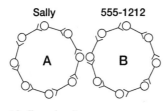

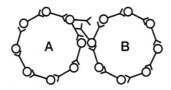

(a) Two circuits

(b) After learning, circuits are stronger and become linked

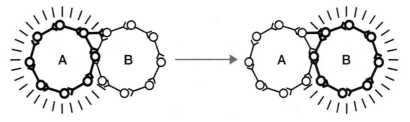

(c) Activity in one circuit can trigger the other

Figure 6.16 How groups of neurons can work together to create a circuit for remembering Sally's phone number. (a) Circuits that represent "Sally" and "Sally's phone number" before learning. (b) Circuits become linked during learning. (c) Later, activation of one circuit can trigger the other one.

Hebb expanded his idea to include larger groups of neurons and suggested that experiences can make a particular *group* of neurons more likely to fire together, and that an experience is therefore represented by the firing this group of neurons.

We can illustrate how this mechanism might operate by considering how groups of neurons could cooperate to create memory for a phone number. Figure 6.16a shows that the neurons in circuit A fire together to represent "Sally," and the neurons in circuit B fire together to represent Sally's phone number. (Simple circular circuits are used for the purposes of this example. The actual circuits in the brain would be far more complex.)

At the beginning of learning, these circuits are weak, so connections between neurons are unreliable and firing isn't strong. However, as learning continues, the circuits become strengthened (Figure 6.16b), and if learning involves associating Sally's name and the phone number, then the circuits become associated so firing in one can trigger firing in the other (Figure 6.16c). Thus, the association between Sally and her phone number is represented by the firing of this new, larger circuit, and the next time you want to remember Sally's phone number, this connection between the circuits is what helps you remember it.

Although linked circuits may provide an explanation for how neural activity helps you remember Sally's phone number, any neural explanation of memory must also explain why you might forget Sally's phone number. While we are far from understanding the complexities of this process, researchers have devoted considerable energy to explaining why our memories can sometimes be disrupted by new experiences or by traumas, such as a blow to the head, that occur shortly after a memory has been formed.

Examples of the traumatic disruption of newly formed memories are easy to find in football. There are many accounts of players who have suffered a concussion during a play and who have no memory for what happened just before they were hit. The loss of memory for what happened prior to the concussion is called **retrograde amnesia.** The occurrence of retrograde amnesia in situations such as this has been linked to a phenomenon called *memory consolidation.*

Memory Consolidation   The fact that memories for recent experiences can be disrupted has led to the idea that the structural changes caused by experience are initially fragile and that it takes time for them to become stamped in more permanently. The strengthening of this neural information is called **memory consolidation.** The period of time needed for this strengthening to occur is called the **consolidation period.** The reason football players experience retrograde amnesia is that the trauma they experience interrupts the consolidation of the newly formed (and therefore fragile) memory traces that were present just before they were hit. As a result, these traces were never consolidated and were therefore lost.

Retrograde amnesia also occurs in people who are given shock treatments, called *electroconvulsive therapy (ECT),* to help relieve severe depression. In these treatments a brief electrical current is passed through the brain, causing loss of consciousness for a few minutes. These patients typically suffer from retrograde amnesia upon awakening—they can't remember things that happened just before the shock (Squire, 1986).

How much time is needed for consolidation to occur? The evidence from accident victims and ECT patients suggests that the consolidation period is short because events that happened several minutes before the trauma are remembered. However, there is also evidence that consolidation may take as long as several years (Squire, 1986). For example, Larry Squire and coworkers (1975) asked participants who had received ECT in 1970 to remember things about TV programs that were on the air for just one season, for the 1967, 1968, 1969, and 1970 seasons. He found that these patients had lost their memories for TV programs that had been on the air for the season just before their treatment, but that their memory for programs that were on the air a few years earlier was not affected (also see Squire & Cohen, 1979). Thus, although long-term memories may form rapidly after an event is experienced, they may be liable to disruption by trauma for a year, or perhaps more.

Consolidation period → how long? variable evidence
brief → a year

Apparently there is a lengthy period of consolidation that is directed by structures in the temporal lobe of the brain (Squire & Zola-Morgan, 1996). One of the structures in the temporal lobe, called the hippocampus, is crucial for forming LTMs. The importance of the hippocampus for memory was discovered by studying patient H.M., whom we described in Chapter 5.

The Hippocampus and Episodic Memory

As we saw in Chapter 5, H.M. had severe epilepsy that did not respond to medication. In an attempt to control H.M.'s seizures, surgeons removed his hippocampus on both sides of the brain (Milner, 1966; Scoville & Milner, 1957). The operation was successful in reducing H.M.'s seizures, but after the operation H.M. could no longer form long-term memories, much like Clive Wearing and Jimmy G. (Milner, 1966). A large number of studies of H.M.'s memory have led to the following conclusions regarding the role of the hippocampus in memory:

1. The hippocampus is not needed for short-term or working memory since H.M. was still able to understand incoming information and remember it briefly.
2. The hippocampus is needed for forming conscious LTMs, since that is the ability that H.M. lost.
3. The hippocampus is not where LTMs are stored, since H.M. could still remember things about his life that occurred long before the operation.
4. The hippocampus is not needed for learning new procedures, since H.M. could learn new skills, such as the incomplete picture test (see Figure 6.7). (Milner et al., 1968).

Although H.M.'s performance improved with practice, he couldn't remember any of his learning trials. This improvement in performance without remembering the practice trials is an example of implicit memory.

Many years after H.M.'s operation, a scan of his brain indicated that his hippocampus *plus* some neighboring structures had been removed. Thus the preceding conclusions describe not just the function of the hippocampus but the functioning of the hippocampus plus some surrounding structures, which, together, are called the medial temporal lobe (MTL) (Figure 6.17). It has also been found from neuropsychological research that damage to just the hippocampus does cause memory loss, but not as severe as that experienced by H.M. (Zola-Morgan et al., 1986).

Brain-imaging experiments have provided further evidence that MTL structures are important for long-term memory. In a number of experiments, activity of MTL structures was measured during encoding, as participants were initially studying stimuli. Then later, when memory for the stimuli was tested, the ones that had generated a larger fMRI response during the study period were more likely to be remembered (Brewer et al., 1998;

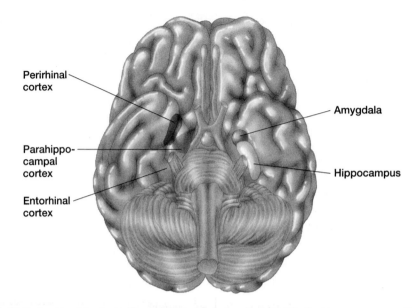

Figure 6.17 Underside of the brain. The structures labeled on the left, plus the hippocampus, are the main structures of the medial temporal lobe (MTL).

Davachi & Wagner, 2002; Wagner et al., 1998; also see the experiment by Lila Davachi and coworkers, 2003, described on page 16 of Chapter 1).

In some of these experiments, increased activity during encoding was also observed in the prefrontal cortex. This is not surprising when we remember that the prefrontal cortex is important for working memory, which we would expect would be involved in encoding new material. These results are exciting because they are measuring what is happening in the brain as memories are being formed, and show that brain activity that occurs during initial exposure to a stimulus can predict whether we will remember the stimulus later or forget it.

We have described just a few of hundreds of research studies that show that the hippocampus and MTL are important for episodic memory. Other structures are involved in establishing memories as well, and in Chapter 7 we will see that highly emotional memories are associated with the amygdala, which is located near the hippocampus.

Even though we are beginning to understand what areas of the brain are activated during encoding, we still don't know where long-term memories are stored. We know that very long-term memories can't be stored in the hippocampus because H.M. and other people with extensive damage to their hippocampus retain memories from their early experiences. Most memory researchers feel that memory is not stored in any one structure, but that information about past events is distributed in a network of neurons across many structures in the brain.

Our emphasis so far has been on how information gets into LTM. We have described memory experiments that demonstrate the importance of elaborative encoding, forming connections with other information, and how material is organized. We have also seen that the formation of memories involves changes at the synapses and that while the hippocampus is important for forming new memories, other structures are likely to be involved in the long-term storage of these memories.

Once memories have been created by effective encoding and physiological storage, we need to be able to retrieve them. The process of retrieval is extremely important because most of our failures of memory are failures of retrieval. These retrieval failures occur when the information is "in there," but we can't get it out. For example, you've studied hard for an exam but can't come up with the answer when you're taking the exam, only to remember it later when the exam is over. Or you can't remember a person's name when you unexpectedly see him or her, but it suddenly comes to you as the two of you are talking. In both of these examples, you possessed the information you needed, but you couldn't access it when you needed it.

Research on retrieval has focused on ways to get information out of storage and into consciousness. One of the most powerful ways to achieve this is to provide retrieval cues for that information. When we introduced retrieval cues on page 198, we defined them as cues that help us to remember information that has been stored in memory. As we now consider these cues in more detail, we will see that this information can come from a number of different sources.

Retrieval Cues

A few weeks ago, while I was in my office at home, I made a mental note to be sure to take my videotape on amnesia to school for my cognitive psychology class. A short while later, as I was about to leave the house, I had a nagging feeling that I was forgetting something but I couldn't remember what it was. Since this is not the first time I've had this problem, I knew exactly what to do. I returned to my office, and as soon as I got there I remembered that I was supposed to take the tape. Returning to the place where I had originally thought about taking the tape helped me to retrieve that thought. Thus, returning to my office provided a retrieval cue for remembering to take the tape.

You may have had similar experiences in which returning to a particular place stimulated memories associated with that place. When I asked students in my class to write about an experience that involved memory, one of my students related the following experience.

> When I was eight years old, both of my grandparents passed away. Their house was sold, and that chapter of my life was closed. Since then I can remember general

things about being there as a child, but not the details. One day I decided to go for a drive. I went to my grandparents' old house and I pulled around to the alley and parked. As I sat there and stared at the house, the most amazing thing happened. I experienced a vivid recollection. All of a sudden, I was eight years old again. I could see myself in the backyard, learning to ride a bike for the first time. I could see the inside of the house. I remembered exactly what every detail looked like. I could even remember the distinct smell. So many times I tried to remember these things, but never so vividly did I remember such detail. (Angela Paidousis)

My experience in my office and Angela's experience outside her grandparents' old house are examples of retrieval cues that are provided by returning to the place where memories were initially formed. The operation of retrieval cues has also been demonstrated in the laboratory. For example, Endel Tulving and Zena Pearlstone (1966) presented participants with a list of words to remember. The words were drawn from specific categories such as "birds" (*pigeon, sparrow*), furniture (*chair, dresser*), and "professions" (*engineer, lawyer*), although the categories were not specifically indicated in the original list (Figure 6.18).

Participants in the "free recall group," who were simply asked to write down as many words as possible, recalled an average of 19 of the 48 words (40 percent). However, participants in the "cued recall group," who were provided with the names of the categories, remembered 36 of the 48 words (75 percent). Thus, the categories functioned as retrieval cues and caused a great increase in the ability to remember the words.

One of the most impressive demonstrations of the power of retrieval cues is provided by Timo Mantyla (1986), who presented his participants with a list of 600 nouns, such as *banana, freedom*, and *tree*. During learning, the participants were told to write down three

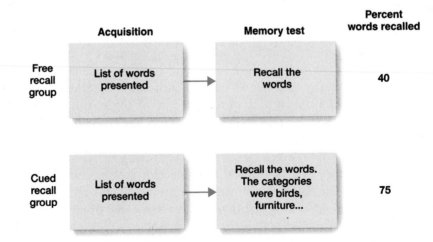

Figure 6.18 Design of the Tulving and Pearlstone (1966) experiment. The results for each group are on the right.

words they associated with each noun. For example, three words for *banana* might be *yellow*, *bunches*, and *edible*. When the participants took a surprise memory test, in which they were presented with the three words they had created and were asked to produce the original word, they were able to remember 90 percent of the 600 words (top bar in Figure 6.19).

Mantyla also ran another group of participants who during the learning part of the experiment were provided with the noun and three cue words that had been generated by someone else. When participants in this condition were later presented with the three cue words in a memory test, they were able to remember 55 percent of the nouns (second bar in Figure 6.19). You might think that it might be possible to guess "bananas" from the three properties, *yellow*, *bunches*, and *edible*, even if you had never been presented with the word *banana*. But when Mantyla ran another control group in which he presented the cue words generated by someone else to participants who had never seen the original nouns, these participants were able to determine only 17 percent of the nouns. Thus, the result of this experiment demonstrates that retrieval cues (the three words) provide extremely effective information for retrieving memories, but that the retrieval cues were more effective if they were created by the person whose memory was being tested. (Also see Wagenaar, 1986, for a description of a study in which Wagenaar was able to remember almost all of 2,400 diary entries he kept over a 5-year period by using retrieval cues.)

The fact that cues are more effective if they are created by the person who will be tested later illustrates the importance of the initial encoding process in establishing memories. We will now see that the relationship between the process of encoding and later retrieval plays a crucial role in determining the effectiveness of retrieval.

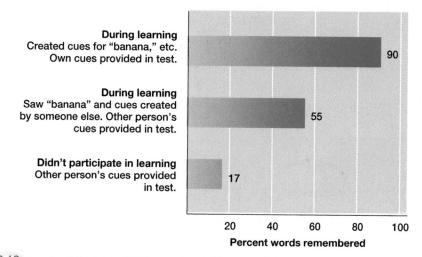

Figure 6.19 Results of Mantyla's (1986) experiment. Memory was best if retrieval cues were created by the person (top bar), not as good when retrieval cues were created by someone else (middle bar), and worst when the cues were created by someone else and the person had never seen them associated with the word (bottom bar).

Transfer-Appropriate Processing — *task-type*

Remember the levels-of-processing theory stated that deeper processing resulted in better memory (see page 195) and that one of the criticisms of the theory was that sometimes this does not occur (page 197). We are now ready to provide the evidence that deeper processing does not always lead to better memory. That evidence is provided by a phenomenon called **transfer-appropriate processing,** in which memory performance is enhanced if the type of encoding that occurs during acquisition matches the type of retrieval that occurs during the memory test. We can understand what this means by considering an experiment by Donald Morris and coworkers (1977).

There were a number of different conditions in Morris's experiment, but we will focus on just two of them, the semantic-acquisition, rhyming-test condition (SA, RT) and the rhyming-acquisition, rhyming-test condition (RA, RT) (Figure 6.20).

In the acquisition part of the experiment, participants in the SA, RT condition heard a fill-in-the-blanks sentence in which the word *blank* was substituted for the target word. Following this sentence, the participants heard the target word, and had to respond "yes" if they thought it fit into the sentence, and "no" if they thought it didn't fit into the sentence.

Example of Semantic Acquisition (SA):
Sentence: The *blank* rode a bicycle.
Target word: Boy
Answer: Yes

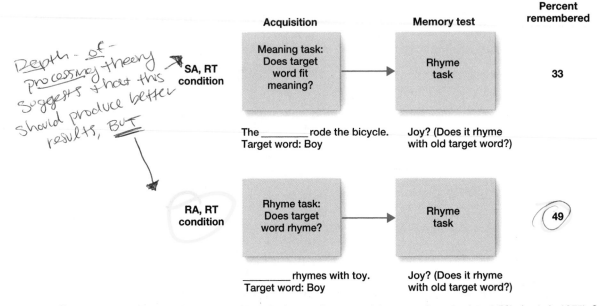

Depth-of-processing theory suggests that this should produce better results, BUT

Figure 6.20 Design and results for transfer-appropriate processing experiment (Morris et al., 1977). SA, RT stands for "semantic acquisition, rhyming test." RA, RT stands for "rhyming acquisition, rhyming test." Notice that performance is better if acquisition and test conditions match.

The idea behind this task is to achieve deep processing by having the participant focus on the target word's meaning.

Participants in the RA, RT condition heard a statement involving rhyming, in which the word *blank* replaced the target word. Following this statement, the participants heard the target word, and had to respond "yes" if the statement was correct and "no" if it wasn't.

Example of Rhyming Acquisition (RA):
Statement: *Blank* rhymes with toy.
Target word: Boy
Answer: Yes

The idea behind this task is to achieve shallower processing by having the participants focus on the target word's sound.

In the rhyming-memory test (RT), participants in both conditions were presented with a rhyming word they had never seen before. Their task was to indicate whether it rhymed with any of the target words they had heard before. For example, if the rhyming word was *joy* they would answer *yes* if they remembered that *boy* was presented earlier, and *no* if they didn't remember a target word that rhymed with *joy*.

The result of this experiment, shown on the right of Figure 6.20, was that participants in the RA, RT group, who were encouraged to focus on the words' sounds during acquisition, were able to remember more words than participants in the SA, RT group, who were encouraged to focus on the words' meanings. This is not the result that levels-of-processing theory would predict, because the SA, RT group, which processed the stimuli most deeply during acquisition, did not perform as well as the RA, RT group, which used "shallower" processing during acquisition, but which achieved transfer-appropriate processing by matching the type of encoding and the type of retrieval. Excellent memory also occurred in the SA, ST condition of this experiment, which we didn't describe here, in which both acquisition and testing were based on meaning.

The Principle of Encoding Specificity → context

Another principle that takes into account the relationship between encoding and retrieval is the principle of **encoding specificity**, which states that we learn information together with its context. This principle is illustrated by the experience of Angela, the student from my class whose visit to her grandparent's house elicited memories of experiences she hadn't thought about for many years.

We presented Angela's experience to illustrate how retrieval cues can facilitate memory. But the most important thing about Angela's experience is that retrieval occurred when the *place* of retrieval matched the *place* at which encoding had originally occurred. This is an example of encoding specificity because childhood experiences such as learning to ride her bike and experiencing specific smells were associated with the context in which they originally occurred (Angela's grandparents' house). This learning of information and context together causes the following two results:

CogLab
Encoding Specificity

1. The context in which learning occurs can be a retrieval cue. This is why Angela's memories came flashing back when she returned to her grandparents' house.
2. Returning to the context where original learning occurred can enhance our memory for the original experience.

The second point can also be stated as follows: *Memory is better if conditions for retrieval are similar to conditions that occurred during encoding.* This has been demonstrated by experiments that manipulate the participants' "state" during encoding and retrieval. This has been achieved in a number of ways, which we will describe in the next section.

State-Dependent Learning

One of the principles that follows from the principle of encoding specificity is the principle of **state-dependent learning**. This principle states that memory is best if a person is in the same state for encoding and retrieval. We will consider experiments that have investigated the effects of place and mood.

Matching Place During Encoding and Retrieval   The effect of matching place during encoding and retrieval is demonstrated by an experiment by D. R. Godden and Alan Baddeley (1975), who had one group of participants put on diving equipment and study a list of words underwater, and had another group study the words on land (Figure 6.21a). Each of these groups was then divided so half of the participants were tested for recall on land and half were tested underwater. The results, shown in Figure 6.21b, indicate that the best recall occurred when encoding and retrieval occurred in the same place.

The results of the diving study, and many others, suggest that a good strategy for test taking would be to study in an environment similar to the environment in which you will be tested. While this doesn't mean you necessarily have to do all of your studying in the classroom where you will be taking the exam, you might want to duplicate, in your study situation, some of the conditions that will occur during the exam.

This conclusion about studying is supported by an experiment by Harry Grant and coworkers (1998), using the design in Figure 6.22a. Participants read an article on psychoimmunology while wearing headphones. The participants in the "silent" condition heard nothing in the headphones. Participants in the "noisy" condition heard a tape of background noise recorded during lunchtime in a university cafeteria (which they were told to ignore). Half of the participants in each group were then given a short-answer test on the article under the silent condition and the other half were tested under the noisy condition.

The results, shown in Figure 6.22b, indicate that participants did better if the testing condition matched the study condition. Since your next cognitive psychology exam will take place under silent conditions, it might make sense to study under silent conditions. (Interestingly, a number of my students report that having outside stimulation such as music or television present helps them study. This idea clearly violates the principle of state-dependent learning. Can you think of some other reasons that students might nonetheless say this?)

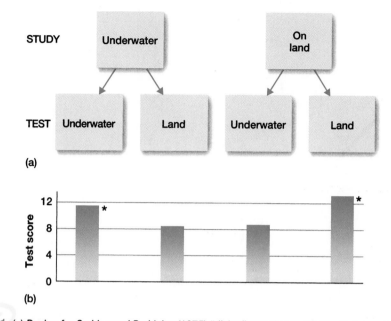

Figure 6.21 (a) Design for Godden and Baddeley (1975) "diving" experiment. (b) Results for each test condition are indicated by the bar directly under that condition. Asterisks indicate situations in which study and test conditions matched.

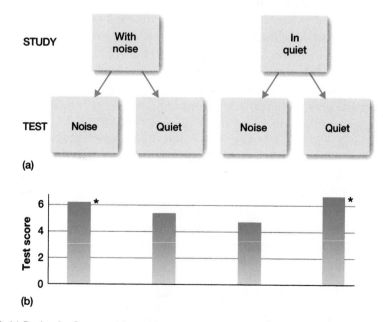

Figure 6.22 (a) Design for Grant et al.'s (1998) "studying" experiment. (b) Results of the experiment. Asterisks indicate situations in which study and test conditions matched.

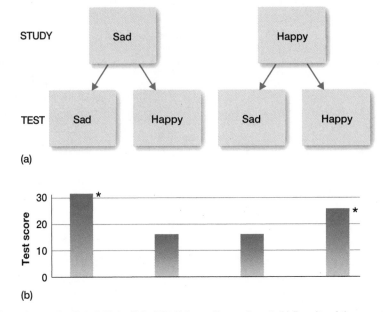

Figure 6.23 (a) Design for Eich & Metcalfe's (1989) "mood" experiment. (b) Results of the experiment.

Matching Mood During Encoding and Retrieval   Experiments on the effect of mood on memory have used the same experimental design as the examples of state-dependent effects we have just described, except positive mood and negative mood are the two variables rather than "underwater" and "land" or "silent" and "noisy." Researchers have devised a number of different ways for achieving positive and negative moods. One method of doing this is called the *continuous music technique*, in which participants are asked to think positive thoughts while listening to "merry" music or depressing thoughts while listening to "melancholic" music (Eich, 1995). Most participants reach an extremely pleasant or extremely unpleasant mood after doing this for about 15–20 minutes.

The results of an experiment by James Eric Eich and J. Metcalfe (1989) in which each participant studied material while in a positive or negative mood and is then tested on the material when in a positive or negative mood are shown in Figure 6.23. This result supports the idea of encoding specificity because people who were happy when they studied did better when they were happy during testing and people who were sad when they studied did better when they were sad during testing.

What Memory Research Tells Us About Studying

While the laboratory research we have been describing may be interesting, you may be more concerned with how to remember all this material about memory for the next exam! Luckily, many of the principles that have been discovered in the laboratory work outside the laboratory as well, and you can use some of them to increase the effectiveness of your studying.

The ideas in this section are presented as suggestions for you to consider. I say this because people's learning styles differ, and what might work for one person might be impractical or ineffective for another. Also, different types of material may require different techniques. One method of studying may work best for memorizing lists or definitions and another method may be better for learning concepts or basic principles. We will consider the following five ways of improving learning and memory.

1. Elaborate
2. Organize
3. Associate
4. Take breaks
5. Match learning and testing conditions

Elaborate   Because the importance of elaboration is one of the themes of this chapter, it should be no surprise that elaboration is an important part of effective studying. One of the mistakes that many students make is that they study using maintenance rehearsal rather than elaborative rehearsal. I have talked with students who have spent many hours studying without achieving positive results because their method was just to read and reread the book and their lecture notes. (Review "Knowing, Learning, and Remembering: Strategies for Successful Learning" on page 19 for further discussion of this problem.)

Reading the material is just the first step toward remembering the material. The step that helps transfer the material you are reading into long-term memory is elaboration— thinking about what you are reading and giving it meaning by relating it to other things that you know. Of course, it is easy to say this, but how can you actually do it?

One of the most effective ways to achieve elaborative studying is to make up questions about the material and then answer them. Research has shown that students who read a text with the idea of making up questions did as well on an exam as students who read a text with the idea of answering questions later, and both groups did better than a group who did not create or answer questions (Frase, 1975).

One way to approach making up questions is to start with general questions and then get more specific. So the question "What is episodic memory?" might be followed by "How does episodic memory differ from semantic memory?" Making up questions is itself a form of elaborative processing, and so is attempting to answer the questions. Of course, once you answer the questions, be sure to get feedback to see if you were correct. Feedback helps track your progress and is in itself a form of elaborative processing.

Finally, beware of highlighting. A survey by Peterson (1992) found that 82 percent of students highlight, and most of them do so while they are reading the material for the first time. The problem with highlighting is that it seems like elaborative processing (you're taking an active role in your reading by highlighting important points), but it often becomes automatic behavior that involves moving the hand, but little deep thinking about the material. A study that compared comprehension for a group who highlighted and a group who didn't found no difference between the performance of the two groups when they were tested on the material (Peterson, 1992). Highlighting may be a good first step for some people, but most students need to take further action to achieve good memory for the material.

Organize   We've seen that memory is better when the material is organized. Organization creates a framework that helps relate some information to other information, and therefore makes the material more meaningful. Organization can be achieved by making "trees," as in Figure 6.13, or outlines or lists that group similar facts or principles together.

Organization also helps reduce the load on your memory. We can illustrate this by looking at a perceptual example. The black and white pattern in Figure 3.26 (in the perception chapter) can be seen as a bunch of black and white areas, or as a dog. Once you've seen this pattern of light and dark as a Dalmatian, you have perceptually organized the pattern into something meaningful, and memory for pictures like this one is much better than memory for patterns that are not meaningful (Wiseman & Neisser, 1974). This relates to the phenomenon of chunking that we discussed in Chapter 5. Grouping small elements into larger more meaningful ones increases memory. Organizing material is one way to achieve this. (Also see page 340 of Chapter 9 for a discussion of how using images to create organization can be used to improve memory.)

Associate   An important aspect of elaborative processing is associating what you are learning to what you already know. The more you learn, the easier this becomes because your prior learning creates a structure on which to hang new information.

Techniques based on association, such as creating images that link two things, as in Figure 6.10, often prove useful for learning individual words or definitions. For example, when I was first learning the difference between proactive interference (old information interferes with learning new information) and retroactive interference (new information interferes with remembering old information), I thought of a "PRO" football player smashing everything in his path as he runs forward in time. I no longer need this image to remember what proactive interference is, but it was helpful when I was first learning this concept.

Take Breaks   Saying "take breaks" is another way of saying, "study in a number of shorter study sessions rather than trying to learn everything at once," or "don't cram." There are good reasons to say these things. The main reason is that research has shown that memory is better if studying the material is broken into a number of short sessions with breaks in between, than if studying occurs in one long session, even if the study time is the same in both groups. This advantage for short study sessions is called the distributed versus massed practice effect (Reder & Anderson, 1982; Smith & Rothkopf, 1984).

The distributed versus massed practice effect occurs for a number of reasons:

1. It is difficult to maintain close attention to material throughout a long study session.

2. Studying after a break gives better feedback about what you actually know. While it may be easy to read over something and to then remember it a few moments later, the real test is whether you remember it a few hours or days later.
3. Studying the same material in a number of different settings can make retrieval less dependent on conditions during the test.

Matching Learning and Testing Conditions   From what we know about encoding specificity, memory should be better if study (encoding) and testing (retrieval) conditions match as closely as possible. To strictly follow this procedure, you would have to do all of your studying in the classroom in which you will be taking the exam. This might, however, be an impractical strategy, not only because of the logistics involved in studying in a room where there are other classes, but also because your classroom might not be a comfortable place to study, and because you might not be highly motivated to spend even more time in your classroom. A solution to this problem is to study in a number of different places. Research has shown that people remember material better if they have learned it in a number of different locations, compared to spending the same amount of time studying in one location (Smith et al., 1978).

Looking at all of these techniques, we can see that many of them involve using more effective encoding strategies. Elaborating, organizing, and associating all encourage deeper processing of the material you are trying to learn. But these techniques can also involve retrieval. Making up questions about the material helps encoding, but answering the questions, which involves retrieval, not only provides feedback about how well you know the material but helps achieve better encoding as well. Thus, as you try remembering something that you've studied, the very act of trying to remember creates stronger encoding of that material (Figure 6.24) (see Buckner et al., 2001).

You may be using some of the study techniques we have described already, or you may benefit from trying them if you aren't. Do you have a study technique that isn't mentioned here, but that works for you and that you can relate to the memory principles we have discussed in this chapter? If so, I invite you to send a description of your technique to me at bruceg@pitt.edu.

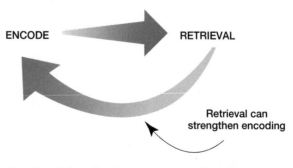

Figure 6.24 Attempting to retrieve information by answering questions about what you have studied can strengthen encoding. This strengthened encoding then increases the likelihood that the next attempt at retrieval will be successful.

1. What is the idea behind the statement "memories are stored at synapses"? What evidence supports this idea?
2. What is the central concept behind the idea that it takes time for memories to become permanent? How long does it take for memories to become more permanent?
3. What has the case of H.M. taught us about the role of the hippocampus and other surrounding structures for memory?
4. Retrieval cues are a powerful way to improve the chances that we will remember something. Why can we say that the better memory that occurs when we use a word in a sentence, create an image, or relate it to yourself (See Test Yourself 6.1, page 203, question 7) all involve retrieval cues? What further evidence from the effectiveness of retrieval cues has been provided by Tulving and Pearlstone and by Mantyla?
5. What is the evidence supporting the idea that the match between encoding and retrieval can influence memory performance? What is this effect called?
6. The relationship between encoding and retrieval has been studied in many different experiments. Describe the experiments on memory and (1) place; (2) study conditions; and (3) mood, that support the idea of encoding specificity.
7. How can concepts established by basic research on memory be used to achieve more effective studying?

Think About It

1. What do you remember about the last five minutes? How much of what you are remembering is in your STM while you are remembering it? Were any of these memories ever in LTM?
2. Not all long-term memories are alike. There is a difference between remembering what you did 10 minutes ago, 1 year ago, and 10 years ago, even though all of these memories are called "long-term memories." What kinds of investigations could you carry out to demonstrate the properties of these different long-term memories?
3. Describe an experience in which retrieval cues led you to remember something. This experience could include things like returning to a place where your memory was initially formed, being somewhere that reminds you of an experience you had in the past, having someone else provide a "hint" to help you remember something, or reading about something that triggers a memory.
4. How do you study? Which study techniques that you use should be effective, according to the results of memory research? How could you improve your study techniques by taking into account the results of memory research? (Also see Chapter 1, page 19.)

KEY TERMS

Alzheimer's disease
Consolidation period
Declarative memory
Deep processing
Depth of processing
Distributed versus mass practice effect
Elaborative rehearsal
Encoding
Encoding specificity
Episodic memory
Implicit memory (nondeclarative memory)
Korsakoff's syndrome
Levels of processing (LOP)
Levels-of-processing theory
Long-term potentiation (LTP)

Maintenance rehearsal
Medial temporal lobe (MTL)
Memory consolidation
Nondeclarative memory
Procedural memory
Propaganda effect
Repetition priming
Retrieval
Retrieval cues
Retrograde amnesia
Self-reference effect
Semantic memory
Shallow processing
State-dependent learning
Transfer-appropriate processing

CogLab To experience these experiments for yourself, go to http://coglab.wadsworth.com. Be sure to read each experiment's setup instructions before you go to the experiment itself. Otherwise, you won't know which keys to press.

Primary Labs

Implicit learning How we can learn something without being aware of the learning (p. 189).

Levels of processing How memory is influenced by depth of processing (p. 194).

Encoding specificity How memory is affected by both conditions at encoding and retrieval, and the relation between them (p. 213).

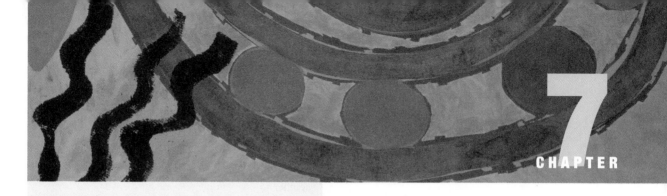

CHAPTER 7

Everyday Memory and Memory Errors

Some Questions We Will Consider

✔ What kinds of events from their lives are people most likely to remember?

✔ Why is it accurate to say that memory is *not* a video recorder?

✔ Why have many innocent people been sent to prison because of inaccurate eyewitness testimony?

■   ■   ■

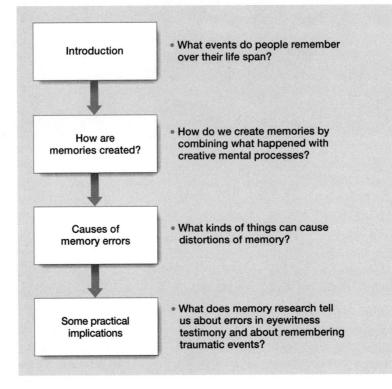

Figure 7.1 Flow diagram for this chapter.

Long-term memory is such a vast topic that it takes more than one chapter to do it justice. Chapter 6 provided a starting point by defining the types of memory (declarative and implicit) and discussing the basic principles of encoding, storage, and retrieval. In this chapter we will continue our discussion of long-term memory by first considering why people remember certain things from their "life stories" and forget others, and then focusing on the main theme of this chapter—that what we remember is determined by a constructive process, so that what you remember involves not just retaining a record of what's "in there," but rather is the outcome of creative mental processes (Figure 7.1).

We will see that this creativity is a gift that helps us determine what happened when not all the information is available, but that this creativity can also lead to errors of memory. There are a number of things that can cause these errors, including people's motivations and needs, and their susceptibility to being influenced by the suggestions offered by others. To end the chapter, we will consider how errors of memory can have unwanted effects on the accuracy of eyewitness testimony about crimes and on people's ability to remember traumatic experiences that happened long ago.

Remembering Personal Experiences

Everyone's life is full of stories. The events that make up these stories are episodic memories, and any time we remember dated events in our lives we are experiencing a type of episodic memory called **autobiographical memory**. Some of the things we classified as episodic memories in the last chapter, such as remembering stimuli presented in memory experiments, would not be autobiographical memories because they are not really part of our "life stories." However, life-story events account for the bulk of our episodic memories.

Autobiographical memories can range from "I went grocery shopping yesterday morning" to "I was in the Marines in Afghanistan." Consider, for example, the following description by the writer Natalie Goldberg of events surrounding her first trip to Washington, DC, to begin her years as a college student at George Washington University.

> I graduated from high school and planned to go away to college. My family never discussed my imminent departure. I simply filled out applications to universities and was accepted at one. I did this all on my own. No one in my immediate family had gone to college and I knew they could not help me.
>
> The end of August arrived. We loaded up my parents' brown Buick convertible and off we went to Washington, DC. I'd never been there before. I was amazed when we arrived. There were big parks and white buildings, but no skyscrapers. Unlike in Manhattan, I didn't have to bend my head all the way back to see the sky between tall rows of apartment houses. My parents helped me carry my suitcases into Thurston Hall and then up the elevator to the eighth floor. One of my roommates—there were four per room—was already there. She was from Shaker Heights, near Cleveland. We all said hello to her, then my parents and I went back down in the elevator and stood looking at each other in the dormitory lobby. What else was there to do? They had delivered me to college. We hugged good-bye and they walked out the door. I stood there. My mother told me years later that she cried, back in the car. (Goldberg, 1993, p. 29)

Goldberg's description of filling out college applications and her arrival at college with her parents illustrates how autobiographical memories can consist of small details that can add up to larger units. Martin Conway (1996) has devised a way to describe autobiographical memories in terms of three layers of knowledge (Figure 7.2). **Event-specific knowledge** consists of individual events that happen on a timescale of minutes or hours. Goldberg's description of her arrival at college is an example of such an event. **General events** are things that happen over days, weeks, or, at the longest, months. Freshman orientation week is an example of a general event. **Lifetime periods** span many years. Goldberg's college years are an example of a lifetime period.

Notice that shorter levels of autobiographical memory are nested within longer levels. A person's lifetime consists of many lifetime periods. Each lifetime period contains many

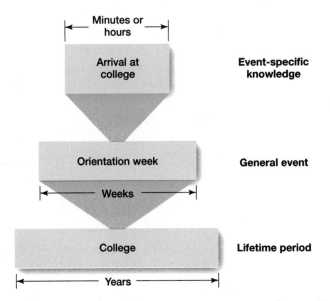

Figure 7.2 Conway's (1996) description of autobiographical memory in terms of layers of knowledge. Notice how brief events (arrival at college) are nested within longer events (orientation week), which are nested within even longer events (college years).

general events, which consist of a great deal of event-specific knowledge. Also, there can sometimes be overlap between lifetime periods, as when "being married to Sandy" overlaps with "my job at Google."

Conway's idea that autobiographical memories represent three levels of knowledge provides a general description of how autobiographical memories can cover time spans ranging from minutes to a large portion of a person's lifetime. But what do people actually remember about events in their lives? Research designed to answer that question shows that we remember some things better than others.

Memory Over the Life Span

What determines which particular life events we will remember years later? Personal milestones such as graduating from college or receiving a marriage proposal stand out, as do highly emotional events such as surviving a car accident (Pillemer, 1998). Events that become significant parts of a person's life story tend to be remembered well. For example, going out to dinner with someone for the first time might stand out if you ended up having a long-term relationship with that person, but the same dinner-date might be far less memorable if you never saw the person again.

Transition points in people's lives appear to be particularly memorable. This is illustrated by what Wellesley College juniors and seniors said when they were asked to recall the most influential event that happened during their freshman year. Most of the responses to this question were descriptions of events that occurred in September. When

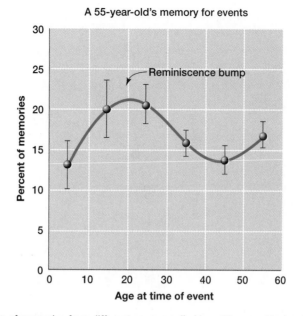

A 55-year-old's memory for events

Figure 7.3 Percentage of memories from different ages, recalled by a 55-year-old, showing the reminiscence bump. (Reprinted from *Journal of Memory and Language, 39,* R. W. Schrauf & D. C. Rubin, "Bilingual Autobiographical Memory in Older Adult Immigrants: A Test of Cognitive Explanations of the Reminiscence Bump and the Linguistic Encoding of Memories," pp. 437–457, Fig. 1, Copyright © 1998 with permission from Elsevier.)

alumni were asked the same question, they remembered more events from September of their freshman year *and* from the end of their senior year (another transition point) (Pillemer et al., 1996).

A particularly interesting result occurs when participants over 40 are asked to remember events in their lives. For these participants, memory is high for recent events and for events experienced from adolescence and early adulthood (between 10 and 30 years of age) (Figure 7.3) (Conway, 1996; Rubin et al., 1998). This enhanced memory for adolescence and young adulthood that can be demonstrated in people over 40 years old is called the **reminiscence bump**. One way the reminiscence bump has been demonstrated is by showing that people over 40 tend to have better memory for things like Academy Award winners, World Series winners, and popular music that occurred during the "bump."

Why are adolescence and young adulthood special times for encoding memories? The **life-narrative hypothesis** states that people assume their life identities during that time. It is the time of "our" generation and the time people return to when they become nostalgic for the "good old days."

Another explanation for the reminiscence bump, called the **cognitive hypothesis**, is that encoding is better during periods of rapid change that are followed by stability. Adolescence and young adulthood fit this description because the rapid changes that occur during these periods are followed by the relative stability of adult life.

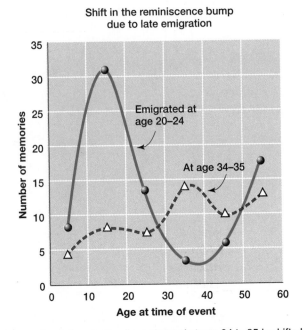

Shift in the reminiscence bump
due to late emigration

Emigrated at
age 20–24

At age 34–35

Figure 7.4 The reminiscence bump for people who emigrated at age 34 to 35 is shifted toward older ages, compared to the bump for people who emigrated between the ages of 20 to 24. (Reprinted from *Journal of Memory and Language, 39,* R. W. Schrauf & D. C. Rubin, "Bilingual Autobiographical Memory in Older Adult Immigrants: A Test of Cognitive Explanations of the Reminiscence Bump and the Linguistic Encoding of Memories," pp. 437–457, Fig. 2, Copyright © 1998 with permission from Elsevier.)

One way to test this hypothesis is to find people who have experienced rapid changes in their lives that occurred at a time past adolescence or young adulthood. The cognitive hypothesis would predict that the reminiscence bump should occur later for these people. To test this idea, Robert Schrauf and David Rubin (1998) determined the recollections of people who had emigrated to the United States in their 20s and in their mid-30s. Figure 7.4, which shows the memory curves for two groups of immigrants, indicates that the reminiscence bump occurs at the normal age for people who emigrated early, but is shifted to 15 years later for those who emigrated later, just as the cognitive change hypothesis would predict.

Flashbulb Memories

What about events that are brief but highly memorable? Everyone reading this book probably has vivid memories of the terrorist attacks of September 11, 2001. Do you remember when you first heard about the attacks? How did you find out? Where were you? What was your reaction? What did you do? I remember walking into the psychology department office and hearing from a secretary that someone had crashed a plane into the

World Trade Center. That was, of course, just the beginning of a day that turned into cancelled classes, the closing of the university, and the unfolding of a story that continues to have repercussions many years after the actual event. Other examples of events that people remember after many years include the space shuttle *Challenger* explosion (January 28, 1986) and the assassination of President John Kennedy (November 22, 1963).

The fact that people can often recall where they were and what they were doing when hearing about such shocking and emotionally charged events caused Roger Brown and James Kulick (1977) to call these memories flashbulb memories. Referring to the lasting memories many people have of the events of November 22, 1963, when President Kennedy was shot, Brown and Kulick state, "For an instant, the entire nation and perhaps much of the world stopped still to have its picture taken."

The Idea of a Special Mechanism Brown and Kulick argue that there is something special about the mechanisms responsible for flashbulb memories. It is not only that they occur under highly emotional circumstances that are remembered for long periods of time, but that they are especially vivid and detailed. Brown and Kulick describe the mechanism responsible for these vivid and detailed memories as a "Now Print" mechanism, as if these memories are created like a photograph that resists fading.

Brown and Kulick propose that one characteristic of events that trigger the "flashbulb" process is that they are high in consequentiality. That is, they have important consequences for a person's life. A study by Martin Conway and coworkers (1994) confirmed this idea by showing that people from Great Britain had much more accurate and long-lasting memories for the day that British Prime Minister Margaret Thatcher resigned (November 22, 1990) than did people from the United States (Figure 7.5). Clearly, Margaret Thatcher's resignation had important consequences for the British people but meant less to people in the United States.

Figure 7.5 People from Great Britain were far more accurate in recalling the day of Margaret Thatcher's resignation than people from the United States (Conway et al., 1994).

Strong Emotions Can Enhance Memory Although flashbulb memories are not always associated with strong emotions (Talarico & Rubin, 2003), there is often an emotional component to "flashbulb" events, and physiological research has demonstrated a link between emotions, memory, and a subcortical structure called the amygdala (see page 27, Chapter 2, and Figure 6.17, page 208).

Stephen Hamann and coworkers (1999) studied this link between emotions and physiology by measuring brain activity using PET while showing people emotionally charged pictures such as appealing people (pleasant) or lethal violence (unpleasant), and neutral pictures such as household scenes. They found that emotionally charged pictures caused greater activation of the amygdala than

neutral ones, and that the pictures that caused the greatest activation of the amygdala were most likely to be remembered later (also see Cahill et al., 1996).

The link between emotions and the amygdala has also been demonstrated by testing a patient, B.P., who had suffered damage to his amygdala. When participants without brain damage viewed a slide show about a boy and his mother in which the boy is injured halfway through the show, these participants had enhanced memory for the emotional part of the story (when the boy is injured). In contrast, B.P.'s memory was the same as that of the non–brain-damaged participants for the first part of the story but was not enhanced for the emotional part (Cahill et al., 1995). It appears, therefore, that emotions may trigger mechanisms in the amygdala that help us remember the event associated with the emotions.

Arguments Against a Special Mechanism   Although events classified as flashbulb memories are often important to a person and are often associated with strong emotions, many psychologists do not agree with the idea that flashbulb memories are caused by a special mechanism. For example, Ulric Neisser (2000) feels that we may remember events like those that happened on 9/11 not because of a special mechanism, but because we rehearse these events after they occur. This idea is called the narrative rehearsal hypothesis.

The narrative rehearsal hypothesis makes sense when we consider the events that followed 9/11 (Figure 7.6). How many times did you see the planes crashing into the World Trade Center replayed on TV? How much did you read about events surrounding 9/11

Figure 7.6 Posters like this one are just one of the many reminders of the terrorist attacks of September 11, 2001, that Americans have experienced since that date.

or talk about them with other people? Neisser argues that if rehearsal is the reason for our memories of significant events, then the term "flashbulb" is misleading.

Another thing that argues against a special flashbulb mechanism is that even though people often report that memories for these events are especially vivid, these memories are often inaccurate. Neisser supports this idea by the results of his study in which participants were asked how they heard about the explosion of the space shuttle *Challenger* that occurred in 1986 (Neisser & Harsch, 1992) (Figure 7.7). Participants filled out a questionnaire within a day after the explosion, and then filled out the same questionnaire 2½ to 3 years later. One participant's response, a day after the explosion, indicated that she had heard about it in class:

> I was in my religion class and some people walked in and started talking about [it]. I didn't know any details except that it had exploded and the schoolteacher's students had all been watching, which I thought was so sad. Then after class I went to my room and watched the TV program talking about it and I got all the details from that.

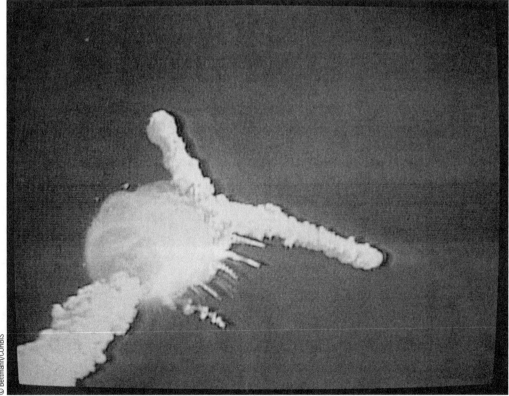

© Bettmann/CORBIS

Figure 7.7 Neisser and Harsch (1992) studied people's memories for the day they heard about the explosion of the space shuttle *Challenger*.

But 2½ years later, her memory had changed to the following:

> When I first heard about the explosion I was sitting in my freshman dorm room with my roommate and we were watching TV. It came on a news flash and we were both totally shocked. I was really upset and I went upstairs to talk to a friend of mine and then I called my parents.

Responses like these, in which participants reported first hearing about the explosion in one place, such as a classroom, and then later remembered that they first heard about it on TV, were common. Right after the explosion, 21 percent of the participants indicated that they first heard about it on TV, but 2½ years later 45 percent of the participants reported that they first heard about it on TV. Reasons for the increase in TV memories could be that the TV reports become more memorable through repetition and because TV is a major source of news. Thus, memory for the *Challenger* explosion had a property that is also a characteristic of memory for less dramatic, everyday, events: It was affected by people's past experiences (people may have seen accounts of the explosion) and their knowledge (people often first hear about important news on TV).

Another example of flashbulb memories that are inaccurate and may have been influenced by past experiences is provided by an experiment in which people were asked how they heard about the October 3, 1995, announcement of the verdict in the O. J. Simpson murder trial (Schmolck et al., 2000). When accuracy of memory was determined by comparing participants' reports long after the event to their reports shortly after the event, it was found that many of the responses at 32 months were inaccurate. For example, compare the 3-day and 32-month responses below:

> *Response at 3 days*: I was in the commuter lounge at college and saw it on TV. As 10:00 approached, more and more people came into the room.

> *Response at 32 months*: I first heard it while I was watching TV at home in my living room. My sister and father were with me. . . .

The large number of inaccurate responses for the *Challenger* and the O. J. Simpson studies suggests that perhaps memories that are supposed to be flashbulb memories may decay just like regular memories. In fact, the authors of the O. J. Simpson study conclude that "it seems unlikely that so-called flashbulb memories differ from ordinary episodic memories in any fundamental way" (Schmolck et al., 2000, p. 44).

This conclusion has been supported by an experiment in which a group of college students was asked a number of questions on September 12, 2001, the day after the terrorist attack on the World Trade Center and the Pentagon (Talarico & Rubin, 2003). Some of these questions were about the terrorist attack ("When did you first hear the news?"). Others were similar questions about an everyday event in the person's life that occurred in the days just preceding the attacks. Some participants were retested 1 week later, some 6 weeks later, and some 32 weeks later by asking them the same questions about the attack and the everyday event.

One result of this experiment was that the participants remembered fewer ⬡ made more errors at longer intervals after the events, with little difference between ults for the flashbulb and everyday memories (Figure 7.8a). This result supports the that there is nothing special about flashbulb memories. However, another result, show in Figure 7.8b, did indicate a difference between flashbulb and everyday memories: people's belief that their memories were accurate stayed high over the entire 32 week period for the flashbulb memories, but dropped for the everyday memories. Ratings of vividness and how well they could "relive" the events also stayed high and constant for the flashbulb memories but dropped for the everyday memories. Thus, the idea that flashbulb memories are special appears to be based at least partially on the fact that people *think* the memories are stronger and more accurate; however, *in reality*, there is little or no difference between flashbulb and everyday memories in terms of the amount remembered and the accuracy of what is remembered.

The question of whether flashbulb memories are "special" has generated a great deal of research, with most of the results indicating that these memories are not as permanent or accurate as the name flashbulb implies. But whether or not there is something special about memory for highly flashbulb-type events, the results of flashbulb memory research suggest an answer to a question that is important for understanding memory in general: How do people arrive at inaccurate memories?

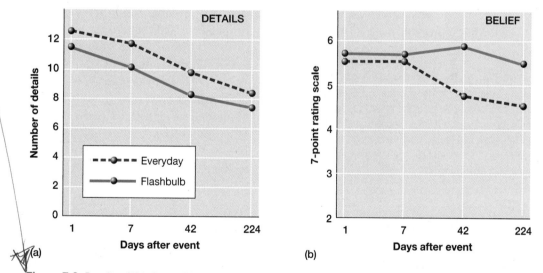

Figure 7.8 Results of Talarico and Rubin's (2003) experiment. (a) The decrease in the number of details remembered was similar for memories of 9/11 and for memories of an everyday event. (b) Participants' belief that their memory was accurate remained high for 9/11, but decreased for memories of the everyday event. (Extracted from "Consistency and Key Properties of Flashbulb and Everyday Memories," by J. M. Talarico & D. C. Rubin, *Psychological Science, 14,* 5, Fig. 1. Copyright © 2003 with permission from the American Psychological Society.)

answer to the question of why people arrive at inaccurate memories is suggested by result of the *Challenger* study in which many of the incorrect responses involved ing television. This same result occurred in the O. J. Simpson study, especially at 32 s, when the participants' memory was the least accurate. But the most significant of the O. J. Simpson study is shown in Figure 7.9, which presents the results in this study for the participants who had the least accurate responses.

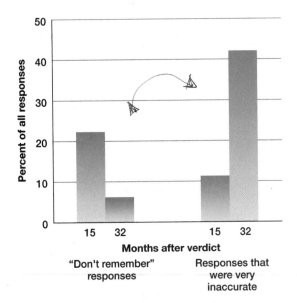

First consider the pair of bars on the left, which indicate the percentage of "don't remember" responses. Contrary to what we might expect, there are fewer "don't remember" responses at 32 months than at 15 months. One way to interpret this result is to propose that memory was better at 32 months. However, the pair of bars on the right, which indicate the percentage of inaccurate responses, suggest that this is not the case because responding at 32 months is far more inaccurate. Thus, what may be happening here is that at 32 months many of the participants may have based their memory reports on what seemed reasonable based on their past experiences in hearing important news stories, and this led them to report that they heard about the verdict on TV, even though they may have actually heard about it from some other source.

The idea that people's memories for an event are determined by things in addition to what actually happened has led many researchers to propose that what people remember is a "construction" that is based on what actually happened plus additional influences.

Figure 7.9 Results of Schmolck et al.'s (2000) study of people's memories for the day the O. J. Simpson verdict was announced. These are the results for people whose memory was least accurate. Notice that at 32 months, these people had fewer "don't remember" responses (left pair of bars), but more inaccurate responses (right pair of bars) than at 15 months.

HOW MEMORY IS CONSTRUCTED

We remember certain things better than others because of their special significance (the events of 9/11, a new job), or because of when they happened in our lives (during a period of change). But what people remember may not match what actually happened. When people report memories for past events they may not only omit things, but they may also distort or change things that happened and in some cases may even report things that never happened at all.

According to the constructive approach to memory, what people report as memories are constructed by the person based on what actually happened plus additional factors, such as other knowledge, experiences, and expectations. This approach is called *constructive* because the mind *constructs* memories based on a number of sources of information. One of the first experiments to suggest that memory is constructive is Bartlett's *War of the Ghosts* experiment.

Bartlett's "War of the Ghosts" Experiment

The British psychologist Fredrick Bartlett conducted a classic study of the constructive nature of memory, which is known as the "War of the Ghosts" experiment. In this experiment, which Bartlett ran before World War I and published in 1932, his participants read the following story from Canadian Indian Folklore.

The War of the Ghosts

One night two young men from Egulac went down to the river to hunt seals, and while they were there it became foggy and calm. Then they heard war-cries, and they thought: "Maybe this is a war-party." They escaped to the shore, and hid behind a log. Now canoes came up, and they heard the noise of paddles, and saw one canoe coming up to them. There were five men in the canoe, and they said:

"What do you think? We wish to take you along. We are going up the river to make war on the people."

One of the young men said: "I have no arrows."

"Arrows are in the canoe," they said.

"I will not go along. I might be killed. My relatives do not know where I have gone. But you," he said, turning to the other, "may go with them."

So one of the young men went, but the other returned home.

And the warriors went on up the river to a town on the other side of Kalama. The people came down to the water, and they began to fight, and many were killed. But presently the young man heard one of the warriors say: "Quick, let us go home; that Indian has been hit." Now he thought: "Oh, they are ghosts." He did not feel sick, but they said he had been shot.

So the canoes went back to Egulac, and the young man went ashore to his house and made a fire. And he told everybody and said: "Behold I accompanied the ghosts, and we went to fight. Many of our fellows were killed, and many of those who attacked us were killed. They said I was hit, and I did not feel sick."

He told it all, and then he became quiet. When the sun rose, he fell down. Something black came out of his mouth. His face became contorted. The people jumped up and cried. He was dead. (Bartlett, 1932, p. 65)

After his participants read this story, Bartlett asked them to recall it as accurately as possible. He then used the technique of repeated reproduction, in which the same participants came back a number of times to try to remember the story at longer and longer intervals after they first read it. This is similar to the repeated remembering technique used in the flashbulb memory experiments.

Bartlett's experiment is considered important because it was one of the first to use the repeated reproduction technique. But the main reason the "War of the Ghosts" experiment is considered important is because of the nature of the errors Bartlett's participants made and how Bartlett interpreted these errors.

Not surprisingly, participants eventually forgot much of the information in the story. Most participants' reproductions of the story were shorter than the original and contained many omissions and inaccuracies. But what interested Bartlett the most were the kinds of changes that occurred in the participants' reproductions. In particular, he noticed that the changes in the stories tended to reflect the participants' own culture. The original story, which came from Canadian folklore, was transformed by many of Bartlett's participants to make it more consistent with their own experience with the culture of Edwardian England. For example, one participant remembered the two men who were out hunting seals as being involved in a sailing expedition, the "canoes" as "boats," and the man who joined the war party as a fighter that any good Englishman would be proud of—ignoring his wounds, he continued fighting and won the admiration of the natives. The original story, which was a folktale that seemed strange to Bartlett's English participants, was "constructed," or "reconstructed," into a story that reflected characteristics of the culture in which they were raised.

Even though Bartlett's experiment was one of the first that considered the idea that changes that occur in memory can be related to a constructive process, it had little impact on psychology when it was published in 1932 because at that time, behaviorism was gaining momentum. Eventually, however, the "War of the Ghosts" experiment came to be considered a classic, and the idea that memory is a constructive process has been confirmed in many other experiments.

Major finding
reconstruction

Educated Guesses About High School Grades

Another example of memory that appears to involve a constructive process is provided by a study in which college students were asked to remember their high school grades (Bahrick et al., 1996). Checking the students' reports against their high school transcripts indicated that the students had accurately remembered *A* grades 89 percent of the time, but accurately remembered *D* grades only 29 percent of the time. Seventy-nine of the 99 students inflated their grades by remembering some of them as being higher than what they actually received.

There are a number of possible reasons for this result. One reason could be that people tend to remember positive events more readily than negative events (Loftus, 1982). Thus, *A*'s or *B*'s would be remembered better than *C*'s or *D*'s. Another reason is related to the idea that memory is constructive. Someone who is a good student, but who doesn't remember what grade they received in 10th grade geometry, might base their guess on the fact that most of their grades were *A*'s and *B*'s. Because a guess of *A* or *B* would have a good chance of being correct, they take a "best guess" approach and guess *A*. Thus, our memory may sometimes be created from guesses that are based on our past experiences with similar events.

educated guess

→what about me?? I remember bad grades...
1) geometry (improved!), 2) analysis, 3) Gaillard essay
definitely really poor, maybe not B's...

Source Monitoring and Source Misattribution

CogLab

Remember/
Know

Memory as a constructive process is also illustrated by **source monitoring**, the process by which we determine the origins of memories, knowledge, or beliefs (M. K. Johnson et al., 1993). Source monitoring is illustrated by the following example. Barbara unexpectedly encounters someone she has met recently. She is able to remember that his name is Roger, but can't remember when she was first introduced to him. Thus, the following thoughts race through her mind, as she is talking to him: *Is he in my cognitive psychology class? No, that was someone else. Did I meet him at that party Saturday night? Oh, right, I remember now. He's the guy I was talking to in the ticket line at the Student Union last Thursday.* Barbara has solved a source monitoring problem by determining when she first met Roger.

Source monitoring provides an example of the constructive nature of memory because when we remember something, we usually retrieve the memory first and then use a decision process to determine where that memory came from, as in this example in which Barbara remembered Roger but then had to consider a number of possibilities for where she met Roger before deciding on the correct one (Mitchell & Johnson, 2000).

We often accurately remember the source of our memories, but sometimes we make errors that lead to **source misattribution,** in which we attribute something we remember to the wrong source. An experiment by Larry Jacoby and coworkers (1989) illustrates how source misattributions can occur (Figure 7.10). In the acquisition part of the experiment, Jacoby had participants read a number of made-up nonfamous names like *Sebastian Weissdorf* and *Valerie Marsh.*

In the *immediate test,* which was presented right after the participants saw the list of nonfamous names, participants were told to pick out the names of famous people from a list containing (1) the nonfamous names they had just seen, (2) new nonfamous names that they had never seen before, and (3) famous names, like Minnie Pearl (a country singer) or Roger Bannister (the first person to run a 4-minute mile), that many people might have recognized in 1988. Just before this test, participants were told that all of the names they had just seen in the first part of the experiment were nonfamous. Because the test was given shortly after the participants had seen the first list of nonfamous names, they correctly identified most of the old nonfamous names (like Sebastian Weissdorf and Valerie Marsh) as being nonfamous.

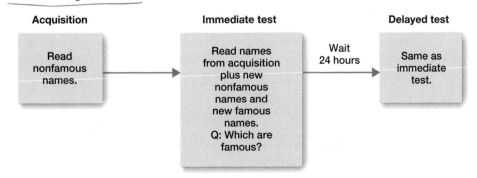

Figure 7.10 Design of Jacoby et al.'s (1989) "becoming famous overnight" experiment.

The interesting result appeared in the *delayed test*, which occurred 24 hours later. When tested on the same names a day later, participants were more likely to identify the old nonfamous names as being famous. Thus, even though they may have identified Sebastian Weissdorf as not being famous in the immediate test, his name was more likely to be labeled as famous on the delayed test 24 hours later. Because of this result, Jacoby's paper is titled "Becoming Famous Overnight."

How did Sebastian Weissdorf become famous overnight? To answer this question, put yourself in the place of one of Jacoby's participants. It is 24 hours since you first saw the names, and you now have to decide whether Sebastian Weissdorf is famous or nonfamous. How do you make your decision? Sebastian Weissdorf doesn't pop out as someone you know of, but the name is familiar. You ask yourself the question: "Why is this name familiar?" This is a source monitoring problem, because to answer this question you need to determine the source of your familiarity. You could be familiar with the name Sebastian Weissdorf because you saw it 24 hours earlier, or because it is the name of a famous person. Apparently, some of Jacoby's participants decided that the familiarity was caused by fame, and so the previously unknown Sabastian Weissdorf became famous!

This example illustrates the constructive nature of memory because it involves a decision process. In this particular example, the cue of familiarity led to source misattribution. In the next section we will continue our discussion of the constructive nature of memory by describing a number of examples in which memory errors (which are often also called *false memories*) can be traced to this constructive process.

KNOWLEDGE FROM PAST EXPERIENCES CAN CREATE FALSE MEMORIES

The way Bartlett's participants changed the "War of the Ghosts" story was influenced by their past experience in growing up in Edwardian England. We will now look at some more examples of how past experiences can result in errors of memory.

Making Inferences   *panding → hammer*

John Bransford and Marcia Johnson (1973) had participants read a number of action statements. Statement 1 below is an example of one of the action statements that was read by participants in the experimental group, and statement 2 is an example of one of the action statements read by participants in the control group (Figure 7.11).

1. *Experimental Group:* John was trying to fix the bird house. He was pounding the nail when his father came out to watch him do the work.
2. *Control Group:* John was trying to fix the bird house. He was looking for the nail when his father came out to watch him do the work.

Both groups were then tested by presenting them with a number of test statements that they had not seen, and were asked to indicate whether they had seen them before. State-

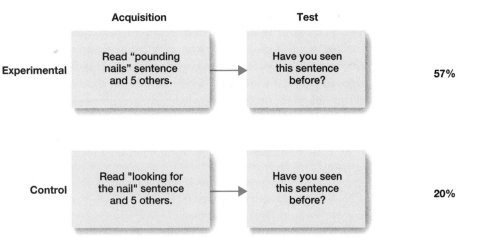

Figure 7.11 Design and results of Bransford and Johnson's (1973) experiment that tested people's memory for the wording of action statements. More errors were made by participants in the experimental group because they identified more sentences as being originally presented, even though they were not.

ment 3 is an example of a test statement that went with statements 1 and 2. Notice that this statement contains the word *hammer*, which was not contained in either of the original sentences.

3. *Experimental and Control Groups:* John was using a hammer to fix the birdhouse. He was looking for the nail when his father came out to watch him.

Participants in the experimental group said they had previously seen 57 percent of the test statements, but participants in the control group said they had previously seen only 20 percent of the test statements. Thus, the participants in the experimental group, who had read the sentence that mentioned *pounding* the nail, were more likely to be misled into thinking that the original sentence had contained the word *hammer*. Apparently, the participants in the experimental group inferred, from the use of the word *pounding*, that a hammer had been used, even though it was never mentioned. This makes sense because we usually pound nails with hammers, but in this case, the participant's inference has caused an error of memory.

Here is the scenario used in another memory experiment, which was designed specifically to elicit inferences based on the participants' past experiences (Arkes & Freedman, 1984):

In a baseball game, the score is tied 1 to 1. The home team has runners on first and third, with one out. A ground ball is hit to the shortstop. The shortstop throws to second base, attempting a double play. The runner who was on third scores, so it is now 2–1 in favor of the home team.

After hearing a story similar to this one, participants were asked to indicate whether the sentence "The batter was safe at first" was part of the passage. From looking at the story, you can see that this sentence was never presented, and most of the participants who didn't know much about baseball correctly indicated this. However, participants who knew the rules of baseball were more likely to say that the sentence had been presented. They based this judgment on their knowledge that if the runner on third had scored, then the double play must have failed, which means that the batter safely reached first. Knowledge, in this example, resulted in a correct inference about what probably happened in the ball game, but in an incorrect inference about whether they had previously seen the sentence in the passage.

Schemas and Scripts

We've seen how a person's knowledge that hammers are used to pound nails and that a runner can score if there is one out and a double play fails can result in inferences that cause errors of memory. We also have knowledge about many other things just from being part of a particular culture and from our day-to-day experience. For example, you are probably quite knowledgeable about college. You know about registering for courses, how course schedules work, studying for exams, and perhaps attending sporting events (depending on your school and your interest in sports). The knowledge of what is involved in a particular experience—be it college, working at a particular job, or being in a campus organization—is called a schema for that experience.

In an experiment that studied how memory is influenced by schemas, participants were seated in an office waiting to be in an experiment (Figure 7.12). When the participants were called into another room, they were told that the experiment was actually a memory experiment, and their task was to write down what they saw while they were sitting in the office (Brewer & Treyens, 1981). The participants responded by writing down many of the things they remembered seeing, but also included some things that were not there but which fit into their "office schema." For example, although there were no books in the office, 30 percent of the participants reported that they saw books.

A script is a type of schema. Like a schema, it is our conception of what a particular experience is usually like, but the key characteristic that makes this conception a *script* is that it is a *sequence of actions* that describe an activity. For example, your script for going to class might include the following sequence: (1) get to class 10 minutes before it is scheduled to start, (2) wait for students from the previous class to leave, (3) enter class and find a seat, (4) take notes on the lecture, and (5) leave when the professor has finished the lecture.

Scripts can influence our memory by setting up expectations about what usually happens in a particular situation. For example, Gordon Bower and coworkers (1979) asked participants to remember short passages like the following.

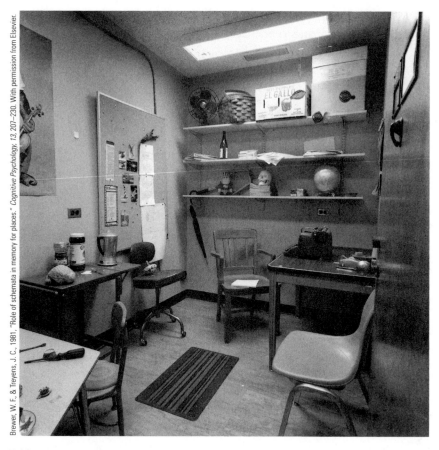

Brewer, W. F., & Treyens, J. C., 1981, "Role of schemata in memory for places." *Cognitive Psychology, 13,* 207–230. With permission from Elsevier.

Figure 7.12 Office in which Brewer and Treyens' (1981) participants waited before being tested on their memory for what was present in the office.

The Dentist

Bill had a bad toothache. It seemed like forever before he finally arrived at the dentist's office. Bill looked around at the various dental posters on the wall. Finally the dental hygienist checked and x-rayed his teeth. He wondered what the dentist was doing. The dentist said that Bill had a lot of cavities. As soon as he'd made another appointment, he left the dentist's office.

The participants read a number of passages like this one, all of which were about familiar activities like going to the dentist, going swimming, or going to a party. After a delay period, the participants were given the titles of the stories they had read and were told to write down what they remembered about each story as accurately as possible. The participants created stories that included much material that matched the original stories, but they also included material that wasn't presented in the original story but which is part of the script for the activity described. For example, for the dentist story some participants reported reading that "Bill checked in with the dentist's receptionist." This statement is part of most people's "going to the dentist" script, but was not included in the original story.

The results of these experiments on schemas and scripts show how knowledge can affect memory, and also shows how semantic memory can influence episodic memory (see page 188). Remember from Chapter 6 that episodic memory is memory for events that a person has experienced, and that semantic memory is memory for knowledge about the world that is not tied to any specific personal experience. A person's knowledge about the world, such as what is usually contained in an office, that hammers are used to pound nails, the rules of baseball, and what it is like to go to the dentist, are all part of semantic memory. Remembering sentences in a story that you just read or the contents of an office you have recently occupied are all examples of episodic memory.

We have described a number of experiments in which people's knowledge of the world has caused errors in their episodic memory. This interaction between semantic memory and episodic memory can also be demonstrated in simple memory experiments in which participants are asked to remember a list of words.

Remembering a List of Words

Try the following demonstration.

■ Demonstration

Memory for a List

Read the following list at a rate of about one item per second then cover the list and write down as many of the words as possible. In order for this demonstration to work, it is important that you complete the memory test before reading past the list of words.

bed, rest, awake, tired, dream
wake, night, blanket, doze, slumber
snore, pillow, peace, yawn, drowsy

Does your list of remembered words include any words that are not on the list above? When I present this list to my class, there are always a substantial number of students who report that they remember the word "sleep." Remembering *sleep* is a false memory because it isn't on the list. This false memory occurs because people associate *sleep* with other words on the list (Deese, 1959; Roediger & McDermott, 1995). This is similar to the effect of schemas, in which people create false memories for office furnishings that aren't present because they associate these office furnishings with what is usually found in offices. Again, constructive processes have created an error in memory.

PERSONAL BIAS CAN AFFECT MEMORY

Memory can be affected, and sometimes distorted, by common biases that are related to personal and social factors such as how people perceive themselves and how they think about events in their lives.

Egocentric Bias

The **egocentric bias** is the tendency for people to see themselves in the best possible light. Rasyid Sanitioso and coworkers (1990) demonstrated this effect by informing one group of participants that research has shown that extraverts (outgoing) people are more academically and professionally successful, and informing another group that introverted people are more successful.

Participants in each group were then asked to explain why they thought extraverts (or introverts) would be more successful, and then they were asked, in what appeared to be an unrelated study, to list autobiographical memories about their own past behaviors, thoughts, and feelings that illustrated extraversion or introversion. The results showed that participants tended to list more experiences that matched the traits they were told were more desirable. Thus, participants who were told that introverted people tended to be more successful included more introverted memories early in their list than did the extravert-success participants. Sanitioso interprets that result to mean that people search through their memory for examples that picture themselves in the best possible light.

what was time elapse?

↳ what about depressed people?? (next pg.)

Consistency Bias

The **consistency bias**—which, like the egocentric bias, is related to how people perceive themselves—refers to people's tendency to perceive their basic attitudes and behaviors as remaining fairly consistent over time. Gregory Marcus (1986) studied this effect by having participants fill out a survey about how they feel about various social issues, such as legalizing marijuana, affirmative action, and women's rights. The participants did this in 1973 and then 9 years later, in 1982. In general, participants' attitudes shifted in a more liberal direction, so while 29 percent of the participants strongly favored equal roles for women in 1973, 43 percent favored equal roles in 1982. This change in attitude from 1973 to 1982 is reflected by the low correlation of 0.39 between the 1973 and 1982 attitudes (left bar in Figure 7.13).

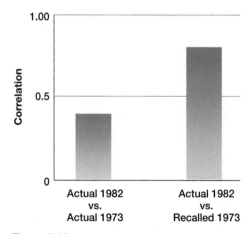

Figure 7.13 Results of Marcus's (1986) experiment that demonstrated the operation of the consistency bias. In 1982, people recalled their attitudes from 1973 as being similar to their attitudes in 1982, as indicated by the high correlation between the two (right bar). However, in reality, the 1982 and 1973 attitudes were often different, as indicated by the lower correlation (left bar).

For the 1982 survey, participants were also asked to look back in time and remember how they felt about those issues in 1973. Rather than remembering the shift in attitudes that actually occurred, participants tended to report that their 1973 attitudes were similar to their present attitudes. This is reflected by the correlation of 0.80 between their 1982 attitudes and their *recalled* 1973 attitudes (right bar in Figure 7.13). This perception that their attitudes remained fairly constant, even though they changed substantially, is an example of the consistency bias.

Positive-Change Bias

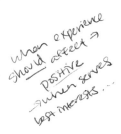

The **positive-change bias** refers to some people's tendency to perceive that "things are getting better." This bias, as well as the egocentric bias, may not hold for everyone. For example, people who are depressed might not see themselves in the best possible light and might not think things are getting better. AitA!

Susan Sprecher (1999) demonstrated the positive-change bias by surveying 101 couples in committed relationships every year for 4 years. Forty-one of the couples were still together at the end of the 4 years and had completed the survey every year. Each year they rated their current level of "love and affection" and other aspects of the relationship, and they also rated how much they thought their feelings had changed since the last survey. The results showed that people tended to perceive each year as better than the previous year, even though their love and affection ratings remained fairly consistent from year to year. (Note that the consistency bias would predict that people would rate their relationships as remaining essentially the same. Apparently, different biases can operate in different situations.) ⟶ So ⟶ beliefs ⟶ Constant

The positive-change bias has been demonstrated in other areas as well. For example, people who took a course to improve their study skills rated their skills as having improved after taking the course, when actually little or no change had occurred (Conway & Ross, 1984). What is particularly interesting about this result is that the participants achieved their perception of positive change by remembering that their study skills used to be worse than they actually were. Thus, in this case, the feeling that things were getting better resulted in a misremembering of how good (or bad) things were in the past.

 ## Test Yourself 7.1

1. What portions of your overall long-term memories would be classified as episodic? What portion of episodic would be autobiographical? How does Conway suggest that you could classify different sections of your life in terms of "layers of knowledge"?

2. What would a plot of "events remembered" versus "age" look like for a 50-year-old person? What theories have been proposed to explain the peak that occurs in this function? How does the "immigrant study" support one of these hypotheses?

3. The idea of flashbulb memories has been debated by psychologists. What is behind the idea that some memories are "special" and are therefore labeled as "flashbulb" memories? What is the evidence that calls the idea of flashbulb memories into question?

4. How do the results of the O. J. Simpson study, Bartlett's "War of the Ghosts" experiment, and the "remembering high school grades" experiment all support the idea of the constructive nature of memory?

5. Source misattributions provide another example of the constructive nature of memory. Describe what source monitoring and source misattribution are and why they are considered "constructive."

6. There have been many experimental demonstrations of how knowledge we have gained from past experience can result in memory errors. Describe how the studies that involved the following questions demonstrated this effect of knowledge, and consider the role of inference in each of these examples: (1) Was John pounding a nail? (2) Was the runner safe at first? (3) What was in the office? (Why is this an example of a schema?) (4) What happened at the dentist? (Why is this an example of a script?)

7. Memory errors can be caused not only by what we know, but by biases that people bring to various situation. Give examples of how the egocentric bias, the consistency bias, and the positive-change bias can result in memory errors.

MEMORY IS NOT A VIDEO RECORDER

Now that we have looked at a number of the things that can cause errors of memory, let's consider the implications of these findings by imagining a conversation about memory you might have with a skeptical friend.

A Hypothetical Conversation

You open the conversation by saying, "I'm learning some interesting things about memory in my cognitive psychology course."

"Right," says your friend. "Memory, as I understand it, basically works like a video recorder. Everything we experience is recorded and stored in the brain."

"Well, if that's the case," you state, "how come we often can't remember things that we once knew?"

"OK," your friend says, "I agree that memory doesn't create a complete playback of a person's experiences, but this occurs because our memory 'recorder' isn't always able to play back all of the information that it has recorded."

"That's closer to the way it works, but it doesn't explain the fact that some of the information that we do play back is different from the information that was originally 'recorded.' Memory is often not a perfect copy of what went in. It is determined by the information that went in, plus other factors, which often distort memory."

After you provide a few examples to support your argument, your friend is finally convinced that memory does not work like a video recorder. But he responds by saying, "What a stupid way to design a system. What's the point of a system in which false constructions and errors occur as part of its normal operation?"

You admit that when you first learned about memory errors and distortions you had similar thoughts yourself, but that you now understand that it might not always be an advantage to have a perfect memory.

Why Does Memory Work That Way?

What could be a disadvantage of having a memory system that can "record" and "play back" everything? One way to answer this question is to consider people whose memory systems do operate like a video recorder. One such person was Shereshevskii (S), whose memory enabled him to remember the exact wording of conversations that had taken place years before. After extensively studying S, the Russian psychologist A. R. Luria (1975) concluded that S's memory was "virtually limitless."

While S's impressive memory made it possible for him to make a living by demonstrating his memory powers on stage, it made many aspects of his life difficult. For one thing, S had trouble forgetting things he no longer needed. His mind was like a blackboard on which everything that happened was written on the board and couldn't be erased. There are many things that flit through our minds briefly and then we don't need them again. Unfortunately for S, these things stayed on his memory "blackboard" even when he wished they would go away.

S also was not good at reasoning that involved drawing inferences or "filling in the blanks" based on partial information. We do this so often that we take this ability for granted, but S's ability to record massive amounts of information, and his inability to erase it, may have hindered his ability to do this.

S's exceptional memory demonstrates that it may not be an advantage to remember everything perfectly. Storing everything that is experienced was apparently annoying to S, but it is also an inefficient way for a system to operate because storing everything that hits the receptors can overload the system. To avoid this "overload," our memory system is designed to selectively remember things that are particularly important to us or that occur often in our environment (Anderson & Schooler, 1991).

S's difficulty in drawing inferences is interesting because we've also seen that our ability to draw inferences sometimes leads our memory astray. But using inference to go beyond the information provided is also one of the hallmarks of intelligent behavior. This intelligence of memory helps us fill in the blanks when we have incomplete information. For example, remember the experiment in which some participants inferred that John was using a hammer after reading that "He was pounding the nail. . . ." Imagine how tiresome it would be if we had to explain everything in excruciating detail in order to know what

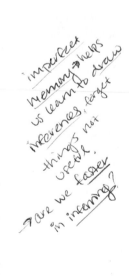
imperfect memory helps us learn to draw inferences, forget things not useful.
are we faster in inferring?

was happening. After all, John *could* be pounding the nail into the birdhouse with a rock! Luckily, we know that a hammer is the tool that is usually used to pound nails.

After listening to all of these arguments your friend is impressed. He now understands that a system designed for intelligent behavior is superior to one that blindly records information, like a video recorder, even if the price is that sometimes a few errors occur. But he has one more point to make.

"OK, I can see why memory doesn't work like a video recorder, but what about those personal biases you told me about? How intelligent is it for someone to remember their attitudes as being consistent when they aren't, or to change their memory so they appear to be functioning better than they really are? Isn't that just denying reality?"

"Yes," you say, "in a way it is, but maybe the purpose of memory is not always to create as accurate a picture of the past as possible. Remember that we're dealing with people here, who have basic needs and motivations. Can you see that recalling events in this way might sometimes make people feel better about themselves?" (Ross & Buehler, 1994).

This idea that memory may not always be used in the service of accuracy, is what novelist Isabel Allende had in mind when she wrote "Memory is fiction. We select the brightest and the darkest, ignoring what we are ashamed of, and so embroider the broad tapestry of our lives" (Allende, 2001, p. 303). Allende's assessment of memory as "fiction" may be overly dramatic, but she is correct in asserting that memory is not a record of everything that has happened in our lives, but is a selective record that may leave out some of the things we find least flattering to ourselves.

memory : in service of self-concept (to some extent!)

The Functionality of Memory

Based on this discussion about why memory doesn't work like a video recorder, you might be tempted to conclude that memory is too prone to error to be useful. But we can reject this conclusion based solely on the fact that a functioning memory is clearly essential for our survival, and that humans, even with their less-than-perfect memories, have survived as a species.

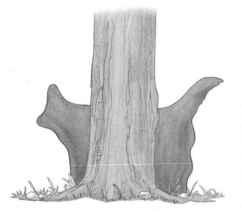

Figure 7.14 The "animal lurking behind a tree" picture from Chapter 3. This looks like an animal, but maybe it isn't.

One way to appreciate the survival value of the memory system is to remember our discussion in Chapter 3 of why we may erroneously perceive the object in Figure 3.37 (repeated here as Figure 7.14) as an animal lurking behind a tree. Our perceptual system, like our memory system, is designed to use partial information to arrive at a "best guess" solution to a perceptual problem, which is correct most of the time. Occasionally, this system comes up with an erroneous perception (see Figure 3.38), but most of the time it provides the correct answer. The few errors we may experience are more than compensated for by a feature of our perceptual system that is essential for our survival—its great speed even when faced with incomplete information.

Our memory system works the same way. Although it may not come up with the correct answers every time, it usually provides us with what we need to know to function rapidly and efficiently, even though we may not always have complete information.

But sometimes our memory system may be called on to do things that it is not designed to do. When a person testifying in court is asked to identify the person whom they saw committing a crime, it is important that they point to exactly the right person, and not someone who looks something like the right person. As we will see shortly, this is a difficult task, not only because perceiving and remembering faces is difficult, but also because our memories can be affected by things that happen between the time we experience something and when we are asked to remember what we have experienced. One of the things that can influence memory is the power of suggestion. In the next section we will consider research that shows how powerful suggestion can be as a way of affecting memory, and we will then look specifically at what this research tells us about eyewitness testimony in court cases.

MEMORY CAN BE MODIFIED OR CREATED BY SUGGESTION

People are suggestible. Advertisements pitching the virtues of different products influence what people purchase. Arguments put forth by politicians, opinion-makers, and friends influence who people vote for. Advertisements and political arguments are examples of things that might influence a person's attitudes, beliefs, or behaviors. We will now see how information presented by others can also influence a person's memory for past events. We first consider a phenomenon called the misinformation effect, in which a person's memory for an event is modified by things that happen after the event has occurred.

The Misinformation Effect

In a typical memory experiment, a person sees or hears some stimulus such as words, or letters, or sentences, and is asked to report what he or she experienced. But what if the experimenter were to add information that went beyond simply asking the person what they remembered? This is the question that Elizabeth Loftus and coworkers asked in a series of pioneering experiments that established the misinformation effect—misleading information presented after a person witnesses an event can change how that person describes that event later. This misleading information is referred to as misleading postevent information, or MPI.

In a typical experiment, participants see a series of slides depicting a traffic accident in which one car runs a stop sign and hits another car (Figure 7.15). Some participants then listen to an accurate description of the event and others hear MPI that the sign at the intersection was a yield sign (rather than the stop sign that the participants actually saw). After hearing the accurate or inaccurate description, participants are given a test on critical details in the story. For example, they would be asked to indicate whether they saw a

Figure 7.15 Picture of a traffic accident similar to one seen by the participants in the Loftus et al. (1978) "misleading postevent information" experiment.

stop sign or a yield sign at the intersection. The misinformation effect is demonstrated by the fact that those in the MPI group were more likely to pick the yield sign than were participants who were not exposed to MPI (Loftus et al., 1978).

Presentation of MPI can alter not only what participants report they saw, but their conclusions about other characteristics of the situation. For example, in another experiment (Loftus & Palmer, 1974), participants who had viewed the car-crash slides were asked either (1) "How fast were the cars going when they smashed into each other?" or (2) "How fast were the cars going when they hit each other?" Although both groups saw the same event, the average speed estimate by participants who heard the word "smashed" was 41 miles per hour, whereas the estimates for participants who heard "hit" was 34 miles per hour. Even more interesting for the study of memory are the participants' responses to the question "Did you see any broken glass?" which Loftus asked one week after they had seen the slide show. Although there was no broken glass in the original presentation, 32 percent of the participants who heard "smashed" before estimating the speed reported seeing broken glass, whereas only 14 percent of the participants who heard "hit" reported seeing the glass (see Loftus, 1993, 1998). *smash = glass →*

The misinformation effect not only shows how false memories can be created by suggestion but also provides an example of how different researchers can interpret the same data in different ways. Remember that the goal of cognitive psychology is to determine mental processes, but that these mental processes must be inferred from the results of behavioral or physiological experiments. The question posed by the misinformation effect is, "What is happening to the participants' memory?" Different researchers have proposed different answers to this question.

Loftus explains the misinformation effect by proposing the memory impairment hypothesis, which states that MPI impairs or replaces memories that were formed during the original experiencing of an event. According to this idea, seeing a stop sign creates a memory trace for a stop sign, but presentation of MPI that a yield sign was present causes the memory for the stop sign to be replaced by a new memory for a yield sign, so the memory for the stop sign is *impaired*.

Another explanation, proposed by Michael McCloskey and Maria Zaragoza (1985), is that the misinformation effect occurs not because the participants' original memory is changed, but because some participants don't form accurate memories in the first place, and so use the MPI to "fill in" these memory gaps. This idea of poor initial memory for details is supported by the experiments on *change blindness* we discussed in Chapter 4 (see page 122), which showed that people are often unable to tell when changes have been made in a picture of an environmental scene.

To support the idea that MPI is filling in memory gaps, McCloskey and Zaragoza showed participants a series of slides that depicted a maintenance man stealing a calculator and sticking the calculator under a hammer in his tool box. After seeing the sequence, one group of participants (the MPI group) read a description of what happened that said that a screwdriver was present at the place where the hammer had appeared in the original story. The screwdriver was MPI. Another group of participants (the control group) read a description that contained neutral information. For example, instead of mentioning the hammer, it said that a *tool* was present.

One way to test participants' memory in this experiment would be to ask them whether a hammer or a screwdriver was present in the original story. If some participants picked the screwdriver, even though they had seen the hammer, this would support Loftus's memory impairment hypothesis. But McCloskey and Zaragoza used a different test procedure: They asked participants in both the MPI (screwdriver) and control (tool) groups whether a hammer or a wrench had been present in the original story. They reasoned that if the MPI had eliminated the memory for the hammer, as the memory impairment hypothesis predicts, then participants would be less likely to choose *hammer*.

The results of the experiment, shown in Table 7.1, indicate that this result did not occur. The hammer was picked equally by the MPI group and the control group. Since presenting the MPI (the screwdriver) did not decrease the likelihood that participants would respond with *hammer*, McCloskey and Zaragoza concluded that MPI does not erase original information, and that the memory impairment hypothesis is, therefore, not correct.

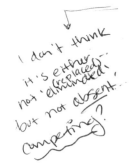

I don't think it's either 'not replaced' or 'eliminated' but not 'absent'? (competing?)

Table 7.1	Design and Results of the McClosky and Zaragoza Experiment		
Group	What They Saw	What They Heard Afterward	% Choosing Hammer
MPI	Hammer in box	"... screwdriver was in the box."	72
Control	Hammer in box	"... tool was in the box."	75

McCloskey and Zaragoza's challenge to Loftus's memory impairment hypothesis has led to a lively debate in which additional evidence for and against the memory impairment mechanism has been presented, and additional explanations for the misinformation effect have been proposed (see Lindsay, 1993; Loftus, 1993; Wright et al., 2001; Zaragoza & McCloskey, 1989).

While the mechanism that causes the misinformation effect is still being discussed by researchers, there is no doubt that the effect is real, and that experimenters' suggestions can influence participants' reports in memory experiments. Some of the most dramatic demonstrations of the effect of experimenter suggestibility are those that have shown that suggestion can cause people to believe that events had occurred early in their lives when in fact these events had never happened.

Creating False Memories for Early Events in People's Lives

Ira Hyman and coworkers (1995) created false memories for long-ago events in an experiment in which they contacted the parents of their participants and asked them to provide descriptions of actual events that happened when the participants were children. The experimenters then also created false events that never happened to their participants, such as a birthday that included a clown and a pizza, and spilling a bowl of punch at a wedding reception.

Participants were given some of the information from the parents' descriptions and were told to elaborate on them. They were also given some of the information from the false events and were told to elaborate on them as well. The result was that 20 percent of the false events were "recalled" and described in some detail by the participants. For example, the following conversation occurred when an interviewer (I) asked a participant (P) what he remembered about the following false event.

> I: At age six you attended a wedding reception and while you were running around with some other kids you bumped into a table and turned a punch bowl over on a parent of the bride.
> P: I have no clue. I have never heard that one before. Age 6?
> I: Uh-huh.
> P: No clue.
> I: Can you think of any details?
> P: Six years old; we would have been in Spokane, um, not at all.
> I: OK.

However, in a second interview that occurred two days later, the participant responded as follows:

> I: The next one was when you were six years old and you were attending a wedding.
> P: The wedding was my best friend in Spokane, T___. Her brother, older brother was getting married, and it was over here in P___, Washington, cause that's where

her family was from and it was in the summer or the spring because it was really hot outside and it was right on the water. It was an outdoor wedding and I think we were running around and knocked something over like the punch bowl or something and um made a big mess and of course got yelled at for it.

I: Do you remember anything else?

P: No.

I: OK.

What is most interesting about this participant's response is that he didn't remember the wedding the first time, but did remember it the second time. Apparently, hearing about the event and then waiting caused the event to emerge as a false memory. One way this can be explained is in terms of familiarity. When questioned about the wedding the second time, the participant's familiarity with the wedding from the first exposure caused him to accept the wedding as having actually happened. Does this sound familiar? Remember Jacoby's "becoming famous overnight" experiment, in which familiarity led participants to erroneously label Sebastian Weissdorf and other nonfamous people as being famous. Both of these cases illustrate source misattribution because the participants interpreted the source of their familiarity to something that never happened.

Yes! link w/ Jacoby

Same misattribution

Suggestion has also succeeded in creating false memories for events that supposedly occurred early in infancy. Susan DuBreuil and coworkers (1998) told participants that they had a personality profile that made it likely that they could remember things from their childhood. They were also told that memories are permanent, and it's just a matter of getting them out of storage. After receiving this information, participants were told that "about the time you were born, hospitals in the United States were influenced by research on the effects of early visual stimulation and so began hanging mobiles over cribs." Participants were then hypnotized, were instructed to go to when they were one day old and lying in their crib, and were asked to describe what they were experiencing. Sixty-one percent of the participants reported seeing a mobile or described something that was consistent with the general characteristics of a mobile, and one-third of them believed their reports were probably or definitely real memories (DuBreuil et al., 1998).

I think this is dumb...

Brain Damage and the Constructive Nature of Memory

We have described many ways in which the constructive processes of memory can create false memories. All of our examples have been from experiments on people with intact, normal memory systems. However, in some people with damage to their prefrontal lobes, and sometimes medial temporal lobes, this process of constructing memories can become exaggerated by confabulation, the process by which outlandish false memories are created. Confabulation is illustrated by the following excerpt from an interview with patient H.W., who had prefrontal cortex damage (Moskovitch, 1995).

Q. Can you tell me a little about yourself? How old are you?

A. I'm 40, 42, pardon me, 62.

Q. Are you married or single?

A. Married.

Q. How long have you been married?

A. About 4 months.

Q. What's your wife's name?

A. Martha.

Q. How many children do you have?

A. Four. (He laughs). Not bad for 4 months!

Q. How old are your children?

A. The eldest is 32, his name is Bob, and the youngest is 22, his name is Joe. (The ages are close to the actual ages).

Q. (He laughs again). How did you get these children in 4 months?

A. They're adopted.

Q. Who adopted them?

A. Martha and I.

Q. Immediately after you got married you wanted to adopt these older children?

A. Before we were married we adopted one of them, two of them. The eldest girl Brenda and Bob, and Joe and Dina since we were married.

Q. Does it all sound a little strange to you, what you are saying?

A. (He laughs.) I think it is a little strange.

Q. Your record says that you've been married for over 30 years. Does that sound more reasonable to you?

A. No.

Q. Do you really believe that you have been married for 4 months?

A. Yes.

(From Moskovitch, 1995, pp. 227–228)

Although the patient's answers to some of the questions may seem absurd (and even the patient acknowledges this!), one characteristic of confabulation is that the patient believes that his statements are true. → looks like another of those inference e.g.'s

One conclusion that has been drawn from cases like this one is that the frontal lobes are involved in evaluating *reasonableness*. Patients without brain damage are able to evaluate their memories for reasonableness, and to therefore reject some possibilities as being unreasonable. However, brain damage can derail this evaluative process and can lead patients to create recollections that are inconsistent with one another, such as H.W.'s statement that he and his wife had 4 older children but they had been married for just 4 months.

While these cases of confabulation due to brain damage are interesting in their own right, they may also tell us something about normal memory because the power to "fill in the blanks" when trying to remember situations for which only partial information is available depends largely on the prefrontal lobes. We have seen that this filling-in process can lead to memory errors. Perhaps having intact frontal lobes helps people create reasonable-sounding memory constructions rather than outlandish ones, as occurs in confabulation.

Why Do People Make Errors in Eyewitness Testimony?

We have seen, from the results of numerous laboratory studies, that memory is fallible. But nowhere is this fallibility more evident and significant than in the area of **eyewitness testimony**—testimony by an eyewitness to a crime about what he or she saw during commission of the crime. As we will see, in numerous cases innocent people have been incarcerated based on mistaken identification by eyewitnesses to a crime. These mistaken identifications occur for a number of reasons—for example, some involve difficulties in perceiving a person's face and others with accurately remembering what was perceived. We will first look at the evidence for errors of eyewitness identification that have occurred in the criminal justice system and have been demonstrated in the laboratory, and we will then ask why these errors have occurred.

Errors of Eyewitness Identification

In the United States, 200 people per day become criminal defendants based on eyewitness testimony (Goldstein et al., 1989). Unfortunately, there are many instances in which errors of eyewitness testimony have resulted in the conviction of innocent people. For example, consider the case of David Webb, who was sentenced to up to 50 years in prison for rape, attempted rape, and attempted robbery based on eyewitness testimony. After serving 10 months he was released after another man confessed to the crimes. Charles Clark went to prison in 1938 for murder, based on eyewitness testimony, which, 30 years after his incarceration, was found to be inaccurate. He was released in 1968 (Loftus, 1979). Lenell Gertner served 16 months for robbing a restaurant based on five "positive" eyewitness identifications. Later, four of the five eyewitnesses identified a different person and Gertner was released (Wells, 1985).

The disturbing thing about these examples is not only that they occurred, but that they suggest that many other innocent people are currently serving time for crimes they didn't commit. This conclusion has recently been confirmed by a number of cases in which innocent people have been exonerated based on DNA evidence that became available after they were convicted. In one survey of 40 such cases, 36 involved identification of innocent people by erroneous eyewitness testimony. In these cases, the innocent persons had served an average of 8.5 years in prison and five had been sentenced to death (Wells et al., 2000).

These miscarriages of justice and many others, some of which have undoubtedly never been discovered, are based on the assumption, made by judges and jurors, that people see and report things accurately. In essence, many people in the criminal justice system have subscribed to the erroneous idea that memory is like a video recorder.

We have seen from laboratory research that memory is definitely not like a video recorder, and research using crime scene scenarios supports this idea. A number of experiments have presented films of actual crimes or of staged crimes to participants, and then have asked the participants to pick the perpetrator from a photospread (photographs of a number of faces, one of which could be the perpetrator). In one study, participants viewed a security videotape in which a gunman was in view for 8 seconds and then were asked to pick the gunman from photographs. Every participant picked someone they thought was the gunman, even though his picture was not included in the photospread (Wells & Bradfield, 1998). In another study, using a similar experimental design, 61 percent of the participants picked someone from a photospread, even though the perpetrator's picture wasn't included (Kneller et al., 2001).

These studies show how difficult it is to accurately identify someone after viewing a videotape of a crime. But things become even more complicated when we consider some of the things that happen during actual crimes.

The Crime Scene and Afterward

Even under ideal conditions, identifying faces is a difficult task and errors occur (Henderson et al., 2001). But other factors can intervene to make the task even more difficult. Emotions often run high during commission of a crime. There can be confusion, rapid actions, and the firing of weapons. All of these things can affect what a person pays attention to and this can affect what the person remembers later. There is some evidence, for example, that the presence of weapons can have such an effect.

Errors Due to the Presence of Weapons

There is some evidence that weapons focus—the tendency to focus attention on a weapon—can affect memory for other things. Claudia Stanny and Thomas Johnson (2000) measured how well participants remembered details of a filmed simulated crime, and found that participants were more likely to recall details of the perpetrator, the victim, and the weapon in the "no-shoot" condition (a gun was present but not fired) compared to the "shoot" condition (the gun was fired). Apparently, the presence of a weapon that was fired distracts attention from other things that are happening (Figure 7.16) (also see Tooley et al., 1987).

Crime scenes not only involve a perpetrator and a victim, but often include innocent bystanders. These bystanders add yet another dimension to the testimony of eyewitnesses.

Errors Due to Familiarity

Is there any danger that a bystander could mistakenly be identified as a perpetrator because they looked familiar? Is there a possibility that someone who wasn't even at the crime scene could be identified because of familiarity from some other context? We might expect, based on what we know about how familiarity can affect memory, that the answer to these questions is "yes," and it is not surprising therefore that there is both real-life and laboratory evidence for errors in eyewitness identification related to familiarity.

A real-life example of misidentification based on familiarity is the case of Donald Thompson, a memory researcher who was talking about memory errors on a TV program at exactly the time that a woman was attacked in her home. The woman, who had been

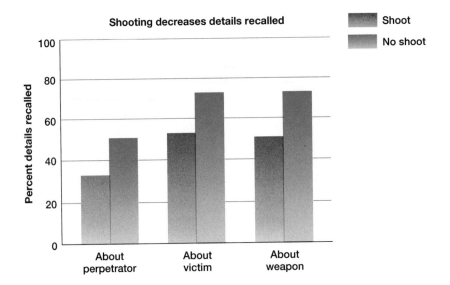

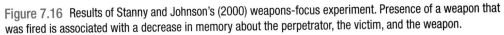

Figure 7.16 Results of Stanny and Johnson's (2000) weapons-focus experiment. Presence of a weapon that was fired is associated with a decrease in memory about the perpetrator, the victim, and the weapon.

[handwritten note in margin: wow, talk about wrong]

watching Thompson on the program, subsequently implicated Thompson as the person who had raped her, based on her memory for his face. Of course, Thompson had a perfect alibi, since the he was in the TV studio at the time of the crime (Schacter, 2001).

In another case, a ticket agent at a railway station was robbed and subsequently identified a sailor from a police lineup as being the robber. Luckily for the sailor, he was able to show that he was somewhere else at the time of the crime. When asked why he identified the sailor, the ticket agent said that he looked familiar. But the reason he looked familiar was not that he was the robber but because he lived near the train station and had purchased train tickets from the agent on a number of occasions. The sailor had, therefore, become transformed, through source misattribution, from a ticket buyer into a holdup man (Ross et al., 1994).

Figure 7.17a shows the design for a laboratory experiment on familiarity and eyewitness testimony (Ross et al., 1994). Participants in the experimental group saw a film of a male teacher reading to students, and participants in the control group saw a film of a female teacher reading to students. Participants in both groups then saw a film of the female teacher getting robbed and were asked to pick the robber from a photospread. The photographs did not include the actual robber, but did include the male teacher, who resembled the robber. The result indicates that the participants in the experimental group were three times more likely to pick the male teacher than participants in the control group (Figure 7.17b). Even when the actual robber's face was included in the photospread, 18 percent of the participants in the experimental group picked the teacher, compared to 10 percent in the control group (Figure 7.17c).

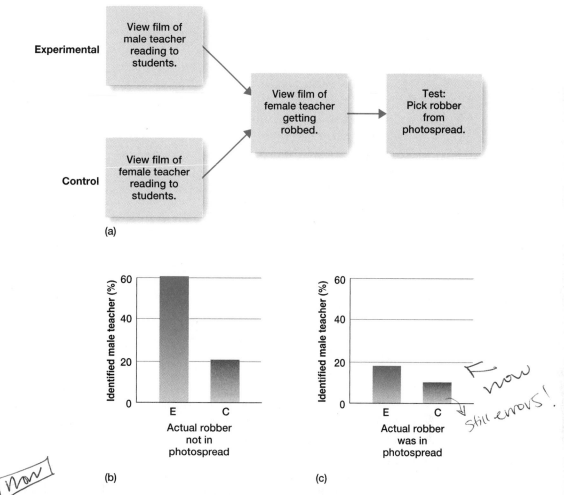

Figure 7.17 (a) Design of Ross et al.'s (1994) experiment on the effect of familiarity on eyewitness testimony. (b) Results of experiment when the actual robber was not in the photospread. In this condition, the male teacher was erroneously identified as the robber 60 percent of the time. (c) Results when the actual robber was in the photospread. In this condition, the male teacher was erroneously identified less than 20 percent of the time.

Errors Due to Suggestion From what we know about the misinformation effect it is obvious that a police officer asking a witness "Did you see the white car . . ." could influence the witness's later testimony about what he or she saw. But suggestibility can also operate on a more subtle level. Consider the following situation. A witness to a crime is looking through a one-way window at a lineup of six men standing on a stage. The police officer says, "Which one of these men did it?" What is wrong with this question?

The problem with the police officer's question is that it includes the implication that the crime perpetrator is in the lineup. This suggestion increases the chances that the witness will pick someone, perhaps using reasoning like, "Well, the guy with the beard looks more like the robber than any of the other men, so that's probably the one." Of course, looking *like* the robber and actually *being* the robber may be two different things, so the result may be identification of an innocent man. A better way of presenting the task is to let the witness know that the crime suspect may or may not be in the lineup.

Here is another situation, taken from a transcript from an actual criminal case, in which suggestion could have played a role.

> Eyewitness to a crime on viewing a lineup: "Oh, my God. . . . I don't know. . . . It's one of those two . . . but I don't know. . . . Oh, man . . . the guy a little bit taller than number two. . . . It's one of those two, but I don't know."
>
> Eyewitness 30 minutes later, still viewing the lineup and having difficulty making a decision: "I don't know . . . number two?"
>
> Officer administering lineup: "Okay."
>
> Months later . . . at trial: "You were positive it was number two? It wasn't a maybe?"
>
> Answer from eyewitness: "There was no maybe about it. . . . I was absolutely positive." (Wells & Bradfield, 1998)

The problem with this scenario is that the police officer's response of "okay" may have influenced the witness to think that he or she had correctly identified the suspect. Thus, the witness's initially uncertain response turns into an "absolutely positive" response. In a paper titled "Good, You Identified the Suspect . . . ," Gary Wells and Amy Bradfield (1998) had participants view a video of an actual crime and then asked them to identify the perpetrator from a photospread that did not actually contain a picture of the perpetrator (Figure 7.18).

All of the participants picked one of the photographs, and following their choice, witnesses either received confirming feedback from the experimenter ("Good, you identified the suspect"), no feedback, or disconfirming feedback ("Actually, the suspect was number __"). A short time later, the participants were asked how confident they were about their identification. The result, shown at the bottom of the figure, indicates that participants who received the confirming feedback were more confident of their choice. Thus, this is another example of how postevent information can influence eyewitness testimony.

Returning to the transcript from the beginning of this section, which indicates that the eyewitness went from being very uncertain to very certain of her choice from a lineup, we should note that her increased confidence at the trial could be attributed not only to the officer's feedback, but to the consistency bias: Once a witness makes a choice, no matter how uncertain at first, he or she wants to be perceived as consistent when questioned later.

right

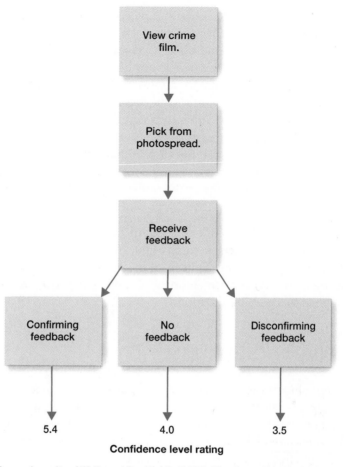

Figure 7.18 Design and results of Wells and Bradfield's (1998) "Good, you identified the suspect" experiment. Feedback from the experimenter influenced the participants' confidence in their identification.

What Is Being Done?

The first step toward correcting problems caused by inaccurate eyewitness testimony is to realize that the problem exists. That step has been taken, largely through the efforts of memory researchers and attorneys and investigators for the unjustly convicted people. The next step is to institute procedural changes that may be contributing to errors in eyewitness testimony. This step was taken in 1997 when then-Attorney General Janet Reno ordered that a panel consisting of memory researchers, police officers, and prosecutors be formed to study the problem of errors in eyewitness testimony. This panel produced a document titled "Eyewitness Evidence: A Guide for Law Enforcement" (available at http://www.ojp.usdoj.gov/nij/pubs-sum/178240.htm), which indicates the best ways to handle evidence and witnesses. Some of the recommendations in this document are:

1. Use open-ended questions when interrogating witnesses. ("What can you tell me about the car?")
2. Avoid leading questions. ("Was the car red?")
3. When assembling people or photographs for a lineup, all of the fillers (people included in addition to the suspect) should resemble the witness's description of the suspect. One of the most common problems in lineups is that fillers are chosen who look so different than the witnesses description that there is little chance they will be chosen.
4. Tell witnesses that the suspect may or may not be in a lineup, to avoid causing the witness to pick someone just because he looks "like" the suspect.
5. Avoid confirming or disconfirming the choice the witness makes when viewing a lineup.

One thing that is striking about these recommendations is that they are the direct outcome of psychological research. Thus, while one goal of cognitive psychology research is to determine basic mechanisms of memory, this research often has practical implications as well. We next consider another example of how cognitive psychology research has been applied to a real-life situation.

Can Lost Memories Be Recovered?

CogLab

I Forgot It
All Along

Beginning in the 1980s, a rash of reports began surfacing of people who, as adults, said they remembered traumatic experiences, such as sexual abuse or witnessing a murder, that had occurred in their childhood, years earlier. These memories have been called recovered memories because they usually occurred when a particular situation caused the person to relive the memory, or because the person was in therapy and the therapist encouraged him or her to remember being abused or witnessing a murder. Following are a few examples of cases that have been publicized.

Cases of Recovered Memories

- Laura Pasley—a 40-year-old secretary in the Dallas police department. In therapy, under the influence of sodium amytal (a drug that has disinhibiting effects), Laura reported that she had been sexually abused by her mother, brother, grandfather, and a neighbor. She later concluded that what she had thought were true memories were in error and sued her therapist.
- Eileen Lipsker was 28 years old in 1989 when, as she watched her young red-haired daughter draw pictures in their family room, suddenly remembered a similar scene from 20 years earlier when, as an 8-year-old, she was playing with her red-haired friend Susan. This memory ended with the image of Eileen's father, George Franklin,

raping and murdering her friend, and then later memories surfaced during therapy, of her father sexually abusing her (Terr, 1994). Based on these reports, George Franklin was convicted of first-degree murder in 1990 and was sentenced to life in prison, a conviction that was later overturned on appeal.

■ A 30-year-old man saw a movie in which the main character grapples with memories of sexual molestation. A few hours later he remembered that a parish priest molested him on a camping trip when he was 11. His story was later corroborated by others who reported similar experiences with the same priest.

These three cases represent many other cases with similar outcomes. In some, such as the Dallas secretary, a patient believes to have recovered a memory, usually in therapy, and then decides it was false. In some cases, such as that of George Franklin, a memory is reported and is accepted as being true by a jury without corroborating evidence, and in others, such as the 30-year-old man, a person recovers a memory and its truth is later confirmed.

Because of cases similar to the first two, many therapists have been sued by patients or patients' families, and the possibility exists that people have been convicted of crimes they did not commit (McElroy & Keck, 1995). This has caused a controversy involving memory researchers, therapists, and patients.

People who believe that all memories of early abuse are accurate propose that after the person experiences the abuse, a process called repression pushes the memory of the abuse into the person's unconscious so he or she can't remember the painful experience. According to this explanation, the memory occurs much later in life, when the repression weakens or some experience brings the memory to the surface.

The problem with this explanation is that there is no convincing evidence that the hypothetical mechanism of repression actually exists. Rather than proposing a special repression mechanism, most psychologists propose that remembering painful experiences from the distant past involves the same mechanisms of memory that we have described in this chapter. Choosing not to think about a disturbing event can be an effective coping mechanism, which could lead people to forget unpleasant events from the past (Anderson et al., 2004). Thus, it is not unusual for people to forget experiences such as automobile crashes or stays in the hospital (Loftus et al., 1994) or being abused sexually as children (Williams, 1994).

We have seen that suggestion can distort memory for actual events or create memories for events that never happened. If the forgetting and later remembering that occurs in cases of abuse is similar to other memory processes, then it is likely that some of the recovered memories are accurate and some are not. The problem is that it is difficult—and in many cases, impossible—to determine which memories are accurate and which are not. Memory researcher Daniel Schacter (1996) summarizes his analysis of the recovered memory debate by stating "The recovered memory controversy . . . is fundamentally a debate about accuracy, distortion, and suggestibility in memory" (p. 251).

Statement of the American Psychological Association

A panel of psychologists from the American Psychological Association have studied the problem of recovered memories and have concluded that there is no question that many people have been abused and have forgotten the abuse and then remembered it later. The problem is that based on what we know about memory, it is sometimes difficult to tell which memories reflect actual abuse and which have been planted in the person's mind by suggestion. Taking all of this into account, the APA's "Working Group on Investigation of Memories of Childhood Abuse" reached the following conclusions.

1. The controversy about adult recollections should not be allowed to obscure the fact that child sexual abuse is a complex and pervasive problem in America that has historically not been acknowledged.
2. Most people who were sexually abused as children remember all or part of what happened to them.
3. It is possible for memories of abuse that have been forgotten for a long time to be remembered. The mechanism by which such delayed recall occurs is not currently well understood.
4. It is possible to construct convincing pseudomemories (false memories) for events that never occurred. The mechanisms by which these pseudomemories occur are currently not well understood.

Test Yourself 7.2

1. If you wanted to convince someone that our memory does not operate like a video recorder, how would you reply to the following: (1) Wouldn't our memory system be better if it could create "photographic memories"? (2) The way personal biases affect memory seems like a flaw in the system.
2. Experiments that have shown that memory can be affected by suggestion have led to the proposal of the misinformation effect. How has the misinformation effect been demonstrated, what mechanisms have been proposed to explain this effect, and what experiments have been done to test these proposed mechanisms?
3. How has it been shown that suggestion can influence people's memories for early childhood experiences?
4. Describe the clinical symptom of confabulation that is created by brain damage. What is the relationship between this clinical symptom and the memory errors made by people who do not have brain damage?
5. What is the evidence both from "real life" and laboratory experiments that eyewitness testimony is not always accurate? Describe how the following factors have been shown to lead to errors in eyewitness testimony: weapons focus, familiarity, leading questions, and feedback from a police officer.

6. How do most psychologists discuss the debate about recovered memories of childhood abuse? What is the American Psychological Association's stance on this issue?

Think About It

1. What do you remember about how you heard about the terrorist attacks of September 11, 2001? How confident are you that your memory of these events is accurate? Given the results of experiments on flashbulb memories described in this chapter, what do you think the chances are that your memories might be in error? Are there any ways that you could check the accuracy of your memories?

2. What do you remember about what you did on the most recent major holiday (Thanksgiving, Christmas, New Year's, your birthday, etc.)? What do you remember about what you did on the same holiday one year earlier? How do these memories differ in terms of (a) how difficult they were to remember, (b) how much detail you can remember, (c) the accuracy of your memory? (How would you know if your answer to (c) is correct?)

3. There are a large number of reports of people who have been unjustly imprisoned due to errors of eyewitness testimony, and more cases are being reported every day based on DNA evidence. Given this fact, how would you react to the proposal that eyewitness testimony should no longer be admitted as evidence in courts of law?

4. Interview people of different ages regarding what they remember about their lives. How does the result you find fit with the results of autobiographical memory experiments, especially the data that supports the idea of a reminiscence bump in older people?

KEY TERMS

Autobiographical memory
Cognitive hypothesis
Confabulation
Consequentiality
Consistency bias
Constructive approach to memory
Egocentric bias
Event-specific knowledge
Eyewitness testimony
Flashbulb memories
General events
Life-narrative hypothesis
Lifetime periods

Memory impairment hypothesis
Misinformation effect
Misleading postevent information (MPI)
Narrative rehearsal hypothesis
Positive-change bias
Recovered memory
Reminiscence bump
Repeated reproduction
Schema
Script
Source misattribution
Source monitoring
Weapons focus

CogLab   To experience these experiments for yourself, go to http://coglab.wadsworth.com. Be sure to read each experiment's setup instructions before you go to the experiment itself. Otherwise, you won't know which keys to press.

Primary Labs

Remember/know   Distinguishing between remembered items in which there is memory for learning the item and items that just seem familiar (p. 236).

False memory   How memory for words on a list sometimes occurs for words that were not presented (p. 242).

Forgot it all along   How it is possible to remember something and also have the experience of having previously forgotten it (p. 260)?

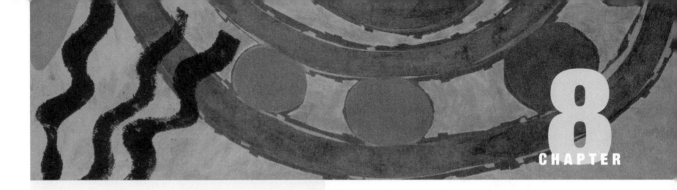

Knowledge

Some Questions We Will Consider

✔ Why do we need to know about categories such as "cars," "people," "mountains," and "birds" in order to make sense of our experiences?

✔ Do people in different cultures categorize objects in the same way?

✔ How are the relationships between various objects "filed away" in the mind?

✔ How is information about different categories stored in the brain?

■　■　■

Imagine that you find yourself in another town, where you have never been before. As you walk down the street, you notice that there are many things that are not exactly the same as what you would encounter if you were in your own town. However, on the other hand, there are lots of things that seem familiar. Cars pass by, there are buildings on either side of the street and a gas station on the corner, and a cat, appearing rather crazed, dashes across the street and makes it safely to the other side. Luckily, you know a lot about cars, buildings, gas stations, and cats, so you have no trouble understanding what is going on.

You know about the various components of this street scene because your mind is full of concepts. A **concept** is a mental representation that is used for a variety of cognitive functions, including memory, reasoning, and using and understanding language (Solomon et al., 1999). Thus, when you think about cats, you are drawing on your concept, or mental representation, of cats, which includes information about what cats are, what they usually look like, how they behave, and so on.

By far the most commonly studied function of concepts is **categorization**, which is the process by which things are placed into groups called **categories**. For example, when you see vehicles in the street you can place them into categories such as cars, SUVs, Chevrolets, Fords, American cars, and foreign cars.

This chapter describes how cognitive psychologists have studied categorization. You might think that this would be simple because placing an object in a particular category would just be a matter of looking up the definition of that category in the dictionary and checking to see if the object fits the definition. However, as we will see, placing objects into categories is not so simple.

This chapter begins by describing why categories are important (Figure 8.1). We then explain why categorization can't be understood by simply looking up a definition. Two approaches to categorization that are based on the idea that we decide whether something belongs in a category by comparing it to a standard are described next. We will then describe another way of looking at categories called the network approach, which considers how categories are organized in the mind, and the chapter concludes by describing how categories are represented in the brain.

Categories Are Essential, but Definitions Don't Work

Categories are not simply convenient ways of sorting objects. They are tools that are essential for our understanding.

Why Categories Are Useful

Using categories to understand individual cases you have never seen before, like the crazed cat crossing the street in the unfamiliar town, is one of the most important functions of categories. Being able to call something a "cat" provides a great deal of information about it (Figure 8.2). Categories have therefore been called "pointers to knowledge"

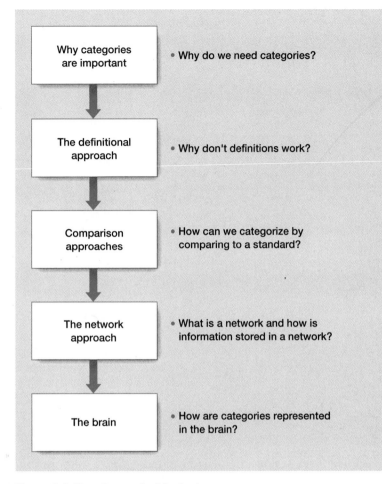

Figure 8.1 Flow diagram for this chapter.

(Yamauchi & Markman, 2000), and so once you know something is in a category, whether it is *cat*, or *gas station*, or *impressionist painting*, you know a lot of general things about it, and can focus your energy on specifying what's special about this particular object (see Spaulding & Murphy, 1996; Solomon et al., 1999).

As we will see later in this chapter, categories not only provide information about the basic properties of things that belong to that category, but also serve as a valuable tool for making inferences about things that belong to other categories. For example, if we know that field mice are being stricken by a particular disease, we might infer that there is a good chance that other rodents, especially those most closely related to field mice, may be carrying the disease as well.

Being able to place things in categories can also help us understand behaviors that we might otherwise find baffling. For example, if we see a man with the left side of his face

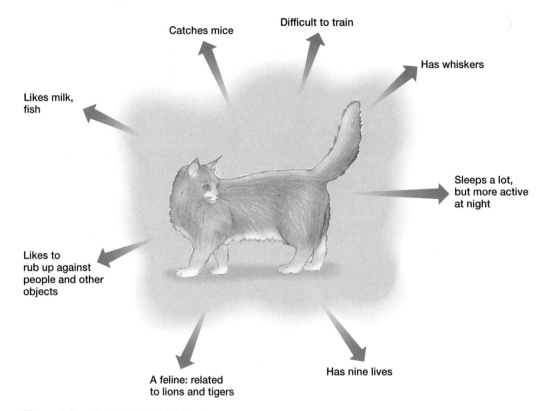

Catches mice

Difficult to train

Has whiskers

Likes milk, fish

Sleeps a lot, but more active at night

Likes to rub up against people and other objects

A feline: related to lions and tigers

Has nine lives

Figure 8.2 Knowing something is in a category provides a great deal of information about it.

painted black and the right side painted gold we might wonder what is going on. However, once we note that the person is heading toward the football stadium and it is Sunday afternoon, we can categorize the person as a "Pittsburgh Steelers fan." Placing him in that category explains his painted face and perhaps other strange behaviors that we might observe as well (Solomon et al., 1999).

These various uses of categories testify to their importance in everyday life. It is no exaggeration to say that if there were no such thing as categories we would have a very difficult time dealing with the world. Consider what it would mean if every time you saw a different object, you knew nothing about it, other than what you could find out by investigating it individually. Clearly, life would become extremely complicated if we weren't able to rely on the knowledge provided to us by categories. Given the importance of categories, cognitive psychologists have been interested in answering the question "How are objects placed in categories?" We will now see that although we are constantly using categories to help us understand the world, we can't simply specify that something belongs to a particular category by looking up a definition.

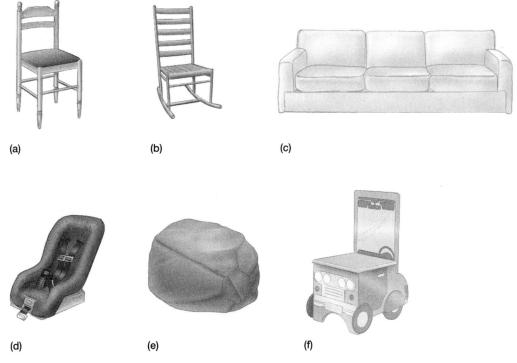

Figure 8.3 Different objects, all "chairs."

(a) (b) (c) (d) (e) (f)

Why Definitions Don't Work for Categories

According to the **definitional approach to categorization** we can decide whether something is a member of a category by determining whether a particular object meets the definition of the category. Definitions work well for some things, such as geometrical objects. Thus, defining a *square* as "a plane figure having four equal sides" works. However, for most natural objects (such as birds, trees, and plants) and many human-made objects (like chairs), definitions do not work well at all.

The problem is that not all of the members of everyday categories have the same features. So, although the dictionary definition of *chair* as "a piece of furniture consisting of a seat, legs, back, and often arms, designed to accommodate one person" may sound reasonable, there are objects we call *chairs* that don't meet that definition. For example, although the objects in Figure 8.3a, b, and c would be classified as chairs by this definition, the ones in Figures 8.3d and e would not. Most chairs may have legs and a back, as specified in the definition, but most people would still call the car seat in d and the beanbag chair in e, a chair. And although most people would not cite an automobile hood as a chair, the "automobile chair" in Figure 8.3f would be accepted as a chair, especially in a playroom.

The philosopher Wittgenstein (1953), noted this problem with definitions and offered a solution:

> Consider for example the proceedings we call "games." I mean board-games, card-games, ball-games, Olympic games, and so on. For if you look at them you will not see something in common to *all*, but similarities, relationships, and a whole series of them at that. I can think of no better expression to characterize these similarities than "family resemblances."

Wittgenstein proposed the idea of **family resemblance** to deal with the fact that definitions often do not include all members of a category. Family resemblance refers to the fact that things in a particular category resemble one another in a number of ways. Thus, instead of setting definite criteria that every member of a category must meet, the family resemblance approach allows for some variation within a category. Chairs may come in many different sizes and shapes and be made of different materials, but every chair does resemble other chairs in some way. Looking at category membership in this way, it is possible to see how a kitchen chair and a car seat could both be called chairs.

You might think, however, that a car seat isn't as good an example of a chair as the kitchen chair. This was the idea behind a program of research that was begun in the 1970s by Eleanor Rosch that incorporated the idea of family resemblance into the *prototype approach* to the study of categorization.

DETERMINING CATEGORIES BY SIMILARITY: USING PROTOTYPES OR EXEMPLARS

The definitional approach to categorization is based on determining whether the properties of a particular object match a definition. We will now consider two approaches that are based on the idea that categorization is based on determining how similar the properties of an object are to standard representations of the category.

The Prototype Approach: Finding the Average Case

CogLab

Prototypes

The basic idea behind the **prototype approach to categorization** is that we decide whether an object belongs to a category by determining whether it is similar to a standard representation of the category called a prototype. A **prototype** is formed by averaging the category members we have encountered in the past (Rosch, 1973). For example, the prototype for the category *birds* might be based on some of the birds you usually see, such as sparrows, robins, and blue jays, but doesn't necessarily look exactly like a particular type of bird. Thus, the prototype is not an actual member of the category, but is an "average" representation of the category (Figure 8.4).

Figure 8.4 Three real birds—a sparrow, a robin, and a blue jay—and a "prototype" bird that is the average representation of the category "birds."

Of course, not all birds are like robins, blue jays, or sparrows. Owls, buzzards, and penguins are also birds. Rosch describes these variations within categories as representing differences in **prototypicality. High-prototypicality** means that the category member closely resembles the category prototype (it is like a "typical" member of the category). **Low-prototypicality** means that the category member does not resemble a typical member of the category. Rosch (1975a) quantified this idea by presenting participants with a category title, such as *furniture*, and a list of about 50 members of the category. The participants' task was to rate the extent to which each member represented the category title on a 7-point scale, with a rating of 1 meaning that the member is a very good example of what the category is, and a rating of 7 meaning that the member fits poorly within the category or is not a member at all.

Typical results for three different categories are shown in Table 8.1. These rankings make sense because most people would agree that a sparrow (rating 1.18) is a better

Table 8.1   TYPICALITY RATINGS FOR MEMBERS OF THREE CATEGORIES

Bird			Furniture		
Category Member	Rank	Rating	Category Member	Rank	Rating
Robin	1	1.02	Chair	1 (tie)	1.04
Sparrow	2	1.18	Sofa	1 (tie)	1.04
Hummingbird	19	1.76	Chest	19	1.89
Raven	27	2.01	China closet	28	2.59
Owl	37	2.96	Drawers	34	3.63
Duck	45	3.24	Mirror	41	4.39
Penguin	53	4.53	Wastebasket	47	5.34
Bat	54	6.15	Telephone	60	6.68

Vehicle		
Category Member	Rank	Rating
Automobile	1	1.02
Ambulance	8	1.62
Bicycle	16	2.51
Tractor	24	3.30
Canoe	36	4.01
Horse	40	4.63
Skis	46	5.40
Elevator	50	5.90

From Rosch, 1975a.

example of a bird than a penguin (rating 4.53). But does an object's prototypicality tell us anything else about the object? To answer this question, we return to the idea of family resemblance that was proposed by Wittgenstein.

Prototypical Objects Have High Family Resemblance   The following demonstration illustrates a characteristic of family resemblance.

Family Resemblance

The following instructions are based on the instructions Rosch and Carolyn Mervis (1975) gave to their participants:

> *For each of the following common objects, list as many characteristics and attributes that you feel are common to these objects. For example, for* bicycles *you might think of things they have in common like two wheels, pedals, handlebars, you ride on them, they don't use fuel, and so on. For* dogs *you might think of things they have in common like having four legs, barking, having fur, and so on. Give yourself about a minute to write down the characteristics for each item.*
>
> *Go.*

| chair | sofa | mirror | telephone | ■ |

If you responded like Rosch and Mervis's participants, you assigned many of the same characteristics to *chair* and *sofa*. For example, chairs and sofas share the characteristics of having legs, having backs, you sit on them, they can have cushions, and so on. It is likely, however, that your list contains far less overlap for *mirror* and *telephone*, which are also members of the category *furniture* (see Table 8.1).

When an item's characteristics have a large amount of overlap with the characteristics of many other items in a category, this means that the family resemblance of these items is high. However, when there is little overlap, the family resemblance is low. But the interesting thing about Rosch and Mervis's results was that they showed that there was a strong relationship between family resemblance and prototypicality, with items high on prototypicality having high family resemblances. Thus, good examples of the category furniture, like chair and sofa, share many attributes with other members of this category, and poor examples, like mirror and telephone, do not.

In addition to the connection between family resemblance and prototypicality, Rosch and coworkers found a number of connections between prototypicality and behavior.

Statements About Prototypical Objects Are Verified Rapidly

Here are two statements. Your task is to answer "yes" if you think the statement is true, and "no" if you think it isn't:

- An apple is a fruit.
- A pomegranate is a fruit.

This task, in which you are asked to determine whether or not a statement is true, is called the **sentence-verification technique.** When Edward Smith and coworkers (1974) used this technique, they found that participants responded faster for objects that are high in prototypicality (like *apple* for the category *fruit*), than they did to objects that are low in

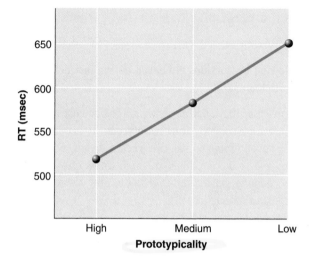

Figure 8.5 Results of E. E. Smith et al.'s (1974) sentence-verification experiment. Reaction times were faster for objects rated higher in prototypicality.

prototypicality (like *pomegranate*) (Figure 8.5). This ability to judge highly prototypical objects more rapidly is called the typicality effect.

Prototypical Objects Are Named First When participants are asked to list as many objects as possible, they tend to list the most prototypical members of the category first (Mervis et al., 1976). Thus *sparrows* would be named before *penguins*.

Prototypical Objects Are Affected More by Priming Priming occurs when presentation of one stimulus facilitates the response to another stimulus that usually follows closely in time. We introduced priming in Chapter 6 by noting that first seeing a word, such as *perfume*, increased the likelihood that a participant will use the word *perfume* to complete the word stem *per*_____ in a later test (see page 191).

Rosch (1975b) demonstrated that prototypical members of a category are affected by a priming stimulus more than are nonprototypical members. The procedure for Rosch's experiment is shown in Figure 8.6. Participants first heard the prime, which was the name of a color, such as *green* or *red*. Two seconds later they saw a pair of colors side by side and indicated by pressing a key, as quickly as possible, whether the two colors were the same or different.

The side-by-side colors were paired in three different ways: (1) Colors were the same and were good examples of the category (primary reds, blues, greens, etc.; Figure 8.6a); (2) Colors were the same, but were poor examples of the category (less rich versions of the good colors, such as light blue, light green, etc.; Figure 8.6b); (3) Colors were different, with the two colors coming from different categories (for example, pairing red with blue; Figure 8.6c).

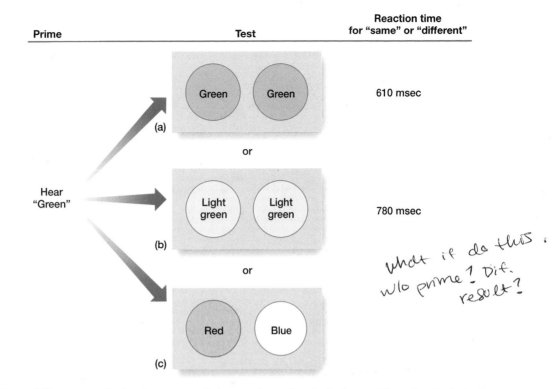

Figure 8.6 Procedure for Rosch's (1975b) priming experiment. Results for the conditions when the test colors were the same are shown on the right. (a) The person's "green" prototype matches the good green, but (b) is a poor match for the light green.

The most important result occurred when the colors were the same because in this condition, priming resulted in faster "same" judgments for the prototypical (good) colors (RT = 610 msec.) than to the nonprototypical (poor) colors (RT = 780 msecs.). Thus, when participants heard the word *green*, they judged two patches of green as being the same more rapidly than two patches of light green.

Rosch explains this result as follows: When the participant hears the word *green* they imagine a "good" (highly prototypical) green. The principle behind priming is that the prime will facilitate the participants' response to a stimulus if it contains some of the information needed to respond to the stimulus. This apparently occurs when the good greens are presented in the test (Figure 8.7b), but not when the poor greens are presented (Figure 8.7c). Thus, the results of the priming experiments support the idea that participants create images of good prototypes in response to color names. Table 8.2 summarizes the various ways, previously discussed, that prototypicality affects behavior.

The prototype approach to categorization, and in particular Rosch's pioneering research, represented a great advance over the definitional approach because it provided a wealth of experimental evidence that all items within a category are not the same. But

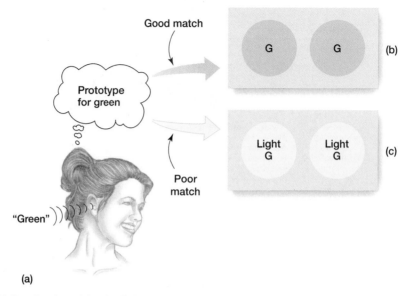

Figure 8.7 How Rosch explains the finding that priming resulted in faster "same" judgments for prototypical colors than for nonprototypical colors.

Table 8.2	SOME EFFECTS OF PROTOTYPICALITY
Effect	**Property of High-Prototypical Items**
Family resemblance	Have more in common with other members of the category.
Typicality	Reaction time to statements like "A _____ is a bird" faster in high prototypical items (like robin) than to low (like ostrich).
Naming	Named first when people list examples of a category.
Priming	Facilitates making same-different color judgments for high-prototypical items.

some research has provided evidence for another approach to categorization, called the exemplar approach, which also takes into account the fact that there is a wide variation among items that belong to a particular category.

The Exemplar Approach: Thinking About Examples

The **exemplar approach to categorization**, like the prototype approach, involves determining whether an object is similar to a standard object. However, whereas the standard for the prototype approach is a single "average" member of the category, the standard for the exemplar approach involves many examples, each one called an exemplar. **Exemplars** are actual members of the category that a person has encountered in the past. Thus, de-

Symptoms of burlosis-correlated condition

Case Study	Swollen eyelids	Splotches on ears	Discolored gums	Nose-bleed
1. R.C.	1	1	1	1
2. R.M.	1	1	1	1
3. J.J.	0	1	0	0
4. L.F.	1	1	1	1
5. A.M.	1	0	1	1
6. J.S.	1	1	0	0
7. S.T.	0	1	1	1
8. S.E.	1	0	0	0
9. E.M.	0	0	1	1

(a) Training cases

Roger	0	1	1	1	← Correlated
Susan	1	1	0	1	← Uncorrelated

(b) Test cases

Figure 8.8 (a) Symptoms for nine hypothetical patients that were presented to the participants in the training phase of Medin et al.'s (1982) "burlosis" experiment. (b) Symptoms for test cases Roger and Susan. (Reprinted from D. L. Medin et al., "Correlated Symptoms and Simulated Medical Classification." From *Journal of Experimental Psychology: Learning, Memory and Cognition, 8,* pp. 37–50, Fig. 1. Copyright © 1982, with permission from the American Psychological Association.)

ciding whether a particular animal is a dog involves comparing it to dogs that have been experienced in the past.

The exemplar approach can explain many of Rosch's results, which were used to support the prototype approach. For example, the exemplar approach explains the typicality effect (in which reaction times for the sentence-verification task are faster for better examples of a category than for less-good examples) by proposing that objects that are like more of the exemplars are classified faster. Thus, a sparrow is similar to many exemplars so it is classified faster than a penguin, which is similar to few exemplars. This is basically the same as the idea of family resemblance that we described for prototypes that states that "better" objects will have higher family resemblance.

An experiment by Douglas Medin and coworkers (1982) sets up a problem that was designed to result in different outcomes depending on whether their participants were using exemplars or prototypes to deal with the problem. Medin's participants were told that their task was to learn as much as possible about a disease called *burlosis* (which, in reality, was a fictitious condition created by the experimenters) by studying descriptions of the symptoms of people with the disease, like the ones in Figure 8.8.

Medin ran two groups of participants. The participants in the *correlated condition* were presented with the descriptions in Figure 8.8a of nine people who had the disease. The

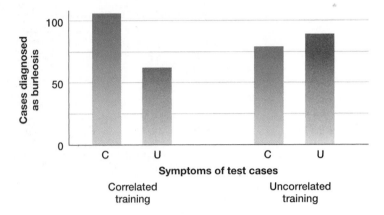

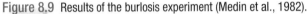

Figure 8.9 Results of the burlosis experiment (Medin et al., 1982).

following four symptoms were associated with burlosis: (1) swollen eyelids; (2) splotches on ears; (3) discolored gums; and (4) nosebleed. However, not all patients had exactly the same symptoms. R.C. had all four symptoms, but S.E. had only swollen eyelids. One thing that all patients did have in common, however, was that the symptoms *discolored gums* and *nosebleed* were correlated—if one occurred, so did the other one. Participants in the *uncorrelated condition* saw a similar list of case descriptions, except that the symptoms of discolored gums and nosebleed were not correlated. Thus, a person could have nosebleed and not have discolored gums.

After studying these cases for 20 minutes, the participants were given pairs of test cases that they had never seen before and were asked to indicate which case in the pair was more likely to have burlosis. Both of the test cases in a pair had the same number of symptoms, but for one case discolored gums and nosebleed were correlated, as in the example of Roger in Figure 8.8b, whereas for the other case, the symptoms were not correlated, as in the example for Susan.

The results of the experiment (Figure 8.9) showed that participants in the correlated condition (left bars) were more likely to diagnosis cases with correlated symptoms, like Roger, as having burlosis than cases with uncorrelated symptoms, like Susan. Participants in the uncorrelated condition (right bars) did not show a significant preference for a particular pattern of symptoms.

These results support the exemplar approach because the participants were apparently basing their diagnoses on the pattern of symptoms. The prototype approach would not predict this because a prototype for burlosis would be an "average case," and because the overall number of symptoms was the same for both the correlated and uncorrelated conditions, the prototype would be the same for both the correlated and uncorrelated conditions.

yes–or something else going on?

Which Approach Works Best: Prototypes or Exemplars?

Which approach—prototypes or exemplars—best describes how people use categories? One advantage of the exemplar approach is that by using real examples, it can more easily take into account atypical cases such as flightless birds. Rather than comparing a penguin to an "average" bird, we remember that there are some birds that don't fly. This ability to take into account individual cases means that the exemplar approach doesn't discard information that might be useful later. Thus, penguins and ostriches and other birds that are not typical can be represented as exemplars, rather than becoming lost in the overall average that creates a prototype. The exemplar approach can also deal more easily with <u>variable categories</u> like games. While it is difficult to imagine what the prototype might be for a category that contains football, computer games, solitaire, marbles, and golf, the exemplar approach requires only that we remember some of these varying examples.

While the results of the burlosis experiment that we just described supports the exemplar approach, other experiments have supported the prototype approach (Minda & Smith, 2001). Some researchers have concluded, based on the results of a number of research studies, that people may use both approaches. It has been proposed that as we initially learn about a category we may average exemplars into a prototype and then later in learning some of the exemplar information becomes stronger (Keri et al., 2002; Malt, 1989). Thus, early in learning we would be poor at taking into account "exceptions," such as ostriches or penguins, but later, exemplars for these cases would be added to the category (Smith & Minda 1998).

Other research indicates that the exemplar approach may work best for small categories such as "U.S. Presidents" or "Mountains taller than 15,000 feet," and that the prototype approach may work best for larger categories, such as "birds" or "automobiles." We can describe this blending of prototypes and exemplars in commonsense terms by the following example: We know generally what cats are (the prototype), but we know specifically our own cat the best (an exemplar) (Minda & Smith, 2001).

IS THERE A PSYCHOLOGICALLY "PRIVILEGED" LEVEL OF CATEGORIES?

As we have considered the prototype and exemplar approaches, we have used examples of categories such as *furniture*, which contains members such as *beds*, *chairs*, and *tables*. But, as you can see in Figure 8.10, the category *chairs* can contain smaller categories such as *kitchen chairs* and *dining room chairs*. This kind of organization, in which larger, more general

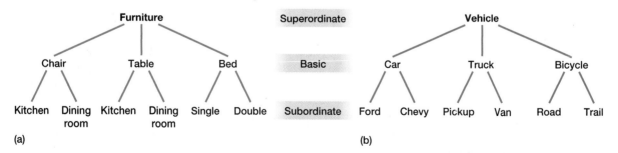

Figure 8.10 Levels of categories for (a) *furniture* and (b) *vehicles*. Rosch provided evidence for the idea that the basic level is "psychologically privileged."

categories are divided into smaller, more specific, categories to create a number of levels of categories, is called a **hierarchical organization.**

One question cognitive psychologists have asked about this organization is whether there is a "basic" level that is more psychologically important or "privileged" than other levels. The research we will describe indicates that there is a basic level of categories with special psychological properties but that, in some cases, the basic level may not be the same for everyone. We begin by describing Rosch's research, in which she introduced the idea of basic-level categories.

Rosch's Approach: What's Special About Basic-Level Categories?

Rosch's research starts with the observation that there are different levels of categories, ranging from general (like *furniture*) to specific (like *kitchen table*), as shown in Figure 8.10, and that when people use categories they tend to focus on one of these levels. She distinguished three levels of categories, the **superordinate level** (for example, *furniture*); the **basic level** (for example, *table*); and the **subordinate level** (for example, *kitchen table*). She proposed that the basic level is psychologically special because it is the level above which much information is lost and below which little information is gained. Before reading further, do the following demonstration.

Rosch: basic 'superiority' hyp.

▨ Demonstration

Listing Common Features

This demonstration is a repeat of the task you did in the Family Resemblance demonstration on page 273, but with different categories. For the following categories, list as many features that would be common to all or most of the objects in the category. For example, for *table* you might list "has legs."

1. furniture
2. table
3. kitchen table

If you responded like the participants in the Rosch, Mervis, and coworkers (1976) experiment, who were given the same task, you listed only a few common features for furniture, but many for table and kitchen table. Rosch's participants listed an average of 3 common features for the superordinate-level category *furniture*, 9 for basic-level categories such as *table*, and 10.3 for subordinate-level categories such as *kitchen table* (right column of Figure 8.11). Thus, we can see that if we start at the basic level and go up to superordinate, we lose a lot of information (9 features versus 3 features). However, when we go from basic to subordinate, we gain only a little information (9 features vs. 10.3 features). Thus, the basic level meets Rosch's criterion for being special (going above the level re-

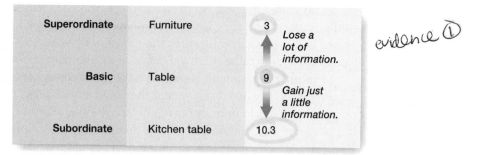

Superordinate	Furniture	3	*Lose a lot of information.*
Basic	Table	9	*Gain just a little information.*
Subordinate	Kitchen table	10.3	

evidence ①

Figure 8.11 Left column: category levels; middle column: examples of each level for *furniture;* right column: average number of common features listed from Rosch, Mervis et al.'s (1976) experiment.

sults in a large loss of information; below results in hardly any gain). Here is another demonstration that is relevant to the idea of a basic level.

◣ Demonstration

Naming Things

Look at Figure 8.12 and, as quickly as possible, write down or say a word that identifies each picture. ◼

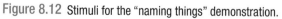

Figure 8.12 Stimuli for the "naming things" demonstration.

What names did you assign to each object? When Rosch and coworkers (1976) did a similar experiment, they found that people tended to pick a basic-level name. So they picked *guitar* (basic level) rather than *musical instrument* (superordinate) or *rock guitar* (subordinate), *fish* rather than *animal* or *trout*, and pants rather than *clothing* or *Levi's*.

In another experiment, Rosch, Simpson, and coworkers (1976) showed participants a category label, like *car* or *vehicle*, and then after a brief delay, presented a picture. The participants' task was to indicate, as rapidly as possible, whether the picture was a member of the category. The results showed that they accomplished this task more rapidly for basic-level categories than for superordinate-level categories. Thus, they would respond "yes" more rapidly if the picture of an automobile was preceded by the word *car* than if the picture was preceded by the word *vehicle*. *how define 'basic'?*

How Knowledge Can Affect Categorization

Rosch's experiments, which were carried out on college undergraduates, showed that there is a level of category, which she called "basic," that reflects people's everyday experience. This has been demonstrated by many researchers in addition to Rosch. Thus, when J. D. Coley and coworkers (1997) asked Northwestern University undergraduates to name, as specifically as possible, 44 different plants on a walk around campus, 75 percent of the responses used labels like "tree," rather than more specific labels like "oak tree."

But if instead of asking college undergraduate to name plants, what if Coley had taken a group of horticulturalists around campus? Do you think they would say "tree" or "oak tree"? An experiment by James Tanaka and Marjorie Taylor (1991) asked a similar question, but for birds. They asked bird experts and nonexperts to name pictures of objects. There were objects from many different categories (tools, clothing, flowers, etc.), but Tanaka and Taylor were interested in how the participants responded to the four bird pictures.

The results (Figure 8.13) show that the experts responded by saying the birds' names (*robin, sparrow, jay,* or *cardinal*), but the nonexperts responded by saying *bird*. Apparently

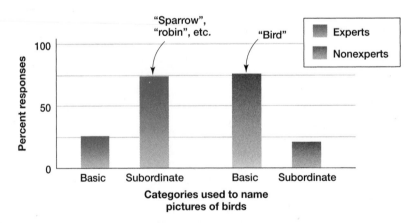

Figure 8.13 Results of J. W. Tanaka and Taylor's (1991) "expert" experiment. Experts (left pair of bars) used more superordinate categories to name birds and nonexperts (right pair of bars) used more basic categories.

the experts have learned to pay attention to features of birds that nonexperts are unaware of. Thus, in order to fully understand how people categorize objects, it is necessary to consider not only the properties of the objects, but the learning and experience of the people perceiving these objects (also see Johnson & Mervis, 1997). From this result we can guess that it is likely that a horticulturist walking around campus would label plants more specifically than people who had little specific knowledge about plants.

How Culture Can Affect Categorization

If being an expert makes people relate to categories at a more specific level, as in the case of Tanaka and Taylor's bird experts, perhaps growing up in a culture that puts a premium on having knowledge about the environment might have a similar effect.

Research studying how members of a traditional village in Guatemala, the Maya Itza, categorize plants, birds, and animals, has shown that culture can, in fact, affect how people categorize. The Itza live in close contact with their natural environment and therefore have a great deal of knowledge about local plants and animals, and identify them at Rosch's subordinate level. That is, an oak tree would be classified as an *oak tree* rather than as a *tree* (Coley et al., 1997).

The effect of culture on categorization has also been studied in another way by Coley (Coley et al., 1997) and Douglas Medin and Scott Atran (2004), who have done a number of experiments investigating how U.S. undergraduates and members of the Itza culture make *inferences* across categories. Participants in these experiments were presented with questions like the following:

If all *oak trees* are susceptible to the disease of the leaf called eta, are all other *trees* susceptible?

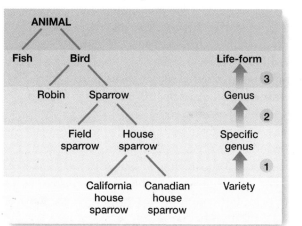

Figure 8.14 A category hierarchy for life forms focusing on birds. The numbers indicate relationships between different levels that correspond to questions (1), (2), and (3) on page 284 (Coley et al., 1997).

There were questions about various plants and animals, with each question always stating that a lower-level category had a disease (*oak tree*, in this example) and asking whether that means members of a higher-level category (*trees*) had the disease. (They also asked some other questions, regarding whether "some," "a few," or "no" members of the higher-level categories had the disease—but we are going to focus on the results for the "all" question.)

We will focus on the three relationships shown in the hierarchy in Figure 8.14. Note that in the right column the levels have been labeled life-form (bird), genus (sparrow), specific genus (house sparrow), and variety (California house sparrow). The sentences corresponding to the three relationships are as follows:

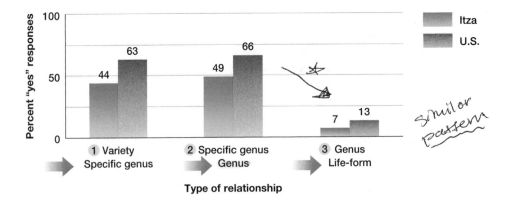

Figure 8.15 Results of Coley et al.'s (1997) experiment showing percentages of "yes" responses to statements like (1), (2), and (3) below. Although U.S. participants produced more "yes" responses than Itza participants, both groups exhibited a large drop in "yes" responses for relationship (3).

1. If all *California house sparrows* are susceptible to disease eta, are all *house sparrows* susceptible?
2. If all *house sparrows* are susceptible to disease eta, are all *sparrows* susceptible?
3. If all *sparrows* are susceptible to disease eta, are all *birds* susceptible?

Figure 8.15 shows the percentage of "yes" responses for the Itza (color bars) and U.S. (gray bars) participants averaged over all of the different animal and plant questions that were presented. For example, 44 percent of Itza responses and 63 percent of the U.S. responses were "yes" to the proposition that if all of the variety category (for example, California house sparrow) was susceptible, then all of the specific genus category (house sparrow) would be susceptible.

What is significant about the results in Figure 8.15 is that Itza and U.S. participants show a similar pattern of responses. For both cultures, inferences were high for relationships (1) and (2) but were low for relationship (3). Thus, participants were willing to make inferences up to the genus level (for example, to sparrows) but not above it (to birds). This result leads to the conclusion that both Itza and U.S. participants treat the genus level as "privileged" in terms of how categories lead to inferences.

These results are surprising when we compare them to the results of earlier categorization experiments. When asked to sort objects into categories, or to name them, the basic level for Itza participants was at the genus level, which would be *sparrow* or *oak tree*. This is similar to the results of the inference experiments, in which the genus level was also "basic" for Itza participants (Figure 8.16, left column). However, for U.S. participants, the life-form level was basic for categorization but the genus level was basic for inference (Figure 8.16, right column). The basic levels for categorization and inference match for Itza participants but do not match for U.S. participants.

Thus, even though most of the U.S. participants might not be able to identify an oak, maple, or hemlock tree in nature, they treat the genus level of trees as basic when asked to

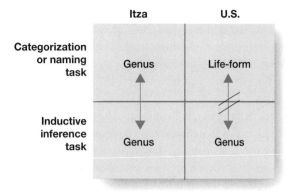

Figure 8.16 Summary of the results of the cross-cultural experiments indicating which levels in the hierarchy in Figure 8.14 are treated as "basic" for tasks involving sorting objects into categories or naming and for tasks involving inference for Itza (left column) and U.S. (right column) participants.

make inferences about them. There may be a number of reasons why this occurs, but one strong possibility is linked to the way the English language labels categories. The genus category is the most general one that contains the same label. For example, the word *sparrow* appears at more specific levels (*California house sparrow*), but not at higher levels (*bird*). Perhaps U.S. participants reason that species with similar names would have similar characteristics, and that is why *sparrow* is basic for inferential reasoning.

These cross-cultural experiments tell us that there are similarities and differences among cultures and that the results are not always obvious before doing the experiment. Who would have guessed that U.S. and Itza participants would reason about biological categories' similarity given the relative ignorance of the U.S. participants about the members of these categories? (Also see Bailenson et al., 2002; Lopez et al., 1997; Proffitt et al., 2000, for some other findings that demonstrate differences among cultures.) But perhaps the most important message of these cross-cultural experiments is that we may not be getting a complete picture of how the human mind operates by just studying U.S. college undergraduates. More cross-cultural research is needed in order to determine the degree to which the cognitive mechanisms we have described in this book hold generally for all humans, or are specific to people in industrialized, Western cultures. We will look at more of this cross-cultural research in the chapters on language (Chapter 10) and reasoning (Chapter 12).

Test Yourself 8.1

1. Why is knowing about categories so important for our day-to-day functioning?
2. Describe the definitional approach to categories. Why does it initially seem like a good way of thinking about categories, but then run into trouble when we consider the kinds of objects that can make up a category?

3. Rosch did a series of experiments investigating the prototype approach to categorization. What is the prototype approach, and what were the experiments that Rosch did that demonstrated connections between prototypicality and behavior?

4. What is the exemplar approach to categorization? How does it differ from the prototype approach, and how might the prototype approach and exemplar approach work together?

5. What does it mean to say that there are different levels within a category? What arguments did Rosch present to support the idea that one of these levels is "privileged"? How has research on how experts and people in traditional cultures categorize led to modifications of Rosch's ideas about which category is "basic" or "privileged"?

6. What has cross-cultural research taught us about how people from different cultures use categories as a way to make inferences?

Representing Relationships Between Categories: Semantic Networks

We have seen that categories can be arranged in a hierarchical organization that represents the levels of categories from general (at the top) to specific (at the bottom). Our main focus in the last section was on deciding which level of the hierarchy is psychologically privileged. In this section, our main concern is to explain how this hierarchical organization can represent how categories are *organized* in the mind. The approach we will be describing, called the **semantic network approach,** proposes that concepts are arranged in networks that represent the way concepts are organized in the mind.

Introduction to Semantic Networks: Collins and Quillian's Model

One of the first semantic network models is based on the pioneering work of Ross Quillian (1967, 1969), whose goal was to develop a model for the structure of human memory that could be run on a computer. We will describe Quillian's approach by looking at a simplified version of his model proposed by Allan Collins and Quillian (1969).

Figure 8.17 shows Collins and Quillian's network. Figure 8.17a, which shows the "skeleton" of Collins and Quillian's model, indicates that the network consists of nodes that are connected by links. Each node represents a category or concept, and concepts are placed in the network so related concepts are connected.

In Figure 8.17b, some concept names have been added to the nodes. The fact that the nodes are connected by links means that they are related to each other in the mind. Thus, the model shown in Figure 8.17b indicates that there is an association in the mind between *canary* and *bird*, and between *bird* and *animal*.

In Figure 8.17c we have filled in the rest of the network by adding concepts *fish*, *shark*, *salmon*, and *ostrich*, and also by including properties of each concept at the nodes. We can illustrate how this network works by considering how we would retrieve the properties of canaries from the network. We start by entering the network at the concept node for *canary*.

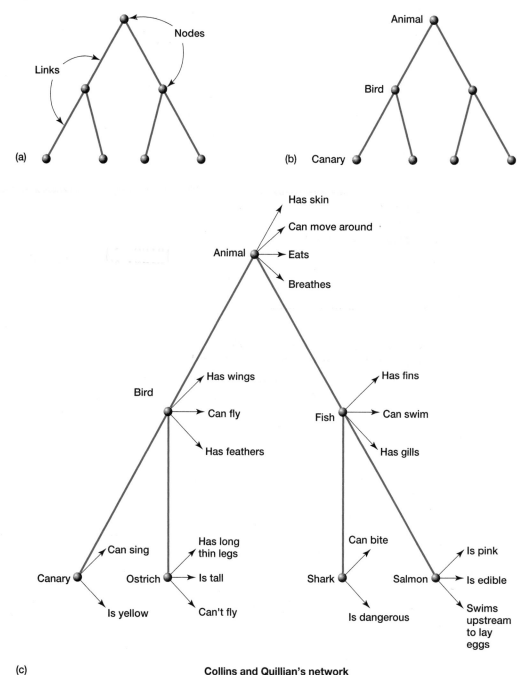

(a)

(b)

(c)   **Collins and Quillian's network**

Figure 8.17 Building a semantic network. (a) The skeleton-nodes connected by links. (b) Adding concept names to the nodes, with more specific ones at the bottom and more general ones at the top. (c) Adding properties of each concept. This is the network proposed by Collins and Quillian (1969). (Reprinted from *Journal of Verbal Learning and Verbal Behavior, 8,* A. M. Collins & M. R. Quillian, "Retrieval Time from Semantic Memory," pp. 240–247, Fig. 1, Copyright © 1969, with permission from Elsevier.)

When we do this we obtain the information that a canary *can sing* and *is yellow*. To access more information about *canary*, we move up the link to *bird* and learn that a *canary* is a *bird* and that a *bird has wings*, *can fly*, and *has feathers*. Moving up another level to *animal*, we find that a *canary* is also an *animal*, which *has skin*, *can move around*, *eats*, and *breathes*.

You might wonder why we have to travel away from canary to find out that a canary can fly. After all, that information could have been placed at the canary node and then we would know it right away. But Collins and Quillian felt that including *can fly* at the node for every bird (*canary, robin, vulture,* etc.) was inefficient and would use up too much storage space. Thus, instead of indicating the properties *can fly* and *has feathers* for every kind of bird, these properties were placed at the node for bird because this property holds for most birds. This way of storing shared properties at a higher-level node is called cognitive economy.

While cognitive economy makes the network more efficient, it does create a problem because not all birds fly. To deal with this problem while still achieving the advantages of cognitive economy, Collins and Quillian added exceptions at lower nodes. For example, to handle the fact that ostriches don't fly, the property *can't fly* is added to the node for ostrich.

Semantic networks look logical, but are they an accurate representation of how concepts are organized in the mind? The beauty of the network's hierarchical organization is that it provides a way to answer this question because it predicts that the time it takes for a person to retrieve information about a concept should be determined by the distance that must be traveled through the network. Thus, the model predicts that by using the sentence-verification technique, in which participants are asked to answer *yes* or *no* to statements about concepts (see page 273), it should take longer to answer "yes" to the statement *a canary is an animal* than to *a canary is a bird*. This prediction follows from the fact that it is necessary to travel along two links to get from *canary* to *animal* but only one to get to *bird* (Figure 8.18).

"A canary is an animal."   "A canary is a bird."

Figure 8.18 The distance between concepts predicts how long it takes to retrieve information about concepts as measured by the sentence-verification technique. Because it is necessary to travel on two links to get from *canary* to *animal* (left), but on only one to get from *canary* to *bird* (right), it should take longer to verify the statement "a canary is an animal."

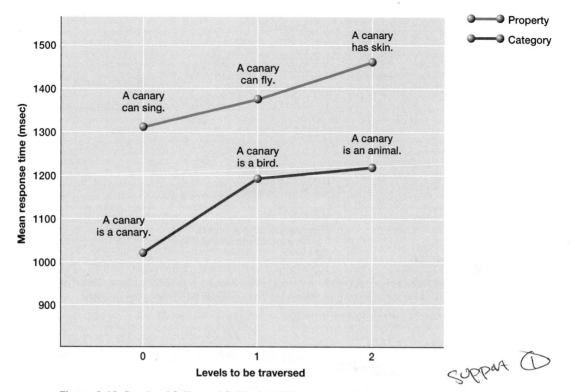

Figure 8.19 Results of Collins and Quillian's (1969) experiment that measured reaction times to statements that involved traversing different distances in the network. Greater distances are associated with longer reaction times, both when verifying statements about properties of canaries (top) and about categories of which the canary is a member (bottom). (Reprinted from *Journal of Verbal Learning and Verbal Behavior, 8,* A. M. Collins & M. R. Quillian, "Retrieval Time from Semantic Memory," pp. 240–247, Fig. 2, Copyright © 1969, with permission from Elsevier.)

Collins and Quillian (1969) tested this prediction by measuring the reaction time to a number of different statements and obtained the result shown in Figure 8.19. As predicted, statements that required further travel from *canary* resulted in longer reaction times.

Another property of the theory, which leads to further predications, is spreading activation. Spreading activation is activity that spreads out along any link that is connected to an activated node. For example, if we move through the network from *canary* to *bird*, the node at *bird* and the link we use to get from *canary* to *bird* are activated, as indicated by the bold arrow in Figure 8.20. This activation then spreads to other nodes in the network, as indicated by the dashed lines. Thus, if the pathway from *canary* to *bird* is activated, activation spreads to concepts that are connected to *bird*, such as *animal* and other types of birds. The result of this spread of activation is that the additional concepts that receive this activation become "primed" and so can be accessed more easily from memory. (We previously discussed priming in conjunction with prototype theory on page 274 and also when we discussed implicit memory in Chapter 6, page 191.)

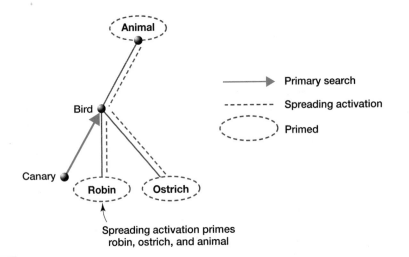

Spreading activation primes
robin, ostrich, and animal

Figure 8.20 How activation can spread through a network as a person searches from *canary* to *bird* (arrow). The dashed lines indicate activation that is spreading from the activated *bird* node. Circled concepts, which have become primed, are easier to retrieve from memory due to the spreading activation.

CogLab

Lexical
Decision

The spreading activation explanation of priming was studied by David Meyer and Roger Schvaneveldt (1971) in a paper published shortly after Collins and Quillian's model was proposed. They used a procedure called the lexical-decision task, in which participants had to decide, as quickly as possible, whether a string of letters was a word or a nonword. They presented two strings of letters, one above the other, and the participants' task was to press the "yes" key if both strings were words or the "no" key if one or both were not words. Thus, the two nonwords shown in Figure 8.21a or the word and nonword in Figure 8.21b would require a "no" response, but the two stimuli in Figure 8.21c and d would require a "yes" response.

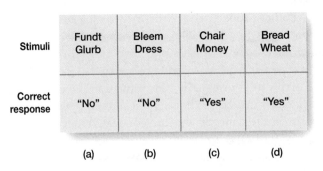

Stimuli	Fundt Glurb	Bleem Dress	Chair Money	Bread Wheat
Correct response	"No"	"No"	"Yes"	"Yes"
	(a)	(b)	(c)	(d)

Figure 8.21 Stimuli and correct responses for Meyer and Schvaneveldt's (1971) priming experiment.

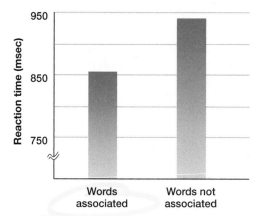

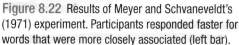

Figure 8.22 Results of Meyer and Schvaneveldt's (1971) experiment. Participants responded faster for words that were more closely associated (left bar).

The key variable in this experiment was the association between the pairs of real words. In some trials the words were closely associated (as for *bread* and *wheat*) and in some trials they were weakly associated (as for *chair* and *money*). The result, shown in Figure 8.22, was that reaction time was faster if the two words were associated. Meyer and Schvaneveldt proposed that this might have occurred because retrieving one word from memory triggers a spread of activation to other nearby locations in a network, and that more activation will spread to words that are related so that the response to the related words will be faster than the response to unrelated words. *What about confounds? word length? similarity? How many trials/prs 1*

Criticism of the Collins and Quillian Model

Although Collins and Quillian's model was supported by the results of a number of experiments, it didn't take long for other researchers to call the theory into question. They pointed out that the theory couldn't explain the typicality effect, in which reaction times are faster for more typical members of a category than for less typical members (see page 274) (Rips et al., 1973). Thus, although the statement *a canary is a bird* is verified more quickly than the sentence *an ostrich is a bird*, the model predicts equally fast reaction times for both, since *canary* and *ostrich* are both just one node away from *bird*. *①*

Researchers also questioned the concept of cognitive economy because of evidence that people may, in fact, store specific properties of concepts (like *has wings* for *canary*) right at the node for that concept (Conrad, 1972). In addition, Lance Rips and coworkers (1973) obtained sentence-verification results such as the following: *②*

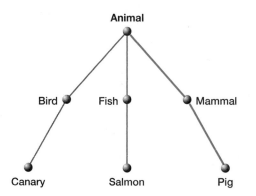

Figure 8.23 Semantic network that shows that *pig* is closer to *mammal* than to *animal*.

- *A pig is a mammal.*   RT = 1,476 msec.
- *A pig is an animal.*   RT = 1,268 msec. → *should be slower*

A pig is an animal is verified more quickly but as we can see from the network in Figure 8.23, the Collins and Quillian model predicts that *a pig is a mammal* should be verified more quickly because a link leads directly from pig to mammal, but to reach animal we need to cross the mammal node and go one link further. Sentence-verification results such as these, plus the other criticisms of the theory, led Collins and Elizabeth Loftus (1975) to propose a new semantic network model designed to handle the results that the Collins and Quillian model couldn't explain.

Collins and Loftus Answer the Critics

Collins and Loftus's (1975) model deals with problems that Collins and Quillian's model had with the typicality effect by using shorter links to connect concepts that are more closely related. For example, the network in Figure 8.24 indicates that *vehicle* is connected to *car*, *truck*, or *bus* by short links (because these are closely related concepts), but is connected to *fire engine* and *ambulance* (which are less typical vehicles than *car*, *truck*, or *bus*) with longer links.

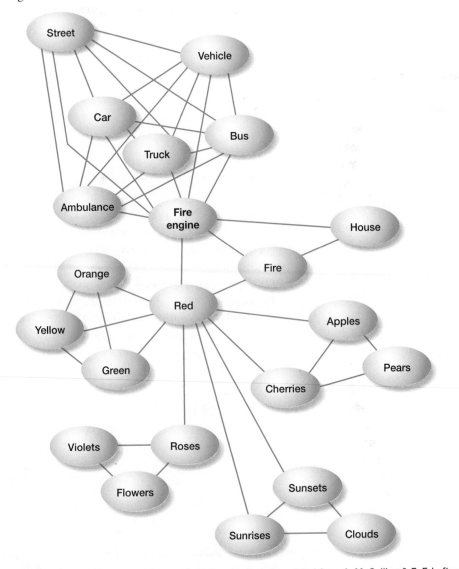

Figure 8.24 Semantic network proposed by Collins and Loftus. (Reprinted from A. M. Collins & E. F. Loftus, "A Spreading-Activation Theory of Semantic Processing." From *Psychological Review, 82,* pp. 407–428, Fig. 1. Copyright © 1975 with permission from the American Physiological Association.)

An important feature of the Collins and Loftus model is that it abandons the hierarchical structure used by Collins and Quillian in favor of a structure based on a person's experience. The spacing between various concepts can differ for various people depending on their experience and knowledge about specific concepts. *→does this get @ culture issue ? too?*

In addition to proposing experientially based links between concepts, Collins and Loftus also proposed a number of additional modifications to the Collins and Quillian model to deal with problems like cognitive economy and the *pig/mammal* problem. The details of their proposed modifications aren't that important. What is important is that these modifications made it possible to explain just about any result of categorization experiments. Collins and Loftus describe their theory as "a fairly complicated theory with enough generality to apply to results from many different experimental paradigms" (1975, p. 427). Although you might think that being able to explain just about any result would be an advantage, this property of the model led some researchers to criticize it.

Assessment of Semantic Network Theories

Why would a model be criticized if it can explain just about any result? We can answer this question by considering the following properties of good psychological theories:

1. *Explanatory power.* The theory can explain why a particular result occurred by making a statement like "Behavior *A* occurred because. . . ."
2. *Predictive power.* The theory can predict the results of a particular experiment by making a statement like "Under these circumstances, behavior *A* will occur."
3. *Falsifiability.* The theory can potentially be shown to be deficient if a particular experimental result occurs. The statement associated with falsifiability is "According to the theory, result *A* will occur, but not result *B*."
4. *Generation of experiments.* Good theories usually stimulate a great deal of research to test the theory, to determine ways of improving the theory, to use new methods suggested by the theory, or study new questions raised by the theory.

When we evaluate the original Collins and Quillian theory against these criteria we find that while it does explain and predict some results (see the data in Figure 8.19), it fails because there are results it can't explain, such as the typicality effect and the longer reaction times for sentences like "a pig is a mammal." These failures to accurately explain and predict are what led Collins and Loftus to propose their theory.

But Collins and Loftus's theory has been criticized for being so flexible that it is difficult to falsify. We can understand why this is a problem by considering the networks in Figure 8.25, which show the node for fire engine and some of its links for two different people. The fire engine node would be more easily activated for the network in (b) than in (a) because the links with other vehicles are shorter in (b). But the lengths of the links can be determined by a number of factors, including a person's past experience with fire engines or other types of vehicles. Unfortunately, there are no definite rules for determining these lengths—or, for that matter, for determining things like how long activation remains after it spreads, or how much total activation is needed to trigger a node. This

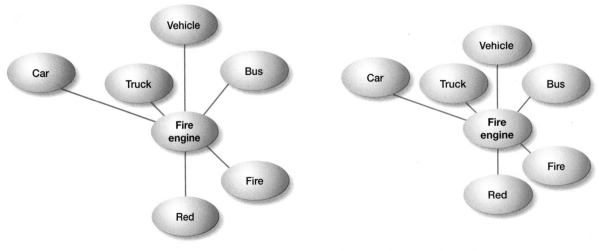

(a) Randy's links to fire engine

(b) Sandra's links to fire engine

Figure 8.25 The node for *fire engine* and some of the concepts to which it is linked for two different people: (a) longer links; (b) shorter links.

means that by appropriately adjusting things like the length of the links and how long activation lasts, the model can "explain" many different results.

But if a theory can explain almost any result by adjusting various properties of the model, what has it really explained? That question is what led P. N. Johnson-Laird and coworkers (1984) to publish a paper that criticized semantic network theories and that concluded that these theories are "too powerful to be refuted by empirical evidence." This is a way of saying that it is difficult to falsify the theories. (See J. R. Anderson & Bower, 1973; Glass & Holyoak, 1975, for additional semantic network theories.)

Although research on semantic network theories was declining by the 1980s, network theories began a resurgence with the publication of a book titled *Parallel Distributed Processing: Explorations in the Microstructure of Cognition* by James McClelland and David Rummelhart (1986). This book proposed a network model of mental functioning called **connectionism.**

REPRESENTING CONCEPTS IN NETWORKS: THE CONNECTIONIST APPROACH

McClelland and Rummelhart proposed that concepts are represented in networks that contain nodes and links like semantic networks, but that operate very differently from semantic networks. The first step in understanding **connectionist networks** is to appreciate that they are modeled after <u>neural networks</u> in the nervous system. Thus, we will begin by reviewing some basic facts of nervous system operation that have been incorporated into connectionist theory.

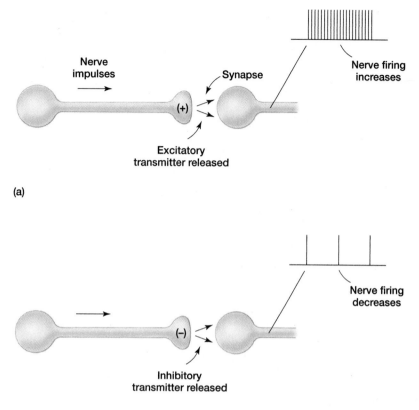

Figure 8.26 Effect of transmitter release at the synapse. (a) Excitatory neurotransmitter increases firing. (b) Inhibitory neurotransmitter decreases firing.

Physiological Bases of Connectionsm

The following principles of nervous system functioning, which we introduced in Chapters 2 and 3, are relevant to connectionism.

Neural Circuits   Information is processed by circuits that are created by neurons that are connected to one another by synapses (Figure 8.26a).

Excitatory and Inhibitory Connections   These synaptic connections between neurons can be excitatory (+) or inhibitory (–). Nerve impulses reaching an excitatory synapse cause the release of transmitter that creates an increase in activity in the next neuron (Figure 8.26a). Nerve impulses reaching an inhibitory synapse cause the release of transmitter that creates a decrease in activity in the next neuron (Figure 8.26b).

Each circle represents a neuron. Darker shading means more firing.

(a) Activity in 5 neurons for Bill's face

Bill

Samantha

(b) Activity in 5 neurons for Samantha's face

Figure 8.27 How five neurons respond to (a) Bill's face; (b) Samantha's face. The pattern of firing across a number of neurons represents a particular face.

Strength of Firing   The number of inputs reaching a neuron and the nature of these inputs (+ or −) determine the rate at which the neuron will fire. A neuron that receives excitatory inputs from many neurons will be more likely to fire than one that receives few excitatory inputs. Similarly, more inhibitory inputs favors lower firing rates.

Distributed Coding   In Chapter 2 we described how the nervous system uses distributed coding to represent different objects so that each object is represented by the pattern of activity across a number of neurons. Thus, Bill's face is indicated by the pattern of activity shown in Figure 8.27a, and Samantha's face is indicated by the pattern shown in Figure 8.27b. The important thing about distributed coding is that to identify a specific object, it is not sufficient to consider activity in an individual neuron. Instead, we must consider the pattern of firing across a number of neurons. Another principle of distributed coding is that objects that are similar cause similar (but not identical) patterns of activity.

Basic Principles of Connectionism

In describing connectionism, it is important to realize that while this model is *based* on the principles of the nervous system like the ones just described, it is not a model of how the

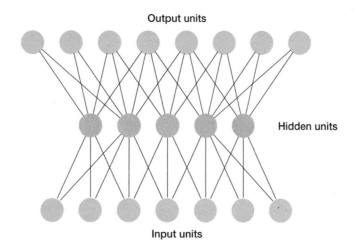

Output units

Hidden units

Input units

Figure 8.28 A parallel distributed processing (PDP) network.

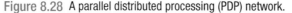

nervous system works. It is a hypothetical system that has the goal of showing how the pattern of activity in a network can represent a specific category. Taking its cue from distributed coding in the nervous system, connectionist theory proposes that the representation of knowledge in our nervous system occurs not in individual units, but in the distributed activity of many units (McClelland et al., 1995). Because the processing in these networks, as in the nervous system, occurs in many parallel lines at the same time, and because the output of these networks is distributed across many units, the connectionist approach is also called the **parallel distributed processing approach,** or **PDP** for short. For convenience, we will use the term *PDP* interchangeably with *connectionist* in the discussion that follows.

This idea of distributed activity is the basis of the PDP network shown in Figure 8.28. The nodes in this network, which have been called "neuronlike processing units" because they are modeled after neurons in the nervous system (McClelland, 1999), are usually called **units,** rather than nodes as they are in semantic networks. There are three kinds of units: **input units** are activated by stimulation from the environment. **Hidden units** receive signals from the input units and pass them along to the **output units.** The pattern of activation of the output units represents the stimulus that was presented to the input units.

The links that connect these units have excitatory and inhibitory connections similar to excitatory and inhibitory synapses in the nervous system. As in the nervous system, these connections can either excite or inhibit the units to which they are connected, and the strength of the connection can vary. The strength of the connection to a unit is called the **weight** of that input, with positive weights meaning that the input is excitatory, and negative weights meaning that the input is inhibitory.

Operation of Connectionist Networks: Representing Canary

How does a PDP network operate? The idea behind PDP networks is that a particular stimulus is represented by a particular pattern of output activity. Thus, the pattern of activity in the output units shown in Figure 8.29a might represent *canary* and the pattern in Figure 8.29b might represent *robin*, and so on. The pattern of output activity depends both on how the input units respond to a stimulus and on the weights of the connections to each of the units.

The idea that a particular concept is represented by a pattern of activity across a number of units is the starting point of PDP theory. But the main question addressed by the theory is, how does this pattern occur? According to connectionism, people are not born with built-in patterns for canary and robin. These patterns are created by learning.

To appreciate how learning can result in a particular output pattern, let's consider how this might work for the concept *canary*. We begin with the network in Figure 8.30a, in which no learning has taken place. Presenting the word *canary* activates the input units, and this activation is transmitted to the hidden units, and from the hidden units to the output units. Note that the input can be the word *canary*, a picture of a canary, a real canary, or even the sound a canary makes. The important thing about this kind of network is that its goal is to create a response across the output units that stands for *canary*.

The signal that reaches the output units is determined by the initial signal generated by the input units and the way this signal is changed by excitation and inhibition as it passes through the network. Eventually, after the signals have worked their way through the network, each of the output units is activated. The response of these output units in this example is +10, +6, +5, and +2, as indicated by the numbers inside the units.

Because no learning has yet occurred in this network, this initial output pattern is different from the pattern that specifies *canary*. The correct pattern, which is +5, +3, +10, and +4, is indicated in the squares above the network. This correct pattern, which in research on PDP networks is often supplied by the experimenter, is the starting point for a process of learning that will eventually result in an output pattern that matches the correct pattern.

The network's learning process begins when the initial output is compared to the correct output, just as you might compare your answers on a practice test to the correct

(a) Input = canary

(b) Input = robin

Figure 8.29 The pattern of activity across a number of output units in a PDP network represents a specific stimulus. Darker shading indicates greater activation. This example shows that *canary* and *robin* are represented by different patterns of activity.

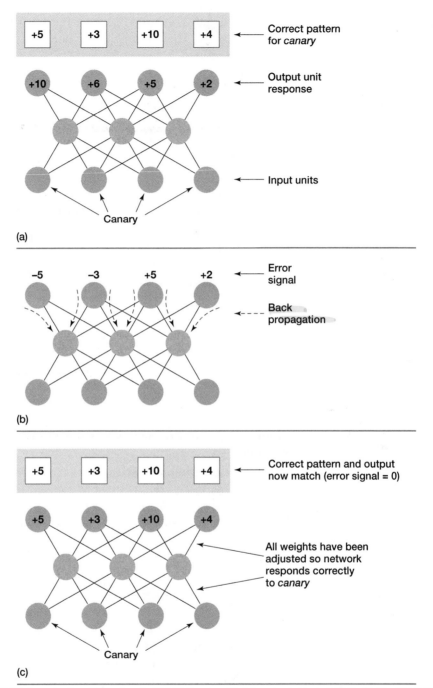

Figure 8.30 Learning in a PDP network. (a) Initially presenting *canary* causes a pattern of activation in the output units that is different than the pattern that stands for *canary*. (b) An error signal is transmitted back through the network to indicate how weights need to be changed to achieve the correct output response. (c) After the processes in (a) and (b) are repeated many times, the network has learned to respond correctly to *canary*.

answers in a study guide. The difference between the actual output pattern and the correct pattern is called the **error signal**. The error signal for our example, which is indicated by the numbers above the output units in Figure 8.30b, is –5, –3, +5 and +2. This error signal provides the feedback that the network can use to learn how to create the correct output pattern for *canary*.

One way this learning can occur is through a process called **back propagation,** in which the error signal is transmitted backward through the circuit. This back propagation of the error signal is symbolized by the dashed arrows in Figure 8.30b. Information provided by the back propagated error signal indicates how the network's weights need to be adjusted so that the output signal will match the correct signal.

From the error signal, we can see that the strength of the inputs to the units on the left need to be decreased and the strength of the inputs to two units on the right need to be increased. This is achieved by changing the weights of the connections between the units. However, this is a complex process because each unit is connected to many units, so changing the weight at one unit can affect the strength of the signals reaching a number of other units. Thus if the weights are changed so the error signal is suddenly reduced to 0 at one place, this could increase the error signal at a number of other places. To prevent this from happening, the back propagation process is tuned to cause only small changes in the weights on any given learning trial.

Because only small changes in the weights occur on a particular trial, this learning process has to be repeated many times before the error signal is reduced to 0. Presenting *canary* again causes signals to travel through the network, generating an output signal and a new error signal that should be slightly smaller than the previous one. This new error signal is back propagated through the circuit, the weights are adjusted again, and the process is repeated until eventually, when the error signal has reached 0, the network has learned the correct pattern for *canary* (Figure 8.30c).

Once the learning process is completed so that presenting *canary* results in the pattern of activity that stands for canary, the circuit is said to contain knowledge about canaries. But where is this knowledge located? Remember that in a semantic network, like the one in Figure 8.17, information is contained at specific nodes. For example, the *animal* node indicates that animals can move and have skin, and this node is connected to other nodes, which contain information about fish, birds, and other animals. Thus, each node in this semantic network provides information similar to what you might find in an encyclopedia or a textbook. Because each location of a semantic network is a rich source of information, we can describe the information in a semantic network as being stored locally.

The situation is quite different in a PDP network because each unit of a PDP network contains little information. Instead, information in a PDP network is *distributed* as a pattern of activity over many units. *Canary*, in our example, is indicated by the pattern of activity in the output units, and perhaps in the hidden units as well.

Our description of how a PDP network learns has focused on one concept—*canary*. Of course, if a network is to be a useful storehouse of knowledge, it needs to contain specific information about canaries, such as "has wings" and "can fly," and also information about many other concepts in addition to canaries. Although creating networks that can do this is a complex process, research using intricate networks and powerful computer-driven calculations has succeeded in creating networks that are able to distinguish among a number of different concepts and to indicate specific properties associated with these concepts (see McClelland et al., 1995).

An issue that connectionist researchers have considered in connection with the learning process we have described, is the common observation that learning often occurs very rapidly, without a large number of learning trials. For example, when Pam parks her car in a parking lot, she simply notes that her car is parked about halfway up aisle 5. Pam does not need a large number of learning trials to know where she parked her car.

It has been proposed that rapid learning such as this is handled by a memory system that is located in the hippocampus, whereas the many-trial learning proposed by PDP theory occurs in the cerebral cortex (McClelland, 2003; McClelland & Rogers, 2003; McClelland et al., 1995). According to this idea, information about where you just parked your car would be stored in the hippocampus, but detailed information about characteristics of different cars would be stored in the cortex (Figure 8.31).

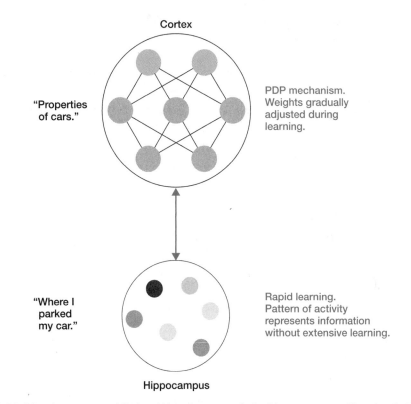

Figure 8.31 It has been proposed that rapid learning occurs in the hippocampus, and learning that requires many trials, as proposed by the PDP model, occurs in the cortex (McClelland, 2003; McClelland & Rogers, 2003; McClelland et al., 1995). This is a very schematic diagram that illustrates this idea.

Connectionism is an approach that many researchers see as providing an important way to study the representation of knowledge and how these representations may be established. However, this approach is still being developed and just like the prototype, exemplar, and semantic network approaches, there is some evidence that supports the theory and some questions that raise problems for it.

Support for PDP Theory   The following arguments have been offered as support for PDP theory:

- *PDP networks are based on the nervous system.* One of the most appealing things about this approach is that it is based on the nervous system. Even though PDP circuits are extremely simplified compared to actual neural circuits (a single neuron in the cortex can receive signals from thousands of other neurons, whereas the units in a PDP circuit receive inputs from a dozen or fewer other units), the basic principles of operation are similar.

- *The system is not totally disrupted by damage.* Because information in the PDP network is not localized at a single place, damage to the system does not completely disrupt its operation. This property, in which disruption of performance occurs only gradually as parts of the system are damaged, is called **graceful degradation,** and is similar to what often happens in actual cases of brain damage.

- *Learning can be generalized.* Because similar concepts have similar patterns, training a system to recognize the properties of one concept (such as *canary*) also provides information about other, related, concepts (such as *robin* and *sparrow*). This is similar to the way we actually learn about concepts because learning about birds in general enables us to predict properties of birds we've never seen. This ability to generalize is the basis of intelligent behavior and the constructive nature of memory (see McClelland et al., 1995).

- *Successful computer models have been developed.* Computer models based on PDP networks have been created that respond to being damaged in ways similar to the response that occurs in actual cases of brain damage in humans. Some researchers have suggested that studying the way networks respond to damage may suggest strategies for rehabilitation of human patients (Farah et al., 1993; Hinton & Shallice, 1991; Olson & Humphreys, 1997).

Problems for PDP Theory   The following have been proposed as problems for PDP theory.

- *The theory explains some things, but not others.* PDP networks perform best for tasks such perceiving objects or recognizing words, but so far can't explain more complex processes like understanding language or solving problems (McClelland, 1988).

- *Learning one concept can interfere with remembering a previously learned concept.* If the network's weights have been adjusted through the training process previously described, so that the network is tuned to create the correct pattern for one concept, these weights can be changed by training the network on another concept (Ratcliff, 1990). Solutions that involve longer training periods have been proposed to deal with this problem (McClelland et al., 1995).

- *It is difficult to explain rapid learning.* The idea that network weights are determined by repetitive experience that takes many trials does not explain how we learn some facts rapidly, without many trials. As we have seen, proponents of PDP have proposed that this rapid learning is handled by the subcortical hippocampus, whereas the gradual learning proposed by PDP occurs in the cortex. This may be what is occurring, but this idea is a hypothesis that requires further research.

Overall Assessment   Opinion regarding PDP networks is divided. Some researchers believe that this approach holds great promise and are especially attracted to working on a system that shares some properties with the nervous system. Other researchers think that there are limits to what PDP networks can explain, and feel that even if these networks may explain some aspects of how we store knowledge, the best way to explain how knowledge is represented in the mind is to combine connectionism with some of the other approaches to semantic memory that we discussed at the beginning of the chapter.

Schacker: dual approach...

CATEGORIES IN THE BRAIN

How are categories represented in the brain? We know from our study of perception (Chapter 3), working memory (Chapter 5), and long-term memory (Chapter 6) that specialization is a basic principle of brain operation, so that different areas of the brain are specialized for different functions, such as recognizing faces, remembering information that has just been experienced, and remembering information that has been stored for a long period of time. But does this principle of specialization apply to categories? Neuropsychological research, brain imaging, and single-neuron recording have provided evidence that areas of the brain are, in fact, selective for categories, although it is unlikely that there is a specific area for each category.

Selectivity of Brain Areas

The first indication that different areas of the brain may be specialized to process information about different categories came from neuropsychological research. Elizabeth Warrington and Tom Shallice (1984) summarized a number of papers that showed that people with damage to their inferior temporal (IT) lobe tend to lose ability to recognize living things, while retaining the ability to recognize human-made artifacts such as tools

Table 8.3	Neuropsychology of Categories	
	Naming	
Cases	Living Things	Nonliving Things
Living Things Deficient*	Deficient	OK
Nonliving Things Deficient†	OK	Deficient

*Caramazza & Shelton (1998); Farah & Wallace (1992); Hart & Gordon (1992); Hart et al., (1985); Hills & Caramazza (1991); Silveri & Gainotti (1988); Warrington & Shallice (1984).

†Sheridan & Humphreys (1993); Warrington & McCarthy (1983).

Source: Caramazza, 2000.

and furniture. (Remember from Chapter 3 that the IT cortex is associated with form perception and the perception of faces). Later research discovered some patients who had difficulty recognizing tools, but not living things. These are examples of a condition called **visual agnosia,** in which people can *see* objects perfectly well, but they cannot *name* these objects. *vs. anomia*

These cases, summarized in Table 8.3, indicate a double dissociation for living things versus nonliving things. Remember from Chapters 2 (page 51) and 6 (page 187) that a double dissociation means that two functions (in this case, categorizing living things and categorizing nonliving things) are served by different and independent mechanisms. However, just to make things interesting, Hills and Caramazza (1991) found a patient who was unable to name nonliving things and some living things, like and fruits and vegetables, but could name other living things, such as animals.

The idea that nonliving and living things are represented in different places in the brain has been confirmed by fMRI research, but with the warning that there is a lot of overlap between activations for different categories (Chao et al., 1999). The fact that different categories activate different areas of the brain but that there is some overlap in the activation for different categories has led to the idea that categories are represented by distributed activity, with categories with similar features causing more similar patterns of brain activity (Low et al., 2003; Martin & Chao, 2001).

Support for PDP

Selectivity of Neurons

Looking at how single neurons in the brain respond to different stimuli reveals that some neurons, called **category-specific neurons,** respond best to objects in specific categories. There are category-specific neurons in the temporal lobe that respond best to objects like the ones shown in Figure 8.32 (Kreiman et al., 2000a). Keep in mind that these neurons don't respond to just one particular object, but to a large number of objects that make up a particular category. Thus, the neuron that responds to the picture of the particular house in Figure 8.32 will also respond to pictures of many other houses as well. What this means

FFA? where in temporal?

Kreiman, G., Koch, C., & Fried, I. (2000a). Category-specific visual responses of single neurons in the human medial temporal lobe. *Nature Neuroscience, 3,* 946–953.

Figure 8.32 There are neurons in the temporal lobe, called category-specific neurons, that respond best to specific objects like the ones shown here (Kreiman et al., 2000a).

is that recognizing a particular house probably involves the firing of a large number of "house" neurons. Thus, just as a particular face is signaled by the pattern of firing across a number of neurons (Figure 8.27), a particular house is probably represented by the pattern of firing across many neurons.

In this chapter, we have described a number of approaches to categorization, each of which has its strengths and weaknesses. Each approach makes some contribution to our understanding of how we store and use knowledge, but more research is needed—especially in the more recently developed areas of connectionist networks and brain mechanisms—before we will really understand how our vast base of knowledge is created and then how it is accessed when we need to use it.

1. What is the basic idea behind the semantic network approach? What is the goal behind this approach, and how did the network created by Collins and Quillian accomplish this goal?
2. What is the evidence for and against the Collins and Quillian model? How did Collins and Loftus modify the model to deal with criticisms of the Collins and Quillian model, and how were these modifications received by other researchers?
3. What are some of the properties of a good psychological theory? How can we apply these properties to the semantic network theories?
4. What is the relationship between the properties of connectionist networks and the real networks that exist in the nervous system?
5. What is the goal of a connectionist network? Describe how a connectionist network would achieve this goal, beginning with the input of a stimulus and ending with the representation of that stimulus in the network. Also consider how the way information is represented in a connectionist network differs from the way it is represented in a semantic network.
6. What is the evidence about how categories are represented in the brain?

Think About It

1. In this chapter we have seen how networks can be constructed that link different levels of concepts. In Chapter 6 we saw how networks can be constructed that organize knowledge about a particular topic (see Figures 6.12 and 6.13). Create a network that represents the material in this chapter by linking together things that are related. How is this network similar to or different from the semantic network in Figure 8.17? Is your network hierarchical? What information does it contain about each concept?

2. Do a survey to determine people's conception of "typical" members of various categories. For example, ask several people to name, as quickly as possible, three typical "birds," or "vehicles," or "beverages." What do the results of this survey tell you about what level is "basic" for different people? What do the results tell you about the variability of different people's conception of categories?

Key Terms

Back propagation

Basic level

Categorization

Category

Category-specific neurons

Cognitive economy

Concept
Connectionism
Connectionist networks
Definitional approach to categorization
Error signal
Exemplar approach to categorization
Examplar
Family resemblance
Graceful degradation
Hidden units
Hierarchical organization
High-prototypicality
Input units
Lexical-decision task
Low-prototypicality

Output units
Parallel distributed processing approach (PDP)
Prototype
Prototype approach to categorization
Prototypicality
Semantic network approach
Sentence-verification technique
Spreading activation
Subordinate level
Superordinate level
Typicality effect
Units
Visual agnosia
Weight

CogLab To experience these experiments for yourself, go to http://coglab.wadsworth.com. Be sure to read each experiment's setup instructions before you go to the experiment itself. Otherwise, you won't know which keys to press.

Primary Labs

Prototypes   A method for studying the effect of concepts on responding (p. 270).

Lexical decision   Demonstration of the lexical-decision task, which has been used to provide evidence for the concept of spreading activation (p. 290).

Related Lab

Absolute identification Remembering labels that have been associated with a stimulus.

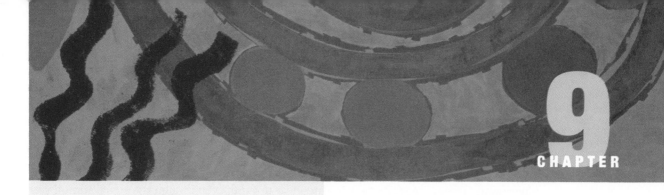

Visual Imagery

Some Questions We Will Consider

✔ How do "pictures in your head" that you create by imagining an object compare to the experience you have when you see the actual object?

✔ What happens in your brain when you create visual images with your eyes closed?

✔ How can we use visual imagery to improve memory?

■   ■   ■

As you look up to observe what's around you, you experience images that are created by nerve impulses that are traveling from your retina to your brain and then to areas in your brain that are responsible for perception. But there is another way to experience images. Consider, for example, what you experience when answering the following questions:

- How many windows are there in front of the house or apartment where you live?
- How is the furniture arranged in your bedroom?
- Are an elephant's ears rounded or pointy?

People often report that they answer questions such as these by forming images in their mind. These images that you create in your mind, even though the actual stimuli you are imagining are not present, are the result of **mental imagery**—experiencing a sensory impression in the absence of sensory input.

WHAT IS IMAGERY, AND WHAT IS IT FOR?

The particular kind of mental imagery involved in the foregoing examples is **visual imagery**—"seeing" in the absence of a visual stimulus. The ability to recreate the sensory world in the absence of physical stimuli also occurs in other senses as well. People also have the ability to imagine tastes, smells, and tactile experiences, and because most people can imagine melodies of familiar songs in their head, it is not surprising that musicians often report strong auditory imagery and that the ability to imagine melodies has played an important role in musical composition. Paul McCartney says that the song "Yesterday" came to him as a mental image, when he woke up with the tune in his head. Another example of auditory imagery is when orchestra conductors use a technique called the "inner audition" to practice without their orchestras by imagining a musical score in their minds. When they do this, they not only imagine the sounds of the various instruments but their locations relative to the podium as well.

In this chapter we will consider visual imagery, because most of the research on mental imagery has focused on visual imagery and because understanding visual imagery provides connections to other cognitive phenomena such as perception, memory, and thinking.

The Uses of Visual Imagery

Just as auditory imagery has played an important role in the creative process of music, visual imagery has resulted in both scientific insights and practical applications. One of the most famous accounts of how visual imagery led to scientific discovery is the story related by the 19th-century chemist Kekule, about how the structure of benzene came to him in a dream in which he saw a writhing chain that formed a circle that resembled a snake, with its head swallowing its tail. This visual image gave Kekule the insight that the carbon atoms that make up the benzene molecule are arranged in a ring.

A more recent example of visual imagery leading to scientific discovery is Albert Einstein's description of how he developed the theory of relativity by imagining himself traveling beside a beam of light (Intons-Peterson, 1993). On a less cosmic level, the golfer

Jack Nicklaus has described how he discovered an error in the way he gripped his club as he was practicing golf swings in a dream (Intons-Peterson, 1993).

One message of these examples is that visual imagery provides a way of thinking that adds another dimension to purely verbal techniques. But the thing that is most important about imagery is that it is associated not only with discoveries by famous people, but with most people's everyday experience. In this chapter, we will consider the basic characteristics of visual imagery and how it relates to other cognitive processes such as thinking, memory, and perception.

The Plan of This Chapter

We will begin our discussion of visual imagery by describing the history of imagery in psychology. We will see how the study of imagery has paralleled the rise, fall, and rebirth of the study of cognition in general (Figure 9.1). We then focus on a debate about the mechanisms

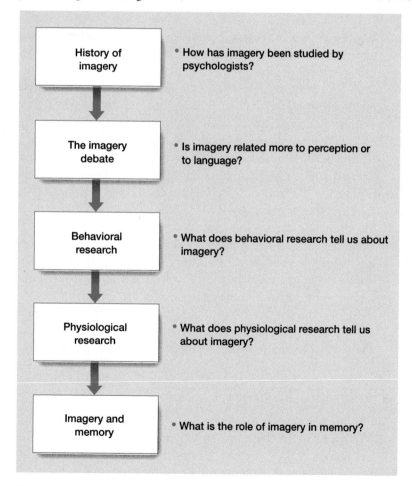

Figure 9.1 Flow diagram for this chapter.

of imagery, in which one group of researchers argue that visual imagery shares mechanisms with perception, and another group argue that imagery is created by mechanisms similar to those involved in language. As we look at arguments for both sides, we will describe experiments involving both the behavioral and physiological approaches to studying imagery. We then consider the relationship between imagery and memory, which suggests how imagery can be used to improve memory. *imagery + memory!*

IMAGERY IN THE HISTORY OF PSYCHOLOGY

We can trace the history of imagery back to the first laboratory of psychology, which was founded by Wilhelm Wundt.

Early Ideas About Imagery

Wundt proposed that images were one of the three basic elements of consciousness, along with sensations and feelings, and he also proposed that because images accompany thought, studying images was a way of studying thinking. This idea of a link between imagery and thinking gave rise to the **imageless-thought debate,** with some psychologists taking up Aristotle's idea that "thought is impossible without an image," and others contending that thinking can occur without images.

Evidence supporting the idea that imagery was not required for thinking was Francis Galton's (1883) observation that people who have great difficulty forming visual images were still quite capable of thinking (also see Richardson, 1994, for more modern accounts of imagery differences between people). Other arguments both for and against the idea that images are necessary for thinking were proposed in the late 1800s and early 1900s, but these arguments and counterarguments ended when behaviorism toppled imagery from its central place in psychology (Watson, 1913) (see Chapter 1, page 9). The behaviorists branded the study of imagery as being unproductive because visual images are invisible to everyone except the person experiencing them. This led the founder of behaviorism, John Watson, to describe images as "unproven" and "mythological" (1928), and therefore not worthy of study. The dominance of behaviorism from the 1920s through the 1950s pushed the study of imagery out of mainstream psychology. However, this situation changed when the study of cognition was reborn in the 1950s.

Imagery and the Cognitive Revolution

The history of cognitive psychology that we described in Chapter 1 recounts events in the 1950s and 1960s that came to be known as the cognitive revolution. One of the keys to the success of this "revolution" was that cognitive psychologists developed ways to measure behavior that could be used to infer cognitive processes. One example of a method that linked behavior and cognition is provided by Alan Paivio's (1963) work on memory in which he showed that it was easier to remember concrete nouns like *truck* or *tree*, that can be imaged, than it is to remember abstract nouns, like *truth* or *justice*, that are difficult to image. As we will see when we describe Paivio's work in more detail at the end of the chapter, this observation led him to propose the *dual-coding theory of memory*, which recognized the important role of imagery in memory.

Whereas Paivio inferred cognitive processes by measuring memory, other researchers inferred cognitive processes by using *mental chronometry*, the determination of the time needed to carry out various cognitive tasks (see Chapter 1, page 6). One way that this method was applied to the study of images is illustrated by the following demonstration.

◧ Demonstration

Comparing Objects

Look at the two pictures in Figure 9.2a and decide, as quickly as possible, whether they represent two different views of the same object ("same") or two different objects ("different"). Also make the same judgment for the two objects in Figure 9.2b. ◼

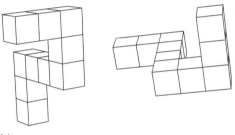

(a)

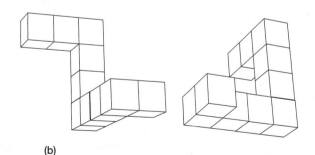

(b)

Figure 9.2 Stimuli for "comparing objects" demonstration. See text for instructions. (Excerpted with permission from "Mental Rotation of Three-Dimensional Objects," by R. N. Shepard & J. Metzler. From *Science, 171,* pp. 701–703, Fig. 1A & B. Copyright © 1971 AAAS.)

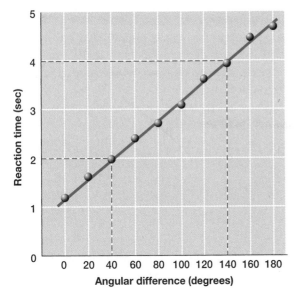

Figure 9.3 Results of Shepard and Metzler's (1971) mental-rotation experiment. The dashed lines have been added to show that the reaction time for two objects that differed in orientation by 40 degrees was 2 seconds, and the reaction time for a 140-degree difference was 4 seconds. (Excerpted from "Mental Rotation of Three-Dimensional Objects," by R. N. Shepard & J. Metzler. From *Science, 171,* pp. 701–703, Fig. 2A. Copyright © 1971 AAAS.)

This demonstration is based on an experiment by Roger Shepard and J. Metzler (1971) which, along with Paivio's memory research, is credited with paving the way toward establishing imagery as an important area in modern cognitive psychology. When Shepard and Metzler measured the time it took for participants to decide whether two objects were the same or different, they found that for objects that were the same, the relationship between the reaction time and the angle between the two views was linear (Figure 9.3). Thus, it took longer to compare two objects that are separated by a large angle, like the ones in (b), then it took to compare two objects that are separated by a smaller angle, like the ones in (a).

From the orderly relationship between reaction time and difference in orientation, Shepard and Metzler inferred that participants were rotating an image of one of the objects in their mind, a phenomenon they called **mental rotation.** From the data in Figure 9.3 we can see that for a difference in orientation of 40 degrees it took 2 seconds to decide a pair was the same shape, but for a difference of 140 degrees it took 4 seconds. Because it took 2 seconds to accomplish a rotation of 100 degrees, this means that participants were rotating the images at a rate of 50 degrees per second.

The reason Shepard and Metzler's experiment was so influential is that it demonstrated a parallel between imagery and perception. Thus, we see an object moving through space when we see a real object actually rotating, and we have a similar experience of movement through space when we rotate an object in our mind. This parallel between imagery and perception suggested that perhaps imagery and perception share the same mechanisms. *Support for perception*

IMAGERY AND PERCEPTION: DO THEY SHARE THE SAME MECHANISMS?

The idea that imagery and perception may share the same mechanisms is based on the observation that although mental images are different from perception because they are not as vivid or long lasting, imagery shares many properties with perception. Shepard and Metzler's results showed that mental and perceptual images both involve spatial analogs of the stimulus. That is, the spatial experience for both imagery and perception match the layout of the actual stimulus. This idea, that there is a spatial correspondence between imagery and perception, is supported by a number of experiments by Stephen Kosslyn involving a task called image scanning, in which participants create mental images and then scan them in their minds.

Kosslyn's Image-Scanning Experiments

Stephen Kosslyn has done enough research on imagery to fill two books (Kosslyn, 1980, 1994), and he has proposed some influential theories of imagery based on parallels between imagery and perception. In one of his early experiments, Kosslyn (1973) asked participants to memorize a picture of an object such as the boat in Figure 9.4, and then to create an image of that object in their mind and to focus on one part of the boat, such as the anchor. They were then asked to look for another part of the boat, such as the motor, and to press the "true" button when they found this part or the "false" button when they couldn't find it.

Figure 9.4 Stimulus for Kosslyn's (1973) image-scanning experiment. (Reprinted from S. M. Kosslyn, "Scanning Visual Images: Some Structural Implications." From *Perception & Psychophysics, 14,* pp. 90–94, Fig. 1. Copyright © 1973 with permission from the Psychonomic Society Publications.)

Kosslyn reasoned that if imagery, like perception, is spatial, then it should take longer for the participants to find parts that are located farther from the initial point of focus because they would be scanning across the image of the object. This is actually what happened, so Kosslyn took this as evidence for the spatial nature of imagery. But as often happens in science, another researcher proposed a different explanation. G. Lea (1975) proposed that the longer reaction times observed by Kosslyn could have been caused by the fact that as participants scanned, they encountered other interesting parts, such as the cabin, which may have increased their reaction time.

To answer this concern, Kosslyn and coworkers (1978) did another scanning experiment, this time asking participants to scan between two places on a map. Before reading about Kosslyn's experiment, try the following demonstration.

◪ Demonstration

Mental Travel Across Your State

Imagine a map of your state that includes three locations, the place where you live, a city that is far away, and another city that is closer but which does not fall on a straight line connecting your location and the far city. For example, for my state, I imagine Pittsburgh, the place where I am now, Philadelphia, all the way across the state (contrary to some people's idea, Pittsburgh is not a suburb of Philadelphia!), and Erie, which is closer than Philadelphia but is not in the same direction (Figure 9.5).

Your task is to create a mental image of your state and starting at your location, to form an image of a black speck moving along a straight line between your location and the closer city. Be

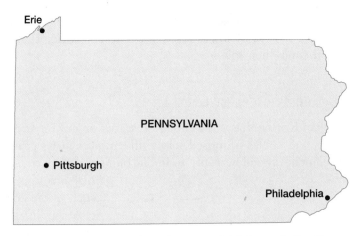

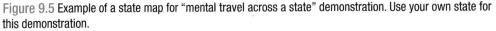

Figure 9.5 Example of a state map for "mental travel across a state" demonstration. Use your own state for this demonstration.

aware of about how long it took to arrive at this city. Then repeat the same procedure for the far city, again noting about how long it took to arrive. ■

Kosslyn's participants used the same procedure as you did for the demonstration, but were told to imagine an island like the one in Figure 9.6a, which contained 7 different locations. By having participants scan between every possible location (a total of 21 trips), Kosslyn determined the relationship between reaction time and distance in Figure 9.6b. Just as for the boat experiment, it took longer to scan between greater distances on the image, a result that supports the idea that visual imagery is spatial in nature. However, as convincing as Kosslyn's results were, Zenon Pylyshyn (1973) proposed another explanation, which started what has been called the imagery debate—a debate about whether imagery is based on spatial mechanisms such as those involved in perception, or is based on mechanisms related to language, which are called *propositional mechanisms*.

The Imagery Debate: Is Imagery Spatial or Propositional?

Much of the research we have described so far in this book is about determining the nature of the mental representations that lie behind different cognitive experiences. For example, when we considered short-term memory in Chapter 5, we presented evidence that information in STM is often represented in auditory form, as when you rehearse a telephone number you have just looked up in the phone book.

Kosslyn interpreted the results of his research on imagery as supporting the idea that the mechanism responsible for imagery involves a spatial representation, a representation in which different parts of an image can be described as corresponding to specific locations in space. But Pylyshyn (1973) disagreed, saying that just because we *experience* imagery as spatial, that doesn't mean that the underlying representation is spatial. After all,

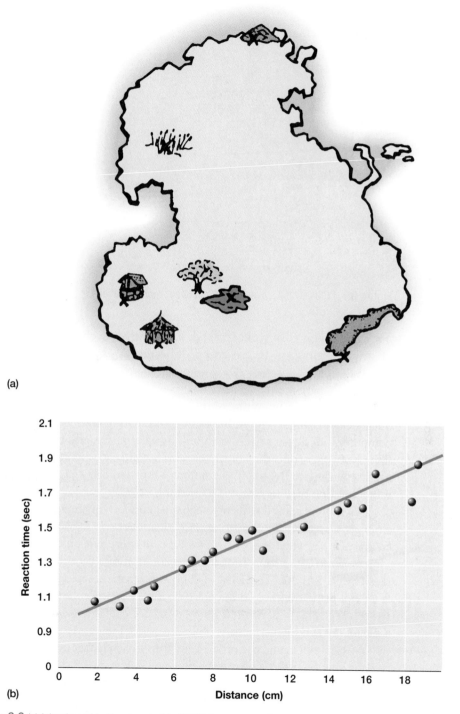

(a)

(b)

Figure 9.6 (a) Island used in Kosslyn et al.'s (1978) image-scanning experiment. Participants mentally traveled between the various locations on the island. (b) Results of the island experiment. (S. M. Kosslyn, T. Ball, & B. J. Reiser, "Visual Images Preserve Metric Spatial Information: Evidence From Studies of Image Scanning." From *Journal of Experimental Psychology: Human Perception and Performance, 4,* pp. 47–60, Figs. 2 & 3. Copyright © 1978 with permission from the American Psychological Association.)

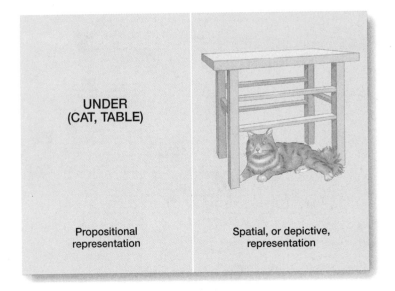

**UNDER
(CAT, TABLE)**

Propositional
representation

Spatial, or depictive,
representation

Figure 9.7 Propositional and spatial, or depictive, representations of "the cat is under the table."

one thing that is clear from research in cognitive psychology is that we often aren't aware of what is going on in our mind. The spatial experience of mental images, argues Pylyshyn, is an **epiphenomenon**—something that accompanies the real mechanism but is not actually part of the mechanism.

An example of an epiphenomenon is lights flashing as a mainframe computer carries out its calculations. The lights may be indicating that *something* is going on inside the computer, but doesn't necessarily tell us what is actually happening. In fact, if all of the light bulbs blew out, the computer would continue operating just as before. Mental images, according to Pylyshyn, are similar—they indicate that something is happening in the mind, but don't tell us *how* it is happening.

Pylyshyn proposed that the mechanism underlying imagery is not spatial but is propositional. A **propositional representation** is one in which relationships can be represented by symbols, as when the words of language represent objects and relationships between objects. Thus, the propositional representation of a cat under a table would be the notation UNDER (CAT, TABLE). In contrast, a spatial representation would involve a spatial layout showing the cat and the table, as can be represented in a picture (Figure 9.7). Spatial relationships represented by pictures are called **depictive representations** because they are *depicted* by the picture.

We can understand the propositional approach better by returning to the depictive representation of Kosslyn's boat from Figure 9.4. Figure 9.8 shows how the visual appearance of this boat can be represented propositionally. The words indicate parts of the boat, the length of the lines indicate the distances between the parts, and the words in parentheses indicate the spatial relations between the parts. A representation such as this would predict that when starting at the motor, it should take longer to find the porthole than to find the anchor because it is necessary to travel through 3 nodes to get to the porthole (dashed line)

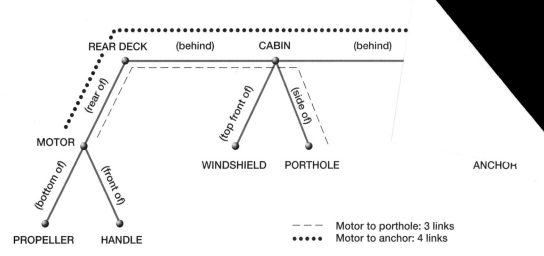

Figure 9.8 How the visual appearance of the boat in Figure 9.4 can be represented propositionally. Paths between motor and porthole (dashed line) and motor and anchor (dotted line) indicate the number of nodes that would be traversed between these parts of the boat. (Reprinted from S. M. Kosslyn, "Mental Imagery," in S. M. Kosslyn & D. N. Osherson, *An Invitation to Cognitive Science,* 2nd edition, volume 2: *Visual Cognition,* pp. 267–296, Fig. 7.6. Copyright © 1995 with permission from MIT Press.)

Figure 9.9 Propositional representation of distances between locations on Kosslyn's island. Each dot is a node. (S. M. Kosslyn, T. Ball, & B. J. Reiser, "Visual Images Preserve Metric Spatial Information: Evidence from Studies of Image Scanning." From *Journal of Experimental Psychology: Human Perception and Performance, 4,* pp. 47–60, Fig. 3. Copyright © 1978 with permission from the American Psychological Association.)

and 4 nodes to get to the anchor (dotted line). This kind of explanation proposes that imagery operates in a way similar to the semantic networks we described in Chapter 8 (see page 286).

Propositional representations can also explain the result of Kosslyn's island experiment by proposing the representation of the island in Figure 9.9. This way of representing the island shows locations on the map as being separated by nodes that represent distances, just as the markings on a ruler represent length.

In addition to suggesting that the results of Kosslyn's boat and island experiments can be explained in terms of propositional representations, Pylyshyn also suggested that one reason that scanning time increases as the distance between two points on an image increases is that the participants are responding to Kosslyn's tasks based on what they know about what usually happens when they are looking at a real scene. In the real world it takes longer to travel longer distances, so that is how participants behave in Kosslyn's experiment. (The same explanation would hold for Shepard and Metzler's mental-rotation experiment.) This is

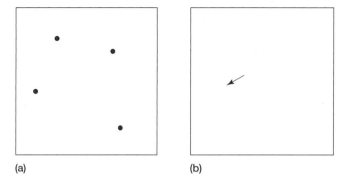

(a)   (b)

Figure 9.10 Stimuli for Finke and Pinker's (1982) experiment. The display in (a) was presented first, followed, after a 2-second delay, by the arrow in (b). The participants' task was to determine whether the arrow pointed to any of the dots that had been presented in the first display. (Reprinted from "Spontaneous Imagery Scanning in Mental Extrapolation," by R. A. Finke & S. Pinker, 1982, *Journal of Experimental Psychology: Learning, Memory and Cognition, 8,* 2, pp. 142–147, Fig. 1, Copyright © 1982 with permission from the American Psychological Association.)

called the **tacit-knowledge explanation,** because it states that participants unconsciously use knowledge about the world in making their judgments.

Although Pylyshyn was in the minority (there were many more researchers who held the spatial representation idea of visual imagery), his criticisms couldn't be ignored, and researchers from the "spatial" camp proceeded to gather more evidence. For example, to counter the tacit-knowledge explanation of Kosslyn's mental-scanning results, Ronald Finke and Stephen Pinker (1982) briefly presented a 4-dot display like the one in Figure 9.10a, and then after a 2-second delay, presented an arrow, as in Figure 9.10b. The participants' task was to indicate whether the arrow was pointing to any of the dots they had just seen.

Although the participants were not told to use imagery or to scan outward from the arrow, they took longer to respond for greater distances between the arrow and the dot. In fact, the results look very similar to the results of other scanning experiments. Finke and Pinker argue that because their participants wouldn't have had time to memorize the distances between the arrow and the dot before making their judgments, it is unlikely that they used tacit knowledge about how long it should take to get from one point to another.

We've discussed two approaches to explaining the results of imagery experiments in some detail because these two explanations provide an excellent example of how data can be interpreted in different ways. Pylyshyn's criticisms stimulated a large number of experiments that have taught us a great deal about the nature of visual imagery (also see Intons-Peterson, 1983). The weight of the evidence supports the idea that imagery is served by a spatial mechanism, and that it shares mechanisms with perception—although Pylyshyn (2001) still disagrees. We will now look at additional evidence that supports the idea of a spatial representation.

spatial/perception seems to be winner!!

View from afar   Move closer

Figure 9.11 Moving closer to an object, such as this car, has two effects: (1) The object fills more of the field of view; and (2) details are easier to see.

Comparing Imagery and Perception

We begin by describing another experiment by Kosslyn. This one looks at how imagery is affected by the size of an object in a person's visual field.

Size in the Visual Field If you were to observe an automobile from far away, it would fill only a portion of your visual field and it would be difficult to see small details such as the door handle. But as you move closer, it fills more of your visual field and you can perceive details like the door handle more easily (Figure 9.11). With these observations about perception in mind, Kosslyn wondered whether this relationship between viewing distance and the ability to perceive details also occurs for mental images.

To answer this question, Kosslyn (1978) asked participants to imagine animals next to each other, such as an elephant and a rabbit, and told them to imagine that they were standing close enough to the larger animal so that it filled most of their visual field (Figure 9.12a). He then posed questions such as "Does a rabbit have whiskers?" and asked his participants to find that part of the animal in their mental image and to answer as quickly as possible. When he repeated this procedure but told participants to imagine a rabbit and a fly next to each other, participants created larger images of the rabbit, as shown in Figure 9.12b. The result of these experiments, shown alongside the pictures, was that participants answered questions about the rabbit more rapidly if it filled more of the visual field.

In addition to asking participants to respond to details in visual images, Kosslyn also asked them to do a **mental-walk task,** in which they were to imagine that they were walking toward their mental image of an animal. Their task was to estimate how far away they were from the animal when they began to experience "overflow"—when the image filled the visual field or when its edges started becoming fuzzy. The result was that participants had to move closer for small animals (less than a foot for a mouse) than for larger animals (about 11 feet for an elephant), just as they would have to do if they were walking toward actual animals. This result therefore provides evidence for the idea that images are spatial, just like perception.

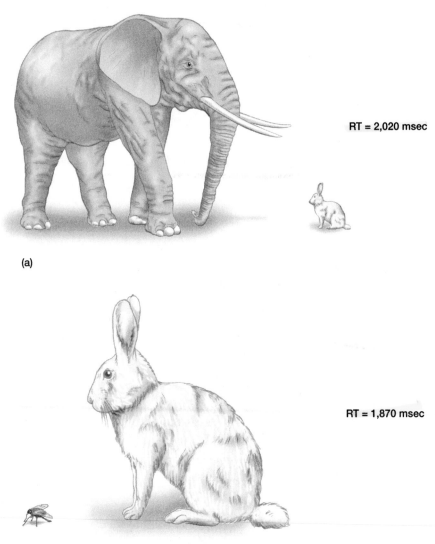

RT = 2,020 msec

(a)

RT = 1,870 msec

(b)

Figure 9.12 These pictures represent images that Kosslyn's (1978) participants created, which filled different portions of their visual field. (a) Imagine elephant and rabbit, so elephant fills the field. (b) Imagine rabbit and fly, so rabbit fills the field. Reaction times indicate how long it took participants to answer questions about the rabbit.

Convincing!

Interactions of Imagery and Perception Another way to demonstrate connections between imagery and perception is to show that they interact with one another. The basic rationale behind this approach is that if imagery affects perception, or perception affects imagery, this means that imagery and perception both have access to the same mechanisms. *→dual task logic!*

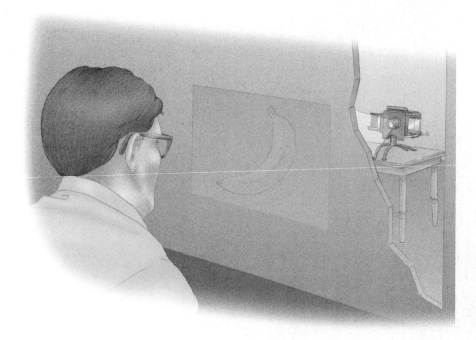

Figure 9.13 Participant in Perky's (1910) experiment. Unbeknownst to the participants, Perky was projecting dim images onto the screen.

The classic demonstration of interaction between perception and imagery dates back to 1910 when Cheves Perky did the experiment pictured in Figure 9.13. Perky asked her participants to "project" visual images of common objects onto a screen, and then to describe this image. Unbeknownst to the participants, Perky was back-projecting a very dim image of this object onto the screen. Thus, when participants were asked to create an image of a banana, Perky projected a dim image of a banana onto the screen. Interestingly, the participants' descriptions of their images matched the images that Perky was projecting. For example, they described the banana as being oriented vertically, just as was the projected image. Even more interesting, not one of Perky's 24 participants noticed that there was an actual picture on the screen. They had apparently mistaken an actual picture for a mental image. *Cool!*

Modern researchers have replicated Perky's result (see Craver-Remly & Reeves, 1992; Segal & Fusella, 1970) and have demonstrated interactions between perception and imagery in a number of other ways. Martha Farah (1985) instructed her participants to imagine either the letter "H" or "T" on a screen (Figure 9.14a). Once they had formed clear images on the screen, they pressed a button that caused two squares to flash, one after the other (Figure 9.14b). One of the squares contained a target letter, which was either an "H" or a "T." The participants' task was to indicate whether the letter was in the first square on the second one. The results, shown in Figure 9.14c, indicate that the target letter was

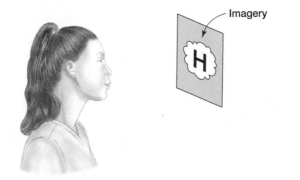

(a) Create image

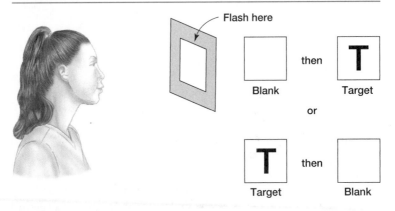

(b) Was target letter flashed first or second?

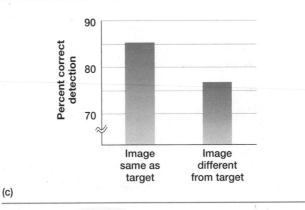

(c)

Figure 9.14 Procedure for Farah's (1985) letter visualization experiment. (a) Participant visualizes "H" or "T" on the screen. (b) Then two squares flash one after the other on the same screen. As shown on the right, the target letter can be in the first square or in the second one. The participants' task is to determine whether the test letter was flashed in the first or in the second square. (c) Results showing that accuracy was higher if the letter in (b) was the same as the one that had been imagined in (a).

detected more accurately if the participant had been imagining the same letter rather than the different letter. Farah interpreted this result as showing that perception and imagery share mechanisms, and many other experiments have demonstrated similar interactions between perception and imagery (see Kosslyn & Thompson, 2000).

Is There a Way to Resolve the Imagery Debate?

You might think, from the evidence of parallels between imagery and perception and of interactions between them, that the imagery debate would have been settled once and for all in favor of the spatial explanation. But John Anderson (1978) warned that despite this evidence, we still can't rule out the propositional explanation, and Martha Farah (1988) pointed out that it is difficult to rule out Pylyshyn's tacit-knowledge explanation just on the basis of the results of behavioral experiments like the ones we have been describing. She argued that it is always possible that participants can be influenced by their past experiences with perception so they could unknowingly be simulating perceptual responses in imagery experiments.

But Farah suggested a way out of this problem: Instead of relying solely on behavioral experiments, we should investigate how the brain responds to visual imagery. The reason Farah was able to make this proposal was that by the 1980s, evidence about the physiology of imagery was becoming available from neuropsychology—the study of patients with brain damage—and from electrophysiological measurements such as the event-related potential (ERP). In addition, beginning in the 1990s, brain-imaging experiments provided additional data regarding the physiology of imagery.

 Test Yourself 9.1

1. Is imagery just a "laboratory phenomenon," or does it occur in real life?
2. Make a list of the important events in the history of the study of imagery in psychology, beginning with the imageless-thought debate from the 1800s, through the studies of imagery that occurred early in the cognitive revolution in the 1960s.
3. How did Kosslyn use the technique of image scanning to demonstrate similarities between perception and imagery? How were Kosslyn's experiments criticized and how did Kosslyn answer this criticism with additional experiments?
4. Describe the spatial (or depictive) and propositional explanations of the mechanism underlying imagery. How can the propositional explanation interpret the results of Kosslyn's boat and island image-scanning experiments?
5. What is the tacit-knowledge explanation of imagery experiments? What experiment was done to counter this explanation?
6. How have experiments demonstrated interactions between imagery and perception? What additional evidence is needed to help settle the imagery debate, according to Farah?

As we look at a number of types of physiological experiments, we will see that there is a great deal of evidence that points to a connection between imagery and perception, but that other evidence shows that the overlap is not perfect. We begin by looking at the results of research that has measured the brain's response to imagery and will then consider how brain damage affects the ability to form visual images.

Event-Related Potentials

We saw in Chapter 2 that event-related potentials (ERPs) measure the activity of thousands of neurons under each recording electrode (see Figure 2.23). Martha Farah, F. Peronnet, and coworkers (1988) measured ERPs while participants read two kinds of lists (Figure 9.15). Some lists contained concrete nouns like *truck* or *house*, and the others contained abstract nouns like *ethics* or *peace*. As they read each list, participants either created a visual image based on the word (image condition), or to just read the word (concrete baseline). You can see from the experimental design in Figure 9.15 that participants were

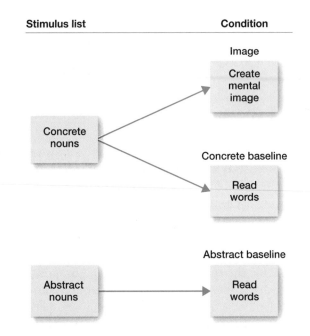

Figure 9.15 Design of Farah et al.'s (1988) ERP experiment. As each word was presented, participants either created an image or just read the word. ERPs were measured as they carried out these tasks. The ERP response to the imagery was determined by subtracting the response to the abstract baseline from the response to the image condition. (The concrete baseline was not used because some participants in this condition may have been creating images as they read the words.) The resulting response is shown in Figure 9.16.

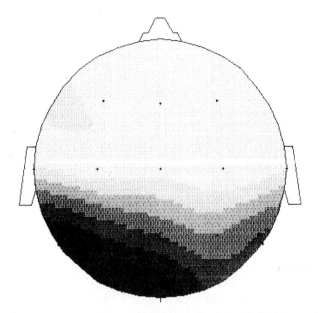

Figure 9.16 Brain's ERP response to images as determined in Farah et al.'s (1988) experiment. Darker areas indicate larger responses. (Reprinted from "Electrophysiological Evidence for a Shared Representational Medium for Visual Images and Precepts," by M. J. Farah et al., 1988, *Journal of Experimental Psychology, 117,* 3, pp. 248–257. Copyright © 1988 with permission from the American Psychological Association.)

not asked to create visual images for the abstract words (try creating an image of *ethics!*). ERPs were recorded during these tasks.

Figure 9.16 shows the brain's response to generating imagery, as determined by subtracting the response generated during the abstract-word baseline condition from the response generated during the concrete-word imagery condition. The key result of this experiment is that the largest imagery response (darker areas) occurred in two areas of cortex that are associated with object perception: (1) the occipital cortex, which contains the primary visual receiving area, V1, and (2) parts of the temporal cortex. (There was not as big a difference between the "concrete image" and "concrete baseline" conditions, possibly because participants may have created images for the concrete words even though they were told just to read them.) From this result, Farah concluded that imagery is created by the same visual system structures that are responsible for perception.

ERPs ... localization ?

Brain Imaging

Beginning in the early 1990s, a large number of brain-imaging experiments were carried out that followed the same general design as the ERP experiments we previously described. Brain activity was measured using either PET or fMRI, as participants were creating visual images or during a baseline condition in which they were not creating images. Subtracting the baseline response from the imagery response indicated which areas of the brain were activated by imagery (see Chapter 2, page 48, for more on the subtraction technique).

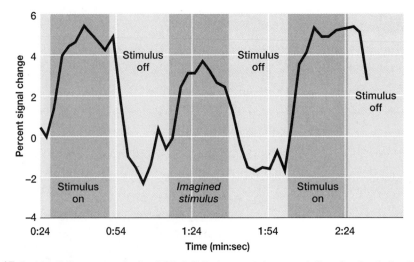

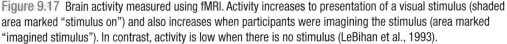

Figure 9.17 Brain activity measured using fMRI. Activity increases to presentation of a visual stimulus (shaded area marked "stimulus on") and also increases when participants were imagining the stimulus (area marked "imagined stimulus"). In contrast, activity is low when there is no stimulus (LeBihan et al., 1993).

[handwritten note: → notice - less V1 activity during imagery]

A number of these experiments have confirmed Farah's ERP result by showing that imagery creates activity in the striate cortex (area V1, the primary visual receiving area) (LiBihan et al., 1993). Figure 9.17 shows how activity in the striate cortex increased both when a person observed presentations of actual visual stimuli (marked "stimulus on"), *and* when the person was imagining the stimulus ("imagined stimulus"). In another brain-imaging experiment, asking participants to think about questions that involve imagery, such as "Is the green of the trees darker than the green of the grass?" generated a greater V1 response than the response generated to nonimagery questions, such as "Is the intensity of electrical current measured in amperes?" (Goldenberg et al., 1989).

Kosslyn and coworkers (1993, 1995) provided more evidence that V1 is involved in imagery by asking participants to create images of different sizes (so a small image fills only a little of the participants' mental field of view and a large image fills more of the field of view). When participants did this, larger areas of visual cortex were activated for the large images, just as would occur if the participants had been observing actual objects.

Although area V1 and the temporal lobe haven't become activated by imagery in all brain-imaging studies (see Mellett et al., 1998), a recent survey of most of the research on brain imaging indicates that V1 is activated when participants are asked to create detailed images (Kosslyn & Thompson, 2000). *[handwritten note: what about if NOT detailed - relying on other strategies? semantic, etc.??]*

Imagery Neurons in the Brain

Studies in which activity is recorded from single neurons in humans are rare. But Gabriel Kreiman and coworkers (2000b) were able to study patients who had electrodes implanted in various areas in their medial temporal lobe (see Figure 6.17) in order to determine the source of severe epileptic seizures that could not be controlled by medication.

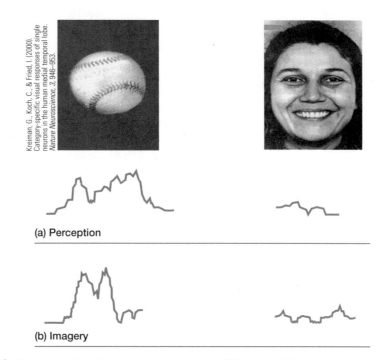

Kreiman, G., Koch, C., & Fried, I. (2000). Category-specific visual responses of single neurons in the human medial temporal lobe. *Nature Neuroscience, 3,* 946–953.

(a) Perception

(b) Imagery

Figure 9.18 Responses of single neurons in a person's medial temporal lobe that (a) responds to perception of a baseball but not to a face; and (b) responds similarly when the person imagines a baseball or a face (Kreiman et al., 2000b).

They found neurons that responded to some objects but not to others. For example, the records in (a) of Figure 9.18 show that the neuron responds to a picture of a baseball, but does not respond to a picture of a face. Neurons that respond to specific objects are called category-specific neurons (see Chapter 8, p. 304; also see Freedman et al., 2001). This neuron is a special type of category-specific neuron because, as shown by the records in (b), it fires in the same way when the person closes his eyes and imagines a baseball (good firing) or a face (no firing). Kreiman calls these neurons imagery neurons.

Neuropsychological Case Studies

How can we use studies of people with brain damage to help us understand imagery? One approach is to determine how brain damage affects imagery. Another approach is to determine how brain damage affects both imagery and perception, and to note whether or not both are affected in the same way.

Removing Part of the Visual Cortex Decreases Image Size
Patient M.G.S. was a young woman who was about to have part of her right occipital lobe removed as treatment for a severe case of epilepsy. Before the operation, Martha Farah and coworkers (1992) had M.G.S. perform the mental-walk task that we described earlier, in which she imagined walking toward an animal and estimated how close she was when the image began to

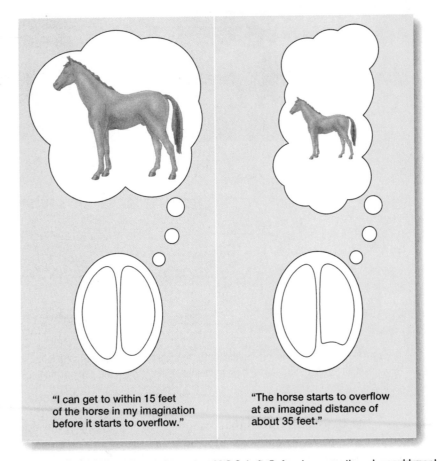

Figure 9.19 Results of mental-walk task for patient M.G.S. Left: Before her operation, she could mentally "walk" to within 15 feet before the image of the horse overflowed her visual field. Right: After removal of the right occipital lobe, the size of the visual field was reduced, and she could mentally approach only to within 35 feet of the horse before it overflowed her visual field. (Reprinted from M.J. Farah, "The Neural Basis of Mental Imagery." In M. Gazzanaga (Ed.), *The Cognitive Neurosciences,* 2nd edition. Cambridge, MIT Press, pp. 965–974 (Fig. 66.2), Copyright © 2000, with permission of The MIT Press.)

overflow her visual field. Figure 9.19 shows that before the operation, M.G.S. felt she was about 15 feet from an imaginary horse before its image overflowed. But when Farah had her repeat this task after her right occipital lobe was removed, M.G.S. could only approach to 35 feet. This occurred because removing part of the visual cortex reduced the size of her field of view, so the horse filled up the field when she was farther away. This result supports the idea that V1 is important for imagery.

Perceptual Problems Are Accompanied by Problems With Imagery

A large number of cases have been studied in which a patient with brain damage has a perceptual problem and also has a similar problem in creating images. For example, people who have lost the ability to see color due to brain damage are also unable to create colors through imagery (DeRenzie & Spinnler, 1967; DeVreese, 1991).

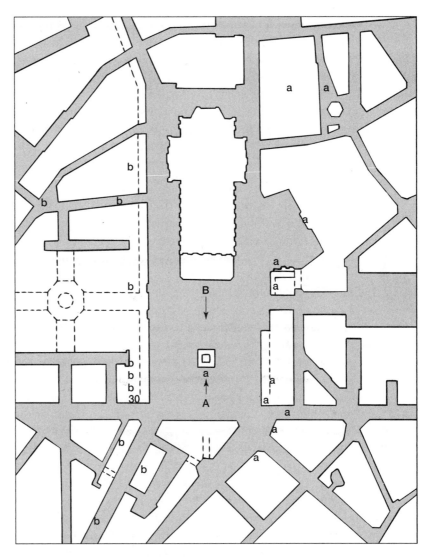

Figure 9.20 Piazza del Duomo in Milan. When Bisiach and Luzzatti's (1978) patient imagined himself standing at A, he could name objects indicated by *a*'s. When he imagined himself at B, he could name objects indicated by *b*'s. (Reprinted from "Unilateral Neglect of Representational Space," by E. Bisiach & G. Luzzatti, 1978, *Cortex, 14,* pp. 129–133. Copyright © 1978 with permission from Cortex.)

We saw in Chapter 4 that damage to the parietal lobes can cause a condition called **unilateral neglect,** in which the patient ignores objects in one half of their visual field, even to the extent of shaving just one side of his face, or eating only the food on one side of her plate (see Figure 4.30).

E. Bisiach and G. Luzzatti (1978) tested the imagery of a patient with neglect by asking him to describe things he saw when imagining himself standing at one end of the Piazza del Duomo in Milan, a place with which he had been familiar before his brain was damaged (Figure 9.20). The patient's responses showed that he neglected the left side of his mental image, just as he neglected the left side of his perceptions. Thus, when he imagined himself standing at A, he neglected the left side and named only objects to his right (small *a*'s). When he imagined himself standing at B, he continued to neglect the left side, this time naming only objects on his right (small *b*'s).

The correspondence between the physiology of mental imagery and the physiology of perception, as demonstrated by brain scans in normal participants and the effects of brain damage in participants with neglect, supports the idea that mental imagery and perception share physiological mechanisms. However, not all physiological results support a one-to-one correspondence between imagery and perception.

Dissociations Between Imagery and Perception   When we discussed memory in Chapters 5 and 6, we described dissociations, in which people with brain damage had one memory function present and another function absent (see pages 154 and 186). Cases have also been reported of dissociations between imagery and perception. For example, C. Guariglia and coworkers (1993) studied a patient whose brain damage had little effect on his ability to perceive but caused neglect in his mental images (his images were limited to just one side, as in the case just described). _fact that imagery harder_

Another case of normal perception but impaired imagery is the case of R.M., who had suffered damage to his occipital and parietal lobes (Farah et al., 1988). R.M. was able to recognize objects and to draw accurate pictures of objects that were placed before him. However, he was unable to draw objects from memory, a task that requires imagery. He also had trouble answering questions that depend on imagery, such as verifying whether the sentence "A grapefruit is larger than an orange" is correct.

Dissociations have also been reported with the opposite result: Perception is impaired but imagery is relatively normal. For example, Marlene Behrmann and coworkers (1994) studied C.K., a 33-year-old graduate student who was struck by a car as he was jogging. C.K. suffered from visual agnosia, the inability to visually recognize objects (see page 304). Thus, he labeled the pictures in Figure 9.21a as a "feather duster" (the dart), a "fencer's mask" (the tennis racquet), and a "rose twig with thorns" (the asparagus). These results show that C.K. could recognize parts of objects but couldn't integrate them into a meaningful whole. But despite his inability to name pictures of objects, C.K., was able to draw objects from memory in rich detail, a task that depends on imagery (Figure 9.21b). Interestingly, when he was shown his own drawings later, he was unable to identify them. *dif. things going on - maybe same resources used preferentially-others don't show up as well - utilized if damaged...*

Making Sense of the Neuropsychological Results   The neuropsychological cases present a paradox: On one hand, there are many cases in which there are close parallels between perceptual deficits and deficits in imagery. On the other hand, there are a number of cases in which perception is normal but imagery is poor, or in which perception is poor but imagery is normal. The cases in which imagery and perception are affected differently by brain damage provide evidence for a double dissociation between imagery and perception (Figure 9.22). The presence of a double dissociation is usually interpreted to

Figure 9.21 (a) Pictures incorrectly labeled by C.K., who had visual agnosia. (b) Drawings from memory by C.K. (Reprinted from "Intact Visual Imagery and Impaired Visual Perception in a Patient with Visual Agnosia," by M. Behrmann et al., 1994, *Journal of Experimental Psychology: Human Perception and Performance, 30,* pp. 1068–1087, Figs. 1 & 6. Copyright © 1994 with permission from the American Psychological Association.)

mean that the two functions (perception and imagery, in this case) are served by different mechanisms (see page 51), a conclusion that contradicts the other evidence we have presented that shows that imagery and perception share mechanisms.

One way to explain this paradox, according to Behrmann and coworkers (1994), is that the mechanisms of imagery and perception overlap only partially, with the mechanism for

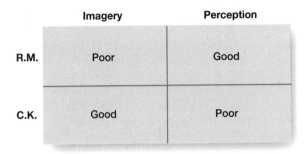

Figure 9.22 The cases of R.M. and C.K. provide evidence for a double dissociation between deficits in perception and imagery.

imagery being located mainly in higher visual centers, and the mechanism for perception being located at both lower and higher centers, as shown in Figure 9.23. According to this idea, perception involves *bottom-up processing*, which originates with an image on the retina and involves processing in the retina, LGN, V1, and higher cortical areas. In contrast, imagery starts as a *top-down process*, which originates when activity is generated in higher visual centers, without the activity generated by an actual stimulus.

Based on this explanation, we can hypothesize that C.K.'s perceptual problems are caused by damage to early processing in the cortex, but that he can still create images because higher-level areas of the brain are intact. Similarly, we can hypothesize that R.M.'s problems with imagery are caused by damage to higher-level areas. Some cases, however, such as M.G.S., the woman who had part of her visual cortex removed (see Figure 9.19), do not fit this explanation because damage early in the visual system caused changes in

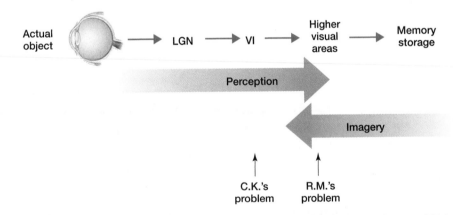

Figure 9.23 Depiction of the idea that mechanisms serving perception are located at lower and higher visual centers and mechanisms serving imagery are located mainly at higher levels (Behrmann et al., 1994). This would explain why C.K. has a perceptual problem but can still create images, and why R.M. can have trouble creating images, but can still perceive.

both perception and imagery. Cases such as this emphasize the challenge of interpreting the results of neuropsychological research. It is likely that further research will lead to modifications in the explanation shown in Figure 9.23, or perhaps a new explanation altogether.

Conclusions From the Imagery Debate

The imagery debate provides an outstanding example of a situation in which a controversy motivated a large amount of research. Most psychologists, looking at the behavioral and physiological evidence, have concluded that imagery and perception are closely related and share some (but not all) mechanisms (but see Pylyshyn, 2001, who doesn't agree).

The idea of shared mechanisms follows from all of the parallels and interactions between perception and imagery. The idea that not all mechanisms are shared follows from some of the neuropsychological results and also from differences in how people experience imagery and perception. For example, perception occurs automatically when we look at something, but imagery needs to be generated with some effort. Also, perception is stable—it continues as long as you are observing a stimulus—but imagery is fragile—it can vanish without continued effort. *differences*

Another example of a difference between imagery and perception is that it is harder to manipulate mental images than images that are created perceptually. This was demonstrated by Deborah Chalmers and Daniel Reisberg (1985), who asked their participants to create mental images of ambiguous figures such as the one in Figure 9.24, which can be seen as a rabbit or a duck. Perceptually, it is fairly easy to "flip" between these two perceptions. However, Chalmers and Reisberg found that participants who were holding a mental image of this figure were unable to flip from one perception to another. Later research has shown that people can manipulate simpler mental images (Finke et al., 1989) or can manipulate mental images when given extra information and "hints" (Mast & Kosslyn, 2002). So the experiments on manipulating images lead to the same conclusion as all of the other experiments we have described: Imagery and perception have many features in common, but there are also differences between them.

Figure 9.24 **What is this, rabbit or duck?**

IMAGERY AND MEMORY: WHAT IS THE CONNECTION?

The history of memory research has been dominated by experiments in which participants are asked to remember lists of words. But lurking behind some of these words are visual images, which can occur even when hearing or reading words, and which have increasingly been studied by memory researchers.

Dual-Coding Theory

At the beginning of the chapter we mentioned Alan Paivio's experiments, which formed the basis of the dual-coding theory of memory. According to **dual-coding theory**, memory is served by two systems. One system is specialized for verbal stimuli and the other for objects and events that are represented nonverbally. Figure 9.25, which shows Paivio's diagram of these two systems, indicates these two systems process verbal and nonverbal stimuli separately, but that there is communication between them.

The communication between the two systems means that some objects and events can be stored as both verbal representations and as visual representations. The verbal representation is symbolic because the objects and events are stored as words, which are symbols, whereas the visual representation preserves the features of the object or scene. Thus, Paivio's conception of imagery is consistent with the spatial or depictive approach that we have just described. What is special about dual-coding theory is that it is concerned with the connection between imagery and memory.

We can appreciate how the idea of dual coding originated from the results of memory research by considering some of Paivio's early experiments. Many of them used the classic memory task of **paired-associate learning,** in which participants are presented with pairs of words, like *boat-hat* or *car-house* during the study period. They are then presented with one of the words during the test period, and are asked to recall the word it had been paired with.

Paivio (1963, 1965) found that memory for concrete nouns, such as *hotel*, *student*, and *garden*, which are likely to evoke images, is much better than memory for abstract nouns,

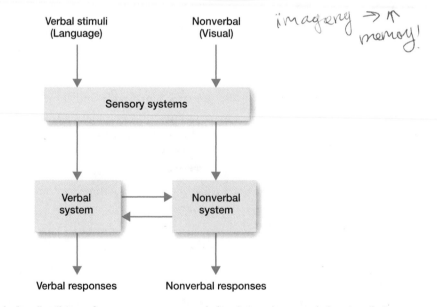

Figure 9.25 Paivio's dual-coding theory of memory proposes a verbal system and a nonverbal system that handle different kinds of information and that can communicate with each other, as shown here.

such as *knowledge, honor,* and *custom,* which are less likely to evoke images. To explain this result, Paivio proposed the **conceptual-peg hypothesis**. According to this hypothesis, concrete nouns create images that other words can "hang onto." For example, if presenting the pair *boat-hat* creates an image of a boat, then presenting the word *boat* later will bring back the boat image, which provides a number of places on which participants can place the hat in their mind.

Some experiments by Ian Begg (1972) provide evidence that concrete items are more likely to become combined with one another than are abstract items. He presented concrete adjective-noun pairs such as *square door* or *rusty engine* and abstract adjective-noun pairs such as *subtle fault* and *absolute truth.* When he used a free-recall test, in which he simply asked participants to recall as many items as possible, he found that participants remembered twice as many of the concrete items.

Was this superior performance for the concrete items caused by the fact that they were more likely to be combined with one another? Begg answered this question by doing another experiment, in which he tested using cued recall rather than free recall. In a cued-recall task, one item is presented (like *subtle*) and the participant's task is to remember the other one (correct answer: *fault*). For this test, performance was better compared to free recall for the concrete words, but performance for the abstract words remained the same. Begg explains this result by suggesting that the concrete words are stored as integrated images, whereas the abstract words are stored as separate words. We will see, at the end of the chapter, how this "binding" effect of imagery has been used as a memory aid.

Paivio's theory and the research associated with it highlighted the role of imagery as a way of encoding material in memory. However, he didn't ignore language. One of the main messages of dual-coding theory is that memory is better if material is encoded in both the verbal (language) and the nonverbal (visual) systems. This idea of two memory systems is similar in many respects to the verbal and visual systems of working memory that we discussed in Chapter 5.

Working Memory

Because we have already described the basic principles of working memory in Chapter 5, we will just review them briefly here. Working memory is a short-term storage and processing system that contains two systems—the phonological loop and the visuospatial sketch pad—that are coordinated by a central executive (see Figure 5.15). One important contribution of the working memory model is that it considers how the phonological loop and the visual spatial sketch pad interact with one another, and it also emphasizes the role of active processing within the working memory system.

According to an updating of the working memory model proposed by Robert Logie (1995), this active processing in the sketch pad is carried out by a number of subcomponents. We will focus on two of them: (1) the **visual buffer,** which is responsible for our conscious experience of images, and (2) the **inner scribe,** which is responsible for manipulating the images that are in the visual buffer (Figure 9.26). One way to illustrate how

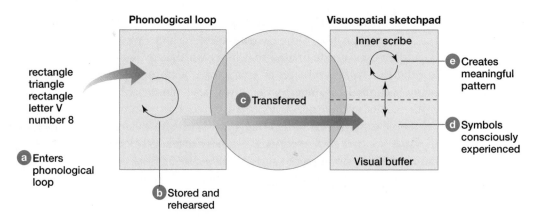

Figure 9.26 Working memory diagram (see Figure 5.15) showing how the phonological loop (left) and the visuospatial sketch pad (right) work together during the mental synthesis task. See text for details. (From Pearson et al., 2001.)

these components operate is to consider what happens during a process called **mental synthesis,** in which patterns are created by manipulating mental images. Try the following demonstration to experience mental synthesis for yourself.

◥ Demonstration

Mental Synthesis

For this demonstration you will be creating a pattern in your mind from symbols. For example, if you were instructed to create a pattern from three circles and a triangle, you might create a snowman by stacking the three circles and placing the triangle in the top circle for the snowman's nose. Your task: Construct a recognizable pattern in your mind by combining the following symbols: rectangle, triangle, rectangle, letter V, number 8.   ∎

Some of the patterns that could be formed from these symbols are shown in Figure 9.28. An explanation based on working memory for the processes involved in this mental synthesis hypothesizes the following steps (see Figure 9.26).

(a) Verbal information is taken in by the phonological loop.
(b) This information is temporarily stored and rehearsed.
(c) The information is transferred to the visual buffer part of the visuospatial sketch pad.
(d) Upon reaching the visual buffer, the symbols are consciously experienced.
(e) These symbols are manipulated by the inner scribe to create a meaningful pattern.

Exactly how the different components within the visuospatial sketch pad operate and work together to process visual information and create the experience of imagery is still being investigated, and the explanation just presented is simpler than the actual process

(Logie, 1995, describes some of the complexities). What is important for our purposes is that the inclusion of a separate processing unit for visual images within working memory takes into account the important role of imagery in memory.

Using Imagery to Improve Your Memory

It is clear that imagery can play an important role in memory. But how can you harness the power of imagery to help you remember things better? To answer this question let's return to our discussion in Chapter 6 of how information can be encoded in long-term memory.

Visualizing Interacting Images Enhances Memory

When we showed, in Chapter 6, that encoding is aided by forming connections with other information, we introduced the idea that these connections can be enhanced by imagery. Participants who created images based on two paired words (like *boat* and *tree*), remembered over twice as many words as participants who just repeated the words (Figure 6.10).

Apparently, visualization is most effective when images of objects are paired in an interactive way, but it is not necessary that these interactions be bizarre, as has been suggested by some authors of books on memory improvement. Wollen and coworkers (1972) showed that bizarreness is not necessary by instructing participants to learn pairs of words that were accompanied by pictures such as those in Figure 9.27. Some of the

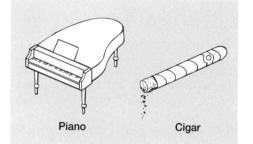

Piano   Cigar

(a) Noninteracting, nonbizarre

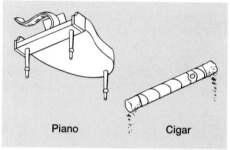

Piano   Cigar

(b) Noninteracting, bizarre

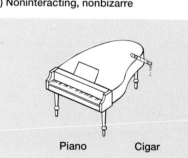

Piano   Cigar

(c) Interacting, nonbizarre

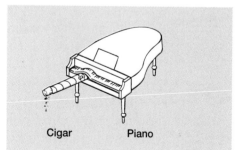

Cigar   Piano

(d) Interacting, bizarre

Figure 9.27   Pictures used by Wollen et al. (1972) to study the role of creating bizarre images in memory. (Reprinted from *Cognitive Psychology*, Volume 3, K. A. Wollen et al., "Bizarreness Versus Interaction of Mental Images as Determinants of Learning," pp. 518–523, Figure 1, Copyright © 1972, with permission from Elsevier.)

SYMBOLS

rectangle, triangle, rectangle, letter V, number 8

EXAMPLES OF LEGITIMATE PATTERNS

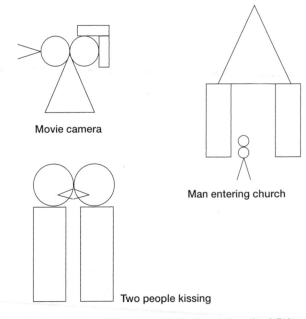

Movie camera

Man entering church

Two people kissing

Figure 9.28 Examples of patterns that could be created in the "mental synthesis" demonstration. (Reprinted from D. G. Pearson, "Imagery and the Visuo-Spatial Sketchpad." In J. Andrade (Ed.) *Working Memory in Perspective,* pp. 33–59, Fig. 2.1. Copyright © 2001 with permission from Psychology Press.)

pictures showed the two objects *separately*, in both (a) nonbizarre and (b) bizarre versions. Other picture showed the two objects *interacting* in both (c) nonbizarre and (d) bizarre versions. Memory was better for the interacting images compared to the noninteracting images, but bizarreness had no effect. Apparently, just creating images and having them interact is enough to improve memory (although creating bizarre images can be more fun!).

The Organizational Effect of Imagery Enhances Memory We also saw in Chapter 6 that organization improves encoding. The mind tends to spontaneously organize information that is initially unorganized, and presenting information that is organized improves memory performance.

The power of imagery to improve memory is tied to its ability to create organized locations upon which memories for specific items can be placed. An example of the organizational function of imagery from ancient history is provided by a story about the Greek poet Simonides. According to legend, 2500 years ago Simonides presented an address at a banquet, and just after he left the banquet, the roof of the hall collapsed, killing most of the people inside. To compound this tragedy, many of the bodies were so severely mutilated that they couldn't be identified. But Simonides realized that as he had looked out over the audience during this address, he had created a mental picture of where each person had been seated at the banquet table. Based on this image of people's locations around the table, he was able to determine who had been killed.

What is important about this rather gory example is that Simonides realized that the technique he had used to help him remember who was at the banquet could also be used to remember other things as well. He found that he could remember things by imagining a physical space, like the banquet table, and by placing, in his mind, items to be remembered in the seats surrounding the table. This feat of mental organization enabled him to later "read out" the items by mentally scanning the locations around the table, just as he had done to identify the people's bodies. Simonides had invented what is now called the **method of loci**—a method in which things to be remembered are placed at different locations in a mental image of a spatial layout.

Method of Loci   This demonstration illustrates how to use the method of loci to remember something from your own experience.

Demonstration

Method of Loci

Pick a place with a spatial layout that is very familiar to you, such as the rooms in your house or apartment, or the buildings on your college campus. Then pick 5–7 things that you want to remember—either events from the past or things you need to do later today. Create an image representing each event and place each image at a location in the house. If you need to remember the events in a particular order, decide on a path you would take while walking through the house or campus, and place the images representing each event along your walking path so they will be encountered in the correct order. After you have done this, retrace the path in your mind and see if encountering the images helps you remember the events. To really test this method, try mentally "walking" this path a few hours from now.   ■

Placing images at locations can help retrieve memories later. For example, to help me remember a dentist appointment later in the day, I could visually place a huge pair of teeth in my living room. To remind myself to go to the gym and work out, I could imagine a Stairmaster stepping-machine on the stairs that lead from the living room to the second floor, and to represent the TV program *West Wing* that I want to watch later tonight, I could imagine a small model of the White House on the landing at the top of the stairs.

Pegword Technique   The **pegword technique** involves imagery, as in the method of loci, but instead of visualizing items in different locations, you associate them with concrete words. The first step is to create a list of nouns, like the following:

one—bun	six—sticks
two—shoe	seven—heaven
three—tree	eight—gate
four—door	nine—mine
five—hive	ten—hen

It's easy to remember these words in order because they were created by rhyming them with the numbers. The next step is to pair each of these things to be remembered with each pegword by creating a vivid image of your item-to-be-remembered with the object represented by the word. Figure 9.29 shows an image I created for the dentist appointment. For the other items I wanted to remember, I might picture a Stairmaster machine inside a shoe, and the White House in a tree. The beauty of this system is that it makes it possible to immediately identify an item based on its order on the list. So if I want to identify the third thing I need to do today, I go straight to *tree*, which translates into my image of the White House in the tree, and this reminds me to watch *West Wing* on TV.

Imagery techniques like the ones just mentioned are often the basis behind books that claim to provide the key to improving your memory (see Crook & Adderly, 1998; Lorayne & Lucas, 1996; Treadeau, 1997). Although these books do provide imagery-based techniques that work, people who purchase these books in the hope of discovering an easy way to develop "photographic memory" are often disappointed because although imagery techniques do work, they do not provide easy "magical" improvements in memory, but rather require a great deal of practice and perseverance (Schacter, 2001).

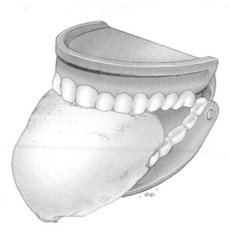

Figure 9.29 An image used by the author to remember a dentist appointment, using the pegword technique.

Test Yourself 9.2

1. Describe how experiments using the following physiological techniques have provided evidence of parallels between imagery and perception: (1) event-related potential; (2) brain imaging; (3) removal of part of the brain; (4) neuropsychology; (5) recording from single neurons.

2. Some of the neuropsychological results demonstrate parallels between imagery and perception, and some results do not. How has Behrmann explained these contradictory results?

3. What are some differences between imagery and perception? What have most psychologists concluded about the connection between imagery and perception?
4. How has imagery and memory been linked by (1) Paivio's dual-coding theory; and (2) a new version of working memory?
5. Under what conditions does imagery improve memory? Describe techniques that use imagery as a tool to improve memory. What is the basic principle that underlies these techniques?

Think About It

1. Look at an object for a minute and then look away, create a mental image of it, and draw a sketch of the object based on your mental image. Then draw a sketch of the same object while you are looking at it. How do the two sketches differ? What kinds of information about the object were you able to include in the sketch that was based on your mental image? What information was omitted, compared to the sketch you created by looking at the object?

2. Write a description of an object as you are looking at it. Then compare the difference between the written description and the information you can obtain by looking at the object or at a picture of the object. Is it true that "a picture is worth a thousand words"? How does your comparison of written and visual representations relate to the discussion of propositional versus depictive representations in this chapter?

3. Try using one of the techniques described at the end of this chapter to create images that represent things you have to do later today or during the coming week. Then, after some time passes (anywhere from an hour to a few days), check to see whether you can retrieve the memories for these images and if you can remember what they stand for.

KEY TERMS

Conceptual-peg hypothesis
Depictive representation
Dual-coding theory
Epiphenomenon
Image scanning
Imageless-thought debate
Imagery debate
Imagery neurons
Inner scribe
Mental imagery
Mental rotation

Mental synthesis
Mental-walk task
Method of loci
Paired-associate learning
Pegword technique
Propositional representation
Spatial representation
Tacit-knowledge explanation
Unilateral neglect
Visual buffer
Visual imagery

To experience these experiments for yourself, go to http://coglab.wadsworth.com. Be sure to read each experiment's setup instructions before you go to the experiment itself. Otherwise, you won't know which keys to press.

Primary Lab

Mental rotation   How a stimulus can be rotated in the mind to determine if its shape matches another stimulus (p. 313).

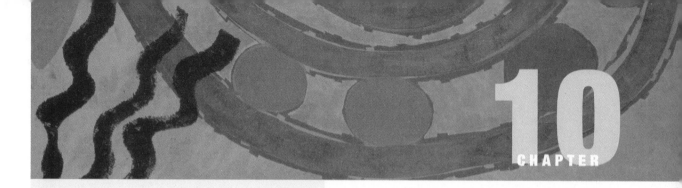

Language

Key Terms

CogLab: Word Superiority; Lexical Decision; Categorical Perception

Some Questions We Will Consider

✔ How do we understand individual words, and how are words combined to create sentences?

✔ How can we understand sentences that have more than one meaning?

✔ When we read a story, how do we relate what happened at the beginning of the story to what happens later in the story?

✔ Is it true that the language that people use in a particular culture can affect the way they think?

■   ■   ■

There are ways to communicate that don't involve language, but language is the most powerful tool we have for transmitting ideas, feelings, and knowledge from one person to another. What exactly is language, and what is it about language that makes it so useful?

WHAT IS LANGUAGE?

We can define **language** as *a system of communication through which we code and express our feelings, thoughts, ideas, and experiences.* This definition includes one of the key features of language—communication. But it is important to differentiate language from other forms of communication. Nonhuman animals communicate by making sounds. My cats "meow" when their food dish is empty. Monkeys have a repertoire of "calls" that stand for things such as "danger" or "greeting," and bees signal through a "waggle-dance" that they perform at the hive to indicate the location of flowers. All of these forms of communication serve valuable functions for these animals, but none has the properties that make human language unique.

The Creativity of Human Language

Human language goes far beyond a series of fixed signals that transmit a single message like "feed me," "danger," or "go that way for flowers." Language provides a way of arranging a sequence of signals—sounds for spoken language, letters and written words for written language, and physical signals for sign language—that provide a wide variety of ways to transmit, from one person to another, things ranging from the simple and commonplace ("My car is over there") to things that have perhaps never been previously written or uttered in the entire history of the world ("I'm thinking of getting a new Mustang because I'm quitting my job in February and taking a trip across the country to celebrate Groundhog Day with my cousin Zelda").

One of the properties of language that makes it possible to create new and unique sentences is that it has a structure that is hierarchical and that is governed by rules. Language is hierarchical because it consists of smaller components, like words, that can be combined to form larger ones, like phrases that can create sentences, which themselves can be components of a larger story. Language is governed by rules that specify permissible ways for these components to be arranged ("What is my cat saying?" is permissible in English; "Cat my saying is what?" is not). These two properties—a hierarchical structure and rules—endow humans with the ability to go far beyond the fixed calls and signs of animals to communicate whatever they want to express.

The Universality of Language

Although people do "talk" to themselves, as when Hamlet wondered "To be or not to be" or when you daydream in class, the predominant staging ground for language is one person conversing with another. Consider the following:

- People's need to communicate is so powerful that when deaf children find themselves in an environment where there are no people who speak or use sign language, they invent a sign language themselves (Goldwin-Meadow, 1982).

- Everyone with normal capacities develops a language and learns to follow its complex rules, even though they are usually not aware of these rules. Although many people find the study of grammar to be very difficult, they have no trouble using language.

- Language is universal across cultures. There are over 5,000 different languages, and there isn't a single culture that is without language. When European explorers first set forth in New Guinea, the people they discovered, who had been isolated from the rest of the world for eons, had developed over 750 different languages, many of them quite different from one another.

- Even though a large number of languages are very different from one another, we can describe them as being "uniquely the same." They are unique because they use different words and sounds, and they may use different rules of combining these words (although many languages use similar rules). They are the same because all languages have words that serve the function of nouns and verbs, and all languages include a system to make things negative, to ask questions, and to refer to the past and present.

All of the above reflect the fact that language is a creation of the human mind. Thus, just as studying perception, attention, and memory reveals various characteristics of the human mind, studying language reveals aspects of the mind as well.

Studying Language

The scientific study of language began in the 1800s, when early psychologists such as Wilhelm Wundt, who founded the first laboratory of psychology, saw language as the mechanism by which thoughts are transformed into sentences. Language was also one of the earliest cognitive capacities to be studied physiologically, as first Paul Broca and then Carl Wernicke showed that damage to specific areas of the brain causes language problems, called **aphasias** (Figure 10.1). Patients with damage to **Broca's area** in the frontal

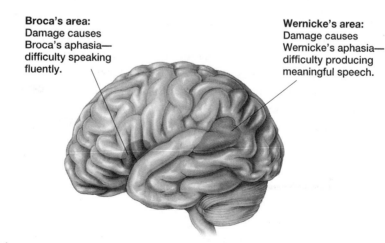

Broca's area:
Damage causes
Broca's aphasia—
difficulty speaking
fluently.

Wernicke's area:
Damage causes
Wernicke's aphasia—
difficulty producing
meaningful speech.

Figure 10.1 Brain showing location of Broca's and Wernicke's areas. Damage to these areas causes language difficulties called aphasias.

lobe produce speech only with great difficulty, and patients with damage to Wernicke's area in the temporal lobe have no trouble producing speech, but what they do produce is not very meaningful.

Although the study of speech disorders continued into the 20th century, the psychological study of language met the same fate as the study of other cognitive abilities—it was largely abandoned in the early 1900s due to the influence of behaviorism (see Chapter 1, page 9).

The modern era of language research began in the 1950s, as the study of the mind was being rediscovered in the "cognitive revolution." Two events that occurred during that time stand out. The first was the 1957 publication of a book by B. F. Skinner, the modern champion of behaviorism. In this book, *Verbal Behavior,* Skinner proposed that language is learned through the mechanism of reinforcement. According to this idea, just as children learn appropriate behavior by being rewarded for "good" behavior and punished for "bad" behavior, children learn language by being rewarded for using correct language and punished (or not rewarded) for using incorrect language.

In the same year, the linguist Noam Chomsky published a book titled *Syntactic Structures.* This book and Chomsky's work that followed proposed that human language was coded in the genes. Thus, just as humans are genetically programmed to walk, they are programmed to acquire and use language. Chomsky's idea that language is preprogrammed into the brain led him to conclude that despite the wide variations that exist across languages, the underlying basis of language is similar across cultures. Most important for our purposes, Chomsky saw studying language as a way to study the properties of the mind and therefore disagreed with the behaviorist idea that the mind is not a valid topic of study for psychology.

Chomsky's disagreement with behaviorism led him to publish a scathing review of Skinner's *Verbal Behavior* in 1959. In his review, he presented arguments that effectively destroyed the behaviorist idea that language can be explained in terms of reinforcements and without reference to the mind. One of Chomsky's most persuasive arguments was that as children learn language they produce sentences that they have never heard, and that have therefore never been reinforced. (A classic example of a sentence that has been created by many children, and which is unlikely to have been taught by parents is, "I hate you, Mommy.") Chomsky's criticism of behaviorism was one of the most important events of both the cognitive revolution and the development of psycholinguistics, the field concerned with the psychological study of language.

The goal of psycholinguistics is to discover the psychological processes by which humans acquire and process language (Gleason & Ratner, 1998; Clark & Van der Wege, 2002). The three major concerns of psycholinguistics are:

1. *Comprehension.* How do people understand spoken and written language? This includes how people process language sounds, how they understand words, sentences, and stories, as expressed both in writing, speech, and sign language, and how people have conversations with one another.

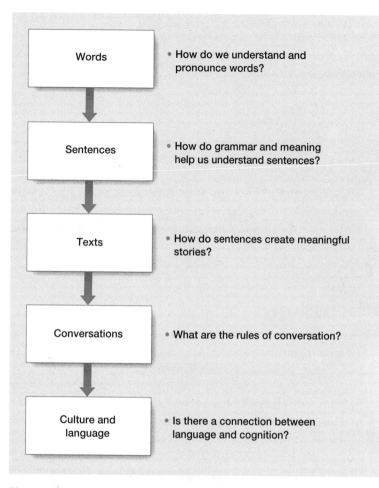

Figure 10.2 Flow diagram for this chapter.

2. *Acquisition.* How do people learn language? This includes not only how children learn language, but how people learn additional languages, either as children or later in life.
3. *Speech production.* How do people produce language? This includes the physical processes of speech production and the mental processes that occur as a person creates speech.

This chapter focuses on the first of these concerns, by describing research on how we understand language. It approaches this research in the same way that many language researchers have approached the study of language—by considering each of the components of language, beginning with small components such as *sounds* and *words* (Figure 10.2), then showing how these words are combined into *sentences*, then showing how we understand *stories* that are created by combining a number of sentences. At the end of the chapter, we describe some of the factors that help people participate in and understand conversations, and, finally, we look at cross-cultural research on language, which considers the role of language in thinking.

HOW DO WE UNDERSTAND WORDS?

One of the most amazing things about words is how many we know and how rapidly we acquire them. Infants produce their first words during their second year (sometimes a little earlier, sometimes later), and after a slow start, begin adding words rapidly, until, when they have become adults, they can understand between 60,000 and 75,000 different words (Altmann, 2001). All of the words a person understands are, together, the person's **lexicon.** We will consider a number of properties of words, beginning with how we perceive and process the individual letters that make up written words.

Perceiving Letters and Words

Each word you are reading is made up of letters. If you were to read these words out loud, you would produce sounds called phonemes, where a **phoneme** is the shortest segment of speech that, if changed, changes the meaning of a word. Thus, the word *bit* contains the phonemes /b/, /i/, and /t/ (phonemes and other speech sounds are indicated by setting them off with slashes), because we can change *bit* into *pit* by replacing /b/ with /p/, to *bat* by replacing /i/ with /a/, or to *bid* by replacing /t/ with /d/.

How we perceive the letters that make up written words and the sounds that create spoken words is a huge topic. We will consider the following two questions within that topic: (1) How does a letter's presence in a word affect our ability to identify it? and (2) How do we perceive separate words within a sentence? We will see that the answers to both of these questions involve meaning. *top-down!*

Letters Are Perceived More Easily in Words: The Word-Superiority Effect
A great deal of research on words has used written words as stimuli. One question that this research has asked is whether we process written words letter by letter, or if we process all of the letters together, in parallel, while we are processing the whole word. Experiments demonstrating the word-superiority effect have helped answer this question.

The **word-superiority effect** refers to the finding that letters are easier to identify when they are part of a word than when they are seen in isolation or in a string of letters that do not form a word. Figure 10.3 shows the procedure that has been used to demonstrate this effect (Reicher, 1969; Wheeler, 1970).

A participant sees a stimulus—either a word, a single letter, or a string of letters that do not create a word—flashed for 25–40 msecs. This stimulus is followed immediately by a masking stimulus (indicated by XXXX) that stops further processing of the stimulus.

CogLab
Word
Superiority

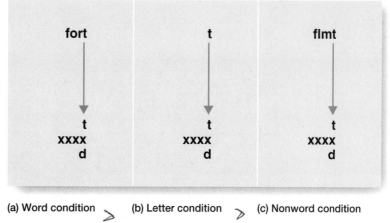

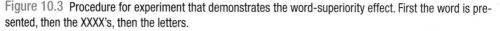

(a) Word condition　　(b) Letter condition　　(c) Nonword condition

Figure 10.3 Procedure for experiment that demonstrates the word-superiority effect. First the word is presented, then the XXXX's, then the letters.

Following the mask, two letters are presented above and below the mask, one that appeared in the stimulus and another that did not appear. When a word has been presented, the letter that did not originally appear spells a new word. Thus, in the example in Figure 10.3, the letter *t* creates the original word *fort* and the letter *d* creates a new word, *ford*.

When participants are asked to choose which of the two letters they saw in the original stimulus, they do so more quickly and accurately when the letter is part of a word, as in Figure 10.3a, than when the letter is presented alone, as in Figure 10.3b, or is part of a nonword, as in Figure 10.3c. This more rapid processing of letters when in a word, the word-superiority effect, means that letters in words are not processed letter by letter but that each letter is affected by its surroundings. Because this enhanced perception of letters occurs for letters in all positions in the word, this means that all of the letters in the word are processed in parallel (Rayner & Clifton 2002).

Perceiving Separate Words in Sentences: Speech Segmentation

The words on this page are easy to recognize. Each word is separated by a space, so it's easy to tell one word from another. However, when people hear words in a conversation, these words are not separated by spaces, or pauses, even though it may sound like they are.

When we look at a record of the physical energy produced by conversational speech, we see that the speech signal is continuous, with either no physical breaks in the signal or breaks that don't correspond to the breaks we perceive between words (Figure 10.4). The fact that there are usually no spaces between words becomes obvious when you listen to someone speaking a foreign language. To someone who is unfamiliar with that language, the words seem to speed by in an unbroken string. However, to a speaker of that language, the words seem separated, just as the words of languages you know seem separated to you. The process of perceiving individual words from the continuous flow of the speech signal

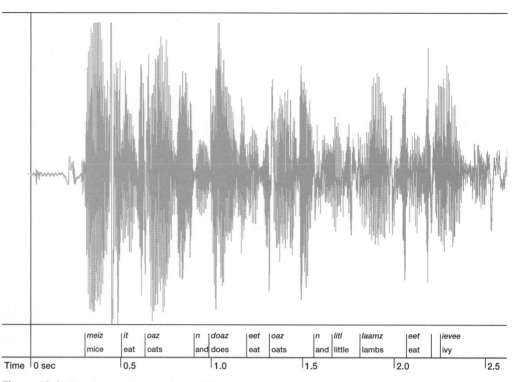

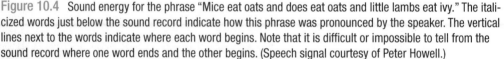

meiz	it	oaz		n	doaz	eet	oaz		n	litl	laamz		eet	ievee
mice	eat	oats		and	does	eat	oats		and	little	lambs		eat	ivy

Time 0 sec   0.5   1.0   1.5   2.0   2.5

Figure 10.4 Sound energy for the phrase "Mice eat oats and does eat oats and little lambs eat ivy." The italicized words just below the sound record indicate how this phrase was pronounced by the speaker. The vertical lines next to the words indicate where each word begins. Note that it is difficult or impossible to tell from the sound record where one word ends and the other begins. (Speech signal courtesy of Peter Howell.)

is called **speech segmentation.** We introduced speech segmentation in Chapter 3 (see page 80), and will now discuss it in more detail.

Our ability to achieve speech segmentation is made more complex by the fact that not everyone produces words in the same way. People talk with different accents and at different speeds, and most important, people often take a relaxed approach to pronouncing words when they are speaking naturally. For example, say the following sentence at the speed you would use in talking to a friend: "This was a best buy." How did you say "best buy"? Did you pronounce the /t/ of best, or did you say "bes buy"? What about "Did you go to the store?" Did you say "did you" or "dijoo"? You have your own ways of producing various words and phonemes and other people have theirs. Analysis of how people actually speak has determined that there are 50 different ways to pronounce the word *the* (Waldrop, 1988).

The way people pronounce words in conversational speech makes about half of the words unintelligible when taken from their fluent context and presented alone. Irwin Pollack and M. Pickett (1964) demonstrated this difficulty in understanding words isolated from their context by recording the conversations of participants who sat in a room, waiting for the experiment to begin. When the participants were then presented with recordings of single words from their own conversations, they could identify only half the words, even though they were listening to their own voices!

There are a number of types of information that listeners can use to deal with the problems posed by words in spoken sentences. One of these is the context, or the meaning of a conversation. The importance of context is illustrated by the results of the Pollack and Pickett experiment, because it showed that when words are taken out of the context provided by other words in a conversation, understanding the words becomes much more difficult.

Our understanding of meaning also helps solve the problem of speech segmentation. An unfamiliar language that sounds like an unbroken string of sounds becomes segmented into individual words once you learn the language. When you learn the language, you not only learn meanings but you also learn that certain sounds are more likely to occur at the ends or beginnings of words. For example, in English, words can end in *rk* (*work, fork*), but not *kr*. However, words can begin with *kr* (*krypton, kremlin*), but not *rk*. There is evidence that people learn these rules about permissible beginnings and endings of words as young children (Gomez & Gerkin, 1999, 2000; Saffran et al., 1999). This knowledge of how words begin and end can be used to help the continuous stream of speech sounds into individual words.

Accessing Words: Frequency Effects

We now move from *perceiving* letters and words to factors that influence our ability to access, or *understand*, words. Our ability to understand words is influenced by a number of factors, including how common the word is and the other words that surround it in a sentence.

Demonstration

Lexical-Decision Task

For each of the following lists, look at each group of letters as quickly as possible and say "yes" if it is a word (like "boat"), or "no" if it is not (like "bort"). You can time yourself for each list, or just notice how difficult it is as you are reading each one.

List 1:

Gambastya, revery, voitle, chard, wefe, cratily, decoy, puldow, faflot, oriole, voluble, boovle, chalt, awry, signet, trave, crock, cryptic, ewe, himpola.

List 2:

Mulvow, governor, bless, tuglety, gare, relief, ruftily, history, pindle, develop, grdot, norve, busy, effort, garvola, match, sard, pleasant, coin, maisle.

The task you have just completed (which is taken from D. W. Carroll, 1999; also see Hirsh-Pasek et al., 1984) is called a **lexical-decision task** because you had to decide whether or not a word is present (see Chapter 8, page 290) (remember that all of the words you know is your *lexicon*). When researchers presented this task under controlled conditions, they found that people read lists of common words faster than lists of less-common words (Savin, 1963). Words that are more common are called *high-frequency words* because they occur with a high frequency in common usage. For example, *cat, coat,* and *square*, which are high-frequency words, occur about 5–15 times more frequently than *low-frequency words* like *ink, jade,* and *prod*. Thus, it is likely that you were able to carry out the lexical decision task more rapidly for list 2 in the demonstration, which contains higher-frequency words than list 1. The faster reading times for high frequency words is called the **word-frequency effect.**

The effect of frequency has also been demonstrated by measuring the time it takes to read sentences such as the following:

When the rhinoceros saw the gnu it was running very fast.
When the supervisor saw the rat it was running very fast.

Because *rhinoceros* and *gnu* are less common than *supervisor* and *rat*, it takes longer to read the first sentence than the second (Underwood & Batt, 1996). This slower response for less-frequent words has also been demonstrated by measuring people's eye movements as they are reading. The eye movements that occur during reading consist of fixations, during which the eye stops on a word for about a quarter of a second (250 msec), and movements, which propel the eye to the next fixation.

In a recent eye-movement study, Keith Rayner and coworkers (2003) had participants read sentences that contained either a high- or a low-frequency target word. For example, the sentence "Sam wore the horrid coat though his pretty girlfriend complained," contains the high-frequency target word *pretty*. The other version of the sentence was exactly the same, but with the high-frequency word *pretty* replaced by the low-frequency word *demure*.

The results, shown in Figure 10.5, indicate that readers looked at the low-frequency words about 40 msec longer than the high-frequency words (left pair of bars). What is even more significant about this result is that it also occurred in a "disappearing text" condition, in which Rayner caused each word in the sentence to disappear 60 msec after the person fixated on it.

Imagine what it would be like to be a participant in the disappearing-word condition. You are reading

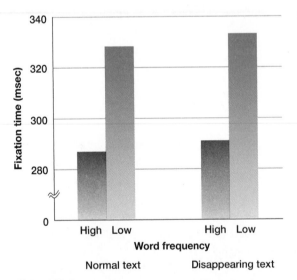

Figure 10.5 Results of Rayner et al.'s (2003) experiment. (a) When participants read normal text, they looked longer at low-frequency words. (b) The same result occurred when the words disappeared 60 msec after the participants looked at them.

a sentence and when you look at a next word, it disappears almost immed[...]
when you move your eye to the next word, it disappears as well. This happens [...]
cause you are reading four words per second. However, even though each wo[...]
briefly visible, the same word-frequency effect occurs as when the words were vis[...]
the time (right pair of bars). Apparently, a 60-msec exposure is long enough for the re[...]
to *see* the word, but after the word disappears, their eyes linger where the word used to [...]
as the reader does the mental processing needed to *understand* the word. Rayner's resul[...]
shows that this processing takes longer for low-frequency words, even if the word is not[...]
physically present as this processing is occurring (also see Rayner & Duffy, 1986, for an
early eye-movement experiment).

Accessing Words: Context Effects

Our ability to access words in a sentence is affected not only by frequency, but also by the
meaning of the rest of the sentence.

It Is Easier to Access Words That Fit the Meaning of a Sentence —expectations

As we will see
when we consider how we understand sentences, we are constantly attempting to figure
out what a sentence means as we are reading it. This process involves both understanding
individual words and understanding how these words fit into the overall meaning of the
sentence. The effect of the sentence on understanding words is demonstrated by the fact
that it takes less time to understand

The Eskimos were frightened by the walrus.

than it takes to understand

The bankers were frightened by the walrus.

Walrus can be accessed more rapidly in the first sentence because it is a better fit to the
meaning of the sentence (Marslen-Wilson, 1990).

Context Helps Clear Up Lexical Ambiguity, but Not Right Away

Words can often
have more than one meaning, a situation called lexical ambiguity. For example, the word
bug can refer to insects, or hidden listening devices, or being annoyed. When ambiguous
words appear in a sentence, we usually use the context of the sentence to determine which
definition applies. For example, if Susan says "My mother is bugging me," we can be
pretty sure that *bugging* refers to the fact that Susan's mother is annoying her, as opposed
to sprinkling insects on her or installing a hidden listening device in her room (although
we might need further context to totally rule out this last possibility).

Often context clears up ambiguity so rapidly that we are not aware of the existence of
the ambiguity. However, David Swinney (1979) did an experiment that showed that people briefly access multiple meanings of ambiguous words before the effect of context takes
over. He did this by presenting participants with a tape recording of a sentence such as the
following:

mor had it that, for years, the government building had been plagued with
blems. The man was not surprised when he found several spiders, roaches, and
bugs in the corner of the room.

to predict which meaning listeners would use for *bugs* in this sentence, *insect*
e logical choice because the sentence mentions spiders and roaches. However,
d that right after the word *bug* was presented, his listeners had accessed two
He determined this by using a lexical-decision task. As participants were hear-
g the word *bugs*, Swinney flashed a test stimulus that was either a word or a nonword
onto a screen, and asked his participants to indicate whether it was a word or nonword.
He measured the reaction times for the test word *ant*, which fits the "insect" meaning, for
the test word *spy*, which fits the "hidden listening device" meaning, and for the word *sky*,
which does not fit either meaning.

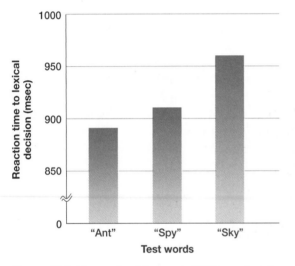

Swinney's result, shown in Figure 10.6, was
that participants responded with nearly the same
speed to both *ant* and *spy* (the small difference between them is not significant), and the response to
both of these words was significantly faster than the
response to *sky*. This faster responding to words associated with two of the meanings of *bug* means that
even though there is information in the sentence indicating that *bug* is an insect, listeners accessed both
meanings of the word as it was being presented. This
effect is, however, short-lived, because when Swinney repeated the same test but waited for two or
three syllables before presenting the test words, the
effect had vanished. Thus, within about 200 msec
after hearing *bug*, the *insect* meaning had been selected from the ones initially activated. Thus, context does have an effect on word meaning, but it ex-
erts its influence only after all meanings have been
briefly accessed.

Figure 10.6 The results of Swinney's (1979) experiment.
The fact that the reaction times to *ant* and *spy* were not
significantly different showed that people briefly accessed
both meanings of the word *bugs* as they read this word in
a sentence.

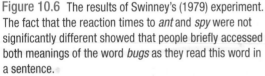

Summary: Words Alone and in Sentences

Figure 10.7 summarizes the results we have described for perceiving letters and words,
and Figure 10.8 summarizes the results for accessing words. Note that for all of the effects
we discussed (except for the word-frequency effect), the meanings of words facilitated perceiving letters and the meaning of sentences facilitated understanding words. The message of these results is an important one because they illustrate one of the main messages
of this chapter: Although the study of language is often described in terms of its individ-

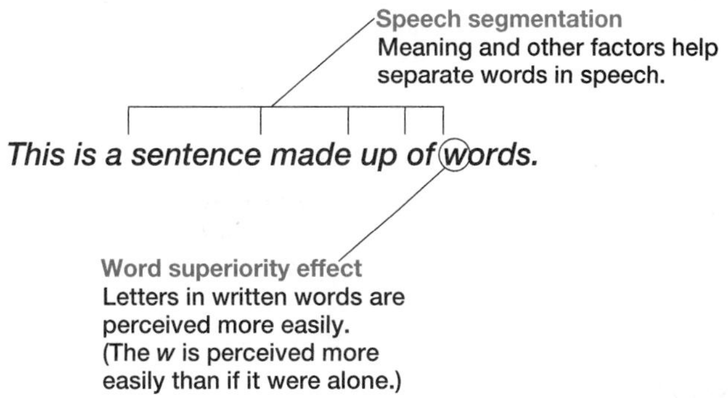

Speech segmentation
Meaning and other factors help
separate words in speech.

This is a sentence made up of words.

Word superiority effect
Letters in written words are
perceived more easily.
(The *w* is perceived more
easily than if it were alone.)

Figure 10.7 Summary of the two effects we described that influence the perception of letters and words:
(1) speech segmentation, and (2) the word-superiority effect.

Lexical ambiguity: short term
All meanings accessed for
ambiguous words—first 200 msec.

Elimination of lexical ambiguity
Context of sentence helps eliminate
lexical ambiguity. (Adding "like ants and
roaches" after bugs makes the meaning
even clearer.)

The class was held even though there were bugs in the basement.

Context provided by the sentence
Word perceived faster if it fits
meaning of sentence (change
basement to *iceberg*
for poor fit).

Word-frequency effect
More frequent words are accessed
faster (change *class* to *vigil* for a
less frequent word).

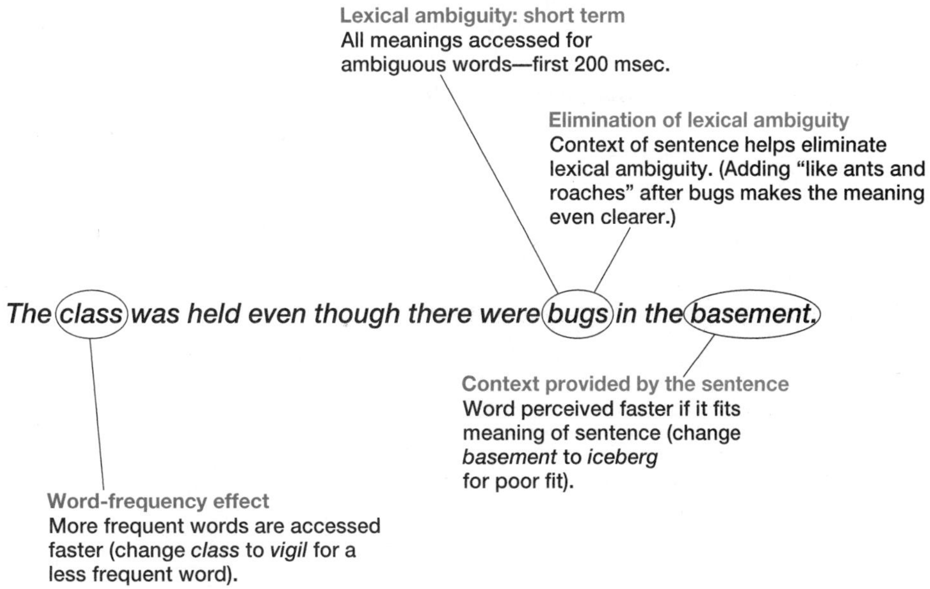

Figure 10.8 Summary of the four effects we described in connection with accessing words: (1) short-term
lexical ambiguity; (2) elimination of lexical ambiguity; (3) how the context of a sentence can cause words to be
perceived faster; and (4) the word-frequency effect.

ual components—such as letters, words, and sentences—these components do not function in isolation. As we discuss how we understand sentences, we will see more examples of how each of these components interacts with and influences one another.

Although the last section was about words, we ended up discussing sentences as well. This isn't surprising because words rarely appear in isolation. They appear together in sentences, with all of the words together creating the meaning of the sentence. To understand how words work together to create the meaning of the sentence, we first need to distinguish between two properties of sentences, semantics and syntax.

Semantics and Syntax

Semantics is the meanings of words and sentences. **Syntax** is the rules for combining words into sentences. Recent experiments have demonstrated a physiological distinction between these two characteristics of words and sentences. For example, semantics and syntax are associated with different components of the event-related potential (ERP). Remember from Chapter 2 (see Figure 2.23), that the ERP is a rapid response that is recorded by an array of electrodes on a person's scalp. The ERP consists of a number of different waves, which are associated with different cognitive functions. Figure 10.9a shows how semantics affects the N400 wave, a negative potential that peaks about

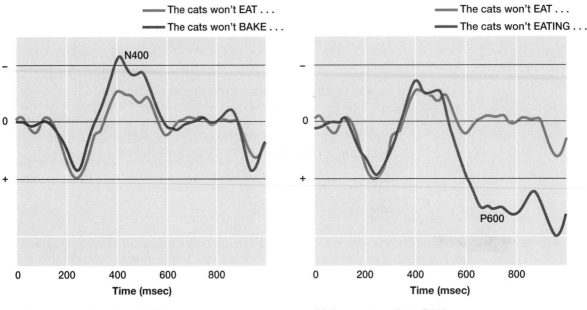

(a) How semantics affects N400

(b) How syntax affects P600

Figure 10.9 (a) The N400 wave of the ERP is affected by semantics. It becomes larger (dark line) when the meaning of a word does not fit the rest of the sentence. (b) The P600 wave of the ERP is affected by syntax. It becomes larger (dark line) when syntax is incorrect. (Reprinted from *Trends in Cognitive Sciences,* Volume 1, Issue 6, Osterhout et al., "Event-Related Potentials and Language," (Figure 1), Copyright © 1997 with permission from Elsevier.)

400 msecs after a stimulus is presented (remember that negative is "up" for ERP records). This component of the ERP is small or nonexistent if a word fits the meaning of a sentence, but becomes larger if a word does not fit the meaning of the sentence. Thus, the response is small for "The cats won't eat . . ." but is larger for "The cats won't bake . . ." (Osterhout et al., 1997; also see Kutas & Federmeier, 2000).

Figure 10.9b shows that the P600 wave is associated with violations of syntax. This wave is small when syntax is correct, but becomes larger when syntax is incorrect. Thus, "The cats won't eating . . ." causes a larger P600 response than "The cats won't eat. . . ." The fact that semantics and syntax are associated with different waves of the ERP supports the idea that they are associated with different mechanisms.

The idea that semantics and syntax are associated with different mechanism has also been supported by brain-imaging studies, which have shown that different areas of the brain are activated by semantics and syntax (Dapretto & Bookheimer, 1999). Also, damage to some areas of the brain causes difficulties in understanding the meanings of words, and damage to other areas causes problems understanding grammar (Breedin & Saffran, 1999).

Semantics and syntax work together to determine the meaning of a sentence. There is more to understanding sentences than simply "adding up" the meanings of words that make up a sentence. The meanings of individual words must fit the overall meaning of the sentence, and the meaning of the sentence is influenced by its structure. As we will see, semantics and syntax interact with one another as a reader or listener works to determine the meaning of a sentence. One of the central processes for determining meaning is **parsing**, the mental grouping of words in a sentence into phrases. *Syntax = grammar*

Parsing a Sentence

The process of parsing normally occurs so automatically that we are not aware of it. To make this process more obvious, psychologists use sentences that can be parsed in more than one way, a situation called **syntactic ambiguity.** Consider the following demonstration.

■ Demonstration

What Does It Mean?

Notice how you first interpret each of the following sentences. Then find another meaning.

> *The spy saw the man with the binoculars.*
> *Flying planes can be dangerous.*
> *Before the police stopped the Toyota disappeared into the night.*
> *They are eating apples.*
> *He read the paper that he received yesterday.*   ■

Each of these sentences provides an example of syntactic ambiguity, in which more than one meaning is possible. We will focus on the first one, about the spy and the binoculars.

There are two ways to parse the sentence about the spy and the binoculars. *The spy* and *with the binoculars* can be grouped together, so the sentence would mean that the spy looked at the man through the binoculars. Alternatively, *the man* and *with the binoculars* could be grouped, so the sentence would mean that the spy saw a man who had some binoculars. Although there is no way to know the correct meaning of this sentence from the information given, there is a tendency for people to interpret this sentence in terms of the first meaning, with the spy being the one with the binoculars.

What causes us to prefer one way of parsing the sentence over another? Psychologists have proposed that there is a mechanism responsible for determining the meaning of the sentence. This mechanism has been called a number of things, including the *language-analysis device* and the *sentence-analyzing mechanism*. We will simply call it the parser. The parser determines the meaning of the sentence, primarily by determining how words are grouped together into phrases. Psychologists are interested in answering the question: "What factors determine how the parsing mechanism works?" Two answers have been proposed to this question, one of which emphasizes the role of syntax, and the other proposes that syntax and semantics works together to determine the meaning of a sentence.

The Syntax-First Approach of Parsing   As its name implies, the syntax-first approach to parsing focuses on how parsing is determined by syntax—the grammatical structure of the sentence. We can appreciate a connection between syntax and sentence understanding by considering the following poem from Lewis Carroll's (1872) *Through the Looking Glass, and What Alice Found There*:

> 'Twas brillig, and the slithy toves
> Did gyre and gimble in the wabe:
> All mimsy were the borogoves,
> And the mome raths outgrabe.

Even though the words in this poem are nonsense, we still have a sense of what the poem is about. The first two lines seem to be about creatures called *slithy toves* doing something called *gyring and gimbling* in a place called *the wabe*. We are able to create meaning out of gibberish because we use syntax to infer meaning (Kako & Wagner, 2001).

The syntax-first approach to parsing states that the parsing mechanism responds to rules that are determined by the grammatical structure of the sentence. There are a number of syntax-based rules. We will focus on one of these rules, called late closure, as an example. The principle of late closure states that when a person encounters a new word, the parser assumes that this word is part of the current phrase (Frazier, 1987). We can illustrate this principle by considering the following sentence:

> Because he always jogs a mile seems like a short distance to him.

Table 10.1 indicates how you may have read this sentence. At first, this sentence seems to be about a man who jogs a mile (a) and (b), but trouble occurs when you get to *seems like* (c) and after reading *a short distance to him* (d), you realize that there is another way to read

Table 10.1	THE PRINCIPLE OF LATE CLOSURE

First Try	
Part of the Sentence	**Probable Reader's Reaction**
(a) Because he always jogs	This is about a man who jogs.
(b) a mile	He jogs a mile.
(c) seems like	This doesn't make sense. How does "seems like" fit in here?
(d) a short distance to him.	OK. I read the sentence incorrectly the first time. I'll try again.

Second Try	
Part of the Sentence	**Probable Reader's Reaction**
Because he always jogs	The man jogs.
a mile seems like a short distance to him.	He is in good shape so a mile doesn't seem like much.

the sentence (see "Second Try," Table 10.1). Because this sentence has led the reader "down the garden path" (down a path that seems right, but turns out to be wrong), this sentence is called a **garden-path sentence** (Frazier & Rayner, 1982).

We can see how this sentence illustrates the principle of late closure by focusing on the words *a mile*. According to the principle, the parser assumes that *a mile* is a continuation of the phrase *because he always jogs*. However, in reality, *a mile* is the beginning of a new phrase. Late closure (so named because it proposes to keep adding new words to the current phrase, so it delays closing off the phrase for as long as possible), leads to the wrong parse—the phrase needed to be closed after *jogs*, so the new phrase can begin. (Note that this would ordinarily be indicated by inserting a comma after *jogs*. For this example, the omission of the comma causes the parser to take us down the garden path.) Because application of the syntactic rule of late closure results in a garden-path sentence, the syntax-first approach to parsing has also been called the **garden-path** model (Frazier & Rayner, 1982).

A number of experiments have supported the idea that parsing is determined by late closure and other syntactic principles (Frazier, 1987). Although the garden-path model of parsing focuses on syntax, it doesn't ignore semantics. It states that if we reach the end of a sentence and find it doesn't make sense, then semantics can be used to clear up the ambiguity. Thus, according to this approach to parsing, syntax is used first, then semantics is called on, if needed, to make sense of the sentence.

We can draw a comparison between this process of determining how words in a sentence are grouped into phrases and how parts of a visual scene become perceptually grouped into objects. Remember from Chapter 3 the example of how the Gestalt principles of organization help cause us to guess that the scene shown in Figure 3.37 might be a creature hiding behind a tree (see page 81). As it turns out, further information provided by looking behind the tree proves that guess to be wrong and so we revise our assessment of the situation from "creature hiding behind a tree" to "strange tree trunks behind a tree" (Figure 3.38).

We used this example in the perception chapter to illustrate the idea that the Gestalt laws of organization are heuristics—rules of thumb that are "best-guess" rules for determining our perceptions. Most of the time, these rules result in perceptions that provide accurate information about what is "out there," and they have the advantage of being fast, which is essential since our very survival depends on quickly reacting to objects and events in the environment.

A similar process occurs when our language system uses a rule such as the principle of late closure to provide a "best guess" about the unfolding meaning of a sentence. Most of the time, this rule leads to the correct conclusion about how the sentence should be parsed. However, in some cases, such as when psychologists create garden-path sentences like the one about the jogger, the rule results in an incorrect parsing, which has to be corrected when more information becomes available at the end of the sentence.

Thus, just as ambiguous visual scenes help perception researchers understand the processes involved in visual perception, garden-path sentences help language researchers determine the processes involved in understanding language. Garden-path sentences accomplish this by showing us what guesses the parser makes, as in the sentence about the jogger (Fodor, 1995).

We have seen that the garden-path model assigns a central place to syntax. We will now describe some experiments that illustrate how semantics can influence how a sentence is processed and we will then describe another approach to parsing.

Semantics Can Influence Sentence Processing   There are a number of situations in which replacing one word in a sentence can make it easier to process the sentence. We will look at a few of these examples, beginning with an early demonstration of how semantics influences sentence processing.

1.   The horse was kicked by the cow.
2.   The fence was kicked by the cow.

Daniel Slobin (1966) compared the speed with which participants were able to understand these two sentences by presenting a picture along with each sentence (see Figure 10.10a). Participants were instructed to respond "true" if the statement described the picture and "false" if it didn't. The result of this experiment indicated that people responded "true" faster to sentence 2 than to sentence 1.

We can understand why participants responded more rapidly to "The fence was kicked by the cow" by considering that to determine the meaning of sentences 1 and 2, it is necessary to determine the identity of the *doer* (who took the action) and the *done to* (who received the action). In sentence 1, the *doer* is the cow and the *done to* is the horse. In sentence 2, the *doer* is the cow and the *done to* is the fence. The difference between these two sentences is that sentence 1 is *reversible*—the roles of *doer* and *done to* could be reversed because horses can kick cows. However, sentence 2 is nonreversible because fences don't

The horse was kicked by the cow.
RT = 1,210 msec

(a)

The fence was kicked by the cow.
RT = 690 msec

The cow was kicked by the fence. (Probably not!)

(b)

Figure 10.10 The participants' task in Slobin's (1966) experiment was to respond "true" if the sentence below the picture accurately described it, or "false" if it did not. (a) The reaction times below the two sentences indicate that people responded faster to "The fence was kicked by the cow" than to "The horse was kicked by the cow." (b) The sentence "The fence was kicked by the cow" is considered nonreversible because its reverse, "The cow was kicked by the fence," is ridiculous.

kick cows (Figure 10.10b). Because there is no need to choose between *doer* and *done to* for sentence 2, it is understood more rapidly. Thus, even though the grammatical structure of these two sentences is the same, the difference in the meaning of one word affects the ability to understand the whole sentence.

Another indication of the role of semantics in understanding sentences is provided by comparing "The spy saw the man with the binoculars" to "The bird saw the man with the binoculars." We have seen that the sentence about the spy has two meanings: The spy could be looking at a man through the binoculars or could be looking at a man who has a pair of binoculars. However, by changing *spy* to *bird*, we create a sentence with only one meaning because the bird wouldn't be looking at the man through binoculars. Thus, in this sentence, it is clear that the man is the one with the binoculars.

Table 10.2	TEMPORARY AMBIGUITY
Phrases	**Reactions While Reading Sentence**
(a) The man recognized	What did the man recognize?
(b) by the spy	Oops! The man didn't recognize anything. The spy recognized the man.
(c) took off down the street.	OK. The man took off.

The ambiguity present in the spy sentence is called standing ambiguity because even after we have all of the information in the sentence, it remains ambiguous. There are other sentences that contain a more subtle kind of ambiguity called temporary ambiguity because the ambiguity occurs in the middle of the sentence and is then cleared up at the end. For example, consider this sentence:

The man recognized by the spy took off down the street.

We can appreciate the ambiguity in this sentence by considering possible meanings that occur as we read the sentence. Table 10.2 follows this process. At the beginning of the sentence the phrase *the man recognized* sets up the expectation that the sentence is going to be about something that the man recognized. However the next phrase, *by the spy*, indicates that instead of the man *doing* the recognizing, the man is the one *being* recognized. At this point, the ambiguity is resolved and the meaning of the sentence is further confirmed by *took off down the street*.

We can illustrate how semantics can influence our interpretation of this sentence by changing the word *man* to *van*, so the sentence becomes:

The van recognized by the spy took off down the street.

As shown in Table 10.3, the word *van* does not lead to the assumption that the van recognized something because vans don't recognize things. No ambiguity is created and there is no confusion when it turns out that the spy was the agent doing the recognizing. Thus, comparing the *man* and the *van* sentences shows how semantics can influence how a reader parses a sentence.

Table 10.3	NO AMBIGUITY
Phrases	**Reactions While Reading Sentence**
The van recognized	Who recognized the van?
by the spy	OK. It was the spy.
took off down the street.	OK. The van took off.

The Interactionist Approach to Parsing We have seen that changing the meaning of a sentence by substituting different words can influence how the sentence is processed and understood. The interactionist approach to parsing starts with the idea that semantics can influence processing and assigns semantics a more central role than it has in the syntax-first approach. The interactionist approach states that all information, both syntactic and semantic, is taken into account as we read a sentence, so any corrections that need to occur in the processing of a sentence take place "on line" as the person is reading the sentence (Altmann, 1998; Altmann & Steedman, 1988; MacDonald et al., 1994). Thus, the crucial question in comparing the syntax-first and interactionist approaches is not *whether* semantics is involved, but *when* semantics comes into play. Is semantics activated only at the end of a sentence after syntax has determined the initial parsing, or does semantics come into play as a sentence is being read?

Recently, a number of studies in which readers' or listeners' eye movements have been measured while they are reading or listening to a sentence have helped answer this question. A property of eye movements that makes them well suited for the task of determining what is happening as a sentence is being read or heard is that they are extremely rapid. The eyes can make 3–4 fixations per second when a person is reading or looking at a scene. In an eye-movement study of reading, John Trueswell and coworkers (1994) measured eye movements as participants read the following two sentences.

1. The defendant examined by the lawyer turned out to be unreliable.
2. The evidence examined by the lawyer turned out to be unreliable.

These sentences may seem familiar because they have the same form as sentences the sentences about the man and the van. Remember that for these sentences, trouble appeared just after the third word (see Table 10.2).

Figure 10.11 shows the amount of time the eyes spent on each part of the two sentences. Notice that the amount of time increases for the phrase *by the lawyer*, and that this increase is larger for sentence 1, which is more ambiguous because it contains *defendant*, since a defendant could *examine* something or *be examined* by someone else, whereas sentence 2 contains *evidence*, which can only *be examined*. This result shows that the meaning of words in the sentence influences processing as the sentence unfolds, a finding that supports the interactionist approach.

Another way to use eye movements to study how people process the information in sentences is to present a picture that illustrates the objects mentioned in a sentence, and to determine *where* participants look while they listen to and are trying to understand the sentence. Michael Tannehaus and coworkers (1995) did such an experiment by presenting the following sentence to participants.

Put the apple on the towel in the box.

The beginning of this sentence (*Put the apple on the towel*) sounds like a straightforward request to put an apple on a towel. But after hearing the last part of the sentence (*in the box*),

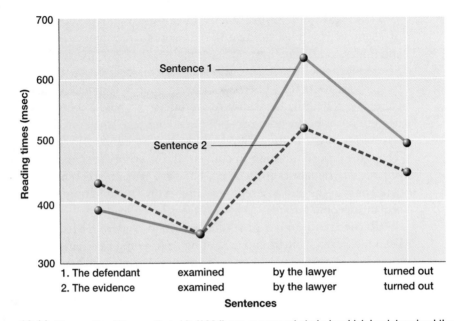

Figure 10.11 The results of Trueswell et al.'s (1994) eye-movement study, in which he determined the amount of time the eyes spent on different parts of sentences 1 and 2 on page 365. Readers spent more time on the phrase *by the lawyer* for sentence 1 ("The defendant . . .") than for sentence 2 ("The evidence . . ."). (Reprinted from *Journal of Memory and Language*, Volume 33, Issue 3, J. C. Trueswell et al., "Semantic Influences on Parsing: Use of Thematic Role Information in Syntactic Ambiguity Resolution," pp. 285–318, Figure 1, Copyright © 1994, with permission from Elsevier.)

two possible meanings emerge: The sentence could be about *where* to put the apple (put it on the towel that's inside the box; Figure 10.12a), or about *which* apple (pick the apple that is on the towel to put in the box; Figure 10.12b).

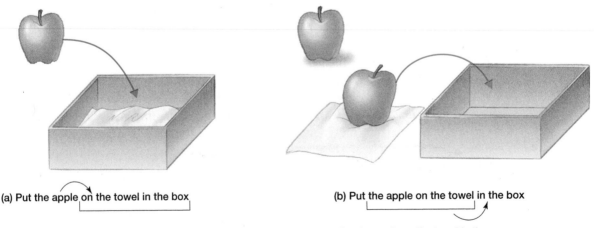

(a) Put the apple on the towel in the box

(b) Put the apple on the towel in the box

Figure 10.12 These two pictures indicate two meanings of the sentence "Put the apple on the towel in the box," which was used in Tannehaus et al.'s (1995) eye-movement study. (a) The apple goes on the towel that's inside the box. (b) The apple on the towel goes in the box.

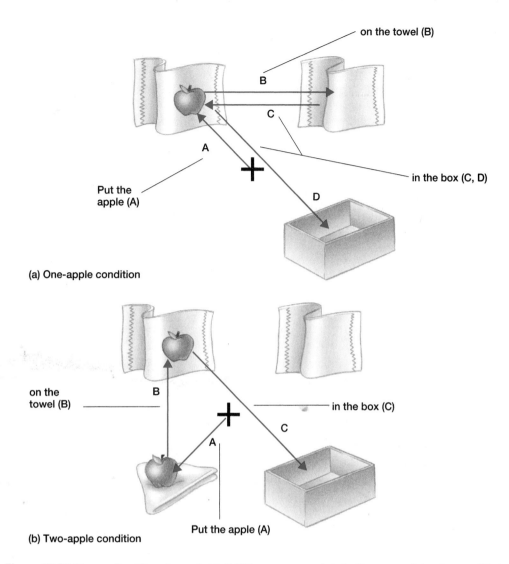

Figure 10.13 The results of Tannehaus et al.'s (1995) eye-movement study. The way participants moved their eyes to different parts of the pictures depended on the information provided by the picture. Note how the eye movements differ in (a), the one-apple condition and (b), the two-apple condition. (Reprinted with permission from "Integration of Visual and Linguistic Information in Spoken Language Comprehension," by M. K. Tanenhaus et al. From *Science, 268,* pp. 1632–1634, Figures 1 & 2. Copyright © 1995 AAAS.)

Tannehaus reasoned that in most real-life situations we hear sentences while we are interacting with the environment. Thus, the purpose of this experiment was to see how the environmental context that accompanies a sentence can influence how a person moves their eyes to fixate on particular objects in the environment. They used two pictures. The picture in Figure 10.13a is the "one-apple condition," in which one apple is shown on a towel. Figure 10.13b is the "two-apple condition," in which one apple is on a towel the other one is on a napkin.

The eye movements for participants looking at the one-apple condition, indicated by the arrows, shows that at the beginning of the sentence, participants moved their eyes to the apple because it is the only apple in the picture (arrow A), and then to the other towel (B) because the sentence seemed to be saying to put the apple on the towel. However, upon hearing the last phrase, *in the box*, the participants apparently realized that the sentence was asking them to move the apple into the box, so they quickly moved their eyes back to the apple (C) and then to the box (D). Thus, when the information in the picture supported the idea that "on the towel" indicated *where* the apple should be placed (one-apple condition), participants' eyes take an incorrect detour to the other towel before making a correction and looking at the box.

Participants in the two-apple condition responded differently. They first moved their eyes to the apple on the napkin (A) and then to the one on the towel (B), because the sentence is telling them to pick the apple on the towel. Then, in response to the last part of the sentence, they moved their eyes directly to the box (C). Thus, when the information in the picture supported the idea that "on the towel" indicated *which* apple to pick, participants moved their eyes straight from the correct apple to the box.

This experiment demonstrates that participants respond immediately as they are thinking about what the sentence means. Thus, for the one-apple condition they changed their response as soon as they received information that indicated that they needed to revise their first interpretation of the sentence. This immediate responding, as they were hearing the sentence, supports the interactionist idea that the reader or listener takes both syntactic and semantic information into account simultaneously. (Also see Altmann & Kamide, 1999, for another demonstration of how the eyes rapidly respond to the meaning of a sentence.)

Although the controversy regarding whether the syntax-first approach or the interactionist approach is correct is still not resolved (Bever et al., 1998; Rayner & Clifton, 2002), evidence such as the eye-movement studies we have described supports the idea that semantics is taken into account earlier than proposed by the syntax-first approach. Furthermore, the result of the "apple in the box" experiment goes beyond the syntax-first approach by showing that information in the environment can help determine what a sentence means. This is important, because in real life we rarely hear sentences in isolation. Rather, we hear sentences within an environment that provides a context for what we are hearing.

This idea that sentences occur within an environment is particularly true of reading because sentences are typically part of a larger text or story. Thus, when we read a particular sentence, we already have picked up a great deal of information about what is happening from what we read before. This brings us to the next level of the study of language—the study of how we understand text and stories (commonly called *discourse processing* or *text processing*). As we will see, most research in text processing is concerned with how readers' understanding of a story is determined by information provided by many sentences taken together.

1. What is special about human language? Consider why human language is unique, and what it is used for.
2. How has language been studied since the 1800s? What events are associated with the beginning of the modern study of language in the 1950s?
3. What is psycholinguistics? What are its concerns, and what part of psycholinguistics does this chapter focus on?
4. What evidence supports the statement that "meaning makes it easier to perceive letters in words, and words in spoken sentences"?
5. How do the frequency of words and the context of a sentence aid in accessing words? How does Swinney's experiment about "bugs" indicate that the meanings of ambiguous words can take precedence over context, at least for a short time?
6. Why do we say that there is more to understanding sentences than simply adding up the meanings of the words that make up the sentence?
7. Describe the syntax-first explanation of parsing, and the interactionist explanation. What are the roles of syntax and semantics in each explanation? What evidence supports the interactionist approach?

HOW DO WE UNDERSTAND TEXT AND STORIES?

Just as sentences are more than the adding up of the meanings of individual words, stories are more than the adding up of the meanings of individual sentences. In a well-written story, sentences in one part of the story are related to sentences in other parts of the story. Thus, the reader's task is to use these relationships between sentences to create a coherent, understandable story.

The materials used in research on text processing are usually excerpts from narrative texts. *Narrative* refers to texts in which there is a story that progresses from one event to another, although stories can also include flashbacks of events that happened earlier. Research on text processing shows that two processes that are important in determining the relationships between various parts of the story are *inference* and *coherence*.

Inference Creates Coherence

Coherence and inference are two key concepts in text processing. **Coherence** refers to the representation of the text in a reader's mind so that information in one part of the text is related to information in another part of the text. Texts that have the property of coherence are usually easier to understand than texts that do not have this property.

Most of the coherence in texts is created by inference. **Inference** refers to the process by which readers create information during reading that is not explicitly stated in the text.

We have had a great deal of experience with inference from our study of memory in Chapter 7. For example, on page 238 we described an experiment in which participants read the passage "John was trying to fix the bird house. He was pounding the nail when his father came out to watch him do the work." We saw that after reading that passage, participants were likely to say that they had previously seen the following passage: "John was using a hammer to fix the birdhouse. He was looking for the nail when his father came out to watch him." The fact that they thought they had seen this passage, even though they had never read that John was using a hammer, occurred because they had inferred that John was using a hammer from the information that he was *pounding the nail* (Bransford & Johnson, 1973). People create coherence as they are reading a text by making a number of different kinds of inferences.

Anaphoric Inference   Inferences that connect an object or person in one sentence to an object or person in another sentence are called **anaphoric inferences.** For example consider the following.

> Riffifi, the famous poodle, won the dog show. She has now won the last three shows she has entered.

Anaphoric inference occurs when we infer that *She* at the beginning of the second sentence and the other *she* near the end both refer to Riffifi. In the previous "John and the birdhouse" example, knowing that *He* in the second sentence refers to *John* is another example of anaphoric inference.

We usually have little trouble making anaphoric inferences because of the way information is presented in sentences and our ability to make use of knowledge we bring to the situation. But here is an example of a quote from a *New York Times* interview with former heavyweight champion George Foreman (who has recently been known for lending his name to a popular indoor grill), which puts our ability to create anaphoric inference to the test.

> What we really love to do on our vacation time is go down to our ranch in Marshall, Texas. We have close to 500 acres. There are lots of ponds and I take the kids out and we fish. And then of course, we grill them. (cited in *The New Yorker*, October 14/21, 2002, page 205)

Based just on the structure of the sentence, we might conclude that the kids were grilled, but we nonetheless know that the chances are pretty good that the fish were grilled, not George Foreman's children! Readers are capable of creating anaphoric inferences even under adverse conditions because they add information from their knowledge of the world to the information provided in the text.

Instrumental Inference   Inferences about tools or methods are **instrumental inferences.** For example, when we read the sentence *William Shakespeare wrote Hamlet while he was sitting at his desk*, we infer from what we know about the time during which Shakespeare lived that he was probably using a quill pen (not a laptop computer!) and that his desk was made of wood. Similarly, inferring from the passage about John that he is using a hammer to pound the nails would be an instrumental inference.

Causal Inference

Inferences that result in the conclusion that the events described in one clause or sentence were caused by events that occurred in a previous sentence are **causal inferences** (Goldman et al., 1999; Graesser et al., 1994; van den Broek, 1994). For example, when we read the sentences

Sharon took an aspirin. Her headache went away.

we infer that the aspirin caused the headache to go away (Singer et al., 1992). This is an example of a fairly obvious inference that most people in our culture would make based on their knowledge about headaches and aspirin.

Other causal inferences are not so obvious and may be more difficult to figure out. For example, what do you conclude from reading the following sentences?

Sharon took a shower. Her headache went away.

You might conclude, from the fact that the headache sentence directly follows the shower sentence, that the shower had something to do with eliminating Sharon's headache, but the connection is not as obvious as in the first pair of sentences. In fact, reading those two sentences might cause you to make up some reasons why the shower might have eliminated Sharon's headache. You might guess that the shower relaxed Sharon, or perhaps her habit of singing in the shower (which you read about earlier) was therapeutic, or you might wonder if there really is a connection between the two sentences.

Causal Connections

Causal inferences create connections that are essential for creating coherence in texts (Goldman et al., 1999; Graesser et al., 1994; van den Broek, 1994). We are now going to describe the connections created by causal inferences in more detail because causal inferences are extremely important in text processing and have generated a great deal of research.

Causal Inference as a Creative Process

Inference is a creative process because it creates information that is not explicitly stated in the text. Consider, for example, this excerpt from Tolstoy's novel *Anna Karenina* (van den Broek, 1994).

The wife had found out about her husband's relationship with the French governess and announced that she could not go on living in the same house with him . . . the wife did not leave her own room, and, the husband stayed from the house all day.

This passage explicitly states a number of facts. We know that the wife found out about the husband's relationship, that the husband had a relationship with the French governess, and so on. However, we can draw a number of conclusions from this passage about things that are not stated at all. From what you know about human behavior, try answering these questions:

- What kind of relationship did the husband have with the governess?
- What was the social class of the wife and husband?
- What is the wife's state of mind?
- Why did the wife stay in her room?
- Why did the husband stay away from home?
- What was the husband doing when he was away from home?

You probably were able to answer some of these questions easily, while others were more difficult. The fact that you can answer these questions, or at least make intelligent guesses, attests to the creativity that readers bring to a text. However, while it is easy to show that people can make inferences that go beyond what they have read, we are also interested in determining the mechanisms behind this creativity. To do this, cognitive psychologists have asked questions such as: (1) What is the relationship between causal connections and memory? and (2) Over what distances in a text do connections occur?

Causal Connections and Memory   For each of these following pairs of sentences, consider the question: What caused Jimmy's bruises?

1. Jimmy's big brother beat him up.
   The next day he was covered with bruises.
2. Jimmy's mother was furious with him.
   The next day he was covered with bruises.
3. Jimmy went to his friend's house.
   The next day he was covered with bruises.

For pair 1, it seems obvious that Jimmy's bruises were caused by the beating he received from his brother. For pair 2, we could conclude that Jimmy's mother was responsible for his bruises because it says she was furious with him, but we might not be as confident about the connection as for the first pair. Finally, there is only a weak connection between the sentences in the third pair, so it is even harder to answer the question.

Pairs of sentences such as these were used in an experiment by Jerome Myers and Susan Duffy (1990). Their participants first read each pair of sentences and then were presented with the first sentence in each pair and asked to recall the second. Memory was worst for pairs like 3, which isn't surprising since there is a low level of connection between the two sentences. Although we might expect that memory would be best for pair 1 because of the strong connection between sentences, that is not what happened. The best memory was for pair 2, which had the intermediate level of connection.

Why do you think memory was better for the intermediate-connection pair than for the high-connection pair? One possible explanation is that drawing a connection in the intermediate pair may involve more mental processing than in the high-connection pair. This would occur because the intermediate pair involves some thought (Would Jimmy's mother really have hit him, even if she was furious?), whereas the connection is so obvious in the high-connection pair that little thought or mental processing is necessary. More research is needed to see if this explanation is correct.

Local and Global Connections   Language researchers distinguish between two kinds of connections. A **local connection** is a connection that occurs between what a person is reading and what they read just 1–3 sentences previously. The limit of 1–3 sentences is determined by the limited capacity of a person's working memory. A **global connection** is a connection between what a person is reading and what they read much earlier. An example of a global connection would be knowing that the sentence "Bob went to work" means that he went to his office at Microtek because we read about Bob's job at Microtek earlier in the text.

Research such as Myers and Duffy's experiments that used the sentence about Johnny being covered with bruises has demonstrated the operation of local connections in text. But what about global connections? Some experiments have suggested that most of the connections that occur as a person reads a text are local and that only under certain special conditions do global connections occur (McKoon & Ratcliff, 1992). However, other experiments have provided evidence for global connections. For example, Jason Albrecht and Edward O'Brien (1993) had participants read a passage that focuses on a specific character. Read the following passage about Mary, and decide how easy it is to follow the story.

> Today, Mary was meeting a friend for lunch. She arrived early at the restaurant and decided to get a table. After she sat down, she started looking at the menu.
>
> This was Mary's favorite restaurant because it had fantastic health food. Mary, a health nut, has been a strict vegetarian for 10 years. Her favorite food was cauliflower. Mary was so serious about her diet that she refused to eat anything which was fried or cooked in grease.
>
> After about 10 minutes, Mary's friend arrived. It had been a few months since they had seen each other. Because of this they had a lot to talk about and chatted for over a half hour. Finally, Mary signaled the waiter to come take their orders. Mary checked the menu one more time. She had a hard time deciding what to have for lunch. Mary ordered a cheeseburger and fries. She handed the menu back to the waiter. Her friend didn't have as much trouble deciding what she wanted. She ordered and they began to chat again. They didn't realize there was so much for them to catch up on.

If you thought it was a little strange that Mary, who was described as a vegetarian at the beginning of the passage, ended up ordering a cheeseburger, then you made a global connection between the information in the first paragraph, which identified Mary as a vegetarian, and the seventh sentence in the last paragraph, which said that she ordered a cheeseburger. Participants who read this passage were in the *inconsistent condition* because ordering a cheeseburger is inconsistent with being a vegetarian.

The key result of Albrecht and O'Brien's experiment was that participants in the inconsistent condition took longer to read the paragraph about the cheeseburger than participants in the *consistent condition*, who read the same passage but with the following paragraph substituted for the second one:

This was Mary's favorite restaurant because it had fantastic junk food. Mary enjoyed eating anything that was quick and easy to fix. In fact, she ate at McDonald's at least three times a week. Mary never worried about her diet and saw no reason to eat nutritious foods.

The fact that participants in the inconsistent group took longer to read the cheeseburger sentence means that they were being influenced by sentences that they had read earlier in the text. Thus, this result provides evidence that people do make global connections as they read a text (also see Huitema et al., 1993).

The idea that people make connections to things they have read earlier in the text has led to an approach to text processing that proposes that readers create something called a *situation model* in their mind as they read a story.

Situation Models

A situation model is a mental representation of what a text is about. This approach proposes that the mental representation people form as they read a story does not indicate information about phrases, sentences, or paragraphs, but does include a representation of the situation in terms of the people, objects, locations, and events that are being described in the story (Graesser & Wiemer-Hastings, 1999; Zwaan, 1999). The situation-model approach also proposes that readers vicariously experience events that are being described in a story and that this experience is often from the point of view of the protagonist—the main character in the story or the character being described at a particular point in the story.

This way of looking at how readers process stories leads to a number of predictions. If we create a situation model and then fit new events into the model as they occur, then we would predict that processing will be slower if we encounter something that doesn't fit the model. This is what occurred in the inconsistent condition of the passage about Mary and the cheeseburger.

According to the situation approach, when people are reading about a particular space, they create a map of that space and then follow the protagonist through it. This leads to the prediction that people will identify an object more rapidly if the object is in the same room as the protagonist.

This prediction was tested by Daniel Morrow and coworkers (1987), who had participants memorize a diagram of a research center (Figure 10.14). They then had the participants read a story that described a man walking through various rooms in the research center. When the man has just walked from the conference room to the laboratory (dashed arrow), participants were presented with the name of an object that was in the laboratory (where the man was located), or in the conference room (where he had just come from), or in the library (which the participants knew about from memorizing the diagram). Their task was to indicate as quickly as possible whether the object was in the same

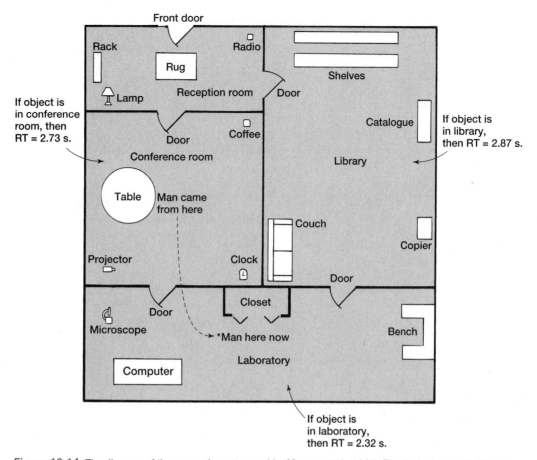

Figure 10.14 The diagram of the research center used by Morrow et al. (1987). The dashed arrow indicates the most recent path of the man, according to the story, and the star indicates his current location (in the laboratory). The reaction times indicate how long it took for participants to indicate whether an object was from the same room as the man or from a different room. Thus, the correct answer for an object in the laboratory was "same," and the correct answer for objects in the conference room or the library was "different." (Reprinted from *Journal of Memory and Language,* Volume 26, D. G. Morrow et al., "Accessibility and Situation Models in Narrative Comprehension," pp. 165–187, Figure 1, Copyright © 1987, with permission from Elsevier.)

room or in a different room than the protagonist. The results, shown in Figure 10.14, indicate that participants responded more quickly for objects closer to the man. In addition, they also made fewer errors for closer objects (also see Glenberg et al., 1987).

   In another experiment, Rolf Zwaan (1996) investigated how readers process information about *time* in a story. He proposed that readers' situation model contains information not only about *where in space* objects are, but also about *when in time* events are happening. According to Zwaan, when the order in which events happen is not explicitly stated in a narrative, readers begin with the assumption that the order in which events are presented in a story corresponds to when the events actually happen in the story, and that the events follow each other closely in time. For example, when we read the sentence

Sam coughed, looked around, and opened the door.

we assume that Sam coughed, he looked around, and then opened the door, in that order, with one event following closely after the one before it.

To take this idea beyond the single sentence, Zwaan did an experiment in which he had participants read a story such as the following.

The Grand Opening
Today was the grand opening of Maurice's new art gallery.
He had invited everybody in town
    who was important in the arts.
Everyone who had been invited had said that they would come.
It seemed like the opening would be a big success.
At seven o'clock, the first guests arrived.
Maurice was in an excellent mood.
He was shaking hands and beaming.
A moment/an hour/a day later, he turned very pale.
He had completely forgotten to invite the local art critic.
And sure enough, the opening was very negatively reviewed in the weekend
    edition of the local newspaper.
Maurice decided to take some Advil and stay in bed the whole day.

Notice that line 9 (italicized here, but not in the actual story the participant read), could be one of the following three sentences: "A moment later he turned very pale," "An hour later he turned very pale," or "A day later he turned very pale." Different groups of participants read different versions of this sentence so that little story time passed for some participants (for the group that had read *a moment later*), and more story time passed for others (for the group that had read *an hour later* or *a day later*).

Zwaan predicted that readers' initial assumption is that each event will immediately follow the other, so when longer time spans occur, they need to make adjustments from what was assumed and this adds to the time readers need to process the sentence. He tested this prediction by measuring the reading times for line 9 for each group of participants. The results show that, in fact, the reading time was fastest for the *moment* group and longer for the other two groups (Figure 10.15).

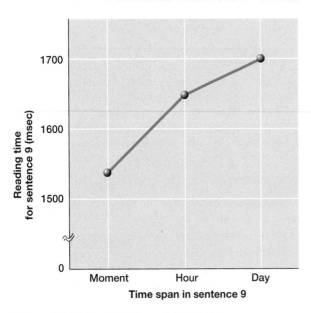

Figure 10.15 Results of Zwaan's (1996) study.

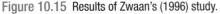

How Do We Understand Conversations?

At the beginning of the chapter, we stated that the staging ground for language is one person conversing with another. Before the relatively recent introduction of written language, this was certainly the case, and it continues to be so today.

Conversations are dynamic interactions between two or more people (Garrod & Pickering, 2004). Two important characteristics of this interaction are that each person brings his or her own knowledge to a conversation and that conversations go more smoothly when the participants bring *shared* knowledge to a conversation. Thus, if people are talking about current events, it helps if everyone has been keeping up with the news, and is more difficult if one of the people has just returned from 6 months of meditation in an isolated monastery.

One of the implications of the idea that it is desirable for people to have shared knowledge about the topic of a conversation is that when someone introduces new information that might not be shared, they have a responsibility to present this information in a way that will enable others to understand it. This idea that participants in a conversation have responsibilities is behind H. P. Grice's (1975) proposal of a basic principle of conversation and four "conversational maxims" that people need to follow in order to have a good conversation.

Grice's Cooperative Principle and Conversational Maxims

Grice's basic principle is called the **cooperative principle.** This principle states that *the speaker and listener agree that the person speaking should strive to make statements that further the agreed goals of the conversation.* The following four **conversational maxims** state ways to achieve the cooperation principle: (1) **Quantity**—be informative. Make your contribution as informative as possible. Do not be either overinformative or underinformative. (2) **Quality**—be truthful. Do not say what you believe to be false, or that for which you lack sufficient evidence. (3) **Manner**—be clear. Avoid being obscure or ambiguous. (4) **Relation**—be relevant. Stay on the topic of the exchange.

Some of these maxims are obvious. If you say "What do you think is going to be on the cognitive psychology exam?" and the person you are talking with responds by saying "I bought a new car yesterday," he or she is not following the maxim of relation.

Other maxims are more subtle. For example, consider the following exchange:

Jason: Howard is meeting a woman for dinner tonight.
Susan: Wow! I wonder what his wife is going to think, if she finds out.
Jason: Actually, the woman he is meeting is his wife.

In this conversation, Jason has violated the maxim of quantity because he provided too little information by simply saying "a woman" rather than "his wife." He is also violating the maximum of manner by being obscure.

An example of a rule of clear conversation that incorporates the maxims of quality (be informative), manner (be clear), and relation (be relevant) is the **given-new contract**, which states that the speaker should construct sentences so they include two kinds of information: (1) *given information*—information that the listener already knows; and (2) *new information*—information that the listener is hearing for the first time (Haviland & Clark, 1974). For example, consider the following two sentences.

1. Ed was given an alligator for his birthday.
   Given information (from previous conversation): Ed had a birthday.
   New information: He got an alligator.
2. The alligator was his favorite present.
   Given information (from sentence 1): Ed got an alligator.
   New information: It was his favorite present.

Notice how the new information in the first sentence becomes the given information in the second sentence. Susan Haviland and Herbert Clark (1974) demonstrated the consequences of not following the given-new contract by presenting pairs of sentences and asking participants to press a button when they felt they understood the second sentence in each pair. They found that it took longer for the participants to comprehend the second sentence in pairs like this one:

We checked the picnic supplies.
The beer was warm.

than it took to comprehend the second sentence in pairs like this one:

We got some beer out of the trunk.
The beer was warm.

The reason comprehending the second sentence in the first pair takes longer is that the given information, that there were picnic supplies, does not mention beer. Thus, when beer is mentioned in the second sentence, the listener has to infer that the picnic supplies included beer. In contrast, this inference is not required in the second pair because the first sentence includes the information that beer is in the trunk. The second pair of sentences, therefore, satisfies Grice's maxims to be informative, clear, and relevant.

Understanding Indirect Statements

People often say things that don't mean what they appear to mean on the surface. If, during an inspection of some barracks, a sergeant says to a soldier, "Do you see that cigarette butt there, soldier?" what thought is he trying to transmit to the soldier? It would be clear to the soldier that the sergeant is not really asking whether or not he can see the cigarette butt; rather, he is telling him to shape up and not leave cigarette butts around in the future. Similarly, when Rodney Hammersmith II, sitting in the drawing room of his mansion, says, "It's stuffy in here, Jeeves" he is doing more than commenting on the atmosphere in the drawing room. Rodney's statement, translated into its true meaning, is "Open the window, Jeeves" or "Turn up the air conditioning, Jeeves." Jeeves, being an intelligent listener, knows exactly what Rodney means. Both Rodney and the sergeant are making indirect statements—statements in which the literal meaning is not the meaning the speaker intends (or the listener hears) (Clark & Lucy, 1975).

There are so many situations in which the literal meaning is not what the speaker intends that we have become experts in figuring out what is really behind what a person is saying. So when someone asks, "Do you have the time?" you know they are asking "What time is it?" Thus, communication between people involves more than simply understanding the sentences they are saying. Cognitive processes that involve taking the context of a statement into account, making inferences and assumptions, and following conversational rules that have been learned from years of practice all help us to communicate clearly and with a minimum of uncertainty. Of course it is important to also realize that people do not always "follow the rules" as they are having a conversation. People can abruptly change the subject, avoid answering questions, talk too much or too little, leave out information that is needed, or be purposely obscure or untruthful.

What is particularly significant about violations of conversational rules is that they often provide information about the intentions and motivations of the speaker. Thus, when you ask your friend Susan, "Do you have the time?" and she says, "Yes," you know that she is actually aware that you were asking, "What time is it?" and you might therefore infer that she is attempting to be funny. On a more serious note, you might wonder why a particular person is not telling the truth or why a person avoided answering a question you asked. Thus, just like other aspects of language, when the rules are being followed, we don't notice them because everything is flowing smoothly. However, when rules are not followed, our cognitive mechanism jumps into action to try to figure out what is going on.

LANGUAGE AND CULTURE

Our survey of language has taken us from letters through words, to sentences, stories, and conversations. Most of the research we have described has been done on English-speaking (American and British) participants, many of them college students. But what about people in other cultures, who speak different languages? Do they use language for different purposes than English speakers? Does their route to understanding language involve the same rules? Despite the evidence that languages across different cultures have many characteristics in common, there is also evidence that there are differences between languages in different cultures, and that some of these differences may be related to differences in cognition.

We have described some of the cultural differences involved in categorization in Chapter 8 (see page 283), and we will describe some differences in the way people in different cultures reason in Chapter 12 (page 440). But our concern in this chapter is language, and we will consider the following two questions about the relation between culture and language: (1) Does culture affect how people use language? and (2) Does language affect cognition? We will see that the answer to both of these questions appears to be "yes."

How Does Culture Affect How People Use Language?

There is good evidence that certain aspects of language usage differ in different cultures. For example, if we return to indirect statements that people make in conversations, we see that speakers across cultures use indirect statements, but if we compare Americans and East Asians, we find that East Asians use statements that are even more indirect than those used by Americans. For example, an American might say, "The door is open" to mean "Please shut the door," whereas a Japanese person might say, "It is somewhat cold today" to accomplish the same result. The Japanese statement is more indirect because it does not refer to the door (Yum, 1991).

Differences have also been observed in the way speakers in different cultures pose questions. For example, when an American speaker inquires whether someone would like a refill of their tea, they would be likely to say, "More tea?" However, a Chinese person would be more likely to say "Drink more?" This difference reflects different ways of looking at the situation. The American reasons that because the person is obviously drinking, it is not necessary to refer to drinking. The Chinese person reasons that it is obvious that tea is involved, so it seems reasonable to inquire about drinking (Nisbett, 2003).

While these examples may seem like minor differences between cultures, there are other differences that reflect the overall orientations of the cultures involved. One contrast between East Asian and Euro-American cultures is that European-Americans are more oriented toward *objects*, and East Asians focus more on *relationships to a group* (Nisbett & Norenzayan, 2002). One way that this difference in orientation could affect language is by influencing what parents teach their children.

In a developmental study in which interactions between mothers and their 6- to 19-month-old children were observed, it was found that American mothers used twice as many object labels as Japanese mothers, and Japanese mothers were twice as likely to talk about how to be polite (Fernald & Morikawa, 1993). Thus, an American mother's conversation might sound like this: "That's a car. See the car? You like it? It's got nice wheels." In contrast, a Japanese mother might say, "Here! It's a vroom vroom. I give it to you. Now give this to me. Yes! Thank you." What these differences in how mothers' behavior toward their children means is that American children are learning that objects are important, and Japanese children are learning that relationships are important (Nisbett, 2003).

The fact that Americans focus more on objects is reflected in adult language as well. For example, when presented with an underwater scene, Americans began by describing individual objects ("There comes a big fish, maybe a trout, moving off to the left"). Japanese, on the other hand, focused on establishing the context within which the action is occurring ("It looked like a pond") (Nisbett, 2003).

If basic cultural orientation and the way parents talk to their children affect what adults attend to in the environment, does this mean we can draw a connection between language in a culture and what people pay attention to, or perhaps even how they perceive and think? The idea of a causal connection between language and cognition has had a varied reception in psychology. As we will see, it was initially rejected, but has recently gained some support.

How Does Language Affect Cognition?

According to the **Sapir-Whorf hypothesis,** which was proposed by anthropologist Edward Sapir and linguist Benjamin Whorf, the nature of a culture's language can affect the way people think (Whorf, 1956). The initial test of this idea were studies of color perception by Eleanor Rosch (the same Eleanor Rosch whose ideas about categorization we described in Chapter 8) (Rosch Heider, 1972; Rosch Heider & Olivier, 1972). Rosch tested color perception and the ability to remember colors in Americans, who have many different color categories (blue, green, red, and so on), and in members of a stone-age agricultural culture in Iran called the Dani, who have only two color categories. The fact that these experiments did not find the large differences in color perception or color memory predicted by the Sapir-Whorf hypothesis caused psychologists to downplay the Sapir-Whorf hypothesis, especially for capacities such as color perception, which are strongly linked to biology.

However, recent research has provided evidence that favors the idea that language can influence cognition. Debi Roberson and coworkers (2000; also see Davidoff, 2001) repeated some of Rosch's experiments on English-speaking British participants and members of the Berinmo from New Guinea. The Berinmo have only five color categories, compared to the Americans' eight. More important than the numbers of color categories are that the borders between the colors are different in the two cultures.

Roberson had the British and Berinmo participants name the colors of 160 Munsell color chips (small color chips similar to those found in paint stores, but scientifically color-calibrated to be used in research). The results of this color naming are shown in Figure 10.16. The British used eight different names and the Berinmo, five. From these figures it is obvious that there are large differences between the way colors are organized in the two cultures. For example, many of the chips that the British called *green* or *blue* were classified as *nol* (which means *live*, and covers green, yellow-green, blue, and purple), *wap* (the term for white and all pale colors), and *kel* (the term for black, charcoal, or anything burnt—and also meaning dirty).

CogLab

**Categorical
Perception**

Roberson made use of a property of categories called **categorical perception,** which states that it is difficult to discriminate between two stimuli that are within a category, and it is easier to discriminate between two stimuli that are in different categories. This means that it is more difficult to tell the difference between two greens than it is to tell the difference between a blue and a green. According to this idea, the British participants would find it more difficult to tell the difference between color chips A and B, which they call *green* (see Figure 10.17), than to tell the difference between *green* chip B and *blue* chip C.

When the ability to tell the difference between colors in the same and different categories was determined for the British and Berinmo, it was found that categorical perception occurred for both groups, but that the results depended on how colors were named in

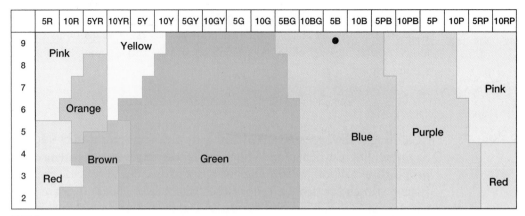

British

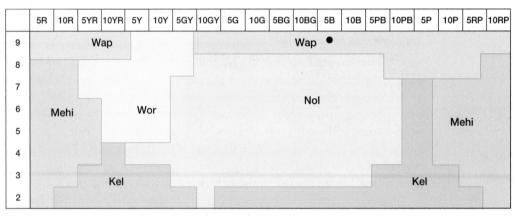

Berinmo

Figure 10.16 Results of Roberson et al.'s (2000) color-naming experiment. The results for British participants are indicated in the top diagram, and for the Berinmo on the bottom diagram. The identity of the colored Munsell chip located at any place on a diagram can be determined by referring to the notations along the top and left sides of the diagrams. For example, the Munsell name of the chip indicated by the dot in each diagram is Chip 5B-9. The color name given to a chip is indicated by the names on the diagrams. For example, Chip 5B-9 was called "blue" by the British participants and "wap" by the Berinmo participants. Chip 5R-2, which is located in the lower left part of the diagrams, was called "red" by the British and "mehi" by the Berinmo. (Reprinted from "Color Categories Are Not Universal: Replications and New Evidence From A Stone-Age Culture," by D. Roberson, et al., 2000, *Journal of Experimental Psychology: General, 129,* pp. 369–398 (Figures 1 & 2), Copyright © 2000 with permission from the American Psychological Association.)

the two cultures. Thus, British participants could discriminate more easily between blue and green than the Berinmo, but the Berinmo could discriminate more easily between between Nol and Wor than the British. This demonstration of a correspondence between language and perception supports the Sapir-Whorf hypothesis (see also Gentner & Goldin-Meadow, 2003).

If reactions to colors can be affected by language, what about thinking? Try the following problem: Which two of the objects in Figure 10.18 would you place together?

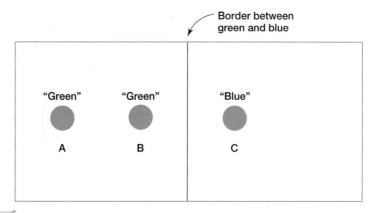

Border between
green and blue

"Green"   "Green"   "Blue"

A   B   C

Figure 10.17 The circles labeled A, B, and C represent colored chips. Chips A and B are called different shades of *green* by the British participants, and Chip C is called *blue*. In a categorical-perception experiment, participants were asked to indicate whether two chips are the same or different. For example, a participant would be asked to respond "same" or "different" when shown Chip A and Chip B, or when shown Chip B and Chip C. For the British participants, Chips B and C are more likely to be judged to be different because they have different color names.

Figure 10.18 Objects like the ones Chiu (1972) used to determine which objects Chinese and American children group together.

When Liang-hwang Chiu (1972) presented problems such as this to American and Chinese children, the Americans tended to pair the cow and chicken because they are both animals. This is called a "taxonomic response." However, the Chinese children were more likely to pair the cow and the grass because cows eat grass. This is called a "relational response." This result makes sense if we remember that Americans are more object-oriented and Asians more relationship-oriented.

To relate this experiment to language, Li-jun Ji and coworkers (2000) presented triads of words such as *panda*, *monkey*, and *banana* to Americans and Chinese. As expected from earlier results, the Americans sorted the items "taxonomically," pairing the panda and the monkey, and the Chinese sorted "relationally," pairing the monkey and the banana. To investigate a possible connection to language, Ji tested bilingual Chinese participants, whose first language was Chinese and who had learned English later. The major finding of this study was that when these participants were tested in Chinese, they grouped the items in terms of relationships. However, when they were tested in English, they were more likely to base their grouping on taxonomy. According to Ji and coworkers (2000) and Nisbett (2003), this result shows that language influences thinking, as the Sapir-Whorf hypothesis predicts.

Results such as these, plus the results of Roberson's color experiments and experiments comparing how Westerners and East Asians think about objects (Iwao & Gentner, 1997), numbers (Lucy & Gaskins, 1997), and space (Levinson, 1996), have supported the idea that language may in fact influence the way people think. When we consider reasoning in Chapter 12, we will describe additional research on cognition in different cultures.

Test Yourself 10.2

1. Why do we say that understanding a story involves more than adding up the meanings of the sentences that make up the story?
2. What is coherence, and how does inference create it? Consider the different kinds of inference and also why causal inference can be described as a creative process, how it is related to memory, and the evidence that inference occurs over both short and long distances in a text.
3. What are the assumptions behind the situation model, and what predictions does this model make?
4. Describe the idea that conversations are based on rules. Consider both what these rules are and what happens if they are violated.
5. How does culture affect how people use language? Consider the results of studies on both children and adults.
6. How does language affect cognition? Consider the history of the Sapir-Whorf hypothesis and why it has recently gained more acceptance.

1. How do the ideas of coherence and connection apply to some of the movies you have seen lately? Have you found that some movies are easy to understand while others are more difficult? In the movies that are easy to understand, does one thing appear to follow from another, whereas in the more difficult ones, some things seem to be left out? What is the difference in the "mental work" needed to determine what is going on in these two kinds of movies? (You can also apply this kind of analysis to books you have read.)

2. Next time you are able to eavesdrop on a conversation, notice how the give-and-take among participants follows (or does not follow) the given-new contract. Also, notice how changes in topic occur, and how that affects the flow of the conversation. One way to "eavesdrop" is to be part of a conversation that includes at least two other people. But don't forget to say something every so often!

3. One of the interesting things about languages is the use of "figures of speech," which people who know the language understand but which nonnative speakers often find baffling. One example is the sentence "He brought everything but the kitchen sink." Can you think of other examples? If you are a speaker of a language other than English, can you identify figures of speech that might be baffling to English speakers?

4. Newspaper headlines are often good sources of ambiguous phrases. For example, consider the following, which were actual headlines: "Milk drinkers are turning to powder," "Iraqi head seeks arms," "Farm bill dies in house," and "Squad helps dog bite victim." See if you can find examples of ambiguous headlines in the newspaper, and try to figure out what it is that makes the headlines ambiguous.

KEY TERMS

Anaphoric inference
Aphasia
Broca's area
Categorical perception
Causal inference
Coherence
Conversational maxim
Cooperative principle
Garden-path model
Garden-path sentence
Given-new contract
Global connection

Indirect statements
Inference
Instrumental inference
Interactionist approach to parsing
Language
Late closure
Lexical ambiguity
Lexical-decision task
Lexicon
Local connection
Manner
Parser

Parsing
Phoneme
Psycholinguistics
Quality
Quantity
Relation
Sapir-Whorf hypothesis
Semantics
Situation model

Speech segmentation
Standing ambiguity
Syntactic ambiguity
Syntax
Syntax-first approach to parsing
Temporary ambiguity
Wernicke's area
Word-frequency effect
Word-superiority effect

CogLab To experience these experiments for yourself, go to http://coglab.wadsworth.com. Be sure to read each experiment's setup instructions before you go to the experiment itself. Otherwise, you won't know which keys to press.

Word superiority	How speed of identifying a letter compares when the letter is isolated or in a word (p. 350).
Lexical decision	Demonstration of the lexical-decision task, which has been used to provide evidence for the concept of spreading activation (p. 354).
Categorical perception	A demonstration of categorical perception using sounds (p. 381).

Problem Solving

Some Questions We Will Consider

✔ How does the ability to solve a problem depend on how the problem is represented in the mind?

✔ How can analogies be used to help solve problems?

✔ Is there anything special about "insight" problems?

✔ What is the difference between how experts in a field solve problems and how nonexperts solve problems?

■　　■　　■

The following is a story about physicist Richard Feynman, who received the Nobel Prize in Physics for his work in nuclear fission and quantum dynamics, and who had a reputation as a scientific genius.

A physicist working at the California Institute of Technology in the 1950s is having trouble deciphering some of Feynman's notes. He asks Murray Gell-Mann, a Nobel Laureate and occasional collaborator of Feynman, "What are Feynman's methods?" Gell-Mann leans coyly against the blackboard and says—"Dick's method is this. You write down the problem. You think very hard." [Gell-Mann shuts his eyes and presses his knuckles periodically to his forehead.] "Then you write down the answer." (adapted from Gleick, 1992, p. 315)

This is an amusing way of describing Feynman's genius, but leaves unanswered the question of what was really going on inside his head while he was thinking "very hard." While we may not know the answer to this question for Feynman, research on problem solving has provided some answers to this question for people in general. In this chapter we will describe some of the answers that have been proposed to explain the mental processes that occur as people work toward determining the solution to a problem.

When I ask students in my cognitive psychology class to indicate some problems they have solved or are currently working on, I get answers such as: problems for math, chemistry, or physics courses; getting writing assignments in on time; dealing with roommates, friends, and relationships in general; deciding what courses to take, what career to go into; whether to go to graduate school or look for a job; how to pay for a new car. There are lots of things that people consider to be problems, but what we are interested in for this chapter is what psychologists consider to be a problem.

One definition of *problem* is *any present situation that differs from a desired goal* (Bransford & Stein, 1984). By this definition, the following would qualify as a problem:

> You are at home at 7:30 AM and need to get to your 9:00 class. You still haven't showered, you have to get your lunch together before leaving, and you've heard that the traffic is bad, so that the trip might take longer than the usual 20 minutes. What do you do?

Although this qualifies as a problem according to the previously stated definition, most psychologists would not classify this as a problem because the solution is too obvious (hurry up, take a shorter shower, leave a little earlier than usual). "Problem" is more commonly defined as involving some difficulty and as having a solution that is not immediately obvious. The following definition emphasizes this quality of **problems:** *A problem occurs when there is an obstacle between a present state and a goal and it is not immediately obvious how to get around the obstacle* (Lovett, 2002).

In this chapter, we will focus on research that is designed to determine the cognitive processes that occur as people try to solve problems for which the solution is not immediately obvious. We will do this by describing the two dominant approaches to studying problem solving: (1) the approach that was originated by the Gestalt psychologists that considers problem solving as involving a process called *restructuring* (Figure 11.1); and (2) the approach that considers problem solving as a process involving *search*. We will then consider how analogies can be used to solve problems, a method that combines

may differ for individuals!

Gestalt → restructuring ⟩ analogies
  · search

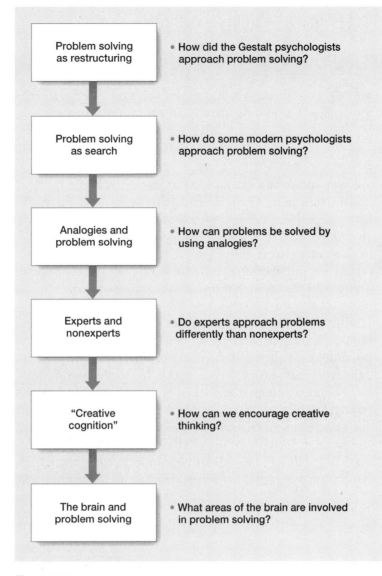

Figure 11.1 Flow diagram for this chapter.

elements of both restructuring and search. We will also consider differences between the way experts and nonexperts solve problems, and a process called creative cognition that is associated with creative thinking. Finally, at the end of the chapter we will describe research designed to determine which areas of the brain are important to solving problems.

The Gestalt Approach: Problem Solving as Representation and Restructuring

We begin our discussion of problem solving by considering the approach of the Gestalt psychologists, who introduced the study of problem solving to psychology in the 1920s.

Representing a Problem in the Mind

We introduced the Gestalt psychologists in Chapter 3 by describing their laws of perceptual organization. The Gestalt psychologists were interested in perception, as well as learning, problem solving, and even attitudes and beliefs (Koffka, 1935). But even as they considered areas of psychology in addition to perception, they took a perceptual approach to these other areas. Thus, problem solving, for the Gestalt psychologists, was about (1) how people represent a problem in their mind, and (2) how solving a problem involves a *reorganization* or *restructuring* of this representation.

The Circle Problem
We can illustrate the idea of representation and restructuring in problem solving by considering Figure 11.2. This problem, which was posed by Gestalt psychologist Wolfgang Kohler, asks us to determine the length of the segment marked *x*, if the radius of the circle has a length *r*. (A number of problems will be posed in this chapter. The answers appear at the end of the chapter. See Figure 11.24 for the answer to the "circle" problem. For this problem, the answer is also stated in the next paragraph, so don't read any further if you want to try to figure it out.)

The key to solving this problem is to create the mental representation of *x* as being a diagonal of the small rectangle. Representing *x* as the diagonal enables us to reorganize the representation by creating the rectangle's other diagonal (Figure 11.24). Once we realize that this diagonal is the radius of the circle, and that both diagonals are the same length, we can conclude that the length of *x* equals the length of the radius, *r*.

What is important about this solution is that it doesn't require mathematical equations. Instead, the solution is obtained by first *perceiving* the object and then *representing* it in a different way. The Gestalt psychologists called the process of changing the problem's representation *restructuring*.

The Gestalt psychologists also introduced the idea that restructuring is associated with insight—sudden realization of the problem's solution. We will now consider a modern experiment that provides evidence that suddenly realizing the solution to a problem occurs for some kinds of problems, but not for others.

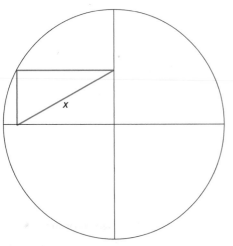

Problem: If the length of the radius is *r*, what is the length of line *x*?

Figure 11.2 The circle problem. See page 424 for the solution.

Insight in Problem Solving

Should there be a separate category of problems called insight problems, as suggested by the Gestalt psychologists? The Gestalt psychologists assumed that people solving their problems were experiencing "insight" because the solutions usually seemed to come to them all of a sudden. Modern researchers have debated this question, with some pointing to the fact that people often experience problem solving as an "Aha!" experience—at one point they don't have the answer and then next minute they have solved the problem—which is one of the characteristics associated with insight problems. However, other researchers have emphasized the lack of evidence, other than anecdotal reports, to support the specialness of the insight experience (Weisberg, 1995; Weisberg & Alba, 1981, 1982).

To deal with this problem, Janet Metcalfe and David Wiebe (1987) hypothesized that there should be a basic difference between how participants feel they are progressing toward a solution as they are working on an insight problem, and how they feel as they are working on a noninsight problem. They predicted that participants working on an insight problem in which the answer appears suddenly should not be very good at predicting how near they are to a solution, but that participants working on a noninsight problem, which involves a more methodical process, would have some knowledge that they are getting closer to the solution.

To test this hypothesis, Mecalfe and Wiebe gave participants insight problems and noninsight problems and had them make "warmth" judgments every 15 seconds, as they were working on the problems. Ratings closer to "hot" (7 on a 7-point scale) were used if they felt they were getting close to a solution, and ratings closer to "cold" (1 on the scale) were used if they didn't feel that they were close to a solution. Here are some examples of the insight problems like the ones they presented.

◧ Demonstration

Two Insight Problems

Triangle Problem The triangle shown in Figure 11.3a points to the top of the page. Show how you can move 3 of the circles to get the triangle to point to the bottom of the page.

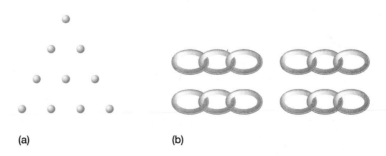

(a)   (b)

Figure 11.3 (a) Triangle problem and (b) chain problem for "two insight problems" demonstration. See page 242 for solutions.

Chain Problem A woman has 4 pieces of chain. Each piece is made up of 3 links, as shown in Figure 11.3b. She wants to join the pieces into a single closed loop of chain. To open a link costs 2 cents and to close a link costs 3 cents. She only has 15 cents. How does she do it? *(Answers to the triangle and chain problems are shown in Figures 11.25 and 11.26 at the end of the chapter.)*

As you work on these problems, see if you can monitor your progress. Do you feel as if you are making steady progress towards a solution, until eventually it all adds up to the answer, or as if you were not really making much progress, but, if you did solve the problem, the solution occurred all of a sudden, like an "Aha!" experience? ∎

For noninsight problems, Metcalfe and Wiebe used algebra problems like the following, which were taken from a high-school mathematics text.

∎ Solve for x: $(1/5)x + 10 = 25$

∎ Factor $16y^2 - 40yz + 25z^2$.

The results of their experiment are shown in Figure 11.4, which indicates the warmth ratings for the minute just before the participants solved the two kinds of problems. If we start at the top of the figure, we can see that 60 seconds before the solution, there is a range of ratings between 1 to 7 for the algebra problems (left column), and as time before the solution decreases, the ratings gradually move toward the right ("hotter"), until, when the problem was solved, all ratings become 7.

For the insight problems, shown in the right column, warmth ratings are clustered near the "cold" end of the scale, and stay there right up until the problem is solved when, suddenly, all of the ratings become "hot." Thus, Metcalfe and Wiebe provided empirical evidence that the solution for problems that have been called insight problems does, in fact, occur suddenly, as measured by people's reports of how close they feel they are to a solution.

The Gestalt psychologists tested their idea that solving insight problems involves a process of restructuring by creating a number of problems for their participants to solve. These problems were used to illustrate how a person's previous experience can make it more difficult to change the representation of the problem and can therefore serve as an obstacle to problem solving.

negative experience!

Obstacles to Problem Solving

We will describe the candle problem, the two-string problem, and the water-jug problem; each illustrates how a person's experience can make problem solving more difficult.

The Candle Problem The **candle problem** was first described by Karl Duncker (1945). In his experiment, he asked participants to use various objects to complete a task. The following demonstration asks you to try to solve Duncker's problem by imagining that you have the specified objects.

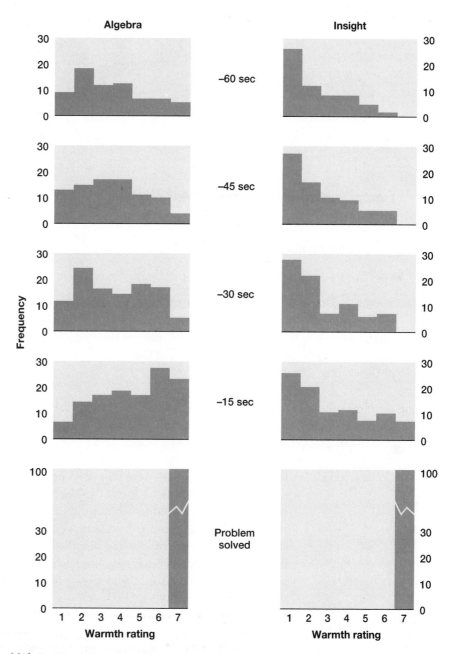

Figure 11.4 Results of Metcalfe and Wiebe's (1987) experiment showing how participants judged how close they were to solving algebra problems (left column) and insight problems (right column). For the algebra problem, warmth ratings move slowly toward the "hot" end of the scale during the minute before the problem is solved. For the insight problems, the solution is sudden.

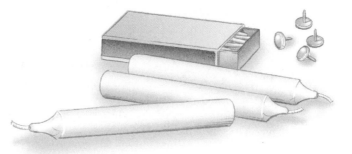

Figure 11.5 Objects for Duncker's (1945) candle problem.

◣ Demonstration

The Candle Problem

You are in a room with a corkboard on the wall. You are given the materials in Figure 11.5—some candles, matches in a matchbox and some tacks. Your task is to mount a candle on the corkboard so it will burn without dripping wax on the floor. Try to figure out how you would solve this problem before reading further, and then check your answer in Figure 11.27 at the end of the chapter on page 425.　　■

The solution to the problem occurs when the person realizes that the match box can be used as a support rather than as a container. When Duncker did this experiment, he presented one group of participants with small cardboard boxes containing the materials (candles, tacks, and matches) and presented another group with the same materials, but outside the boxes, so the boxes were empty. When he compared the performance of the two groups, he found that the group that had been presented with the boxes as containers found the problem more difficult than did the group that was presented with empty boxes. Robert Adamson (1952) reran Duncker's experiment and obtained the same result: Participants who were presented with empty boxes were twice as likely to solve the problem than participants who were presented with boxes that were used as containers (Figure 11.6).

The decrease in performance that occurred when the boxes were used as containers led the Gestalt psychologists to propose the idea of functional fixedness—ideas a person holds about an object's function can inhibit the person's ability to use the object for a different function. Thus, seeing the boxes as containers inhibited using them as supports. Another demonstration of functional fixedness is provided by the two-string problem.

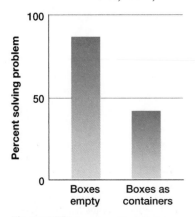

Figure 11.6 Results of Adamson's (1952) replication of Duncker's candle problem.

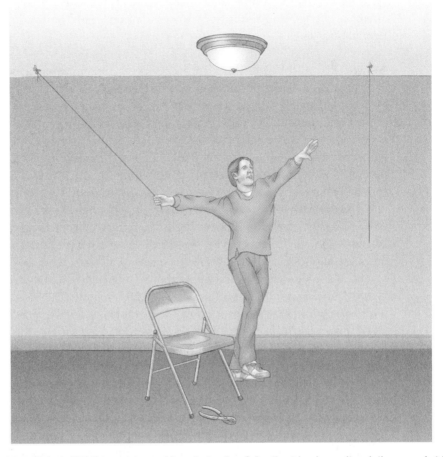

Figure 11.7 Maier's (1931) two-string problem. As hard as Sebastian tries, he can't grab the second string. How can he tie the two strings together?

Functional Fixedness and the Two-String Problem

In Maier's (1931) **two-string problem,** the participants' task was to tie together two strings that were hanging from the ceiling. This is difficult, because the strings are separated so it is impossible to reach one of them while holding the other (Figure 11.7). Other objects available for solving this problem were a chair and a pair of pliers.

To solve this problem, participants needed to tie the pliers to one of the strings to create a pendulum, which could be swung to within the person's reach. There are two things that are particularly significant about this problem. First, 60 percent of the participants did not solve the problem because they did not think of using the pliers as a weight. Second, when Maier set the string into motion by "accidentally" brushing against it, 23 of 37 participants who hadn't solved the problem after 10 minutes proceeded to solve it within

60 seconds. Maier's "hint," which many of the participants claimed not to be aware of, had apparently triggered the insight that the pliers could be used as a weight to create a pendulum.

Mental Set and the Water-Jug Problem   The functional fixedness involved in the candle and two-string problems illustrate mental set—a person's tendency to respond in a certain manner based on past experience. Thus, they considered full boxes to be containers and pliers to be a tool. Functional fixedness creates mental set by causing the person to focus on a particular *function* of an object. We illustrated mental set in another way with the rat-man demonstration from Chapter 3 (see Figure 3.8), in which presenting a picture of a rat caused a person to see an ambiguous picture as a rat, or presenting a picture of a man's face caused the person to see the same picture as a face.

A. S. Luchins (1942) demonstrated mental set by showing how having participants solve one set of problems can influence their attempts to solve another problem. In the water-jug problem, participants were given three jugs of different capacities and were required to use these jugs to measure out a specific quantity of water, as shown in Figure 11.8.

Problem 1 is solved by first filling the 127-cup jug (B) and then pouring the water from B into A once and into C two times, thereby subtracting 27 cups and leaving 100 in jug B. This solution, which can be stated by the formula $B - A - 2C$ = desired quantity, works for all of the problems in Figure 11.8. However, problems 7 and 8 can also be solved using fewer steps than this (see problem 7's solution in Figure 11.28 at the end of the chapter).

Luchins had some participants begin with problem 1 and do each problem in sequence (the mental set group), and had other participants begin with problem 7 (the non-mental set group). Figure 11.9 compares the performance of the two groups. All of the participants in the *no mental set group* used the shorter solution for problems 7 and 8, whereas only 23 percent in the *mental set group* used this solution for these problems.

All of the problems we have presented illustrate the Gestalt idea of restructuring. Table 11.1 summarizes the problems we have considered, by indicating (1) the way the problem was initially represented and (2) the new representation, which led to the solution of the problems. In addition, the Gestalt idea of functional fixedness and mental set emphasized the role of prior learning and experience on achieving this restructuring.

Table 11.1	GESTALT RESTRUCTURING SUMMARY	
Problem	Initial Representation	New Representation
Circle (Figure 11.2)	Diagonal of rectangle	Diagonal is radius
Candle (Figure 11.5)	Box is a container for candles	Box is a support for candles
Two-string (Figure 11.7)	Stationary strings	Swinging strings
Water-jug (Figure 11.8)	Pour in this sequence: $B - A - 2C$	Pour in this sequence: $A + C$ or $A - C$

Capacities (cups)

Problem	Jug A	Jug B	Jug C	Desired quantity
1	21	127	3	100
2	14	163	25	99
3	18	43	10	5
4	9	42	6	21
5	20	59	4	31
6	23	49	3	20
7	15	39	3	18
8	28	59	3	25

Solution to Problem 1

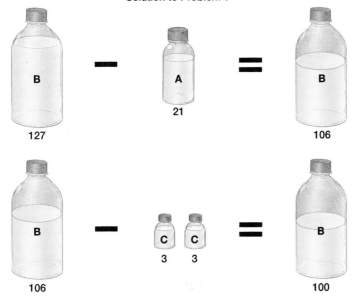

Figure 11.8 Luchins's (1942) water-jug problem. Each problem specifies the capacities of jugs A, B, and C, and a final desired quantity. The task is to use the jugs to measure out the final quantity. The solution to problem 1 is shown. All of the other problems can be solved using the same pattern of pourings, but there are more efficient solutions to problems 7 and 8.

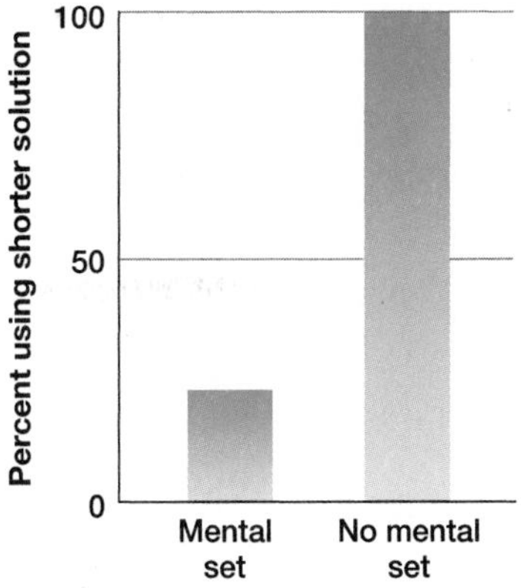

Figure 11.9 All of the participants who began the Luchins water-jug problem with problem 7 used the shorter solution (right bar), but less than a quarter who had established a mental set by beginning with problem 1 used the shorter solution to solve problem 7 (left bar).

Modern Research on Problem Solving: What Happens During the Search for a Solution?

The Gestalt psychologists were the pioneers of problem-solving research. Between about 1920 and 1950 they devised clever problems that illustrated factors such as functional fixedness and mental set that affect problem solving. In addition, many of these problems provide examples of how solving a problem involves creating a new representation. But questions about what actually happens as a person solves a problem still remained unanswered when the modern era of cognitive psychology began in the late 1950s.

In our description of the history of cognitive psychology in Chapter 1, we noted that in 1956 there were two important conferences, one at the Massachusetts Institute of Technology and one at Dartmouth University, which brought together researchers from many disciplines to discuss new ways to study the mind. At both of these conferences, Alan Newell and Herbert Simon reported on their efforts to design computer programs that could solve problems. This marked the beginning of a research program that was based on the idea that problem solving is a process that involves *search*. That is, instead of just considering the initial structure of a problem and then the new structure that is achieved when the problem is solved, as the Gestalt psychologists did, Newell and Simon described problem solving in terms of a search that occurs between the posing of the problem and its solution.

The idea of problem solving as a search is part of our language. People commonly talk about problems in terms of "searching for a way to reach a goal," "getting around roadblocks," "hitting a dead end," and "approaching a problem from a different angle" (Lakoff & Turner, 1989). Newell and Simon describe search in problem solving in terms of a problem space.

Newell and Simon's Approach: Searching a Problem Space

What path do people take as they attempt to solve a problem? Newell and Simon (1972) describe selection of a path as occurring within a problem space that consists of the following four problem elements:

1. The **initial state**—the conditions at the beginning of the problem.
2. The **goal state**—the condition at the end of the problem.
3. The **intermediate states**—the various conditions that exist along the pathways between the initial and goal states.
4. The **operators**—permissible moves that can be made toward the problem's solution.

We can think of the problem space as a maze of pathways between the initial and goal states. According to this concept, solving a problem involves starting at the initial state

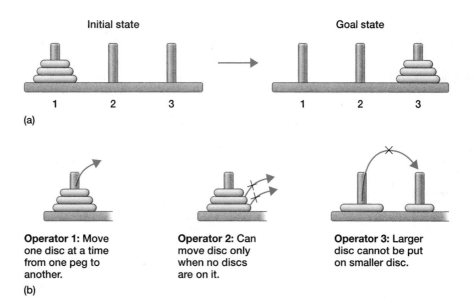

Initial state   Goal state

1   2   3   1   2   3

(a)

Operator 1: Move
one disc at a time
from one peg to
another.

Operator 2: Can
move disc only
when no discs
are on it.

Operator 3: Larger
disc cannot be put
on smaller disc.

(b)

Figure 11.10 (a) Initial and goal states for the Tower of Hanoi problem. (b) Operators that govern the Tower of Hanoi problem.

and then finding a path from one intermediate state to another, which eventually ends up at the goal state. If this path is efficient, a problem is solved in a small number of steps.

How do people determine which pathways to take? Newell and Simon propose that many problems can be solved using a strategy called means-end analysis. The primary goal of means-end analysis is to reduce the difference between the initial and goal states. This is achieved not by jumping directly from the initial to the goal state, but by creating subgoals—goals that create intermediate states that are closer to the goal.

We can illustrate this process by considering the initial and goals states of the Tower of Hanoi problem shown in Figure 11.10a. The initial state is a large, a medium, and a small disc stacked on the left peg. The goal state is the same three discs on the right peg. Figure 11.10b shows the operators that govern this problem: operator 1: discs are moved one at a time from one peg to another; operator 2: a disc can be moved only when there are no discs on top of it; and operator 3: a large disc can never be placed on top of a smaller disc.

This problem is called the Tower of Hanoi problem because of a legend that states that there are monks in a monastery near Hanoi who are working on this problem. Their version of it is, however, vastly more complex than ours, with 64 discs on peg 1. According to the legend, the world will end when the problem is solved. Luckily, this will take close to a trillion years to accomplish even if the monks make one move every second and every move is correct (Raphael, 1986).

Now let's apply means-end analysis to our 3-disc version of the problem. The first thing we see is that there is a difference between the initial state (all discs on peg l) and the

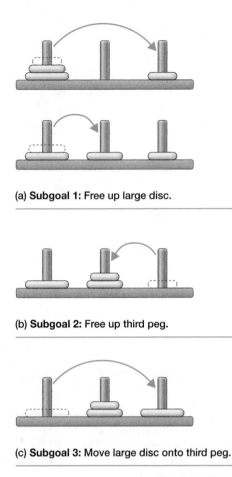

(a) Subgoal 1: Free up large disc.

(b) Subgoal 2: Free up third peg.

(c) Subgoal 3: Move large disc onto third peg.

Figure 11.11 Initial steps in solving the Tower of Hanoi problem, showing how the problem can be broken down into subgoals.

goal state (all discs on peg 3). Our goal is to reduce the size of this difference. However, if we are to obey the operators, we can't accomplish this in just one step (we can only move one disc at a time). Thus, we first set the subgoal of freeing up the large disc so we can move it onto peg 3. To accomplish this, we remove the small disc and place it on the 3rd peg. Then we remove the medium disc and place it on the 2nd peg (Figure 11.11a). This completes the subgoal of freeing up the large disc. Our next goal is to free up the 3rd peg so we can move the large disc onto it. We do this by moving the small disc onto the medium one (Figure 11.11b). We now achieve subgoal 3, which is to move the large disc onto peg 3 (Figure 11.11c). We continue in this way, setting subgoals and achieving them until we reach our final goal.

Means-end analysis is important because it is the way people often go about solving everyday problems. For example, let's say that you realize that your car's radiator is leaking and so the car needs to be taken in for service. The initial state is "leaking car" and the goal state is "fixed car." But because you can't immediately drive the car to the mechanic, you need to set subgoals. First, you call to make an appointment. You get an appointment for next week, so another subgoal is to find a way to keep driving during the coming week. You achieve this subgoal by buying some coolant and adding enough every day to make up for the leakage. Another subgoal is to find a way to get home after you drop your car off, so you arrange to have a friend follow you to the mechanic. By approaching the problem in terms of a number of smaller steps, each of which gets you a little closer to the goal, you eventually reach the final goal of getting the car fixed.

Here's another problem that involves an initial state, a goal state, and operators. Try doing it, and then we will discuss what this problem illustrates about means-end analysis.

◼ Demonstration

The Hobbits-and-Orcs Problem

On the left bank of a river are three hobbits and three orcs (Figure 11.12). They have a boat on their side that is capable of carrying two creatures at a time across the river. The goal is to transport all six creatures across to the right side of the river. At no point on either side of the river can orcs outnumber hobbits, because if that happens the orcs will kill the hobbits. The problem is to find a method of transporting all six creatures across the river without the hobbits ever being

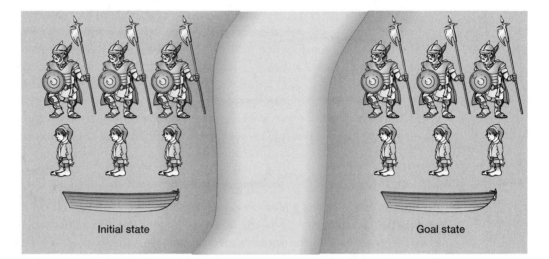

Figure 11.12 Initial and goal states for the hobbits-and-orcs problem. See the end of the chapter, page 426, for the solution (but try doing it first!).

outnumbered. Remember that in order to cross the river the boat must be piloted by at least one creature.

Try to solve this problem before reading further.

How did you do the problem? If you solved it, were you able to apply the rules of means-end analysis? From the solution in Figure 11.29 at the end of the chapter, we can see that at one point in the problem it is necessary to violate one of the rules of means-end analysis. The first three trips to the right bank reduce the difference between the current and goal states. Trip 1 leaves 4 creatures on the left bank, trip 2 leaves 3 creatures and trip 3 leaves 2 creatures. However, following trip 3, 2 creatures return to the left bank, increasing the population to 4; and after trip 4, 2 creatures remain on the left bank, the same number as were left after trip 3. Thus, to reach our final goal we need to temporarily put aside the rule that we should strive to reduce the difference between the current state and the goal state. Participants who are trying to solve this problem often make errors just after trip 3 because they resist making a move that seems to be increasing the distance to the solution (Greeno, 1974).

The **hobbits-and-orcs problem** shows that means-end analysis sends us in the right direction most of the time, but not always. In this case and in others, the procedure of always doing what is necessary to reduce the distance between where you are and a goal usually works, but occasionally some **backtracking** is necessary. When means-end analysis has been modified to allow occasional backtracking, it has proven to be an excellent way to think about problem solving, and computer programs based on means-end analysis have been able to solve a wide variety of problems (Lehman et al., 1998).

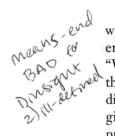

means-end
BAD for
1) insight
2) ill-defined

Although means-end analysis has proven to be successful for many problems, it is not well-suited to problems for which it is difficult to specify a clear goal state or specific operators. Such problems, called **ill-defined problems,** are common in everyday life. "Which college should I attend?" "Should I go to graduate school?" and "How can I make this relationship work?" are examples of ill-defined problems. Means-end analysis is also difficult to apply to some insight problems, like the ones posed by the Gestalt psychologists. Notice that the Tower of Hanoi and hobbits-and-orcs problems are not insight problems because it is possible to work methodically toward the solution.

Knowing How to Look for a Solution: The Importance of How a Problem Is Stated

In addition to considering how people search a problem space, modern researchers have paid particular attention to how the way a problem is stated can affect a person's ability to solve the problem. A difficulty with many problems is that sometimes the person doesn't even know where to begin. Figuring out how to start a problem is often the hardest part, and once that is accomplished, the solution often follows easily. Research by Craig Kaplan and Herbert Simon (1990) has used a problem called the **mutilated-checkerboard problem** to study how the way a problem is stated can affect a person's ability to get started on the solution. Here is the problem they presented to the participants in their experiment.

▊ Demonstration

The Mutilated-Checkerboard Problem

A checkerboard consists of 64 squares. These 64 squares can be completely covered by placing 32 dominos on the board so each domino covers two squares. If we eliminate two corners of the checkerboard, as shown in Figure 11.13, can we now cover the remaining squares with 31 dominos?

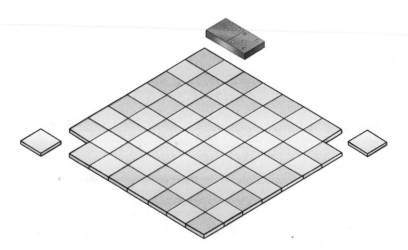

Figure 11.13 Mutilated-checkerboard problem. See demonstration for instructions.

See if you can solve this problem. A solution would be either a "yes" or "no" answer plus a statement of the rationale behind your answer. If you have trouble with this problem, you are not alone. Kaplan and Simon's participants found this problem extremely difficult, with many needing hints in order to solve it. ∎

There were four conditions in Kaplan and Simon's experiment. Each group received a different version of the problem. The four conditions, shown in Figure 11.14, were (1) *blank*: a board with all blank squares; (2) *color:* alternating black and pink squares as might appear on a regular checkerboard; (3) *black and pink:* the words *black* and *pink* on the board; and (4) *bread and butter:* the words *bread* and *butter* on the board.

The four conditions:

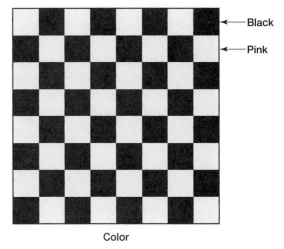

Blank

Color

black	pink	black	pink	black	pink	black	pink
pink	black	pink	black	pink	black	pink	black
black	pink	black	pink	black	pink	black	pink
pink	black	pink	black	pink	black	pink	black
black	pink	black	pink	black	pink	black	pink
pink	black	pink	black	pink	black	pink	black
black	pink	black	pink	black	pink	black	pink
pink	black	pink	black	pink	black	pink	black

Black and pink

butter	bread	butter	bread	butter	bread	butter	bread
bread	butter	bread	butter	bread	butter	bread	butter
butter	bread	butter	bread	butter	bread	butter	bread
bread	butter	bread	butter	bread	butter	bread	butter
butter	bread	butter	bread	butter	bread	butter	bread
bread	butter	bread	butter	bread	butter	bread	butter
butter	bread	butter	bread	butter	bread	butter	bread
bread	butter	bread	butter	bread	butter	bread	butter

Bread and butter

(Note: Boards not drawn to actual size.)

Figure 11.14 Conditions in Kaplan and Simon's (1990) study of the mutilated-checkerboard problem. (Reprinted from *Cognitive Psychology,* Volume 22, C. A. Kaplan & H. A. Simon, "In Search of Insight," pp. 374–419, Figure 2. Copyright © 1990, with permission from Elsevier.)

The key to solving the problem is that participants have to arrive at what Kaplan and Simon call the *parity representation*. The parity representation takes into account the fact that each square can be paired with its neighbor. Shifting to this representation makes it easier for the participants to realize that when a domino is placed on the board so it covers just two squares, it is always covering two squares that are different (pink and black, for example). There is no way to place a domino so it covers two pink squares or two black squares. Therefore, for 31 dominos to cover the board there must be 31 pink squares and 31 black squares. However, this isn't the case, because two pink squares were removed. Thus, the board can't be covered by 31 dominos.

Most of the participants in this experiment did not start with the parity representation. They often started by focusing on how many squares remain after two are removed, so they would be thinking along the lines of "OK. There were 64 squares and 2 were taken away, leaving 62. There are 31 dominos, which is half of 62, and each domino can cover two squares."

Thinking about the numbers of squares in this way usually does not result in a solution, but shifting to the parity representation makes a solution more likely. Here is an example of what one of the participants in the bread-and-butter condition said as he described his thought processes as he was working on the problem:

> Participant: Just by trial and error I can only find 31 places. . . . I dunno, maybe someone else would have counted the spaces and just said that you could fit 31, but if you try it out on the paper, you can only fit 30. (Pause)
>
> Experimenter: Keep trying.
>
> Participant: Maybe it has to do with the words on the page? I haven't tried anything with that. Maybe that's it. OK, dominos, umm, the dominos can only fit . . . alright, the dominos can fit over two squares, and no matter which way you put it because it cannot go diagonally, it has to fit over a butter and a bread. And because you crossed out two breads, it has to leave two butters left over so it doesn't . . . only 30, so it won't fit. Is that the answer?

Notice that the person was stuck at first, and then suddenly got the answer after realizing that the words *bread* and *butter* were important. The key result of the experiment was that participants who were presented with representations of the board that emphasized the difference between adjoining squares found the problem to be easier. The bread-and-butter condition emphasized the difference the most, because bread and butter are very different but are also associated with each other. The blank board had no information about the difference, since all squares were the same. Participants in the bread-and-butter group solved the problem twice as fast as those in the blank group and required fewer hints, which the experimenter provided when participants appeared to be at a "dead end." The bread-and-butter group required an average of 1 hint, and the blank group required an average of 3.14 hints. The performance of the color and the black-and-pink groups fell between these two. This shows that solving a problem becomes easier when information is provided that helps point people toward the correct representation of the problem.

Thus, the key to solving problems is sometimes in how we perceive the different elements of the problem. This idea is very similar to what the Gestalt psychologists were proposing. For example, remember the "circle problem" in Figure 11.2. The key to solving that problem was realizing that the line x was the same length as the radius of the circle. Similarly, the key to solving the mutilated-checkerboard problem is realizing that adjoining squares are paired, because a domino always covers two different-colored squares in a normal checkerboard.

Kaplan and Simon used two different colors to help their participants realize that pairing of adjacent squares is important. But this has also been achieved in another way—by telling the following story, which has parallels to the checkerboard problem.

> In a small Russian village, there were 32 bachelors and 32 unmarried women. Through tireless efforts, the village matchmaker succeeded in arranging 32 highly satisfactory marriages. The village was proud and happy. Then one drunken night, two bachelors, in a test of strength, stuffed each other with pirogies and died. Can the matchmaker, through some quick arrangements, come up with 31 heterosexual marriages among the 62 survivors? (adapted from Hayes, 1978, p. 180)

The answer to this problem is obvious. Losing two males makes it impossible to arrange 31 heterosexual marriages. Of course, this is exactly the situation in the mutilated-checkerboard problem, except instead of males and females being paired up, light and dark squares are. People who read this story are usually able to solve the mutilated-checkerboard problem if they realize the connection between the couples in the story and the black and white squares in the checkerboard. The idea that recasting a problem in a different form can make solving the problem easier, by making a connection between one problem and another one is also illustrated by the following demonstration.

◪ Demonstration

The Monk-and-the-Mountain Problem

An old monk leaves the monastery at exactly 6 AM to climb a trail that leads to a mountain peak. He arrives at 4 PM. After a night of sleep and meditation, he leaves the mountain peak at 6 AM and starts down the same trail he climbed the day before. He walks faster going down than climbing up, but stops at a few places along the way to rest and enjoy the views. Is there some point on the mountain trail that he passes at exactly the same time each day? ■

The answer to this problem might not be immediately obvious. Consider this problem, which is stated in a different way, but is analogous to the monk-and-the-mountain problem.

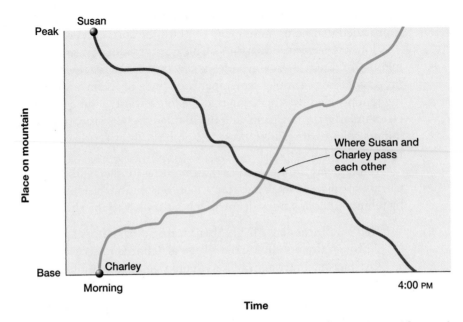

Figure 11.15 Progress of Charley, who starts climbing up the mountain in the morning, and Susan, who starts climbing down at the same time, showing that at some point in time they are both at the same place on the mountain, just as the monk in the "monk and the mountain" problem is, during his ascent and descent.

Assume that Charley leaves the base of the mountain at exactly the same time Susan leaves the peak and begins climbing down the same trial. Charley reaches the peak at 4 PM and Susan reaches the base of the mountain at 4 PM. Is there some point on the mountain trail that Charley and Susan pass at exactly the same time?

Whereas the monk problem is difficult, the answer to the two-hikers problem is so trivial that it isn't really much of a problem. Of course, Charley and Susan must pass each other at some point because they are walking on the same trail (Figure 11.15). Returning to the old monk problem, we can think of the monk's ascent as equivalent to Charley's ascent, and the monk's descent as equivalent to Susan's descent. Clearly, just as Charley and Susan must pass the same point at a particular time, the monk must also be at a particular point at the same time each day.

Our examples of the mutilated-checkerboard problem and the monk-and-the-mountain problem both show how restating problems can make them easier to solve. Demonstrations such as these reflect the fact that drawing analogies between two problems can lead to solutions of difficult-to-solve problems. In the next section, we will describe research that considers the role of analogy in problem solving.

1. What is the psychological definition of a problem? Give some examples of situations that meet the definition of a problem, and some situations that may appear to be problems, but which do not meet the definition.

2. What is the basic principle behind the Gestalt approach to problem solving? (Hint: R & R.) Describe how the following problems illustrate this principle, and also what else these problems demonstrate about problem solving: the circle (radius) problem; the candle problem; the two-string problem; the water-jug problem.

3. What is insight, and what is the evidence that insight does, in fact, occur as people are solving a problem?

4. Describe Newell and Simon's approach to problem solving, in which "search" plays a central role. How does means-end analysis as applied to the Tower of Hanoi problem illustrate this approach? What does the solution to the hobbits-and-orcs problem tell us about the means-end approach? Does this approach work for all types of problems?

5. How does Kaplan and Simon's experiment, using the mutilated-checkerboard problem, illustrate that the way a problem is stated can affect a person's ability to solve the problem? How does this idea also apply to the monk-and-the-mountain problem?

USING ANALOGIES TO SOLVE PROBLEMS

Analogies occur when there are parallels between two different situations. Thus, when the boxer Muhammad Ali said that he "floats like a butterfly, stings like a bee" he was drawing an analogy between his footwork and a floating butterfly and between his punch and a stinging bee. Analogies also give meaning to processes that may be invisible to us, such as when William Harvey compared the action of the heart to a hydraulic pump, and when electrons orbiting atoms are described as being like small solar systems. As we saw for the mutilated-checkerboard problem, presenting an analogy can often facilitate arriving at the solution to a problem.

Restructuring Through Analogy

When we described the Gestalt approach, we saw that one route to solving problems is to create a change in the way the problem is represented, a process called *restructuring*. One way to achieve restructuring is through analogical problem solving, in which a solution to one problem is presented that is analogous to the solution of another problem that we are trying to solve. The following demonstration consists of a problem to solve, followed by a story that provides a hint at the solution to the problem.

■ Demonstration

Duncker's Radiation Problem

The following **radiation problem** was posed to participants by the Gestalt psychologist Karl Duncker (1945) (who also originated the candle problem).

> *Suppose you are a doctor faced with a patient who has a malignant tumor in his stomach. It is impossible to operate on the patient, but unless the tumor is destroyed the patient will die. There is a kind of ray that can be used to destroy the tumor. If the ray reaches the tumor at a sufficiently high intensity, the tumor will be destroyed. Unfortunately, at this intensity the healthy tissue that the ray passes through on the way to the tumor will also be destroyed. At lower intensities the ray is harmless to healthy tissue, but it will not affect the tumor either. What type of procedure might be used to destroy the tumor with the rays and at the same time avoid destroying the healthy tissue? (Gick & Holyoak, 1980)*

Before reading further, see if you can come up with a solution to this problem. ■

If after thinking about this problem for a while, you haven't come up with a suitable answer, you are not alone. Most of Duncker's participants could not solve this problem without hints. Duncker had his participants talk aloud to describe their attempts at solving the problem, and some of the solutions included sending the ray down the esophagus in order to avoid contact with healthy tissue (won't work because the esophagus is curved) and decreasing the intensity of the ray as it was passing through the healthy tissue (won't work because it is not possible to decrease activity at one place and not at the other). Whether or not you think you've solved this problem, consider the following story. (If you haven't solved the problem, it might help.)

The General

A small country was ruled from a strong fortress by a dictator. The fortress was situated in the middle of the country, surrounded by farms and villages. Many roads led to the fortress through the countryside. A rebel general vowed to capture the fortress. The general knew that an attack by his entire army would capture the fortress. He gathered his army at the head of one of the roads, ready to launch a full-scale direct attack. However, the general then learned that the dictator had planted mines on each of the roads. The mines were set so that small bodies of men could pass over them safely, since the dictator needed to move his troops and workers to and from the fortress. However, any large force would detonate the mines. Not only would this blow up the road, but it would also destroy many neighboring villages. It therefore seemed impossible to capture the fortress.

However, the general devised a simple plan. He divided his army into small groups and dispatched each group to the head of a different road. When all was ready he gave the signal and each group marched down a different road. Each group continued down its road to the fortress so that the entire army arrived together at the fortress at the same time. In this way, the general captured the fortress and overthrew the dictator. [See Figure 11.16.]

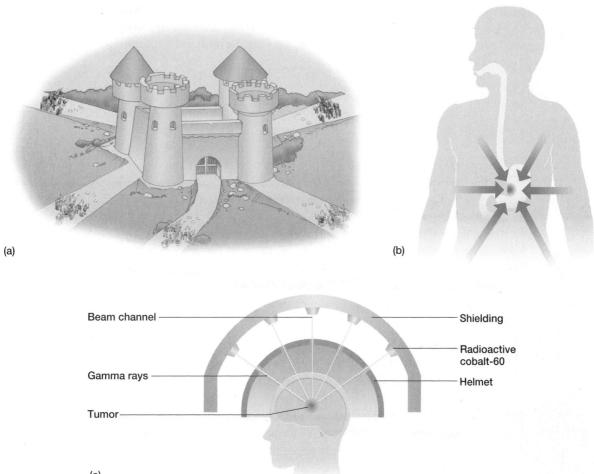

(a)

(b)

Beam channel ————————————————————— Shielding

————————————— Radioactive
cobalt-60

Gamma rays ——————————————————— Helmet

Tumor ——————————

(c)

Figure 11.16 (a) How the general solved the problem of how to capture the fortress. (b) Solution to the radiation problem. Bombarding the tumor, shown in the center, with a number of low-intensity rays from different directions destroys the tumor without damaging the tissue it passes through. (c) Radiosurgery, a modern medical technique for irradiating brain tumors with a number of beams of gamma rays, uses the same principle. The actual technique uses 201 gamma-ray beams.

Did reading this story give you any insight into the solution to the radiation problem? "The General," which is called the **source problem,** is analogous to the radiation problem, which is called the **target problem.** As you can see from the solution to the radiation problem in Figure 11.16b, the dictator's fortress corresponds to the tumor and the small groups of soldiers sent down different roads correspond to the of low-intensity rays that can be directed at the tumor.

Notice how the radiation problem and its solution fit with the Gestalt idea of representation and restructuring. The initial representation of the problem is a single ray that destroys the tumor but also destroys healthy tissue, and the restructured solution involves dividing the single ray into many smaller rays. In fact, the solution to this problem is actually the procedure used in a modern procedure called radiosurgery, in which a tumor is bombarded with 201 gamma ray beams that intersect at the tumor (Tarkan, 2003) (Figure 11.16c).

When Mary Gick and Keith Holyoak (1980, 1983) presented Duncker's radiation problem to a group of participants, only 10 percent were able to solve the problem. They also had another group of participants read and memorize "The General" story, giving them the impression that the purpose was to test their memory for the story. However, once they had read the story, they were told to begin work on the radiation problem. Thirty percent of the people in this group were able to solve the radiation problem, so reading the story helped some of the participants. However, what is significant about this experiment was the small number of participants who solved the problem, even when provided with the analogous story.

Apparently, just presenting the story wasn't enough. Most of Gick and Holyoak's participants had to be given a hint to make them aware that they could use "The General" story to help solve the radiation problem. When this hint was provided, 75 percent of the participants were able to solve the problem. These results led Gick and Holyoak to propose that the process of analogical problem solving involves the following three steps (Figure 11.17):

1. *Noticing* that there is an analogous relationship between the source story and the target problem. This step is obviously crucial in order for analogical problem solving to work. However, as we have seen, most participants need some prompting before they notice the connection between the source problem and the target problem. Gick and Holyoak consider this *noticing* step to be the most difficult of the three steps to achieve. A number of experiments have shown that the most effective source stories are those that are most similar to the target problems (Catrambone & Holyoak, 1989; Holyoak & Thagard, 1995). This similarity could make it easier to notice the analogical relationship between the source story and the target problem, and could also help achieve the next step—mapping.

2. *Mapping* the correspondence between the source story and the target problem. To use the story to solve the problem, the participant has to map corresponding parts of the story onto the test problem by connecting elements in one story (for example, the dictator's fortress) to elements in the problem (the tumor).

3. *Applying* the mapping to generate a parallel solution to the target problem. This would involve, for example, generalizing from the many small groups of soldiers approaching the fortress from different directions to the idea of using many weaker rays which would approach the tumor from different directions.

Once they determined that analogies can help with problem solving, but that hints are required to help participants notice the presence of the source problem, Gick and Holyoak (1983) proceeded to look for factors that help facilitate the *noticing* and *mapping* steps.

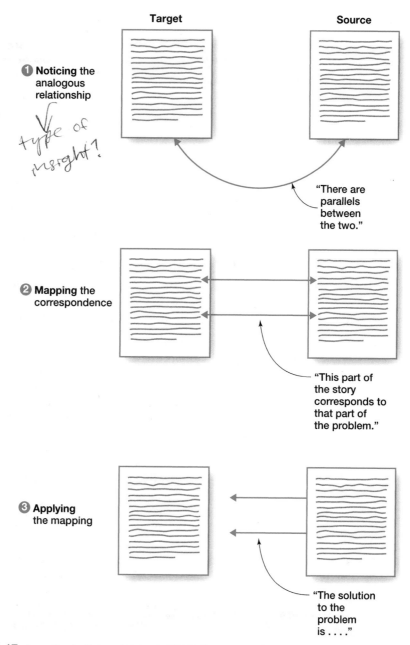

Target **Source**

1 Noticing the analogous relationship

type of insight?

"There are parallels between the two."

2 Mapping the correspondence

"This part of the story corresponds to that part of the problem."

3 Applying the mapping

"The solution to the problem is . . . ."

Figure 11.17 According to Gick and Holyoak (1980), the process of analogical problem solving involves these three steps.

Schemas and Analogy

One procedure they found effective was to help participants discover the basic concept that links the source problem and the target problem. This concept is called the problem schema, and the process of activating a schema is called schema induction.

One way Gick and Holyoak achieved schema induction was to present two stories and to give participants the task of writing brief summaries of each story and describing ways in which the stories were similar. The task of describing ways in which the stories were similar was designed to help participants map similarities between the stories, which could form the basis of a schema. They used "The General" plus three other stories, but each participant read just two of these stories. One of the other stories was "The Fire Chief."

The Fire Chief

One night a fire broke out in a wood shed full of timber on Mr. Johnson's place. As soon as he saw flames he sounded the alarm, and within minutes dozens of neighbors were on the scene armed with buckets. The shed was already burning fiercely, and everyone was afraid that if it wasn't controlled quickly the house would go up next. Fortunately, the shed was right beside a lake, so there was plenty of water available. If a large volume of water could hit the fire at the same time, it would be extinguished. But with only small buckets to work with, it was hard to make any headway. The fire seemed to evaporate each bucket of water before it hit the wood. It looked like the house was doomed.

Just then the fire chief arrived. He immediately took charge and organized everyone. He had everyone fill their bucket and then wait in a circle surrounding the burning shed. As soon as the last man was prepared, the chief gave a shout and everyone threw their bucket of water at the fire. The force of all the water together dampened the fire right down, and it was quickly brought under control. Mr. Johnson was relieved that his house was saved, and the village council voted the fire chief a raise in pay.

After reading the two stories and determining their similarities, participants were told to solve the radiation problem. The results showed that using two stories was better than one, because 52 percent of the participants solved the radiation problem without any hints. Remember that only 30 percent of the participants in the other experiment, who read only "The General" story, solved the problem without hints. But the most interesting result of this experiment was that there was a relationship between the quality of the schemas that the participants created and the participants' ability to solve the problem. Gick and Holyoak classified the schemas into three groups, *good*, *intermediate*, and *poor*. Here are some examples of each:

- *Good schema:* "Both stories used the same concept to solve a problem, which was to use many small forces applied together to add up to one large force necessary to destroy the object." (21 percent of participants)

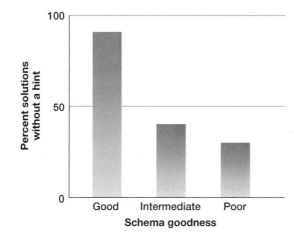

Figure 11.18 Results of Gick and Holyoak's (1983) schema-induction experiment, showing that participants who developed good schemas by reading two stories, were more likely to solve a target problem than those who did not develop good schemas.

- *Intermediate schema:* "In both cases many small forces were used. (20 percent)

- *Poor schema:* "In both stories the hero was rewarded for his efforts." (59 percent)

When participants' schemas were each rated for goodness, the relationship shown in Figure 11.18 emerged. Ninety-one percent of participants who had created good schemas solved the radiation problem without hints, whereas only 30 percent of those who had created poor schemas solved the problem. Thus, apparently using two analogs to create a schema helps participants notice important similarities and also helps in mapping these similarities onto the target problem. Note, however, that only 21 percent of the participants created good schemas.

Research on analogical problem solving has shown that thinking in terms of analogies can be helpful in problem solving. However, in the research we have described, the experimenters provided source problems and the participants often needed hints to help them realize that the source problem was analogous to the target problem. When analogies and hints are not available, it is up to the problem-solver to be aware that analogies can be helpful and to create their own analogies. This is a problem-solving skill that requires practice and a base of knowledge in a particular area. We will see that experts in a field often approach problems by looking for general principles that link one problem to another.

Although we understand some of the mental processes that occur as a person works toward the solution to a problem, what actually happens is still somewhat mysterious. We do know, however, that one factor that can sometimes make problem solving easier is practice or training. Some people can become very good at solving certain kinds of problems, because through practice and training they become experts in an area. We will now consider what it means to be an expert and how being an expert affects problem solving.

HOW EXPERTS SOLVE PROBLEMS

Experts are people who, by devoting a large amount of time to learning about a field and practicing the application of that learning, have become acknowledged as being extremely knowledgeable or skilled in the particular field. For example, by spending

10,000–20,000 hours playing and studying chess, some chess players have reached the rank of grand master (Chase & Simon, 1973a, b). Not surprisingly, experts tend to be better at solving problems in their field than are nonexperts. Research on the nature of expertise has focused on determining differences between the way experts and nonexperts go about solving problems.

Some Differences Between How Experts and Novices Solve Problems

Experts in a particular field usually solve problems faster with a higher success rate than do novices (people who are beginners or who have not had the extensive training of experts) (Chi et al., 1982; Larkin et al., 1980). But what is behind this faster speed and greater success? Are experts smarter than novices? Are they better at reasoning in general? Do they approach problems in a different way? Cognitive psychologists have answered these questions by comparing the performance and methods of experts and novices, and have reached the following conclusions.

Experts Possess More Knowledge About Their Fields   In Chapter 5 we discussed Chase and Simon's (1973a, b) research on how well chess masters and novices can reproduce positions on a chessboard that they have seen briefly. The results showed that experts excelled at this task when the chess pieces were arranged in actual game positions, but were no better than novices when the pieces were arranged randomly (see Figure 5.13). The reason for the experts' good performance for actual positions is that the chess masters were able to recognize specific arrangements of pieces from actual game positions. A chess master has about 50,000 patterns in their memory, compared to 1,000 patterns for a good player and few or none for a poor player (Bedard & Chi, 1992). But what is important for the purposes of problem solving is not just that the experts' mind contains lots of knowledge, but that this knowledge is *organized* so it can be accessed when needed to work on a problem.

Experts' Knowledge Is Organized Differently From Novices'   The difference in organization between experts and novices is illustrated by an experiment by Michelene Chi and coworkers (1982; also see Chi et al., 1981). They presented 24 physics problems to a group of experts (physics professors) and a group of novices (students with one semester of physics) and asked them to sort the problems into groups based on their similarities. Figure 11.19 shows diagrams of problems that were grouped together by an expert and by a novice. We don't need a statement of the actual problems to see from the diagrams that the novice sorted the problems based on how similar the *objects* in the problem were. Thus, two problems that included inclined planes were grouped together, even though the physical principles involved in the problems were quite different.

The expert, in contrast, sorted problems based on general principles. The expert perceived two problems as similar because they both involved the principle of conservation of energy, even though the diagrams indicate that one problem involved a spring and an-

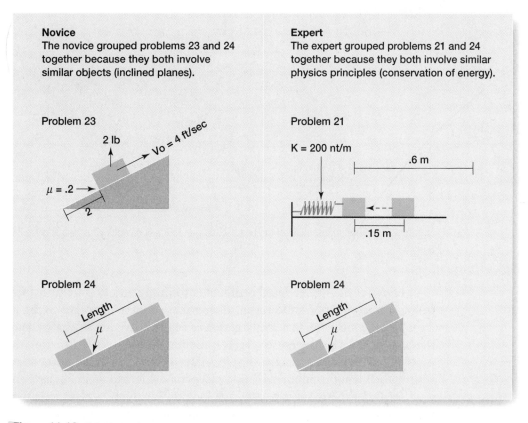

Novice
The novice grouped problems 23 and 24 together because they both involve similar objects (inclined planes).

Expert
The expert grouped problems 21 and 24 together because they both involve similar physics principles (conservation of energy).

Problem 23

2 lb
$V_0 = 4$ ft/sec
$\mu = .2$
2

Problem 21

$K = 200$ nt/m
.6 m
.15 m

Problem 24

Length
μ

Problem 24

Length
μ

Figure 11.19 The kinds of physics problems that were grouped together by novices (left) and experts (right) (Chi et al., 1981).

other an inclined plane. Thus, novices categorized problems based on their *surface structure* (what the objects looked like) and the experts categorized them based on their *deep structure* (the underlying principles involved). Experts' ability to organize knowledge has been found to be important not only for chess masters and physics experts, but for experts in many other fields as well (Egan & Schwartz, 1979; Reitman, 1976).

Experts Spend More Time Analyzing Problems   Experts often get off to what appears to be a slow start on a problem because they spend time trying to understand the problem, rather than immediately trying to solve it. Here is an interesting problem that has not been used to compare experts and novices, but which does illustrate the value of stopping for a moment to analyze a problem, rather than immediately starting to search for a solution.

A board was sawed into two pieces. One piece was two-thirds as large as the whole board and was exceeded in length by the second piece by 4 feet. How long was the board before it was cut? (Paige & Simon, 1966)

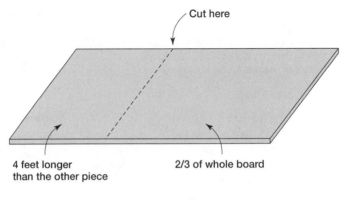

Figure 11.20 The impossibility of the board-cutting problem is obvious when we analyze it by drawing a picture.

One way to approach this problem is to immediately start transforming the word problem into equations. However, solving these equations results in the interesting (and impossible) conclusion that the larger piece of the board has a negative length. If, instead, the person takes a moment to create a mental picture of the situation described in the problem, it becomes apparent that it is impossible for a piece to account for 2/3 of the board's total length and for the other piece to be 4 feet longer (Figure 11.20).

The way experts spend some time looking for the best representation of a problem may slow them down, right at the beginning. However, in the long run, this strategy usually pays off in a more effective approach to the problem.

Experts Are Often No Better Than Novices When Given Problems Outside of Their Field

When James Voss and coworkers (1983) posed a real-world problem involving Soviet agriculture to expert political scientists, expert chemists, and novice political scientists, they found that the expert political scientists performed best and that the expert chemists performed as poorly as the novice political scientists. In general, experts are experts only within their own field, and perform like anyone else outside of their field (Bedard & Chi, 1992). This makes sense when we remember that the superior performance of experts occurs largely because they possess a larger and more well organized store of knowledge about their specific field.

Before leaving our discussion of expertise, we sshould note that being an expert is not always an advantage. One disadvantage to being an expert is that knowing about the established facts and theories in a field may make experts less likely to be open to new ways of looking at problems. This may be why younger and less experienced scientists in a field are often the ones responsible for revolutionary discoveries (Kuhn, 1970; Simonton, 1984). In line with this, it has been suggested that one situation in which being an expert would be a disadvantage is when solving a problem that involves flexible thinking, that might involve rejecting the usual procedures for solving the problem in favor of other procedures that might not normally be used (Frensch & Sternberg, 1989).

CREATIVE COGNITION: AN EXERCISE IN DIVERGENT THINKING

Our survey of problem solving has focused on ways to arrive at solutions to specific problems that have "right answers." We have seen how people can arrive at these answers by restructuring, by searching, and by being aware of analogies. This is pretty serious stuff—like trying to determine the correct answer on a cognitive psychology exam! So now it's time to have a little fun, while at the same time considering another approach to problem solving that does not require that the problem solver find a "correct answer," but which instead encourages a process of creativity—hence the name *creative cognition* (Finke, 1990). As you will see from the following demonstration, the initial goal is not to arrive at a specific answer, but to create something.

◼ Demonstration

Creating an Object

Figure 11.21 shows 15 object parts and their names. Close your eyes and touch the page three times, in order to randomly pick three of these object parts. After reading these instructions take one minute to construct a new object using these three parts. The object should be interesting-looking and possibly useful, but try to avoid making your object correspond to a familiar object, and don't worry what it might be used for. You can vary the size, position, orientation, and material of the parts, just so you don't alter the basic shape (except for the wire and the tube, which can be bent). Once you come up with something in your mind, draw a picture of it. ◼

This exercise is patterned after one devised by Ronald Finke (1990, 1995), who randomly selected three of the object parts from Figure 11.21 for his participants. After the participants had created an object, they were provided with the name of one of the object categories from Table 11.2 and were given one minute to interpret their object, which Finke called a *preinventive form*, as a practical object or device within that category. For example, if the category was tools and utensils, the person had to interpret their preinventive form as a screwdriver, a spoon, or some other tool or utensil. To do this for your preinventive form, pick a category and then decide what your object could be used for and describe how it functions. Figure 11.22 shows how a single preinventive form that was constructed from the half-sphere, wire, and handle could be interpreted in terms of each of the eight categories in Table 11.2.

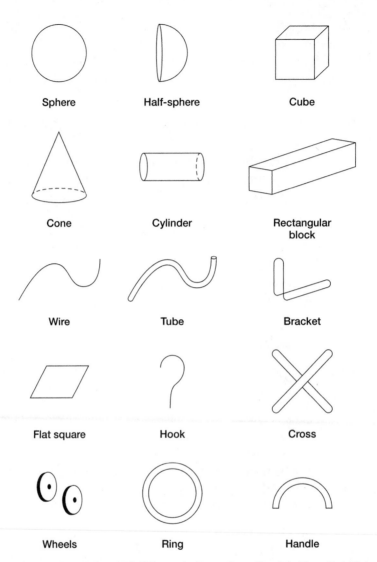

Figure 11.21 Objects used by Finke (1990). See text for instructions. (Reprinted from R. A. Finke, "Creative Insight and Preinventive Forms," from *The Nature of Insight,* by R. J. Sternberg & J. E. Davidson, Eds., pp. 255–280, Figure 8.1. Copyright © 1995 with permission from the MIT Press.)

In an experiment in which 360 objects were created, Finke (1990, 1995) found that a panel of judges rated 120 of these objects as being "practical inventions" (they were given high ratings for "practicality") and rated 65 as "creative inventions" (the objects received high ratings for both practicality and for originality). What is remarkable about this result is that Finke's participants received no training or practice, and were not pre-selected for "creativity." It is apparently not necessary to be an expert or an inventor to think creatively.

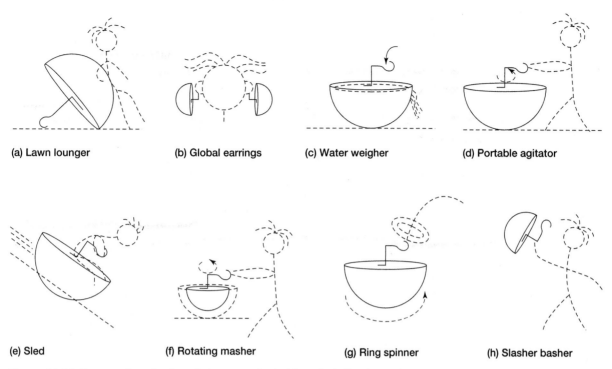

(a) Lawn lounger   (b) Global earrings   (c) Water weigher   (d) Portable agitator

(e) Sled   (f) Rotating masher   (g) Ring spinner   (h) Slasher basher

Figure 11.22 How a preinventive form that was constructed from the half-sphere, wire, and handle can be interpreted in terms of each of the eight categories in Table 11.2. (Reprinted from R. A. Finke, "Creative Insight and Preinventive Forms," from *The Nature of Insight,* by R. J. Sternberg & J. E. Davidson, Eds., pp. 255–280, Figure 8.6. Copyright © 1995 with permission from the MIT Press.)

Table 11.2	OBJECT CATEGORIES IN PREINVENTIVE FORM STUDIES
Category	Examples
(a) Furniture	Chairs, tables, lamps
(b) Personal items	Jewelry, glasses
(c) Scientific instruments	Measuring devices
(d) Appliances	Washing machines, toasters
(e) Transportation	Cars, boats
(f) Tools and utensils	Screwdrivers, spoons
(g) Toys and games	Baseball bats, dolls
(h) Weapons	Guns, missiles

Adapted from Finke, 1995.

Divergent and Convergent Thinking

Finke's "creative cognition" exercise provides an example of **divergent thinking**—thinking that is open-ended and for which there are a large number of potential "solutions" and no "correct" answer (although some proposals might work better than others) (see Guilford, 1956; Ward et al., 1997). Divergent thinking can be contrasted with **convergent thinking,** which is thinking that works toward finding a solution to a specific problem that usually has a correct answer. In this case, thinking *converges* onto the correct answer.

Although divergent thinking has often been associated with creativity, it has been difficult to determine clear connections between divergent thinking and measures of creativity. One measure of divergent thinking, developed by J. P. Guilford (1956), involved asking participants to determine as many uses as possible for familiar objects. For example, how many different uses can you think of for a brick? Unfortunately, the correlations between performance on tasks such as this and other measures of creativity are only modest (Guilford, 1967). Research that has explored other approaches to creativity seem to indicate that although divergent thinking can lead to the creation of many ideas, the processes that have led to original and practical inventions often involve not only the uninhibited kind of divergent thinking involved in Finke's object production task, but also other processes such as searching for solutions, being aware of structure, and looking for analogies, which we have discussed in this chapter.

PROBLEM SOLVING AND THE BRAIN

Which areas of the brain are involved in problem solving? One answer to this question is that a particular problem activates many different areas. For example, when Paolo Nichelli and coworkers (1994) used PET to measure the brain activity of chess players as they viewed a chessboard and solved various chess problems ("Can the white knight capture the black rook?" "Can the white side achieve checkmate in one more move?"), they found that brain activity was associated with the following components of the chess task (Figure 11.23):

Task	*Location of Brain Activity*
■ Identifying chess pieces	Pathway from occipital lobe to temporal lobe
■ Determining location of pieces	Pathway from occipital lobe to parietal lobe
■ Thinking about making a move	Premotor area
■ Remembering a piece's moves	Hippocampus
■ Planning and executing strategies	Prefrontal cortex

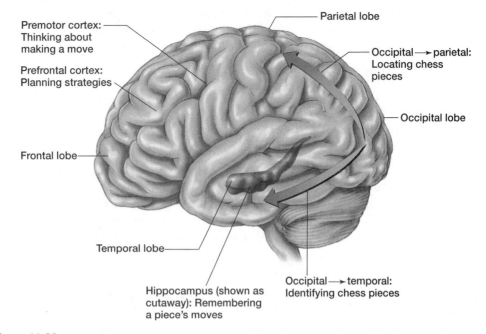

Premotor cortex:
Thinking about
making a move

Prefrontal cortex:
Planning strategies

Frontal lobe

Temporal lobe

Hippocampus (shown as
cutaway): Remembering
a piece's moves

Parietal lobe

Occipital → parietal:
Locating chess
pieces

Occipital lobe

Occipital → temporal:
Identifying chess pieces

Figure 11.23 Areas of the brain that are activated by playing chess, according to Nichelli et al. (1994).

It is not surprising that many brain areas are involved in solving a complex problem because solving most problems involves a number of different types of tasks. But one area has been identified as being particularly important for one of the key tasks in problem solving—planning and executing strategies. That area is the prefrontal cortex (PFC).

The PFC has been linked to problem solving in a number of ways. Damage to the PFC interferes with people's ability to act flexibly, a key requirement for solving problems. One symptom of PFC damage is a behavior called **perseveration,** in which patients have difficulty in switching from one pattern of behavior to another (Hauser, 1999; Munakata et al., 2003). For example, patients with damage to PFC have difficulty when the rules change in a card-sorting task. Thus, if they begin by successfully separating out the blue cards from a pack, they continue picking the blue cards even after the experimenter tells them to shift to separating out the brown cards. Clearly, perseveration would play havoc with attempts to solve complex problems for which it is necessary to consider one possible solution and then shift to another possibility if the first one doesn't work.

One of the earliest reports of the effect of frontal lobe damage on functioning was the case of a young homemaker who had a tumor in her frontal lobe that made it impossible for her to prepare a family meal, even though she was capable of cooking the individual dishes (Penfield & Evans, 1935). Results such as this led to the conclusion that the PFC plays an important role in planning future activities (Owen et al., 1990).

Because damage to the PFC results in perseveration and poor ability to plan, it is not surprising that PFC damage decreases performance on tasks such as the Tower of London problem (a task similar to the Tower of Hanoi problem that involves moving colored beads between two vertical rods) (Carlin et al., 2000; Owen et al., 1990), the Tower of Hanoi problem (Morris et al., 1997), and the Luchins water-jug problem (Colvin et al., 2001). Brain imaging has also shown that problem solving activates the PFC in normal participants (Rowe et al., 2001).

The picture that emerges from all of this research is that the PFC is important for problem solving, and other research has shown that the PFC is important for a number of cognitive tasks involving planning, reasoning, and making connections among different parts of a problem or a story. For example, when Tiziana Zalla and coworkers (2002) tested patients with PFC damage, she found that these patients were able to understand individual words and could identify events that were described in stories, but they could not follow the story as a whole, because they were unable to follow the order of events in the story or to make inferences that connected different parts of the story (see Chapter 10, page 369). In the next chapter we will see that the PFC is also involved in reasoning and making decisions.

Test Yourself 11.2

1. What is the basic idea behind analogical problem solving? How effective is it to present a source problem and then the target problem, without indicating that the source problem is related to the target problem?
2. What are the three steps in the process of analogical problem solving? Which of the steps appears to be the most difficult to achieve?
3. How did Gick and Holyoak apply the idea of schemas to help people discover the basic concept that links the source problem and the target problem?
4. What is an expert? What are some differences between the way experts and nonexperts go about solving problems? How good are experts at solving problems outside of their field?
5. What is convergent thinking? What is divergent thinking? How do these two types of thinking relate to the problems we have discussed in this chapter and to Finke's "creative cognition" demonstration involving preinventive forms?
6. Why would it be inaccurate to say that one particular area of the brain is the "center" for problem solving? What is one behavioral outcome of damage to the prefrontal cortex that suggests that this area is important for problem solving?

Think About It

1. Pick a problem you have had to deal with (like the "getting the car fixed" example in the book) and analyze the process of solving it into subgoals, as is done in means-end analysis.

2. Have you ever experienced a situation in which you were trying to solve a problem, but stopped working on it because you couldn't come up with the answer? Then, after a while, when you returned to the problem, you got the answer right away? What do you think might be behind this process?

3. On August 14, 2003, a power failure caused millions of people in the northeast and midwest United States and in eastern Canada to lose their electricity. A few days later, after most people had their electricity restored, experts still did not know why the power failure occurred and said it would take weeks to determine the cause. Imagine that you are a member of a special commission that has the task of solving this problem, or some other major problem. How could the processes described in this chapter be applied to finding a solution? What would the shortcomings of these processes be for solving this kind of problem?

4. Think of some examples of situations in which you overcame functional fixedness by finding a new use for an object.

KEY TERMS

Analogical problem solving
Analogy
Candle problem
Convergent thinking
Divergent thinking
Experts
Functional fixedness
Goal state
Hobbits-and-orcs problem
Ill-defined problem
Initial state
Insight
Intermediate states
Means-end analysis
Mental set

Mutilated-checkerboard problem
Operators
Perseveration
Problem
Problem schema
Problem space
Radiation problem
Schema induction
Source problem
Subgoal
Target problem
Tower of Hanoi problem
Two-string problem
Water-jug problem

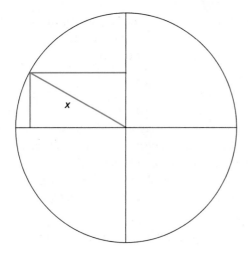

Solution: The length of the line *x* is *r*.

Figure 11.24 Solution to the circle problem.

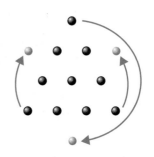

Figure 11.25 Solution to the triangle problem. Arrows indicate movement; colored circles indicate new positions.

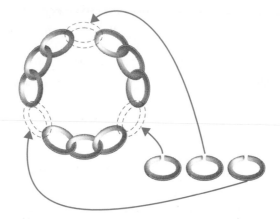

Figure 11.26 Solution to the chain problem. All the links in one chain are cut and separated (3 cuts @ 2 cents = 6 cents). Then each separated link is used to connect the other three pieces and are then closed (3 closings @ 3 cents = 9 cents). Total = 15 cents.

Figure 11.27 Solution to the candle problem.

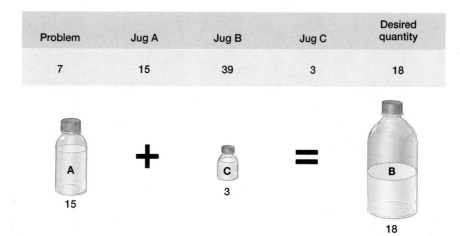

Problem	Jug A	Jug B	Jug C	Desired quantity
7	15	39	3	18

Figure 11.28 Solution to problem 7 of the Luchins water-jug problem. Problem 8 can also be solved using just jugs A and C.

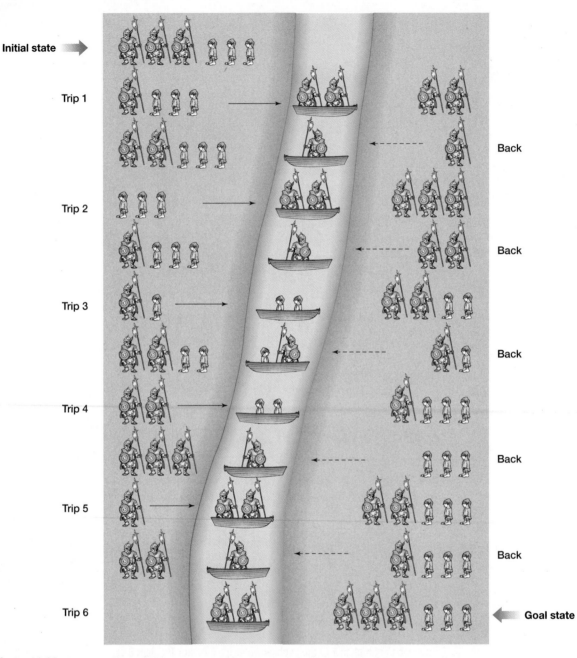

Initial state

Trip 1

Back

Trip 2

Back

Trip 3

Back

Trip 4

Back

Trip 5

Back

Trip 6

Goal state

Figure 11.29 Solution to the hobbits-and-orcs problem. Each trip indication on the left (trip 1, trip 2, etc.) indicates the number of hobbits and orcs that remain after the trip. The hobbits and orcs in the next row down indicate how many hobbits and orcs there are each time the boat comes back.

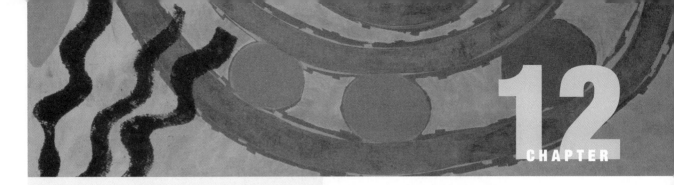

CHAPTER 12

Reasoning and Decision Making

Some Questions We Will Consider

✔ Do people reason logically, or do they make errors in reasoning?

✔ How does reasoning operate in the discoveries made by scientists?

✔ What kinds of reasoning "traps" do people get into when reasoning and when making decisions?

✔ How does the fact that people sometimes feel a need to justify their decisions affect the process by which they make these decisions?

What is **reasoning**? One definition is *cognitive processes by which people start with information and come to conclusions that go beyond that information* (Kurtz et al., 1999). If you think about what we've covered in this book, this definition applies to material in just about every chapter. For example, in Chapter 3, on perception, we saw that perceiving an object can involve inference from incomplete information (Figure 12.1); in Chapter 6, on long-term memory, we saw that our memories of events from the past are created by a process of construction, also from incomplete information; and in Chapter 10, on language, we saw how understanding one part of a story can depend on inferences based on what you know has happened before.

As these examples show, reasoning is involved in a large portion of what we study in cognitive psychology. In this chapter we are going to focus on how cognitive psychologists have studied the processes of reasoning by focusing on two specific types of reasoning, deductive reasoning and inductive reasoning. We first consider **deductive reasoning,** which involves syllogisms in which a conclusion logically follows from premises (Figure 12.2). For example, if we are given the information that to graduate from State U., you need to have at least a C average, and that Josie is graduating from State U., we can logically conclude that Josie had at least a C average.

We then consider **inductive reasoning,** in which we arrive at conclusions about what is *probably* true, based on evidence. Thus, if we know that Richard attended State U. for four years and that he is now the vice president of a bank, we might conclude that it is likely that he graduated. Notice, however, that in this example, we cannot say that he *definitely* graduated (maybe he never completed all the requirements and his father, who is president of the bank, made him a vice president). Thus, we can make *definite* conclusions based on deductive reasoning and *probable* conclusions based on inductive reasoning. Studying both kinds of reasoning provides insights both about how the mind works and about everyday thinking.

We will also consider **decisions,** which usually involve making choices between alternatives, and which can involve both inductive and deductive reasoning. Finally, we will describe how the brain is involved in reasoning.

DEDUCTIVE REASONING: THINKING CATEGORICALLY

Aristotle is considered to be the father of deductive reasoning because he introduced the basic form of deductive reasoning called the *syllogism.* A **syllogism** includes two statements, called **premises,** followed by a third statement, called the **conclusion.** We will first consider syllogisms that are called **categorical syllogisms,** in which the premises and conclusion describe the relation between two categories by using statements that begin with *all, no,* or *some.* We will refer to categorical syllogisms as simply *syllogisms* in the discussion that follows.

There are two approaches to studying syllogisms. The **normative approach** indicates which forms of syllogisms are logically valid and which are not valid. Studying this

COGNITION	REASONING
Chapter 3: Perception "That's an animal lurking."	Animal is inferred from ambiguous shapes.
Chapter 6: Long-Term Memory "I remember, on the first day of class. . . ."	Memories are constructed from what we remember, plus perhaps other information.
Chapter 10: Language "To be or not to be . . ." "I understand what he is saying."	Meaning is created by using knowledge we obtained earlier to help interpret Hamlet's statement.

Figure 12.1 Some examples of processes that fit the definition of "reasoning" that we have encountered in previous chapters.

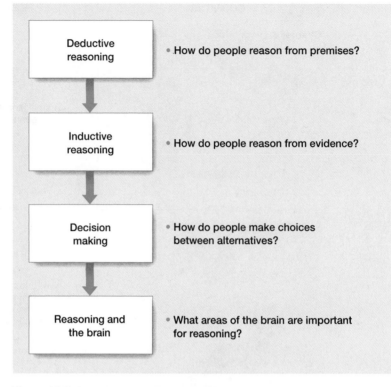

Figure 12.2 Flow diagram for this chapter.

approach involves logic, not psychology. The **descriptive approach** does involve psychology because it is concerned with how well people can evaluate whether a syllogism is valid.

The Normative Approach: Which Syllogisms Are Valid and Which Are Not?

The basic form of a syllogism is two premises followed by a conclusion, as in this example:

Premise 1:   All A are B.
Premise 2:   All B are C.
Conclusion: Therefore, all A are C.

The conclusion begins with "therefore," to indicate that it follows from the two premises. For brevity, we will omit the *therefore* in the rest of the syllogisms, with the understanding that in valid syllogisms the conclusion always follows from the premises.

Syllogisms can be stated abstractly, in terms of A, B, and C, as just shown, or more concretely, using meaningful terms, as in this example:

1. All birds are animals.
   All animals eat food.
   All birds eat food.

Although syllogisms may seem like an artificial way of studying thinking, the advantage of using them is that we can construct syllogisms that are either **valid** (the conclusion follows logically from the two premises), or not valid (the conclusion does not follow from the premises). These syllogisms can then be used to determine how well people are able to evaluate validity.

Validity and Truth in Syllogisms
The first principle of deductive reasoning is:

> *Principle 1*: If the two premises are true, the conclusion of a valid syllogism must be true.

Syllogism 1 above has been called Aristotle's "perfect" syllogism because it was introduced by Aristotle, and because it is almost immediately obvious that the conclusion follows from the two premises (Manktelow, 1999). This syllogism is valid because the conclusion logically follows from the two premises. In this particular example, both premises are true, so according to Principle 1, the conclusion must be true.

Another principle of deductive reasoning is the following:

> *Principle 2*: The validity of a syllogism is determined only by its form, not its content.

According to this principle, the following syllogism, which has exactly the same form as syllogism 1, is also valid:

2. All birds are ants.
   All ants have four legs.
   All birds have four legs.

In this example, premise 1 is clearly false, but because the syllogism has a valid form, the syllogism is still valid. Notice that even though the syllogism is valid, the conclusion is not true. Remember that the first basic principle of deductive reasoning states that *if the two premises are true*, then the conclusion of a valid syllogism is true. Because the first premise in this example is not true, there is no guarantee that the conclusion will be true. It is, however, possible to start with false premises yet reach a true conclusion, as in syllogism 3 below, in which the first premise is false, the syllogism is valid, and the conclusion is true.

3. All birds are ants.
   All ants eat food.
   All birds eat food.

The message of these examples bears repeating: *The validity of a syllogism depends on its form, not its content.* Given this principle, we can now ask how we can determine if a syllogism is valid. Although it is easy to see that the conclusion logically follows from the premises in syllogism 1, so it is valid, the validity of other forms of syllogism is not always so obvious. One way to determine whether or not a syllogism is valid is to use a device called Euler circles.

Determining Validity Using Euler Circles   Is syllogism 4, below, valid or invalid?

4. Some people are athletes.
   All athletes exercise.
   Some people exercise.

One way to determine the validity of this syllogism is to use Euler circles. Euler circles are diagrams that graphically depict the relationships between the various items in a syllogism to determine whether or not a syllogism is valid. Figure 12.3 shows how Euler circles work for syllogism 1. Figure 12.4 applies Euler circles to syllogism 4. Before reading further, study the description in these two figures of how to use Euler circles. Then try your own hand at Euler circles in the following demonstration.

◪ Demonstration

Euler Circles

Before looking at the answer in Figure 12.5, try using Euler circles to determine whether this syllogism is valid:

5. All athletes are people.
   Some people are college students.
   Some athletes are college students.

This syllogism is more difficult to evaluate than the syllogisms we have considered so far. You might want to try reasoning this one out and then try drawing the Euler circles for this syllogism to see what they tell you.

What did your circles tell you? Check Figure 12.5 to be sure you drew the Euler circles correctly. Notice that it is important that you draw all *possible* circles, because for a syllogism to be valid, the conclusion must be supported by *every version* of the diagram. ∎

Euler circles provide a tool that makes it possible to determine the validity of most syllogisms. But the most important thing to take away from this last demonstration of Euler circles is yet another principle of deductive reasoning:

Principle 3: For a syllogism to be valid, the conclusion must follow for every possible case. If there is even one exception, then the syllogism is not valid.

Some of the errors people make in judging validity in deductive reasoning can be traced to a failure to follow one or more of the three basic principles.

All birds are animals. (B = Birds; A = Animals)
All animals eat food. (F = Food)
All birds eat food.

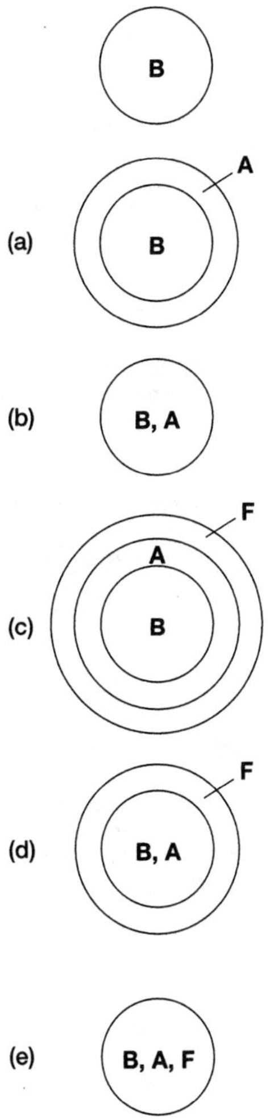

How to draw Euler circles for the above syllogism:

1 Draw a circle to represent the first category in the first premise.

Here is the circle for birds. Everything inside this circle is a bird.

2 Draw another circle to indicate the relationship indicated by the first premise. For

• **All birds are animals**

we draw a large circle, for animals, around the bird circle, as shown in (a). Because everything within the bird circle is also inside the animal circle, these two circles represent "All birds are animals." We can also repeat this, as shown in (b), in which the bird and animal circles are the same. This also stands for "All birds are animals."

3 Add another circle for the second premise. For

• **All animals eat food**

in (c), we draw a large circle, for food, around the animal circle. Because everything within the animal circle is also inside the food circle, this represents "All animals eat food." We can also create two more diagrams, (d) and (e), by adding the food circle to diagram (b) above.

4 Check to see if the conclusion is represented by the circles in c, d, and e.

These circles all fit the conclusion,

• **All birds eat food**

because the bird circle is enitirely within the food circle for all versions of the circles that we drew. Thus, this syllogism is valid.

(a)
(b)
(c)
(d)
(e)

Figure 12.3 How to draw Euler circles, using syllogism 1 as an example.

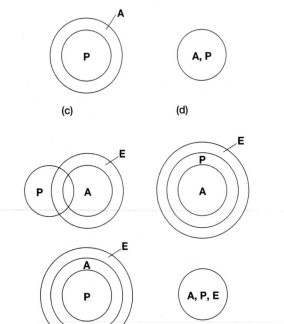

There are four ways to diagram the premise

• Some people are athletes

Notice that for the first two, shown in (a) and (b), some (but not all) of the people are athletes. For these two circles, some of the people fall within the athlete circle. The people outside the athlete circle are not athletes.

For the second two circles, shown in (c) and (d), all of the people are athletes. It is important to note that from the point of view of logic, "some" means at least one, up to all. Thus, if "some people are athletes," it is also logically possible that all of the people could be athletes.

We indicate the second premise

• All athletes exercise

by drawing the exercise circle around the athlete circle for each of the cases above.

All of these diagrams fit the conclusion,

• Some people exercise

because some or all of the people circle is covered by the exercise circle (remember that "some" is at least one, up to all). Thus, this syllogism is valid.

Figure 12.4 Drawing Euler circles for syllogism 4.

The Descriptive Approach: How Well Can People Judge Validity?

We are now ready to consider the *psychology* of categorical syllogisms. That is, we are going to shift from the normative approach, which specifies the correct answers to deductive reasoning problems (i.e., whether a particular syllogism is valid or invalid), to the descriptive approach, which asks how well people can actually judge validity. But before we answer this question, let's consider why we would be interested in doing this.

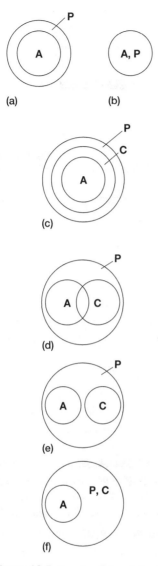

All athletes are people. (A = Athletes; P = People)
Some people are college students. (C = College students)
Some athletes are college students.

- **All athletes are people**

is indicated by the fact that the circle for athletes fall within the circle for people in (a), or is the same as the circle for people, in (b).

- **Some people are college students**

We have shown four different ways to draw this. In (c), (d), and (e), we have drawn a "college student" circle inside the "people" circle, with different amounts of overlap with the athlete circle. There is total overlap in (c), partial overlap in (d), and no overlap in (e). In (f) the "college student" and "people" circles overlap completely.

We now look at these diagrams to see if the conclusion,

- **Some athletes are college students**

follows from the two premises. We can see that diagrams (c), (d), and (f) are all consistent with the statement "some athletes are college students." However, this conclusion is not represented by diagram (e), in which there is no overlap between "college students" and "athletes." Because this diagram does not match the conclusion, we conclude that the syllogism is not valid.

Figure 12.5 Drawing Euler circles for syllogism 5.

One reason to be interested in determining how well people can judge validity is to help answer the question, "Do people think logically?" One approach to this question was taken by early philosophers, who said that people's minds work logically, and so if they do make errors in judging validity it means that they were being careless or were not paying attention.

Another approach, which has been adopted by most cognitive psychologists, is that logic is not necessarily built into the human mind, and so if people do make errors, these errors tell us something about how the mind operates. Psychologists are interested in determining what errors occur and what contributes to these errors.

People's performance in judging syllogisms has been determined using two methods: (1) *Evaluation:* Present two premises and a conclusion, and ask people to indicate if the conclusion logically follows from the premises; (2) *Production:* Present two premises and ask people to indicate what conclusion logically follows from the premises, or if no conclusion logically follows. We will focus our attention on the evaluation task because a great deal of the research on deductive reasoning has used this method.

When people are tested using the evaluation method, they generally have no problem indicating that Aristotle's "perfect" syllogism (syllogism 1, shown previously) is valid, but make errors on all other forms of syllogisms. The exact error rate depends on a number of factors, including whether the syllogism is stated abstractly (in terms of A's, B's, and C's) or in real-world terms (for example, in terms of athletes and people). People make errors for all syllogisms except for syllogism 1, and for some syllogisms the error rate can be as high as 70–80 percent (Gilhooly, 1988).

What Are the Sources of Errors in Syllogisms?

There are many reasons that people make errors in syllogisms. We will focus on two sources that have been widely studied, the atmosphere effect and the belief bias. The **atmosphere effect** states that the words *All, Some,* and *No* in the premises creates an overall "mood" or "atmosphere" that can influence the evaluation of the conclusion. According to the atmosphere effect, two *All*'s generally suggests an *All* conclusion. One or two *No*'s suggest a *No* conclusion; and one or two *Some*'s suggest a *Some* conclusion. If you look back at the syllogisms we have considered so far, you can see that application of these ideas often leads to a correct evaluation. For example, syllogisms 1–4 all follow the rules of atmosphere and are all valid. However, note that in syllogism 5, the atmosphere effect would lead to the incorrect conclusion that this invalid syllogism is valid. Thus, just considering the initial terms of premises can often lead to the correct evaluation, but also leads to some errors.

According to the **belief bias**, if a syllogism's conclusion is true or agrees with a person's beliefs, this increases the likelihood that the syllogism will be judged as valid. In addition, if the conclusion is false, this increases the likelihood that the syllogism will be judged as invalid. The belief bias could lead to the erroneous conclusion that syllogism 5 is valid because most people know that the conclusion "some athletes are college students" is true. Here are two other examples that have the same form as syllogism 5:

6. All of the students are tired.
   Some tired people are irritable.
   Some of the students are irritable.

7. All of the men are tired.
   Some tired people are women.
   Some of the men are women.

When people are presented with these two syllogisms, they do not hesitate to indicate that syllogism 7 is invalid because the conclusion is not believable, but will often indicate that syllogism 6 is valid because the conclusion is believable. The results of a study in which people were presented with valid and invalid syllogisms with both believable and not-

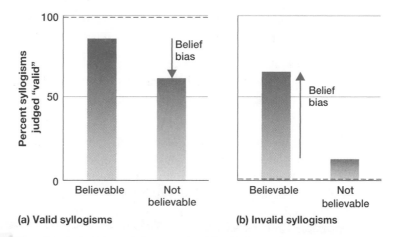

Figure 12.6 Effect of the belief bias on judgments of validity. (a) Results for valid syllogisms. The dashed lines indicate the percent of syllogisms that were actually valid. The arrows indicate the effect of the belief bias (Evans et al., 1983).

believable conclusions are shown in Figure 12.6 (Evans et al., 1983). Figure 12.6a shows the results for valid syllogisms, which, if people judge validity correctly, should result in 100 percent "valid" responses, as indicated by the dashed line. It is no surprise that when the conclusion is believable, 86 percent of the judgments were "valid." However, when the conclusion was not believable, the rates of "valid" responses dropped to 62 percent. This decrease in "valid" responses due to the unbelievability of the conclusion is an example of the belief bias.

Figure 12.6b shows the results for invalid syllogisms (Evans et al., 1983). In this case the belief bias has a huge effect. Even though the syllogism is invalid (so the percent of "valid" responses should be 0, as shown by the dashed line at the bottom of the graph), 62 percent of the responses with believable conclusions were judged to be "valid."

The belief bias illustrates a violation of Principle 2, which states that the validity of a syllogism is determined by its form. The data in Figure 12.6 indicate that people are influenced by the believability of the conclusion, and therefore they do not always follow the rules of logic.

Mental Models of Deductive Reasoning

We have presented some data on deductive reasoning, but we still haven't considered what mental processes might be occurring as people are trying to determine if a syllogism is valid. We saw that one way to test the validity of a syllogism is to use Euler circles, like the ones in Figures 12.3, 12.4, and 12.5, but Phillip Johnson-Laird (1999) wonders whether people would use these circles naturally if they hadn't been taught about them, and also points out that Euler circles don't work for some of the more complex syllogisms.

So what could people be doing? To begin a discussion of this question, Johnson-Laird (1995) posed a problem similar to this one (try it):

> On a pool table there is a black ball directly above the cue ball. The green ball is on the right side of the cue ball, and there is a red ball between them. If I move so the red ball is between me and the black ball, the cue ball is to the _____ of my line of sight.

How did you go about solving this problem? (See the end of the chapter for the correct answer.) Johnson-Laird points out that the problem can be solved by applying logical rules, but that most people solve it by imagining the way the balls are arranged on the pool table. This idea that people will imagine situations is the basis of Johnson-Laird's idea that people use mental models to solve deductive reasoning problems.

A **mental model** is a specific situation that is represented in a person's mind that can be used to help determine the validity of syllogisms in deductive reasoning. We can illustrate how this would work for a categorical syllogism by using the following example (from Johnson-Laird, 1999a):

> None of the artists are beekeepers.
> All of the beekeepers are chemists.
> Some of the chemists are not artists.

We can illustrate how mental models can be used to determine if this syllogism is valid by imagining that we are visiting a meeting of the Artists, Beekeepers, and Chemists Society (the ABC Society, for short). We know that everyone who is eligible to be a member of the ABC Society must be an artist, a beekeeper, or a chemist, and that they must also follow the following rules, which correspond to the first two premises of the syllogism above: (1) *No artists can be beekeepers*; and (2) *All of the beekeepers must be chemists*. The Keeper of the Records of the ABC Society has determined, by applying the rules of logic, that one outcome of these membership regulations is that *Some of the chemists are not artists*.

We can create mental models for this syllogism by imagining that we are meeting ABC Society members at the annual ABC "mixer." We first meet Susan, who is an artist (but who isn't a beekeeper, which follows membership rule 1). We then meet Roger, who is a beekeeper and a chemist (see rule 2). Figure 12.7 shows the model we can create based on these two people. Model 1 supports the conclusion that *None of the artists is a chemist*.

However, one of the requirements of mental models theory is that we need to check all possibilities to see if there are other models that might refute this conclusion. As it turns out, you meet Cyrus, who happens to be an artist and a chemist, which is allowed by the membership regulations. Adding Cyrus enables us to create a new model, Model 2. From this model we can see that the conclusion *None of the artists is a chemist* is not true, but that the conclusion *Some of the chemists are not artists* could be true.

We now try to find some other people in the room who might refute this conclusion and we come across Natasha, who is just a chemist, which is allowed by the membership regulations. But this case does not refute our conclusion, and after more searching, we

MODELS OF THE ABC SOCIETY

Susan	Artist		
Roger		Beekeeper	Chemist

Model 1: This model supports the conclusion, *None of the artists is a chemist.*

But then we meet Cyrus, and so we create a new model that includes him.

Susan	Artist		
Roger		Beekeeper	Chemist
Cyrus	Artist		Chemist

Model 2: This model supports the conclusion, *Some of the chemists are not artists.*

We also meet Natasha.

Natasha	Chemist

Adding Natasha to Model 2 doesn't change our conclusion.

Figure 12.7 Mental models for the ABC Society based on meeting members of the society at the annual ABC Society mixer.

can't find anyone else in the room whose existence would refute this syllogism's conclusion, so we accept it. This example illustrates the basic principle behind the mental model theory: A conclusion is valid only if it *cannot* be refuted by any model of the premises.

The mental model theory is attractive because it can be applied without training in the rules of logic, and because it makes predictions that can be tested. For example, the theory predicts that syllogisms that require more models will be more difficult to solve, and this prediction has been confirmed in experiments (Buciarelli & Johnson-Laird, 1999).

There are other proposals about how people might go about testing syllogisms (see Rips, 1995, 2002), and there isn't agreement among researchers regarding the correct approach. We have presented the mental model theory because it is supported by the results of a number of experiments and because it is one of the models that is easiest to explain. However, a number of problems face researchers who are trying to determine how people reason about syllogisms. These problems include the fact that people use a variety of different strategies in reasoning, and that some people are much better at solving syllogisms than others (Buciarelli & Johnson-Laird, 1999). Thus, the question of how people go about solving syllogisms remains to be answered.

Effects of Culture on Deductive Reasoning

So far we have seen that people are good at judging validity for one type of syllogism, not as good for others, and can be influenced by content, rather than just focusing on logic. Psychologists have wondered whether people from different cultures reason differently. To answer this question, psychologists have done cross-cultural experiments, in which reasoning problems were presented to people in different cultures. An early cross-cultural experiment was done by Sylvia Scribner (1977), who studied how the Kepelle, a traditional tribe in Liberia, deal with syllogisms. She presented two premises of the syllogism and then asked a question which could, logically, be answered from the premises. For example, here is the question, presented by the experimenter (E), and the ensuing discussion between the experimenter and the participant (P).

Premise 1: If Sumo or Saki drinks palm wine, the Town Chief gets vexed.
Premise 2: Sumo is not drinking palm wine. Saki is drinking palm wine.
Question: Is the Town Chief vexed?

P: The Town Chief was not vexed on that day.
E: The Town Chief was not vexed? What is the reason?
P: The reason is that he doesn't love Sumo.
E: He doesn't love Sumo? Go on with the reason.
P: The reason is that Sumo's drinking is a hard time. That is why when he drinks palm wine, the Town Chief gets vexed. But sometimes when Saki drinks palm juice he will not give a hard time to people. He goes to lie down to sleep. At that rate people do not get vexed with him. But people who drink and go about fighting— the Town Chief cannot love them in the town. (p. 487)

Scribner observed that the man gave the wrong answer to the question if the question is considered purely in terms of formal logic. However, he *did* use logic in justifying his answer. In logical format the participant's reasoning is as follows:

Sumo's drinking gives people a hard time.
Saki's drinking does not give people a hard time.
People do not get vexed when they are not given a hard time.
The Town Chief is a person.
Therefore, the Town Chief is not vexed at Saki.

What is happening here is that the participant is using evidence from his own experience with Saki and Sumo (empirical evidence) and is ignoring evidence presented in the syllogism (theoretical evidence). The fact that people often base their responses on empirical evidence becomes clear when we ask them to explain their answers. For example, consider the following problem, presented to an illiterate woman from a remote area in Central Asia called Uzbekistan (Schribner, 1977).

Premise 1:	In the far north all bears are white.
Premise 2:	Novaya Zemyla is in the far north.
Question:	What color are the bears there?

The participant's response to this problem was, "You should ask the people who have been there and seen them. We always speak of only what we see, we don't talk about what we haven't seen." The woman's response makes it clear that she has a style of thinking that puts a high value on what one can know through direct experience. She did not see the question as a logical puzzle, but as a question to be answered empirically.

Much of the early cross-cultural work, such as Scribner's, compared people from traditional cultures, who were often uneducated, to educated people in the United States. Recently, a number of studies have compared the performance of U.S. participants to educated participants from a modern culture. Ara Norenzayan and coworkers (2002) compared reasoning in European American and Korean participants on a number of tasks. One task tested for the effects of the belief bias on reasoning. Participants were presented with valid and invalid syllogisms that had believable or nonbelievable conclusions. Here are two examples:

Valid syllogism: Believable conclusion

Premise 1:	No police dogs are old.
Premise 2:	Some highly trained dogs are old.
Conclusion:	Therefore, some highly trained dogs are not police dogs.

Valid syllogism: Nonbelievable conclusion

Premise 1:	All things that are made of plants are good for health.
Premise 2:	Cigarettes are made of plants.
Conclusion:	Therefore, cigarettes are good for health.

The participants read each syllogism and answered "yes" if they thought it was valid and "no" if they thought it wasn't. The results, shown in Figure 12.8, indicate that the Koreans were more affected by the believability of the conclusions. The figure, which shows results for the valid arguments, indicates that there was a slight drop in "valid" judgments when the conclusion was not believable for the European American participants, but a bigger drop for the Korean participants. (Note that there was no difference between cultures for the invalid syllogisms. Both groups had more valid responses to syllogisms with believable conclusions.)

Norenyazan interprets these results as showing that the European American participants were more likely to base their judgments on logic, whereas the Koreans used a more intuitive strategy. We will look further at possible reasons for cultural differences in a moment. First, let's consider a study that compares how European Americans, Asian Americans, and Korean participants performed on another task. For this task, participants were presented with deductive arguments, such as the following, that involved a typical member of a category:

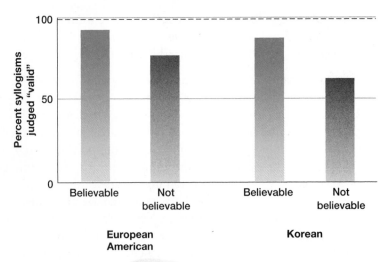

Figure 12.8 Cross-cultural study of the belief bias for valid syllogisms. If all answers were correct, all bars would be at 100 percent, as indicated by the dashed line. The lower level of "valid" responses for not believable conclusions compared to believable conclusions indicates an effect of the belief bias. The effect is slightly stronger for Korean participants (right pair of bars) than for European American participants (left pair of bars) (Norenzayan et al., 2002).

> All birds have an ulnar artery.
> Therefore, all eagles have an ulnar artery.

Participants also read other arguments that involved nontypical members of a category:

> All birds have an ulnar artery.
> Therefore, all penguins have an ulnar artery.

Participants were presented with one argument at a time and were told: "Read the argument. Assume that the facts are true and evaluate how convincing you believe each argument is. Rate convincingness on an 11-point scale." The results, in Figure 12.9, show that whether items were typical (like an eagle) or not typical (like a penguin) made no difference to the European American participants (the left pair of bars are about the same), but made some difference to the Asian Americans (compare the middle pair of bars), and even more difference to the Koreans (the right bars). This result was similar to the results for belief bias, in that the European American participants relied more on logic and less on content than the Koreans.

We do not yet fully understand why these differences among cultures occur, but it seems likely that some cultural differences between Asians and Westerners are caused by how children in these cultures are raised. Richard Nisbitt (2003), in a book aptly titled *The Geography of Thought*, suggest that East Asians are brought up in a culture that focuses on the social environment and is more collective or group oriented. In contrast, Westerners are less focused on social relations, more concerned with individuals and objects, and are encouraged to develop categories and rules to govern them.

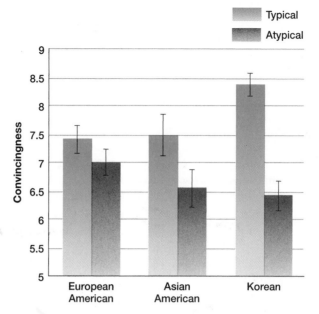

Figure 12.9 The effect of "typicality" on judging the convincingness of deductive arguments. Typicality has little effect on European American participants, but does have an effect on Asian American and Korean participants. All of the deductive arguments presented in this experiment were valid. (Reprinted from A. Norenzayan et al., "Cultural Preferences for Formal Versus Intuitive Reasoning," from *Cognitive Science, 26,* pp. 653–684, Figure 6. Copyright © 2002 with permission from the Cognitive Science Society.)

Nisbett relates these differences in culture to many different cognitive behaviors. For the experiments just described, the European Americans focusing on rules may be making them less susceptible to the belief bias (Figure 12.7) and less susceptible to having the type of bird (or other category) make any difference in their reasoning (Figure 12.8). Whatever the reason for cultural differences, experiments such as these strengthen the idea that people in different cultures may, for some kinds of problems, use different strategies for reasoning.

The categorical syllogisms we have been considering so far have premises and conclusions that begin with *All*, *Some*, or *No*. We will now consider another type of syllogism called conditional syllogisms, in which the first premise has the form "If . . . then."

DEDUCTIVE REASONING: THINKING CONDITIONALLY

Conditional syllogisms have two premises and a conclusion, like the ones we have been discussing, but the first premise has the form "If . . . then." This kind of deductive reasoning is common in everyday life. For example, let's say that you lent your friend Steve $20 but he has never paid you back. Knowing Steve, you might say to yourself that you knew this would happen. Stated in the form of a syllogism, your reasoning might look like this:

If I lend Steve $20, then I won't get it back.
I lent Steve $20.
Therefore, I won't get my $20 back.

Forms of Conditional Syllogisms

There are four major types of conditional syllogisms. Each of them is listed in the demonstration that follows, as real-life examples, along with abstract terms *p* and *q* indicated in parenthesis. For conditional syllogisms, the notations *p* and *q* are typically used instead of *A* and *B*, with *p*, the first, or "If," term in "If p then q" being called the antecedent, and *q*, the second, or "then," term, being called the consequent.

◼ Demonstration

Conditional Syllogisms

All four of the syllogisms that follow begin with the following first premise:

If I study, then I'll get a good grade on the exam. (if p then q)

Each syllogism is indicated by a second premise and a conclusion. Indicate which are valid and which ones are not valid.

1. I studied. (p)
   Therefore, I got a good grade on the exam. (q)
2. I didn't get a good grade. (not q)
   Therefore, I didn't study. (not p)
3. I didn't study. (not p)
   Therefore, I didn't get a good grade. (not q)
4. I got a good grade. (q)
   Therefore, I studied. (p)

The answers, shown in Figure 12.10 and Table 12.1, indicate that the first two syllogisms, 1 and 2, are valid and the last two, 3 and 4, are invalid. The two valid syllogisms have names. Syllogism 1 is called *modus ponens,* which means *method of affirming* in Latin (because the antecedent, p, in the second premise is affirmed). Syllogism 2 is called *modus tollens,* which means *method of denying* in Latin (because the consequent, q, in the second premise is negated—not q). We will return to these two types of syllogisms when we consider how well people are able to determine the validity of syllogisms, but first let's consider why 3 and 4 are not valid.

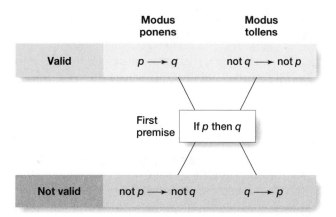

Figure 12.10 The first premise of a conditional syllogism is shown in the middle. Four different second premises and conclusions are shown above and below the box. For example p → q stands for "p occurred" (second premise), therefore "q occurred" (conclusion). The two conditions on the top, called *modus ponens* and *modus tollens*, are valid. The two on the bottom are not valid.

	Table 12.1	BASIC FORMS OF CONDITIONAL SYLLOGISMS			

The first premise, *If p then q*, is the same in all four cases.

No.	Second Premise	Conclusion	Type	Valid?	% Correct
1	p	q	*Modus ponens* (method of affirming)	Yes	97
2	Not q	Not p	*Modus tollens* (method of denying)	Yes	60
3	Not p	Not q	Denying the antecedent	No	40
4	q	p	Affirming the consequent	No	40

From Evans et al., 1993.

Syllogism 3 is called denying the antecedent, because p is negated (not p) in the second premise. This conclusion is invalid, because even though you didn't study, it is still possible that you could have received a good grade. Can you think of any situations in which you didn't study, but got a good grade on the exam anyway? Perhaps you didn't study, but the exam was easy, or maybe you knew the material because it was about experience you gained in your job. If that explanation is not convincing, consider the following syllogism, which has the same form as 3:

5. If the chicken walks across the road, it will get to the other side. (if p then q)
   The chicken did not walk across the road. (not p)
   Therefore, the chicken is not on the other side. (not q)

In this case, the conclusion does not follow because even if the chicken didn't walk across the road, perhaps a big gust of wind blew it across, or someone carried it across.

Syllogism 4 is called **affirming the consequent,** because q is affirmed in the second premise. As for syllogism 3, studying is not always associated with getting a good grade, therefore the conclusion is not valid (try the chicken scenario for this one).

How well did you evaluate the syllogisms in the demonstration? The results shown in the right column of Table 12.1 indicate that most people (close to 100 percent in most experiments) correctly judge that *modus ponens* is valid, but that performance is lower on *modus tollens* (which is also valid) and the other two (which are not). These figures are the average results from many studies in which the letters p and q were used for the antecedent and the consequent. As we will see in the next section, people's performance in conditional reasoning tasks can be greatly affected by whether the task is stated abstractly or concretely, and also by knowledge possessed by the person who is evaluating the syllogism.

Why People Make Errors in Conditional Reasoning: The Wason Four-Card Problem

If reasoning from conditional syllogisms depended only on applying rules of formal logic, then it wouldn't matter whether the syllogism was stated in terms of abstract symbols, such as *p*'s and *q*'s, or in terms of real-world items, such as people studying or chickens crossing a road. However, we know that people are often better at judging the validity of syllogisms when real-world items are substituted for abstract symbols, and we also know that real-world items can sometimes lead to errors, as when people are influenced by the belief bias. Evidence for the effect of using real-world items in a conditional-reasoning problem is provided by a series of experiments involving the **Wason four-card problem.** Try this task in the following demonstration.

◼ Demonstration

CogLab Wason Four-Card Problem

Wason Selection Task

Four cards are shown in Figure 12.11. There is a letter on one side of each card and a number on the other side. Your task is to indicate the minimum number of cards you would need to turn over to test the following rule: If there is a vowel on one side, then there is an even number on the other side. ◼

If vowel, then even number.

Figure 12.11 The Wason four-card problem (Wason, 1966). Follow the directions in the demonstration and try this problem.

Which cards did you pick? After writing down your answer, try the following problem:

Four cards are shown in Figure 12.12. Each card has an age on one side and the name of a beverage on the other side. Imagine you are a police officer who is applying the rule "If a person is drinking beer, then he or she must be over 19 years old." Which of the cards in Figure 12.12 must be turned over to determine whether the rule is being followed?

If drinking beer, then over 19 years old.

Figure 12.12 The beer/drinking-age version of the four-card problem (Griggs & Cox, 1982)

Which cards did you pick for this one? Did you find it easier to decide which cards to pick when the task was posed in terms of drinking beer rather than in the more abstract statement in terms of letters and numbers? When Wason (1966) posed the letter-number task (which we will call the abstract task from now on), 53 percent of his participants indicated that the E must be turned over. This is correct because turning over the E directly tests the rule. (If there is an E, then there must be an even number, so if there is an odd number on the other side, this would prove the rule to be false.) However, another card needs to be turned over to fully test the rule. Forty-six percent of Wason's participants indicated that in addition to the E, the 4 would need to be turned over. The problem with this answer is that if a vowel is on the other side of the card, this is consistent with the rule, but if a consonant is on the other side, turning over the 4 has tells us nothing about the rule, since having a consonant on one side and a vowel on the other does not violate the rule. As shown in Figure 12.13a, only 4 percent of Wason's participants came up with the

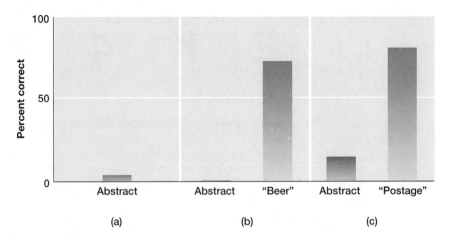

Figure 12.13 Performance on different versions of the four-card problem. (a) Abstract version in Figure 12.11. (b) Abstract version and the Beer version in Figure 12.12. (c) Abstract version and the postage version in Figure 12.14. Performance is better on concrete versions of the problem.

correct answer that the card with the 7 also needs to be turned over. Turning over the 7 is important because revealing a vowel would disconfirm the rule.

The key to solving the card problem is to be aware of the **falsification principle:** *To test a rule, it is necessary to look for situations that falsify the rule.* As you can see from Table 12.2, the only two cards that have the potential to achieve this are the E and the 7. Thus, these are the only two cards that need to be turned over to test the rule.

Table 12.2	OUTCOMES OF TURNING OVER EACH CARD IN THE WASON TASK

The Rule: If there is a vowel on one side, then there is an even number on the other side.

If turn over . . .	And the result is . . .	Then this _____ the rule.
E	even	confirms
E	odd	**falsifies**
K	even	is irrelevant to*
K	odd	is irrelevant to
4	vowel	confirms
4	consonant	is irrelevant to
7	vowel	**falsifies**
7	consonant	is irrelevant to

*This outcome is irrelevant because the rule does not say anything about what should be on the card if a consonant is on one side. Similar reasoning holds for all of the other irrelevant cases.

Stating the Four-Card Task in Real-World Terms: The Role of "Regulations"

The Wason task has generated a great deal of research. One reason for the degree of interest in this problem is because it is a conditional-reasoning task. (Note that the problem is stated as an "If . . . then" statement.) But the main reason researchers are interested in this problem is that they want to know why participants make so many errors.

One way researchers have gone about answering this question is to determine how participants perform when the problem is restated in real-world terms. In one of these experiments Richard Griggs and James Cox (1982) used the beer/drinking-age problem from the demonstration, which is identical to the abstract version except that concrete everyday terms (beer, soda, and ages) are substituted for the letters and numbers. They found that 73 percent of their participants provided the correct response: It is necessary to turn over the "beer" and the "16 years" cards. In contrast, none of their participants answered the abstract task correctly (Figure 12.13b). Why is the concrete task easier than the abstract task? Apparently, being able to relate the beer task to regulations about drinking makes it easier to realize that the "16 years" card must be turned over. (The participants in this experiment were from Florida, where the drinking age was 19 at the time.)

The idea that knowing about regulations helps solve the Wason task has also been demonstrated using the cards in Figure 12.14 and the following instructions:

> Pretend you are a postal worker sorting letters. According to postal regulations, if a letter is sealed, it must have a 5d stamp on it (*d* is pence in Great Britain). Which of the four envelopes in Figure 12.14 would you have to turn over to determine whether the rule is being obeyed?

The answer to the English postal version of the problem is that the sealed envelope and the one with a 4d stamp on it must be turned over to check the rule. When Philip Johnson-Laird and coworkers (1972) presented this problem to English participants who were familiar with an actual postal regulation similar to the one stated in the problem, performance was 81 percent correct, compared to 15 percent for the standard task (Figure 12.13c). When Griggs and Cox (1982) tested American participants on the postal regulation task, they did not observe the large improvement in performance observed for the English participants. The reason for this result appears to be that the American participants were not familiar with postal regulations that specified different postage for opened and sealed envelopes.

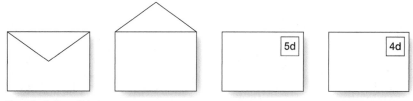

If sealed, then 5d stamp.

Figure 12.14 Postage version of the four-card problem (Johnson-Laird et al., 1972).

Pragmatic Reasoning Schemas in the Wason Task: The Role of "Permissions"

Patricia Cheng and Keith Holyoak (1985) took the idea that understanding regulations improves performance in real-world versions of the Wason task a step further by proposing the concept of pragmatic reasoning schemas. A **pragmatic reasoning schema** is a way of thinking about cause and effect in the world that is learned as part of experiencing everyday life. One schema that people learn is the **permission schema,** which states that if a person satisfies condition A, then they get to carry out action B. The permission schema for the drinking problem, "If you are 19 then you got to drink beer," is something that most of the participants in this experiment had learned, so they were able to apply that schema to the card task.

This idea that people apply a real-life schema like the permissions schema to the card task makes it easier to understand the difference between the abstract version of the card task and the "drinking beer" or "postal regulation" versions. The abstract task is set up so that participants approach it as a problem in which their goal is to indicate whether an abstract statement about letters and numbers is true. But the drinking-beer task and postal-regulation tasks are set up so participants approach it as problems in which their goal is to be sure that a person has permission to drink alcohol or mail a letter. Apparently, activating the permission schema helps people to focus attention on the far right card, which participants often ignore for the abstract task.

To test this idea that a permissions schema may be involved in reasoning about the card task, Chung and Holyoak ran an experiment with two groups of participants who both saw the cards on Figure 12.15. One of the groups was read the following directions:

> You are an immigration officer at the International Airport in Manila, capital of the Philippines. Among the documents you have to check is a sheet called Form H. One side of this form indicates whether the passenger is entering the country or in transit, and the other side of the form lists names of tropical diseases. You have to make sure that if the form says "Entering" on one side, that the other side includes cholera among the list of diseases.* Which of the following forms would you have to turn over to check? Indicate only those that you need to check to be sure. [*The asterisk is explained in the text that follows.]

Sixty-two percent of the participants in this group chose the correct cards ("Entering" and "Typhoid, Hepatitis"). Participants in the other group saw the same cards and heard

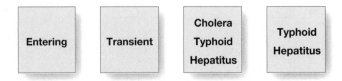

If entering, then cholera is listed.

Figure 12.15 Cholera version of the four-card problem (Cheng & Holyoak, 1985).

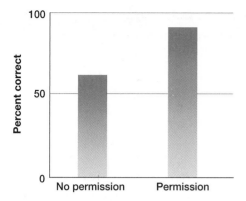

Figure 12.16 Results of Cheng and Holyoak's (1985) experiment that used two versions of the cholera problem. When "permissions" are implied by the instructions, performance is better.

the same instructions as the first group, but with the following changes: Instead of saying that the form listed tropical diseases, it said that the form listed *inoculations the travelers had received in the past 6 months*. In addition, the following sentence was added where indicated by the *: *This is to ensure that entering passengers are protected against the disease.*

The changes in the instructions were calculated to achieve a very important effect: Instead of just checking to see if the correct diseases are listed on the form, the immigration officer is checking to see whether the travelers have the inoculations necessary to *give them permission* to enter the country. The idea behind these instructions was to activate the participants' permissions schema, and apparently this did happen, because 91 percent of the participants in this condition picked the correct cards (Figure 12.16).

An Evolutionary Approach to the Four-Card Problem: The Role of "Cheating"

One of the things we have learned in considering various results from cognitive psychology research is that one set of data can be interpreted in different ways by different investigators. We saw this in the case of the misinformation effect in Chapter 7, in which memory errors were caused by presenting misleading postevent information (MPI) after a person witnessed an event. We saw that one group of researchers explained these errors by stating that the MPI distorted existing memories (Loftus, 1993), but that another group claimed that the effect was due to the formation of entirely new memories (McClosky & Zarogoza, 1985).

Our consideration of the Wason four-card problem has now led us to another controversy, in which different explanations have been offered to explain the results of various experiments. For example, a proposed alternative to the idea of a permissions schema is that performance on the Wason task is governed by a built-in cognitive program for detecting cheating. Let's consider the rationale behind this idea.

Leda Cosmides and John Tooby (1992) are among psychologists who have an **evolutionary perspective on cognition.** They argue that we can trace many properties of our minds to the evolutionary principles of natural selection. According to natural selection, adaptive characteristics—characteristics that help a person or animal survive to pass their genes to the next generation—will, over time, become a basic characteristic of humans (see Chapter 3, page 91, for a discussion of this idea, as applied to perception). This idea was originally proposed by Charles Darwin based on observations of physical characteristics. For example, Darwin observed that birds in a specific area had beaks with shapes that were adapted to enable them to obtain the food available in that area.

Applying this idea to cognition, it follows that a highly adaptive feature of the mind would, through a similar evolutionary process, become a basic characteristic of the mind. One such characteristic, according to the evolutionary approach, is related to the idea of social-exchange theory, which states that an important aspect of human behavior is the ability for two people to cooperate in a way that is beneficial to both people. Thus, when caveman Morg lends caveman Eng his carving tool in exchange for some food that Eng has brought back from the hunt, both people benefit from the exchange.

Everything works well in social exchange as long as each person is receiving a benefit for whatever he or she is giving up. However, problems arise when someone cheats. Thus, if Morg gives up his carving tool, but Eng fails to give him the food, this does not bode well for Morg. It is essential, therefore, that people be able to detect cheating behavior so they can avoid it. According to the evolutionary approach, people who can do this will have a better chance of surviving, so "detecting cheating" has become a part of the brain's cognitive makeup.

The evolutionary approach proposes that the Wason problem can be understood in terms of cheating. Thus, people do well in the postal version of the four-card problem (Figure 12.14) because they can detect cheaters—someone who mails a letter with incorrect postage. Similarly, people do well in the cholera task (Figure 12.15) because they can detect someone who cheats by entering the country without a cholera shot.

To test the idea that cheating (and not permissions) is the important variable in the four-card problem, Cosmides and Tooby (1992) devised a number of four-card scenarios that involved cheating. A feature of these scenarios is that they involved unfamiliar situations. Remember that one idea behind the permissions schema is that people perform well because they are familiar with various rules.

To create unfamiliar situations, Cosmides and Tooby created a number of experiments that took place in a culture called the Kulwane. Participants in these experiments read a story about this culture, which led to the conditional statement, "If a man eats cassava root, then he must have a tattoo on his face." Participants saw the following four cards: (1) eats cassava roots; (2) eats molo nuts; (3) tattoo; and (4) no tattoo. Their task was to determine which cards they needed to turn over to determine whether the conditional statement above was being adhered to. This is a situation unfamiliar to the participants, and one in which cheating could occur, because a man who eats the cassava root without a tattoo would be cheating.

Cosmides and Tooby found that participants' performance was high on this task, even though it was unfamiliar. They also ran other experiments in which they showed that participants did better for statements that involved cheating than for other statements that could not be interpreted in this way (Cosmides, 1989; also see Gigerenzer & Hug, 1992).

However, in response to this proposal, other researchers have created scenarios that involve unfamiliar permissions rules. For example, Ken Manktelow and David Over (1990) tested people using a rule that said, "If you clean up spilt blood, you must wear gloves." Even though this "permission" statement is one that most people have not heard before, and which does not involve cheating, stating the problem in this way caused an increase in performance, just like many of the other examples of the Wason task that we have described.

The controversy among those who feel permissions are important, those who focus on cheating, and researchers who have proposed other explanations for the results of the

Wason task has yet to be resolved, because evidence has been presented for and against every mechanism that has been proposed (Johnson-Laird, 1999b; Manktelow, 1999). What we are left with is the important finding that the context within which conditional reasoning occurs makes a big difference. Stating the four-card problem in terms of situations that are familiar or that bring into play certain ways of thinking about a problem can often generate better reasoning than statements that are stated abstractly, or that people cannot relate to in some way. However, familiarity is not always necessary for conditional reasoning (as in the tattoo problem), and situations have also been devised in which people's performance is not improved, even in familiar situations (Griggs, 1983; Manktelow & Evans, 1979).

Sometimes controversies such as this one are frustrating to read about because after all, aren't we looking for "answers"? But another way to look at controversies such as this is that they illustrate the complexity of the human mind and the challenge facing cognitive psychologists who are working to understand this complexity. Remember, that this book began by describing an experiment by Donders, which involved simply indicating when a light was presented or whether the light was presented on the right or on the left. We described Donders's experiment to illustrate the basic principle that cognitive psychologists must infer the workings of the mind from behavioral observations. It is fitting, therefore, that in this, the last chapter of the book, we are now describing a task that involves complex reasoning, but which illustrates exactly the same principle—that the workings of the mind must be inferred from behavioral observations.

What we are seeing in this controversy over how people deal with the Wason task is a situation in which a number of different hypotheses about what is happening in the mind can be plausibly inferred from the behavioral evidence. Perhaps, in the end, the actual mechanism will be something that has yet to be proposed, or perhaps the mind, in its complexity, has a number of different ways of approaching the Wason task, depending on the situation.

 Test Yourself 12.1

1. What is deductive reasoning? What does it mean to say that the conclusion to a syllogism is "valid"? How can a conclusion be valid but not true? True but not valid?
2. How can the validity or nonvalidity of a categorical syllogism be determined by Euler circles?
3. What is the difference between the normative and descriptive approaches to studying deductive reasoning?
4. How well can people judge the validity of syllogisms? Why are psychologists interested in the errors that people make in judging validity?
5. What are the atmosphere effect and belief bias?
6. What is a mental model for reasoning? Explain how this model can be applied to the Artists, Beekeepers, and Chemists syllogism on page 438.

7. What do the results of cross-cultural studies indicate about the effect of culture on the belief bias? What do cross-cultural studies tell us about the degree to which people from different cultures are influenced by the content of syllogisms, as opposed to the logical structure of the syllogism?

8. What is a conditional syllogism? Which of the four types of syllogisms described in the chapter are valid, which are not valid, and how well can people judge the validity of each type?

9. What is the Wason four-card problem, and what do the results of experiments that have used abstract and concrete versions of the problem indicate about the roles of (a) concreteness; (b) knowledge of regulations; and (c) permissions schemas in solving this problem?

10. How has the evolutionary approach to cognition been applied to the Wason four-card problem? What can we conclude from all of the experiments on the Wason problem?

INDUCTIVE REASONING: REACHING CONCLUSIONS FROM EVIDENCE

We have seen that problems that require deductive reasoning have a specific form and that the task in deductive reasoning is to determine whether a certain conclusion follows from the premises. In deductive reasoning conclusions follow directly from premises and it is possible to determine with logical certainty whether a conclusion arrived at using deductive reasoning is or is not valid.

The Nature of Inductive Reasoning

While in deductive reasoning each premise is stated as a fact, such as "All ants have four legs," in inductive reasoning the premises are based on observation of one or more specific cases, and we generalize from these cases to a more general conclusion. This is illustrated by these three inductive arguments:

Observation: All the crows I've seen in Pittsburgh are black, and recently I visited my brother in Washington, DC, and the crows I saw there are black too.

Conclusion: I think it is a pretty good bet that all crows are black.

Observation: Every time the Boston Red Sox have been in first place in June or July and the Yankees have been in second place, the Yankees have gone on to win the pennant. It's now July and the Red Sox are in first place and the Yankees are in second place.

Conclusion: I think it is inevitable that the Yankees will win the pennant this year.

Observation: Here in Nashville, the sun has risen every morning.

Conclusion: The sun is going to rise in Nashville tomorrow.

Notice that there is a certain logic to each of these arguments, but that some of the arguments are more convincing than others. How would you rank these arguments from weakest to strongest?

Determining the Strength of an Inductive Argument

In evaluating inductive arguments, we do not consider validity, as we did for deductive arguments, but instead we decide how strong the argument is. Strong arguments are more likely to result in conclusions that are true, weak arguments, to result in conclusions that are not as likely to be true. Remember that for inductive arguments we are dealing with what is *probably* true, not what is *definitely* true.

There are a number of factors that can contribute to the strength of an inductive argument. Among them are the following:

- *Number of observations:* The argument about the crows is made stronger by adding the Washington, DC, observations to the Pittsburgh observations. Adding more observations would strengthen it further. The conclusion about the sun rising in Nashville is extremely strong because it is supported by a very large number of observations.

- *Representativeness of observations:* How well do the observations about a particular category represent all of the members of that category? Clearly, the crows example suffers from a lack of representativeness because it does not consider crows from other parts of the country. If there is a rare blue crow in California, then the conclusion is not true. For the Red Sox/Yankees example, we can ask whether the situation this year is similar to the ones observed in the past. Perhaps this year the Red Sox have some hot new players, and some of the Yankee stars are injured, so the Sox might have a better chance of winning it all.

- *Quality of the evidence:* Stronger evidence results in stronger conclusions. For example, although the conclusion that "The sun will rise in Nashville" is extremely strong because of the number of observations, it becomes even stronger when we consider scientific descriptions of how the earth rotates on its axis and revolves around the sun. Thus, adding the observation that "scientific measurements of the rotation of the earth indicate that every time the earth rotates the sun will appear to rise" strengthens the conclusion even further.

The idea of bringing in scientific evidence to support an inductive argument illustrates the connection between inductive and deductive reasoning because the scientific observation about the rotation of the earth can be stated as the following deductive syllogism:

If the earth rotates around its axis, then the place where Nashville is located will experience sunrise for each rotation.
The earth rotates on its axis.
Therefore, Nashville will experience sunrise for each rotation.

The possibility of using scientific evidence in both inductive and deductive arguments illustrates that although it is important to distinguish between the two types of reasoning, the borderline between them can sometimes become fuzzy. We will describe the link between inductive and deductive reasoning further as we consider how inductive reasoning is used in science.

Inductive Reasoning in Science   Inductive reasoning is the basic procedure used to make scientific discoveries. The goal in science is to discover something new. To achieve this, we often make systematic observations. These observations can include taking a poll about political attitudes, observing social behavior in a shopping mall, or doing a laboratory experiment on the Wason four-card problem. If these observations yield interesting data, these observations can be generalized to a larger population and perhaps be used to create a theory that goes beyond the specific observations.

In most scientific research, and especially in psychology, we base our conclusions on more than one observation. We test a large number of participants, and may run an experiment in a number of different ways. Added participants and obtaining similar results in variations of an experiment all strengthen our conclusions. The strength of scientific conclusions also depends on the representativeness of our observations.

An obvious example of the importance of representative observations is determining attitudes by polling. It would clearly be a mistake to draw conclusions about political attitudes in the United States based on a poll of Oklahoma high school seniors. To make a statement about attitudes in the United States it is necessary to elicit opinions from a representative cross-section of people in the United States. Similarly, conclusions from laboratory experiments in cognitive psychology can be safely generalized only to the population represented in the sample of people who participate in the experiment. Thus, it would be a mistake to say that the results for the beer/drinking-age version of the Wason four-card experiment will generalize to people in a society in which there are no laws regulating drinking.

Inductive reasoning is not only used to make the jump from specific observations to more general conclusions, but to create hypotheses for further experiments. An example of how inductive reasoning has been used to devise scientific experiments is provided by the way Cheng and Holyoak devised the cholera experiment we described on page 450 (Holyoak, 2003). The first step was to observe that people's performance on the Wason task improves when the task is stated in terms of receiving "permission" to do something, as is the case in the beer/drinking-age and stamp/sealed-envelope versions of the task.

Based on this observation, Cheng and Holyoak reasoned that making people more aware that permissions are involved when they are trying to solve the Wason task should improve their performance. They devised a way to test this idea by creating the scenario for the cholera problem, which included one condition in which permissions were not emphasized and another condition in which they were. We can state the reasoning behind their thinking about this experiment (which, as we have described above, was created using inductive reasoning), by the following *deductive* syllogism:

If a permissions schema is activated, then performance on the Wason task should improve.

In this experiment, one of the groups will read a sentence that will activate a permissions schema.

Therefore, the performance of this group will improve.

As we saw when we described the Chung and Holyoak "cholera" experiment on page 450, adding a sentence that was designed to activate a permissions schema did, in fact, increase performance, thereby confirming the "If . . . then" premise of the conditional argument. Thus, inductive reasoning can be used to generate a hypothesis about what might be going on, and deductive reasoning sets forth the rationale of the experiment that is designed to test this hypothesis.

Inductive Reasoning in Everyday Life

Inductive reasoning is not used just for creating scientific experiments, but for determining many of the choices we make in everyday life. For example, Sarah has observed, from a course she took with Professor X, that he asked a lot of questions about experimental procedures on his exams. Based on this observation, Sarah concludes that the exam she is about to take in another of Professor X's courses will probably be similar. Or Sam has bought merchandise from mail-order company Y before and got good service, so he places another order based on the assumption that he will continue to get good service. Thus, anytime we make a prediction about *what will happen* based on our observations about *what has happened in the past*, we are using inductive reasoning.

The idea that we make predictions and choices based on past experience makes sense, especially when stated in terms of familiar situations such as studying for an exam or buying merchandise by mail. However, we make so many assumptions about the world, based on past experience, that we are using inductive reasoning constantly, often without even realizing it. For example, did you run a stress test on the chair you are sitting in to be sure it wouldn't collapse when you sat down? Probably not. You assumed, based on your past experience with chairs, that it would not collapse. This is an example of the kind of inductive reasoning you do every day that is so automatic that you are not aware that any kind of "reasoning" is happening at all. Think about how time consuming it would be if you had to approach every experience as if you were having it for the first time. Inductive reasoning provides the mechanism for using past experience to guide present behavior.

When people use past experience to guide present behavior, they often use shortcuts to help them reach conclusions rapidly. After all, we don't have the time or energy to stop and gather every bit of information that we need to be 100 percent certain that every conclusion we reach is correct. These shortcuts take the form of heuristics, which are "rules of thumb" that are likely to provide the correct answer to a problem, but which are not foolproof.

The idea of using heuristics may sound familiar because we have seen that people use heuristics to help them understand what they are seeing (Chapter 3, page 82), what happened in the past (Chapter 7, page 247), and what a sentence means (Chapter 10, page 362).

check out heuristics!!

There are a number of heuristics that people use in reasoning that often lead to the correct conclusion, but that sometimes do not. We will now describe two of these heuristics, the availability heuristic and the representative heuristic.

The Availability Heuristic

◣ Demonstration

Which Is More Prevalent?

Try the following two problems.

- Which is more prevalent, words that begin with the letter *r*, or words in which *r* is the third letter?
- Each item in the following list consists of two different possible causes of death. Your task is to judge which cause of death you consider more likely for people in the United States. Think about this question in this way: Imagine you randomly picked someone in the United States. Will that person be more likely to die next year from cause A or cause B?

Cause A	Cause B
Homicide	Appendicitis
Auto-train collision	Drowning
Measles	Smallpox
Botulism	Asthma
Asthma	Tornado
Appendicitis	Pregnancy

Things That Are More Easily Remembered Are Judged to Be More Prevalent

When faced with a choice, we are often guided by what we remember from the past. The availability heuristic states that we base our judgments of the frequency of events on what events come to mind. Another way of defining the availability heuristic is that events that are more easily remembered are judged as being more probable than events that are less easily remembered (Tversky & Kahneman, 1973). Consider, for example, the problems we posed in the demonstration. When participants were asked to judge whether there are more words with *r* in the first position or the third, 70 percent stated that there are more words that begin with *r*, even though in reality there are three times more words that have *r* in the third position (Tversky & Kahneman, 1973).

Figure 12.17 shows the results of experiments in which participants were asked to judge the relative prevalence of various causes of death (Lichtenstein et al., 1978). The height of the bars indicates the percentage of participants who picked the least likely alternative. The key below the graph indicates the pairs for each bar, with the least likely cause indicated first, followed by the more likely cause. The number in parenthesis indicates the relative frequency of the more-likely cause compared to the less-likely cause. For example, the far

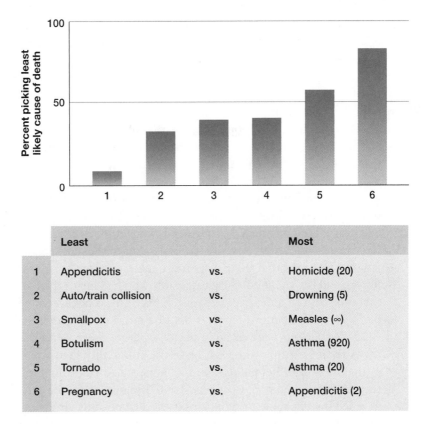

Figure 12.17 Likely-causes-of-death experiment results. Pairs of "causes of death" are listed below the graph, with the least likely cause on the left. The number in parentheses on the right indicates how many more times more people were actually killed by the cause on the right. The bars in the graph indicate the number of people who judged the *least likely* alternative in each pair as causing the most deaths. (Adapted from Lichtenstein et al., 1978.)

left bar indicates that 9 percent of the participants thought it was more likely that a person would die from appendicitis compared to homicide. However, actual mortality data indicate that 20 times more people die from homicide than from appendicitis. Thus, in this case, 9 percent of the participants made an incorrect judgment, but most of the participants made an accurate judgment regarding the most likely cause of death.

For the other causes of death, a substantial proportion of the participants misjudged which cause is more likely. In these cases, large numbers of errors were associated with causes that were publicized by the media. For example, 58 percent thought that more deaths were caused by tornados than by asthma, when in reality, 20 times more people die from asthma than from tornados. Particularly striking is that fact that 41 percent of the participants thought that botulism caused more deaths than asthma, even though 920 times more people die of asthma.

The explanation for these misjudgments appears to be linked to availability. When you try to think of words that begin with *r* or that have *r* in the third position, it is much easier to think of words that begin with *r* (run, rain, real . . .) than words that have *r* in their third position (word, car, arranged . . .). When someone dies of botulism or tornados it is front-page news, whereas deaths from asthma go virtually unnoticed by the general public (Lichtenstein et al., 1978).

An experiment by Stuart McKelvie (1997) demonstrates the availability heuristic in another way. McKelvie presented lists of 26 names to participants. In the "famous men" condition, 12 of the names were famous men (Ronald Reagan, Mick Jagger) and 14 were nonfamous women. In the "famous women" condition, 12 of the names were famous women (Tina Turner, Beatrix Potter) and 14 were nonfamous men. When participants were asked to estimate whether there were more males or more females in the list they had heard, their answer was influenced by whether they had heard the male-famous list or the female-famous list. Seventy-seven percent of the participants who had heard the male-famous list stated that there were more males in their list (notice that there were actually fewer), and 81 percent of the participants who had heard the female-famous list stated that there were more females in their list. This result is consistent with the availability heuristic, because the famous names would be more easily remembered and would stand out when participants were asked to decide whether there were more male or female names.

A recent example of operation of the availability heuristic in everyday life is the drop in the number of people flying on commercial airlines that occurred after the 9/11 terrorist attacks. The persistent images of airplanes smashing into the World Trade Center have led many people to avoid air travel in favor of driving even though, according to the National Transportation Safety Board, the fatality rate is about 500 times greater for driving than for flying in a commercial airplane. While factors other than thinking about safety are undoubtedly involved in the drop in air travel, it is likely that the ready availability of images and descriptions of this disaster is one of the factors involved.

Illusory Correlations   We are often aware of correlations between the occurrences of two events. You might, for example, know from past observations that when it is cloudy and there is a certain smell in the air, it is likely to rain later in the day. Being aware of correlations can be extremely useful. If you have observed that your boss is more likely to grant your requests if he or she is in a good mood, you can use this knowledge to determine the best time to ask for a raise.

While knowledge of correlations between events can be useful, sometimes people fall into the trap of creating illusory correlations. **Illusory correlations** occur when a correlation between two events appears to exist, but in reality the correlation doesn't exist or is much weaker than you assume it to be.

Illusory correlations can occur when we expect two things to be related, and so we fool ourselves into thinking they are related even if they are not. These expectations often take the form of **stereotypes**—an oversimplified generalization about a group or class of people that often focuses on the negative. Often, people's stereotype about the characteristics of a particular group leads them to pay particular attention to behaviors associated with that stereotype, and this attention creates an illusory correlation, which reinforces the stereotype. This is related to the availability heuristic because selective attention to the stereotypical behaviors makes these behaviors more "available" (Chapman & Chapman, 1969; Hamilton, 1981).

We can appreciate how illusory correlations reinforce stereotypes by considering the stereotype that gay males are effeminate. A person who believes this stereotype might pay particular attention to effeminate gay characters on TV programs or in movies, and to situations in which they see a person who they know is gay acting effeminate. Although these observations support a correlation between being gay and being effeminate, the person has ignored the large number of cases in which gay males are not effeminate. This may be because these cases do not stand out or because the person chooses not to pay attention to them. Whatever the reason, selectively taking into account only the situations that support the person's preconceptions can create the illusion that a correlation exists, when there may be only a weak correlation or none at all.

The Representativeness Heuristic

The representativeness heuristic is based on the idea that people often make judgments based on how much one event resembles another event.

Making Judgments Based on Resemblances   The **representativeness heuristic** states that the probability that an event A comes from class B can be determined by how well A resembles the properties of class B. To put this in more concrete terms, consider the following demonstration.

CogLab

**Typical
Reasoning**

◣ Demonstration

Judging Occupations

We randomly pick one male from the population of the United States. That male, Robert, wears glasses, speaks quietly, and reads a lot. Is it more likely that Robert is a librarian or a farmer? ■

When Amos Tversky and Daniel Kahneman (1974) presented this question in an experiment, more people guessed that Robert was a librarian. Apparently the description of Robert as wearing glasses, speaking quietly, and reading a lot matched these people's image of a typical librarian. Thus, they were influenced by the representativeness heuristic into basing their judgment on how closely they think Robert's characteristics (which correspond to "A" in our definition of the representativeness heuristic) match those of a "typical" librarian ("B"). However, in doing this they were ignoring another important source of information—the base rates of farmers and librarians in the population. The **base rate** is the relative proportion of different classes in the population. In 1972, when this experiment was carried out, there were many more male farmers than male librarians in the United States, and this base rate leads to the conclusion that it is much more likely that Robert is a farmer (remember that he was randomly chosen from the population).

One reaction to the farmer–librarian problem might be that the participants might not have been aware of the base rates for farmers and librarians, and so didn't have the information they needed to make a correct judgment. The effect of knowing the base rate has been demonstrated by presenting participants with the following problem:

> In a group of 100 people, there are 70 lawyers and 30 engineers. What is the chance that if we pick one person from the group at random that the person will be an engineer?

Participants given this problem correctly guessed that there would be a 30 percent chance of picking an engineer. However, for some participants the following description of the person was added:

> Jack is a 45-year-old man. He is married and has four children. He is generally conservative, careful, and ambitious. He shows no interest in political and social issues and spends most of his free time on his many hobbies, which include home carpentry, sailing, and mathematical puzzles.

Adding this description caused participants to greatly increase their estimate of the chances that the randomly picked person was an engineer. Apparently, when only base-rate information is available, people use that information to make their estimates. However, as soon as descriptive information is available, people disregard the base-rate information. In many cases this causes errors in reasoning, although it is important to note that descriptive information can sometimes be rich enough to justify giving it more weight than base-rate information. For example, if we also know that the person graduated from the University of Michigan with a degree in engineering, then it would make sense to guess that the person was an engineer, even though the base rate is only 30 percent.

Following is a demonstration that illustrates another characteristic of the representativeness heuristic.

◣ Demonstration

The Feminist Bank Teller

Linda is 31 years old, single, outspoken, and very bright. She majored in philosophy. As a student, she was deeply concerned with issues of discrimination and social justice, and also participated in antinuclear demonstrations. Which of the following alternatives is more probable?

1. Linda is a bank teller.
2. Linda is a bank teller and is active in the feminist movement.   ■

The correct answer to this problem is that it is more likely that Linda is a bank teller, but when Tversky and Kahneman (1983) posed this problem to their participants, 85 per-

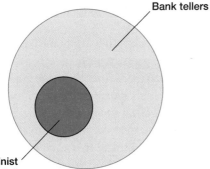

Bank tellers

Feminist bank tellers

Figure 12.18 Because feminist bank tellers are a subset of bank tellers, it is always more likely that someone is a bank teller than a feminist bank teller.

cent picked statement 2. It is easy to see why they did this. They were influenced by the representativeness heuristic, because the description of Linda fits people's idea of a typical feminist. However, in doing this they violated the **conjunction rule,** which states that the probability of a conjunction of two events (A and B) cannot be higher than the probability of the single constituents (A alone or B alone). For example, the probability that Anne has a red Corvette cannot be greater than the probability that she has a Corvette, because the two constituents together (red *and* Corvette) define a smaller number of cars than one constituent (Corvette) alone. Similarly, there are fewer feminist bank tellers than bank tellers, so stating that Linda is a bank teller *includes* the possibility that she is a *feminist* bank teller (Figure 12.18).

People tend to commit the conjunction fallacy even when it is clear that they understand the conjunction rule. The culprit is the representativeness heuristic; in the example just cited, the participants saw Linda's characteristics as more representative of *feminist bank teller* than *bank teller.*

Incorrectly Assuming That Small Samples Are Representative   People also make errors in reasoning by ignoring the importance of the size of the sample on which observations are based. The following demonstration illustrates the effect of sample size.

Demonstration

Male and Female Births

A certain town is served by two hospitals. In the larger hospital about 45 babies are born each day, and in the smaller hospital about 15 babies are born each day. As you know, about 50 percent of all babies are boys. However, the exact percentage varies from day to day. Sometimes it may be higher than 50 percent, sometimes lower.

For a period of 1 year, each hospital recorded the days on which more than 60 percent of the babies born were boys. Which hospital do you think recorded more such days?

- The larger hospital?
- The smaller hospital?
- About the same (that is, within 5 percent of each other)?

When participants were asked this question in an experiment (Tversky & Kahneman, 1974), 22 percent picked the larger hospital, 22 percent picked the smaller hospital, and 56 percent stated that there would be no difference. The group that thought there would be no difference was presumably assuming that the birthrate for males and females in both hospitals would be representative of the overall birthrate for males and females. However, the correct answer is that there would be more days with over 60 percent male births in the small hospital.

We can understand why this result would occur by considering a statistical rule called the **law of large numbers,** which states that the larger the number of individuals that are randomly drawn from a population, the more representative the resulting group will be of the entire population. Conversely, samples of small numbers of individuals will be less representative of the population. Thus, in the hospital problem it is more likely that the percentage of boys born on any given day will be near 50 percent in the large hospital and farther from 50 percent in the small hospital. To make this conclusion clear, imagine that there is a very small hospital that records only one birth each day. Over a period of a year there will be 365 births, with about 50 percent being boys and 50 percent being girls. However, on any given day, there will be either 100 percent boys or 100 percent girls—clearly percentages that are not representative of the overall population. The problem for reasoning, however, is that people often assume representativeness holds for small samples, and this results in errors in reasoning. (See Gigerenzer & Hoffrage, 1995; Gigerenzer & Todd, 1999, for additional perspectives on how statistical thinking and heuristics operate in reasoning.)

The Confirmation Bias

One of the major roadblocks to accurate reasoning is the **confirmation bias,** our tendency to selectively look for information that conforms to our hypothesis and to overlook information that argues against it. This effect was demonstrated by Wason (1960), who presented participants with the following instructions:

> You will be given three numbers which conform to a simple rule that I have in mind. . . . Your aim is to discover this rule by writing down sets of three numbers together with your reasons for your choice of them. . . . After you have written down each set, I shall tell you whether your numbers conform to the rule or not. . . . When you feel highly confident that you have discovered the rule, you are to write it down and tell me what it is. (p. 131)

After Wason presented the first set of numbers, *2, 4,* and *6,* the participants began creating their own sets of three numbers and receiving feedback from Wason. Note that Wason told participants only whether their numbers fit his rule. The participants did not find out whether their *rationale* was correct until they felt confident enough to actually announce their rule. The most common initial hypothesis was "increasing intervals of two." Because the actual rule was "three numbers in increasing order of magnitude," the rule "increasing intervals of two" is incorrect even though it creates sequences that satisfy Wason's rule.

The secret to determining the correct rule is to try to create sequences that *don't* satisfy the person's current hypothesis, but which *do* satisfy Wason's rule. Thus, determining that the sequence 2, 4, 5 is correct, allows us to reject our "increasing intervals of two" hypothesis and formulate a new one. The few participants whose rule was correct on their first guess followed the strategy of testing a number of hypotheses by creating sequences that were designed to *disconfirm* their current hypothesis. In contrast, participants who didn't guess the rule correctly on their first try tended to keep creating sequences that confirmed their current hypothesis.

The confirmation bias acts like a pair of blinders—we see the world according to rules we think are correct and are never dissuaded from this view because we seek out only evidence that confirms our rule. The confirmation bias is so strong that it can affect people's reasoning by causing them to ignore relevant information. Charles Lord and coworkers (1979) demonstrated this in an experiment that tested how people's attitudes are affected by exposure to evidence that contradicts the attitudes.

By means of a questionnaire, Lord identified one group of participants in favor of capital punishment and another group against it. Each participant was then presented with descriptions of research studies on capital punishment. Some of the studies provided evidence that capital punishment had a deterrent effect on murder; others provided evidence that capital punishment had no deterrent effect. When the participants reacted to the studies, their responses reflected the attitudes they had at the beginning of the experiment. For example, an article presenting evidence that supported the deterrence effect of capital punishment was rated as "convincing" by proponents of capital punishment and "unconvincing" by those against capital punishment. This is the confirmation bias at work—people's prior beliefs caused them to focus only on information that agreed with their beliefs and to disregard information that didn't.

Culture, Categories, and Inductive Reasoning

When we discussed categories in Chapter 8, we described research comparing the way Itza and American participants think about categories. We saw that Itza and American participants have different ideas about which level of categories is "basic," with Itza focusing on the level "sparrow, oak" and Americans focusing on the level "bird, tree." We also saw that there are similarities, with both American and Itza using categories similarly for an inductive-reasoning task (see page 283).

We now return to these two groups to consider some further comparisons of how they use categories in reasoning. Let's start with a demonstration.

◣ Demonstration

Questions About Animals

The following two questions are about animals that live on an island.

Question 1:
> Porcupines have a disease.
> Squirrels have another disease.
> Do you think all other mammals on the island have the disease of *porcupines* or the disease of *squirrels*?

Question 2:

Wolves and deer have a disease.

Wolves and coyotes have another disease.

Do you think all other mammals on the island have the disease of *wolves and deer* or of *wolves and coyotes*?

■

The preceding questions both involve induction, because they require reasoning from specific observations to more general conclusions, and because the answer is a "probably" answer rather than a "definitely" answer. These items are based on a model of reasoning about categories called the **similarity-coverage model** (Osherson et al., 1990). The goal of this model is to explain how people's conceptions of different categories influence the strength of inductive arguments. We will discuss this model by posing a few more problems, and will then return to the questions posed in the demonstration. One principle of the model, called *typicality*, is illustrated by the following problem.

Which of the following is most likely to be true?

Premise: Robins have a higher potassium concentration in their blood than humans.

Conclusion 1: Therefore, all birds have a higher potassium concentration in their blood than humans.

Premise: Penguins have a higher potassium concentration in their blood than humans.

Conclusion 2: Therefore, all birds have a higher potassium concentration in their blood than humans.

According to the principle of **typicality**, the argument with the most typical example of a category in the premise is the strongest argument. Thus, if people think robins are more typical of birds than penguins, they will pick conclusion 1 as more likely to be true.

Here is an example that illustrates another principle. Which of the following arguments are more likely to be true?

Premise: Hippopotamuses have an ulnar artery.

      Hamsters have an ulnar artery.

Conclusion 1: All mammals have an ulnar artery.

Premise: Hippopotamuses have an ulnar artery.

      Rhinoceroses have an ulnar artery.

Conciusion 2: All mammals have an ulnar artery.

According to the principle of **diversity**, the argument with the greatest coverage of a category is stronger. Since hippopotamus and hamster are more diverse than hippopotamus and rhinoceros, they have higher coverage of the category *mammal*. Therefore, according to the principle of diversity, conclusion 1 is stronger.

Now return to the demonstration "Questions About Animals," and decide which argument illustrates typicality and which illustrates diversity. (Note that the questions in the

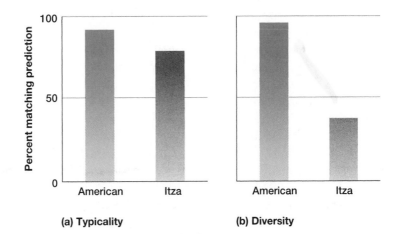

Figure 12.19 (a) Percentage of judgments of inductive arguments that follow the principle of typicality, for American and for Itza participants. (b) Percentage of judgments that follow the principle of diversity for American and Itza participants (Lopez et al., 1997).

demonstration are stated differently from the examples we have just considered, but it is still possible to determine which principles apply. Stop and decide, before reading further.)

When Alejandro Lopez and coworkers (1997) presented problems like question 1 in the demonstration to Itza and U.S. participants, they found that the overall responses of both groups agreed with the principle of typicality (Figure 12.19a; picking *squirrel* rather than *porcupine*). Thus, both groups' answers reflected the animals in the premises that they thought were more typical.

Although the results for typicality were similar for both groups, the results for diversity were different. Thus, when the two groups were presented with problems like question 2 in the demonstration, almost all of the U.S. participants (96 percent) gave an answer that corresponded to the principle of diversity (picking *wolves and deer*), whereas only 38 percent of the Itza participants gave an answer that corresponded to this principle (Figure 12.19b).

What does this result mean? Why do Itza ignore diversity in making their choices? One reason is that the Itza, but not the U.S. participants, are influenced by ecological considerations. For example, one Itza participant was presented with the following problem.

Rats and pocket mice have a disease.
Tapirs and squirrels have a disease.
Do you think all other mammals on the island would have the disease of rats and pocket mice or the disease of tapirs and squirrels?

The person chose "rats and pocket mice," even though the principle of diversity predicts that tapirs and squirrels, which are more different, would be chosen. The person explained that tapirs and squirrels are less likely to pass on the disease because they probably got it from another agent, such as a bat biting them, whereas rats and pocket mice are similar enough so they don't need an agent like a bat biting them to both get the disease. Thus, the Itza participant was not being illogical. Rather, she was using logic that was based on her knowledge of the animals in their environment.

Interestingly, similar effects of knowledge on reasoning about categories have been observed for different groups of U.S. participants. For example, when asked to sort trees into different categories, taxonomists (who are schooled in scientific biology) sorted the trees by their scientific biological category, whereas park maintenance workers (who are responsible for maintaining the trees) sorted the trees based on their experience in taking care of trees. When tested for the diversity principle, the park maintenance workers rejected the diversity principle in favor of ecologically based reasoning—just like the Itza (Medin et al., 1997)!

These cross-cultural and cross-occupational studies emphasize that in studying cognition, we can't assume that people always think in exactly the same way or use the same information to support their thinking.

DECISION MAKING: CHOOSING AMONG ALTERNATIVES

We make decisions every day, from relatively unimportant ones (what clothes to wear, what movie to see) to those that can have great impact on our lives (what college to attend, whom to marry, what job to choose). The process of decision making can involve both inductive and deductive reasoning, so we have already considered some of the principles that apply to the study of how people make decisions.

When we discussed the availability and representativeness heuristics we used examples in which people were asked to make judgments about things like causes of death or people's occupations. As we discuss decision making, our emphasis will be on how people make judgments that involve choices between different courses of action. These choices can be concerned with personal decisions, such as deciding what school to attend or whether to fly or drive to a destination, or they can be concerned with decisions that a person might make in conjunction with their profession, such as "Which advertising campaign should my company run?" or "What is the best economic policy for the United States?" We begin by considering one of the basic properties of decision making: Decisions involve both benefits and costs.

The Utility Approach to Decisions

Much of the early theorizing on decision making was influenced by economic theories, which stated that optimal decision making occurs when the outcome of the decision causes the maximum expected utility. Utility refers to outcomes that are desirable because they are in the person's best interest (Manktelow, 1999; Reber, 1995). The economists who studied decision making thought about utility in terms of monetary value, with the goal of good decision making being to make choices that resulted in the maximum monetary payoff.

One of the advantages of the utility approach is that it specifies procedures that make it possible to determine which choice would result in the highest monetary value. For example, if we know the odds of winning when playing a slot machine in a casino, and also know the cost of playing and the size of the payoff, it is possible to determine that, in the long run, playing slot machines is a losing proposition. Thus, in terms of monetary payoff, it would be unwise to play the slots.

A Problem for the Utility Approach: People Do Not Necessarily Act to Maximize Monetary Value

Even though most people realize that in the long run the casino wins, the huge popularity of casinos indicates that many people have decided to patronize casinos anyway. Observations such as this, as well as the results of many experiments, have led psychologists to conclude that people do not always make decisions that maximize their monetary outcome. This does not necessarily mean that people are irrational, but that they find value in things other than money. Thus, for some people the fun of gambling might outweigh the probable loss of some money, and, of course, there's the thrill of thinking about the possibility of "beating the odds" and being the one who hits the jackpot.

Another problem with the utility approach is that many decisions do not involve payoffs that can be calculated. As the popular television advertisement for a credit card says, *Tickets to the ball game, $60; Hot dogs, $10; Your team's baseball cap, $20; Seeing the game with your son or daughter, "priceless."* Thus, utility is not always reducible to dollars and cents, but is often in the mind of the person.

The idea that utility can be in the person's mind brings up another potential problem with the utility approach. When people have to make decisions that will affect their lives, they often create mental simulations, which can sometimes be misleading (Kahneman & Tversky, 1982; Dunning & Parpal, 1989). **Mental simulations** are models that people create about what will happen following different decisions. For example, if Roberta is trying to decide whether to go to "Excellent Private University" or "Good State University," she may imagine what it would be like attending each school. In doing this she may imagine life at "Private U" to be intellectual, with the other students being very smart and with many famous professors. Or, shifting attention to "State University," she may imagine that football weekends would be fun and that she might find it easier to get good grades, although the classes will probably be larger.

While the procedure of creating mental simulations can be useful, there is a danger that it may not lead to accurate predictions. After all, Roberta hasn't actually attended either school and has no experience with college, so she is just guessing what each school would be like. In fact, people often make inaccurate predictions about what will happen in a particular situation. For example, when people win the lottery, they may initially see nothing but positive outcomes, such as being able to quit their job, buy a new house, and finance their children's college educations. Later, however, they become aware of negative aspects, such as being hounded by other people who want a piece of the action, lack of privacy, losing friends, and worries about what's happening to their investments in the stock market. Events that people imagine will occur are often different from the events that actually do occur (T. D. Wilson et al., 2000).

People Are Often Not Good at Predicting Their Emotional Reactions to Events

T. D. Wilson and coworkers (2000) point out that even if people were able to accurately predict what would happen, they are often poor at predicting how happy or unhappy the event will cause them to feel. One of the things responsible for this lack of accuracy in predicting their emotions is called the **focusing illusion,** which occurs when people focus their attention on just one aspect of a situation and ignore other aspects of a situation that may be important. For example, when college students were asked the questions "How happy are you?" and "How many dates did you have last month?" their answers depended on the order in which the questions were asked. When the happiness question was asked first, the correlation between the answers to the two questions was 0.12, but if the dating question was asked first, the correlation rose to 0.66. Apparently, asking the dating question first caused participants to focus on dating as being an important determinant of happiness, and so they rated themselves as happier if they had a large number of dates.

The focusing illusion has also been demonstrated in a study that considered people's perceptions of how satisfied a target person would be if they lived in different locations. The participants for this study were students at two Midwestern universities (the University of Michigan and the University of Ohio) and at two California universities (the University of California at Irvine and UCLA).

There were two groups, the *self* group and the *other* group. The self group rated *themselves* on overall life satisfaction. The *other* group predicted how a hypothetical *target person* who was similar to themselves would rate their life satisfaction if they lived in California and if they lived in the Midwest. (Both groups also rated other things as well, but for our purposes we will focus on overall life satisfaction.)

The results of this study showed that there was no difference in how the California and Midwest students in the *self* group rated their own overall life satisfaction, but both California and Midwest students in the *other* group predicted that their hypothetical target person would be happier in California (Table 12.3).

Table 12.3	FOCUSING-ILLUSION EXPERIMENT
Group	Life Satisfaction Rating
Self	*Own Life Satisfaction*
	No difference in self-ratings for California and Midwest students.
Other	*Target-Person Life Satisfaction*
	Both California and Midwest students rate hypothetical target person as being higher in life satisfaction if in California.

Why did both California and Midwest students in the *other* group predict that their target person would be happier in California? The experimenters, David Schkade and Daniel Kahneman (1998), suggest that the higher ratings for California was probably caused by the participants' tendency to focus on the most easily observed and distinctive differences between the two locations, such as good weather and natural beauty (which people generally associate with California), when making their predictions of overall happiness, and to ignore other factors, such as job prospects, academic opportunities, and financial situation, which tend to be more similar in the two locations. The message here is that before you decide that moving to California will make you happier, it is important to consider a wide range of outcomes from this decision—not just that the weather will be better.

All of the evidence above supports the idea that people often make decisions that do not result in maximizing monetary value, and in situations in which monetary value is not a factor, they may not be able to accurately predict what outcome a particular decision will bring or how they will feel about the outcome when it happens. We will now consider research on decision making that has shown that people's evaluation of different choices can depend on the way these choices are presented.

Framing Effects

CogLab
Risky Decision

We saw for deductive and inductive reasoning that reasoning is affected by many things in addition to just the facts of the situation. This also occurs in decision making, when a person's judgments are affected by the way choices are stated, or *framed*.

Demonstration

What Would You Do?

Imagine that the United States is preparing for the outbreak of an unusual Asian disease, which is expected to kill 600 people. Two alternative programs to combat the disease have been proposed. Assume that the exact scientific estimates of the consequences of the programs are as follows:

- If Program A is adopted, 200 people will be saved.
- If Program B is adopted, there is a 1/3 probability that 600 people will be saved, and a 2/3 probability that no people will be saved.

Which of the two programs would you favor?

Now consider the following additional proposals for combating the same disease:

- If Program C is adopted, 400 people will die.
- If Program D is adopted, there is a 1/3 probability that nobody will die, and a 2/3 probability that 600 people will die.

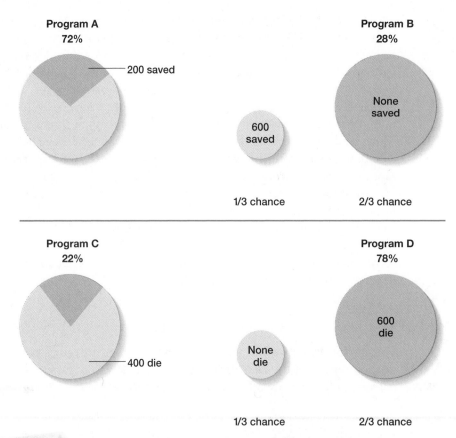

Program A
72%

200 saved

600
saved

Program B
28%

None
saved

1/3 chance   2/3 chance

Program C
22%

400 die

None
die

Program D
78%

600
die

1/3 chance   2/3 chance

Figure 12.20 How framing affects decision making. These pie charts diagram the conditions set forth for Programs A, B, C, and D in the text. Note that the number of deaths and probabilities for programs A and B are exactly the same as for programs C and D. The percentages indicate the percentage of participants who picked each program when given choices between A and B or between C and D (Tversky & Kahneman, 1981).

For the first pair of proposals, Program A was chosen by 72 percent of the students in an experiment by Tversky and Kahneman (1981) and the rest picked Program B (Figure 12.20). The choice of Program A represents a **risk-aversion strategy.** The idea of saving 200 lives with certainty is more attractive than the risk that no one will be saved. However, when Tversky and Kahneman presented the descriptions of Programs C and D to another group of students, 22 percent picked Program C and 78 percent picked Program D. This represents a **risk-taking strategy.** The certain death of 400 people is less acceptable than a 2 in 3 chance that 600 people will die. Tversky and Kahneman concluded that, in general, when a choice is framed in terms of gains (as in the first problem, which is stated in terms of saving lives) people use a risk-aversion strategy, and when a choice is framed in terms of losses (as in the second problem, which is stated in terms of losing lives), people use a risk-taking strategy.

But if we look at the four programs closely, we can see that they are identical pairs (Figure 12.20). Programs A and C both result in 200 people living and 400 people dying. Yet 72 percent of the participants picked program A and only 22 percent picked program C. A similar situation occurs if we compare programs B and D. Both lead to the same number of deaths, yet one was picked by 28 percent of the participants and the other by 78 percent. These results show that decisions are influenced both by the objective outcome of the decision and by how the problem is stated.

Justification in Decision Making

To end our consideration of decision making, we will consider yet another factor that influences how people go about making decisions. This factor is the need to justify the decision. We can illustrate what this means by considering an experiment by Tversky and Eldar Shafir (1992), in which they presented the following problem to two groups of students. The "pass" group read the words that are underlined, and the "fail" group had these words replaced by the words in italics (which the pass group did not see).

> Imagine that you have just taken a tough qualifying examination. It is the end of the semester, you feel tired and run-down, and you find out that you passed the exam/[failed the exam. You will have to take it again in a couple of months—after the Christmas holidays]. You now have the opportunity to buy a very attractive 5-day Christmas vacation package to Hawaii at an exceptionally low price. The special offer expires tomorrow. Would you:
>
> ■ buy the vacation package?
> ■ not buy the vacation package?
> ■ pay a $5 nonrefundable fee in order to retain the rights to buy the vacation package at the same exceptional price the day after tomorrow?

The results for the two groups are shown in the columns headed "passed" and "failed" in Table 12.4. Notice that there is no difference between the two groups. Fifty-four percent of the participants in the "pass" group opt to buy the vacation package, and 57 percent of the participants in the "fail" group opt for the package. The interesting result

Table 12.4	CHOICE BEHAVIOR AND KNOWLEDGE OF EXAM OUTCOME		
Choice	Passed	Failed	Don't Know Result of Exam Yet
Buy vacation package	54%	57%	32%
Don't buy	16	12	7
$5 to keep open option to buy later	30	31	61

happened when a third group received the same problem as above, except these participants were told that the outcome of the exam wouldn't be available for two more days. Notice that only 32 percent of these participants opted for the package and that 61 percent decided they would pay the $5 so they could put off making the decision until they knew if they had passed or failed the exam.

Apparently what happened in this experiment is that 61 percent of the participants in the "no result" group did not want to make a decision about the trip until they found out whether they passed or failed, even though the results for the other two groups indicates that passing or failing actually made no difference in the decision about the vacation packages. *Crazy!*

To explain this result, Tversky and Shafir suggest that once the students know the outcome they can then assign a reason for deciding to buy the vacation. Participants who passed could see the vacation as a reward; participants who failed could see the vacation as a consolation that would provide time to recuperate before taking the exam again.

Although there are other possible interpretations for these results, there is a great deal of other evidence that the decision-making process often includes looking for justification so the person can state a rationale for his or her decision. This is why doctors may carry out medical tests that might not lead to different treatments but that provide additional evidence for the treatment they have recommended, thereby making it easier to justify the treatment to themselves, their patients, and, if necessary, to the courts (Tversky & Shafir, 1992).

Reasoning and the Brain

How is the brain involved in reasoning? One way to answer this question is to return to our consideration of problem solving, which involves cognitive skills similar to those involved in reasoning. Because the prefrontal cortex (PFC) is important for understanding problem solving, it is not surprising that this area of the brain is also important for reasoning.

One reason the PFC is important for reasoning is because it plays a role in working memory. Remember from Chapter 5 that damage to the PFC decreases the ability to hold information for short periods of time, and that there are neurons in the PFC that continue firing after a stimulus is terminated (see page 173).

In this chapter we noted that complex syllogisms place more load on working memory than do simpler syllogisms and so they are harder to evaluate. In line with this idea, brain-imaging research has shown that as reasoning problems become more complex, reasoning takes longer and activates larger areas of the PFC (Kroger et al., 2002).

Reasoning does not involve only the PFC. As for any complex cognitive task, other areas are involved as well. For example, measuring brain activity as a participant carries out a reasoning task that involves remembering how a series of geometrical figures are ordered relative to one another in space reveals activity in both the PFC and parietal cortex (Acuna et al., 2002). The fact that there is activity in the parietal cortex fits with the fact that damage to this area of the brain causes difficulty in processing information about the locations of objects in space (Milner & Goodale, 1995).

Studies of patients with brain damage also indicate that the PFC is important for reasoning. This has been demonstrated by presenting a deductive-reasoning task to people with PFC damage. Participants were presented with relationships such as the following: *Sam is taller than Nate; Nate is taller than Roger*, and their task was to arrange the names in order of the people's heights. When James Waltz and coworkers (1999) presented these tasks to patients with PFC damage and control groups of normal participants and patients with temporal lobe damage, they found that all of these groups did well when the task was easy, like the previous one about Sam, Nate, and Roger (Figure 12.21a). However, when the task was made more difficult by scrambling the order of presentation (example: *Beth is taller than Tina; Amy is taller than Beth*), then the patients without brain damage and the patients with temporal lobe damage still did well, but the PFC patients performed poorly (Figure 12.21b). This result confirms the conclusion of the brain-imaging studies, which showed that the PFC is important for reasoning that involves holding and manipulating relationships in memory.

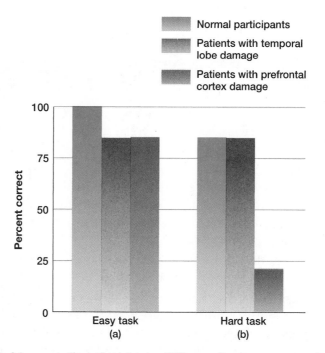

Figure 12.21 Effect of damage to the prefrontal cortex (PFC) on performance on a reasoning task. Participants without brain damage, participants with temporal lobe damage and participants with PFC damage can all solve the easy task (left bars), but the PFC group's performance drops to a low level when the task is made more difficult (Waltz et al., 1999).

Test Yourself 12.2

1. What is inductive reasoning, and how is it different from deductive reasoning?
2. How is inductive reasoning involved in the practice of science? How do inductive and inductive reasoning work together in scientific research?
3. How is inductive reasoning involved in everyday experience?
4. How do the following cause errors in reasoning: availability heuristic; illusory correlations; representativeness heuristic; confirmation bias?
5. How can failure to take into account base rates and small sample sizes cause errors in reasoning?
6. What is the cross-cultural evidence regarding how U.S. and Itza participants use typicality and diversity when making inferences about categories? How are the behaviors of these two groups similar? Different? What is an explanation for the differences?
7. What is the utility approach to decisions? What are some problems with the utility approach? As you consider this, take into account mental simulations and the focusing illusion.
8. How do framing and the need to justify decisions affect the decisions people make?
9. How is the brain involved in reasoning? Cite evidence from brain-imaging research and studies of brain damage to support your answer.

 **Think About It**

1. Astrology is popular with many people because they perceive a close connection between astrological predictions and events in their lives. Explain factors that might lead to this perception, even if a close connection does not, in fact, exist.

2. Think about a decision you have made recently. It can be a minor one, such as deciding which restaurant to go to on Saturday evening, or a more major one, such as picking an apartment or deciding to move to a new city. Analyze this decision, taking into account the processes you went through to arrive at it, and how you justified it in your mind as being a good decision.

3. Create deductive syllogisms and inductive arguments that apply to the decision you analyzed in the previous question.

4. Johanna has a reputation for being extremely good at justifying her behavior by a process that is often called "rationalization." For example, she justifies the fact that she eats anything she wants by saying "Ten years ago this food was supposed to be bad for you and now they are saying it may even have some beneficial effects, so what's the point of listening to the so-called health experts?" or "That movie actor who was really into red meat lived to be 95." Analyze Johanna's arguments by stating them as inductive or deductive arguments or, better yet, do that for one of your own rationalizations.

5. From watching the news or reading the paper, what can you conclude about how the availability heuristic can influence our conceptions of the nature of the lives of different groups of people (for example, movie stars, rich people, various racial, ethnic, or cultural groups), and how accurate these conceptions might actually be?

KEY TERMS

Affirming the consequent
Antecedent
Atmosphere effect
Availability heuristic
Base rate
Belief bias
Categorical syllogism
Conclusion
Conditional syllogism
Confirmation bias
Conjunction rule
Consequent
Decisions
Deductive reasoning
Denying the antecedent
Descriptive approach
Diversity principle
Euler circles
Evolutionary perspective on cognition
Falsification principle
Focusing illusion
Illusory correlation

Inductive reasoning
Law of large numbers
Mental model
Mental simulation
Modus ponens
Modus tollens
Normative approach
Permission schema
Pragmatic reasoning schema
Premises
Reasoning
Representativeness heuristic
Risk-aversion strategy
Risk-taking strategy
Similarity-coverage model
Social-exchange theory
Stereotype
Syllogism
Typicality principle
Utility
Valid
Wason four-card problem

CogLab To experience these experiments for yourself, go to http://coglab.wadsworth.com. Be sure to read each experiment's setup instructions before you go to the experiment itself. Otherwise, you won't know which keys to press.

Primary Labs

Wason selection task	Two versions of the Wason four-card problem (p. 446).
Typical reasoning	How the representativeness heuristic can lead to errors of judgment (p. 461).
Risky decisions	How decision making is influenced by framing effects (p. 471).

Monty Hall   A simulation of the Monty Hall 3-door problem, which involves an understanding of probability.

Answer to mental models cue ball problem from page 438:
The cue ball is to the *left* of your line of sight.

(Number in parentheses is the chapter in which the term first appears.)

Action potential Electrical potential that travels down a neuron's axon. (2)

Affirming the consequent A conditional syllogism in which the first premise is "If p, then q," the second premise is "q," and the conclusion is "p." This is an invalid form of conditional syllogism. See also **Denying the antecedent;** *Modus ponens; Modus tollens.* (12)

Algorithm A procedure that is guaranteed to solve a problem. (3)

Alzheimer's disease A condition that eventually results in severe memory deficits, especially affecting the ability to form new long-term memories. (6)

Amygdala A subcortical structure that is involved in processing emotional aspects of experience. (2)

Analogical problem solving The use of analogies as an aid to solving problems. Typically, a solution to one problem, the source problem, is presented that is analogous to the solution to another problem, the target problem. (11)

Analogy Drawing a comparison in order to show a similarity between two different things. (11)

Analytic introspection The procedure used by early psychologists in which trained participants described their experiences and thought processes elicited by stimuli presented under controlled conditions. (1)

Anaphoric inference An inference that connects an object or person in one sentence to an object or person in another sentence. See also **Causal interference; Instrumental inference.** (10)

Antecedent In a conditional syllogism, the term "p" in the conditional premise "If p then q." See also **Consequent.** (12)

Aphasia A general term that encompasses a number of different kinds of problems in understanding and using language that are usually associated with brain damage. (10)

Articulatory suppression Interference with operation of the phonological loop that occurs when a person repeats an irrelevant word such as "the" as he or she is carrying out a task that requires the phonological loop. (5)

Atmosphere effect The idea that the words *All,* *Some,* and *No* in the premises of a syllogism create an overall "mood" or "atmosphere" that can influence the evaluation of the validity of the conclusion. According to this idea, two *All*'s suggest an *all* conclusion, one or two *No*'s suggests a *no* conclusion, and one or two *Some*'s suggests a *some* conclusion. (12)

Attention Focusing on specific features of the environment or on certain thoughts or activities. (4)

Attenuation theory of attention Anne Treisman's model of selective attention, that proposes that selection occurs in two stages. In the first stage, an attenuator analyzes the incoming message and lets through the attended message—and also the unattended message, but at a lower (attenuated) strength. (4)

Autobiographical memory Memory for dated events in a person's life. Autobiographical memory is a type of episodic memory. (7)

Automatic processing Processing that occurs automatically without the person intending to do it, and which also uses few cognitive resources. Automatic processing is associated with easy or well-practiced tasks. (4)

Availability heuristic We base our judgments of the frequency of events on what events come to mind. (12)

Axon Part of the neuron that transmits signals from the cell body to the synapse at the end of the axon. (2)

Back propagation A process by which learning can occur in a connectionist network, in which the error signal is transmitted backward through the circuit. This backward-transmitted error signal provides the information needed to adjust the weights in the circuit to achieve the correct output signal for a stimulus. (8)

Base rate The relative proportions of different classes in a population. Failure to consider base rates can often lead to errors of reasoning. (12)

Basic level In Rosch's categorization scheme, the level below the superordinate level that would correspond to *table* or *chair* for the superordinate category of *furniture*. According to Rosch, the basic level is psychologically special because it is the level above which much information is lost and below which little is gained. See also **Subordinate level; Superordinate level.** (8)

Behavioral approach to the study of the mind When the mind is studied by measuring a person's behavior and by explaining this behavior in behavioral terms. (1)

Behaviorism The approach to psychology, founded by John B. Watson, which stated that observable behavior is the only valid data for psychology. A consequence of this idea is that consciousness and unobservable mental processes were considered not worthy of study by psychologists. (1)

Belief bias The idea that if a syllogism's conclusion is true or agrees with a person's beliefs, this increases the likelihood that the syllogism will be judged to be valid. Also, if the conclusion is viewed as false, this increases the likelihood that the syllogism will be judged as invalid. (12)

Bottom-up processing Processing that starts with information received by the receptors; can also be called data-based processing. See also **Top-down processing.** (3)

Brain imaging Techniques such as functional magnetic resonance imaging (fMRI) and positron emission tomography (PET) that result in images of the brain that represent the brain activity caused by specific cognitive tasks. (2)

Brain lesioning Removal or destruction of a portion of the brain, usually carried out as an experimental or surgical procedure. (2)

Broca's aphasia Problem in language processing caused by damage to Broca's area that is characterized by difficulty in producing fluent speech. (2)

Broca's area Area in the frontal lobe that is specialized for processing aspects of language. A person with damage to Broca's area suffers from Broca's aphasia. (2, 10)

Candle problem A problem first described by Duncker in which a person is given a number of objects and is given the task of mounting a candle on a wall so it can burn without dripping wax on the floor. (11)

Categorical perception It is difficult to discriminate between two stimuli that are within a category, and it is easier to discriminate between two stimuli that are in different categories. (10)

Categorical syllogism A syllogism in which the premises and conclusion describe the relationship between two categories by using statements that begin with *all*, *no*, or *some*. (12)

Categorization The process by which objects are placed in categories. (8)

Category Groups of objects that belong together because they belong to the same class of objects, such as "houses," "furniture," or "schools." (8)

Category-specific neurons Neurons in the temporal lobe that respond best to objects in a specific category. (8)

Causal inference An inference that results in the conclusion that the events described in one clause or sentence were caused by events that occurred in a previous sentence. See also **Anaphoric inference; Instrumental inference.** (10)

Cell body Part of a cell that contains mechanisms that keep the cell alive. In some neurons the cell bodies, and the dendrites associated with it, receive information from other neurons. (2)

Central executive The part of working memory that coordinates the activity of the phonological loop and the visuospatial sketch pad. (5)

Cerebral cortex The 3-mm-thick outer layer of the brain, which contains the mechanisms responsible for higher mental functions such as perception, language, thinking, and problem solving. (2)

Change blindness Difficulty in detecting changes in scenes that are presented one after another. The changes are often easy to see once attention is directed to them, but are usually undetected in the absence of appropriate attention. (4)

Choice reaction time Reacting to one of two or more stimuli. For example, in Donder's experiment (see Chapter 1), participants had to make one response to one stimulus, and a different response to another stimulus. (1)

Chunk Used in connection with the idea of chunking in memory, a chunk is a collection of elements that are strongly associated with each other, but are weakly associated with elements in other chunks. (5)

Chunking Combining small units into larger ones, such as when individual words are combined into a meaningful sentence. Chunking can be used to increase the capacity of memory. (5)

Cocktail party phenomenon The ability to focus attention on one message and ignore others. The name is taken from the ability to pay attention to one conversation at a crowded party without attending to other conversations that are happening at the same time. (4)

Coding The form in which stimuli are represented in the mind. For example, information can be represented in visual, semantic, and phonological forms. See also **Neural code,** which refers to how stimuli are represented in the firing of neurons. (5)

Cognition The mental processes involved in perception, attention, memory, language, problem solving, reasoning, and making decisions. (1)

Cognitive economy A feature of some semantic network models in which properties of a category that are shared by many members of a category are stored at a higher-level node in the network. For example, the property *can fly* would be stored at the node for *bird* rather than at the node for *canary*. (8)

Cognitive hypothesis An explanation for the reminiscence bump, which states that memories are better for adolescence and early adulthood because encoding is better during periods of rapid change that are followed by stability. (7)

Cognitive psychology The branch of psychology concerned with the scientific study of the mental processes involved in perception, attention, memory, language, problem solving, reasoning, and decision making. In short, cognitive psychology is concerned with the scientific study of the mind and mental processes. (1)

Cognitive science The interdisciplinary approach to the study of the mind. Cognitive science includes a wide net of disciplines including computer science, linguistics, neuroscience, artificial intelligence, philosophy, and psychology. (1)

Coherence The representation of text in a reader's mind so that information in one part of the text is related to information in another part of the text. (10)

Common fate, law of Law of perceptual organization that states that things moving in the same direction appear to be grouped together. (3)

Complex cells A type of neuron in the visual cortex that responds best to a moving, oriented bar of light. Often responding occurs to a specific direction of movement. (2)

Concept A mental representation used for a variety of cognitive functions, including memory, reasoning, and using and understanding language. An example of a concept would be the way a person mentally represents "cat" or "house." (8)

Conceptual-peg hypothesis A hypothesis associated with Paivio's dual coding theory that states that concrete nouns create images that other words can hang onto, and that this enhances memory for these words. (9)

Conclusion The final statement in a syllogism, which follows from the two premises. (12)

Conditional syllogism Syllogisms with two premises and a conclusion, like categorical syllogisms, but the first premise is an "If . . . then" statement. (12)

Confabulation The creation of outlandish false memories. Confabulation is associated with damage to the prefrontal, and sometimes temporal, lobes. (7)

Confirmation bias The tendency to selectively look for information that conforms to a hypothesis and to overlook information that argues against it. (12)

Conjunction rule The probability of the conjunction of two events (such as feminist and bank teller) cannot be higher than the probability of the single constituents (feminist alone or bank teller alone). (12)

Connectionism A network model of mental operation that proposes that concepts are represented in connectionist networks, which are modeled after neural networks. This approach to describing the mental representation of concepts is also called the *parallel distributed processing approach*. See also **Connectionist network.** (8)

Connectionist network The type of network proposed by the connectionist approach to the representation of concepts. Connectionist networks are based on neural networks, but are not necessarily identical to them. One of the key properties of a connectionist network is that a specific category is represented by activity that is distributed over many units in the network. This contrasts with semantic networks, in which specific categories are represented at individual nodes. (8)

Consequent In a conditional syllogism, the term "q" in the conditional premise "If p then q." See also **Antecedent.** (12)

Consequentiality An event that has important consequences for a person's life. It has been hypothesized that this quality is a characteristic of events that become flashbulb memories. (7)

Consistency bias The tendency for people to perceive their basic attitudes and behaviors as remaining fairly consistent over time. This bias can affect people's memory for events in their lives. See also **Egocentric bias; Positive change bias.** (7)

Consolidation period The time that it takes for memory consolidation to occur. (6)

Constructive approach to memory. The idea that what people report as memories are constructed by the person based on what actually happened plus additional factors, such as expectations, other knowledge, and other life experiences. (7)

Control processes In Atkinson and Shiffrin's modal model of memory, active processes that can be controlled by the person and may differ from one task to another. Rehearsal is an example of a control process. (5)

Controlled processing Processing that involves close attention. This term is especially associated with Schneider and Shiffrin's (1977) experiment, which showed that controlled processing was needed in the difficult, varied mapping condition of their experiment, even after extensive practice. (4)

Convergence Synapsing of a number of neurons onto one neuron. (2)

Convergent thinking Thinking that works toward finding a solution to a specific problem that usually has a correct answer. Can be contrasted with divergent thinking. (11)

Conversational maxims A number of principles that help achieve Grice's cooperation principle. See also **Given-new contract; Manner; Quality; Quantity; Relation.** (10)

Cooperative principle Grice's principle of conversation, which states that the speaker and the listener agree that the person speaking should strive to make statements that further the agreed goals of the conversation. See also **Conversational maxim; Given-new contract.** (10)

Decisions Making choices between alternatives. (12)

Declarative memory Memory that involves conscious recollections of events or facts that we have learned in the past. (6)

Deductive reasoning Reasoning that involves syllogisms in which a conclusion logically follows from premises. See also **Inductive reasoning.** (12)

Deep processing Processing that involves attention to meaning and relating an item to something else. Deep processing is usually associated with elaborative rehearsal. See also **Depth of processing; Shallow processing.** (6)

Definitional approach to categorization The idea that we can decide if something is member of a category by determining whether the object meets the definition of the category. See also **Family resemblance.** (8)

Delayed-response task A task in which information is provided, a delay is imposed, and then memory is tested. This task has been used to test monkeys' ability to hold information about the location of a food reward during a delay. (5)

Dendrites Structures that branch out from the cell body to receive electrical signals from other neurons. (2)

Denying the antecedent A conditional syllogism in which the first premise is "If p then q," the second premise is "not p," and the conclusion is "not q." This is an invalid form of conditional syllogism. See also **Affirming the consequent;** *Modus ponens; Modus tollens.* (12)

Depictive representation Corresponds to spatial representation. So called because a spatial representation can be depicted by a picture. (9)

Depth of processing The idea that the processing that occurs as an item is being encoded into memory can be deep or shallow. Deep processing involves attention to meaning and is associated with elaborative rehearsal. Shallow processing involves repetition with little attention to meaning, and is associated with maintenance rehearsal. (6)

Descriptive approach The approach to studying syllogisms that involves psychology, because it is concerned with how well people can evaluate whether a syllogism is valid. See also **Normative approach.** (12)

Dichotic listening The procedure of presenting one message to the left ear and a different message to the right ear. (4)

Dictionary unit A component of Treisman's attenuation theory of attention. This processing unit contains stored words and thresholds for activating the words. The dictionary unit helps explain why we can sometimes hear a familiar word, such as our name, in an unattended message. (4)

Digit span The number of digits a person can remember. Digit span is used as a measure of the capacity of short-term memory. (5)

Discriminability In recognition-by-components theory, the property that geons can be distinguished from each other from almost all viewpoints. (3)

Dissociations A situation that occurs in cases of brain damage, in which the damage causes a problem in one function while not affecting other functions. (2)

Distributed activation of the brain Simultaneous activation of a number of areas of the brain by a specific object or experience. (2)

Distributed coding Representation of an object or experience by the pattern of firing of a number of neurons. (2)

Distributed versus mass practice effect Memory is better if learning occurs in a number of short study sessions, with breaks in between, than if learning occurs in one long session. (6)

Divergent thinking Thinking that is open-ended and for which there are a large number of potential solutions. Can be contrasted with convergent thinking. (11)

Diversity principle The inductive argument with the greatest coverage of a category is stronger. See also **Similarity-coverage model; Typicality.** (12)

Divided attention The ability to pay attention to, or carry out, two or more different tasks simultaneously. (4)

Double dissociation A situation in which a single dissociation can be demonstrated in one person, and the opposite type of single dissociation can be demonstrated in another person (i.e., Person 1: function A is present; function B is deficient; Person 2: function A is deficient; function B is present). (2)

Dual-coding theory A theory proposed by Paivio that memory is served by two systems, one that is specialized for verbal stimuli, and the other that is specialized for objects and events that are represented non-verbally. (9)

Early-selection model Model of attention that explains selective attention by early filtering-out of the unattended message. In Broadbent's model, the filtering step occurs before the message is analyzed to determine its meaning. (4)

Echoic memory. Brief sensory memory for auditory stimuli that lasts for a few seconds after a stimulus is extinguished. (5)

Egocentric bias The tendency for people to see themselves in the best possible light. This bias can affect people's memory for events in their lives. See also **Consistency bias; Positive change bias.** (7)

Elaborative rehearsal Rehearsal that involves thinking about the meaning of an item to be remembered or making connections between that item and prior knowledge. Compare to **Maintenance rehearsal.** (6)

Encoding The process of acquiring information and transferring it into memory. (6)

Encoding specificity The principle that we learn information together with its context. This means that presence of context can lead to enhanced memory for the information. See also **State-dependent learning.** (6)

End-stopped cells Neurons in the visual cortex that respond to oriented bars of light of a particular length moving in a particular direction. (2)

Epiphenomenon A phenomenon that accompanies a mechanism, but is not actually part of the mechanism. An example of an epiphenomenon is lights that flash on a mainframe computer as it operates. (9)

Episodic memory Memory for specific events that have happened to the person having the memory. These events are usually remembered as a personal experience that occurred at a particular time and place. Episodic and semantic memory, together, make up declarative memory. (6)

Error signal During learning in a connectionist network, the difference between the output signal generated by a particular stimulus and the output that actually represents that stimulus. (8)

Euler circles A graphical procedure for determining whether or not a syllogism is valid. (12)

Event-related potential (ERP) An electrical response recorded with disc electrodes placed on the scalp that record the firing of thousands of neurons to specific stimuli or events. This response consists of a number of waves, each of which indicates a different aspect of cognitive processing. (2)

Event-specific knowledge As proposed by Conway, individual events in a person's life that happen on a time scale of minutes or hours. See also **General events; Lifetime periods.** (7)

Evolutionary perspective on cognition Based on the idea that many properties of our minds can be traced to the evolutionary principles of natural selection. See also **Social-exchange theory.** (12)

Excitation An effect caused by excitatory neurotransmitter that increases the rate of nerve firing or the likelihood of nerve firing. (2)

Excitatory neurotransmitter Neurotransmitter that causes an excitatory effect on a membrane. This excitatory effect causes an increase in firing or in the likelihood of firing.

Exemplar In categorization, members of a category that a person has experienced in the past. (8)

Exemplar approach to categorization The approach to categorization in which members of a category are judged against exemplars, which are examples of members of the category that the person has encountered in the past. (8)

Experience-dependent plasticity A mechanism that causes neurons to develop so they respond best to the type of stimulation that they experience. (3)

Expert Person who, by devoting a large amount of time to learning about a field and practicing application of that learning, has become acknowledged as being extremely skilled or knowledgeable about that field. (11)

Eyewitness testimony Testimony by eyewitnesses to a crime about what they saw during commission of the crime. (7)

Falsification principle The reasoning principle that to test a rule, it is necessary to look for situations that falsify the rule. (12)

Familiarity, law of Law of perceptual organization that states that things are more likely to form groups if the groups appear familiar or meaningful. (3)

Family resemblance In considering the process of categorization, the idea of family resemblance states that things in a particular category resemble each other in a number of ways. This approach can be contrasted with the definitional approach, which states that an object belongs to a category only if it meets a definite set of criteria. (8)

Feature analysis stage The initial stage of a feature analysis model of object perception, which consists of feature units that each respond to a specific feature of the object. (3)

Feature approach to object perception An approach that describes object perception as beginning with an initial stage in which the object is analyzed into its individual features. (3)

Feature detectors Neurons that respond to specific visual features, such as orientation or size or the more complex features that make up environmental stimuli. (2)

Feature integration theory An approach to object perception developed by Anne Treisman that proposes that object perception occurs in a sequence of stages in which features are first analyzed and then combined to result in perception of an object. (3)

Feature units A unit in the feature analysis model of object perception that is activated by a specific feature. (3)

Filter model of attention A model of attention that proposes that selective attention is achieved by a filtering out of unattended messages. The first filter model of attention was proposed by Donald Broadbent. (4)

Flanker-compatibility task A procedure in which participants are instructed to respond to a target stimulus that is flanked, or surrounded, by distractor stimuli that they are supposed to ignore. The degree to which the distractor interferes with responding to the target is taken as an indication of whether the distractor stimuli are being processed. (4)

Flashbulb memories Memories of emotionally charged or especially memorable events that have been claimed to be particularly vivid and accurate. See **Narrative rehearsal hypothesis** for another viewpoint. (7)

Focused attention stage The second stage of Treisman's feature integration theory. According to the theory, attention causes the combination of features into perception of an object. (3)

Focusing illusion When people focus their attention on just one aspect of a situation and ignore other aspects of a situation that may be important, this can lead to lack of accuracy in predicting emotional reactions to events. (12)

Frontal lobe The lobe in the front of the brain that serves higher functions such as language, thought, memory, and motor functioning. (2)

Functional fixedness An effect that occurs when the ideas a person has about an object's function inhibits the person's ability to use the object for a different function. (11)

Functional magnetic resonance imaging (fMRI) A brain-imaging technique involving the measurement of blood flow changes to cognitive activity. Unlike positron emission tomography, this technique does not involve the injection of a radioactive tracer. (2)

Fusiform face area (FFA) An area in the temporal lobe that contains many neurons that respond selectively to faces. (3)

Garden-path model See **Syntax-first approach to parsing.** (10)

Garden-path sentence A sentence in which the meaning that seems to be implied at the beginning of the sentence turns out to be incorrect, based on information that is present later in the sentence. (10)

General events As proposed by Conway, events in a person's life that happens over days, weeks, or months. See also **Event-specific knowledge; Lifetime periods.** (7)

Geon The basic feature unit of the recognition-by-components approach to object perception. Geons are basic three-dimensional volumes. (3)

Gestalt psychologists A group of psychologists who disagreed with the structuralist approach to perception, and who proposed the laws of perceptual organization. (3)

Given-new contract A speaker should construct sentences so that they contain both given information (information that the listener already knows) and new information (information that the listener is hearing for the first time). (10)

Global connection A connection that occurs between what a person is reading and what they read much earlier. (10)

Goal state In problem solving, the condition at the end of a problem. (11)

Good continuation, law of Law of perceptual organization stating that connected points that result in straight or smoothly curving lines, are seen as belonging together. In addition, lines tend to be seen as following the smoothest path. (3)

Good figure, law of See **Pragnanz, law of.** (3)

Graceful degradation Disruption of performance due to damage to a system, which occurs only gradually as parts of the system are damaged. This occurs in some cases of brain damage and also when parts of a connectionist network are damaged. (8)

Heuristic A "rule of thumb" that provides a best-guess solution to a problem. (3)

Hidden units Units in a connectionist network that located between input units and output units. See also **Connectionist network; Input units; Output units.** (8)

Hierarchical organization Organization of categories in which larger, more general categories are divided into smaller, more specific categories. These smaller categories can, in turn, be divided into even more specific categories to create a number of levels. (8)

High-prototypicality A category member that closely resembles the category prototype. See also **Prototypicality.** (8)

Hippocampus A subcortical structure that is important in forming memories. (2)

Hobbits-and-orcs problem A problem involving transporting hobbits and orcs across a river that has been used to illustrate how the means-end strategy must sometimes be violated in order to solve a problem. (11)

Iconic memory Brief sensory memory for visual stimuli that lasts for a fraction of a second after a stimulus is extinguished. This corresponds to the sensory memory stage of the modal model of memory. (5)

Ill-defined problem A problem in which it is difficult to specify a clear goal state or specific operators. Many real-life problems are ill-defined problems. (11)

Illusory conjunctions A situation that has been demonstrated in experiments by Anne Treisman, in which features from different objects are inappropriately combined. (3)

Illusory correlation A correlation between two events that appears to exist, when in reality there is no correlation or it is weaker than it is assumed to be. (12)

Image scanning A procedure in which a person creates a mental image and then scans the image in his or her mind. (9)

Imageless-thought debate The debate about whether thought was possible in the absence of images. (9)

Imagery debate The debate about whether imagery is based on spatial mechanisms such as those involved in perception, or on propositional mechanisms that are related to language. (9)

Imagery neurons A type of category-specific neuron is activated by imagery. (9)

Implicit memory Memory that occurs when an experience affects a person's behavior, even though the person is not aware that he or she had the experience. Also called nondeclarative memory. (6)

Indirect statements Statements in which the literal meaning is not the meaning that the speaker intends. (10)

Inductive reasoning Reasoning in which a conclusion follows from a consideration of evidence. This conclusion is stated as being probably true, rather than definitely true, as can be the case for the conclusions from deductive reasoning. (12)

Inference The process by which people reach conclusions based on incomplete or partial information. (7, 10)

Inferotemporal cortex Area in the temporal lobe that is specialized to process information about form. (2)

Information-processing approach The approach to psychology, developed beginning in the 1950s, in which the mind is seen as processing information through a sequence of stages. (1)

Inhibition An effect caused by inhibitory neurotransmitter that decreases the rate of nerve firing or the likelihood of nerve firing. (2)

Inhibitory neurotransmitter Neurotransmitter that causes an inhibitory effect on a membrane. This inhibitory effect causes a decrease in firing or in the likelihood of firing. (2)

Initial state In problem solving, the conditions at the beginning of a problem. (11)

Inner scribe Part of the visuospatial sketch pad in the updated version of the working memory model that is responsible that for manipulating images that are in the visual buffer. See also **Visual buffer.** (9)

Input units Units in a connectionist network that are activated by stimulation from the environment. See also **Connectionist network; Hidden units; Output units.** (8)

Insight Sudden realization of a problem's solution. (11)

Instrumental inference An inference about tools or methods that occurs during reading or listening to speech. See also **Anaphoric inference; Causal inference.** (10)

Interactionist approach to parsing The approach to parsing that takes into account all information—both semantic and syntactic—to determine parsing as a person reads a sentence. This approach to parsing assigns more weight to semantics than does the syntax-first approach to parsing. (10)

Intermediate states In problem solving, the various conditions that exist along the pathways between the initial and goal states. (11)

Inverse projection problem The ambiguity of the retinal image caused by the fact that a particular image could be caused by an infinite number of objects, with different sizes, shapes, orientations, and located at different distances from the eye. (3)

Korsakoff's syndrome A condition caused by prolonged vitamin B1 deficiency that leads to destruction of areas on the frontal and temporal lobes, which causes severe impairments in memory. (6)

Language A system of communication through which we code and express our feelings, thoughts, ideas, and experiences. (10)

Late closure, principle of When a person encounters a new word, the parser assumes that this word is part of the current phrase. (10)

Late-selection model of attention A model of selective attention that proposes that selection of stimuli for final processing does not occur until after the information in the message has been analyzed for its meaning. (4)

Law of large numbers The larger the number of individuals that are randomly drawn from a population, the more representative the resulting group will be of the entire population. (12)

Law(s) of common fate, familiarity, good continuation, good figure, nearness, perceptual organization, Pragnanz, proximity, similarity, simplicity See inverted entries (e.g., **Common fate, law of**).

Letter units Units in the feature analysis model of object perception that respond to specific letters. (3)

Letter-analysis stage A stage in the feature analysis model of object perception consisting of a bank of letter units that respond to specific letters. (3)

Levels of processing Part of levels of processing theory that states that there are different depths of processing that can be achieved information is being encoded. See also **Levels of processing theory; Depth of processing.** (6)

Levels-of-processing theory The idea that memory depends on how information is encoded, with better memory being achieved when processing is deep than when processing is shallow. Deep processing involves attention to meaning and is associated with elaborative rehearsal. Shallow processing involves repetition with little attention to meaning and is associated with maintenance rehearsal. (6)

Lexical ambiguity The condition that exists when a word can have more than one meaning. (10)

Lexical-decision task A procedure in which a person is asked to decide as quickly as possible, whether a particular stimulus is a word or a nonword. (8, 10)

Lexicon All of the words that a person understands—the person's vocabulary. (10)

Life-narrative hypothesis An explanation for the reminiscence bump, which states that memories are better for adolescence and early adulthood because people assume their life identities during that time. (7)

Lifetime periods As proposed by Conway, events in a person's life that span many years. See also **Event-specific knowledge; General events.** (7)

Light-from-above heuristic The assumption that light is coming from above. (3)

Local connection A connection that occurs between what a person is reading and what they read 1–3 sentences previously. (10)

Localization of function Location of specific functions in specific areas of the brain. For example, areas have been identified that are specialized to process information involved in the perception of movement, the perception of form, speech, and different aspects of memory. See also **Modules.** (2)

Location-based attention Models of attention that propose that attention operates on whatever stimuli are at a particular location. This contrasts with object-based attention, in which attention is focused on a particular object. (4)

Long-term memory A memory mechanism that can hold large amounts of information for long periods of time. Long-term memory is one of the stages in the modal model of memory. (5)

Long-term potentiation (LTP) The increased firing that occurs in a postsynaptic neuron due to prior activity at the synapse. (6)

Low-prototypicality A category member that does not resemble the category prototype. See also **Prototypicality**. (8)

Maintenance rehearsal Rehearsal that involves repetition without any consideration of meaning or making connections to other information. Compare to **Elaborative rehearsal.** (6)

Manner Grice's conversational maxim that states that participants in a conversation should be clear, and so should avoid being ambiguous. (10)

Means-end analysis A problem-solving strategy in which the goal is to reduce the difference between the initial and goal state. This is achieved by working to achieve subgoals that move the process of solution closer to the goal. (11)

Medial temporal area Area in the temporal lobe that is specialized to process information about movement. (2)

Medial temporal lobe (MTL) An area in the temporal lobe that consists of the hippocampus and a number of surrounding structures. Damage to the MTL causes problems in forming new long-term memories. (6)

Memory The processes involved in retaining, retrieving, and using information about stimuli, images, events, ideas, and skills, after the original information is no longer present. (5)

Memory consolidation Strengthening of the neural information representing a memory over time. See also **Consolidation period.** (6)

Memory impairment hypothesis The explanation of the misinformation effect that states that misleading postevent information impairs or replaces the memories that were formed during the original experiencing of an event. (7)

Mental chronometry Measuring the time-course of mental processes. (1)

Mental imagery Experiencing a sensory impression in the absence of sensory input. (9)

Mental model In reasoning, a mental model is a specific situation that is represented in a person's mind that can be used to help determine the validity of syllogisms in deductive reasoning. (12)

Mental set A person's tendency to respond in a certain manner, based on past experience. (11)

Mental simulation Models that people create about what will happen following different decisions. (12)

Mental synthesis A process in which patterns are created by manipulating mental images. (9)

Mental-walk task A task used in imagery experiments in which participants are asked to form a mental image of an object and to imagine that they are walking toward this mental image. (9)

Method of loci A method for remembering things in which things to be remembered are placed at different locations in a mental image of a spatial layout. See also **Pegword technique.** (9)

Microelectrodes Small wires that are used to record electrical signals from the axons of neurons. (2)

Misinformation effect Occurs when misleading information presented after a person witnesses an event can change how that person describes the event later. (7)

Misleading postevent information (MPI) The misleading information that causes the misinformation effect. (7)

Modal model of memory The model proposed by Atkinson and Shiffrin describing memory as a mechanism that involves processing information through a series of stages, which include short-term memory and long-term memory. It is called the *modal model* because of the great influence it has had on memory research. (5)

Modules A brain area specialized to process information related to a specific function. See also **Localization of function.**

Modus ponens *Method of affirming.* A conditional syllogism in which the first premise is "If p then q," the second premise is "p," and the conclusion is "q." This is a valid form of conditional syllogism. See also **Affirming the consequent; Denying the antecedent;** *Modus tollens.* (12)

Modus tollens *Method of denying.* A conditional syllogism in which the first premise is "If p then q," the second is "not q," and the conclusion is "not p." This is a valid form of conditional syllogism. See also **Affirming the consequent; Denying the antecedent;** *Modus ponens.* (12)

Motion agnosia Condition caused by brain damage in which a person cannot perceive the movement of objects. (2)

Mutilated-checkerboard problem A problem that has been used to study how the statement of a problem influences a person's ability to reach a solution. (11)

Narrative rehearsal hypothesis The idea that we remember some life events better because we rehearse them. This idea was proposed by Neisser as an explanation for "flashbulb" memories. (7)

Natural selection, theory of The idea that genetically based characteristics that enhance an animal's ability to survive and reproduce will be passed on to future generations. (3)

Nearness, law of Law of perceptual organization that states that things that are near to each other appear to be grouped together. (3)

Nerve fiber See **Axon.** (2)

Neural circuits Groups of interconnected neurons that are responsible for neural processing. (2)

Neural code The representation of specific stimuli or experiences by the firing of neurons. (2)

Neural processing Interactions between neurons that cause a target neuron or group of neurons to respond to specific stimuli. (2)

Neurons Cells that are specialized to receive and transmit information in the nervous system. (2)

Neuropsychology The study of the behavioral effects of brain damage in humans. (2)

Neurotransmitter Chemical that is released at the synapse in response to incoming action potentials. (2)

Nondeclarative memory See **Implicit memory.** (6)

Normative approach The approach to studying syllogisms that indicates which forms of syllogisms are logically valid and which are not valid. This approach involves the rules of logic, but does not involve psychology. See also **Descriptive approach.** (12)

Object-based attention Model of attention proposing that the enhancing effects of attention can be located on a particular object. This contrasts with *location-based attention*, in which attention is focused on a location. (4)

Occipital lobe The lobe at the back of the brain that is devoted primarily to analyzing incoming visual information. (2)

Occlusion heuristic When a large object is occluded by a smaller one, we perceive the large object as continuing behind the smaller one. (3)

Operators In problem solving, permissible moves that can be made toward a problem's solution. (11)

Output units Units in a connectionist network that contain the final output of the network. See also **Connectionist network; Hidden units; Input units.** (8)

Paired-associate learning Learning that occurs when a participant is presented with pairs of words during a study period and then is tested when one of the words is presented and the task is to recall the other word. (9)

Parallel distributed processing approach (PDP) See **Connectionism; Connectionist network.** (8)

Parietal lobe The lobe at the top of the brain that contains mechanisms responsible for sensations caused by stimulation of the skin, and also some aspects of visual information. (2)

Parser The mechanism for determining the way words are grouped together into phrases; has also been called the *language-analysis device* and the *sentence-analyzing mechanism*. (10)

Parsing The mental groping of words in a sentence into phrases. (10)

Partial-report procedure The procedure used in Sperling's experiment in which he was studying the properties of the visual icon. His participants were instructed to report only some of the stimuli in a briefly presented display. See also **Sensory memory; Whole-report procedure.** (5)

Pegword technique A method for remembering things in which the things to be remembered are associated with concrete words. See also **Method of loci.** (9)

Perception Conscious experience that results from stimulation of the senses. (3)

Perceptual organization The process of organizing elements of the environment into separate objects. (3)

Perceptual organization, laws of Rules proposed by the Gestalt psychologists that specify how we perceptually organize parts into wholes. (3)

Permission schema A pragmatic reasoning schema that states that if a person satisfies condition A, then they get to carry out action B. The permission schema has been used to explain the results of the Wason four-card problem. (12)

Perseveration Difficulty in switching from one behavior to another, which can hinder a person's ability to solve problems that require flexible thinking. Perseveration is observed in cases in which the prefrontal cortex has been damaged. (11)

Persistence of vision The continued perception of light for a fraction of a second after the original light stimulus has been extinguished. Perceiving a trail of light from a moving sparkler is caused by the persistence of vision. (5)

Phoneme The shortest segment of speech that, if changed, changes the meaning of a word. (10)

Phonological coding Coding in the mind in auditory form. An example of phonological coding would be remembering something in terms of its sound. For example, since the letters "t" and "p" sound the same, they have similar phonological codes. See also **Semantic coding; Visual coding.** (5)

Phonological loop The part of working memory that holds and processes verbal and auditory information. See also **Central executive; Visuospatial sketch pad; Working memory.** (5)

Phonological similarity effect An effect that occurs when letters or words that sound similar are confused. For example, "T" and "P" are examples of two similar-sounding letters that could be confused. (5)

Physiological approach to the study of the mind When the mind is studied by measuring physiological and behavioral responses, and when behavior is explained in physiological terms. (1)

Pop-out A situation in which, in a visual search task, the target stimulus is detected immediately (it "pops out"). When pop-out occurs, the speed of detection of the target stimulus is independent of the number of distractors. (3)

Positive-change bias The tendency for people to perceive that "things are getting better." See also **Consistency bias; Egocentric bias.** (7)

Positron emission tomography (PET) A brain-imaging technique involving the injection of a radioactive tracer. (2)

Pragmatic reasoning schema A way of thinking about cause and effect in the world that is learned as part of experiencing everyday life. See also **Permission schema.** (12)

Pragnanz, law of Law of perceptual organization that states that every stimulus pattern is seen in such as way that the resulting structure is as simple as possible. Also called the *law of good figure* and the *law of simplicity.*

Preattentive stage The first stage of Treisman's feature integration theory, in which an object is analyzed into its features. (3)

Precueing procedure A procedure in which participants are given a cue which will, usually, help them carry out a subsequent task. This procedure has been used in visual attention experiments in which participants are presented with a cue that tells them where to direct their attention. (4)

Premises The first two statements in a syllogism. (12)

Primacy effect In a memory experiment in which a list of words is presented, enhanced memory for words presented at the beginning of the list. See also **Recency effect.** (5)

Proactive interference A situation in which information learned previously interferes with learning new information. (5)

Problem A situation that occurs when there is an obstacle between a present state and a goal state and it is not immediately obvious how to get around the obstacle. (11)

Problem schema In analogical problem solving, the basic concept that links the source problem and the target problem. See also **Schema induction.** (11)

Problem space The mental space within which solution of a problem occurs. The idea of a problem space, which is associated with Newell and Simon, states that the problem space consists of the following four components: initial state, goal state, intermediate states, and operators. The problem space can be thought of as a maze of pathways between the initial and goal state. (11)

Procedural memory Memory for how to carry out highly practiced skills. Procedural memory is a type of implicit memory, because although people can carry out a skilled behavior, they often cannot explain exactly how they are able to carry out this behavior. (6)

Propaganda effect When people are more likely to rate statements they have read or heard before as being true, just because of prior exposure to the statements. (6)

Propagated A property of action potentials. Once they are generated, they travel unchanged down the length of an axon. (2)

Propositional representation A representation in which relationships are represented by symbols, as when the words of language represent objects and the relationships between objects. (9)

Prospagnosia Condition caused by brain damage in which a person cannot recognize the faces of familiar people. (2)

Prototype A standard used in categorization that is formed by averaging the category members a person has encountered in the past. (8)

Prototype approach to categorization The idea that we decide whether something is a member of a category by determining whether it is similar to a standard representation of the category called a prototype. (8)

Prototypicality The degree to which a particular member of a category matches the prototype for that category. See also **High-prototypicality; Low-prototypicality.** (8)

Proximity, law of Law of perceptual organization that states that things that are near to each other appear to be grouped together. (3)

Psycholinguistics The field concerned with the psychological study of language. (10)

Quality Grice's conversational maxim that states that a participant in a conversation should be informative, and so should not be either over-informative or underinformative. (10)

Quantity Grice's conversational maxim that states that participants in a conversation should be truthful, and so should not say things that are false or for which they lack sufficient evidence. (10)

Radiation problem A problem posed by Duncker that is difficult to solve, but becomes easier when participants are exposed to an analogous source problem. (11)

Rat-man demonstration Demonstration in which presentation of a "rat-like" or "man-like" stimulus picture can bias perception of another picture that is presented immediately afterward, so that it is more likely to be perceived as a rat or as a man. This is an example of the technique of priming. (3)

Reaction time The time it takes for a person to react to a stimulus. This is usually determined by measuring the time between presentation of a stimulus and the person's response to the stimulus. Examples of responses are pushing a button, saying a word, moving the eyes, and appearance of a particular brain wave. (1)

Reasoning Cognitive processes by which people start with information and come to conclusions that go beyond that information. See also **Deductive reasoning; Inductive reasoning.** (12)

Recency effect. In a memory experiment in which a list of words is presented, enhanced memory for words presented at the end of the list. See also **Primacy effect.** (5)

Receptors Neurons that are specialized to receive information from the environment. (2)

Recognition-by-components approach A feature-based approach to object perception that proposes that the recognition of objects is based on three-dimensional features called geons. (3)

Recovered memory A term used to refer to the situation in which memories of traumatic experiences, such as childhood abuse, are recalled after many years during which the person was not aware of these memories. The idea that these memories are "recovered" due to a special mechanism is controversial; many psychologists interpret this effect in terms of normal mechanisms of forgetting and remembering. (7)

Rehearsal The process of repeating a stimulus over and over, usually for the purpose of remembering it, by keeping it active in short-term memory. (5)

Relation Grice's conversational maxim that states that participants in a conversation should be relevant, and so should stay on the topic of the conversation. (10)

Release from proactive interference A situation in which conditions occur that eliminate or reduce the decrease in performance caused by proactive interference. See Wilkens's experiment described in Chapter 5. (5)

Reminiscence bump The empirical finding that people over 40 years old have enhanced memory for events from adolescence and early adulthood, compared to other periods of their lives. (7)

Repeated reproduction A method of measuring memory in which a person recalls a stimulus on repeated occasions so his or her memory is tested at longer and longer intervals after the original presentation of the material to be remembered. (7)

Repetition priming When an initial presentation of a stimulus affects the person's response to the same stimulus when it is presented later. (6)

Representativeness heuristic The idea that the probability that an event A comes from class B can be determined by how well A resembles the properties of class B. (12)

Resistance to visual noise In recognition-by-components theory, the property that geons can be perceived under "noisy" conditions that obscure part of the geon. (3)

Retina A network of neurons that lines the back of the eye. Transduction and the initial processing of visual information occur in the retina. (2)

Retrieval The process of remembering information that has been stored in long-term memory. (5)

Retrieval cues Cues that help a person remember information that is stored in memory. (6)

Retrograde amnesia. Loss of memory for something that happened prior to an injury or traumatic event such as a concussion. (6)

Risk-aversion strategy A decision-making strategy that is governed by the idea of avoiding risk. Often used when a problem is stated in terms of gains. See also **Risk-taking strategy.** (12)

Risk-taking strategy A decision-making strategy that is governed by the idea of taking risks. Often used when a problem is stated in terms of losses. See also **Risk-aversion strategy.** (12)

Sapir-Whorf hypothesis The idea that the nature of language in a particular culture can affect the way people in that culture think. (10)

Schema A person's knowledge about what is involved in a particular experience. For example, a person's knowledge about what usually happens when they go to the dentist's office is their "dentist's office" schema. See also **Script.** (7)

Schema induction The process of activating the problem schema in analogical problem solving. See also **Problem schema.** (11)

Script A type of schema. The conception of the sequence of actions that describe a particular activity. For example, the sequence of events that are associated with going to class would be a "going to class" script. See also **Schema.** (7)

Selective attention The ability to focus on one message and ignore all others. (4)

Self-reference effect Memory for a word is improved by relating the word to the self. (6)

Semantic coding Coding in the mind in the form of meaning. An example of semantic coding would be remembering the meaning of something you have read, as opposed to what the letters or words looked like (visual coding) or sounded like (phonological coding). (5)

Semantic memory Memory for knowledge about the world that is not tied to any specific personal experience. Semantic and episodic memory, together, make up declarative memory. (6)

Semantic network approach The approach to concepts in which concepts are arranged in networks that represent the way the concepts are organized in the mind. (8)

Semantics The meanings of words and sentences. Distinguished from **Syntax.** (10)

Sensations Small elementary units that, according to the structuralists, are added together to create perceptions. (3)

Sensory memory A brief stage of memory that holds information for seconds or fractions of a second. It is the first stage in the modal model of memory. See also **Visual icon; Echoic memory.** (5)

Sentence-verification technique A technique in which the participant is asked to indicate whether or not a particular sentence is true or false. For example, sentences like "an apple is a fruit" have been used in studies on categorization. (8)

Serial-position curve In a memory experiment in which a number of participants are presented with a list of words, the serial position curve is a plot of the percentage of participants remembering each word, versus the position of that word in the list. See also **Primacy effect; Recency effect.** (5)

Shadowing The procedure of repeating a message out loud as it is heard. Shadowing is commonly used in conjunction with studies of selective attention that use the dichotic-listening procedure. (4)

Shallow processing Processing that involves repetition with little attention to meaning. Shallow processing is usually associated with maintenance rehearsal. See also **Deep processing; Depth of processing.** (6)

Short-term memory A memory mechanism that can hold a limited amount of information for a brief period of time, usually around 30 seconds, unless there is rehearsal (such as repeating a telephone number) that can maintain information in long-term memory. Short-term memory is one of the stages in the modal model of memory. (5)

Similarity, law of Law of perceptual organization that states that similar things appear to be grouped together. (3)

Similarity-coverage model A model designed to explain how people's conceptions of different categories influences the strength of inductive arguments. Two basic principles of the model are typicality (the argument with the most typical example of a category in the premise is the strongest argument) and diversity (the argument with the greatest coverage of a category is stronger). (12)

Simple cells A type of neuron in the visual cortex that responds best to presentation of an oriented bar of light. (2)

Simple reaction time Reacting to the presence or absence of a single stimulus (as opposed to having to choose between a number of stimuli before making a response). (1)

Simplicity, law of See **Pragnanz, law of.** (3)

Single dissociation A dissociation in which one function is present and another is absent. (2)

Single-unit recording Recording electrical signals from single neurons. This is accomplished by a microelectrode placed inside or near the neuron. (2)

Situation model A mental representation of what a text is about. (10)

Social-exchange theory An important aspect of human behavior is the ability for two people to cooperate in a way that is beneficial to both people. According to the evolutionary perspective on cognition, application of this theory can lead to the conclusion that detecting cheating is an important part of the brain's cognitive makeup. This idea has been used to explain the results of the Wason four-card problem. (12)

Source misattribution Errors of source monitoring in which people attribute something they remember to the wrong source. (7)

Source monitoring. The process by which people determine the origins of memories, knowledge, or beliefs. Remembering that you heard about something from a particular person would be an example of source monitoring. (7)

Source problem A problem that is analogous to the target problem and which therefore provides information that can lead to a solution to the target problem. (11)

Spatial representation A representation in which different parts of an image can be described as corresponding to specific locations in space. See also **Depictive representation.** (9)

Speech segmentation The ability to organize the sounds of speech into individual words. (3)

Speech segmentation The process of perceiving individual words from the continuous flow of the speech signal. (10)

Spotlight model of attention The model of visual attention that conceives of attention as having an effect similar to a spotlight that, when directed at different locations, increases the efficiency for which signals at that location can be processed. (4)

Spreading activation Activity that spreads out along any link in a network that is connected to an activated node. (8)

Standing ambiguity Ambiguity that persists even after reading an entire sentence. Context or other information is needed in order to resolve this type of ambiguity. See also **Temporary ambiguity.** (10)

State-dependent learning The principle that memory is best if a person is in the same state for encoding and retrieval. This principle is related to encoding specificity. (6)

Stereotype An oversimplified generalization about a group or class of people that often focuses on negative characteristics. See also **Illusory correlation.** (12)

Stroop effect An effect originally studied by J. R. Stroop, using a task in which a person is instructed to respond to one aspect of a stimulus, such as the color of ink that a word is printed in, and ignore another aspect, such as what the word spells. The Stroop effect refers to the fact that people find this task difficult because the ink color differs from what the word spells. (1, 4)

Structural features In the modal model of memory, structural features are the various stages of the model, such as sensory memory, short-term memory, and long-term memory. (5)

Structuralism. An approach to psychology that explained perception as the adding-up of small elementary units called sensations. (3)

Subcortical structures Brain structures located beneath the cerebral cortex. Subcortical structures that are important for cognition are the amygdala, hippocampus, and thalamus. (2)

Subgoal In the means-end analysis approach to problem solving, subgoals are goals that create intermediate states that move the process of solution closer to the goal. (11)

Subordinate level The level in Rosch's categorization scheme that is a level below the basic level, and so would correspond to *kitchen table* for the basic category of *table*. See also **Basic level; Superordinate level.** (8)

Subtraction technique The technique used in brain imaging in which baseline activity is subtracted from the activity generated by a specific task. The result is the activity due only to the task that is being studied. (2)

Superordinate level The highest level in Rosch's categorization scheme that corresponds to general categories such as *furniture* or *vehicles*. See also **Basic level; Subordinate level.** (8)

Syllogism A series of three statements, two premises followed by a conclusion. The conclusion can follow from the premises based on the rules of logic. See also **Categorical syllogism; Conditional syllogism.** (12)

Synapse Space between the end of an axon and the cell body or dendrite of another neuron. (2)

Syntactic ambiguity Sentences that are ambiguous because they can be parsed in more than one way. (10)

Syntax The rules for combining words into sentences. Distinguished from semantics. (10)

Syntax-first approach to parsing The approach to parsing that emphasizes the role of syntax in determining parsing. See also **Interactionist approach to parsing.** (10)

Tacit-knowledge explanation An explanation proposed to account for the results of some imagery experiments that states that participants unconsciously use knowledge about the world in making their judgments. This explanation has been used as one of the arguments against describing imagery as a depictive or spatial representation. (9)

Target problem A problem to be solved. In analogical problem solving, solution of this problem can become easier if the problem solver is exposed to an analogous source problem. (11)

Task load How much of a person's cognitive resources are used to accomplish a task. The idea of task load is important for some explanations of selective attention and also for explanations of how people process information in working memory. (4)

Temporal lobe The lobe on the side of the brain that contains mechanisms responsible for language, memory, hearing, and vision. (2)

Temporary ambiguity Ambiguity that occurs in the middle of a sentence, but is resolved when the information at the end of the sentence becomes available. (10)

Thalamus A subcortical structure that is important for processing information from the senses of vision, hearing, and touch. (2)

Top-down processing Processing that involves a person's knowledge or expectations; can also be called knowledge-based processing. See also **Bottom-up processing.** (3)

Tower of Hanoi problem A problem involving moving discs from one set of pegs to another set. It has been used to illustrate the process involved in means-end analysis. (11)

Transduction The transformation of one form of energy into another. In the nervous system, environmental energy is transformed into electrical energy. (2)

Transfer-appropriate processing When the type of encoding that occurs during acquisition matches the type of encoding that occurs during acquisition. This type of processing can result in enhanced memory. (6)

Two-string problem A problem first described by Maier in which a person is given the task of attaching two strings together that are too far apart to be reached at the same time. This task was devised to illustrate the operation of functional fixedness. (11)

Typicality effect The ability to judge the truth or falsity of sentences involving high-prototypical members of a category more rapidly than sentences involving low-prototypical members of a category. See also **Sentence-verification technique.** (8)

Typicality principle The inductive argument with the most typical example of a category in the premise is the strongest argument. See also **Diversity; Similarity-coverage model.** (12)

Unconscious inference Helmholtz's idea that some of our perceptions are the result of unconscious assumptions that we make about the environment. (1)

Unilateral neglect A condition that is usually associated with damage to the right parietal lobe, in which the person ignores stimuli presented in the left half of the visual field. Neglect is usually described as a lack of attention to the left side of space. (4)

Units "Neuron-like processing units" in a connectionist network. See also **Hidden units; Input units; Output units.** (8)

Utility An approach to decision making that states that optimal decision-making occurs when the outcome of the decision causes the maximum expected utility, where utility refers to outcomes that are desirable. (12)

Valid or **Validity** A situation that occurs in syllogisms when the conclusion follows logically from the premises. (12)

View invariance In recognition-by-components theory, the idea that geons can be identified when viewed from many different angles. (3)

View invariant properties In recognition-by-components theory, properties that give geons the property of view invariance. (3)

Visual agnosia. A condition associated with brain damage in which a person can see an object but cannot name the object. (8)

Visual buffer Part of the visuospatial sketch pad in the updated version of the working memory model, which is responsible for our conscious experience of images. See also **Inner scribe.** (9)

Visual coding Coding in the mind in the form of a visual image. An example of visual coding, would be remembering something by conjuring up an image of it in your mind. See also **Phonological coding; Semantic coding.** (5)

Visual icon Brief sensory memory for visual stimuli, which lasts for a fraction of a second after a stimulus is extinguished. The visual icon is associated with the sensory memory stage of the modal model of memory. (5)

Visual imagery A type of mental imagery involving vision, in which an image is experienced in the absence of a visual stimulus. (9)

Visual search A procedure in which the task involves finding a specific target object among other, distractor, objects. (3)

Visuospatial sketch pad The part of working memory that holds and processes visual and spatial information. See also **Central executive; Phonological loop; Working memory.** (5)

Wason four-card problem A conditional-reasoning task involving four cards that was developed by Wason. Various versions of this problem have been used to determine the mechanisms that determine the outcomes of conditional-reasoning tasks. (12)

Water-jug problem A problem first described by Luchins that illustrates how mental set can influence the strategies that people use to solve a problem. (11)

Weapons focus A situation that occurs in which eyewitnesses to a crime tend to focus attention on a weapon, which causes poorer memory for other things that are happening. (7)

Weight The strength of a connection between units in a connectionist network. (8)

Wernicke's area Area of the brain in the temporal lobe involved in language. Damage to Wernicke's area typically produces speech that is confused and not meaningful. (10)

Whole-report procedure The procedure used in Sperling's experiment in which he was studying the properties of the visual icon. His participants were instructed to report all of the stimuli they saw in a brief presentation. See also **Partial-report procedure; Sensory memory.** (5)

Word-frequency effect The phenomenon of faster reading time for high-frequency words compared to low-frequency words. (10)

Word-length effect The finding that it is more difficult to remember a list of long words than a list of short words. (5)

Word-superiority effect The idea that letters are easier to identify when they are part of a word than when they are seen in isolation or in a string of letters that do not form a word. (10)

Working memory A limited capacity system for temporary storage and manipulation of information for complex tasks such as comprehension, learning, and reasoning. (5)

Zoom lens model A model of selective attention that conceives of attention as being like a zoom lens, in which attention can be spread over large areas or "zoomed in" to be focused on smaller areas. See also **Spotlight model of attention.** (4)

References

Abel, T., & Lattal, K. M. (2001). Molecular mechanisms of memory acquisition, consolidation, and retrieval. *Current Opinion in Neurobiology, 11,* 180–187.

Acuna, B. D., Eliassen, J. C., Donoghue, J. P., & Sanes, J. N. (2002). Frontal and parietal lobe activation during transitive inference in humans. *Cerebral Cortex, 12,* 1312–1321.

Adamson, R. E. (1952). Functional fixedness as related to problem solving. *Journal of Experimental Psychology, 44,* 288–291.

Albrecht, J. E., & O'Brien, E. J. (1993). Updating a mental model: Maintaining both local and global coherence. *Journal of Experimental Psychology: Learning, Memory, and Cognition, 19,* 1061–1070.

Allende, I. (2001). *Portrait in sepia.* New York: HarperCollins.

Altmann, G. T. M. (1998). Ambiguity in sentence processing. *Trends in Cognitive Sciences, 2,* 146–152.

Altmann, G. T. M. (2001). The language machine: Psycholinguistics in review. *British Journal of Psychology, 92,* 129–170.

Altmann, G. T. M., & Kamide, Y. (1999). Incremental interpretation at verbs: Restricting the domain of subsequent reference. *Cognition, 73,* 247–264.

Altmann, G. T. M., & Steedman, M. J. (1988). Interaction with context during human sentence parsing. *Cognition, 30,* 191–238.

American Psychological Association (1996). Interim report of the working group on investigation of memories of childhood abuse. In K. Pezelek & W. P. Banks (Eds.), *The recovered memory/false memory debate* (pp. 371–392). San Diego: Academic Press.

Anderson, C. A., & Bushman, B. J. (2001). Effect of violent video games on aggressive behavior, aggressive cognitions, aggressive affect, physiological arousal, and prosocial behavior: A meta-analytic review of the literature. *Psychological Science, 12,* 353–359.

Anderson, M. C., Ochsner, K. N., Kuhl, B., Cooper, J., Robertson, E., Gabrieli, S. W., Glover, G. H., & Gabrieli, J. D. E. (2004). Neural systems underlying the suppression of unwanted memories. *Science, 303,* 232–235.

Anderson, J. R. (1978). Arguments concerning representation for mental imagery. *Psychological Review, 85,* 249–277.

Anderson, J. R., & Bower, G. H. (1973). *Human associative memory.* Washington, DC: V. H. Winston.

Anderson, J. R., & Schooler, L. J. (1991). Reflections of the environment in memory. *Psychological Science, 2,* 396–408.

Andrade, J. (Ed.). (2002). *Working memory in perspective.* Philadelphia: Psychology Press.

Annenberg/CPB Project/WNET-TV (2000). *The Mind Video,* 2nd ed. F. J. Vattano, T. L. Bennett, & M. Butler (Eds.), Module 11: Clive Wearing, part 2: Living without memory.

Arkes, H. R., & Freedman, M. R. (1984). A demonstration of the costs and benefits of expertise in recognition memory. *Memory & Cognition, 12,* 84–89.

Atkinson, R. C., & Shiffrin, R. M. (1968). Human memory: A proposed system and its control processes. In K. W. Spence & J. T. Spence (Eds.), *The psychology of learning and motivation.* New York: Academic Press.

Baddeley, A. D. (1996). Exploring the central executive. *Quarterly Journal of Experimental Psychology, 49A,* 5–28.

Baddeley, A. D. (2000). Short-term and working memory. In E. Tulving & F. I. M. Craik (Eds.), *The Oxford handbook of memory* (pp. 77–92). New York: Oxford University Press.

Baddeley, A. D., & Hitch, G. J. (1974). Working memory. In G. A. Bower (Ed.), *The psychology of learning and motivation* (pp. 47–89). New York: Academic Press.

Baddeley, A. D., Lewis, V. F. J., & Vallar, G. (1984). Exploring the articulatory loop. *Quarterly Journal of Experimental Psychology, 36,* 233–252.

Baddeley, A. D., Thomson, N., & Buchanan, M. (1975). Word length and the structure of short-term memory. *Journal of Verbal Learning and Verbal Behavior, 14,* 575–589.

Bahrick, H. P., Hall, L, L., & Berger, S. A. (1996). Accuracy and distortion in memory for high school grades. *Psychological Science, 7,* 265–271.

Bailenson, J. N., Shum, M. S., Atran, S., Medin, D. L., & Coley, J. D. (2002). A bird's-eye view: Biological categorization and reasoning within and across cultures. *Cognition, 84,* 1–53.

Barrow, H. G., & Tannenbaum, J. M. (1986). Computational approaches to vision. In K. R. Boff, L. Kaufman, & J. P. Thomas (Eds.), *Handbook of perception and human performance* (Chapter 35). New York: Wiley.

Bartlett, F. C. (1932). *Remembering: A study in experimental and social psychology.* Cambridge, UK: Cambridge University Press.

Baylis, G. C., & Driver, J. (1993). Visual attention and objects: evidence for hierarchical coding of location. *Journal of Experimental Psychology: Human Perception and Performance, 19,* 451–470.

Bechtel, W., Abrahamsen, A., & Graham, G. (1998). The life of cognitive science. In W. Bechtel & G. Graham (Eds.), *A companion to cognitive science* (pp. 2–104). Oxford, UK: Blackwell.

Beck, J. (1982). Textural segmentation. In J. Beck (Ed.), *Organization and representation in perception.* Hillsdale, NJ: Erlbaum.

Beck, J., Hope, B., & Rosenfeld, A. (Eds.). (1983). *Human and machine vision.* New York: Academic Press.

Bedard, J., & Chi, M. T. H. (1992). *Current Directions in Psychological Science, 1,* 135–139.

Begg, I. (1972). Recall of meaningful phrases. *Journal of Verbal Learning and Verbal Behavior, 11,* 431–439.

Begg, I., Anas, A., & Farinacci, S. (1992). Dissociation of processes in belief: Source recollection, statement familiarity, and the illusion of truth. *Journal of Experimental Psychology: General, 121,* 446–458.

Behrmann, M., Moscovitch, M., & Winocur, G. (1994). Intact visual imagery and impaired visual perception in a patient with visual agnosia. *Journal of Experimental Psychology: Human Perception and Performance, 30,* 1068–1087.

Behrmann, M., & Tipper, S. P. (1994). Object-based attentional mechanisms: Evidence from patients with unilateral neglect. In C. Umilta & M. Moscovitch (Eds.), *Attention and performance XV: Conscious and nonconscious information processing* (pp. 351–375). Cambridge, MA: MIT Press.

Behrmann, M., & Tipper, S. P. (1999). Attention accesses multiple reference frames: evidence from visual neglect. *Journal of Experimental Psychology: Human Perception and Performance, 25,* 83–101.

Bensley, L., & VanEewyk, J. (2001). Video games and real life aggression: Review of the literature. *Journal of Adolescent Health, 29,* 244–257.

Bever, T. G., Sanz, M., & Townsend, D. J. (1998). The emperor's psycholinguistics. *Journal of Psycholinguistic Research, 27,* 261–284.

Biederman, I. (1981). On the semantics of a glance at a scene. In M. Kubovy & J. Pomerantz (Eds.), *Perceptual organization.* Hillsdale, NJ: Erlbaum.

Biederman, I. (1987). Recognition by components: A theory of human image understanding. *Psychological Review, 94,* 115–147.

Biederman, I. (2001). Recognizing depth-rotated objects: A review of results of research and theory. *Spatial Vision, 13,* 241–253.

Biederman, I., & Cooper, E. E. (1991). Priming contour deleted images: Evidence for intermediate representations in visual object recognition. *Cognitive Psychology, 23,* 393–419.

Biederman, I., Cooper, E. E., Hummel, J. E., & Fiser, J. (1993). Geon theory as an account of shape recognition in mind, brain, and machine. In J. Illingworth (Ed.), *Proceedings of the Fourth British Machine Vision Conference* (pp. 175–186). Guildford, Surrey, UK: BMVA Press.

Biegler, R., McGregor, A., Krebs, J. R., & Healy, S. D. (2001). A larger hippocampus is associated with longer-lasting spatial memory. *Proceedings of the National Academy of Science, USA, 98,* 6941–6944.

Bisiach, E., & Luzzatti, G. (1978). Unilateral neglect of representational space. *Cortex, 14,* 129–133.

Blakemore, C., & Cooper, G. G. (1970). Development of the brain depends on the visual environment. *Nature, 228,* 477–478.

Boring, E. G. (1942). *Sensation and perception in the history of experimental psychology.* New York: Appleton-Century-Crofts.

Bower, G. H., Black, J. B., & Turner, T. J. (1979). Scripts in memory for text. *Cognitive Psychology, 11,* 177-220.

Bower, G. H., Clark, M., C., Lesgold, A. M., & Winzenz, D. (1969). Hierarchical retrieval schemes in recall of categorized word lists. *Journal of Verbal Learning and Verbal Behavior, 8,* 323–343.

Bower, G. H. & Winzenz, D. (1970). Comparison of associative learning strategies. *Psychonomic Science, 20,* 119–120.

Brandimonte, M. A., Hitch, G. J., & Bishop, D. V. M. (1992). Influence of short-term memory codes on visual image processing: Evidence from image transformation tasks. *Journal of Experimental Psychology: Learning, Memory, and Cognition, 18,* 157–165.

Bransford, J. D., & Johnson, M. K. (1972). Contextual prerequisites for understanding: Some investigations of comprehension and recall. *Journal of Verbal Learning and Verbal Behavior, 11,* 717–726.

Bransford, J. D., & Johnson, M. K. (1973). Consideration of some problems of comprehension. In W. C. Chase (Ed.), *Visual information processing* (pp. 383–438). New York: Academic Press.

Bransford, J. D., & Stein, B. S. (1984). The IDEAL problem solver. New York: Freeman.

Breedin, S. D., & Saffran, E. M. (1999). Sentence processing in the face of semantic loss: A case study. *Journal of Experimental Psychology: General, 128,* 547–562.

Bregman, A. S. (1981). Asking the "what for" question in auditory perception. In M. Kubovy & J. R. Pomerantz (Eds.), *Perceptual organization* (pp. 99–119). Hillsdale, NJ: Erlbaum.

Breland, K., & Breland, M. (1961). The misbehavior of organisms. *American Psychologist, 16,* 631–684.

Brewer, J. G., Zhao, Z., Desmond, J. E., Glover, G. H., & Gabrieli, J. D. E. (1998). Making memories: Brain activity that predicts whether visual experience will be remembered or forgotten. *Science, 281*, 1185–1187.

Brewer, W. F., & Treyens, J. C. (1981). Role of schemata in memory for places. *Cognitive Psychology, 13*, 207–230.

Broadbent, D. E. (1958). *Perception and communication*. London: Pergammon.

Brooks, L. (1968). Spatial and verbal components of the act of recall. *Canadian Journal of Psychology, 22*, 349–368.

Brown, C. M. (1984). Computer vision and natural constraints. *Science, 224*, 1299–1305.

Brown, J. (1958). Some tests of the decay theory of immediate memory. *Quarterly Journal of Experimental Psychology, 10*, 12–21.

Brown, R., & Kulik, J. (1977). Flashbulb memories. *Cognition, 5*, 73–99.

Brown, S. C. & Craik, F. I. M. (2000). Encoding and retrieval of information. In E. Tulving & F. I. M. Craik (Eds.), *The Oxford Handbook of Memory* (pp. 93–107). New York: Oxford University Press.

Buciarelli, M., & Johnson-Laird, P. N. (1999). Strategies in syllogistic reasoning. *Cognitive Science, 23*, 247–303.

Buckner, R. L., & Wheeler, M. E. (2001). The cognitive neuroscience of remembering. *Nature Reviews, 2*, 624–634.

Burton, A. M., Young, A. W., Bruce, J., Johnston, R. A., & Ellis, A. W. (1991). Understanding covert recognition. *Cognition, 39*, 129–166.

Butterworth, B., Shallice, T., & Watson, F. L. (1990). Short-term retention without short-term memory. In G. Vallar & T. Shallice (Eds.), *Neuropsychological impairments of short term memory* (pp. 187–213). Cambridge: Cambridge University Press.

Cahill, L., Babinsky, R., Markowitsch, H. J., & McGaugh, J. L. (1995). The amygdala and emotional memory. *Nature, 377*, 295–296.

Cahill, L., Haier, R. J., Fallon, J., Alkire, M. T, Tang, C., Keator, D., Wu, J., & McGaugh, J. L. (1996). Amygdala activity at encoding correlated with long-term free recall of emotional information. *Proceedings of the National Academy of Sciences, USA, 93*, 8016–8021.

Cahill, L., & McGaugh, J. L. (1998). Mechanisms of emotional arousal and lasting declarative memory. *Trends in Neurosciences, 21*, 294–299.

Caramazza, A. (2000). The organization of conceptual knowledge in the brain. In M. A. Gazzanaga (Ed.). *The Cognitive Neurosciences*, (2nd ed., pp. 1037–1046). Cambridge: MIT Press.

Caramazza, A., & Shelton, J. R. (1998). Domain-specific knowledge systems in the brain: The animate-inanimate distinction. *Journal of Cognitive Neuroscience, 10*, 1–34.

Carlin, D., Bonerba, J., Phipps, M., Alexander, G., Shapiro, M., & Grafman, J. (2000). Planning impairments in frontal lobe dementia and frontal lobe lesion patients. *Neuropsychologia, 38*, 655–665.

Carroll, D. W. (1999). *Psychology of language* (3rd ed.). Pacific Grove, CA: Brooks/Cole.

Carroll, L. (1872). *Through the looking glass, and what Alice found there*. New York: Macmillan.

Catrambone, R., & Holyoak, K. J. (1989). Overcoming contextual limitations on problem-solving transfer. *Journal of Experimental Psychology: Learning, Memory, and Cognition, 15*, 1147–1156.

Chalmers, D., & Reisberg, D. (1985). Can mental images beambiguous? *Journal of Experimental Psychology: Human Perception and Performance, 11*, 317–328.

Chao, L. L., Haxby, J. V., & Martin, A. (1999). Attribute-based neural substrates in temporal cortex for perceiving and knowing about objects. *Nature Neuroscience, 2*, 913–919.

Chapman, L. J., & Chapman, J. P. (1969). Genesis of popular but erroneous psychodiagnostic observations. *Journal of Abnormal Psychology, 74,* 272–280.

Chase, W. G., & Simon, H. A. (1973a). Perception in chess. *Cognitive Psychology, 4,* 55–81.

Chase, W. G., & Simon, H. A. (1973b). The mind's eye in chess. In W. G. Chase (Ed.), *Visual information processing.* New York: Academic Press.

Cheng, P. W., & Holyoak, K. J. (1985). Pragmatic reasoning schemas. *Cognitive Psychology, 17,* 391–416.

Cherry, E. C. (1953). Some experiments on the recognition of speech, with one and with two ears. *Journal of the Acoustical Society of America, 25,* 975–979.

Chi, M. T. H., Feltovich, P. J., & Glaser, R. (1981). Categorization and representation of physics problems by experts and novices. *Cognitive Science, 5,* 121–152.

Chi, M. T. H., Glaser, R., & Rees, E. (1982). Expertise in problem solving. In R. J. Sternberg (Ed.), *Advances in the psychology of human intelligence.* Hillsdale, NJ: Erlbaum.

Chino, Y., Smith, E., Hatta, S., & Cheng, H. (1997). Postnatal development of binocular disparity sensitivity in neurons of the primate visual cortex. *Journal of Neuroscience, 17,* 296–307.

Chiu, L-H. (1972). A cross-cultural comparison of cognitive styles in Chinese and American children. *International Journal of Psychology, 7,* 235–242.

Chomsky, N. (1957). *Syntactic structures.* The Hague: Mouton.

Chomsky, N. (1959). A review of Skinner's *Verbal behavior. Language, 35,* 26–58.

Chun, M. M., & Wolfe, J. M. (2001). Visual attention. In E. B. Goldstein (Ed.), *Blackwell's Handbook of Perception* (pp. 272–310). Oxford, UK: Blackwell.

Clark, H. H., & Lucy, P. (1975). Understanding what is meant from what is said: A study in conversationally conveyed requests. *Journal of Verbal Learning and Verbal Behavior, 14,* 56–72.

Clark, H. H., & Van der Wege, M. M. (2002). Psycholinguistics. In H. Pashler & S. Yantis (Eds.), *Stevens' Handbook of Experimental Psychology* (3rd ed., pp. 209–259). New York: Wiley.

Colby, C. L., Duhamel, J.-R, & Goldberg, M. E. (1995). Oculocentric spatial representation in parietal cortex. *Cerebral Cortex, 5,* 470–481.

Coley, J. D., Medin, D. L., & Atran, S. (1997). Does rank have its privilege? Inductive inferences within folkbiological taxonomies. *Cognition, 64,* 73–112.

Collins, A. M., & Loftus, E. F. (1975). A spreading-activation theory of semantic processing. *Psychological Review, 82,* 407–428.

Collins, A. M., & Quillian, M. R. (1969). Retrieval time from semantic memory. *Journal of Verbal Learning and Verbal Behavior, 8,* 240–247.

Colvin, M. K., Dunbar, K., & Grafman, J. (2001). The effects of frontal lobe lesions on goal achievement in the water jug task. *Journal of Cognitive Neuroscience, 13,* 1129–1147.

Colman, A. W. (2001). *Dictionary of psychology.* Oxford, UK: Oxford University Press.

Conrad, C. (1972). Cognitive economy in semantic memory. *Journal of Experimental Psychology, 92,* 149–154.

Conrad, R. (1964). Acoustic confusion in immediate memory. *British Journal of Psychology, 55,* 75–84.

Conway, M. A. (1996). Autobiographical memory. In E. L. Bjork & R. A. Bjork (Eds.), *Handbook of Perception and Cognition* (2nd ed., pp. 165–194). *Volume: Memory.* New York: Academic Press.

Conway, M. A., Anderson, S. J., Larsen, S. F., Donnelly, C. M., McDaniel, M. A., McClelland, A. G. R., Rawles, R. E., & Logie, R. H. (1994). The formation of flashbulb memories. *Memory and Cognition, 22,* 326–343.

Conway, M. A., & Ross, M. (1984). Getting what you want by revising what you had. *Journal of Personality and Social Psychology, 47,* 738–748.

Coppola, D. M., White, L. E., Fitzpatrick, D., & Purves, D. (1998). Unequal distribution of cardinal and oblique contours in ferret visual cortex. *Proceedings of the National Academy of Sciences, 95,* 2621–2623.

Cosmides, L. (1989). The logic of social exchange: Has natural selection shaped how humans reason? Studies with the Wason selection task. *Cognition, 31,* 187–226.

Cosmides, L., & Tooby, J. (1992). Cognitive adaptations for social exchange. In J. H. Barkow, L. Cosmides, & J. Tooby (Eds.), *The adapted mind* (pp. 179–228). Oxford, UK: Oxford University Press.

Courtney, S. M., Petit, L., Maisog, J. M., Ungerleider, L. G., & Haxby, J. V. (1998). An area specialized for spatial working memory in human frontal cortex. *Science, 279,* 1347–1351.

Craik, F. I. M., & Lockhart, R. S. (1972). Levels of processing: A framework for memory research. *Journal of Verbal Learning and Verbal Behavior, 11,* 671–684.

Craik, F. I. M., & Tulving, E. (1975). Depth of processing and retention of words in episodic memory. *Journal of Experimental Psychology: General, 104,* 268–294.

Craver-Lemley, C., & Reeves, A. (1992). How visual imagery interferes with vision. *Psychological Review, 99,* 633–649.

Crook, T. H., & Adderly, B. (1998). *The memory cure.* New York: Simon & Schuster.

Dapretto, M., & Bookheimer, S. Y. (1999). Form and content: Dissociating syntax and semantics in sentence comprehension. *Neuron, 24,* 427–432.

Darwin, C. J., Turvey, M. T., & Crowder, R. G. (1972). An auditory analogue of the Sperling partial report procedure: Evidence for brief auditory storage. *Cognitive Psychology, 3,* 255–267.

Davachi, L., Mitchell, J. P., & Wagner, A. C. (2003). Multiple routes to memory: Distinct medial temporal lobe processes build item and source memories. *Proceedings of the National Academy of Sciences, 100,* 2157–2162.

Davachi, L., & Wagner, A. D. (2002). Hippocampal contributions to episodic encoding: Insights from relational and item-based learning. *Journal of Neurophysiology, 88,* 982–990.

Davidoff, J. (2001). Language and perceptual categorization. *Trends in Cognitive Sciences, 5,* 382–387.

Deese, J. (1959). On the prediction of occurrence of particular verbal intrusions in immediate recall. *Journal of Experimental Psychology, 58,* 17–22.

DeGroot, A. (1965). *Thought and choice in chess.* The Hague: Mouton.

DeRenzi, E., Liotti, M., & Nichelli, P. (1987). Semantic amnesia with preservation of autobiographic memory: A case report. *Cortex, 23,* 575–597.

DeRenzi, E., & Spinnler, H. (1967). Impaired performance on color tasks inpatients with hemispheric lesions. *Cortex, 3,* 194–217.

Desimone, R., Miller, E. K., Chelazzi, L., & Lueschow, A. (1995). Multiple memory systems in the visual cortex. In M. Gazzanaga (Ed.), *The Cognitive Neurosciences* (pp. 475–486). Cambridge, MA: MIT Press.

Deutsch, J. A., & Deutsch, D. (1963). Attention: Some theoretical considerations. *Psychological Review, 70,* 80–90.

DeVreese, L. P. (1991). Two systems for colour-naming defects: Verbal disconnection vs. colour imagery disorder. *Neuropsychologia, 29,* 1–18.

Donders, F. C. (1868/1969). Over de snelheid van psychische processen [Speed of mental processes]. Onderzoekingen gedann in het Psyciologish Laboratorium der Utrechtsche Hoogeschool (W. G. Koster, Trans.). In W. G. Koster (Ed.), Attention and performance II. *Acta Psychologica, 30,* 412–431.

Driver, J., & Baylis, G. C. (1989). Movement and visual attention: The spotlight metaphor breaks down. *Journal of Experimental Psychology: Human Perception and Performance, 15,* 448–456.

Driver, J., & Baylis, G. C. (1998). Attention and visual object segmentation. In R. Parasuraman (Ed.), *The attentive brain* (pp. 299–325). Cambridge, MA: MIT Press.

DuBreuil, S. C., Garry, M., & Loftus, E. F. (1998). Tales from the crib. In S. J. Lynn & K. M. McConkie (Eds.), *Truth in memory* (pp. 137–160). New York: Guilford.

Duncker, K. (1945). On problem solving. *Psychological Monographs 58* (Whole No. 270).

Dunning, D., & Parpal, M. (1989). Mental addition versus subtraction in counterfactual reasoning: On assessing the impact of personal actions and life events. *Journal of Personality and Social Psychology, 57,* 5–15.

Duzel, E., Cabeza, R., Picton, T. W., Yonelinas, A. P., Scheich, H., Heinze, H.-J., & Tulving, E. (1999). Task-related and item-related brain processes of memory retrieval. *Proceedings of the National Academy of Sciences, USA, 96,* 1794–1799.

Egan, D. E., & Schwartz, B. J. (1979). Chunking in recall of symbolic drawings. *Memory and Cognition, 7,* 149–158.

Egly, R., Driver, J., & Rafal, R. D. (1994). Shifting visual attention between objects and locations: Evidence from normal and parietal lesion subjects. *Journal of Experimental Psychology: General, 123,* 161–177.

Eich, E. (1995). Searching for mood dependent memory. *Psychological Science, 6,* 67–75.

Eich, E., & Metcalfe, J. (1989). Mood dependent memory for internal vs. external events. *Journal of Experimental Psychology: Learning, Memory and Cognition, 15,* 443–455.

Ellis, N., & Hennelly, R. A. (1980). A bilingual word-length effect: Implications for intelligence testing and the relative ease of mental calculation in Welsh and English. *British Journal of Psychology, 71,* 43–52.

Ericsson, K. A., Chase, W. G., & Falloon, F. (1980). Acquisition of a memory skill. *Science, 208,* 1181–1182.

Ericsson, K. A., & Kintsch, W. (1995). Long-term working memory. *Psychological Review, 102,* 211–245.

Eriksen, B. A., & Eriksen, C. W. (1974). Effects of noise letters upon the identification of a target letter in a nonsearch task. *Perception and Psychophysics, 16,* 143–149.

Eriksen, C. W., & Yeh, Y.-Y. (1985). Allocation of attention in the visual field. *Journal of Experimental Psychology: Human Perception and Performance, 11,* 583–597.

Eriksen., C. W., & St. James, J. D. (1986). Visual attention within and around the field of focal attention: A zoom lens model. *Perception and Psychophysics, 40,* 225–240.

Evans, J. St. B. T., Barston, J. L., & Pollard, P. (1983). On the conflict between logic and belief in syllogistic reasoning. *Memory and Cognition, 11,* 295–306.

Evans, J. St. B. T., Newstead, S. E., & Byrne, R. M. J. (1993). *Human reasoning: The psychology of deduction.* Hove, UK: Lawrence Erlbaum.

Farah, M. J. (1985). Psychophysical evidence for a shared representational medium for mental images and percepts. *Journal of Experimental Psychology: General, 114,* 91–103.

Farah, M. J. (1988). Is visual imagery really visual? Overlooked evidence from neuropsychology. *Psychological Review, 95,* 307–317.

Farah, M. J., Levine, D. N., & Calvanio, R. (1988). A case study of mental imagery deficit. *Brain and Cognition, 8,* 147–164.

Farah, M. J., O'Reilly, R. C., & Vecera, S. P. (1993). Dissociated overt and covert recognition as an emergent property of a lesioned neural network. *Psychological Review, 100*, 571–588.

Farah, M. J., Peronnet, F., Gonon, M. A., & Girard, M. H. (1988). Electrophysiological evidence for a shared representational medium for visual images and percepts. *Journal of Experimental Psychology, 117*, 248–257.

Farah, M. J., Peronnet, F., Weisberg, L. L., & Monheit, M. A. (1989). Brain activity underlying mental images: Event-related potentials during image generation. *Journal of Cognitive Neuroscience, 1*, 302–316.

Farah, M. J., Soso, M. J., & Dasheiff, R. M. (1992). The visual angle of the mind's eye before and after unilateral occipital lobectomy. *Journal of Experimental Psychology: Human Perception and Performance, 18*, 241–246.

Farah, M. J., & Wallace, M. A. (1992). Semantically bound amnesia: Implications for the neural implementation of naming. *Neuropsychologia, 30*, 609–621.

Fernald, A., & Morikawa, H. (1993). Common themes and cultural variations in Japanese and American mothers' speech to infants. *Child Development, 64*, 637–656.

Fiez, J. A. (2001). Bridging the gap between neuroimaging and neuropsychology: Using working memory as a case study. *Journal of Clinical and Experimental Neuropsychology, 23*, 19–31.

Finke, R. A. (1990). *Creative imagery: discoveries and inventions in visualization.* Hillsdale, NJ: Erlbaum.

Finke, R. A. (1995). Creative insight and preinventive forms. In R. J. Sternberg & J. E. Davidson (Eds.), *The nature of insight* (pp. 255–280). Cambridge, MA: MIT Press.

Finke, R. A., & Pinker, S. (1982). Spontaneous imagery scanning in mental exploration. *Journal of Experimental Psychology: Learning, Memory and Cognition, 8*, 142–147.

Finke, R. A., Pinker, S., & Farah, M. J. (1989). Reinterpreting visual patterns in visual imagery. *Cognitive Science, 13*, 51–78.

Fodor, J. D. (1995). Comprehending sentence structure. In L. R. Gleitman & M. Liberman (Eds.), *An invitation to cognitive science, Vol. 1.* Cambridge, MA: MIT Press, pp. 209–246.

Frase, L. T. (1975). Prose processing. In G. H. Bower (Ed.), *The psychology of learning and motivation* (Vol. 9). New York: Academic Press.

Frazier, L. (1987). Sentence processing: A tutorial review. In M. Coltheart (Ed.), *Attention and performance: Vol. XII. The psychology of reading* (pp. 559–586). Hove: Erlbaum.

Frazier, L., & Rayner, K. (1982). Making and correcting errors during sentence comprehension: Eye movements in the analysis of structurally ambiguous sentences. *Cognitive Psychology, 14*, 178–210.

Freedman, D. J., Riesenhuber, M., Poggio, T., & Miller, E. K. (2001). Categorical representations of visual stimuli in the primate prefrontal cortex. *Science, 291*, 312–316.

Freedman, M. L., & Martin, R. C. (2001). Dissociable components of short-term memory and their relation to long-term learning. *Cognitive Neuropsychology, 18*, 193–226.

Frensch, P. A., & Sternberg, R. J. (1989). Expertise and intelligent thinking: When is it worse to know better? In R. J. Sternberg (Ed.), *Advances in the psychology of human intelligence, Vol. 5.* Hillsdale, NJ: Erlbaum.

Funahashi, S., Bruce, C. J., & Goldman-Rakic, P. S. (1989). Mnemonic coding of visual space in the primate dorsolateral prefrontal cortex. *Journal of Neurophysiology, 61*, 331–349.

Furmanski, C. S., & Engel, S. A. (2000). An oblique effect in human primary visual cortex. *Nature Neuroscience, 3*, 535–536.

Galton, F. (1883). *Inquiries into human faculty and its development.* London: Macmillan.

Gardner, H. (1974). *The shattered mind*. New York: Vintage.

Garrod, S., & Pickering, M. J. (2004). Why is conversation so easy? *Trends in Cognitive Sciences, 8*, 8–11.

Gauthier, I., Skudlarski, P., Gore, J. C., & Anderson, A. W. (2000). Expertise for cars and birds recruits brain areas involved in face recognition. *Nature Neuroscience, 3*, 191–197.

Gauthier, I., Tarr, M. J., Anderson, A. W., Skudlarski, P., & Gore, J. C. (1999). Activation of the middle fusiform "face area" increases with expertise in recognizing novel objects. *Nature Neuroscience, 2*, 568–573.

Gazzaniga, M. S. (2000). In E. Tulving & F. I. M. Craik (Eds.). *The Oxford Handbook of Memory*, back cover quotation. New York: Oxford University Press.

Gentner, D., & Goldin-Meadow, S. (2003). *Language in mind*. Cambridge, MA: M. I. T. Press.

Gick, M. L., & Holyoak, K. J. (1980). Analogical problem solving. *Cognitive Psychology, 12*, 306–355.

Gick, M. L., & Holyoak, K. J. (1983). Schema induction and analogical transfer. *Cognitive Psychology, 15*, 1–38.

Gigerenzer, G., & Hoffrage, U. (1995). How to improve Bayesian reasoning without instruction: Frequency formats. *Psychological Review, 98*, 506–528.

Gigerenzer, G., & Hug, K. (1992). Domain-specific reasoning: Social contracts, cheating, and perspective change. *Cognition, 43*, 127–171.

Gigerenzer, G., & Todd, P. M. (1999). *Simple heuristics that make us smart*. Oxford, UK: Oxford University Press.

Gilhooly, K. J. (Ed.). (1988). *Thinking: Directed, undirected and creative* (2nd ed.). San Diego, CA: Academic Press.

Glanzer, M., & Cunitz, A. R. (1966). Two storage mechanisms in free recall. *Journal of Verbal Learning and Verbal Behavior, 5*, 351–360.

Glass, A. L., & Holyoak, K. J. (1975). Alternative conceptions of semantic memory. *Cognition, 3*, 313–339.

Gleason, J. B., & Ratner, N. B. (1998). *Psycholinguistics* (2nd ed.). Orlando, FL: Harcourt.

Gleick, J. (1992). *Genius: The life and science of Richard Feynman*. New York: Pantheon.

Glenberg, A. M., Meyer, M., & Lindem, K. (1987). Mental models contribute to foregrounding during text comprehension. *Journal of Memory and Language, 26*, 69–83.

Gobet, F., Land, P. C. R., Croker, S., Cheng, P. C.-H., Jones, G., Oliver, I., & Pine, J. M. (2001). Chunking mechanisms in human learning. *Trends in Cognitive Science, 5*, 236–243.

Godden, D. R., & Baddeley, A. D. (1975). Context-dependent memory in two natural environments: On land and underwater. *British Journal of Psychology, 66*, 325–331.

Goldberg, N. (1993). *Long quiet highway*. New York: Bantam.

Goldenberg, G., Podreka, I., Steiner, M., Willmes, K., Suess, E., & Deecke, L. (1989). Regional cerebral blood flow patterns in visual imagery. *Neuropsychologia, 27*, 641–664.

Goldman, S. R., Graesser, A. C., & Van den Broek, P. (Eds.). (1999). *Narrative comprehension, causality, and coherence*. Mahwah, NJ: Erlbaum.

Goldman-Rakic, P. S. (1992, September). Working memory and the mind. *Scientific American*, 111–117.

Goldstein, A. G., Chance, J. E., & Schneller, G. R. (1989). Frequency of eyewitness identification in criminal cases: A survey of prosecutors. *Bulletin of the Psychonomic Society, 27*, 71–74.

Goldwin-Meadow, S. (1982). The resilience of recursion: A study of a communication system developed without a conventional language model. In E. Wanner & L. R. Gleitman (Eds.), *Language acquisition: The state of the art* (pp.

51–77). Cambridge: Cambridge University Press.

Gollin, E. S. (1960). Developmental studies of visual recognition of incomplete objects. *Perceptual and Motor Skills, 11*, 289–298.

Gomez, R. L., & Gerken, L. A. (1999). Artificial grammar learning by one-year-olds leads to specific and abstract knowledge. *Cognition, 70*, 109–135.

Gomez, R. L., & Gerken, L. (2000). Infant artificial language learning and language acquisition. *Trends in Cognitive Sciences, 4*, 178–186.

Graesser, A., Singer, M., & Trabasso, T. (1994). Constructing inferences during narrative text comprehension. *Psychological Review, 101*, 371–395.

Graesser, A. C., & Wiemer-Hastings, K. (1999). Situation models and concepts in story comprehension. In S. R. Goldman, A. C. Graesser, & P. Van den Broek (Eds.), *Narrative comprehension, causality, and coherence* (pp. 77–92). Mahwah, NJ: Erlbaum.

Grant, H., Bredahl, L. S., Clay, J., Ferrie, J., Goves, J. E., Mcdorman, T. A., & Dark, V. J. (1998). Context-dependent memory for meaningful material: Information for students. *Applied cognitive Psychology, 12*, 617–623.

Gray, J. A., & Wedderburn, A. I. (1960). Grouping strategies with simultaneous stimuli. *Quarterly Journal of Experimental Psychology, 12*, 180–184.

Green, C. S., & Bavelier, D. (2003). Action video game modifies visual selective attention. *Nature, 423*, 534–537.

Greeno, J. G. (1974). Hobbits and orcs: Acquisition of a sequential concept. *Cognitive Psychology, 6*, 270–292.

Grice, H. P. (1975). Logic and conversation. In P. Cole & J. L. Morgan (Eds.), *Syntax and semantics: Vol. 3. Speech acts* (pp. 41–58). New York: Seminar.

Griggs, R A. (1983). The role of problem content in the selection task and in the THOG problem. In J. St. B. T. Evans (Ed.), *Thinking and reasoning: Psychological approaches.* London: Routledge & Kegan Paul.

Griggs, R. A., & Cox, J. R. (1982). The elusive thematic-materials effect in Wason's abstract selection task. *British Journal of Psychology, 73*, 407–420.

Guariglia, C., Padovani, A., Pantano, P., & Pizzamiglio, L. (1993). Unilateral neglect restricted to visual imagery. *Nature, 364*, 235–237.

Guilford, J. (1956). The structure of intellect. *Psychological Bulletin, 53*, 267–293.

Guilford, J. (1967). *The nature of human intelligence.* New York: Scribner.

Haber, R. N. (1983). The impending demise of the icon: A critique of the concept of iconic storage in visual information processing. *The Behavioral and Brain Sciences, 6*, 1–11.

Hafner, K. (1999, July 29). Road daze: A hand on the wheel and an ear to the phone. *New York Times*, p. G8.

Haigney, D., & Westerman, S. J. (2001). Mobile (cellular) phone use and driving: A critical review of research methodology. *Ergonomics, 44*, 132–143.

Hamann, S. B., Ely, T. D., Grafton, S. T., & Kilts, C. D. (1999). Amygdala activity related to enhanced memory for pleasant and aversive stimuli. *Nature Neuroscience, 2*, 289–293.

Hamilton, D. L. (1981). Illusory correlation as a basis for stereotyping. In D. L. Hamilton (Ed.), *Cognitive processes in stereotyping and intergroup behavior.* Hillsdale, NJ: Erlbaum.

Hart, J., Berndt, R. S., & Caramazza, A. (1985). Category-specific naming deficit following cerebral infarction. *Nature, 316*, 439–440.

Hart, J., & Gordon, B. (1992). Neural subsystems for object knowledge. *Nature, 359*, 60–64.

Hauser, M. D. (1999). Perseveration, inhibition and the prefrontal cortex: A new look. *Current Opinion in Neurobiology, 9*, 214–222.

Haviland, S. E., & Clark, H. H. (1974). What's new? Acquiring new information as a process in comprehension. *Journal of Verbal Learning and Verbal Behavior, 13*, 512–521.

Hays, J. R. (1978). *Cognitive psychology.* Homewood, IL: Dorsey Press.

Hebb, D. O. (1948). *Organization of behavior.* New York: Wiley.

Hecaen, H., & Angelerques, R. (1962). Agnosia for faces (prospagnosia). *Archives of Neurology, 7,* 92–100.

Helmholtz, H. von (1866). *Treatise on physiological optics.* Leipzig: Voss.

Helson, H. (1933). The fundamental propositions of Gestalt psychology. *Psychological Review, 40,* 13–32.

Henderson, A., Bruce, V., & Burton, A. M. (2001). Matching the faces of robbers captured on video. *Applied Cognitive Psychology, 15,* 445–464.

Henderson, J. M., & Hollingworth, A. (2003). Global transsaccadic change blindness during scene perception. *Psychological Science, 14,* 493–497.

Hills, A. E., & Caramazza, A. (1991). Category-specific naming and comprehension impairment: A double-dissociation. *Brain, 114,* 2081–2094.

Hillyard, S. A., & Anllo-Vento, L. (1998). Event-related brain potentials in the study of visual selective attention. *Proceedings of the National Academy of Sciences, USA, 95,* 781–787.

Hillyard, S. A., Hink, R. F., Schwent, V. L., & Picton, T. W. (1973). Electrical signs of selective attention in the human brain. *Science, 182,* 177–180.

Hinton, G. E., & Shallice, T. (1991). Lesioning an attractor network: Investigations of acquired dyslexia. *Psychological Review, 98,* 74–95.

Hirsh-Pasek, K., Reeves, L. M., & Golinkoff, R., (1993). Words and meaning: From primitives to complex organization. In J. B. Gleason & N. B. Ratner (Eds.), *Psycholinguistics* (p. 138). Fort Worth, TX: Harcourt Brace Jovanovich.

Hochberg, J. E. (1971). Perception. In J. W. Kling & L. A. Riggs (Eds.), *Experimental psychology* (3rd ed., pp. 396–450). New York: Holt, Rinehart and Winston.

Hoffman, E. J., Phelps, M. E., Mullani, N. A., Higgins, C. S., & Ter-Pogossian, M. M. (1976). Design and performance characteristics of a whole-body positron tranaxial tomography. *Journal of Nuclear Medicine, 17,* 493–502.

Holyoak, K. J. (2003). Personal communication to the author.

Holyoak, K. J., & Koh, K. (1987). Surface and structural similarity in analogical transfer. *Memory and Cognition, 15,* 332–340.

Holyoak, K. J., & Thagard, P. (1995). Analogical mapping by constraint satisfaction. *Cognitive Science, 13,* 295–355.

Hubel, D. H. (1995). *Eye, brain and vision.* New York: Scientific American Books.

Hubel, D. H., & Wiesel, T. N. (1961). Integrative action in the cat's lateral geniculate body. *Journal of Physiology, 155,* 385–398.

Hubel D. H., & Wiesel, T. N. (1965). Receptive fields and functional architecture in two non-striate visual areas (18 and 19) of the cat. *Journal of Neurophysiology, 28,* 229–289.

Huesmann, L. R., Moise, T. J., Podolski, C. L., & Eron, L. D. (2003). Longitudinal relations between children's exposure to TV violence and their aggressive and violent behavior in young adulthood: 1977–1992. *Developmental Psychology, 39,* 201–222.

Huitema, J. S., Dopkins, S., Klin, C. M., & Myers, J. L. (1993). Connecting goals and actions during reading. *Journal of Experimental Psychology: Learning, Memory and Cognition, 19,* 1053–1060.

Hyde, T. S., & Jenkins, J. J. (1969). Differential effects of incidental tasks on the organization of a list of highly associated words. *Journal of Experimental Psychology, 82,* 472–481.

Hyman, I. E. Jr., Husband, T. H., & Billings, J. F. (1995). False memories of childhood experiences. *Applied Cognitive Psychology, 9,* 181–197.

Intons-Peterson, M. J. (1983). Imagery paradigms: How vulnerable are they to experimenters' expectations? *Journal of Experimental Psychology: Human Perception and Performance, 9,* 394–412.

Intons-Peterson, M. J. (1993). Imagery's role in creativity and discovery. In B. Roskos-Ewoldson, M. J. Intons-Peterson, & R. E. Anderson (Eds.), *Imagery, creativity, and discovery: A cognitive perspective* (pp. 1-37). New York: Elsevier.

Iwao, M., & Gentner, D. (1997). A cross-linguistic study of early word meaning: Universal ontology and linguistic influence. *Cognition, 62,* 169–200.

Jacoby, L. L., Kelley, C. M., Brown, J., & Jaseckko, J. (1989). Becoming famous overnight: Limits on the ability to avoid unconscious inferences of the past. *Journal of Personality and Social Psychology, 56,* 326–338.

James, W. (1890). *The principles of psychology* (Vol. 1). New York: Henry Holt & Co. (Reprinted, 1981, Harvard University Press.)

Jenkins, J. J., & Russell, W. A. (1952). Associative clustering during recall. *Journal of Abnormal and Social Psychology, 47,* 818–821.

Ji, L., Peng, K., & Nisbett, R. E. (2000). Culture, control, and perception of relationships in the environment. *Journal of Personality and Social Psychology, 78,* 943–955.

Johnson, K. E., & Mervis, C. B. (1997). Effects of varying levels of expertise on the basic level of categorization. *Journal of Experimental Psychology: General, 126,* 248–277.

Johnson, M. K., Hashtroudi, S., & Lindsay, D. S. (1993). Source monitoring. *Psychological Bulletin, 114,* 3–28.

Johnson-Laird, P. N. (1995). Inference and mental models. In S. E. Newstead & J. St. B. T. Evans (Eds.), *Perspectives on thinking and reasoning. Essays in honour of Peter Wason.* Hove, UK: Erlbaum.

Johnson-Laird, P. N. (1999a). Formal rules versus mental models in reasoning. In R. Sternberg (Ed.), *The nature of cognition* (pp. 587–624). Cambridge, MA: MIT Press.

Johnson-Laird, P. N. (1999b). Deductive reasoning. *Annual Review of Psychology, 50,* 109–135.

Johnson-Laird, P. N., Herrmann, D. J., & Chaffin, R. (1984). Only connections: A critique of semantic networks. *Psychological Bulletin, 96,* 292–315.

Johnson-Laird, P. N., Legrenzi, P., & Legrenzi, M. S. (1972). Reasoning and a sense of reality. *British Journal of Psychology, 63,* 395–400.

Jones, M. R., & Yee, W. (1993). Attending to auditory events: The role of temporal organization. In S. McAdams & E. Bigand (Eds.), *Thinking in sound: The cognitive psychology of human audition* (pp. 69–112). Oxford, England: Oxford University Press.

Julesz, B. (1984). A brief outline of the texton theory of human vision. *Trends in Neuroscience, 7,* 41–45.

Kahneman, D. (1973). *Attention and effort.* Englewood Cliffs, NJ: Prentice-Hall.

Kahneman, D., & Tversky, A. (1982). The simulation heuristic. In D. Kahneman, P. Slovic, & A. Tversky (Eds.), *Judgment under uncertainty: Heuristics and biases* (pp. 201–208). New York: Cambridge University Press.

Kako, E., & Wagner, L. (2001). The semantics of syntactic structures. *Trends in Cognitive Sciences, 5,* 102–108.

Kandel, E. R. (2001). A molecular biology of memory storage: A dialogue between genes and synapses. *Science, 294,* 1030–1038.

Kaplan, C. A., & Simon, H. A. (1990). In search of insight. *Cognitive Psychology, 22,* 374–419.

Keppel, G., & Underwood, B. J. (1962). Proactive inhibition in short-term retention of single items. *Journal of Verbal Learning and Verbal Behavior, 1*, 153–161.

Keri, S., Janka, Z., Benedek, G., Aszalos, P., Szatmary, B., Szirtes, G., & Lorincz, A. (2002). Categories prototypes and memory systems in Alzheimer's disease. *Trends in Cognitive Sciences, 6*, 132–136.

Keysers, C., Xiao, D. K., Foeldiak, P., & Perrett, D. I. (2001). The speed of sight. *Journal of Cognitive Neuroscience, 13*, 90–101.

Kleffner, D. A., & Ramachandran, V. S. (1992). On the perception of shape from shading. *Perception and Psychophysics, 52*, 18–36.

Kneller, W., Memon, A., & Stevenage, S. (2001). Simultaneous and sequential lineups: Decision processes of accurate and inaccurate eye witnesses. *Applied Cognitive Psychology, 15*, 659–671.

Koffka, K. (1935). *Principles of Gestalt psychology.* New York: Harcourt Brace & World.

Kolb, B., & Wishaw, I. Q. (1990). *Fundamentals of human neuropsychology* (3rd ed.). New York: Freeman.

Kosslyn, S. M. (1973). Scanning visual images: Some structural implications. *Perception & Psychophysics, 14*, 90–94.

Kosslyn, S. M. (1978). Measuring the visual angle of the mind's eye. *Cognitive Psychology, 10*, 356–389.

Kosslyn, S. M. (1980). *Image and mind.* Cambridge, MA: Harvard University Press.

Kosslyn, S. M. (1994). *Image and brain: The resolution of the imagery debate.* Cambridge, MA: MIT Press.

Kosslyn, S. M., Alpert, N. M., Thompson, W. L., Maljkovic, V., Weise, S. B., Chabris, C. F., Hamilton, E., Rauch, S. L., & Buonanno, F. S. (1993). Visual mental imagery activates topographically organized/visual cortex: PET investigations. *Journal of Cognitive Neuroscience, 5*, 263–287.

Kosslyn, S. M., Ball, T., & Reiser, B. J. (1978). Visual images preserve metric spatial information: Evidence from studies of image scanning. *Journal of Experimental Psychology: Human Perception and Performance, 4*, 47–60.

Kosslyn, S. M., & Thompson, W. L. (2000). Shared mechanisms in visual imagery and visual perception: Insights from cognitive neuroscience. In M. Gazzanaga (Ed.), *The Cognitive Neurosciences* (2nd ed., pp. 975–985). Cambridge: MIT Press.

Kosslyn, S. M., Thompson, W. L., Kim, I. J., & Alpert, N. M. (1995). Topographical representations of mental images in primary visual cortex. *Nature, 378*, 496–498.

Kreiman, G., Koch, C., & Fried, I. (2000a). Category-specific visual responses of single neurons in the human medial temporal lobe. *Nature Neuroscience, 3*, 946–953.

Kreiman, G., Koch, C., & Fried, I. (2000b). Imagery neurons in the human brain. *Nature, 408*, 357–361.

Kroger, J. K., Sabb, F. W., Fales, C. L., Bookheimer, S. Y., Cohen, M. S., & Holyoak, K. J. (2002). Recruitment of anterior dorsolateral prefrontal cortex in human reasoning: a parametric study of relational complexity. *Cerebral Cortex, 12*, 477–485.

Kroll, N. (1970). Short-term memory while shadowing: Recall of visually and aurally presented letters. *Journal of Experimental Psychology, 85*, 220–224.

Kuhn, T. (1970). *The structure of scientific revolution* (2nd ed.). Chicago: University of Chicago Press.

Kurtz, K. J., Gentner, D., & Gunn, V. (1999). Reasoning. In B. M. Bly & D. E. Rumelhart (Eds.), *Cognitive science:. Handbook of perception and cognition.* (2nd ed.; pp. 145–200). San Diego, CA: Academic Press.

Kutas, M., & Federmeier, K. D. (2000). Electrophysiology reveals semantic memory use in language comprehension. *Trends in Cognitive Sciences, 4,* 463–470.

Lakoff, G., & Turner, M. (1989). *More than cool reason: The power of poetic metaphor.* Chicago: Chicago University Press.

Lamble, D., Kauranen, T., Laakso, M., & Summala, H. (1999). Cognitive load and detection thresholds in car following situations: Safety implications for using mobile (cellular) telephones while driving. *Accident Analysis and Prevention, 31,* 617–623.

Lamprecht, R., & LeDoux, J. (2004). Structural plasticity and memory. *Nature Reviews Neuroscience, 5,* 45–54.

Larkin, J. H., McDermott, J., Simon, D. P., & Simon, H. A. (1980). Expert and novice performance in solving physics problems. *Science, 208,* 1335–1342.

Lavie, N. (1995). Perceptual load as a necessary condition for selective attention. *Journal of Experimental Psychology: Human Perception and Performance, 21,* 451–486.

Lavie, N., & Driver, J. (1996). On the spatial extent of attention in object-based visual selection. *Perception & Psychophysics, 58,* 1238–1251.

Lavie, N., Ro, T., & Russell, C. (2003). The role of perceptual load in processing distractor faces. *Psychological Science, 15,* 510–515.

Lea, G. (1975). Chronometric analysis of the method of loci. *Journal of Experimental Psychology: Human Perception and Performance, 2,* 95–104.

LeBihan, D., Turner, R., Zeffiro, T. A., Cuenod, A., Jezzard, P., & Bonnerdot, V. (1993). Activation of human primary visual cortex during visual recall: A magnetic resonance imaging study. *Proceedings of the National Academy of Sciences, USA, 90,* 11802–11805.

Lehman, J. F., Laird, J. E., & Rosenbloom, P. (1998). A gentle introduction to Soar: An architecture for human cognition. In D. Scarborough & S. Sternberg (Eds.), *An invitation to cognitive science,* (Vol. 4, 2nd ed., pp. 212–249). Cambridge, MA: MIT Press.

Levin, D., & Simons, D. (1997). Failure to detect changes in attended objects in motion pictures. *Psychonomic Bulletin and Review, 4,* 501–506.

Levinson, S. C. (1996). Language and space. *Annual Review of Anthropology, 25,* 353–382.

Li, F. F., VanRullen, R., Koch, C., & Perona, P. (2002). Rapid natural scene categorization in the near absence of attention. *Proceedings of the National Academy of Sciences, USA, 99,* 9596–9601.

Lichtenstein, S., Slovic, P., Fischoff, B., Layman, M., & Combs, B. (1978). Judged frequency of lethal events. *Journal of Experimental Psychology: Human Learning and Memory, 4,* 551–578.

Lindsay, D. S. (1993). Eyewitness suggestibility. *Current Directions in Psychological Science, 2,* 86–89.

Loftus, E. F. (1979). *Eyewitness testimony.* Cambridge, MA: Harvard University Press.

Loftus, E. F. (1982). Memory and its distortions. In Kraut, A. G. (Ed.), *The G. Stanley Hall lecture series* (Vol. 2, pp. 123–154). Washington, DC: American Psychological Association.

Loftus, E. F. (1993). Made in memory: Distortions in recollection after misleading information. In D. L. Medin (Ed.), *The psychology of learning and motivation: Advances in theory and research* (pp. 187–215). New York: Academic Press.

Loftus, E. F. (1998). Imaginary memories. In M. A. Conway, S. E. Gathercole, & C. Cornoldi (Eds.), *Theories of memory II* (pp. 135–145). Hove, UK: Psychology Press.

Loftus, E. F., Garry, M., & Feldman, J. (1994). Forgetting sexual trauma: What does it mean when 38% forget? *Journal of Consulting and Clinical Psychology, 62,* 1177–1181.

Loftus, E. F., Miller, D. G., & Burns, H. J. (1978). Semantic integration of verbal information into visual memory. *Journal of Experimental*

Psychology: Human Learning and Memory, 4, 19–31.

Loftus, E. F., & Palmer, J. C. (1974). Reconstruction of an automobile destruction: An example of the interaction between language and memory. *Journal of Verbal Learning and Verbal Behavior, 13,* 585–589.

Loftus, E. F., & Pickerel, J. E. (1995). The formation of false memories. *Psychiatric Annals, 25,* 720–725.

Logie, R. H. (1995). *Visuo-spatial working memory.* Hove, UK: Erlbaum.

Lopez, A., Atran, S., Coley, J. D., Medin, D. L., & Smith, E. E. (1997). The tree of life: Universal and cultural features of folkbiological taxonomies and inductions. *Cognitive Psychology, 32,* 251–295.

Lorayne, H., & Lucas, J. (1996). *The memory book.* New York: Ballantine Books.

Lord, C. G., Ross, L., & Lepper, M. (1979). Biased assimilation and attitude polarization: The effects of prior theories on subsequently considered evidence. *Journal of Personality and Social Psychology, 46,* 1254–1266.

Lovett, M. C. (2002). Problem solving. In D. L. Medin (Ed.), *Stevens' Handbook of Experimental Psychology* (3rd ed., pp. 317–362). New York: Wiley.

Low, A., Bentin, S., Rockstroh, B., Silberman, Y., Gomolla, A., Cohen, R., & Elbert, T. (2003). Semantic categorization in the human brain: Spatiotemporal dynamics revealed by magnetoencephalography. *Psychological Science, 14,* 367–372.

Luchins, A. S. (1942). Mechanization in problem solving—the effect of Einstellung. *Psychological Monographs, 54* (No. 6), 195.

Luck, S. J., Chelazzi, L., Hillyard, S. A., & Desimone, R. (1997). Neural mechanisms of spatial selective attention in areas V1, V2, and V4 of macaque visual cortex. *Journal of Neurophysiology, 77,* 24–42.

Luck, S. J., & Vecera, S. P. (2002). Attention. In H. Pashler & S. Yantis (Eds.), *Stevens' Handbook of Experimental Psychology* (3rd ed., pp. 235–286). New York: Wiley.

Lucy, J. A., & Gaskins, S. (1997). Grammatical categories and the development of classification preferences: A comparative approach. In S. C. Levinson & M. Bowerman (Eds.), *Language acquisition and conceptual development.* Cambridge: Cambridge University Press.

Luria, A. R. (1968). *The mind of a mnemonist* (L. Solotaroff, Trans.). New York: Basic Books.

MacDonald, M. C., Pearlmutter, N. J., & Seidenberg, M. S. (1994). Lexical nature of syntactic ambiguity resolution. *Psychological Review, 101,* 676–703.

MacKay, D. G. (1973). Aspects of the theory of comprehension, memory and attention. *Quarterly Journal of Experimental Psychology, 25,* 22–40.

Maier, N. R. F. (1931). Reasoning in humans: II. The solution of a problem and its appearance in consciousness. *Journal of Comparative Psychology, 12,* 181–194.

Malenka, R. C., & Nicoll, R. A. (1999). Long-term potentiation—A decade of progress? *Science, 285,* 1870–1874.

Malt, B. C. (1989). An on-line investigation of prototype and exemplar strategies in classification. *Journal of Experimental Psychology: Learning, Memory and Cognition, 4,* 539–555.

Manktelow, K. (1999). *Reasoning and thinking.* Hove, UK: Psychology Press.

Manktelow, K. I., & Evans, J. St. B. T. (1979). Facilitation of reasoning by realism: effect or non-effect? *British Journal of Psychology, 70,* 477–488.

Manketelow, K. I., & Over, D. E. (1990). Deontic thought and the selection task. In K. J. Gilhooly, M. T. G., Keane, R. H., Logie, & G. Erdos (Eds.), *Lines of thinking: Reflections on the psychology of thought* (Vol. 1). Chichester, UK: Wiley.

Mansfield, R. J. (1974). Neural basis of orientation perception in primate vision. *Science, 186*, 1133–1135.

Mantyla, T. (1986). Optimizing cue effectiveness: Recall of 500 and 600 incidentally learned words. *Journal of Experimental Psychology: Learning Memory, and Cognition, 12*, 66–71.

Marcus, G. B. (1986). Stability and change in political attitudes: "Observe, recall, and explain." *Political Behavior, 8*, 21–44.

Marslen-Wilson, W. (1990). Activation, competition, and frequency in lexical access. On G. T. M. Altmann (Ed.), *Cognitive models of speech processing: Psycholinguistic and computational perspectives*. Cambridge, MA: MIT Press.

Martin, A., & Chao, L. L. (2001). Semantic memory and the brain: Structure and processes. *Current Opinion in Neurology, 11*, 194–201.

Mast, F. W., & Kosslyn, S. M. (2002). Visual mental images can be ambiguous: Insights from individual differences in spatial transformation abilities. *Cognition, 86*, 57–70.

McArthur, D. J. (1982). Computer vision and perceptual psychology. *Psychological Bulletin, 92*, 283–309.

McClelland, J. L. (1988). Connectionist models and psychological evidence. *Journal of Memory and Language, 27*, 107–123.

McClelland, J. L. (1995a). Constructive memory and memory distortions: A parallel-distributed processing approach. In D. L. Schacter (Ed.), *Memory distortion* (pp. 69–90). Cambridge, MA: Harvard University Press.

McClelland, J. L. (1995b). Why there are complementary learning systems in the hippocampus and neocortex: Insights from the successes and failures of connectionist models of learning and memory. *Psychological Review, 102*, 419–457.

McClelland, J. L. (1999). Cognitive modeling, connectionist. In R. W. Engel (Ed.), *M.I.T. Encyclopedia of Cognitive Science* (pp. 137–141). Cambridge, MA: MIT Press.

McClelland, J. L., (2003). Why is it heard to learn? Insights from models of how learning occurs in the brain. Lecture at Carnegie-Mellon University, November 17.

McClelland, J. L., McNaughton, B. L., & O'Reilly, R. C. (1995). Why there are complementary learning systems in the hippocampus and neocortex: Insights from the successes and failures of connectionist models of learning and memory. *Psychological Review, 102*, 419–457.

McClelland, J. L., & Rogers, T. T. (2003). The parallel-distributed processing approach to semantic cognition. *Nature Reviews Neuroscience, 4*, 310–322.

McClelland, J. L., & Rummelhart, D. E. (1986). *Parallel distributed processing*. Cambridge, MA: MIT Press.

McCloskey, M., & Zaragoza, Z. (1985). Misleading postevent information and memory for events: Arguments and evidence against memory impairment hypothesis. *Journal of Experimental Psychology: General, 114*, 3–18.

McElroy, S. L., & Keck, P. E. (1995). Recovered memory therapy: False memory syndrome and other complications. *Psychiatric Annals, 25*, 731–735.

McKelvie, S. L. (1997). The availability heuristic: effects of fame and gender on the estimated frequency of male and female names. *Journal of Social Psychology, 137*, 63–78.

McKoon, G., & Ratcliff, R. (1992). Inference during reading. *Psychological Review, 99*, 440–466.

Medin, D. L., Altom, M. W., Edelson, S. M., & Freko, D. (1982). Correlated symptoms and simulated medical classification. *Journal of Experimental Psychology: Learning, Memory, and Cognition, 8*, 37–50.

Medin, D., & Atran, S. (2004). The native mind: Biological categorization, reasoning, and decision making in development and across cultures. *Psychological Review*, in press.

Medin, D., Lynch, E., Coley, J., & Atran, S. (1997). Categorization and reasoning among tree experts: Do all roads lead to Rome? *Cognitive Psychology, 32*, 49–96.

Mellett, E., Tzourino, N., Denis, M., & Mazoyer, B. (1998). Cortical anatomy of mental imagery of concrete nouns based on their dictionary definition. *Neuroreport, 9*, 803–808.

Mervis, C. B., Catlin, J., & Rosch, E. (1976). Relationships among goodness-of-example, category norms and word frequency. *Bulletin of the Psychonomic Society, 7*, 268–284.

Merzenich, M. M., Recanzone, G., Jenkins, W. M., Allard, T. T., & Nudo, R. J. (1988). Cortical representational plasticity. In P. Rakic & W. Singer (Eds.), *Neurobiology of neocortex* (pp. 42–67). Berlin: Wiley.

Metcalfe, J., & Wiebe, D. (1987). Intuition in insight and noninsight problem solving. *Memory and Cognition, 15*, 238–246.

Meyer, D. E., & Schvaneveldt, R. W. (1971). Facilitation in recognizing pairs of words: Evidence of a dependence between retrieval operations. *Journal of Experimental Psychology, 90*, 227–234.

Miller, G. A. (1956). The magical number seven, plus or minus two: Some limits on our capacity for processing information. *Psychological Review, 63*, 81–97.

Milner, A. D., & Goodale, M. A. (1995). *The visual brain in action.* New York: Oxford University Press.

Milner, B. (1966). Amnesia following operation on the temporal lobe. In C. W. M. Whitty & O. L. Zangwill (Eds.), *Amnesia* (pp. 109–133). London: Butterworth & Co.

Milner, B., Corkin, S., & Teuber, H-L. (1968). Further analysis of hippocampal amnesic syndrome: 14-year follow-up study of H.M. *Neuropsychologia, 6*, 215–234.

Minda, J. P., & Smith, J. D. (2001). Prototypes in category learning: The effect of category size, category structure, and stimulus complexity. *Journal of Experimental Psychology: Learning, Memory, and Cognition, 27*, 775–799.

Misiak, H., & Sexton, V. (1966). History of psychology: An overview. New York: Grune & Stratton.

Mitchell, K. J., & Johnson, M. K. (2000). Source monitoring. In E. Tulving and F. I. M. Craik, *The Oxford handbook of memory* (pp. 179–195). New York: Oxford University Press.

Moore, C. M., Yantis, S., & Vaughan, B. (1998). Object-based visual selection: Evidence from perceptual completion. *Psychological Science, 9*, 104–110.

Moray, N. (1959). Attention in dichotic listening: Affective cues and the influence of instructions. *Quarterly Journal of Experimental Psychology, 11*, 56–60.

Morris, C. D., Bransford, J. D., & Franks, J. J. (1977). Levels of processing versus transfer appropriate processing. *Journal of Verbal Learning and Verbal Behavior, 16*, 519–533.

Morris, R. G., Miotto, E. C., Feigenbaum, J. D., Bullock, P., & Polkey, C. E. (1997). The effect of goal-subgoal conflict on planning ability after frontal- and temporal-lobe lesions in humans. *Neuropsychologia, 35*, 1147–1157.

Morrow, D. G., Greenspan, S. L., & Bower, G. H. (1987). Accessibility and situation models in narrative comprehension. *Journal of Memory and Language, 26*, 165–187.

Moscovitch, M. (1995). Confabulation. In D. L. Schacter (Ed.), *Memory distortion* (pp. 226–251). Cambridge, MA: Harvard University Press.

Mowbray, G. H. (1953). Simultaneous vision and audition: The comprehension of prose passages with varying levels of difficulty. *Journal of Experimental Psychology, 46*, 365–372.

Munakata, Y., Morton, J. B., & Stedron, J. M. (2003). The role of prefrontal cortex in perseveration: Developmental and computational explorations. In P. Quinlan (Ed.), *Connectionist models of development.* East Sussex: Psychology Press.

Munakata, Y., Morton, J. B., & Yerys, B. E. (2003). Children's perseveration: Attentional inertia and alternative accounts. *Developmental Science, 6*, 471–473.

Murdoch, B. B., Jr. (1962). The serial position effect in free recall. *Journal of Experimental Psychology, 64*, 482–488.

Murray, D. J. (1968). Articulating and acoustic confusability in short-term memory. *Journal of Experimental Psychology, 78*, 679–684.

Myers, J. L., & Duffy, S. A. (1990). Causal inferences and text memory. In *The psychology of learning and motivation, Vol. 25.* New York: Academic Press.

Neisser, U. (1964). Visual search. *Scientific American, 210*, 94–107.

Neisser, U. (1967). *Cognitive psychology.* New York: Appleton-Century-Crofts.

Neisser, U. (1988). New vistas in the study of memory. In U. Neisser & E. Winograd (Eds.), *Remembering reconsidered: Ecological and traditional approaches to the study of memory* (pp. 1–10). Cambridge: Cambridge University Press.

Neisser, U., & Harsch, N. (1992). Phantom flashbulbs: False recollections of hearing the news about *Challenger.* In E. Winograd & U. Neisser (Eds.), *Affect and accuracy in recall: Studies of "flashbulb" memories* (pp. 9–31). New York: Cambridge University Press.

Newell, A., & Simon, H. A. (1956). The logic theory machine: A complex information processing system. *Transactions on information theory* (Institute of Radio Engineers), *IT-2*, No. 3, 61–79.

Newell, A., & Simon, H. A. (1972). *Human problem solving.* Englewood Cliffs, NJ: Prentice-Hall.

Newman, L. S., & Baumeister, R. F. (1998). Abducted by aliens. In S. J.Lynn and K. M. McConkie (Eds.), *Truth in memory* (pp. 284–303). New York: Guilford Press.

Nichelli, P., Grafman, J., Pietrini, P., Always, D., Carton, J. C., & Miletich, R. (1994). Brain activity in chess playing. *Nature, 369*, 191.

Nicoletta, B., Pizzourusso, T., Gian-Michele, R., & Maffei, L. (2003). Molecular basis of plasticity in the visual cortex. *Trends in Neurosciences, 26*, 369–378.

Nisbett, R. E. (2003). *The geography of thought.* New York: Free Press.

Nisbett. R. E., & Norenzayan, A. (2002). Culture and cognition. In D. L. Medin (Ed.), *Stevens' Handbook of Experimental Psychology* (3rd ed.). New York: Wiley.

Norenzayan, A., Smith, E. E., Kim, B. J., & Nisbett, R. E. (2002). Cultural preferences for formal versus intuitive reasoning. *Cognitive Science, 26*, 653–684.

Norman, D. (1968). Toward a theory of memory and attention. *Psychological Review, 75*, 522–536.

Nyberg, L., McIntosh, A. R., Cabeaa, R., Habib, R., Houle, S., & Tulving, E. (1996). General and specific brain regions involved in encoding and retrieval of events: What, where and when. *Proceedings of the National Academy of Sciences, USA, 93*, 11280–11285.

Olesen, P. J., Westerberg, H., & Klingberg, T. (2004). Increased prefrontal and parietal activity after training of working memory. *Nature Neuroscience, 7*, 75–79.

Olson, A. C., & Humphreys, G. W. (1997). Connectionist models of neuropsychological disorders. *Trends in Cognitive Sciences, 1*, 222–228.

Orban, G. A., Vandenbussche, E., & Vogels, R. (1984*).* Human orientation discrimination tested with long stimuli. *Vision Research, 24*, 121–128.

Osherson, D. N., Smith, E. E., Wilkie, O., Lopez, A., & Shafir, E. (1990). Category-based induction. *Psychological Review, 97*, 185–200.

Osterhout, L., McLaughlin, J., & Bersick, M. (1997). Event-related brain potentials and human language. *Trends in Cognitive Sciences, 1,* 203–209.

Owen, A. M., Downes, J. J., Sahakian, B. J., Polkey, C. E., & Robbins, T. W. (1990). Planning and spatial working memory following frontal lobe lesions in man. *Neuropsychologica, 28,* 1021–1034.

Paige, J. M., & Simon, H. A. (1966). Cognitive processes in solving word problems. Reprinted in H. A. Simon (Ed.), *Models of thought.* New Haven: Yale University Press (1979).

Paivio, A. (1963). Learning of adjective-noun paired associates as a function of adjective-noun word order and noun abstractness. *Canadian Journal of Psychology, 17,* 370–379.

Paivio, A. (1965). Abstractness, imagery, and meaningfulness in paired-associate learning. *Journal of Verbal Learning and Verbal Behavior, 4,* 32–38.

Paivio, A. (1986). *Mental representations: A dual coding approach.* New York: Oxford University Press.

Palmer, S. E. (1975). The effects of contextual scenes on the identification of objects. *Memory and Cognition, 3,* 519–526.

Parkin, A. J. (1996). *Explorations in cognitive neuropsychology.* Oxford, England: Blackwell.

Penfield, W., & Evans, J. (1935). The frontal lobe in man: A clinical study of maximum removals. *Brain, 58,* 115–133.

Perfect, T. J., & Askew, C. (1994). Print adverts: Not remembered but memorable. *Applied Cognitive Psychology, 8,* 693–703.

Perky, C. W. (1910). An experimental study of imagination. *American Journal of Psychology, 21,* 422–452.

Perret, D. I., Hietanen, J. K., Oram, M. W., & Benson, P. J. (1992). Organization and function of cells responsive to faces in the temporal cortex. *Transactions of the Royal Society of London, B225,* 23–30.

Petersen, S. E., Fox, P. T., Posner, M. I., Minturn, M., & Raichle, M. E. (1988). Positron emission tomographic studies of the cortical anatomy of single-word processing. *Nature, 331,* 585–589.

Peterson, L. R., and Peterson, M. J. (1959). Short-term retention of individual verbal items. *Journal of Experimental Psychology, 58,* 193–198.

Peterson, M. A. (1994). Object recognition processes can and do operate before figure-ground organization. *Current Directions in Psychological Science, 3,* 105–111.

Peterson, S. W. (1992). The cognitive functions of underlining as a study technique. *Reading Research and Instrumentation, 31,* 49–56.

Pillemer, D. B. (1998). *Momentous events, vivid memories.* Cambridge, MA: Harvard University Press.

Pillemer, D. B., Picariello, M. L., Law, A. B., & Reichman, J. S. (1996). Memories of college: The importance of specific educational episodes. In D. C. Rubin (Ed.), *Remembering our past: Studies in autobiographical memory* (pp. 318–337). Cambridge, England: Cambridge University Press.

Poggio, T. (1984, April). Vision by man and machine. *Scientific American,* 106–116.

Pollack, I., & Pickett, J. M. (1964). Intelligibility of excerpts from fluent speech: Auditory vs. structural context. *Journal of Verbal Learning and Verbal Behavior, 3,* 79–84.

Posner, M. I., & Keele, S. W. (1967). Decay of visual information from a single letter. *Science, 158,* 137–139.

Posner, M. I., Snyder, C. R. R., & Davidson, B. J. (1980). Attention and the detection of signals. *Journal of Experimental Psychology: General, 109,* 160–174.

Proffitt, J. B., Coley, J. D., & Medin, D. L. (2000). Expertise and category-based induction. *Journal of Experimental Psychology: Learning, Memory and Cognition, 26,* 811–828.

Pylyshyn, Z. W. (1973). What the mind's eye tells the mind's brain: A critique of mental imagery. *Psychological Bulletin, 80,* 1–24.

Pylyshyn, Z. W. (2001). Is the imagery debate over? If so, what was it about? In E. Dupoux (Ed.), *Language, brain, and cognitive development* (pp. 59–83). Cambridge, MA: MIT Press.

Quillian, M. R. (1967). Word concepts: A theory and simulation of some basic semantic capabilities. *Behavioral Science, 12,* 410–430.

Quillian, M. R. (1969). The Teachable Language Comprehender: A simulation program and theory of language. *Communications of the ACM, 12,* 459–476.

Raphael, B. (1976). *The thinking computer.* New York: Freeman.

Ratcliff, R. (1990). Connectionist models of recognition memory: Constraints imposed by learning and forgetting functions. *Psychological Review, 97,* 285–308.

Rayner, K., & Clifton, C. (2002). Language processing. In H. Pashler & S. Yantis (Eds.), *Stevens' Handbook of Experimental Psychology* (3rd ed., pp. 261–316). New York: Wiley.

Rayner, K., & Duffy, S. A. (1986). Lexical complexity and fixation times in reading: Effects of word frequency, verb complexity, and lexical ambiguity. *Memory and Cognition, 14,* 191–201.

Rayner, K., Liersedge, S. P., White, S. J., & Vergilino-Perez, D. (2003). Reading disappearing text: Cognitive control of eye movements. *Psychological Science, 14,* 385–388.

Reber, A. S. (1995). *Penguin dictionary of psychology* (2nd ed.). New York: Penguin.

Redelmeier, D. A., & Tibshirani, R. J. (1997). Association between cellular-telephone calls and motor vehicle collisions. *New England Journal of Medicine, 336,* 453–458.

Reder, L. M., & Anderson, J. R. (1982). Effects of spacing and embellishment for the main points of a text. *Memory and Cognition, 10,* 97–102.

Reicher, G. M. (1969). Perceptual recognition as a function of meaningfulness of stimulus material. *Journal of Experimental Psychology, 81,* 275–280.

Reitman, J. (1976). Skilled perception in Go: Deducing memory structures from inter-response times. *Cognitive Psychology, 8,* 336–356.

Rensink, R. A. (2002). Change detection. *Annual Review of Psychology, 53,* 245–277.

Rensink, R. A., O'Regan, J. K., & Clark, J. J. (1997). To see or not to see: The need for attention to perceive changes in scenes. *Psychological Science, 8,* 368–373.

Richardson, A. (1994). *Individual differences in imaging: Their measurement, origins, and consequences.* Amityville, NY: Baywood.

Rips, L. J. (1995). Deduction and Cognition. In E. Smith & D. N. Osherson (Eds.), *An invitation to cognitive science* (Vol. 2, pp. 297–343). Cambridge, MA: MIT Press.

Rips, L. J. (2002). Reasoning. In D. L. Medin (Ed.), *Stevens' Handbook of Experimental Psychology* (3rd ed., pp. 363–411). New York: Wiley.

Rips, L. J., Shoben, E. J., & Smith, E. E. (1973). Semantic distance and the verification of semantic relations. *Journal of Verbal Learning and Verbal Behavior, 12,* 1–20.

Roberson, D., Davies, I., & Davidoff, J. (2000). Color categories are not universal: Replications and new evidence from a stone-age culture. *Journal of Experimental Psychology: General, 129,* 369–398.

Robertson, L. C., & Rafal, R. (2000). Disorders of visual attention. In M. Gazzanaga (Ed.), *The Cognitive Neurosciences* (2nd ed., pp. 633–649). Cambridge, MA: MIT Press.

Roediger, H. L., Guynn, M. J., & Jones, T. C. (1994). Implicit memory: A tutorial review. In G. d'Ydewalle, P. Eallen, & P. Bertelson (Eds.), *International perspectives on cognitive science* (Vol. 2, pp. 67–94). Hillsdale, NJ: Erlbaum.

Roediger, H. L., & McDermott, K. B. (1995). Creating false memories: Remembering words not presented in lists. *Journal of Experimental Psychology: Learning, Memory, and Cognition, 21,* 803–814.

Rogers, T. B., Kuiper, N. A., & Kirker, W. S. (1979). Self-reference and the encoding of personal information. *Journal of Personality and Social Psychology, 35,* 677–688.

Rosch, E. H. (1973). On the internal structure of perceptual and semantic categories. In T. E. Moore (Ed.), *Cognitive development and the acquisition of language* (pp. 111–144). New York: Academic Press.

Rosch, E. H. (1975a). Cognitive representations of semantic categories. *Journal of Experimental Psychology: General, 104,* 192–233.

Rosch, E. H. (1975b). The nature of mental codes for color categories. *Journal of Experimental Psychology: Human Perception and Performance, 1,* 303–322.

Rosch, E. H., & Mervis, C. B. (1975). Family resemblances: Studies in the internal structures of categories. *Cognitive Psychology, 7,* 573–605.

Rosch, E. H., Mervis, C. B., Gray, W. D., Johnson, D. M., & Boyes-Braem, P. (1976). Basic objects in natural categories. *Cognitive Psychology, 8,* 382–439.

Rosch, E., Simpson, C., & Miller, R. S. (1976). Structural bases of typicality effects. *Journal of Experimental Psychology: Human Perception and Performance, 2,* 491–502.

Rosch Heider, E. (1972). Universals in color naming and memory. *Journal of Experimental Psychology, 93,* 10–20.

Rosch Heider, E., & Olivier, D. C. (1972). The structure of color space in naming and memory for two languages. *Cognitive Psychology, 3,* 337–354.

Ross, D. F., Ceci, S. J., Dunning, D., & Toglia, M. P. (1994). Unconscious transference and mistaken identity: When a witness misidentifies a familiar but innocent person. *Journal of Applied Psychology, 79,* 918–930.

Ross, M., & Buehler, R. (1994). Creative remembering. In U. Neisser & R. Fivish (Eds.), *The remembering self: Construction and accuracy in the self-narrative* (pp. 205–235). New York: Cambridge University Press.

Ross, M., & Makin, V. S. (1999). Prototype versus exemplar models in cognition. In R. J. Sternberg (Ed.), *The nature of cognition* (pp. 205–241). Cambridge, MA: MIT Press.

Rowe, J. B., Owen, A. M., Johnsrude, I. S., & Passingham, R. E. (2001). Imaging the mental components of a planning task. *Neuropsychologia, 39,* 315–327.

Rubin, D. C., Rahhal, T. A., & Poon, L. W. (1998). Things learned in early adulthood are remembered best. *Memory and Cognition, 26,* 3–19.

Sachs, J. (1967). Recognition memory for syntactic and semantic aspects of a connected discourse. *Perception & Psychophysics, 2,* 437–442.

Sacks, O. W. (1985). *The man who mistook his wife for a hat and other clinical tales.* New York: Summit Books.

Saffran, J. R., Aslin, R. N., & Newport, E. L. (1999). Statistical learning of tone sequences by human infants and adults. *Cognition, 70,* 27–52.

Sanitioso, R., Kunda, Z., & Fong, G. T. (1990). Motivated recruitment of autobiographical memories. *Journal of Personality and Social Psychology, 59,* 229–241.

Savin, H. B. (1963). Word-frequency effects and errors in the perception of speech. *Journal of the Acoustical Society of America, 35,* 200–206.

Schacter, D. (2001). *The seven sins of memory.* New York: Houghton Mifflin.

Schacter, D. L. (1996). *Searching for memory: The brain, the mind, and the past.* New York: Basic Books.

Schkade, D. A., & Kahneman, D. (1998). Does living in California make people happy? *Psychological Science, 9,* 340–346.

Schmolck, H., Buffalo, E. A., & Squire, L. R. (2000). Memory distortions develop over time: Recollections of the O.J. Simpson trial verdict after 15 and 32 months. *Psychological Science, 11,* 39–45.

Schneider, W. & Shiffrin, R. M. (1977). Controlled and automatic human information processing: I. Detection, search, and attention. *Psychological Review, 84,* 1–66.

Schrauf, R. W., & Rubin, D. C. (1998). Bilingual autobiographical memory in order adult immigrants: A test of cognitive explanations of the reminiscence bump and the linguistic encoding of memories. *Journal of Memory and Language, 39,* 437–457.

Schweickert, R., & Boruff, B. (1986). Short-term memory capacity: Magic number or magic spell? *Journal of Experimental Psychology: Learning, Memory and Cognition, 12,* 419–425.

Scoville, W. B., & Milner, B. (1957). Loss of recent memory after bilateral hippocampal lesions. *Journal of Neurology, Neurosurgery, and Psychiatry, 20,* 11–21.

Scribner, S. (1977). Modes of thinking and ways of speaking: culture and logic reconsidered. In Johnson-Laird, P. N., & Wason, P. C. (Eds.), *Thinking: Readings in cognitive science* (pp. 483–500). Cambridge: Cambridge University Press.

Segal, S. J., & Fusella, V. (1970). Influence of imaged pictures and sounds on detection of visual and auditory signals. *Journal of Experimental Psychology, 83,* 458–464.

Shallice, T., & Warrington, E. K. (1970). Independent functioning of verbal memory stores: A neuropsychological study. *Quarterly Journal of Experimental Psychology, 22,* 261–273.

Shepard, R. N., & Metzler, J. (1971). Mental rotation of three-dimensional objects. *Science, 171,* 701–703.

Sheridan, J., & Humphreys, G. W. (1993). A verbal-semantic category-specific recognition impairment. *Cognitive Neuropsychology, 10,* 143–184.

Sherry, J. L. (2001). The effects of violent video games on aggression: A meta-analysis. *Human Communication Research, 27,* 409–431.

Shiffrin, R. M., & Schneider, W. (1977). Controlled and automatic human information processing: II. Perceptual learning, automatic attending, and a general theory. *Psychological Review, 84,* 127–190.

Silveri, M. C., & Gainotti, G. (1988). Interaction between vision and language in category-specific impairment. *Cognitive Neuropsychology, 5,* 677–709.

Simonton, D. K. (1984). *Genius, creativity, and leadership.* Cambridge, MA: Harvard University Press.

Singer, M., Andrusiak, P., Reisdorf, P., & Black, N. L. (1992). Individual differences in bridging inference processes. *Memory & Cognition, 20,* 539–548.

Skinner, B. F. (1938). *The behavior of organisms.* New York: Appleton Century.

Skinner, B. F. (1957). *Verbal behavior.* New York: Appleton-Century Crofts.

Slobin, D. I. (1966). Grammatical transformations and sentence comprehension in childhood and adulthood. *Journal of Verbal Learning and Verbal Behavior, 5,* 219–227.

Smith, E. E., Schoben, E. J., & Rips, L. J. (1974). Structure and process in semantic memory. *Psychological Review, 81,* 214–241.

Smith, J. D., & Minda, J. P. (1998). Prototypes in the mist: The early epochs of category learning. *Journal of Experimental Psychology: Learning, Memory, and Cognition, 24,* 1411–1436.

Smith, J. D., & Minda, J. P. (2000). Thirty categorization results in search of a model. *Journal of Experimental Psychology: Learning, Memory, and Cognition, 26,* 3–27.

Smith, S. M, Glenberg, A. M., & Bjork, R. A. (1978). Environmental context and human memory. *Memory & Cognition, 6,* 342–353.

Smith, S. M., & Rothkopf, E. Z. (1984). Contextual enhancement and distribution of practice in the classroom. *Cognition and Instruction, 1,* 341–358.

Solomon, K. O., Medin, D. L., & Lynch, E. (1999). Concepts do more than categorize. *Trends in Cognitive Science, 3,* 99–105.

Spalding, T. L., & Murphy, G. L. (1996). Effects of background knowledge on category construction. *Journal of Experimental Psychology: Learning, Memory and Cognition, 22,* 525–538.

Spelke, E., Hirst, W., & Neisser, U. (1976). Skills of divided attention. *Cognition, 4,* 215–230.

Spence, C., & Read, L. (2003). Speech shadowing while driving: On the difficulty of splitting attention between eye and ear. *Psychological Science, 14,* 251–256.

Sperling, G. (1960). The information available in brief visual presentations. *Psychological Monographs, 74* (Series 498).

Sprecher, S. (1999). "I love you more today than yesterday": Romantic partners' perceptions of changes in love and related affect over time. *Journal of Personality and Social Psychology, 76,* 46–53.

Squire, L. R. (1986). Mechanisms of memory. *Science, 232,* 1612–1619.

Squire, L. R., & Cohen, N. (1979). Memory and amnesia: Resistance to disruption develops for years after learning. *Behavioral and Neural Biology. 25,* 115–125.

Squire, L. R., & Zola-Morgan, S. (1996). Structure and functioning of declarative and nondeclarative memory systems. *Proceedings of the National Academy of Science, 93,* 13515–13522.

Squire, L. R., & Zola-Morgan, S. (1998). Episodic memory, semantic memory, and amnesia. *Hippocampus, 8,* 205–211.

Squire, L. R., Slater, D. C., & Chace, P. M., (1975). Retrograde amnesia: Temporal gradient in very long term memory following electroconvulsive therapy. *Science, 187,* 77–79.

Srinivasan, M. V., & Ventatesh, S. (Eds.). (1997). *From living eyes to seeing machines.* New York: Oxford.

Stanny, C. J., & Johnson, T. C. (2000). Effects of stress induced by a simulated shooting on recall by police and citizen witnesses. *American Journal of Psychology, 113,* 359–386.

Strayer, D. L., & Johnston, W. A. (2001). Driven to distraction: Dual-task studies of simulated driving and conversing on a cellular telephone. *Psychological Science, 12,* 462–466.

Stroop, J. R. (1935). Studies of interference in serial verbal reactions. *Journal of Experimental Psychology, 18,* 643–662.

Styles, E. A. (1997). *The psychology of attention.* Hove, UK: Psychology Press.

Super, H., Spekreijse, H., & Lamme, V. A. F. (2001). A neural correlate of working memory in the monkey primary visual cortex. *Science, 293,* 120–124.

Swinney, D. A. (1979). Lexical access during sentence comprehension: (Re)considerations of context effects. *Journal of Verbal Learning and Verbal Behavior, 18,* 645–659.

Talarico, J. M., & Rubin, D. C. (2003). Confidence, not consistency, characterizes flashbulb memories. *Psychological Science, 14,* 455–461.

Tanaka, J. W., & Taylor, M. (1991). Object categories and expertise: Is the basic level in the eye of the beholder? *Cognitive Psychology, 23,* 457–482.

Tanaka, K. (1993). Neuronal mechanisms of object recognition. *Science, 262,* 684–688.

Tannehaus, M. K., Spivey-Knowlton, M. J., Beerhard, K. M., & Sedivy, J. C. (1995). Integration of visual and linguistic information in spoken language comprehension. *Science, 268,* 1632–1634.

Tarkan, L. (2003, April 29). Brain surgery, without knife or blood, gains favor. *New York Times,* p. F5.

Ter-Pogossian, M. M., Phelps, M. E., Hoffman, E. J., & Mullani, N. A. (1975). A positron-emission tomography for nuclear imaging (PET). *Radiology, 114,* 89–98.

Terr, L. C. (1994). Unchained memories: The stories of traumatic memories lost and found. New York: Basic Books.

Tipper, S. P., & Behrmann, M. (1996). Object-centered not scene-based visual neglect. *Journal of Experimental Psychology: Human Perception and Performance, 22,* 1261–1278.

Toni, N., Buchs, P-A., Nikonenko, I., Bron, C. R., & Muller. D. (1999). LTP promotes formation of multiple spine synapses between a single axon terminal and a dendrite. *Nature 402,* 421–425.

Tooley, V., Bringham, J. C., Maass, A., & Bothwell, R. K. (1987). Facial recognition: Weapon effect and attentional focus. *Journal of Applied Social Psychology, 17,* 845–859.

Treadeau, K. (1997). *Mega Memory.* New York: William Morrow.

Treisman, A. (1986). Features and objects in visual processing. *Scientific American. 225,* 114–125.

Treisman, A. M. (1964a). Selective attention in man. *British Medical Bulletin, 20,* 12–16.

Treisman, A. M. (1964b). Contextual cues in selective listening. *Quarterly Journal of Experimental Psychology, 12,* 242–245.

Treisman, A. M., & Schmidt, H. (1982). Illusory conjunctions in the perception of objects. *Cognitive Psychology, 14,* 107–141.

Trueswell, J. C., Tannehaus, M. K., & Garnsey, S. M. (1994). Semantic influences on parsing: Use of thematic role information in syntactic ambiguity resolution. *Journal of Memory and Language, 33,* 285–318.

Tulving, E. (1962). Subjective organization in free recall of "unrelated" words. *Psychological Review, 69,* 344–354.

Tulving, E. (1972). Episodic and semantic memory. In E. Tulving and W. Donaldson (Eds.), *Orga-nization of memory* (pp. 381–403). New York: Academic Press.

Tulving, E., & Markowitsch, H. J. (1998). Episodic and declarative memory: Role of the hippocampus. *Hippocampus, 8,* 198–204.

Tulving, E., & Pearlstone, Z. (1966). Availability versus accessibility of information in memory for words. *Journal of Verbal Learning and Verbal Behavior, 5,* 381–391.

Tversky, A., & Kahneman, D. (1973). Availability: A heuristic for judging frequency and probability. *Cognitive Psychology, 5,* 207–232.

Tversky, A., & Kahneman, D. (1974). Judgment under uncertainty: Heuristics and biases. *Science, 185,* 1124–1131.

Tversky, A., & Kahneman, D. (1981). The framing of decisions and the psychology of choice. *Science, 185,* 1124–1131.

Tversky, A., & Kahneman, D. (1983). Extensional versus intuitive reasoning: The conjunction fallacy in probability judgment. *Psychological Review, 90,* 293–315.

Tversky, A., & Shafir, E. (1992). Choice under conflict: The dynamics of deferred decision. *Psychological Science, 3,* 358–361.

Tyler, S. W., Hertel, P. T., McCallum, M. C., & Ellis, H. C. (1979). *Journal of Experimental Psychology: Human Learning and Memory, 6,* 607–617.

Underwood, G., & Batt, V. (1996). *Reading and understanding.* Oxford, UK: Blackwell.

Vallar, G., & Baddeley, A. D. (1984). Fractionation of working memory: Neuropsychological evidence for a phonological short-term store. *Journal of Verbal Learning and Verbal Behavior, 23,* 151–161.

Van den Broek, P. (1994). Copmprehension and memory of narrative texts. In M. A. Gernsbacher (Ed.), *Handbook of psycholinguistics* (pp. 539–588). San Diego: Academic Press.

Van Rullen, R., & Thorpe, S. J. (2001). The time course of visual processing: From early perception to decision-making. *Journal of Cognitive Neuroscience, 13,* 454–461.

Vargha-Khadem, F., Gadian, D. G., Watkins, K., Connolly, A., Van Paesschen, W., & Mishkin, M. (1997). Differential effects of early hippocampal pathology on episodic and semantic memory. *Science, 277,* 376–380.

Vecera, S. P., & O'Reilly, R. C. (2000). Graded effects in hierarchical figure-ground organization: Reply to Peterson (1999). *Journal of Experimental Psychology: Human Perception and Performance, 26,* 1221–1231.

Violanti, J. M. (1998). Cellular phones and fatal traffic collisions. *Accident Analysis and Prevention, 28,* 265–270.

Voss, J. F., Greene, T. R., Post, T., & Penner, B. C. (1983). Problem-solving skill in the social sciences. In G. Bower (Ed.), *The psychology of learning and motivation.* New York: Academic Press.

Wagenaar, W. A. (1986). My memory: A study of autobiographical memory over six years. *Cognitive Psychology, 18,* 225–252.

Wagner, A. D., Schacter, D. L., Rotte, M., Koutstaal, W., Maril, A., Dale, A. M., Rosen, B. R., & Buckner, R. L. (1998). Building memories: Remembering and forgetting of verbal experiences as predicted by brain activity. *Science, 281,* 1188–1191.

Waldrop, M. M. (1998). A landmark in speech recognition. *Science, 240,* 1615.

Waltz, J. A., Knowlton, B. J., Holyoak, K. J., Boone, K. B., Mishkin, F. S., Santos, M. de M., Thomas, C. R., & Miller, B. L. (1999). A system for relational reasoning in human prefrontal cortex. *Psychological Science, 10,* 119–124.

Ward, T. B., Smith, S. M., & Vaid, J. (Eds.). (1997). *Creative thought: An investigation of conceptual structures and processes.* Washington, DC: American Psychological Association.

Warrington, E. K., & McCarthy, R. (1983). Category specific access dysphasia. *Brain, 106,* 859–878.

Warrington, E. K., & Shallice, T. (1969). The selective impairment of auditory verbal short-term memory. *Brain, 92,* 885–896.

Warrington, E. K., & Shallice, T. (1984). Category specific semantic impairments. *Brain, 107,* 829–854.

Warrington, E. K., & Weiskrantz, L. (1968). New method of testing long-term retention with special reference to amnesic patients. *Nature, 217,* 972–974.

Wason, P. C. (1960). On the failure to eliminate hypotheses in a conceptual task. *Quarterly Journal of Experimental Psychology, 12,* 129–140.

Wason, P. C. (1966). Reasoning. In B. Foss (Ed.), *New horizons in psychology.* Harmonsworth, UK: Penguin.

Watson, J. B. (1913). Psychology as the behaviorist views it. *Psychological Review, 20,* 158–177.

Watson, J. B. (1928). *The ways of behaviorism.* New York: Harper and Brothers.

Watson, J. B., & Rayner, R. (1920). Conditioned emotional reactions. *Journal of Experimental Psychology, 3,* 1–14.

Waugh, N. C., & Norman, D. A. (1965). Primary memory. *Psychological Review, 72,* 69–104.

Weisberg, R. W. (1995). Prolegomena to theories of insight in problem solving: A taxonomy of problems. In R. J. Sternberg & J. E. Davidson (Eds.), *The nature of insight.* (pp. 157–196). Cambridge, MA: MIT Press.

Weisberg, R. W., & Alba, J. W. (1981). An examination of the alleged role of "fixation" in the solution of several "insight" problems. *Journal of Experimental Psychology: General, 110,* 169–192.

Weisberg, R. W., & Alba, J. W. (1982). Problem solving is not like perception: More on Gestalt theory. *Journal of Experimental Psychology: General, 111*, 326–330.

Wells, G. L. (1985). Verbal descriptions of faces from memory: Are they diagnostic of identification accuracy? *Journal of Applied Social Psychology, 14*, 89–103.

Wells, G. L., & Bradfield, A. L. (1998). "Good, you identified the suspect": Feedback to eyewitnesses distorts their reports of the witnessing experience. *Journal of Applied Psychology, 83*, 360–376.

Wells, G. L., Malpass, R. S., Lindsay, R. C. L., Fisher, R. P., Turtle, J. W., & Fulero, S. M. (2000). From the lab to the police station. *American Psychologist, 55*, 581–598.

Wheeler, D. D. (1970). Processes in word recognition. *Cognitive Psychology, 1*, 59–85.

Whitaker, B. (2003, June 10). California may restrict vehicle cellphone use. *New York Times*, p. A25.

Whorf, B. J. (1956). The relation of habitual thought and behavior to language. In J. B. Carroll (Ed.), *Language, thought and reality: Essays by B. L. Whorf* (pp. 35–270). Cambridge, MA: MIT Press.

Wickelgren, W. A. (1965). Acoustic similarity and retroactive interference in short-term memory. *Journal of Verbal Learning and Verbal Behavior, 4*, 53–61.

Wickens, D. D., Dalezman, R. E., & Eggemeier, F. T. (1976). Multiple encoding of word attributes in memory. *Memory & Cognition, 4*, 307–310.

Williams, L. M. (1994). Recall of childhood trauma: A prospective study of women's memories of child sexual abuse. *Journal of Consulting and Clinical Psychology, 62*, 1167–1176.

Wilson, B., & Baddeley, A. (1988). Semantic, episodic, and autobiographical memory in a postmeningitic amnesic patient. *Brain and Cognition, 8*, 31–46.

Wilson, T. D., Wheatley, T., Meyers, J. M., Gilbert, D. T., & Axsom, D. (2000). Focalism: A source of durability bias in affective forecasting. *Journal of Personality and Social Psychology, 78*, 821–836.

Wiseman, S., & Neisser, U. (1974). Perceptual organization as a determinant of visual recognition memory. *American Journal of Psychology, 87*, 675–681.

Wittgenstein, L. (1953). *Philosophical investigations* (G. E. M. Amnscombe, Trans.). Oxford, UK: Blackwell.

Wollen, K. A., Weber, A., & Lowry, D. H. (1972). Bizarreness versus interaction of mental images as determinants of learning. *Cognitive Psychology, 3*, 518–523.

Wood, N., & Cowan, N. (1995). The cocktail party phenomenon revisited: How frequent are attention shifts to one's name in an irrelevant auditory channel? *Journal of Experimental Psychology: Human Perception and Performance, 21*, 255–260.

Wright, D. B., Loftus, E. F., & Hall, M. (2001). Now you see it; now you don't: Inhibiting recall and recognition of scenes. *Applied Cognitive Psychology, 15*, 471–482.

Yamauchi, T., & Markman, A. B. (2000). Inference using categories. *Journal of Experimental Psychology: Learning, Memory and Cognition, 26*, 776–795.

Yost, W. A., & Sheft, S. (1993). Auditory processing. In W. A. Yost, A. N. Popper, & R. R. Fay (Eds.), *Handbook of auditory research* (Vol. 3). New York: Springer-Verlag.

Yum, J. O. (1991). The impact of Confucianism on interpersonal relationships and communication patterns in East Asia. In L. A. Samovar & R. E. Porter (Eds.), *Intercultural communication* (6th ed., pp. 66–78). Belmont, CA: Wadsworth.

Zalla, T., Phipps, M., & Grafman, J. (2002). Story processing in patients with damage to the prefrontal cortex. *Cortex, 38*, 215–231.

Zaragoza, M. S., & McCloskey, M. (1989). Misleading postevent information and the memory impairment hypothesis: Comment on Belli and reply to Tversky and Tuchin. *Journal of Experimental Psychology: General, 118*, 92–99.

Zhang, G., & Simon, H. A. (1985). STM capacity for Chinese words and idioms: Chunking and acoustical loop hypotheses. *Memory and Cognition, 13*, 193–201.

Zihl, J., von Cramon, D., & Mai, N. (1983). Selective disturbance of movement vision after bilateral brain damage. *Brain, 106*, 313–340.

Zihl, J., von Cramon, D., Mai, N., & Schmid, C. (1991). Disturbance of movement vision after bilateral posterior brain damage. *Brain, 114*, 2235–2252.

Zola-Morgan, S., Squire, L., & Amaral, D. G. (1986). Human amnesia and the medial temporal region: enduring memory impairment following a bilateral lesion limited to field CA1 of the hippocampus. *Journal of Neuroscience, 6*, 2950–2967.

Zwaan, R. A. (1996). Processing narrative time shifts. *Journal of Experimental Psychology: Learning, Memory and Cognition, 22*, 1196–1207.

Zwaan, R. A. (1999). Situation models: The mental leap into imagined worlds. *Current Directions in Psychological Science, 8*, 15–18.

CREDITS

This page constitutes an extension of the copyright page. We have made every effort to trace the ownership of all copyrighted material and to secure permission from copyright holders. In the event of any question arising as to the use of any material, we will be pleased to make the necessary corrections in future printings. Thanks are due to the following authors, publishers, and agents for permission to use the material indicated.

Chapter 2. **47:** Reprinted from *Trends in Cognitive Sciences*, Volume 1, Issue 6, Osterhout et al., "Event-Related Potentials and Language" (figure 1), Copyright © 1997 with permission from Elsevier.

Chapter 3. **61:** Adapted from "The Role of Frequency in Developing Perceptual Sets," by B. R. Bugelski et al., 1961, *Canadian Journal of Psychology*, 15, pp. 205–211, Copyright © 1961 by the Canadian Psychological Association. **62:** Reprinted from "The effects of contextual scenes on the identification of objects," by S. E. Palmer, 1975, *Memory and Cognition*, 3, pp. 519–526, Copyright ©1975 with permission from the author and the Psychonomic Society Publishers. **63:** Adapted from "The Role of Frequency in Developing Perceptual Sets," by B. R. Bugelski et al., 1961, *Canadian Journal of Psychology*, 15, pp. 205–211, Copyright © 1961 by the Canadian Psychological Association. **65:** Adapted from "The Role of Frequency in Developing Perceptual Sets," by B. R. Bugelski et al., 1961, *Canadian Journal of Psychology*, 15, pp. 205–211, Copyright © 1961 by the Canadian Psychological Association. **71:** Adapted from "Recognition-by-Components: A Theory of Human Image Understanding," by I. Biederman, 1987, *Psychological Review*, 24 (2), pp. 115–147 (figures 3, 6, 7 and

11), Copyright © 1987 with permission from the author and the American Psychological Association. **72: 3.23** Reprinted from "Recognition-by-Components: A Theory of Human Image Understanding," by I. Biederman, 1987, *Psychological Review*, 24 (2), pp. 115–147 (figure 26), Copyright © 1987 with permission from the author and the American Psychological Association; **3.24** Reprinted from "Recognition-by-Components: A Theory of Human Image Understanding," by I. Biederman, 1987, *Psychological Review*, 24 (2), pp. 115–147 (figure 25), Copyright © 1987 with permission from the author and the American Psychological Association. **73:** Reprinted from "Recognition-by-Components: A Theory of Human Image Understanding," by I. Biederman, 1987, *Psychological Review*, 24 (2), pp. 115–147 (figure 13), Copyright © 1987 with permission from the author and the American Psychological Association. **79:** Reprinted with permission of The Greenwich Workshop. **87:** Reprinted from "Asking the 'what for' question in auditory perception," A. Bregman, in *Perceptual Organization*, M. Kubovy & J. R. Pomerantz (Eds.), 1981, pp. 99–119. Copyright © 1981 with permission from Lawrence Erlbaum Associates, Inc. **92:** Reprinted from "Development of the brain depends on the vi-

sual environment," by C. Blakemore et al., 1970, *Nature, London*, 228, pp. 477–478, Copyright © 1970 with permission from Nature Publishing Group. **93:** Reprinted from "Activation of the middle fusiform 'face area' increases with expertise in recognizing novel objects," by I. Gauthier et al., from *Nature Neuroscience*, 2, pp. 568–573. Copyright © 1999 with permission of the author and Nature Publishing Group.

Chapter 4. 108: Reprinted from "Electrical signs of selective attention in the human brain," by S. A. Hillyard et al., 1973, *Science*, 182, pp. 177–180. Copyright © 1973 AAAS. **110:** From "Action video game modifies visual selective attention," by C. S. Green, et al., From *Nature*, 423 (6939), pp. 534–537, Copyright © 2003 by C. S. Green et al. Reprinted with permission of the authors and Nature Publishing Group. **115:** Reprinted from "Controlled and automatic human information processing: Perceptual learning, automatic attending, and a general theory," by R. M. Shiffrin & W. Schneider, *Psychological Review*, 84, pp. 127–190. Copyright © 1977 with permission from the American Psychological Association. **119:** Reprinted from "Spatial and Verbal Components of the Act of Recall," by L. Brooks, *Canadian Journal of Psychology*, 22, pp.

Experimental Psychology: Human Perception and Performance, 4, pp. 47–60 (figures 2 & 3). Copyright © 1978 with permission from the American Psychological Association. **319: 9.8:** Reprinted from S. M. Kosslyn. "Mental Imagery" in S. M. Kosslyn & D. N. Osherson. *An Invitation to Cognitive Science*—2nd edition, volume 2: Visual Cognition, pp. 267–296 (figure 7.6). Copyright © 1995 with permission from MIT Press; **9.9:** S. M. Kosslyn, T. Ball, & B. J. Reiser. "Visual Images Preserve Metric Spatial Information: Evidence from Studies of Image Scanning." From *Journal of Experimental Psychology: Human Perception and Performance*, 4, pp. 47–60 (figure 3). Copyright © 1978 with permission from the American Psychological Association. **320:** Reprinted from "Spontaneous Imagery Scanning in Mental Extrapolation," by R. A. Finke & S. Pinker, 1982, *Journal of Experimental Psychology: Learning, Memory and Cognition*, 8 (2), pp. 142–147 (figure 1), Copyright © 1982 with permission from the American Psychological Association. **327:** Reprinted from "Electrophysiological Evidence for a Shared Representational Medium for Visual Images and Precepts," by M. J. Farah et al., 1988, *Journal of Experimental Psychology*, 117 (3), pp. 248–257. Copyright © 1988 with permission from the American Psychological Association. **330:** Reprinted from M. J. Farah. "The Neural Basis of Mental Imagery." In M. Gazzanaga (Ed.), *The Cognitive Neurosciences*, 2nd edition. Cambridge, MIT Press, pp. 965–974 (figure 66.2), Copyright © 2000, with permission of The MIT Press. **331:** Reprinted from "Unilateral Neglect of Representational Space," by E. Bisiach et al., 1978, *Cortex*, 14, pp. 129–133. Copyright © 1978 with permission from *Cortex*. **333:**

Reprinted from "Intact Visual Imagery and Impaired Visual Perception in a Patient with Visual Agnosia," by M. Behrmann et al., 1994, *Journal of Experimental Psychology: Human Perception and Performance*, 30. pp. 1068–1087 (figures 1 & 6). Copyright © 1994 with permission from the American Psychological Association. **339:** Reprinted from *Cognitive Psychology*, Volume 3, Wollen et al., "Bizarreness Versus Interaction of Mental Images as Determinants of Learning," pp. 518–523 (figure 1), Copyright © 1972, with permission from Elsevier. **340:** Reprinted from D. G. Pearson, "Imagery and the Visuo-Spatial Sketchpad." In J. Andrade (Ed.), *Working Memory in Perspective*, pp. 33–59 (figure 2.1). Copyright © 2001 with permission from Psychology Press.

Chapter 10. 358: Reprinted from *Trends in Cognitive Sciences*, Volume 1, Issue 6, Osterhout et al., "Event-Related Potentials and Language" (figure 1), Copyright © 1997 with permission from Elsevier. **366:** Reprinted from *Journal of Memory and Language*, Volume 33, Issue 3, Trueswell et al., "Semantic Influences on Parsing: Use of Thematic Role Information in Syntactic Ambiguity Resolution," pp. 285–318 (figure 1), Copyright © 1994, with permission from Elsevier. **367:** Reprinted with permission from "Integration of Visual and Linguistic Information in Spoken Language Comprehension," by M. K. Tanenhaus et al. From *Science*, 268, pp. 1632–1634 (figures 1 & 2). Copyright © 1995 AAAS. **375:** Reprinted from *Journal of Memory and Language*, Volume 26, Morrow et al., "Accessibility and Situation Models in Narrative Comprehension," pp. 165–187 (figure 1), Copyright © 1987, with permission from Elsevier.

382: Reprinted from "Color Categories Are Not Universal: Replications and New Evidence from A Stone-Age Culture," by D. Roberson et al., 2000, *Journal of Experimental Psychology: General*, 129, pp. 369–398 (figures 1& 2), Copyright © 2000 with permission from the American Psychological Association.

Chapter 11. 403: Reprinted from *Cognitive Psychology*, Volume 22, Kaplan et al., "In search of insight," pp. 374–419 (figure 2). Copyright © 1990, with permission from Elsevier. **418:** Reprinted from R. A. Finke, "Creative Insight and Preinventive Forms," from *The Nature of Insight*, by R. J. Sternberg & J. E. Davidson (Eds.), pp. 255–280 (figure 8.1). Copyright © 1995 with permission from the MIT Press. **419:** Reprinted from R. A. Finke, "Creative Insight and Preinventive Forms," from *The Nature of Insight*, by R. J. Sternberg & J. E. Davidson (Eds.), pp. 255–280 (figure 8.6). Copyright © 1995 with permission from the MIT Press.

Chapter 12. 443: Reprinted from A. Norenzayan et al., "Cultural Preferences for Formal Versus Intuitive Reasoning," from *Cognitive Science*, 26, pp. 653–684 (figure 6). Copyright © 2002 with permission from the Cognitive Science Society.

Photo Credits

Inside Cover (Right). Top: Brewer, J. G., Zhao, Z., Desmond, J. E., Glover, G. H., & Gabrieli, J. D. E. (1998). "Making memories: Brain activity that predicts whether visual experience will be remembered or forgotten." *Science*, *281*, 1185–1187. **Bottom:** Gauthier, I., Tarr, M. J., Anderson, A. W., Skudlarski, P., & Gore, J. C. (1999). "Activation of the middle fusiform 'face area' increases with expertise in recognizing novel objects." *Nature Neuroscience, 2,* 568–573.

Chapter 2. 29: top, © Science Pictures Limited/CORBIS. **47:** bottom left, photograph courtesy Natasha Tokowicz. **49:** top, © Leif Skoogfors/CORBIS.

Chapter 3. 56: top, *The Lord of the Rings™: the Fellowship of the Ring™.* Copyright MMI, New Line Productions, Inc.™ The Saul Zaentz Company d/b/a Tolkien Enterprises under license to New Line Productions, Inc. All rights reserved. Photo by Pierre Vinet. Photo appears courtesy of New Line Productions, Inc. **72:** top, photograph by the author. **74:** top, R. C. James. **79:** bottom, *The Forest Has Eyes* © 1984 Bev Doolittle, courtesy of The Greenwich Workshop, Inc. **81:** top, photograph by the author. **84:** top, Ian Macaulay. **85:** bottom left, © Mary Ann McDonald/CORBIS. **86:** top, photograph by the author. **88:** top, photograph by Barbara Goldstein.

90: top, © Richard Hamilton Smith/CORBIS. **93:** top left, Gauthier, I., Tarr, M. J., Anderson, A. W., Skudlarkski, P. L., & Gore, J. C. (1999). "Activation of the middle fusiform 'face area' increases with experience in recognizing novel objects." *Nature Neuroscience, 2,* 568–573.

Chapter 4. 121: bottom, photograph by the author. **122:** bottom, photograph by the author. **123:** center, from "Failure to detect changes in attended objects in motion pictures" by D. Levin and D. Simons, 1997, *Psychonomic Bulletin and Review,* 209.

Chapter 5. 142: top left, © Bazuki Muhammad/Reuters Newsmedia Inc./CORBIS.

Chapter 6. 181: bottom, *Memento* still photo © CORBIS SYGMA.

Chapter 7. 230: bottom, photograph by the author. **231:** bottom, © Bettmann/CORBIS. **241:** top,

Brewer, W. F., & Treyens, J. C. (1981), "Role of schemata in memory for places." *Cognitive Psychology, 13,* 207–230. With permission from Elsevier.

Chapter 8. 271: top right, © Tim Zurowski/CORBIS. **271:** bottom left, © Gary W. Carter/CORBIS. **271:** top left, © Roger Tidman/CORBIS. **305:** top, Kreiman, G., Koch, C., & Fried, I. (2000). "Category-specific visual responses of single neurons in the human medial temporal lobe." *Nature Neuroscience, 3,* 946–953.

Chapter 9. 327: top, Farah, M. J., Peronnet, F., Weisberg, L. L. & Monheit, M. A. (1989). "Brain activity underlying mental imagery: Event-related potentials during image generation." *Journal of Cognitive Neuroscience, 1,* 302–316. **329:** top left, Kreiman, G., Koch, C., & Fried, I. (2000). "Category-specific visual responses of single neurons in the human medial temporal lobe." *Nature Neuroscience, 3,* 946–953.

Name Index

SUBJECT INDEX

Action potentials, 31–32
Advertising and implicit memory, 191–192
Affirming the consequent, 446
Agnosia, 42
  motion, 42
  visual 304, 332–333
Algorithm, 82
Alzheimer's disease, 187
Amaphoric inference 370
Ambiguity
  imagery and, 335
  lexical, 355–357
  perceptual stimulus and, 83–84
  sentence processing and, 359–368
  standing, 364
  temporary, 364
Ambiguous figure and imagery, 335
American Psychological Association, statement on recovered memory, 262
Amnesia, retrograde, 206, 208, 229–230
Amygdala, 27–28, 45
  emotions and, 208
  emotions and memory, 45, 229–230
Analogical approach to problem solving, 407–413
Analytic introspection, 8–9
Antecedent in conditional syllogism, 444
Aphasia, 41, 347–348
Articulatory suppression, 166–167
Atmosphere effect, 436–437
Attention, 3, 4, 99–134
  attenuation theory of, 106–107
  cell phone use and, 118–119
  divided, 113–120
  early selection models of, 103–109
  filter model of, 102–106
  late selection model of, 108–109
  location-based, 124–127

memory and, 132, 139
object based 128–131
perception and, 120–123, 132
physiological mechanisms, 46, 108, 125–126
response-dependent, 119–120
selective 12, 101–112
single unit recording and, 44–47, 125–126
spotlight model of, 124–125, 127
task load and, 110–112
top-down processing and, 125, 131
visual, 120–131
zoom-lens model of, 126–127
Attenuation theory of attention, 106–107
Automatic processing, 114–117
Autobiographical memory, 225–234
Availability heuristic, 458–461

Back propagation, 299–300
Basic level of categories, 279–285
Behavioral approach to the study of cognition, 15–17, 19
Behaviorism, 9–10, 312, 348
  cognition and, 9–10
  imagery and, 312
  language and, 348
Belief bias, 436–437
  culture and, 442–443
Berinmo culture and language, 383–383
Bias
  memory, affected by, 243–244
  reasoning, affected by, 436–437, 464–465
Biological constraints on learning, 11
Bottom-up processing 58–60, 70, 334
  attention and, 131
  feature integration theory and, 70
  imagery and, 334
  object analysis and, 62–73, 95
  perception and, 58–61, 334

Brain. *See* Physiology
Brain damage, effect of. *See* Neuropsychology
Brain imaging, 18, 48–50, 82–90
  categorization and, 304
  imagery and, 327–328
  language and, 359
  memory and, 18, 175, 207–208, 229–230
  perception and, 92–94
  problem solving and, 422
  reasoning and, 474–475
  working memory and, 175
Brain lesioning, 50–51. *See also* Neuropsychology
Broca's aphasia, 41, 347–348
Broca's area, 41, 347

Candle problem, 392, 394, 425
Categorical perception of colors, 381–383
Categorical syllogism, 428
Categorization, 266–303
  connectionist approach to, 294–303
  culture and, 283–285, 465–466
  definitional approach to, 268–270
  hierarchical organization of, 280
  levels of, 279–285
  network approach to, 286–303
  physiological mechanisms, 52, 303–305
  prototype approach to, 270–279
  semantic networks and, 286–294
  usefulness of, 266–268
Category, 266–285
Category-specific neurons, 304–305
Causal connections and memory, 372–374
Causal inference, 371–374
Cell phones and driving, 118–119
Central executive, 163–165, 172
Cerebral cortex, 26